D0221429

09 N$ 51.05

ECONOMIC ANALYSIS

Theory and Application

**Irwin Publications
in Economics**

Advisory Editor
Martin S. Feldstein
Harvard University

Economic Analysis

Theory and Application

S. Charles Maurice
Professor of Economics
Texas A&M University

Owen R. Phillips
Assistant Professor of Economics
University of Wyoming

Fifth Edition

1986

Homewood, Illinios 60430

© RICHARD D. IRWIN, INC., 1970, 1974, 1978, 1982, and 1986

All rights reserved. No part of this publication may be
reproduced, stored in a retrieval system, or transmitted,
in any form or by any means, electronic, mechanical,
photocopying, recording, or otherwise, without the prior
written permission of the publisher.

ISBN 0-256-03343-9
Library of Congress Catalog Card No. 85-81038
Printed in the United States of America

3 4 5 6 7 8 9 0 D O 3 2 1 0 9 8 7

To
Ray Battalio and Charles Smithson,
colleagues and friends

Preface

This textbook is designed for undergraduate courses in basic micro-economics—the theory of market value and distribution. Throughout all of its editions, this text has held to two major objectives. The primary goal is to present the basic fundamentals of price theory. A secondary, but quite important, purpose is to illustrate how the fundamentals of price theory can be applied to the solution of real-world, decision-making problems and to give students experience in solving these problems.

To meet these goals we continue to combine the theory of markets with numerous topical applications of the analytical tools developed in each chapter. These applications are of two basic forms. They are either designed to emphasize the importance of a theoretical concept with a related real-world event that illustrates the presence of the concept in actual markets, or the applications are presented in terms of a contextual problem to help us think and reason like economists. Economics is a science because it has a well-defined body of theory that describes how markets work. But anyone exposed to this theory is exposed to a way of thinking, and thinking is an art. In discussing economics as a science, we are committed to developing the art of problem-solving.

In this edition we stress the economic approach to issues. In particular, whenever seeking the optimal level of any activity a decision maker should set marginal benefit equal to marginal cost. After reviewing the fundamental concepts of supply and demand in Chapters 2 and 3, Chapter 4 is completely devoted to generalizing and applying this principle. We use this chapter as a door through which utility maximization and production efficiency are introduced. Time and again equating marginal cost with marginal benefit is emphasized. It runs as a unifying theme through each topic covered, until finally, in Chapter 19, we end with a discussion of social marginal benefit and cost in the context of externalities.

Some things have not changed in this fifth edition, and some things have. To get the reader to apply the concepts presented, we remain committed to application topics in each chapter and numerous problems at the end of each chapter to cement ideas and challenge thinking. No other text offers as many different and interesting problems at the end of each chapter. To reinforce the feeling that economics is useful, we have added chapters to the text that have a more applied flavor. For instance,

Chapter 3 on markets, 7 on consumer behavior, 12 on the model of perfect competition, and 14 on monopoly are applied theory chapters that expand on the more theoretical discussions in the preceding chapters.

As evidenced by the Table of Contents this change in style naturally leads to a topical grouping of chapters. Chapters 2 through 4 deal with market basics, 5 through 7 discuss consumer behavior, 8 through 10 production and cost, 11 through 15 market structures, 16 and 17 address input demands, and the last two chapters cover welfare analysis. Altogether this edition has been expanded to 19 chapters. The book is not much longer than previous editions, which means chapters are shorter and more focused.

We have undertaken some bold changes in this edition. In Chapter 12 for example, we apply the model of perfect competition in a discussion that distinguishes the strategic importance of fixed and variable costs. We introduce a breakeven chart to show the effect of fixed and variable costs on profit. In an application of the principle, we take sections of a short story from "The Devil" by Guy De Maupassant. This story illustrates how choosing between a fixed cost and variable cost can arise in everyday situations.

Advertising is another topic we treat differently than other texts. In Chapter 7, several applied topics are discussed after indifference theory is presented in Chapters 5 and 6. One of these topics is advertising. We illustrate how advertising increases sales by changing the slope of indifference curves and shifting them to the left, much in the way technology has an impact on the production function.

In our chapters on imperfect competition we have made two changes that make our text unique. First, in discussing long-run monopoly profits we argue strongly that these profits should be capitalized like rents in competition. Thus the presence of monopoly cannot be judged by the profits a firm earns. Secondly, we recognize that the theory of oligopoly has typically been difficult to discuss in an intermediate microeconomic course without the use of calculus. We have, without the calculus, written an illuminating discussion of oligopoly behavior through the introduction of a "payoff table." Without getting into mechanics we identify and discuss the various oligopoly equilibria as points on a payoff table. For various equilibria we are able to compare relative price, output, and profits.

All in all, *Economic Analysis* remains a fundamental text in the basics of microeconomic theory. We are committed to writing the best intermediate undergraduate text without the use of calculus. We believe the changes we have made in this edition continue to move us in this direction. We would very much appreciate hearing comments and criticisms from instructors and students. We can either be reached through our publisher or directly by writing to the department of economics at Texas A&M University or the University of Wyoming.

We are grateful for the many suggestions we have received from students and instructors who have used *Economic Analysis* in the past. We wish to thank our colleagues at Texas A&M for their help with this revision. Ray Battalio, David Hancock, Carl Kogut, and Charles Smithson have been especially helpful to us with ideas about new problems and applications. We also thank Jack Adams (University of Arkansas, Little Rock), Dwayne Barney (Montana State University), George Dery (University of Lowell), Michael Hare (Consultant, Toronto, Canada), Wayne Jesswein (University of Minnesota, Duluth), J. William Levedahl (North Carolina State University, Raleigh), George Palumbo (Canisius College), and Chris Thomas (University of South Florida) for their excellent reviews and suggestions.

S. Charles Maurice
Owen R. Phillips

CONTENTS

PART I: INTRODUCTION

1. Scope of Economics   2

Introduction. The Science of Economics: (Application: The Development of Synthetic Rubber.) Uses of Economics. Purpose of Theory. Structure of the Course. Style of Text. Summary.

PART II: MARKET BASICS

2. Demand and Supply   14

Introduction. Individual and Market Demand Schedules: *Aggregating and Graphing Demand Schedules. Changes in Demand.* Demand Elasticity: *Algebraic Computation of Elasticity. Graphical Computation of Elasticity. Factors Affecting Demand Elasticity.* (Application: Some Uses of Demand Elasticities in the Automobile Industry.) Supply Schedules: *Graphing Supply Schedules. Factors Influencing Supply. Changes in Supply.* Supply Elasticity: *Computation. Determinants of Supply Elasticity.* Market Determination of Price and Quantity: *Equilibrium. Demand and Supply Shifts.* (Application: An Unexpected Recovery in Housing.) Summary.

3. Supply and Demand Analysis   55

Introduction. Supply and Demand in Real Markets: *Prices in Markets.* Floor and Ceiling Prices: *Price Ceilings. Price Floors.* (Application: Price Supports for Peanuts.) Excise Taxes: *Market Effect of a Unit Tax. Ad Valorem Taxes. Government Revenue.* Cost-Benefit Analysis: *The Paradox of Value. Consumer's Surplus and the Area under the Demand Curve.* (Application: The Sale of

Gasoline Rationing Tickets.) *Producer's Surplus*. *Total Surplus and Cost-Benefit Studies*. (Application: Federal Regulation of Natural Gas.) Estimating Demand Schedules: *Estimating Problems*. *Estimating Procedures*. Summary.

4. *Theory of Optimizing Behavior: Static and Dynamic Analysis*   91*

Introduction. Unconstrained Optimization: *Unconstrained Maximization*. *Unconstrained Minimization*. Constrained Optimization: *Constrained Maximization*. *Constrained Minimization*. Multiperiod Analysis: *The Role of Interest*. *Future Value*. *Present Value*. *Discounting and Consumption Expenditures*. (Application: Lease or Buy an Automobile?) Summary.

PART III: CONSUMER BEHAVIOR

5. *Theory of Consumer Behavior: Preferences and Constraints*   124*

Introduction. *Determinants of Consumer Choice*. Basic Assumptions: *Information and Ranking*. *Ordinal versus Cardinal Utility*. Indifference Curves. Characteristics of Indifference Curves. Marginal Rate of Substitution: *Substitution in Consumption*. *Diminishing MRS*. *Marginal Utility Approach*. *The Value of Indifference Curve Theory*. Budget Lines. *Income Constraints*. *Shifting the Budget Line*. Utility Maximization: *Maximizing Satisfaction Subject to a Limited Money Income*. *Marginal Utility Interpretation of Optimization*. *Zero Consumption of a Good*. *Unusual Preference Maps*. (Application: Fringe Benefits and Taxation.) Summary.

6. *Theory of Consumer Behavior: Changes in Income and Price*   163*

Introduction: *Basic Principles*. Changes in Money Income: *Engel Curves and Income Elasticity*. *Normal and Inferior*

Goods. (Application: Income Elasticities of Housing.)
Demand Curves: *Price-Consumption Curves. Derivation of
Demand Curves from Price-Consumption Curves. Demand
Elasticity and the Price-Consumption Curve.* Substitution
and Income Effects: *Substitution Effect. Income Effect.*
Why Demand Slopes Downward: *Demand for Normal
Goods. Demand for Inferior Goods. The Law of Demand.*
Summary.

7. *Applying Consumer Behavior Theory*   **192**

Introduction. The Real Effect of Inflation: *The Consumer
Price Index. True Effect of Inflation. Deflation.* The
Labor-Leisure Choice: *The Labor-Leisure Map. Labor-
Leisure Choices.* (Application: Effects of Progressive and
Flat Rate Income Tax.) Advertising and Indifference
Curves: *Informative Advertising. Image Advertising.*
(Application: When Information is Advertising: *THE NEW
YORK TIMES* BEST SELLER LIST.) Consumption Over
Time: *Income Allocation Over Time.* Summary.

PART IV: PRODUCTION AND COST

8. *Theory of Production*   **228**

Introduction: *Source of Production Cost. Production-
Possibility Frontier.* Production Functions: *Economic
Efficiency in Production. Short and Long Runs. Fixed or
Variable Proportions.* (Application: Fixed-Proportions
Production and the Timber Crisis.) Production with One
Variable Input: *Total, Average, and Marginal Product:
Arithmetic Approach. Total, Average, and Marginal
Product: Graphical Approach. Law of Diminishing
Marginal Product. Three Stages of Production.* Production
with Two or More Variable Inputs: *Production Isoquants.
Relation of MRTS to Marginal Products.* Optimal
Combination of Resources: *Input Prices and Isocost
Curves. Production of a Given Output at Minimum Cost.
Production of Maximum Output with a Given Level of
Cost. Expansion Path. Returns to scale.* Summary.

9. Theory of Cost   269

Introduction: *Definition of Cost. Opportunity Cost and
Accounting Cost*. Planning Horizon and Long-Run Costs:
*Derivation of Long-Run Cost Schedules from a Production
Function. Long-Run Average and Marginal Costs.
Economics and Diseconomies of Scale*. (Application: Are
Diseconomies of Scale a Real Problem?) Theory of Cost
in the Short Run: *Short-Run Total Cost. Average and
Marginal Costs*. (Application: Refinery Cost Functions
from Engineering Data.) Relations between Short-Run and
Long-Run Average and Marginal Costs. Summary.

**10. Input Price Changes and
Technological Change   312**

Introduction. Changes in Input Prices—Substitution
Effect: *Graphical Analysis*. (Application: The Effect of
Rate-of-Return Regulation.) *Elasticity of Substitution.
Elasticity of Substitution and Changes in Relative Input
Shares*. Changes in Input Prices—The Output Effect for a
Profit Maximizer: *Profit Maximization on the Expansion
Path. The Output Effect*. Technological Change and Input
Usage: *Classification of Technological Change.
Technological Change and Factor Usage. Input Price
Changes and Technological Change*. (Application:
Adapting to Changes in Technology and Input Prices—
The Effect of Time.) Summary.

PART V: Market Structures

11. Theory of Perfectly Competitive Markets   338

Introduction: *Why Firms Exist*. The Concept of Profit
Maximization: *Profit Maximization. Economic Profit*.
Perfect Competition: *Free Markets. Small Size, Large
Numbers. Homogeneous Products. Free Mobility of
Resources. Perfect Knowledge about Markets. Conclusion*.
Demand Facing a Perfectly Competitive Firm: *Demand for*

a Price Taker. *Average Revenue*. Short-Run Profit
Maximization: *Numerical Example*. (Application: Decision
Making and Fixed Costs at the Margin.) *Graphical
Exposition of Short-Run Equilibrium*. *Profit, Loss, and the
Firm's Short-Run Supply Curve*. (Application: How Long
Can a Firm Suffer Losses?) *Short-Run Supply of the Firm*.
Short-Run Industry Supply Curve. Long-Run Equilibrium
of a Competitive Firm: *Profit Maximization in the Long
Run*. *Zero and Negative Profit Situations*. *Graphical
Exposition of Long-Run Equilibrium*. *Long-Run
Equilibrium and Rent*. Constant-, Increasing-, and
Decreasing-Cost Industries: *Constant-Cost Industries*.
Increasing-Cost Industries. *Decreasing-Cost Industries*.
Summary.

**12. *The Model of Perfect Competition
in Practice and Perspective*   379**

Introduction. The Adjustment Process in Competitive
Markets: *Long-Run Effects of a Price Ceiling on Coal*.
Allocation of Fixed and Variable Cost in a Competitive
Environment: *The Break-Even Chart*. *Choosing a Cost
Structure*. (Application: Choosing between a Fixed and
Variable Cost.) Perfect Competition as a Goal:
Desirability of Perfect Competition. *Incentive Effects of
Being Small*. *Product Variety*. Perfect Competition and
Consumer's Surplus: *Competition and Maximum Surplus*.
Consumer's Surplus and Imperfect Competition.
Summary.

13. *Theory of Price under Monopoly*   403

Introduction: *Monopoly and Profit Maximization*.
Monopoly Power Measured: *Elasticity of Demand*. *Cross-
Price Elasticity of Demand*. (Application: United States v.
E.I. du Pont de Nemours & Company.) Demand and
Marginal Revenue under Monopoly. Short-Run Monopoly
Profit Maximization: *Cost under Monopoly*. *Short-Run
Equilibrium*. *Monopoly Supply*. *Numerical Illustration*.
Long-Run Equilibrium under Monopoly: *Long-Run*

Equilibrium Process for a Monopoly. Capitalized Profits.
Multiplant Monopoly: (Application: Nonconventional
Mineral Extraction.) Summary.

14. *Monopoly Behavior and Performance*   431

Introduction. Examples of Entry Barriers: *Economies of
Scale. Fixed Costs. Barriers Created by Government.
Input Barriers. Brand Loyalties.* Entry Limiting Strategies:
Entry Limit Pricing. (Application: Entry Limit Pricing.)
*Capacity Barriers to Entry. Multiproduct Cost Barriers.
New Product Development as a Barrier to Entry.
Summary of Strategies.* Price Discrimination: *Price
Discrimination in Theory—Third Degree.* (Application:
Some Examples of Price Discrimination.) *First-Degree
Price Discriminiation—Perfect Price Discrimination.
Second-Degree Price Discrimination.* Market Performance
of Monopoly: *Comparison with Perfect Competition.
Surplus Loss from Monopoly. Welfare Loss from
Monopoly in the United States. A Caveat.* Monopoly
Regulation: *Price Regulation. Taxation.* Summary.

15. *Imperfect Competition*   469

Introduction. Fundamentals of Monopolistic Competition.
*Demand under Monopolistic Competition. Short-Run
Equilibrium. Long-Run Equilibrium. The Long-Run
Equilibrium in Comparison with Perfect Competition.*
Nonprice Competition: *Product Quality. Advertising.*
(Application: Nonprice Competition in the Decaffeinated
Coffee Market.) Interdependence in Oligopoly Behavior:
*Types of Behavior. Tacit Collusion. Competition in
Oligopoly.* Theories of Oligopoly Rivalry: *A Pay-Off
Table. Oligopoly Equilibrium.* Oligopoly and Cartels:
*Cartels and Profit Maximization. Cartels and Market
Sharing. Short and Turbulent Life of Cartels.*
(Application: An Unsuccessful Cartel in Real Estate.)
Summary.

PART VI: INPUT DEMAND

16. *Markets for Variable Inputs*   506

Introduction. One Variable Input and Perfect Competition in Input Markets: *Demand of a Perfectly Competitive Firm. Monopoly in the Commodity Market.* (Application: The Marginal Product of Irrigation Water.) Demand for a Productive Resource with More than One Variable Input: *Parameters for Marginal Revenue Product. Adjusted Demand When More Than One Input Varies.* Industry Demand for an Input. Supply of a Variable Productive Service: *Intermediate Goods and Natural Resources. Labor Supply.* (Application: The Shortage of Nurses.) Market Equilibrium and Returns to Inputs: *Market Equilibrium for Variable Inputs. Fixed Inputs and Quasi-Rent. The Full-Wage Equilibrium.* (Application: Effect of Improved Working Conditions in Mining Industries.) Effects of Labor Unions and Minimum Wages: *Labor Unions. Minimum Wages.* Monopsony: Monopoly in the Input Market: *Marginal Factor Cost under Monopsony. Price and Employment under Monopsony. Bilateral Monopoly.* Summary.

17. *Demand for Fixed Inputs: Theory of Investment*   549

Introduction. Theory of Investment: *Investment Decision Making. The Firm's Demand for Investment.* (Application: Evaluation of Investment Projects.) *Industry Demand for Investment. Monopoly in Capital Markets. Monopsony in Capital Markets. Demand for Capital in Summary.* Inflation and Investment: *Theoretical Effects of Inflation. Actual Effects of Inflation.* (Application: The Effects of Inflation on Public Utilities.) Depletion of Natural Resources: Pricing over Time: *Rates of Extraction.* Effects of Risk and Uncertainty: *Expected Value. Risk Effects in Investment.* Summary.

PART VII: WELFARE ANALYSIS

18. Welfare and Competition   578

Introduction. Social Welfare: *The Concept of Social Welfare. Pareto Optimality. Consumer's Surplus and Pareto Efficiency.* Pareto Optimality in Consumption and Production: *The Gains from Exchange. The Edgeworth Box. Equilibrium of Exchange.* (Application: Uses of the Theory: Goods-in-Kind and Water Rationing.) *Equilibrium of Production.* General Equilibrium and Perfect Competition: *Pareto Optimality across Consumers and Producers. Equilibrium in Perfect Competition.* Summary.

19. Exchange Inefficiencies and Welfare   605

Introduction. Public Goods: *The Free Rider Problem. Public Goods and Marginal Cost. The Role of Government.* Imperfect Competition: *Monopoly Inefficiency. Theory of Second Best.* Information and Market Failure: *Insufficient Information and Prices. Rules of Thumb: The Akerlof Model. Evaluating Product Quality.* Externalities: *Definition of Externalities.* (Application: Externalities and Urban Renewal.) *Property Rights and Externalities. Nonowned or Community-Owned Property.* (Application: Property Rights and Fishing for Striped Bass.) *The Assignment of Property Rights and Externalities.* (Application: Subsidizing Organ Transplants: The Case of an External Benefit.) Summary.

Index   635

PART I

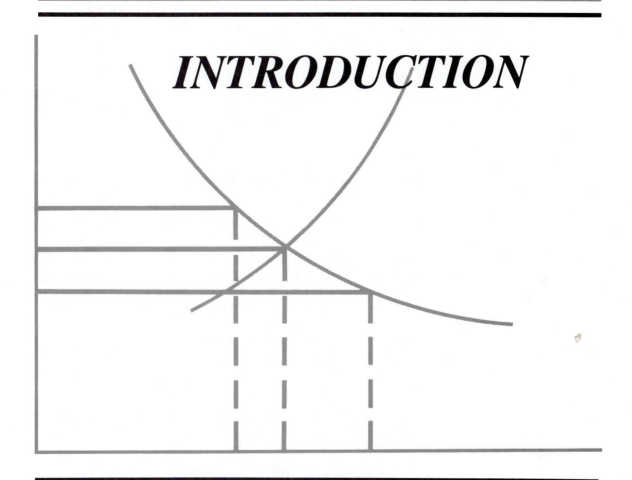

INTRODUCTION

■ *Scope of Economics*

Chapter 1

Scope of Economics

1.1 INTRODUCTION

You are beginning a course in microeconomic theory and analysis. Many of you have had a beginning Principles course; for others, this is your first course. In the Principles course, you were exposed to some economic theory, but you were also probably taught a great deal about economic institutions, such as how government operates, certain characteristics of businesses, and so forth.

In this course, you will be concerned with learning the basics of economic theory—the fundamental tools used by economists—and with using the theory to analyze real economic problems. The theories you will learn are relatively simple but very relevant and applicable to the solution of many important economic problems. Let us emphasize at the very beginning that, simple as the theories may be, they are similar to the theoretical methods used by well-paid professional economists in government, business, and universities to analyze important real-world problems. The analytical techniques used by these economists are more advanced, but the fundamentals of the theoretical structure are frequently quite similar.

You will apply the theories you learn to analyze such problems as the impact of cartels like OPEC, the reasons for shortages, and some effects of taxation. These are the same types of questions now being analyzed by winners of Nobel Prizes in economics, such as Paul Samuelson and Milton Friedman. You will analyze problems similar to those that now concern economists who, at this time, are high-ranking government officials. You will be concerned with decision-making problems similar to those now being considered by top analysts employed by the nation's largest banks and industrial firms.

This is a different situation from that encountered by undergraduate students in other fields. Students in undergraduate chemistry and physics courses do not work on the same types of problems being addressed by Nobel Prize winners in chemistry and physics. Beginning mathematics students are many years away from using the techniques employed by their professors to solve problems. This, however, is not the case with beginning or intermediate economics students.

Let us reemphasize: *the basic theoretical tools, the fundamental methods of analysis, and the overall approaches to the solution of economic problems for the professional economist are those that you will learn and use in this course.* Economic theory is essentially a way of thinking about problems. The economic way of thinking does not change fundamentally as one acquires more sophisticated tools.

1.2 THE SCIENCE OF ECONOMICS

Thomas Carlyle, a Scottish historian of some repute, was fond of criticizing economists. He referred to Malthus and Ricardo as "the respectable professors of the dismal science," thereby giving economics a name it has never quite overcome—possibly, as John Kenneth Galbraith has said, because it has never quite deserved to. In one sense, economics remains a dismal science in that economists all note that there is no such thing as a free lunch—though most economists no longer make the dire predictions about the inevitable poverty of society that were being made at the time Carlyle coined his phrase.

The dismal nature of economics stems from the definition of economics. As most beginning texts avow, economics is a study of the method of allocating scarce physical and human resources among unlimited wants or competing ends. In other words, economics is the study of scarcity, which results when people want more than can be produced. Since wants are unlimited for society, and the resources used to produce things to satisfy the wants are finite or limited, all wants cannot be satisfied. To satisfy some desires, the fulfillment of others must be sacrificed. Alternative uses for resources make them valuable, and this is what leads to cost.

Those who know economics tend to be a somewhat cynical lot. They have a habit of asking what something will cost—cost in the sense of what will have to be sacrificed. People with some economic expertise tend to scoff when politicians promise more schools, more police, more buildings, more of everything, at no additional cost to society. To have more of some goods, society must give up other goods.

Thus, economics has become fundamentally the science of making choices. Most, if not all, basic theory is designed to aid in making decisions and in understanding the consequences of economic decisions made by others. These economic decisions are necessary because of scarcity. Thus societies and individuals must make choices between desirable goals, because all goals cannot be met. How nice it would be if society and individuals could have more of the good things without giving up anything. To the extent that economists continually point out the costs of these "good things," economics still merits the title "dismal science."

From another point of view, however, those who know some economics see a rather optimistic side to the allocation problem. Economists have recently begun to present arguments counter to the current fad of "doomsday" philosophies. Those who espouse the doomsday approach are fond of pointing out that some natural resource such as water will be totally depleted in a specific number of years if society continues to use the resource at the current rate. Or they prophesy shortages of resources in the future. They say that, in a few years, society will need a certain amount of the resource, but this amount will not be available.

Economists are quick to point out flaws in such doomsday arguments. The major flaw, they say, is ignoring the functioning of the market. As society uses up some resource, the amount of that resource decreases, causing the resource to become more and more scarce. This increasing scarcity, as we know, drives up the price of the resource. The increased price causes consumers to economize on their consumption of the good. The increased price also induces an increased search for substitutes. It causes alternatives that were once unprofitable to become more attractive, thus adding to the number of substitutes available. Finally, the higher price brings about research and development in other areas in search of a substitute commodity. Much of our theoretical analysis in the text deals with the fundamentals behind such processes. In any case, those who understand the operation of economic markets argue that, when something becomes more scarce, prices rise to ration the commodity among buyers along with bringing forth additional products from producers. When a "crisis" occurs, economists often point out that there are fundamental economic forces at work that offer a solution. In this context, economics is not a dismal science.

APPLICATION

The Development of Synthetic Rubber

The economic history of the development of synthetic rubber provides a fascinating application of how the market finds a solution to the burdensome problem of scarcity. True, prices and costs, the elements of any market, are a result of scarcity. But when prices rise and prevent some buyers from participating in the market, they look for substitutes. The search for substitutes is often the silver lining in an otherwise dismal economic cloud.

As early as 1909, the German Bayer Company demonstrated the possibility of making a synthetic rubber. Unfortunately, the finished product lacked the strength and flexibility of natural rubber. Despite these handicaps, the product was invaluable to a resource-starved Germany during World War I. For tires, cables, and especially submarine storage batteries, the substitute was indispensable. The commercialization of the

1909 development did not come about until Germany was at war and natural rubber was virtually impossible to obtain. After the war, when the price of natural rubber returned to normal levels, the future of synthetic substitutes looked dim. Synthetic rubber was more expensive and of lower quality than natural rubber, so the product fell into obscurity.

In the mid-1920s, the price of natural rubber rose again. Demand for crude rubber was increasing dramatically because of the growth of the automobile industry. Great Britain had formed a rubber cartel to restrict worldwide natural rubber supply. In 1926, Thomas Midgley, a research scientist at General Motors, approached Alfred Sloan, president of the company, concerning a research project on synthetic rubber. General Motors was interested. In the words of Sloan, natural rubber was "most unsatisfactory from the standpoint of erratic costs. . . . "[1] In other words, prices were often too high for the company's tastes. For two years, Midgley investigated the properties of natural rubber in an effort to duplicate them, but the investigation was commercially unsuccessful and General Motors canceled the project.

Then in 1933, at almost the same time Great Britain was attempting to form a second rubber cartel, General Tire and Goodyear began separate investigations into the feasibility of a synthetic rubber tire. After a year of research, both companies lost interest. General's final report on the research concluded that synthetic rubber was unsuitable for "handling in standard factory equipment, and the quality of the product was definitely inferior to natural rubber."[2] In 1937, Standard Oil Development Company, the research branch of Standard Oil of New Jersey, perfected a synthetic rubber christened "Butyl." The quality was comparable to that of natural rubber, but it was still much too expensive (relative to natural rubber) to produce. World War II brought about the motivation to commercially develop a high-quality synthetic at a price close to that of natural rubber.

At the outbreak of World War II, the U.S. War Department was worried about threatened supplies of natural rubber and the increased demand for the substance if the United States should become involved in the war. In 1939, the five largest tire companies in the United States were contacted by the War Department about the impending danger, and because natural rubber prices were rising quickly they took the warning seriously. The companies were encouraged to look for a commercially feasible synthetic. Research support for their efforts was promised to them by the War Department. This was one of several joint projects between private enterprise and the government during the war. By 1942, the rubber companies had commercially developed several kinds of high-quality synthetic rubber. Natural rubber was virtually impossible to obtain at this time because

---

[1] S. Leslie, "Thomas Midgley and the Politics of Industrial Research," *Business History Review,* Winter 1980, p. 490.

[2] F. Howard, *Buna Rubber* (New York: D. Van Nostrand, 1947), p. 39.

of the war with Japan. Interestingly, the post-war price of synthetic rubber was not higher than that of natural rubber. In 1947, standard-grade natural rubber ranged from 9.9 to 23 cents per pound, while "Buna-S," the standard grade of synthetic rubber, was priced between 15 and 20 cents per pound. Today, synthetic rubbers remain a viable substitute for the natural product.

1.3 USES OF ECONOMICS

The major reason for studying economic theory is that it is practical. Very few students who take this course go on to a Ph.D. in economics. Everyone, however, must make economic decisions every day. We all will continue to face the problems of scarcities and, consequently, must continue to make choices. Everyone will, therefore, find economics useful in their private and professional lives.

Students who choose business as a career will find economics particularly helpful. A knowledge of economics is extremely important in decision making if profit is a motivation. For example, one way economics is useful in business is in predicting what the effect of an external change will be. What would be the impact of higher gasoline prices? A change in the tax laws? Stricter antitrust laws? An increase in the minimum wage? Further, economics is useful in deciding whether or not to expand and whether to sell an asset or hold it in anticipation of a future price increase. Decisions concerning whether or not to stay open extra hours or produce additional output are also economic decisions.

More and more students are going to work in government—federal, state, or local. A knowledge of economics is of great use in many of these occupations. People who work for all branches of government frequently forecast the effect of some action to be taken by that branch of government. At the local level, for example, what will be the effect of a change in zoning regulations? Stricter pollution standards? Changes in tax rates? Increased urban renewal? At the state level, deciding the allocation of funds between education and highways is of great importance. And what would be the effect of a state minimum wage higher than the federal minimum? At the federal level, economic theory is used when considering the effect of changes in income tax and welfare laws. For another example, what would be the effect of stricter enforcement of laws concerning illegal drugs? Economic theory is probably the most important tool used by policymakers in making predictions. Throughout this text, we will develop and apply many of the tools needed to analyze questions relevant to government policymakers.

Many students take positions in nonprofit institutions other than government—in hospitals, universities, and foundations. Since these institutions are greatly affected by economic forces, decision makers must have a good economic understanding. Although these institutions are not motivated by profit, they do make decisions based on economic principles. Often, nonprofit groups work with a fixed budget. Managers desire to maximize the quantity and quality of their service subject to keeping expenditures within their budget. Choices must be made, and economic theory has a good deal to say about the best way to make them.

Finally, a good understanding of economics is important in a person's private life. Obviously, to be a well-informed citizen and voter, one needs to know economics. We stressed that economics is the science of decision making; people make decisions in their private lives, as well as in their business lives. Many of these decisions are also based on economic factors. The type of home appliance to install is, in large part, based on economic variables, such as the interest rate and the price of electricity. Economic factors, such as predicted employment opportunities for women, influence the decisions of families to have children. This does not, of course, mean that other, noneconomic variables do not affect such decisions, but economic forces play an important part. A decision to leave a job and return to school to train for a different job requires economic analysis, as does the decision to go on to graduate school.

We have barely skimmed the surface, mentioning only a few types of decisions where economic reasoning is extremely useful in making the correct choice. We will bring up many more examples and analyze these problems throughout the entire text. As you increase your expertise in applying economics, you will have the satisfaction of actually solving the problems yourself. Through practice you will increase your ability to analyze problems.

1.4 PURPOSE OF THEORY

Since this course is basically concerned with microeconomic theory, we might take the time to explain what theory is. No doubt you have heard statements such as "That's OK in theory, but how about the real world?" Theory *is* designed to apply to the real world; it allows us to gain insights into the economy that would otherwise be impossible. We can make predictions from theory that hold in the real world, even though theoretical structures abstract from most actual characteristics of the world. Theory is abstraction—a way of simplifying things. Its purpose is to make sense out of confusion. The real world is a very complicated place and has an infinite number of variables in continual change. Theory is concerned with knowing those variables that are important to the issue at hand and those that are not. Theoretical structures allow us to concentrate on a few important forces and ignore the many, many variables that are not important. In other words, when using theory, we ignore the irrelevant.

It is this ability to abstract—to cast aside all factors insignificant to the problem—that allows us to come to grips with the issue at hand without becoming bogged down in unimportant issues. We reach conclusions using very simple assumptions, while ignoring forces that *could* affect the consequences but in all likelihood will not. Not only economists, but people in business, government, and everyday life make predictions using similar principles. With the use of economic theory, we have a more formalized structure, or method of analysis, for handling economic questions.

Using a formal but simple theoretical model, we can answer thousands of questions, such as those mentioned above. These questions are important both to individuals and governments; and they can be given answers that are *approximately* correct. In carrying out our analysis, we must remember that, while everything depends on everything else, most things depend in an essential way on only a *few other things*. We usually ignore the general interdependence of everything and concentrate only on the *close interdependence* of a few variables. If pressed far enough, the price of beef depends not only on the prices of pork and other meats and fowls, but also on the prices of butane, color televisions, and airline tickets. As a first approximation, we ignore the prices of butane, TVs, and so on. We temporarily hold *other things constant,* and concentrate our attention on a few closely related variables.

In this text, we adopt that basic approach. We assume that *most,* but not all, of the economic interrelations can be ignored. We analyze our problems and realize that our answers are first approximations. We carry out our analysis from assumptions based on real-world conditions, and then we go through a purely logical analysis. Before we make any definite statements or predictions about the real world, we must go through the interpretation stage. Here, it is necessary to realize that we have held many "other things" constant. We must conclude that a freeze in Florida, for instance, will *tend* to cause an increase in the price of oranges. If our theory is sound, the answers, even though first approximations, will be qualitatively correct. This is about all one can demand of economic theory. Quantitative results are up to the econometricians; that is, those interested in testing economic theories. This text consists mostly of the theory and applications, but the testing aspect will not be totally ignored.

1.5 STRUCTURE OF THE COURSE

We might briefly examine what types of material will and will not be covered in this text. Economic theory is generally divided into two major branches—macroeconomics and microeconomics. Microeconomics, the subject of this book, is concerned with organizing individual behavior, or the behavior of small groups of individuals. Some examples are analyses of the forces that determine the price and the amount of beef consumed by a group of customers, the reasons for a natural gas shortage, why the price of small computers has fallen as most other prices have been rising, and why price must increase for firms to be induced to supply more output. Macroeconomics, on the other hand, is concerned with aggregates over the economy as a whole; for example, the total level of unemployment in a society, the rate of inflation, the effect of changing the supply of money in a society, the forces affecting the level of interest rates, per capita rates of consumption, and so on.

By way of contrast, in microeconomics we study the forces that affect relative prices—why the price of oil rises relative to the price of coal, even though both are increasing. Macroeconomics courses analyze why the entire price level, the "cost of living," rises or falls. In this course, we will study the reasons why wage rates in a particular industry change relative to rates in other industries. This contrasts with the macro approach, which analyzes reasons for changes in the wage level for the whole economy. To summarize, we will be concerned with analyzing behavior of individuals and groups of individuals but not the behavior of aggregates in the economy as a whole, such as all households or all businesses. We will concentrate on the causes and effects of changes in relative prices, knowing that inflation may be causing all prices to rise in a given period.

Typically, a course in microeconomics is divided into three major sectors, and this text follows that approach. The first area is the behavior of individual consumers and groups of consumers that determines the demand for goods and services. The second major area is the theories of firms and industries. Among these are the theories of production and cost. The behavior of firms and industries determines the supplies of goods and services. The third major area is theories of distribution. In this area, we study the forces that affect the payment to the owners of resources—labor, capital, land, management. The owners of these resources receive wages, salaries, rents, profits, and interest from those firms that purchase the resources.

Sometimes economists simplify the economy by thinking of it as being divided into two sectors: (1) households composed of individuals who purchase and consume commodities produced by the other sector, and (2) firms. The households must have income to purchase the goods and services produced and sold by the firms, which must in turn hire the resources owned by the households if they are to produce the goods. We can think of the economy as consisting of resource owners who sell their resources to firms in order to attain income to buy their consumption goods. This is a rather simplistic view, of course, but it does provide a beginning idea of how the economy functions.

The major factor limiting the amount of goods and services that such a society produces and consumes is the amount of resources in the society available to produce goods and services. Clearly, as either the technology improves or as the resources owned by the society increase, the society can have more of some goods without giving up some other goods. During any one period of time, the total supply of resources limits the total amount of goods possible; and if the society wishes more of certain things, it must give up some other things that are also desired. The society experiences scarcity, and scarcity is the subject of study for economists. We will deal with this concept more completely in Chapter 8 where the amount of goods and services a society can have at any one time is analyzed, considering the production possibilities of the society as a whole.

1.6 STYLE OF TEXT

We have tried to make this text as easy to understand as possible. This is not to say that everything you read will be simple. On the contrary, you will encounter some difficult concepts, but they will be presented in an understandable fashion.

To help you grasp the important ideas presented in each chapter, we have identified and classified them as *definitions, relations,* or *principles*. Often, these concepts will be listed at the end of a chapter as a summary. They are very important in your study of microeconomics.

You will also encounter sections in each chapter set aside as *applications*. You encountered the first one a few pages ago. The purposes of applications are to emphasize the value of the theory and to stress the importance of the arguments presented just before the application. There is a connection between the real world and the curves and symbols used in abundance throughout this text. Occasionally, an application will even extend the theory in the context of a real-world issue.

Finally, each chapter, except Chapter 1, ends with two sets of problems. The first set falls under the heading of "technical problems." Here, the solutions are generally expressed in quantities or a money unit. They are designed to ensure your understanding of market mechanics. The second set is given the name "analytical problems." These problems are more thought provoking. They are intended to make you apply the theory presented in the chapter in a wide variety of market contexts. These analytical problems are more difficult, and you might not be able to answer all of them. They are learning tools to keep you thinking and to promote discussion with your fellow students and instructor.

Of course, each chapter, including this one, will conclude with a summary to help tie things together.

1.7 SUMMARY

We emphasized at the beginning of this introductory chapter that economics is the science of decision making. These decisions arise because of the important concept of scarcity. Without scarcity, there would be no problems of economic decision making—no decision about what to produce and what to consume would be necessary. Everyone could have everything desired. But scarcity does exist, and economic decisions are necessary; people make such decisions about production and consumption every day. The study of economics enables us to understand how and why individuals make these decisions. It allows us to predict the consequences of such decisions and helps us make better decisions.

We have discussed only the scope and structure of economics. We have mentioned what economics is and what it can do. Now we will begin developing the basic theory and applying that theory to problems. We will show how economists have used theories as simple as those to be developed here to solve interesting, sophisticated, and highly relevant business and social problems. We will be dealing with problems as vast as pollution, conservation of natural resources, and the consequences of price supports. We will also discuss how economics is used in decision making by business and households, and give examples for both.

We should stress that the purely theoretical sections make up a large part of the text and form a self-contained unit. Very little new theoretical material is introduced in the applications. The applications can even be omitted—they are easily spotted because they are marked off—if one is interested only in theory. The applications are designed to show how theory is used—they are offered primarily to give you practice in using the theory. After all, in economics, as in mathematics, riding a bike, playing baseball, dancing, speaking a foreign language, and so on, one learns by doing. If practice doesn't make perfect, it will at least make you better. Finally, the applications are designed to give you some fun, as you become better and better at doing the analysis yourself. At the end of each chapter, you will find some problems that will allow you plenty of practice.

PART II

MARKET BASICS

- **Demand and Supply**

- **Supply and Demand Analysis**

- **Theory of Optimizing Behavior: Static and Dynamic Analysis**

Chapter 2

Demand and Supply

2.1 INTRODUCTION

Economics is concerned with the problem of scarcity. Goods are scarce because the resources used to produce them have alternative uses. When there is free exchange, prices will allocate scarce goods and services. A fundamental task of economics is to analyze the factors that determine the prices and quantities of commodities sold. The determinants of price and quantity are usually separated into two categories: those affecting demand for a good and those affecting supply. The purpose of this chapter is to explain what demand and supply are and show how they determine price and the quantity sold in markets. We will also show how the concepts of demand and supply reveal consumers' and producers' sensitivity to price change.

Thomas Carlyle, the man who named economics "the dismal science," stated: "It is easy to train an economist: teach a parrot to say Demand and Supply." This is another epigram that has survived because it is humorous and contains a certain amount of truth. Demand and supply are such important tools of analysis that we will devote several chapters to investigating the underlying forces behind them. In this chapter, however, we will discuss what demand and supply are and, more specifically, how they determine prices in markets.

2.2 INDIVIDUAL AND MARKET DEMAND SCHEDULES

An *individual's* (or a household's) demand schedule for a specific commodity is the quantity of that commodity the person (or household) is willing and able to purchase at each possible price during a particular time period. For example, if someone is willing and could afford to buy, during some time period (say, a week), 6 units of a particular item at $6 each, 10 units at $5 each, or 15 units at $4 each, these combinations would be part of that person's demand schedule for the commodity. To get the full schedule we would have to extend the list of prices upward and downward.

Consumers are usually willing and able to buy more at lower prices. Such behavior is so pervasive it is referred to as the *law of demand*. If you

14

doubt the law of demand, try to think of a specific item you would buy in larger amounts if its price were higher. A major reason for the inverse relationship between price and quantity purchased is that consumers tend to substitute—they buy more of a less expensive good and less of a more expensive good when prices change. Since considerable portions of later chapters are devoted to analyzing the law of demand and this "substitution effect," we now assume the following is correct: people are willing and able to buy more at lower than at higher prices.

Principle

An individual's demand schedule is a list of prices and corresponding quantities that an individual is willing and able to buy in some time period. Quantity demanded per time period varies inversely with price.

Aggregating and Graphing Demand Schedules

Suppose a very large group of people gathers together to buy its weekly supply of some commodity. An auctioneer in the market requests that each person turn in a list indicating the amount of the good he or she is willing and able to purchase that day at each price: $1, $2, $3, $4, $5, $6, and so forth. The auctioneer then adds up the amounts that each person is willing and able to buy at each of the prices and gets the figures shown in Table 2–1. The table shows a list of prices and corresponding quantities that consumers demand per period of time at each price on the list. This list of prices and quantities is called a *market demand schedule*. It is the *sum* of the demand schedules of all individuals in the market. Since people are willing to buy more at lower prices than at higher prices, quantity demanded and price vary inversely in the market.

Principle

The market demand schedule is the sum of the quantities that all individual consumers in the market demand at each price. In the market, quantity demanded varies inversely with price.

TABLE 2–1   **Market demand schedule**

Quantity demanded	Price per unit ($)
1,000	6
1,500	5
2,500	4
4,500	3
7,000	2
9,000	1

Someone untrained in economic reasoning might accuse economists of ignoring style and taste and saying that price is the only thing that affects consumer purchases. This criticism can be concisely stated by using the letter f for the symbol "function of" or "depends upon." If we let X_d represent the quantity of a certain good and P_x its price, then the accusation that economists think X_d is only a function of P_x is mathematically represented as:

$$X_d = f(P_x).$$

This claim is not really valid. All economists recognize that many forces other than price determine the quantity demanded. A fundamental analytical method used in economics is to hold all other influences constant and focus on one important variable. Economists do not say price is the *sole* influence on purchases—but they say that price generally has a *very important effect* on quantity purchased. To analyze the effect of price, economists hold constant other variables and concentrate on the relation between quantity demanded and price—the relation shown by a demand schedule. In this way, attention can be focused on the effect of price. However, when using demand curves, you should be aware of the other things that influence quantity demanded but are held constant when deriving demand.

First, a consumer's income affects the amount demanded at any price. For some commodities, an increase in income would cause consumers to demand more of a particular commodity at a particular price. For other commodities, an increase in income would cause consumers to demand less at some given price. Thus, the effect of income on quantity purchased can be the same as price or just the opposite. We generally hold income constant when deriving demand.

Second, the prices of other goods must be held constant because they affect how much of a good is purchased at a given price. For example, suppose both beef and pork have been selling for $2 a pound, and the price of beef falls to $1 per pound. Consumers would probably buy less pork when beef is cheaper than they would when beef and pork are the same price.

Third, changes in consumer's tastes can affect how much of a good is demanded at a given price. If some influential movie or television stars are photographed wearing a certain style of clothing, consumers who wish to imitate them would probably be willing to buy more of that style at the prevailing price. Since changes in tastes affect the demand for commodities, economists hold tastes constant when deriving demand.

Finally, people's expectations affect demand. When people think the price of a good is going to rise, they have an incentive to increase their rates of purchase before the price rises. On the other hand, expecting prices to fall causes some purchases to be postponed.

Therefore, economists do not believe that quantity demanded is simply a function of price, but if we let M represent the consumer's income, P_o, the prices of other goods, T, tastes, and V, expectations, economists know that

$$X_d = f(P_x, M, P_o, T, V).$$

When economists draw up demand schedules such as the one shown in Table 2–1, they do so *ceteris paribus*, or under the assumption that other things remain the same. Economists do not think price is the sole determinant of the quantity that people purchase, but they are interested in *isolating* the effect of price changes.

Quite often, it is more convenient to work with a graph of demand, rather than a table. Figure 2–1 is the graph of the demand schedule shown in Table 2–1. Each price-quantity combination ($6–1,000, $5–1,500, and so on) is plotted, then the six points are connected by the curve labeled *DD'*. This *demand curve* indicates the quantity of the good consumers are

FIGURE 2–1   **Market demand curve**

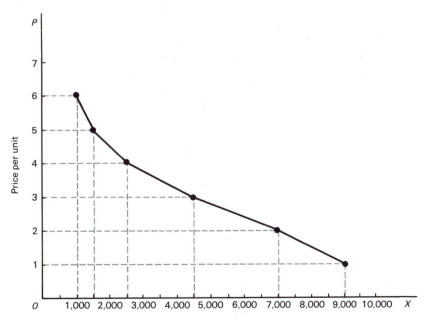

Quantity of *X* demanded per unit of time

willing and able to buy per unit of time at *every* price from \$6 to \$1. Since consumers demand more at lower prices, the curve slopes downward. When deriving a demand curve from a set of price-quantity data, we assume that price and quantity are infinitely divisible. Price can be *any* number between \$6 and \$1; quantity demanded can also be any number between 1,000 and 9,000. This assumption sacrifices some realism since consumers usually cannot buy fractions of units, but this sacrifice is more than counterbalanced by the gain in analytical convenience of having smooth curves in the graphs.

Whenever we draw a demand curve, price will always be on the vertical axis and quantity on the horizontal axis. By convention, when graphs are drawn the variable on the vertical scale is dependent on the one measured by the horizontal scale, so we have reversed the role of P_x and X from our discussion above, and drawn the graph in such a way that P_x is a function of X, rather than X a function of P_x. Technically, the curve in Figure 2–1 is an inverse demand curve. We will continue, however, to refer to it as the demand curve.

Changes in Demand

When price falls (rises) and consumers purchase more (less) of a good, other things remaining the same, we say that *quantity demanded* increases (decreases). We do not say that demand increases or decreases, which refers to a complete shift of the schedule. Demand is a *list* or schedule of prices and quantities demanded at each price. Demand increases or decreases only if one or more of the factors held constant when deriving demand changes. For example, if the incomes of consumers change, causing them to demand more of a good at each price than they did previously, we say the demand for that good increases. If the change in income causes consumers to demand less of a good at each price than they did before, then demand decreases.

Figure 2–2 illustrates changes in demand. Assume that the demand curve for a good is $D_0 D_0'$. At a price of \$12 per unit, consumers purchase 2,100 units per period of time; if price falls to \$8, *quantity demanded* on the same demand curve increases to 2,500 units. Now, begin once more with demand at $D_0 D_0'$ and a price of \$12. Assume that tastes change and demand decreases (shifts to the left) to $D_1 D_1'$. Now consumers demand only 1,000 units per period of time at the price of \$12. In fact, at every price, consumers are willing and able to buy less of the good after the shift than before. This shows a *decrease in demand*. Now, let something previously held constant change causing demand to increase (shift to the right) to $D_2 D_2'$. At \$12, consumers purchase 3,500 units per period, and at every other relevant price they buy more than before. This shows an *increase in demand*. It is worthwhile to repeat, if demand is $D_0 D_0'$ and

FIGURE 2–2 **Shifts in demand**

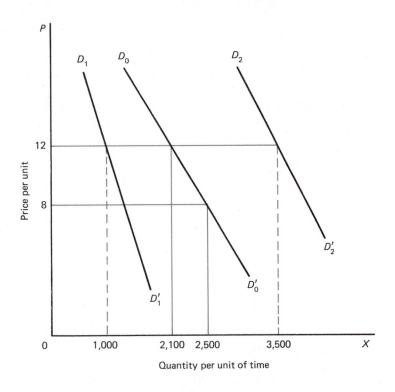

price falls from \$12 to \$8, other things remaining the same, we say that *quantity demanded* changes from 2,100 to 2,500, but demand does not change. An increase or decrease in demand means the entire schedule has shifted to the right or left. The distinction between a change in quantity demanded and a change in demand may be summarized as follows:

Relation
When price falls (rises), other things remaining the same, quantity demanded rises (falls). When something held constant in deriving the demand curve changes, demand increases or decreases. An increase in demand indicates that consumers are willing and able to buy more at each price on the schedule. A decrease in demand indicates they are willing and able to buy less at each price. Changes in demand are represented by shifts in the demand curve; changes in quantity demanded are shown by movements along the original demand curve.

2.3 DEMAND ELASTICITY

Those who use economics in decision making are frequently interested in the shape of the demand schedule because this determines how total expenditures for a commodity change when there is a movement along the curve. Total expenditure, or total revenue (R), is simply price times quantity demanded, or

$$R = P_x \times X.$$

In Figure 2-2, we can calculate total revenue for any point on demand curve $D_0 D_0'$. At a price of \$8, market sales are 2,500 units. Total revenue is, therefore, $R = \$8 \times 2,500 = \$20,000$. When sales fall to 2,100 units after the price goes to \$12, revenue becomes $\$12 \times 2,100 = \$25,200$, an increase over the revenue at the lower \$8 price. Along any downward sloping demand curve, P_x and X move in opposite directions and, consequently, have offsetting effects on revenue. Specifically, an increase in price alone would tend to increase expenditures, whereas the resulting decrease in quantity would tend to decrease expenditures. The effect on total expenditure depends on which force dominates—the increase in price or the decrease in quantity demanded.

The change in price dominates if the percentage increase in price exceeds the percentage decrease in quantity demanded; in such cases total expenditure will rise. Total expenditure falls, however, if the percentage increase in price is less than the percentage decrease in quantity demanded. The effect of a price change therefore depends on the relative sensitivity of quantity demanded to price along a demand curve. The measure of this relative sensitivity along a given demand curve is called the *elasticity of demand*.

This concept is of great interest to both economists and business people. Obviously, in business, one would like to know the effect of a change in price on sales revenue and what determines such an effect. For some products, a small change in price over a certain range of the demand curve results in a significant change in quantity demanded. In this case, quantity demanded is very responsive to changes in price, and the total revenue collected by a seller will rise when price decreases. For other products, or perhaps for the same product over a different range of the demand curve, a relatively large change in price leads to a correspondingly small change in quantity demanded. That is, quantity demanded is not particularly responsive to price changes. In this case total expenditure would rise when price increases.

A graph can help us visualize how price and quantity interact to determine the effect on total revenue of a movement along the demand curve. In Figure 2-3, a seller sets a price of p, and operates at point b on the demand curve. Price is then raised by the amount Δp, where Δ means "a change in," until the seller is at point a on the curve and sells Δx fewer

FIGURE 2-3   **Change in revenue from a price increase**

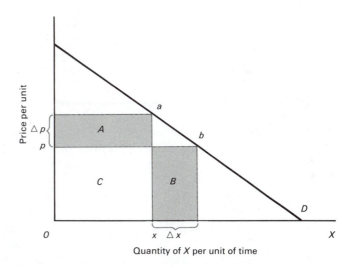

units. We refer to total sales at this point as x. Before the price change, revenue or total expenditure on the seller's commodity was the sum of the two areas $B + C$. After the price change, revenue becomes the areas $A + C$. The difference in revenue is easily seen to be the difference between shaded areas A and B. For a price increase, total revenue rises if area A is greater than area B, it falls if area A is less than area B, and stays the same if area A equals area B.

Economists have a precise way of classifying demand according to the sensitivity of quantity demanded to a price change and the effect of changes in price on total revenue. Demand is said to be elastic if revenue falls with a price increase and rises with a price decrease; it is inelastic if total revenue rises with a price increase and falls with a price decrease. We can talk about changes in total revenue or total expenditure in response to changes in price through the concepts of demand elasticity or inelasticity.

Suppose the price change "outweighs" the quantity change in terms of percent, that is, quantity demanded is not particularly sensitive to price. In this case, when price rises and quantity falls, total revenue to the seller increases. Demand is said to be inelastic. If price decreases and quantity demanded increases, under the inelastic demand total expenditure falls. On the other hand, if demand is elastic, the percentage change in quantity demanded exceeds the percentage change in price. In this case, when

TABLE 2–2   **Relations between demand elasticity and total expenditure (*TE*)**

	Elastic demand $\|\%\Delta X\| > \|\%\Delta P\|$	*Unitary elasticity* $\|\%\Delta X\| = \|\%\Delta P\|$	*Inelastic demand* $\|\%\Delta X\| < \|\%\Delta P\|$
Price rises	*TE* falls	No change in *TE*	*TE* rises
Price falls	*TE* rises	No change in *TE*	*TE* falls

price rises and quantity falls, total revenue falls because of the greater quantity effect. Clearly, a price decrease leads to an increase in quantity demanded, and, with an elastic demand, total revenue rises. Finally, we classify a demand curve as having unitary elasticity when the percentage change in price is exactly offset by the percentage change in quantity demanded. In this case, a change in price results in no change in total expenditure. All of these relations are summarized in Table 2–2. In the table the terms $|\%\Delta P|$ and $|\%\Delta X|$ are the absolute values of the percentage changes in price and quantity. The Δ symbol means "the change in." These expressions refer only to the change in magnitude of price and quantity, respectively, and not the direction of change.

Algebraic Computation of Elasticity

We have explained elasticity and inelasticity only in very general terms. It is often useful to have a specific measure of relative responsiveness rather than speaking of demand as being elastic or inelastic. This measure will show us that it is usually not accurate to say that a given demand curve is wholly elastic or inelastic. In many cases, demand curves have both an inelastic and an elastic range, along with a point or range of unitary elasticity. With this measure we can also determine, over a certain range of prices, which of two demand curves is more elastic. This proves very helpful in analyzing many public policy issues. The measure or coefficient of price elasticity (*E*) is:

$$E = -\%\Delta X / \%\Delta P = -\frac{\Delta X / X}{\Delta P / P} = -\frac{\Delta X}{\Delta P} \cdot \frac{P}{X},$$

where Δ, as always, means "the change in," and *P* and *X* denote price and quantity demanded.

Since price and quantity vary inversely, a minus sign is used in the formula to make the coefficient positive. From the formula, we see that the relative responsiveness of quantity demanded to changes in price measures the ratio of the proportional change in quantity demanded to the proportional change in price. If E is less than one, demand is inelastic, $|\%\Delta X| < |\%\Delta P|$. If E is greater than one, demand is elastic, $|\%\Delta X| > |\%\Delta P|$. If E equals one, demand has unitary elasticity, or $|\%\Delta X| = |\%\Delta P|$.

We can return to Figure 2–3 and show that, for a price increase, if total expenditure goes up, then demand is truly inelastic. If total revenue rises as price rises in Figure 2–3, then area $A >$ area B, or

$$x \cdot (\Delta p) > p \cdot (\Delta x).$$

Dividing the right side by the left side gives

$$1 > \frac{\Delta x}{\Delta p} \cdot \frac{p}{x} = E.$$

This proves that when total expenditures rise after a price increase, demand elasticity is less than one. If total revenue goes down, then we reverse the inequality, area $A <$ area B, and

$$x \cdot (\Delta p) < p \cdot \Delta x.$$

Again, dividing the right side by the left side

$$1 < \frac{\Delta x}{\Delta p} \cdot \frac{p}{x} = E.$$

So demand elasticity is indeed greater than one when total revenue falls for a price increase. It is left as an exercise for the student to show $E = 1$ when area $A = $ area B.

The process of deriving the coefficient of elasticity between two price-quantity relations is a relatively simple computation. Certain biases come up, however, from selecting the price (p) and quantity (x) used in the calculation. As an example, consider the demand schedule given in Table 2–3. Suppose price falls from $1 to 50 cents, and the quantity demanded rises from 100,000 to 300,000. Total expenditure then rises to $150,000. By the analysis in Table 2–3, demand is elastic since total expenditure increases.

TABLE 2–3   **Demand and elasticity**

Price	Quantity demanded	Total expenditure	Elasticity
$1.00	100,000	$100,000	ELASTIC
.50	300,000	150,000	UNITARY
.25	600,000	150,000	INELASTIC
.10	1,000,000	100,000	

Let us now compute E for $X = 100,000$ and $P = \$1$:

$$E = -\frac{\Delta X/X}{\Delta P/P} = -\frac{(100,000 - 300,000) \div 100,000}{(\$1 - \$0.50) \div \$1} = -\frac{-2}{1/2} = 4.$$

As expected, the coefficient is greater than one. But some caution must be exercised. The changes in X and P are definitely known from Table 2–3, but often we do not know whether to use the values $X = 100,000$ and $P = \$1$ or the values $X = 300,000$ and $P = \$0.50$ for the starting quantity and price. Try the computation with $P = \$0.50$ and $X = 300,000$:

$$E = -\frac{(300,000 - 100,000) \div 300,000}{(\$0.50 - \$1) \div \$0.50} = \frac{2}{3}.$$

It actually looks as though demand is inelastic, despite the fact that we know it is elastic from the total expenditure calculation.

The difficulty lies in the fact that elasticity has been computed over a segment of the demand curve and not at a specific point. We can get a much better approximation by using the *average* values of P and X over the range in which they change. That is, for large changes such as this, we should compute elasticity using what is known as the "arc formula." Arc elasticity $\overline{E}$ is

$$\overline{E} = -\frac{X_1 - X_0}{(X_1 + X_0)/2} \div \frac{P_1 - P_0}{(P_1 + P_0)/2} = -\frac{X_1 - X_0}{X_1 + X_0} \div \frac{P_1 - P_0}{P_1 + P_0},$$

where subscripts 0 and 1 refer respectively to the initial and the new prices and quantities demanded. Using this formula, we obtain

$$\overline{E} = -\frac{(300,000 - 100,000) \div (300,000 + 100,000)}{(\$0.50 - \$1) \div (\$1 + \$0.50)} = \frac{3}{2}.$$

Demand is indeed elastic when allowance is made for the discrete, or finite, changes in price and quantity demanded. As a rule, when measuring elasticity along a segment of the demand schedule we should use the arc formula, or $\overline{E}$. If we calculate elasticity at or very near to a point on the demand curve, we should use the formula for E. Frequently this ratio is referred to as the "point" elasticity formula.

Principle.
Demand is said to be elastic, of unitary elasticity, or inelastic according to the value of E. If $E > 1$, demand is elastic; a given percentage change in price results in a greater percentage change in quantity demanded. Small price changes result in more significant changes in quantity demanded. When $E = 1$, demand has unitary elasticity, meaning that the percentage changes in price and quantity demanded are precisely the same. Finally, if $E < 1$, demand is inelastic. A given percentage change in price results in a smaller percentage change in quantity demanded.

Graphical Computation of Elasticity

The formula for E can be rewritten and expressed in geometric terms, to allow us to compute demand elasticity from a sketch of the curve. We can then immediately compare the relative price sensitivity of two demand curves and have a way of estimating elasticity at a point on a curve of any shape.

Let us consider the case of a linear demand curve such as that shown in Figure 2–4. The point elasticity at any price and quantity, such as P and X at point B, can be computed as the ratio of XC/OX, or OP/AP. These ratios are estimates of the elasticity at a point for very small changes in price and quantity, and each proves useful in different contexts. To prove that these ratios measure elasticity, recall that $E = \Delta X/\Delta P \cdot P/X$. The ratio P/X is geometrically OP/OX, but, since $OX = PB$, P/X is also equal to the ratio OP/PB. We know the slope of the curve is $\Delta P/\Delta X$, the inverse of $\Delta X/\Delta P$. Referring to Figure 2–4, $\Delta P/\Delta X = AP/PB$, so for the inverse we have $\Delta X/\Delta P = PB/AP$. Therefore,

$$E = \frac{\Delta X}{\Delta P} \cdot \frac{P}{X} = \frac{PB}{AP} \cdot \frac{OP}{PB} = \frac{OP}{AP}.$$

Similarly, since we may also set $OP = BX$, the ratio OP/OX is equal to BX/OX, and from the figure we see that slope $\Delta P/\Delta X$ may also be written as BX/XC, giving

FIGURE 2–4   **Estimation of point elasticity**

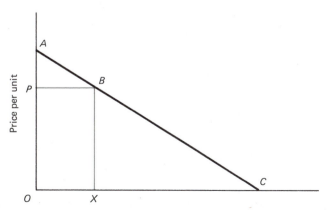

FIGURE 2–5   **Ranges of demand elasticity for linear demand curve**

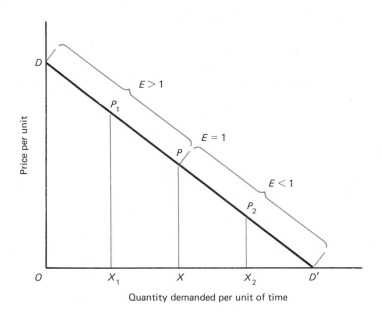

$$E = \frac{\Delta X}{\Delta P} \cdot \frac{P}{X} = \frac{XC}{BX} \cdot \frac{BX}{OX} = \frac{XC}{OX}.$$

With these two geometric expressions for elasticity of demand we can readily show how elasticity along a linear demand curve changes. At the midpoint of a linear schedule, elasticity is unitary. We can locate a point on DD', the linear demand curve in Figure 2–5, where $OX = XD'$. This is the midpoint of a linear curve. It is also the point where demand has unitary price elasticity, since $E = XD'/OX = 1$. Next, consider any point to the left of X such as X_1. At X_1, $E = X_1D'/OX_1 > 1$. The coefficient of price elasticity is greater than unity at any point to the left of X. Finally, at any point to the right of X, say X_2, the coefficient of price elasticity is $E = X_2D'/OX_2 < 1$. Over this range, demand is inelastic. These observations deserve to be highlighted:

Relation
For a linear demand curve: (1) demand is elastic at higher prices, (2) has unitary elasticity at the midpoint, and (3) is inelastic at lower prices. Therefore, in the case of linear demand, elasticity declines as one moves downward along the curve.

When demand is not linear, as in the case of DD' in Figure 2–6, we can easily approximate point elasticity in the following manner. Suppose we want to compute the elasticity of DD' at point R. First, draw the straight line AB tangent to DD' at R. For very small movements away from R along DD', the slope of AB is a relatively good estimate of the slope of DD'. We may estimate the elasticity at R by using either of the above elasticity ratios

$$E = \frac{XB}{OX} = \frac{OP}{AP} \gtreqless 1.$$

These formulas also help us compare the relative elasticities of two or more demand schedules. Figure 2–7 illustrates two intersecting demand curves. To intersect, they must have different slopes. While elasticity is

FIGURE 2–6　　　**Computation of point elasticity for nonlinear demand curve**

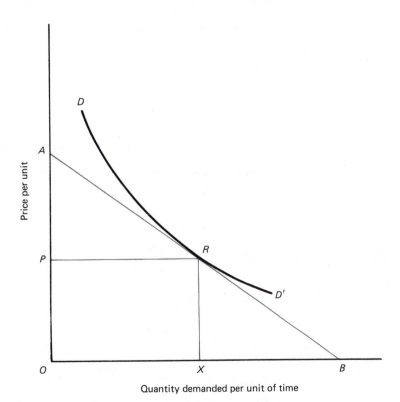

FIGURE 2–7   **Relative elasticities of two intersecting demand curves**

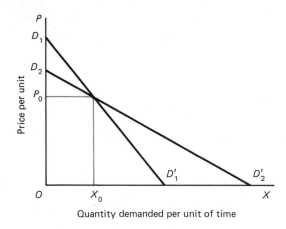

FIGURE 2–8   **Relative elasticities of two nonintersecting demand curves**

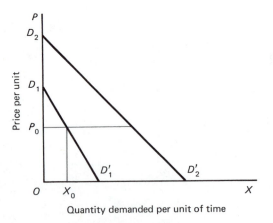

not the same as slope, it is possible to show, in this example, that the demand curve with the steeper slope is less elastic. It is a straightforward application of the geometric ratios for elasticity. By applying either formula, we see that D_1D_1' is less elastic for any price and quantity than D_2D_2'. For instance, let E_1 be the elasticity of the steep schedule and E_2 the elasticity of the flat demand schedule. Then at P_0, the intersection of the schedule,

$$E_1 = \frac{X_0D_1'}{OX_0} < \frac{X_0D_2'}{OX_0} = E_2 \qquad \text{or } E_1 = \frac{OP_0}{P_0D_1} < \frac{OP_0}{P_0D_2} = E_2.$$

You can pick any other point on the price or quantity axis and apply either formula to get the same result.

The curves in Figure 2–8 do not intersect nor are they necessarily parallel. By now, observation should tell us which curve is more elastic. At price P_0, for demand curve D_1D_1', $E_1 = OP_0/P_0D_1$, but for the curve D_2D_2', $E_2 = OP_0/P_0D_2$. The numerators are equal for both ratios, but the denominator is smaller for DD_1'. Hence, at any given price DD_1' is the more elastic schedule. As long as linear schedules do not share the same endpoints, the curve with the smaller quantity demanded at every price has the greater elasticity of demand. These results may be summarized by the following principle:

Principle
Slope is not elasticity; at any price, demand curves with different slopes may have the same elasticity, while curves with the same slope may have different elasticities.

Factors Affecting Demand Elasticity

Whether demand is elastic or inelastic is an important consideration in making government policy and business decisions. For example, if demand for wheat is elastic, an increase in the price of wheat would result in a proportionately greater reduction in quantity demanded. Farmers would obtain smaller total revenue from the sale of wheat. If the government established a minimum wheat price above the market equilibrium price, wheat sales would be reduced (as would farmers' incomes, unless the price support were accompanied by a minimum sales guarantee). On the other hand, if the demand for wheat is inelastic, as it probably is over the relevant range, a minimum price above the equilibrium price would increase farmers' total revenue.

Price elasticities can take a wide range of values. For any given demand curve, two basic factors determine price elasticity: the availability of good substitutes and the time period of adjustment. These factors are related: a long adjustment period gives consumers more time to shop for suitable substitutes in the event of a price increase. If the adjustment period is sufficiently long, substitutes can be developed when none was present earlier.

The more and better the substitutes for a specific good, the greater its price elasticity will be at a given set of prices. Goods with few and poor substitutes—wheat and salt, for example—will always tend to have low price elasticities. Goods with many substitutes (wool, for example, can be replaced by cotton and manmade fibers) will have higher elasticities.

Substitutability implies that there is a great deal of difference between the market elasticity of demand for a good and the elasticity of demand faced by one seller in the market. For example, if all of the gasoline stations in a city raised the price of gasoline five cents a gallon, total sales would undoubtedly fall off, but in the absence of close substitutes, probably not very much. If all of the Exxon stations—but no others—raised the price a nickel, the sales of Exxon gasoline would probably fall substantially. There are many good substitutes for one brand of gasoline at the lower price. If only one service station raised price, its sales in the long run would probably fall almost to zero. Some might continue buying there (perhaps the owner's close relatives), but the availability of so many easily accessible substitutes would encourage most customers to trade elsewhere, since the cost of finding a substitute service station is so small.

Time also affects the demand for a commodity. Consider the following example. Congress has recently passed legislation to deregulate the price of natural gas piped across state lines. Suppose the immediate effect of deregulation is an increase in the average price of a cubic foot of natural gas. What predictions would you make, using your knowledge of demand theory and information about the real world, on the effect higher prices will have on the quantity of natural gas demanded immediately after deregulation, and then after a rather long period of time, say two to five years?

We examine first the very near future, say within a year after deregulation. The theory of demand says that when the price of something increases, people demand less. In most cases, however, businesses and households already have their gas-using appliances and equipment installed. During a very short period of adjustment, households and businesses will respond by decreasing their use of natural gas, but it is difficult to quickly switch to an alternative fuel. We would expect the use of natural gas not to be particularly responsive to an increase in price.

Given a longer period of adjustment, users of natural gas can decrease consumption much more. Even though manufacturing plants that use gas are already built, some can convert to alternative fuel use. In the last 10 years, many industrial and utility boilers have, in fact, been designed to switch between two fuels. Households, with some time, can replace gas furnaces and air conditioners with electricity. Builders of new homes can insulate better. People can increase the insulation in older homes and install storm windows. In summary, if people think the price increase is permanent, the longer the time period that consumers have to adapt to a price change, the more elastic is the demand for the product. This adaptation can be in response to a price increase or decrease.

APPLICATION

Some Uses of Demand Elasticities in the Automobile Industry

Many important business and policy decisions require estimating demand elasticities. This application shows the value of such estimates in two contexts involving the automobile industry.

One obvious use of demand elasticity in decision making is forecasting changes in price from projected changes in quantity, or changes in quantity from projected changes in price. For example, at the request of the U.S. government, the Japanese government in the early 1980s limited the number of automobiles it exported to the United States. Certainly governmental policymakers wanted to predict the effect of the decreased imports on domestic automobile prices. Suppose the best estimate of the elasticity of demand for automobiles is approximately 1.5—a 1 percent increase in price leads to a 1.5 percent fall in quantity purchased. Suppose the percentage reduction from voluntary import restrictions was 9 percent. Assuming American manufacturers do not make up the difference, what would be the expected increase in the average price of automobiles? Using our definition of elasticity

$$E = -\frac{\%\Delta X}{\%\Delta P},$$

we can solve for

$$\%\Delta P = -\frac{\%\Delta X}{E} = \frac{.09}{1.5} \cong .06,$$

where the sign $\cong$ means "approximately equal to." This indicates that a 9 percent reduction in the number of new automobiles sold each year would cause a 6 percent increase in price. We know that American manufacturers will attempt to increase sales, so the 6 percent hike in real prices is an upper bound. If we multiply the dollar value of this 6 percent increase in price by the expected number of new cars sold, we would have an estimate of how much the import restrictions would cost consumers. Policymakers could use this estimate of cost to weigh against the perceived benefits of import restrictions.

Another historical example from the automobile industry illustrates a neglect of demand elasticities that might have jeopardized government policy. In a 1977 speech to the nation, President Jimmy Carter released his plan for energy conservation. One of the more important points of this plan was a large tax on the purchase of "gas guzzlers," automobiles that had low miles-per-gallon ratings. This was combined with a subsidy on the purchase of new automobiles that had miles-per-gallon ratings higher than a particular level. The plan was designed to raise the price of gas guzzlers and lower the price of small cars that are gas efficient. It was thought that this would, in the long run, effectively increase the average gasoline mileage of automobiles being driven in the United States and decrease gasoline consumption in the country. No one questioned this postulated effect for some time. In an article appearing in the May 23, 1977 issue of the *National Observer,* it was pointed out that, when relative demand elasticities are taken into account, the heavy tax on large cars combined with the subsidy on small cars could cause *more rather than less* gasoline to be consumed, even though the tax-subsidy scheme would increase the average gasoline mileage of cars on the road. The argument was based on the difference in demand elasticities for small cars and large cars. Most studies indicate that the demand for large, gas-inefficient cars is relatively inelastic, while the demand for small, gas-efficient cars is relatively elastic.

If this is the case, people would decrease their purchases of larger cars in response to the higher price as demand theory predicts. Potential Cadillac or Lincoln purchasers might step down a little in response to higher prices caused by taxes, but they would not move all the way down to subcompacts. If the demand for the large cars is not very elastic, even inelastic, the purchase of the larger cars would not fall much.

On the other hand, the subsidy on smaller cars would tend to lower their prices. If the demand for small cars is rather elastic, this lower price would cause a substantial increase in the purchase of small cars. People could be induced by the lower price to buy a second car. Some who previously used public transportation would be marginally induced to buy a car.

If the sales of the gas guzzlers did not decrease substantially, and the sales of small cars increased significantly, the *number* of cars on the road might increase even though the average gas mileage increased. More cars being driven, even with better gas mileages, might *increase rather than decrease the total gasoline consumption.* The issue is, of course, an empirical one and one we will never know the answer to since the 1977 tax and subsidy scheme never went into effect. The point we want to make here, however, is that the difference in relative demand elasticities should have at least been considered. That difference could make a policy designed to have one effect—conserving gasoline—have an entirely different effect—increasing the use of gasoline.

2.4 SUPPLY SCHEDULES

To gain an understanding of supply, suppose a large number of farmers sell cabbage in the same market. One particular farmer is willing to grow and sell 1,000 cabbages per season if the price per head of cabbage is 25 cents. If the price of cabbage were 35 cents, the farmer would grow more—say, 2,000 heads. The higher price induces the farmer to take land out of the cultivation of other crops and grow the more lucrative cabbage. A still higher price, 50 cents perhaps, would be required to induce 3,000 cabbages, and so on. The farmer allocates time and land to make as much money as possible. It naturally follows that higher prices are required to induce the farmer to reallocate more time and land to cabbage production.

A portion of the farmer's cabbage supply schedule might, therefore, be as follows:

Price	Quantity supplied
$0.25	1,000
.35	2,000
.50	3,000
.75	4,000
1.25	5,000

This table shows the *minimum price* that induces the farmer to supply each amount on the list. Note that, in contrast to demand analysis, where price and quantity demanded vary inversely, price and quantity supplied are directly related. We must postpone the explanation of this direct relation until Chapter 11, after we have analyzed cost and production. For the present, we assume that the supply schedule shows the minimum price necessary to induce producers to voluntarily offer each possible quantity for sale. We also assume that an increase in price is required to induce an increase in quantity supplied.

Just as the market demand schedule is the sum of the quantities demanded by all consumers, the market supply schedule shows the sum of the quantities that suppliers (firms) supply at each price. If all cabbage farmers had the same supply schedule as that shown in the table and there were 10,000 cabbage farmers, then 10 million heads would be supplied at 25 cents, 20 million at 35 cents, and so on. Our definition of supply is analogous to that of demand.

Definition

Supply is a list of prices and the quantities that a supplier or group of suppliers (firms) are willing and able to offer for sale at each price in the list per period of time.

TABLE 2–4   **Market supply schedule**

Quantity supplied (units)	Prices (dollars)
7,000	$6
6,500	5
6,000	4
4,500	3
3,000	2
1,000	1

FIGURE 2–9   **Market supply curve**

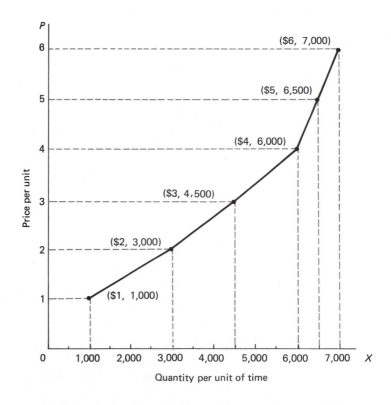

Graphing Supply Schedules

Consider the supply schedule in Table 2–4. This table shows the minimum price necessary to induce firms to supply, per unit of time, each of the six quantities listed. In order to induce greater quantities, price must rise, or, in other words, if price increases from $4 to $5, firms will increase quantity supplied from 6,000 units to 6,500 units. Remember that we are assuming a large number of competing firms; in the case of a single firm supplying the entire market, a different principle applies (shown in Chapter 13). Figure 2–9 shows a graph of the schedule in Table 2–4.

Factors Influencing Supply

As in the case of demand, we might ask why the supply schedule in Table 2–4 is what it is. Why, for example, does a price of $5 rather than a price of $4 induce a quantity supplied of 6,500? Why isn't a lower quantity supplied at each price in the list? A much more thorough discussion of supply is undertaken in Chapter 11. For now, we will only mention briefly four factors that affect supply. These are the factors generally held constant when drawing a supply curve.

First, technology is assumed to be unchanged. If a more efficient method of production is discovered, firms generally change the amounts they are willing to supply at each price. Second, the prices of factors of production are usually held constant. For example, a change in wage rates or in the prices of raw materials will change the supply curve. Third, the prices of related goods (in production) are held constant. If the price of corn rises while the price of wheat remains the same, some farmers will switch from growing wheat to growing corn, and less wheat will be supplied. Fourth, the expectations of producers are assumed not to change.

Changes in Supply

When price rises and firms are induced to offer a greater quantity of a good for sale, we say that *quantity supplied changes,* and in this case increases. When one or more of the factors mentioned above change, the entire schedule moves and firms are induced to offer more or less at each price on the schedule. In this case, *supply changes.* Consider Figure 2–10 in which S_0S_0' is the initial supply curve. If price falls from p to p', the quantity supplied decreases from x_0 to x_0', other things remaining the same. We have simply moved down the existing schedule. On the other hand, if technology changes and supply increases to S_2S_2', firms now wish to offer x_2 at price p, and they wish to offer more units for sale at each price in the entire range of prices. A shift from S_0S_0' to S_1S_1', in contrast,

FIGURE 2–10   **Shifts in supply**

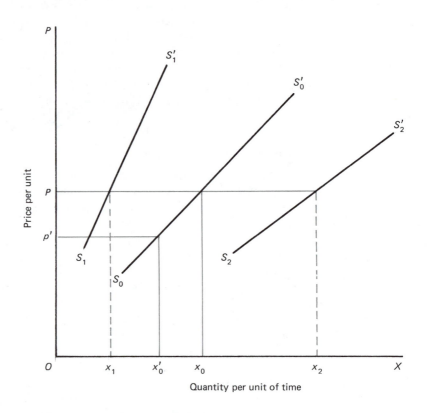

indicates a decrease in supply, and firms then wish to offer less for sale at each price.

Relation

When price rises (falls), other things remaining the same, quantity supplied rises (falls). When something that was held constant in deriving supply changes, for example the prices of inputs or technology, supply increases or decreases. If firms are induced to offer more (less) at each price, supply has increased (decreased).

2.5 SUPPLY ELASTICITY

As in demand, the coefficient of supply elasticity measures the relative responsiveness of quantity supplied to changes in price *along a given supply schedule*. The computation technique is essentially the same as that used for demand elasticity.

Computation

The coefficient of supply elasticity is defined as

$$E_s = \frac{\Delta X/X}{\Delta P/P} = \frac{\Delta X}{\Delta P} \cdot \frac{P}{X},$$

where ΔX is the change in quantity supplied, ΔP is the change in price, and P and X are price and quantity supplied. Since X and P are assumed to change in the same direction, that is, if P falls (rises), quantity supplied falls (rises), the term E_s is always a positive number. Similar to demand, supply curves can be elastic, unitary, and inelastic. If the percentage change in quantity supplied exceeds the percentage change in price, supply is elastic and $E_s > 1$. If the two percentages are equal, supply has unitary elasticity and $E_s = 1$. If the percentage change in price exceeds the percentage change in quantity, supply is inelastic, and $E_s < 1$.

The more elastic is supply, the more responsive is quantity supplied to price changes. This tells us something about the shape of a supply schedule. If E_s is large, the supply curve will be a relatively horizontal schedule, and as the curve becomes perfectly horizontal, the coefficient will approach infinity. A small E_s indicates the supply curve is steep, and as the curve becomes vertical, the coefficient gets closer to zero. Table 2–5 shows the elasticity of supply for the schedule illustrated in Figure 2–9, based on Table 2–4. The elasticities shown have been calculated by using the average quantity and price to determine the percentage changes between two points. For example, when the price changes from $6 to $5, the elasticity of supply is

$$E_s = \frac{7{,}000 - 6{,}500}{(7{,}000 + 6{,}500)/2} \div \frac{\$6 - \$5}{(\$5 + \$6)/2} = .41.$$

As we move down the supply schedule elasticity increases, and goes from being inelastic to unitary and then elastic. In Figure 2–9 this corresponds to the schedule becoming increasingly flat as price gets lower. Elasticity of supply is thus a summary measure of a curve's shape. It is important to mention that, unlike demand, we cannot relate elasticity of

TABLE 2–5   **Supply and elasticity**

Quantity supplied	Price	Elasticity
7,000	$6	.41
6,500	5	.36
6,000	4	1.00
4,500	3	1.00
3,000	2	1.50
1,000	1	

FIGURE 2–11   **Calculating supply elasticity**

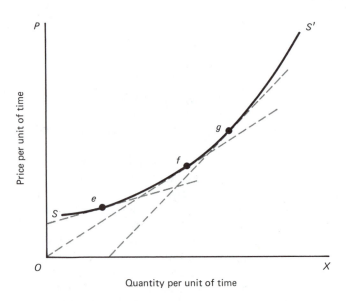

supply to the change in revenue. After all, price and quantity vary directly. An increase in price increases quantity supplied and, hence, increases revenue at that price and quantity whether supply is elastic or inelastic.

Geometrically, it is possible to tell whether a supply curve at a certain point is elastic, inelastic, or unitary at a glance. Consider the curve in Figure 2–11, with points $e, f,$ and g along the corresponding tangent lines at each point. For any point on a supply curve, if the tangent line intersects the vertical axis above the origin, supply is elastic at that point; if it passes through the origin, it has unitary elasticity; and if it cuts the horizontal axis, supply is inelastic.[1] We can see from Figure 2–11 without

---

[1] Proof: Each of the tangent lines in Figure 2–11 is of the form $P = b + aX$. For such linear forms, the slope, $\Delta P/\Delta X$, is "a" and the intercept is "b." If we divide both sides of the linear equation by X, after rearranging the order of terms we get:

$$\frac{P}{X} = a + \frac{b}{X}$$

Since the elasticity of the supply curve at each point approximately equals the elasticity of the tangent at that point, this information helps us determine the elasticity of the supply curve. Observe for a positive supply slope ($a > 0$):

$$E_s = \frac{\Delta X}{\Delta P}\frac{P}{X} = \frac{1}{\Delta P/\Delta X}\frac{P}{X} = \frac{1}{a}\left(a + \frac{b}{X}\right) = 1 + \frac{b}{aX}.$$

(cont.)

any computation, that e is a point with elastic supply, point f is unitary elasticity, and g describes a point on the supply schedule that is inelastic.

Determinants of Supply Elasticity

The responsiveness of quantity supplied to changes in price depends, in a very large measure, on the ease with which resources can be drawn into the production of the good in question, in the case of a price increase, or withdrawn from production of that good and attracted into production of other goods, in the case of a price decrease. If additional quantities can be produced only at much higher costs, then a very large increase in price is needed to induce much more quantity supplied. In these cases, supply is rather inelastic. On the other hand, if more can be produced at a very small increase in cost, quantity supplied is quite responsive to price changes, and supply is rather elastic. To summarize, suppose the price of a particular good increases. If the resources used to produce that good are readily accessible, in the sense that more of the resources can be purchased without substantially increasing their prices, and if production can be increased easily, supply would be more elastic than would be the case if the additional resources are obtainable only at sharply increasing prices. For a price decrease, elasticity depends on how rapidly resources can be released from production of the good in question and moved into the production of other goods.

One can also think of the elasticity of the supply of people to an occupation. For some occupations, a small increase in the average wage or salary induces rapid entry into that occupation. Thus, supply is elastic if entry is easy. For other occupations, the supply is more inelastic because entry is induced only at a much higher wage. The elasticity of persons to an occupation depends on how easily people can enter the occupation after a wage increase and how willing they are to enter that occupation. In the case of wage decreases, elasticity depends on how rapidly people leave the occupation.

The length of the adjustment period is a crucial determinant of supply elasticity, either in the case of goods and services, or entrants into an occupation. Clearly, if suppliers have more time to adapt to a change in price, the quantity supplied is more responsive, and supply is more elastic. Over a very short period of time, supply is generally quite inelastic.

Economists frequently distinguish between momentary, short-run, and

---

At point e in Figure 2–11 the intercept, b, is positive, thus $E_s = 1 + (b/a)X > 0$ and the supply curve is elastic. More generally, if the tangent at a point intersects the vertical axis, supply is elastic at that point. If we knew "a" and "b", we could even estimate the elasticity. At point f, $b = 0$, so $E_s = 1$. If the tangent line goes through the origin, we know the elasticity of supply is unitary. Finally, at point g, the intercept is negative for the tangent line and $E_s < 1$, and a tangent cutting the horizontal axis means the supply curve is inelastic.

FIGURE 2–12   **Effect of time of adjustment on supply elasticity**

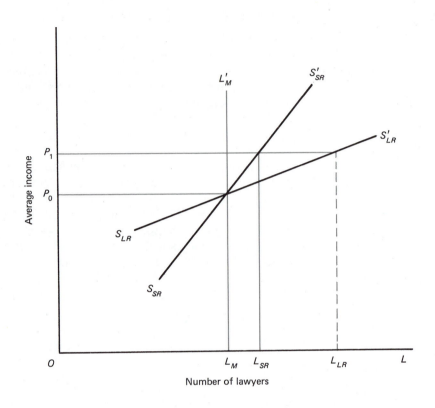

long-run supply elasticity. For example, consider the supply of lawyers. Three supply curves for lawyers are shown in Figure 2–12. $L_M L'_M$ is the momentary supply of lawyers. At any moment, there are L_M lawyers, and this number cannot be instantaneously changed. Suppose the average income of lawyers rises from p_0 to p_1. At that moment, or over a very short period of time, the number of lawyers cannot be increased. Since quantity does not respond at all, the vertical supply curve $L_M L'_M$ is infinitely inelastic.

Within a reasonably short period of time, however, the increase in the average income of lawyers will induce an increase in the number of lawyers, perhaps from L_M to L_{SR}. The increase in income will induce some retired lawyers to begin practice again, and some business people with law degrees will be induced to leave their companies and enter practice. The resulting short-run supply curve is $S_{SR}S'_{SR}$, the supply curve when a reasonably short period of adjustment is permitted. This curve is more elastic than is $L_M L'_M$ because, when some adjustment time is permitted, quantity supplied is more responsive to price changes.

The long-run supply curve is $S_{LR} S'_{LR}$, which allows sufficient time for *all* adjustments to be made. (We shall define short run and long run more precisely in Chapter 8.) In our example, higher average incomes will induce more college graduates to enter law school, and the period of adjustment is long enough to permit them to begin practicing law. Alternatively, if average income declines relative to those of other professions requiring similar periods of training, the number of lawyers will decline appreciably. The long-run supply curve $S_{LR} S'_{LR}$ is more elastic than is $S_{SR} S'_{SR}$ because quantity is more responsive to price when sufficient adjustment time is permitted.

2.6 MARKET DETERMINATION OF PRICE AND QUANTITY

The study of supply and demand prepares us to analyze their interaction, which determines market price and quantity. A primary reason for separating them is to isolate the factors that determine each so that we can analyze the market effects of changing these factors. In this section we combine the supply and demand curves and examine their interaction in the market.

Equilibrium

Suppose that in the market for a good, demanders and suppliers have the particular schedules set forth in Tables 2–1 and 2–4, respectively. These schedules are combined in Table 2–6. An auctioneer, who does not know the schedules, is assigned the task of finding a price that clears the market; a price where quantity demanded equals quantity supplied. The auctioneer does not know the market-clearing price since the schedules change from time to time. The auctioneer begins by picking some price at

TABLE 2–6 **Market demand and supply**

Price	Quantity supplied	Quantity demanded	Excess supply ($+$) or demand ($-$)
$6	7,000	1,000	$+6,000$
5	6,500	1,500	$+5,000$
4	6,000	2,500	$+3,500$
3	4,500	4,500	0
2	3,000	7,000	$-4,000$
1	1,000	9,000	$-8,000$

random and announcing this price to the demanders and suppliers, who then tell him the amounts they wish to purchase or sell at that price. The first price chosen may or may not clear the market. If it does, exchange takes place. If not, the auctioneer must choose another price but this time he does not proceed purely at random.

The auctioneer knows from experience that, if quantity demanded exceeds quantity supplied (we call this situation excess demand), an increase in price will cause quantity demanded to decrease and quantity supplied to increase; that is, excess demand will decrease when price rises. The auctioneer also knows that, if quantity supplied exceeds quantity demanded (called excess supply), a reduction in price causes a reduction in quantity supplied and an increase in quantity demanded; that is, a price reduction reduces excess supply.

Suppose the first price chosen is $5 and 1,500 units are demanded. If 6,500 units are offered for sale, there is an excess supply of 5,000 units at that price. To reduce excess supply, the auctioneer reduces the price to $1. Since consumers demand 9,000 and producers are willing to supply only 1,000, excess demand is 8,000. The auctioneer raises the price to $4, and quantity supplied exceeds quantity demanded by 3,500. He therefore reduces the price to $3. Quantity demanded equals quantity supplied, and the market is cleared. The equilibrium price and quantity are $3 and 4,500 units.

We can also express the equilibrium solution graphically. In Figure 2–13, DD' and SS' are the market demand and supply curves. (These are not graphs of the schedules in Table 2–6.) It is clear that p_e and x_e are the market-clearing, or equilibrium, price and quantity. Only at p_e does quantity demanded equal quantity supplied. In this model, we don't need the auctioneer. Consumers and producers themselves bid the price up or down if the market is not in equilibrium.

Suppose price happens to be $\bar{p}$, greater than p_e. At $\bar{p}$, producers supply $\bar{x}_s$, but only $\bar{x}_d$ is demanded. An excess supply of $\bar{x}_d\bar{x}_s$ develops. This surplus accumulates for the producers, and producers are induced to lower price to keep from accumulating unwanted surpluses. (This is the same thing our auctioneer would have done.) Note that at any price above p_e, there is an excess supply, and producers will lower price. On the other hand, suppose price is $\hat{p}$. Demanders are willing and able to purchase $\hat{x}_d$, while suppliers are only willing to offer $\hat{x}_s$ units for sale. Some consumers are not satisfied, and there is an excess demand of $\hat{x}_s\hat{x}_d$ in the market. Since their demands are not satisfied, consumers bid the price up. Again, this is what our auctioneer would have done if a shortage existed. As consumers continue to bid up the price, quantity demanded decreases and quantity supplied increases until price reaches p_e and quantity is x_e. Any price below p_e causes a shortage, and the shortage causes consumers to bid up the price. Given no outside influences that prevent price from

FIGURE 2–13   **Market equilibrium**

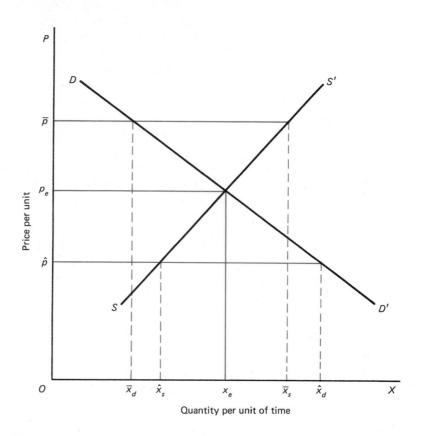

being bid up or down, an equilibrium price and quantity are attained. This equilibrium price is the price that clears the market, and both excess demand and excess supply are zero in equilibrium. Equilibrium is attained in the market because of the following:

Principle

When price is above the equilibrium price, quantity supplied exceeds quantity demanded. The resulting excess supply induces sellers to reduce price in order to sell the surplus. If price is below equilibrium, quantity demanded exceeds quantity supplied. The resulting excess demand causes the unsatisfied consumers to bid up price. Since prices below equilibrium are bid up by consumers and prices above equilibrium are lowered by producers, the market will converge at the equilibrium price-quantity combination.

Demand and Supply Shifts

So long as the determinants of demand and supply do not change, the price-quantity equilibrium described above will not change. Before finishing our study of the market, we must see how this equilibrium is disturbed when there are changes in one or more of the factors held constant in deriving demand and supply.

A bit of intuitive reasoning may ease the transition to the complicated graphical analysis that follows. Consider the career you plan after graduation. Suppose you plan to become an economist, and prior to your graduation, Congress passes a law requiring that everyone who buys a share of stock or a bond must, for protection, consult with an economist. Would this law please you? Why, or why not? Does it seem logical that economists' salaries would rise after this law is passed? People now must consult economists when previously they did not have to. How could they bid away the necessary economists from jobs in academics or government? They would do so simply by offering higher salaries. Before long, economists' salaries would rise since universities, government, and businesses must meet the increasing bids of potential investors. Or, in terms developed in this chapter, the demand for economists rises. With a given supply of economists, salaries must rise. Of course, after a while, the higher salaries may lure others into the profession and drive salaries back down again.

Consider another example. Does a cotton farmer bringing his crop to

FIGURE 2–14   **Changes in equilibrium prices and quantities**

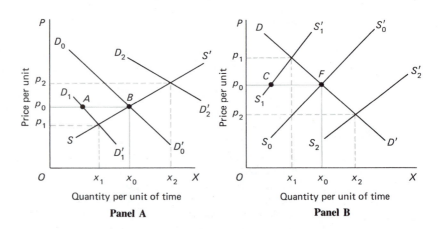

Panel A

Panel B

market want a large or small amount of cotton marketed at the same time? Obviously, a small amount because if a large amount of cotton is available, the price of cotton will be lower. It should be clear that, with a given demand, the greater the supply, the greater will be the quantity sold—but the lower the price will be. The greater the demand—for economists, cotton, or anything else—the greater both *quantity* and *price* will be. These relations can be refined by the following graphical analysis.

In Panel A, Figure 2-14, p_0 and x_0 are the equilibrium price and quantity when demand and supply are $D_0 D_0'$ and SS'. Suppose income falls and demand decreases to $D_1 D_1'$. At p_0, quantity supplied exceeds the new quantity demanded by AB, that is, excess supply at p_0 is AB. Faced with this surplus, sellers reduce price until the new equilibrium is reached at p_1 and x_1. Now, suppose the price of some substitute good increases so that demand increases to $D_2 D_2'$. At price p_1, quantity demanded far exceeds quantity supplied, and a shortage occurs. The excess demand causes consumers to bid the price up until the new equilibrium at p_2 and x_2 is reached. We can see that, if supply remains fixed and demand decreases, quantity and price both fall; if demand increases, price and quantity both rise. This direct relation between price and quantity would be expected since the movements take place *along* the supply curve, which is positively sloped.

Panel B, Figure 2-14, shows what happens to price and quantity when demand remains constant and supply shifts. Let demand be DD' and supply $S_0 S_0'$. The original equilibrium occurs at price p_0 and quantity x_0. Now, let input prices rise so that supply decreases to $S_1 S_1'$. The shortage of CF at p_0 causes consumers to bid up price until equilibrium is reached at p_1 and x_1. Now, let technology improve so that supply increases to $S_2 S_2'$. The surplus at p_1 causes producers to lower price. Equilibrium occurs at p_2 and x_2. If demand remains constant and supply decreases, price rises and quantity falls; if supply increases, price falls and quantity increases. This inverse relation is expected, since in Panel B, Figure 2-14, the movement is *along* a negatively sloped demand curve.

The direction of change is not always immediately apparent when both supply and demand change simultaneously. In Panel A, Figure 2-15, $D_0 D_0'$ and $S_0 S_0'$ are the initial demand and supply curves. Their intersection determines the equilibrium price and quantity, p_0 and x_0. Now, suppose supply increases to $S_1 S_1'$ and demand increases to $D_1 D_1'$; price rises to p_1, and quantity rises to x_1. While quantity always increases when both demand and supply increase, price may increase, decrease, or even remain the same. Suppose supply shifts to $S_1 S_1'$, but demand shifts only to the position indicated by the dashed demand curve crossing $S_1 S_1'$ at A. With this shift, quantity still rises (although by a lesser amount), but price falls to p_2. Furthermore, by constructing the change in supply or demand still differently, we can cause price to remain at p_0 while quantity increases.

FIGURE 2–15   **Effects of supply and demand shifts**

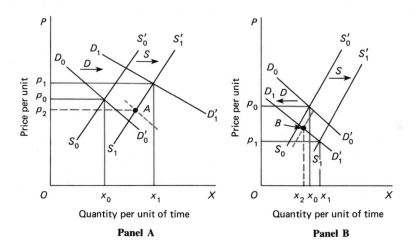

Panel A   **Panel B**

To see the effect of a decrease in both supply and demand, consider D_1D_1' and S_1S_1' in Panel A as the original schedules. Next, let them both decrease to D_0D_0' and S_0S_0'. Quantity and price decrease from x_1 and p_1 to x_0 and p_0. While quantity always decreases when both curves decrease, price need not fall.

Panel B, Figure 2–15, shows the effect of an increase in one curve accompanied by a decrease in the other. Let supply *increase* from S_0S_0' to S_1S_1', and let demand *decrease* from D_0D_0' to D_1D_1'. Price falls from p_0 to p_1 and quantity rises from x_0 to x_1. While price *must* fall when supply increases and demand decreases, quantity need not increase. Suppose that, while demand went to D_1D_1', supply increased only to the position indicated by the dashed line crossing D_1D_1' at B. The new equilibrium entails a price reduction (although not so large as before), but now quantity decreases to x_2 rather than rising to x_1. To see the effect of a decrease in supply accompanied by an increase in demand, simply assume that demand shifts from D_1D_1' to D_0D_0' and supply from S_1S_1' to S_0S_0'. Price must rise. In this illustration, quantity decreases, but depending on the size of the shifts in the curves, quantity may change in either direction. In summary:

Principle

(1) When demand increases (decreases), and supply remains constant, both price and quantity increase (decrease). (2) When supply increases (decreases), and demand remains constant, price falls (rises) and quantity rises (falls).

(3) When both demand and supply increase (decrease) quantity increases (decreases), but price can either increase or decrease, depending on the relative magnitude of the shifts. (4) When supply and demand shift in opposite directions, the change in quantity is indeterminant, but price always changes in the same direction as the shift in demand.

APPLICATION

An Unexpected Recovery in Housing

From mid-1982 until fall 1983 the housing industry experienced a substantial expansion in sales, an expansion that was expected by very few observers prior to the recovery. Lindey H. Clark, Jr., in his column "Speaking of Business," in *The Wall Street Journal* of August 9, 1983, described the housing situation that had existed in July 1982, just prior to the recovery.[2]

According to Mr. Clark, in 10 out of the 11 preceding months, housing starts had been below 1 million. In only seven months over the previous 30 years had housing starts been so low. Indeed, Congress was debating legislation to save the ailing building industry.

Moreover, Mr. Clark noted that, in July 1982, the savings and loan industry was practically "on the brink of extinction." Interest rates had exploded in 1979, and about 500 S & Ls had disappeared. They were carrying portfolios of loans at 10 percent interest rates and were having to borrow at much higher rates.

But in spite of all the adversity, housing began to expand in the late summer of 1982. What happened? Were there changes occurring in the economy that would have permitted people to forecast the housing boom and to profit from their knowledge? As it turned out, there were such changes; and some people did profit from the knowledge.

Writing a year after the expansion began, Mr. Clark cited several of these changes that had begun in mid-1982: (1) In response to monetary policy, interest rates had begun to decline. Since most homes are financed by borrowing, this decrease in interest rates, particularly mortgage rates, reduced the cost of financing a home. (2) The economy was beginning to recover from an extremely severe recession. Since many people had postponed purchasing a home during the recession there was a great deal of pent up demand for housing. (3) Inflation was slowing down appreciably, and people were beginning to believe that the purchasing power of their income was not going to continue to be eroded by increases in the

---

[2] Reprinted by permission of *The Wall Street Journal.* © Dow Jones & Company, Inc. 1983. All rights reserved.

cost of living. (4) The housing recovery was reinforced by declining house prices.

Since we know that supply and demand determine both price and quantity sold in a market, what can we say about the effect of these changes on the demand and supply of housing? Let's translate the changes in the housing market noted by Mr. Clark into shifts in the demand for and supply of housing. In Figure 2–16, let the quantity of housing (possibly new housing) in a particular area be measured along the horizontal axis and the price per unit on the vertical. We denote the original (i.e., 1982) demand and supply for housing as respectively D_0D_0' and S_0S_0'. The price and quantity per period prior to the recovery are therefore p_0 and x_0.

Now we can isolate the effects of the changes mentioned by Clark to see what happened. First consider the decline in interest rates. This change would probably affect both demand and supply. In the case of

FIGURE 2–16   **Recovery in the housing market**

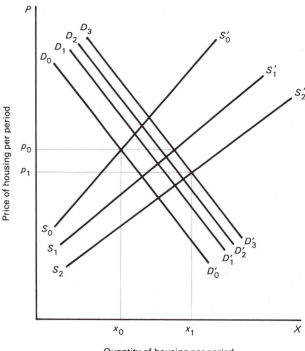

Quantity of housing per period

demand, the decline in interest rates (more specifically mortgage interest rates) made it easier for some people to obtain mortgage loans. Since most people do not pay cash for a house, they purchase the home and the financing together. As home mortgages decrease in price or become easier to obtain, the demand for housing should increase. We illustrate this effect in Figure 2–16 as a shift in demand from D_0D_0' to D_1D_1'. This shift by itself would have the effect of increasing both the price and the quantity sold of housing. In the case of supply, the decrease in interest rates would lower the price of inputs used in the production (construction) of new houses. Builders find that it is cheaper to borrow funds to finance construction projects and purchase new capital equipment. As the builders' costs of acquiring physical or money capital declined, the price of inputs would fall and supply would be expected to increase. This effect is illustrated as the shift from S_0S_0' to S_1S_1'.

We would expect the economic recovery, along with the large reduction in the rate of inflation, to affect demand. The real income of potential purchasers would increase and would result in an increase in the demand for housing. In Figure 2–16 we show the increase in demand resulting from the increase in real income as the shift from D_1D_1' to D_2D_2'.

Finally, on the demand side, Clark refers to the "pent up demand for housing." This must mean that potential purchasers put off buying homes when economic conditions were bad, not knowing how long the recession would last. The recovery, if Clark is correct, must have changed people's expectations about future economic conditions. As expectations concerning the future improved, people who had postponed buying houses began to purchase under the expectation of higher real income in the future. We show the effect of improved expectations as the shift from D_2D_2' to D_3D_3'.

As we have drawn in Figure 2–16, the effect of shifting demand to D_3D_3' and supply to S_1S_1' would have increased the quantity of housing sold, while keeping the price the same. But Clark noted that the increase in housing purchases was due to a fall in housing prices. Unless the shift from S_0S_0' to S_1S_1' was greater than we have shown, something else must have occurred to increase supply even further. This shift could have occurred because of a change in expectations by suppliers.

It is generally recognized that housing is almost always one of the first industries to recover as the economy pulls out of a recession. Clark noted this fact in his article. Builders must have recognized this also. As the recovery began they would have changed their expectations about future housing demand. Thus, improved expectations about the future would have increased the supply of housing, shown in Figure 2–16 as the shift from S_1S_1' to S_2S_2'.

While many other forces were at work at the time, those we have isolated are probably the most important—improved expectations about the future, reduced interest rates, and higher real income. In our figure, the new equilibrium occurs at the intersection of D_3D_3' and S_2S_2'. The quantity of housing sold per period increases to x_1 and the price falls slightly from p_0 to p_1. All of the forces we have isolated would have had the effect of increasing quantity sold. In Figure 2–16 we showed a small decrease in price; but since both demand and supply increased, price could have remained constant or even risen, depending on the relative strength of the shifts in supply and demand. We drew our figure to be consistent with Clark's discussion of the decline in housing prices.

2.7 SUMMARY

Demand is a list of prices and of the corresponding quantities that consumers are willing and able to buy at each price. Quantity demanded varies inversely with price. The entire demand schedule changes when something held constant in deriving demand changes. Among these are income, tastes, the prices of other goods, and expectations.

Demand elasticity measures the responsiveness of quantity demanded to price changes. The more (less) responsive quantity demanded is to price, the more elastic (inelastic) is demand. An increase in price causes total revenue to increase if demand is inelastic and to decrease if demand is elastic. The effects are opposite for a price decrease. In case of unitary elasticity, there is no change in total revenue for a change in price. Elasticity is affected by the availability of substitutes and adjustment time.

Supply is the list of prices and the corresponding quantity that will be supplied at each price on the list. Changes in technology, the price of inputs, and the prices of related (in production) goods will shift the entire schedule. Supply elasticity measures the responsiveness of quantity supplied to changes in price. The time period of adjustment is one of the principal determinants of elasticity.

When price in a market is such that quantity demanded equals quantity supplied, the market is in equilibrium. Prices below equilibrium cause excess demand (or a shortage). If prices are not artificially fixed, they will be bid up. Prices above equilibrium cause excess supply (or a surplus). If prices are not fixed, they will be bid down. When supply and demand change, equilibrium price and quantity will change.

Every day, economists use simple demand and supply analysis to solve complex problems and to answer questions dealing with these curves. However, one must be careful about deciding how these underlying factors affect market price and output. In the next chapter, we apply the model of supply and demand in selected market problems. We do this to gain more familiarity with the model and to extend the theory in certain directions.

In all cases there are two fundamental concepts to remember. First, on the demand side of the market, when the price of something falls, more is taken; when the price of something rises, less is taken. Second, for supply, as prices rise, more will be offered for sale; when prices fall, less will be offered. The supply curve is a schedule of *minimum* prices necessary to produce any particular quantity.

TECHNICAL PROBLEMS

1. In Table 2–3, compute $\overline{E}$ for a change in price from \$.25 to \$.10 and from \$.50 to \$.25. Use the arc elasticity formula.

2. Assume the following demand and supply functions:

$$X_d = 60 - 2P$$
$$X_s = -12 + 4P$$

   a. Plot these functions on a graph.
   b. What are the equilibrium price and quantity?
   c. Supply shifts to

$$X_s = -24 + 4P$$

   What are the new equilibrium price and quantity?

3. The following are the demand and supply functions for a hypothetical product

$$X_d = -.6P + 8$$
$$X_s = .4P - 2.0$$

   a. Plot these functions on a graph.
   b. Find the equilibrium price.
   c. Calculate the elasticity of demand and supply at the equilibrium.
   d. At what price and quantity is the demand elasticity equal to 1?

4. Given a supply curve defined by the equation $X = 4P - 20$,
   a. Draw the supply curve.
   b. Calculate the point elasticity of supply at $P = 10$.
   c. What happens to elasticity of supply along this supply curve as the price rises? Derive a general expression relating the elasticity of this supply schedule to the price of the product.

5. "I earn \$20 a week and spend it all on beer no matter what the price of beer is." Exactly what is this person's elasticity of demand for beer?

6. "Federal officials would be quite happy if severe weather reduced the size of the (1980 grain) crop," says Russel Arndt, president of the National Corn Growers' Association. "The pickup in price would bail (farmers) out." (*Business Week*, July 21, 1980.) If Mr.

Arndt means a rise in income would bail farmers out, what must be true about the elasticity of demand for grain?

7. Casio, a large Japanese watchmaker, aims to win market share by slashing prices to the bone. This spring, Casio unwrapped its new F–7 model, which retails for $15.75. "Our average revenue may be going down, but the increase in volume compensates for that," claims Kazno Kashio, executive managing director at Casio. What can an economist say about the elasticity of Casio's demand schedule? As Casio's market share increases at any price, explain what happens to demand elasticity.

8. Seltzer Company sells spring water at a desert oasis, its costs are virtually zero. Seltzer knows that its demand function is $X_d = 25 - (3/2)P$. Presently, it charges a price of $2 per gallon of water. You are hired as a consultant to help Seltzer maximize total revenue. Do you recommend a price change? If so, calculate and explain at what price the firm ought to sell its water.

9. Suppose the demand schedule for umbrellas is $X_d = 50 - (4/5)P$, where X_d is the quantity demanded in millions of umbrellas and P is price in dollars per umbrella. Calculate the price elasticity of demand for umbrellas. If you have trouble, what piece of information is missing? Can you show that you need to know more?

10. Draw a typical supply and demand diagram showing equilibrium price and quantity. Now illustrate how the effects of each of the following could be shown in such a diagram.
    a. An increase in consumer income.
    b. An improvement in technology.
    c. A decrease in the price of a product buyers regard as a close substitute for this one.

11. Derive a general expression for price elasticity of demand in terms of X for the following demand schedule: $X = 100 - 5P$.

12. An athletic director at a college recently raised ticket prices form $12 to $15 per game. Sales went down 8 percent. The director said ". . . with the 25 percent increase in ticket prices, dollar volume has increased about 16 percent." Is this claim consistent with what you know about demand elasticity? Find the elasticity of demand in this case, assuming the demand schedule is stable.

ANALYTICAL PROBLEMS

1. Suppose that a disease attacks the nation's beef cattle but has no effect on its pork production. What effect will this have on:
    a. The market supply curve for pork?
    b. The market demand curve for pork?
    c. The equilibrium price of pork?

2. Manufacturers expect to sell 15 percent more color televisions in 1986 than 1985. Growth rates in sales look even better in the years ahead. What are some of the reasons for improved sales? Consider
   a. Videocassette recorders.
   b. Home computers.
   c. Cable television.
   d. Pay TV (e.g., HBO and Showtime).
   e. Stereo television.

3. An urban researcher collects data on wages across urban areas. Adjusting for labor quality, the data indicate that average real wages per worker are systematically higher in large cities than in small cities. Suggest *two* alternative explanations as to why average wages for labor would be higher in large than in small cities.

4. Can a price clear the market in the sense that sellers sell everything they offer and the market still not be in equilibrium?

5. Why can't we use the slope of a demand curve as an equivalent to price elasticity of demand? Why would a linear demand curve not have a constant price elasticity of demand?

6. Even though the market demand schedule for a product may have a low price elasticity, an individual producer of that product may find itself confronted with a highly elastic demand schedule for its own output. How is this possible?

7. Distinguish between a change in demand and a movement along a given demand schedule. Explain the chief causes of each. Now distinguish between a change in supply and a movement along a given supply schedule. Explain the chief causes of each.

8. Evaluate the following comment in a letter to Ann Landers using supply and demand schedules.

   I am a hairdresser who wishes to speak my piece. My remarks are for the women who think they are paying too much for a haircut, and those who try to save money by cutting their own hair. The reason haircuts are rather costly these days is because so many people are cutting their own hair and others wait three months between haircuts. [*Dallas Morning News*, January 17, 1985, p. 83.]

   Does the statement make sense?

9. According to recent studies at M.I.T. and the University of Michigan, a 10 percent increase in the price of cigarettes leads to a 14 percent drop in sales to teenagers. What is the elasticity of demand for cigarettes among teenagers? Would you expect it to be this high for older smokers? Explain your answer.

10. Suppose you are looking for a place to park your car in the business district of a large city. Parking is a problem. You see two lots across

the street from each other. One charges $3.50 per hour to park and the other $4.00 per hour.

    a.   What are some possible explanations for the price differences observed?

    b.   Do the lots provide the same service?

    c.   Does the absence of one ''market-clearing'' price imply that the parking market is not in equilibrium?

11. Between August of 1979 and August of 1981, the price of housing rose approximately 18 percent, while money income rose only 14 percent. Interest rates for mortgage loans during the same period rose from 10 percent to roughly 15 percent. Payments on a $60,000, 30-year mortgage went from $526.54 to $895.23 per month, a 70 percent increase. Given this information, what would you expect happened to

    a.   The demand for owner-occupied housing?

    b.   The size of houses built during this period?

    c.   The demand for rental housing?

    d.   The demand for household appliances?

12. It is illegal to carry handguns in many states. In New York anyone found with a handgun is sentenced to a mandatory one-year jail term. There is still a black market for guns. Is the price of guns higher or lower in states where they are outlawed? Explain your answer.

Chapter 3

Supply and Demand Analysis

3.1 INTRODUCTION

Now that we have discussed the basic theoretical concepts of supply and demand, we want to spend some time discussing how these tools are useful to decision makers of all types. We will apply our understanding of how markets work to some broad economic problems to extend and improve our understanding of markets.

As we work through the sections of this chapter, a theme will become evident. Markets work best when they are allowed to find their equilibrium at the intersection of the supply and demand curve. Frequently this equilibrium is impeded. We will discuss some of the causes here and return to the notion of market failure in Chapters 18 and 19 after discussing imperfect competition. In general, markets are prevented from finding their natural equilibrium when prices are fixed either above or below the price determined by the intersection of supply and demand. Usually the fixing is done in order to transfer income. This is indeed the goal, for example, of price supports to farmers.

Government intervention in markets is not the only influence that makes prices and quantities diverge from what they otherwise would be. There sometimes exist conditions within markets that also effectively transfer income. Monopoly is a kind of market structure where one seller seeks to transfer income from buyers to the seller. In monopoly markets, prices diverge away from the equilibrium in much the same way as when there is government intervention. Prices are higher and the quantity sold less than would be the case if supply and demand were allowed to freely interact. A full analysis of monopoly will be set forth in Chapter 13, but keep in mind that government intervention is not the only cause of divergence from the market equilibrium.

3.2 SUPPLY AND DEMAND IN REAL MARKETS

Some students may question the relevance of demand and supply analysis to real-world problems. What if sellers do not know the demand or the supply schedules? In fact, do they even know what demand and supply are? It may be useful to show how demand and supply determine price and allocate output in the absence of perfect knowledge about the schedules.

Prices have two social functions: They are a rationing device among consumers of the product, and they serve as an inducement for producers to produce more or less of a product. High prices restrict consumption to those who have a willingness and ability to pay a price at least equal to the going price. For the producer, since supply is upward sloping, a higher price causes more to be produced; a lower price causes less to be produced. An example should help give us a better idea of how prices allocate goods and services and control production.

Prices in Markets

Suppose that all newspapers print a scientific report stating that eating rhubarb makes people more healthy. Now we know that the demand for rhubarb will increase. But perhaps some grocers who have not read Chapter 2 do not know this. How does the market allocate under these conditions?

First, consider what happens to the stock of rhubarb in the grocery stores. Assuming that demand increases, grocers find that what had previously been a week's supply of rhubarb at the established price now lasts only until Thursday morning. Customers complain that they cannot get rhubarb. We can use demand analysis to examine the situation *even though buyers and sellers are completely unaware of demand and supply curves.*

Panel A, Figure 3–1, shows what happens in the retail market. Price is p_r, and x_r per week is the rate of sales when demand is D_r^0. Demand increases to D_r^1. At p_r, consumers now want x_r' units per week. Grocery stores consequently run out of rhubarb before the week is over. The profitable thing for grocers to do is order more rhubarb from wholesalers. When they do, the wholesalers sell more rhubarb and their stocks begin to run low. This is shown in Panel B. The original demand is D_w^0; this is the demand by grocers for wholesale rhubarb. When demand at retail increases, demand at wholesale also increases. Before the shift in demand, retail grocers wanted x_w at a wholesale price of p_w; they now want x_w'.

As their inventories run low, wholesalers instruct their buyers in the farm market to buy more rhubarb. At any one time, however, there is a limit to the amount of rhubarb available. Therefore, as the buyers try to

FIGURE 3–1   **Supply and demand analysis of real markets**

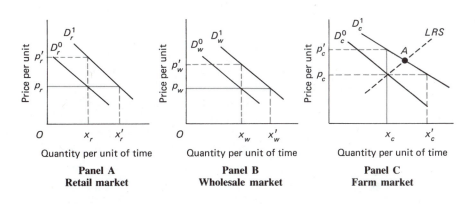

Panel A	Panel B	Panel C
Retail market	**Wholesale market**	**Farm market**

increase their purchases, they bid against one another and force price up. Panel C indicates what happens in the farm market. The old demand of wholesalers for rhubarb was D_c^0 and price was p_c. Suppose the quantity available is x_c (the supply at the moment). When wholesalers' demand rises to D_c^1 a shortage of $x_c x_c'$ develops at price p_c. Price rises to p_c' to ration the available rhubarb among the competing buyers. (It might be well to note that the scales of the graphs in Figure 3–1 are different).

Wholesalers now pay a higher price in the farm market and, consequently, raise their price to grocers to p_w'. As they tell the grocers, their costs have risen and they are forced to raise prices. Since grocers now pay the wholesale price of p_w', they raise the retail price to p_r'. They tell their complaining customers that costs have risen and they are forced to raise prices. Costs to the grocers and to the wholesalers have, of course, risen, but ultimately it was the increased demand that caused the price rise. Price must rise until it rations the available rhubarb to those prospective buyers who are both willing and able to pay the price.

Everything that occurs in the transition period occurs not because we draw some curves, but because of individual actions in the market. We use demand and supply curves only to analyze more clearly what takes place in the market.

We can take the analysis a few steps further. Suppose the higher price in the farm market induces farmers to increase their rhubarb crop or convinces farmers growing other crops to switch to rhubarb. Remember x_c and p_c make up only one point on the long-run supply curve. Assume there is an upward sloping long-run supply *(LRS)* passing through point A in Panel C. In the farm market, price falls and quantity increases after all adjustments are made (point A, Panel C). The increased quantity supplied causes price to fall and quantity sold to rise in the wholesale and retail markets.

3.3 FLOOR AND CEILING PRICES

Excess demand or excess supply can occur after a demand or a supply shift. But market forces over time tend to eliminate shortages and surpluses. In fact, it is the very existence of these excess demands and supplies, reflecting changes in market conditions, that allows the market to work. There are, however, certain shortages (excess demands) and surpluses (excess supplies) that market forces do not eliminate. These are more permanent in nature and result from interferences with the market mechanism.

There are two things that governments knows how to do: create a shortage, and create a surplus. Shortages and surpluses can be created simply by legislating a price below or above equilibrium. Governments have, in the past, and probably will in the future, decided that the price of a particular commodity is or will be either "too high" or "too low" and proceed to set a "fair" price. Without evaluating the desirability of such interference, we can use demand and supply curves to analyze the economic effects of the two types of interference: the setting of minimum and maximum prices.

Price Ceilings

If the government imposes a maximum, or ceiling, price on a good, the effect is to cause a shortage of that good (and frequently create a black market that rations the quantity available). In Figure 3–2, a ceiling price, p_c, is set on good X. No one can legally sell X for more than p_c, per unit, which is below the equilibrium price, p_e. At the ceiling price, only x_e is offered for sale; that is, the *momentary* supply is the vertical line at x_e. But x_d is demanded. Over a period of time, the shortage grows worse. After a suitable period of adjustment, suppliers decrease the quantity supplied still more, to x_s, and excess demand becomes $x_s x_d$. Since quantity supplied is less than quantity demanded at the ceiling price, there must be some method of allocating the limited quantity among all those who are willing and able to buy a larger amount. The sellers may devise the method—perhaps consumers have to stand in line, with suppliers deciding who comes first in the line on the basis of under-the-counter offers. Black markets may develop. In any case, when price ceilings are set, the allocation is either based on nonmarket considerations or the market mechanism functions less effectively outside the law.

FIGURE 3–2   **Effect of ceiling price**

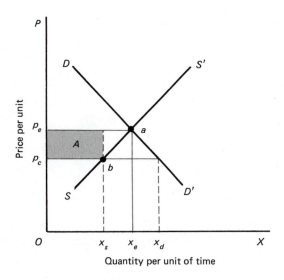

Aside from the cost of these additional means of allocating the commodity, some consumers benefit from price ceilings. Those who are fortunate enough to get the x_s units pay less. Figure 3–2 shows the income transfer away from the producers to the consumers. Before the price ceiling, buyers paid p_e for all units they purchased. When the lower price is installed, they pay p_c. Area $A = (p_e - p_c) \cdot x_s$ represents income buyers originally gave to sellers, but now keep because prices are lower. Buyers as a group do not unambiguously gain from price ceilings because not all buyers can purchase the quantity they want. There is a shortage of $x_d x_s$ units that buyers would be willing to purchase at a price above the minimum price at which the good is supplied. Also, we must not forget the costs involved from standing in line, or avoiding the law if black markets should arise, to allocate the good. Sellers clearly lose on price ceilings. They sell fewer units at a lower price, so total revenue must go down. In the figure, before the ceiling, revenue was the area $Op_e a x_e$; afterward it becomes just the area $Op_c b x_s$.

Price Floors

In contrast to price ceilings, the government may feel that the suppliers of the good are not earning as much income as they ''deserve'' and,

FIGURE 3–3   **Effect of floor price**

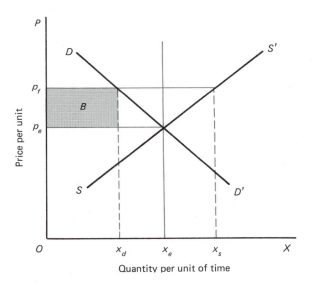

therefore, sets a minimum, or floor price. We can see the results of such actions in Figure 3–3. Dissatisfied with the equilibrium price and quantity, p_e and x_e, the government sets a minimum price of p_f. Since the law of demand could not concurrently be repealed, consumers demand less (x_d), and, immediately, excess supply of $x_d x_e$ develops. In order to maintain the price p_f, the government must find some way to limit supply, or it must agree to purchase the excess. As firms are induced to supply more and as new firms are enticed into the industry by the higher price, the quantity supplied at p_f increases. If SS' is the long-run supply curve, the increased quantity supplied causes a greater amount of unsold goods, $x_d x_s$, which the government must now buy. The alternative is to find some way to make producers keep output at x_d; that is, the government could simply restrict production at x_d by law. The vertical dashed line at this output then becomes the new supply curve, and a price of p_f would clear the market.

For those producers lucky enough to sell the x_d units of output, area B represents an income transfer, $p_f - p_e$ more revenue is earned on every unit sold. Some producers will not benefit because the quantity supplied is restricted by $x_e x_d$ units, and no revenue is earned on this output unless the government buys it. This loss could be as great as the area $(x_d - x_e) \cdot p_e$ in Figure 3–3. On the other side of the market, buyers are not helped by price floors. No matter how many units are purchased, they pay more per unit.

We should recognize that certain temporary shortages or surpluses may not be governmentally caused. For example, cities will experience serious natural gas shortages during extreme cold spells. Many people have blamed these shortages on the fact that gas shipped interstate is subject to a regulated ceiling price below the market equilibrium. It is true that more households and firms will want and use gas than would be the case with a market-determined price, but some shortages probably would, and even should, occur with no ceiling price.

Why? Consider when a gas shortage occurs, always during an extreme cold spell—for example, a 50-year low in temperatures. Clearly, a publicly or privately owned gas company would not construct pipelines and storage capacity to accommodate all users during such a cold spell. This would not be economical. Also think of the political implications if the city or even a private utility drastically raised prices to consumers during a freezing blizzard. Citizens would march on city hall and vote different in the next election. Therefore, cities or utilities rely on a gas capacity sufficient to handle the vast majority of winters, but not the extremes. When one of the rare, extremely cold periods occurs, they generally ration by eliminating or reducing some industrial users and asking for voluntary reductions from customers.

The situation is analogous to the problem of snow removal in the Sunbelt. Every few years, the South gets a snow storm—light by most Northern standards, paralyzing by local standards. Practically everything comes to a standstill until the snow melts. Would snow removal equipment be economical? Of course not. Such an expense to alleviate some inconvenience every few years would be very costly.

Similarly, during the summer of 1980, Dallas, Texas, experienced the hottest two months in its recorded history. Heavy air-conditioning usage caused periodic shortages of electricity. Should the electric company have increased prices to consumers? Over 100 people died from the heat. What do you think the reaction would have been to a large price increase?

Similar conditions apply to businesses. Movie theaters sometimes turn away customers from a popular movie. They also have a surplus, sometimes a very large surplus, of seats for other movies. Prices could be used more effectively to ration seats, but theaters would be constantly changing them, depending on the movie and the time it was shown. Such behavior would cause poor public relations. Movie goers, uncertain of the price they would pay, might prefer entertainment with more stable prices, and the long-run profits of theaters could fall. Similarly, retailers face the problem of the proper size of inventory to hold. Too much stock can get very costly to store, too little turns customers away. Over the long run, an inventory is held to maximize profits, but because there is a cost of storage, shortages can occur at the going price.

APPLICATION

Price Supports for Peanuts

The U.S. peanut program is designed to help peanut farmers. Each year, the Department of Agriculture decides what size the peanut crop in the coming season should be, then tells the approximately 53,000 growers, who hold the legal right to grow peanuts, how much acreage they can plant. Anyone who markets peanuts commercially without a government "allotment" can be fined or sent to jail.

"Loans," that really are not loans, are provided to guarantee that farmers receive a set price for their peanuts. In 1981, for instance, the government advanced a peanut farmer $455 per ton of peanuts if the crop could not be sold for at least that amount in the open market. Later, if the crop could be sold for $455 or more per ton, the loan had to be repaid. If prices stayed below the $455 mark, the government took the crop, and the farmer did not have to give the money back. In essence, the government set a price floor for peanuts at $455 per ton.

FIGURE 3–4   **Price floors for peanuts**

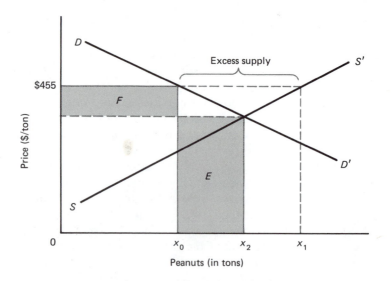

The federal peanut program can be modeled in a simple supply and demand setting. Figure 3–4 shows the main features of the program. We can easily see why the Department of Agriculture restricts the peanut acreage. At \$455 per ton, there would be an excess supply, equal to $x_0 x_1$, that the government would have to purchase at the agreed price if there were no restrictions.

Does the income of peanut farmers rise because of the price floor? On the surface, it appears that it does. The answer really depends on the elasticity of demand. Suppose the acreage restriction is just sufficient to limit quantity supplied to x_0; thus at \$455 there is no excess supply. Clearly, peanut farmers gain if the area F in Figure 3–4 exceeds area E, the revenue lost by not being able to sell at the freely determined market price. We know that F is greater than E if demand is inelastic over the relevant quantity range. From the diagram, peanut farmers would want price supports and restrictions if, and only if, demand is inelastic. Otherwise they are better off in unregulated markets.

The situation is, in reality, a bit more complex for policy makers. Even with the restrictions, farmers with acreage allotments have become very successful at increasing their yield per acre. The acreage restriction notwithstanding, price floors have brought about excess supply in the market as farmers have increased productivity. In fiscal 1981, the government paid an estimated \$51 million in "loans" for peanut crops that could not be sold. The government then has to take the crops and store them. This shows that, even with restrictions, excess supply can occur if the restrictions are not perfect.

A more fundamental problem arises when we think of the long-run benefits to farmers from price supports. Those lucky enough to receive an acreage allotment from the government have the promise of an increased stream of earnings over the years they sell their crops; this amount might be the difference in areas $F-E$ for a typical year. This makes an allotment a valuable license. Now suppose someone wants to grow peanuts and does not have an allotment. If the government does not pass out any more, they will have to buy one. What should its price be? The price of a peanut license should reflect the stream of the increased income it grants the present owner. New or entering peanut farmers must pay another farmer to exit from the market. That payment will help the farmer gertting out of business, but not the new farmer, who pays a price that probably just captures the gain $F-E$ in Figure 3–4 over the years the farm is operated. In the long run, we must conclude that price supports will help the generation of farmers who are the first beneficiaries, but do not guarantee higher levels of income to the industry as entry and exit of farmers from the industry takes place.

3.4 EXCISE TAXES

An excise tax is a tax directly related to either the number of units sold or the price of a particular commodity. Excise taxes are always collected through the seller. If the tax is based on the number of units sold, it is often called a *unit tax*. The classic example of a unit tax is the excise tax collected on gasoline sold to motorists. It is not based on the price of gasoline, but on the number of gallons pumped. Alternatively, the tax may be a fixed percent of the sales price, in which case the excise tax is also known as an *ad valorem tax*. Sales taxes on consumer goods in most cities and states are examples of ad valorem taxes.

We will use supply and demand to study the market effects of excise taxes, looking first at the unit tax and then turning to ad valorem taxes.

Market Effect of a Unit Tax

Suppose your state legislature is debating the establishment of a state excise tax on gasoline. Typical claims made by legislators are that such a tax will cause motorists to conserve on gasoline, and the added tax revenue is necessary for road improvement and construction. On the other hand, some lawmakers may oppose the tax on grounds that sellers will pass the full tax on to the consumer, who is taxed heavily enough already. Economic tools we have already developed will shed some light on these arguments and controversies surrounding excise taxes.

Let us turn to a theoretical analysis of a unit tax with the tools of supply and demand. Suppose DD' in Figure 3–5 is the state economy's demand for gasoline. SS' is the present supply of gasoline prior to the tax imposition. Therefore, x_0 and p_0 are, respectively, the equilibrium quantity and price.

A unit tax simply means that for every gallon of gasoline sold, the seller must pay a stipulated amount to the state. This payment shifts the supply curve upward (decreases supply). Demand does not shift. The consumer who pays $1.25 for a gallon of gasoline presumably does not care what portion of the price goes to the seller and what portion goes to the government. Consumers demand so much at $1.25 and at every other price, no matter what part goes to the government. Sellers do care what portion of the price goes to the government and what portion they can keep. For example, suppose at a price of $1.25 a gallon, stations are induced to supply a million gallons per week to the market. This means that they themselves must receive $1.25 a gallon to supply this amount. Now, let a tax of 10 cents a gallon be imposed. In order to induce suppliers to supply one million gallons a week, the price must be $1.35 a gallon, because only in this way can suppliers keep $1.25 for themselves. At every quantity, suppliers must receive 10 cents a gallon more to induce them to supply the same amount.

FIGURE 3–5   **Price effect of an excise tax**

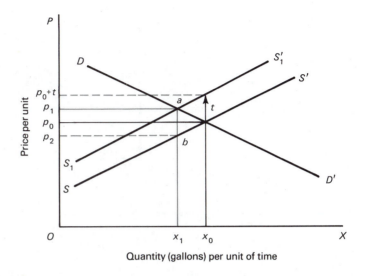

Quantity (gallons) per unit of time

In terms of Figure 3–5, suppose the unit tax being debated is t cents per gallon. By the argument presented above, the original supply SS' shifts upward by t cents to $S_1 S_1'$. At the old price of p_0, there is excess demand; consequently, price is bid up to p_1. The new quantity sold declines from x_0 to x_1. The extent of the price rise and quantity decrease depends on the elasticity of supply and demand. Note that price does not rise by the full amount of t cents. Price rises by the amount $p_1 - p_0 = \Delta p$, which is less than t. Consumers absorb some of the tax in the form of higher prices, and sellers absorb the remainder of the tax. In fact, the burden or incidence of the unit tax on consumers is simply the portion they pay:

$$\text{Tax incidence} = \frac{\Delta p}{t} \leq 1.$$

The only time consumers pay the entire tax is when demand is perfectly inelastic, as shown in Figure 3–6. In general, the more inelastic is demand, the heavier the tax burden on consumers. This should not be a surprising conclusion. Inelastic goods are insensitive to price—when prices rise, consumers are willing to pay the increase rather than forego the commodity. Suppose demand was highly elastic. Now the quantity purchased is sensitive to price. Rather than pay the tax, consumers reduce consumption. It stands to reason that, under these conditions, the seller ends up paying most of the tax. A diagram similar to Figure 3–6 but with a very elastic demand can be constructed to prove this point. For

FIGURE 3-6   **Price effect of an excise tax when demand is perfectly inelastic**

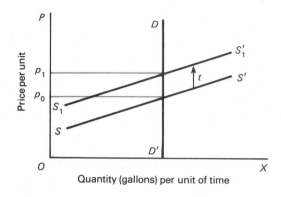

practice, check to see who pays the tax when the demand is perfectly elastic, or horizontal.

In summary, the more inelastic is demand, the greater is the tax burden on consumers and the smaller is the change in quantity purchased. Conversely, the more elastic is demand, the smaller is the tax burden on the buyer, and the greater is the change in quantity purchased. It is never correct to suggest that a tax placed on a particular commodity is always paid by the final consumer.

The fact that the tax burden depends on the elasticity of demand is a difficult concept for people to accept. It is frequently claimed that taxes are fully passed on to consumers, that is, the tax is added to the old price p_0 and everyone is forced to pay it. But suppose gasoline dealers did this. Returning to Figure 3–5 sellers would like to charge a price of $p_0 + t$, yet if they did, excess supply would result. Inventories would build up and eventually price would fall to p_1. The willingness of consumers to pay does not allow suppliers to sell x_0 at $p_0 + t$.

Turning now to the effect of supply elasticity, we can show that the more inelastic is the supply curve, the less is the burden of a unit tax on consumers. Figure 3–7 is similar to Figure 3–5 except that the supply curve is noticeably steeper. The demand curves have exactly the same slope in Figures 3–5 and 3–7. Comparing the two figures reveals that the difference between $p_0 + t$ and p_1 is greater in Figure 3–7. In other words, the consumer pays a smaller portion of the tax.

Although this is easy to see in the graphs, the reasoning behind this conclusion is worth putting into words. The key to understanding why price does not change much when supply is inelastic, as shown in Figure 3–7, is to see that when a unit tax is imposed there is not much of a leftward (as opposed to upward) shift in the supply curve. As a conse-

FIGURE 3-7　　　　**Price effect of a unit tax when supply is relatively inelastic**

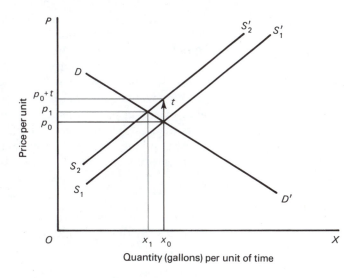

Quantity (gallons) per unit of time

quence, there is only a small movement along the demand curve, and there tends to be little overall change in price and quantity exchanged. By comparing Figure 3–5 and 3–7 you can see what happens when supply is relatively elastic (shown in Figure 3–5). The leftward shift is larger the more elastic is supply. When supply is elastic, sellers are more willing to adjust the quantity supplied rather than pay the tax themselves. In contrast, when supply is inelastic, the quantity sold adjusts very little, so sellers tend to absorb the tax.

Ad Valorem Taxes

The analysis is conceptually the same for an ad valorem tax. The tax shifts the supply curve upward, and the incidence of the tax depends on the elasticities of demand and supply. However, with a percentage tax, the amount of tax depends on the price of the commodity. Let us focus our attention on the supply curve, which tells us how much sellers offer at each possible price. If we placed a 10 percent ad valorem tax on sellers, they would need their old price plus 10 percent to supply the same amount.

Supply curves have a positive slope, meaning that higher prices are necessary for sellers to offer larger quantities in a market. As prices rise to induce larger quantities, the absolute amount of the tax, t, must rise. Remember t is a constant percentage of the sales price; as the price rises, so does the amount of tax paid. If the sales tax on a bicycle is 10 percent, then a $100 price tag means the tax is $10, but if the price jumps to $150, the tax becomes $15.

Figure 3–8 shows a market supply and demand schedule. With an ad valorem tax, t gets larger as we move up the supply curve SS'. The new equilibrium is defined by the intersection of $S_1 S'_1$ and DD'. Compared to the old equilibrium, prices are higher, and the quantity sold is less.

The incidence of the tax, once again, does not fall entirely on the buyer. Figure 3–8 shows that $\Delta p = p_1 - p_0 < t$ at the new equilibrium. The rise in price would get closer to t as demand became more inelastic or supply more elastic at p_0, just as it was for a unit tax. Unlike a unit tax, however, as demand becomes more inelastic in this case, both the incidence of the tax on buyers and the total amount of the tax rises. Consumers would therefore pay a higher percentage of a larger tax.

Government Revenue

The amount of tax revenue collected by the government is always equal to the tax, t, times the numbers of units sold. Letting T be tax revenue, then

FIGURE 3–8   **The market effect of an ad valorem tax**

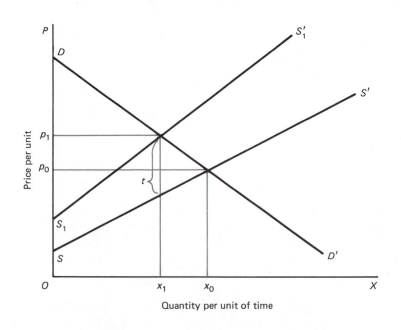

Quantity per unit of time

$$T = t \cdot x.$$

In Figure 3–5, T is the rectangular area abp_2p_1. For any t, tax revenue is less, the greater the fall in quantity sold when the tax is imposed. Tax authorities prefer to tax goods that are not very sensitive to tax rates, e.g., gasoline, cigarettes, and liquor. These kinds of goods represent reliable sources of income to governments, because they tend to have market demand schedules that are relatively inelastic.

The point can be made more forcefully by comparing the tax revenue collected on a good with two contrasting elasticities of demand. Figure 3–9 illustrates the relative revenue-generating power of a commodity when demand is elastic as opposed to when it is inelastic. In both cases, the same tax is collected on the units sold, but when demand is relatively inelastic, more units are sold and tax revenue is higher. The difference in revenue collected is clearly $t \cdot (x_0 - x_1)$ in Figure 3–9.

3.5 COST-BENEFIT ANALYSIS

In applied studies, supply and demand schedules can be used as tools to estimate the costs and benefits of market activity. In this section we explain how the area under a demand curve gives us an estimate of a commodity's value to consumers. At the same time the area under the supply curve is an estimate of the resource cost of producing a product. We can use supply and demand to gauge the impact of moving away from a market equilibrium. Only a rudimentary description of cost-benefit

FIGURE 3–9   **Revenue depends on the elasticity of demand**

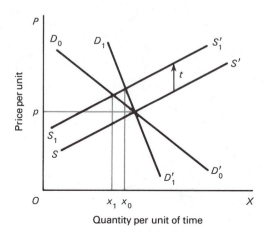

analysis is presented here, but the elements necessary for any such analysis remain basically the same, though they are used at higher levels of sophistication by economists.

The Paradox of Value

In his 1776 book, *The Wealth of Nations,* Adam Smith was troubled by the disparity between price and value. He asked: How is it that water, which is so very useful that life is impossible without it, has such a low price, while diamonds, a luxury, have such a high price? This question is known as the *paradox of value.* We can beg its answer by pointing out that the demand and supply for water intersect at a low price, while the market equilibrium for diamonds is established at a high price. Diamonds are scarce relative to demand, but water is plentiful.

Smith would probably not have been satisfied with this answer. Even though demand and supply curves had not been invented yet, he knew that scarcity led to high prices, and abundance to low prices. What bothered him was why something valuable to buyers did not fetch a high price in spite of its abundance. In 1776 economists had not yet comprehended that price in a market is determined by the value of the *last unit*

FIGURE 3–10   **The value of a commodity**

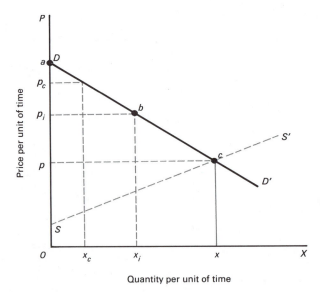

Quantity per unit of time

exchanged. We know from our description of demand schedules and demand curves in Chapter 2 that the value individuals place on each unit of a commodity falls as they consume more. Value is conceptually a much broader notion than price.

Figure 3–10 helps us visualize the distinction between value and price. Let's think of each point on the demand curve as a measure of what an individual would pay for that unit of the good. So for unit x_c, and no other unit, the consumer would pay as much as p_c, and for the x_i unit the value to the buyer is p_i. These points on the demand curve reveal the maximum willingness to pay of a buyer. The demand curve tells us how much a buyer is willing to pay for any number of units purchased of a particular good.[1] The total value of x_i units, for instance, is the sum of how much the consumer would be willing to pay up to and including the x_ith unit. Value in the figure would be the area under the demand schedule, $Oabx_i$.

We know that demand slopes downward, as shown in Figure 3–10. This means that the value of the last unit consumed is less than the value of those units previously consumed. If the market price of x is p, the consumer will make purchases out to the xth in Figure 3–10. As long as value is greater than price, more will be bought. The value of the last unit—in this case the xth unit—is exactly equal to p, but units purchased up to the xth unit have the combined value equivalent to area $Oacx$. This is the difference between price and value. Price is the value of the last unit, not total value. The area under the demand schedule is an estimate of total value.

Consumer's Surplus and the Area under the Demand Curve

Economists who work on public policy problems frequently use a tool called consumer's surplus, measured as the difference between the maximum amount a consumer is willing to pay—or value—and the dollar amount actually paid for a commodity. To illustrate the concept of consumer's surplus, suppose you visit the grocery store to buy some apples. The grocer is capable of charging a sufficiently high price that you do not make any purchases, but at lower prices you will buy apples, and the lower the price the more you buy. In other words, your demand curve for apples is downward sloping. Points on the demand curve have been tabulated in Table 3–1. We show a maximum willingness to pay for the first five apples. The value of the first apple is relatively high, $1.00, and then falls to $.20 with the fifth apple. The demand curve that this table is constructed from is shown in Figure 3–11.

---

[1] This is not a precise claim because of what is called the "income effect" when price changes. A better measure of willingness to pay would compensate the consumer for the income effect. A more thorough discussion of demand is undertaken in Chapters 5 and 6.

TABLE 3–1   **A consumer's willingness to pay for apples**

Apple	Willingness to pay for the last apple	Grocer's price	Consumer's surplus
1	$1.00	.40	$ .60
2	.80	.40	.40
3	.60	.40	.20
4	.40	.40	.00
5	.20		
Total consumer's surplus			$1.20

Suppose the grocer sells all apples at $.40. Regardless of whether the consumer is purchasing his or her first or fifth apple, the price is the same, as shown in Table 3–1. From the consumer's point of view the supply curve is a horizontal schedule at the price of $.40. All the apples they could conceivably purchase are sold at this constant price. Consumer's surplus is the difference between what you are willing and able to pay and the asking price. Since you are just willing and able to pay $.40 for the fourth apple and the price of apples is $.40 each, you stop buying apples at this point on your demand schedule in Figure 3–11. For the first through third apples however, Table 3–1 shows that you gain consumer's surplus

FIGURE 3–11   **Willingness to pay and consumer's surplus**

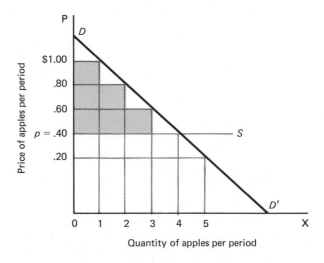

from making the purchases. Total consumer's surplus is $1.20. For emphasis we repeat the definition of consumer's surplus and relate it to demand curves.

Definition

Consumer's surplus is the difference between a buyer's willingness to pay and the market price. It is estimated by the area between the demand curve and price.

Consumer's surplus is graphed in Figure 3–11, where the consumer buys just four apples. This is where the grocer's supply curve intersects demand. It is important to understand that the consumer does not buy four apples because four apples are valued at $.40 each by the consumer. On the contrary, all but the fourth apple are valued more highly than $.40. A consumer buys four because the consumer's willingness to pay for the fourth apple is just equal to the price of apples. More than four are not bought, because he or she is willing to pay only $.20 cents for the fifth while the price is $.40.

We see that Table 3–1 has actually subtracted price from the willingness to pay to get an exact measure of consumer's surplus. Adding up these amounts tells us that the consumer's surplus from buying four apples is $1.20. This is also represented by the shaded region in Figure 3–11. If we had taken the area under the demand curve above $.40, we would have overestimated the surplus by the unshaded triangular areas between the price line and *DD'*. The estimate, however, becomes more exact as units of measure for the quantity become smaller. Say the grocer charged $.20 for each apple half. The consumer depicted in Figure 3–11 would then buy eight halves, and as the units are made smaller, the area between the price and the demand curve would become a much better estimate of consumer's surplus.

APPLICATION

The Sale of Gasoline Rationing Tickets

During the Carter administration, one plan to make consumers conserve energy was gasoline rationing. Motorists would be issued rationing tickets, that would be presented to the station attendant when they purchased gasoline. There was controversy among public officials over whether it should be legal to sell the tickets after they were issued. A major concern was that those people who could afford to buy extra tickets would benefit at the expense of those who could not. The theory of consumer's surplus helps us analyze the issue and decide whether the sale of ration tickets should be permitted in the event of rationing.

If tickets were sold, people could be divided into three groups: (1) those who sold tickets, (2) those who bought tickets, and (3) those who did neither. The last group is unaffected by the buying and selling of tickets, so they do not enter the analysis. The issue is whether those who buy and sell tickets are helped or harmed.

Suppose all motorists were given weekly coupons allowing them to purchase 10 gallons of gasoline. The government allocates tickets equally among households at no charge. Mr. Adams and Ms. Jones drive the same amount each week, but for some reason—it could be that Jones is richer—Jones would be willing to pay more than Adams for the 10th coupon if a market for the coupons existed. Figures 3–12 and 3–13 show, respectively, the amounts Adams and Jones would be willing to pay for each additional ration coupon i.e., their demands for coupons. We can see that Adams is willing is pay $1.10 for the 10th coupon, while Jones is willing to pay $2.25.

Suppose a market for coupons does exist and trading is allowed. After a few months, a price of $1.50 prevails. Adams would be willing to keep only 6 coupons at that price and would therefore wish to sell 4 of his 10 coupons. Jones would like to purchase four more tickets at this price. Clearly, trade would be beneficial to both. The benefit to Jones from being able to purchase four more tickets at $1.50 each is the consumer's surplus shown by the area *J.* This area represents the difference between what she is willing to pay for each additional ticket and what she actually pays, and can be estimated by using the formula for the area of a triangle

FIGURE 3–12   **Adams's willingness to pay for rationing tickets**

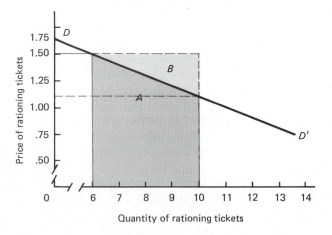

FIGURE 3-13   **Jones's willingness to pay for rationing tickets**

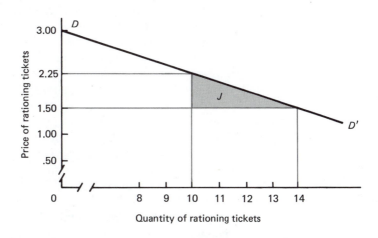

$$Area = 1/2 \cdot b \cdot h,$$

where b is the base and h is the height of the triangle. Substituting the numbers shown in Figure 3-13, consumer's surplus for Jones is $1/2 \cdot (\$2.25 - 1.50) \cdot (14 - 10) = \$1.50$.

Adams benefits also. Since the tickets cost him nothing, his consumer's surplus from tickets 6 through 10 is the entire area A under his demand curve. This is shown as the diagonally shaded region in Figure 3-12. If he is not worse off by selling the four tickets to Jones, he must receive an amount greater than or equal to the amount represented by area A. He does, in fact, receive $\$1.50 \times 4 = \$6.00$ in income from selling the tickets represented by the sum of areas A and B. Adams is made better off from selling the tickets by an amount represented by the area B above his demand curve. This area represents sales income above the total value of the tickets if the ticket were kept.

Applying the concept of consumer's surplus, we see that both the buyer and the seller of rationing tickets benefit regardless of who is richer or poorer, while those who do not trade are neither helped nor hurt by trading. The conclusion of this very simple benefit-cost study is that some groups of individuals are helped by trading, and no one is harmed. The trading of rationing tickets is therefore beneficial for motorists.

Producer's Surplus

A concept related to consumer's surplus, and used in conjunction with the measure, is producer's surplus. Thinking about the supply curve now, recall from Chapter 2 that supply is defined as a schedule of *minimum prices* necessary for the provision of particular levels of production. The schedule, in other words, represents the lowest prices that persuade producers to offer certain amounts of a commodity. The upward slope of supply curves tells us that higher prices are necessary to coax more output from producers. It is because the supply curve slopes upward that there is a difference between the revenue a seller collects and the minimum amount it would have taken to produce a particular level of output. This difference is referred to as producer's surplus.

Figure 3–14 illustrates producer's surplus. The vertically shaded area under the supply curve shows the minimum expenditure necessary to coax *x* units of output from a seller. This area represents the value of the product to the seller, or more exactly, it is the value of the resources necessary to produce *x* units of output. We discuss supply curves in more detail when we explore cost more fully in Chapter 9. The upward slope of the supply curve tells us that an increasingly higher price is necessary to make a seller produce an additional unit of output. For instance, the seller

FIGURE 3–14   **Producer's surplus**

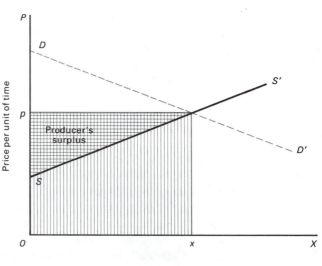

Quantity per unit of time

would need at least the price p to provide the xth unit of output. This is more than that needed to produce those units before the last x unit. When output is sold however, all units sell at the same price. That is, revenue to a seller for a total of x units of production is $p \cdot x$. This is the entire rectangular shaded area in Figure 3–14. We see that this is greater than the area under supply by the region marked producer's surplus. Producer's surplus is the dollar amount sellers receive in the form of revenue above that necessary to induce a producer to sell its output.

To summarize we emphasize the definition of producer's surplus:

Definition
Producer's surplus is the difference between total revenue and the value of a product to a producer, represented by the area under the supply curve. It is estimated by the area between price and the supply curve in a graph.

Total Surplus and Cost-Benefit Studies

Cost-benefit studies look at the change in consumer's and producer's surplus from a public policy point of view. Markets are said to be efficient when total surplus, the sum of consumer's and producer's surplus, is maximized. Most government policies—e.g. taxes and price supports—generate losses in total surplus. We can show, however, that this is an inevitable price to pay when income redistribution is desired, or governments seek to collect revenue by taxing commodities. In many cases the goal is to minimize the amount of inefficiency created in the form of lost surplus.

As an example of the impact of government policy on market efficiency, we can illustrate what happens to total surplus when a unit tax of $\$t$ is put on a commodity. In Figure 3–15 we show supply and demand before a tax in Panel A. Consumer's surplus is the shaded area E and producer's surplus is the area F. Total surplus is the sum $E + F$. As we discussed earlier, a unit tax of $\$t$ will shift supply upward to SS' in Panel B by the distance t from the old supply curve S_0S_0'. The quantity sold falls to x and price rises to p. The government collects revenue equal to $\$t \cdot x$, or the area G in the figure.

This area represents a transfer of consumer's and producer's surplus to the government. By comparing Panels A and B in Figure 3–15, parts of area E and F become government revenue G. The new surplus areas in Panel B fall to E' for the consumer and F' for the producer. Between the quantities x and x_0 in Panel B we see that the tax drives a wedge between the old supply curve and demand. In this wedged area H represents a net loss in consumer's surplus and area I is a net loss in producer's surplus.

The sum of these areas in a cost-benefit study, should be counted as part of the total cost of levying the tax. It represents a net decrease in total market benefit. Why? Look at the difference between DD' and S_0S_0' in

FIGURE 3–15   **Loss of total surplus from a tax**

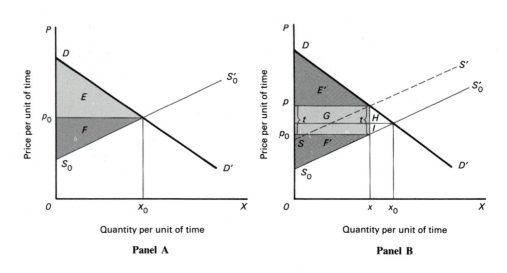

Panel A

Panel B

Panel B of Figure 3–15 at the quantity x. A consumer, without the tax, is willing to pay more than the amount necessary to make a producer supply the product, but because the producer must pay the tax and the effective supply curve moves up to SS' less is produced and the sum of consumer's and producers surplus declines. Total market benefit, including government revenue collected, declines when the tax is paid. Economists argue that when governments seek to collect revenue they should minimize the degree of market distortion caused by the tax. Generally, the closer x is to x_0, the smaller are areas $H + I$ in Figure 3–15. Stated a different way, the most inelastic is demand for a commodity the lower the distortion cost of taxation.

Surplus analysis can be used to show, somewhat more generally, that any time prices and quantities are not determined by the intersection of supply and demand there will be a loss of total surplus. Think about a price that is either lower or higher than the equilibrium price. We picture the case in Figure 3–16.[2] When prices are below the equilibrium p_0, the supply curve determines the quantity sold, in which case there may be excess demand. When they are above p_0, demand determines the quantity supplied, and there may be excess supply. The "above equilibrium" price

---

[2] As discussed earlier in the chapter, price ceilings and floors may be the cause of prices diverging from the market equilibrium defined by the intersection of supply and demand.

FIGURE 3–16   **Loss of surplus when prices diverge from the market equilibrium**

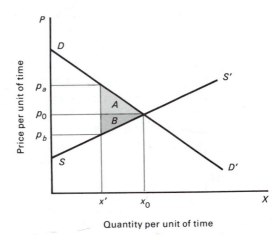

Quantity per unit of time

and "below equilibrium: price are shown as p_a and p_b, respectively. Suppose we pick these prices to reduce quantity by the same amount. In both cases then, moving prices away from the equilibrium generates losses in total surplus equivalent to the shaded region. The figure shows part of the loss (area A) is consumer's surplus and part (area B) is producer's surplus. Any price, and consequently any quantity sold, that is not freely determined by the interaction of supply and demand will cause losses in total surplus. Total surplus is maximized at the intersection of supply and demand.

APPLICATION

Federal Regulation of Natural Gas

Consumer's and producer's surplus can be combined to analyze the effects of the price ceiling that was imposed on natural gas. For illustration, we use the years between 1960 and 1973 and assume we have only one consumer and one seller of natural gas.

In 1938, Congress passed the Natural Gas Act which gave the Federal Power Commission (later called the Federal Energy Regulatory Commission) the right to set "just and reasonable" rates for interstate sales of natural gas. From 1960 to 1973, the commission froze the wellhead price of natural gas at its 1959–60 level. Taking account of inflation, the price of natural gas to residential customers declined by almost 20 percent from 1960 to 1973.[3]

There is strong evidence that this price was below the market equilibrium that would have been established by the intersection of the supply and demand curves. Before the price of gas was fixed, the average number of wells drilled annually between 1948 and 1960 was 662. Between 1960 and 1973, the number fell to 641, and after 1973, when the ceiling was raised, the average number of wells drilled increased dramatically to 1,370 per year.[4] Furthermore, natural gas suppliers were having difficulty meeting their contract obligations. In 1970, curtailments on old contracts represented .5 percent of total production; by 1974, they were 9.6 percent of production. Many new contracts were, of course, not being written, since gas suppliers were not even meeting existing obligations.

Figure 3–17 shows a familiar diagram. Price p_c represents the price set by the Federal Power Commission; p_e is the equilibrium price for natural gas. At first, p_e and p_c were probably about equal, but in the early 1970s,

FIGURE 3–17   **Price ceilings on natural gas**

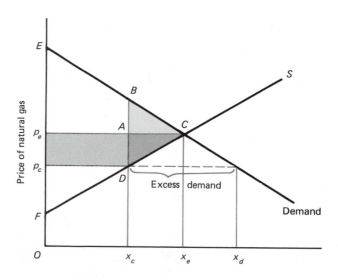

[3] *Annual Report to Congress,* Vol. 2, (Washington, D.C.: Department of Energy, 1978), p. 85.

[4] Ibid., p. 27.

the size of curtailments indicates there was a large excess demand at the artifically low price, p_c. The curtailments do not even include those contracts that might have been made if more gas had been available. At p_c, excess demand is the distance $x_c x_d$ in Figure 3–17.

Does a consumer or producer benefit from a price ceiling? The question can be answered in terms of consumer's and producer's surplus.

Without the price ceiling, a consumer would have purchased x_e natural gas and would have paid p_e. Consumer's surplus would have been the area ECp_e. A price ceiling restricts the output of a producer to x_c. Under these conditions, surplus for the consumer becomes area $EBDp_c$. The consumer gains if $p_e ADp_c > ABC$ and loses surplus if $ABC > p_e ADp_c$. So, it is not clear whether the consumer gains or loses on balance from the ceiling.

A clearer answer emerges for the producer. Producer's surplus is the area between price and the supply schedules. Before regulation, producer's surplus was $p_e CF$; afterward, it is $p_c DF$. It is obvious that $p_c DF < p_e CF$. The producer loses area ADC. We do not know whether surplus for the consumer goes up or down, but for the producer, it goes down.

What about the combined consumer's and producer's surplus? What happens to total market surplus when a price ceiling is set? Before regulation, the sum of producer's and consumer's surplus was $p_e CF + ECp_e = ECF$. Once the price ceiling came into effect, it was $p_c DF + EBDp_c = EBDF$. We see that total surplus falls by the amount BCD. A price ceiling, in general, will reduce total surplus in a market.

We can see that, if the consumer gains surplus from the ceiling price, the result is a wealth transfer from the producer to the consumer. Since there is a net total loss of surplus, both could be made better off if price was raised to the equilibrium, p_e, and the producer paid the consumer an amount that made this change desirable. Suppose $p_e ADp_c - ABC = T$. This difference is the gain in consumer's surplus from the price ceiling. Then, if the producer paid the consumer slightly more than T, both would be willing to have prices at p_e. The producer could easily do this, since he gains all of area $p_e ADp_c$ and area ACD when the price is raised to p_e. Of course, if $ABC > p_e ADp_c$, both the producer and consumer could be made better off without a transfer if the ceiling were removed.

3.6 ESTIMATING DEMAND SCHEDULES

While theoretical or graphical derivation of consumer demand is simple, the statistical estimation of actual demand curves is quite difficult. It is, however, these real-world demands that decision makers are interested in. Those in business are willing to pay large amounts of money to have the demand for their products estimated. Certainly, a knowledge of this type of demand is of primary importance in business decision making. Anyone in business wishes to know how sales will vary when price varies.

Governmental decision makers make many important decisions based on statistical estimates of commodity demand curves. Estimates of demand elasticities for gasoline and petroleum have had a significant impact on government policy concerning these commodities. In some cases the estimates proved accurate; in other cases the results were far off. Estimates of demand play an important role in the decision to levy taxes on certain commodities.

Those working for nonprofit institutions make long-range plans based on estimates of demand also. For example, the demand for hospital services plays an important role in the plans of hospital administrators. University presidents like to have good estimates about the demand for classroom space. Decision makers, in general, can frequently make better decisions when they have a reasonably accurate estimate of the demand for the relevant goods and services.

FIGURE 3–18   **Price-quantity observations from a time series**

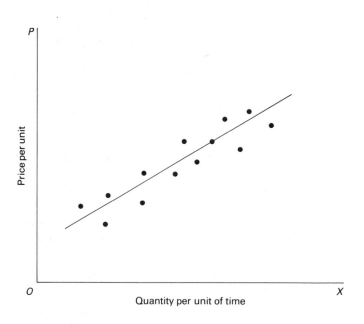

Estimating Problems

Estimating problems begin with statisticians using actual data. In theory, we hold everything but price and quantity constant when deriving demands; in actual investigations, economists may have strong reason to believe that other things have changed during the time that they have collected their data. It is not enough to go out into the world and gather data on price and quantity sold, plot these data, and from those plotted points estimate a demand curve. A series of price-quantity observations collected over time may, for instance, give the series of points plotted in Figure 3–18. The line drawn through the points appears to fit the data rather well. Its positive slope, however, is not evidence that the market demand for X is upward sloping. The points plotted in the figure may well designate different points of equilibrium. Supply and demand could have shifted many times during the period of observation because of changes in

FIGURE 3–19   **Changing equilibria over time**

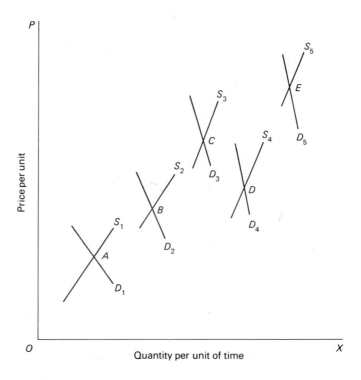

other variables. Each indicated point would then be a point of equilibrium. Without knowledge of the way these other variables change and the way they affect supply and demand, one cannot really say what the line indicates.

Supply and demand may have shifted over time in the way illustrated by Figure 3–19. S_1 and D_1 determine equilibrium point A, S_2 and D_2 determine B, and so forth. From five observations, we observe only points A through E. We cannot tell from the observations how these points were generated. Even though some observed points actually indicate an inverse relation between price and quantity, these points do not necessarily set forth a demand curve. Again, they may simply be points of equilibrium. There are, however, some techniques that economists and statisticians have used to estimate actual demands from actual data.

Estimating Procedures

A widely used technique for estimating demand from price-quantity data is called multiple regression. Economists or statisticians set up a model of equations with two or more independent variables. They solve the model to obtain estimating equations. One example of this type is

$$X = b_0 + b_1 P_x + b_2 W + b_3 P_0,$$

where X is the total quantity sold, P_x is the per-unit price of the good, W is an average wage rate, and P_0 is some index of related prices. The b's are the parameters to be estimated by multiple regression techniques. (Such techniques are generally taught in beginning statistics classes.) In this way, the effect of changes in W and P_0 can be isolated while one attempts to analyze the effect of just P_x on X. Of course, the effect of any other variables that affect supply and demand is not isolated, and such an omission could cause misleading interpretation. Another problem is the frequent difficulty of obtaining sufficient and accurate data so that meaningful results can be obtained.

In using the above method, the economist must assume that the relations are reasonably linear and that the estimating equation specifies what is actually happening. The problems concerned with making such types of estimates make up an entire branch of economics. This branch is known as econometrics—the use of statistics in economic theory. Many government agencies and businesses employ econometricians for estimating and forecasting.

Another interesting, though expensive and difficult, technique for estimating demand and demand elasticity is the controlled market experiment. The experimenter attempts to hold everything constant during the experiment except the price of the good. Many such experiments have been undertaken to gain information for the agricultural sector of the economy.

Those carrying out these market experiments display the products in several different grocery stores over a period of time. They make sure that there are always sufficient amounts available at each price to satisfy consumers over a period of time. In this way, the effect of changes in supply is removed. There is generally no advertising. During the period of the experiment, price is changed in reasonably small increments over a range, and sales are recorded at each price. Therefore, many of the effects of changes in other things can be removed, and a reasonable approximation of actual demand is estimated. We must mention again, however, that this is a difficult and expensive process.

As we noted above, in market experiments to determine demand, advertising is generally omitted. Frequently, however, retail merchants are interested in the effect of both price and advertising. One such controlled experiment was carried out by the Agricultural Experiment Station of Oregon State University.[5] A grocery chain of 20 stores participated in the experiment, which lasted about five years.

The experiment was designed to determine whether sales revenue was higher from advertising a particular good, in this case fish, with or without a price reduction. Clearly a store advertises a good in the hope of increasing revenue from that good. But if, in conjunction with the ad, the price of the good is reduced, revenues may be either larger or smaller than if the good is advertised without a price decrease. The result would depend on the price elasticity of demand.

Over the five-year period, several types of fish were advertised in the 20 stores. Sometimes there was no price reduction. At other times, the advertising was done in connection with price reductions that varied over the relevant range. In this way, the retailers learned the price response for various items. The results were rather surprising (to us, at least). For some fish—for example, salmon—advertising with a price discount created more revenue than advertising without a price decrease; for others—sole and snapper—revenue from advertising was greater without a price discount than with one.

This example shows that there are many ways to estimate the effect of price changes on sales under various circumstances, and there are many groups, public and private, that specialize in such estimation. The example demonstrates the application of statistical methods to economic theory in making business decisions.

An alternative method of derivation, the questionnaire or survey approach, is a much cheaper method, but far less reliable. Potential or actual consumers are simply questioned about how much of certain goods they *would* buy at several prices, or what they consider a reasonable price.

---

[5] "Fresh Fish Sales as a Function of Promotion in a Portland, Oregon, Grocery Chain," Agricultural Experiment Station, Special Report 372 (Corvallis: Oregon State University, October 1972).

These surveys may provide some useful indirect information, but the imprecision and ambiguity is extremely high. What consumers say they would do or would buy often differs from how they actually act. In fact, consumers may not even know their future reactions. What people being questioned say may also depend on the images they wish to convey to the questioner. That is, they may not wish to appear miserly and, therefore, say price would not affect their purchases. According to marketing experts, these techniques are not very reliable.

A relatively new technique, laboratory experimentation, attempts to create the essential features of a market under study. Volunteers are paid to behave like buyers and sellers, and this creates the laboratory market. The experimenter can change relative prices and the basic market conditions during a session to study the behavior of participants. Studies have found it a trivial exercise to show that demand is downward sloping. Downward sloping demand curves have even been found for animal consumers. In these tests the experimenter is the seller of food and liquid. Prices are changed by changing the number of lever presses necessary for the release of a substance or changing the amount released when the right number of presses is made. Most experiments presently done are studying broader questions, many of them with public policy importance, e.g., exploring the impact of certain selling practices on collusive behavior.

Going a step further, some economists—with the help of psychologists—have conducted experiments on consumer behavior in mental institutions and in drug centers by setting up a token economy (which, incidentally, is supposed to have therapeutic value). Patients receive tokens for jobs performed. They can exchange these tokens for goods and services. The experimenters can change prices and incomes and, thereby generate demand curves. Their properties are then compared with the theoretical properties of such curves. These types of experiments are in very early stages.

All of this discussion is not meant to teach you how to estimate actual demands. This is the task of your marketing and econometrics classes. In these classes, you will actually be shown how estimates are made. But to do such estimating, you should have a thorough foundation in the theoretical underpinnings of demand theory.

3.7 SUMMARY

We have selected several applied topics in economics to better see how markets operate. In the arena of public policy we examined the impact of price supports and unit taxes. These forms of government intervention cause distortions in market outcomes, and, taking a very simple cost-benefit approach to these policies, we concluded that they cause total surplus in the market to decline. This loss of surplus ought to be counted as part of the cost of carrying out the policy. Minimizing these costs should also be a goal, given the policy desired. This depends on accurately estimating the supply and demand schedules in a market, and, as we saw in the last section, this is a formidable problem.

Even when market participants are completely unaware of how supply and demand interact, forces operate to move price and quantity to the equilibrium intersection. We discussed this in Section 3.2 of this chapter. Unless we are aware of impediments to the tendency toward equilibrium, we may safely assume that markets are moving toward and operate at prices and quantities close to the intersection of supply and demand. Markets may not operate precisely at this intersection since we know that demand and supply are often affected by exogenous factors that redefine an equilibrium. Once demand and/or supply change, the adjustment process begins anew.

The continual tendency towards equilibrium tells us that for some purposes we do not need to know what supply and demand curves look like to understand the relative impact of a public policy. It is important to know the elasticity of supply and demand at the equilibrium—or near equilibrium—prices and quantities. Government interference in relatively inelastic markets will cause less distortion and loss of surplus than policies carried out in markets with elastic supply and demand.

TECHNICAL PROBLEMS

1. A subsidy is the opposite of a tax; that is, the government gives a certain payment to each purchaser of a good that the government thinks people should consume more of. Begin with an original set of supply and demand curves. Show equilibrium. Next show graphically the effect of the subsidy on market price and on equilibrium quantity. Discuss the way that the slopes of demand and supply affect the change in equilibrium price and quantity.

2. Suppose a unit tax is placed on sellers in a market. Describe the change in price and quantity sold, and carefully explain why price usually does not rise by the full amount of the tax.

3. By using a graph showing shifts in supply and demand evaluate the following information about the dairy industry.
   a. Demand has fallen since 1980.
   b. Supply has increased since 1980.
   c. The equilibrium price should have decreased.
   d. A support price has kept price above the equilibrium price.
   e. A huge surplus of dairy products now exists.

4. Oscar Wilde once wrote, "A cynic is a man who knows the price of everything and the value of nothing." Explain the difference between price and value, using the concept of consumer's surplus.

5. The demand schedule for beer is $X_d = 25 - 1P$, where X_d is the quantity demanded of beer in millions of barrels per year and P is the price in dollars per barrel.

a. If the supply curve for beer is $X_s = -20 + 4P$, what is the equilibrium price of a barrel of beer?

b. What would the effect on the price of a barrel of beer if a tax of $4 per barrel is imposed by the government.

c. How much revenue does the government collect?

d. What is the reduction in total surplus due to the tax? (Hint: use consumer's and producer's surplus and calculate a dollar amount).

6. Assume the following demand and supply schedules exist:

$$X_d = 100 - 2P$$
$$X_s = -20 + 4P$$

a. Find the equilibrium price and quantity.

b. Calculate consumer's and producer's surplus at this equilibrium.

c. Now suppose a price ceiling is imposed at $15. What is the new quantity sold? Recalculate consumer's and producer's surplus.

d. By how much does consumer's surplus rise?

e. What is the decrease of total surplus in the market?

7. Use Figure E.3–1 to answer the following questions:

FIGURE E.3–1

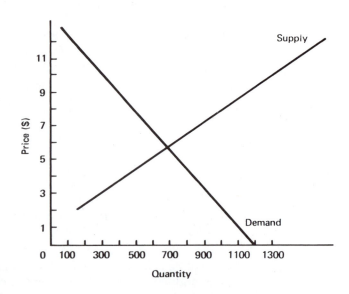

    a. In equilibrium price is $ _____ , and quantity sold in the market is _____ units.

    b. A governmentally mandated price of $4 will cause a _____ of _____ units.

    c. A governmentally mandated price of $8 will cause a _____ of _____ units.

    d. The imposition of a $2 per unit excise tax will change equilibrium price to $ _____ .

    e. $ _____ of the tax is paid by producers, and $ _____ is shifted to consumers of the good.

ANALYTICAL PROBLEMS

1. Excise tax authorities find themselves torn between the need to tax items that promise a high and steady flow of revenue and not taxing "necessities." Explain this conflict. On items that provide a good tax base, who bears the burden? Explain.

2. Suppose the price of materials and labor used in the construction of refrigerators goes up 6 percent. Using simple supply and demand curve analysis, do you expect the price of refrigerators to go up this much? What is the maximum price increase you would expect? Under what market conditions would this happen?

3. Some cities license taxicabs. The cities also fix the rate that taxis may charge. If, after several years, no new licenses are issued, an "unofficial" market for licenses generally arises.

    a. Discuss the factors that determine the price of a license.

    b. Would a change in the allowed fare raise or lower the price of a license?

    c. Who would benefit and who would lose from an expansion in the number of licenses issued by the city?

4. Here is another problem about taxicabs. In most big cities taxi fares are fixed by local government. At peak times some people are known to wave money at a cab instead of their hand. The money is paid to the driver, in addition to the regular fare plus tip [See *The New York Times*, January 26, 1985]. What does this practice tell you about the effectiveness of price ceilings? Is it *fair* that the person willing to pay more gets the cab?

5. Some people say that, without government price support programs, farmers could not afford to grow some crops like cotton; therefore, the country would have no cotton without the support program. Analyze.

6. Some legislators want to put higher taxes on liquor and cigarettes because they assert that people, particularly poor people, spend too much of their income on liquor and cigarettes and not enough on other goods, such as food. If extra taxes are levied on liquor and cigarettes, people would spend less on the "bad" things and more on other "good" things. Evaluate this statement.

7. Assume first an effective government-imposed maximum price is placed on a particular good. The price is set below equilibrium. Let the price ceiling be removed. Consumer spending on the good will increase only if demand is inelastic. Evaluate. (This is a tricky one.)

8. The president signed an executive order deregulating petroleum products. Before this, the price of gasoline was set by law below the equilibrium. As a result of the order, what will happen to price and quantity sold?

9. The airline industry is now deregulated. Previously, the Civil Aeronautics Board (CAB) kept a price floor on airline fares. When a price floor is eliminated, predict the effect on market price and output. Are your predictions consistent with your observations of what occurred in the airline industry?

10. Recently, Texas outlawed the practice of scalping tickets before major sports events and concerts. Scalping is selling tickets to an event at a higher price than face value. The practice was considered "unfair" by legislators. Analyze who gains and loses from such a practice using the concept of consumer's surplus. Are you opposed to the practice?

11. During the Christmas seasons of 1983 and 1984 Cabbage Patch dolls were extremely popular. Two large department stores advertised the dolls for under $30, but told customers they could not fill any orders. Local toy shops had waiting lists of 8 to 12 weeks. Yet the dolls were available in "antique" and pawn shops. They could also be purchased through classified newspaper ads. Prices ranged between $60 and $80. Suppose toy stores offer the doll for $26. Graphically depict this disequilibrium using supply and demand. Is it wrong to be a lucky buyer at $26 and then resell the doll at a higher price? Apply the concepts of consumer's and producer's surplus.

Chapter 4

Theory of Optimizing Behavior: Static and Dynamic Analysis

4.1 INTRODUCTION

A vast number of economic problems and a large part of this text are concerned with how individuals and firms can best utilize what they have. We call this optimization behavior. For example, consumers try to obtain the maximum satisfaction from a given income; producers want to produce a given output at the lowest possible cost; firms attempt to maximize profits; investors want to obtain the maximum discounted stream of net returns from a variety of potential investments. We could go on and on.

Since optimization plays an important role in this text, and in the whole body of economic analysis, some fundamental principles of optimizing behavior should be considered before going further in the analysis. A thorough understanding of these principles will significantly decrease difficulties in understanding the theoretical material set forth in later chapters.

All optimizing behavior falls into two classifications: constrained and unconstrained optimization. In these two types of behavior, the objective is either to maximize a goal or to minimize a cost.

A firm's attempt to choose a level of output that maximizes profit is an example of unconstrained maximization. Another example is a firm's attempt to minimize the total cost of product damage, including both the cost in lost sales and repairs of this damage and the cost of reducing the damage. The solutions to all such unconstrained optimization problems involve the same fundamental principle.

In the case of constrained optimization, individuals try to maximize or minimize, subject to some restriction on their behavior. An example of a constrained maximization problem is an individual's attempt to choose and purchase the bundle of goods and services that leads to the highest level of satisfaction possible, given a fixed level of income. Another constrained optimization problem is a firm's attempt to choose levels of input usage to minimize the cost of producing some chosen level of output. The solution to all such constrained optimization problems involves identical principles.

All economic problems that involve only a single period of time are classified as static analysis. For example, in the preceding chapters we discussed demand and supply within a single period. Consumers or producers will demand or supply a given amount at each price *per period of time*—i.e., in a single period. As we will see, much of the development of consumer behavior theory and the theory of the firm is under the single-period, decision-making framework.

Just because single-period analysis is called "static", don't assume that such an approach is somehow inferior to multiperiod, or dynamic analysis. Indeed, the large majority of analysis in this book—and in fact a large majority of all economic theory—involves single-period analysis. Most economic problems can be solved under this type of framework and the solution is simpler than one from a dynamic model.

Some economic problems must be analyzed by considering more than one period of time, for example, the theory of investment. Capital investment, such as the purchase of factories and machinery, is expected to yield a return not just during the period when the investment is undertaken, but many periods into the future. Also, the payments for such investments are frequently spread over several periods. Although an individual obtains satisfaction from some goods (such as steaks or hamburgers) only during the consumption period, goods like automobiles or household appliances yield satisfaction over many periods. At times it is useful to use multiperiod analysis when analyzing the latter type of consumption decision. As we will emphasize, the rate of interest is an extremely important concept in all economic theory involving time.

We will first develop the concept of unconstrained optimization; then turn to constrained. The fundamental principles that are in all such economic problems are set forth. You will be using these principles in a large part of the material covered in this text. Finally, we develop the principles that are used in multiperiod optimization, with particular emphasis on the role of the rate of interest.

4.2 UNCONSTRAINED OPTIMIZATION

The theory of unconstrained optimization is quite simple. The fundamental concept is equating costs and benefits at the margin. Once this principle is understood everything follows directly. To demonstrate, let's look first at the maximization decision.

Unconstrained Maximization

Suppose that some activity yields benefits—measured in dollars of income. The greater the level of the activity, the greater the benefits over the relevant range; the higher the level of the activity, the higher the cost in dollars. For each additional unit of the activity chosen, the individual receives added benefits, but has to pay additional costs. Let's call the additional benefits from an additional unit of the activity the marginal benefit. The additional cost from increasing the activity by one more unit is the marginal cost of that unit.

The task of the decision maker is to choose the level of activity that maximizes the total benefit received less the total cost of the activity. This maximizes the net value of the benefits received.

Suppose the decision maker is presently choosing a zero level of the activity but is considering whether to choose one unit. Should this one unit be chosen? Yes, if this unit is expected to add more benefit (say, income) than it costs. No, if the benefit from this one unit is less than the cost. In other words, add this unit if the marginal benefit exceeds the marginal cost; don't add this unit if the marginal benefit is less than the marginal cost. Rather simple so far.

Suppose one unit is chosen; should a second unit be added? Following the same kind of reasoning, it should be added if the marginal benefit exceeds the marginal cost. The same thing holds for every additional unit of the activity. As long as the additional benefit from each additional unit of the activity is greater than the additional cost, the level of the activity should be expanded. As soon as the level is reached where the additional cost of adding one more unit is greater than the additional benefit from that unit, no more should be added. In this way the total net return (total benefit minus total cost) is maximized. This, of course, is because net total return increases when the additional benefit exceeds the additional cost, and net return declines when the additional benefit is less than the additional cost.

The following principle follows logically:

Principle

To maximize the net return from an activity, the decision maker should choose the level of the activity where the marginal benefit from the last unit chosen equals the marginal cost of that unit.

We illustrate this principle graphically in Figure 4–1. The marginal benefit curve is downward sloping to reflect positive but decreasing marginal benefits from additional units of the activity. The marginal cost curve is positively sloped, indicating that the marginal cost increases as the level of the activity increases.

A maximizing decision maker would choose $\overline{A}$ as the optimal level of the activity, the optimal level being the amount of the activity that

FIGURE 4-1   **Principle of unconstrained maximization**

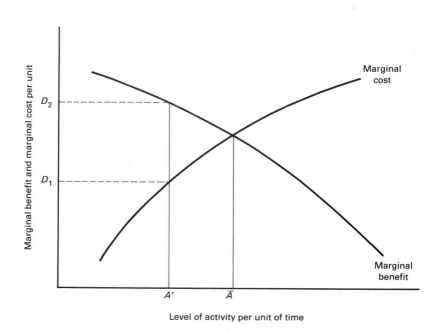

Level of activity per unit of time

maximizes net return. At any level less than $\overline{A}$ an additional unit of the activity would add more benefit than it costs. For example, at A' one more unit of the activity would add slightly more than D_1 to cost but would add slightly less than D_2 to benefits. Clearly, the net return would increase with one more unit since D_2 is greater than D_1. The decision maker would not increase the activity beyond $\overline{A}$, because each additional unit would add more to cost than to benefit, and would therefore decrease the net return. Maximization requires that marginal benefit must equal marginal cost for the last unit of the activity.

This general principle holds for many types of economic decisions. For example, a firm chooses its level of output to maximize profit, which is total revenue minus total cost. Each additional unit of output produced and sold increases both total revenue and total cost. The manager would increase output so long as the added revenue from each additional unit is greater than the added cost of producing that unit. If the cost is greater than the revenue, that unit would not be produced. In this way profit is maximized. We will develop this concept further in later chapters.

A similar situation holds when the firm decides how much of each input in the production process to hire. An additional unit of an input increases the level of output and therefore increases revenue. Each additional unit also adds to cost—for example, the wages that must be paid in the case of labor. Clearly a firm would hire more of the input as long as additional revenue exceeds additional cost. It would hire no more of the input if the additional revenue is less than the additional cost. For every input employed—labor, capital, land, etc.—the firm would employ the amount that makes the additional revenue of the last unit equal to the additional cost of that unit. Marginal benefit must equal marginal cost in order to maximize the net return.

Unconstrained Minimization

The principle of unconstrained minimization is identical to that of maximization. In this case the decision maker wishes to minimize the net cost of some activity rather than maximize the net return. To illustrate, suppose a firm is experiencing a considerable amount of product damage in its shipping department. The engineers recommend an extensive program of inspection and damage control. How much damage control should the firm undertake?

Assuming that we can divide the damage control activity into units—number of inspectors, units of handling equipment, etc.—each additional unit of damage control reduces the amount of breakage and therefore reduces the cost of breakage to the firm. But each unit of control costs the firm money—the inspectors must be paid a salary. Should the firm add more units of damage control? Yes, if an additional unit of control reduces the cost of breakage damage by more than the cost of that unit. Clearly, the firm would not employ another unit of damage control if that unit costs more than the resulting reduction in cost. The firm would increase damage control until the marginal benefit (reduction in breakage cost) equals the marginal cost (additional cost of the damage control).

The same principle applies to many other cost-reducing activities, such as spilling ore during unloading, reducing shoplifting in a store, or even the cost of polluting the environment. In all such activities the following principle applies:

Principle

The optimal amount of a cost-reducing activity is the level where the marginal benefit or marginal cost reduction of the last unit of the activity equals the marginal cost of undertaking that activity.

4.3 CONSTRAINED OPTIMIZATION

Constrained and unconstrained optimization are similar in the sense that the decision maker wishes to maximize some benefit or minimize the cost from some activity. The two concepts are different because in constrained optimization the maximization or minimization takes place under some imposed restriction.

Constrained Maximization

Let's take a general case as an example. Suppose an individual wants to maximize the benefits (output, satisfaction, etc.) that can be produced using two activities, call them A and B. The constraint or restriction is that the activities can only be obtained at a price, P_A and P_B, and there is only a limited money budget, M, available for purchasing the activities. The constraint could be written as

$$M = P_A A + P_B B.$$

This shows that the total expenditure on the activities must equal the amount of income available—M.

We make the assumption that as each activity is increased, holding the other constant, the marginal benefit, MB_A and MB_B, from each additional unit is positive but at incrementally smaller amounts. We can write the marginal benefit per dollar of each unit of the activity as MB_A/P_A and MB_B/P_B. That is, if an additional unit of A adds 10 units of benefit ($MB_A = 10$) and if the price of a unit of A is \$2 ($P_A = \$2$), then the marginal benefit per dollar spent on that unit of A is 5 ($MB_A/P_A = 5$). Each dollar spent on that unit of A adds five units of benefit.

If the decision maker is spending the entire budget on A and B and

$$\frac{MB_A}{P_A} > \frac{MB_B}{P_B},$$

is this person obtaining the maximum benefit from the given budget? Clearly not. The marginal benefit from the last dollar spent on A exceeds that forthcoming from the last dollar spent on B. The person should reallocate the budget, taking dollars away from B and adding to A. Total benefit would increase since each dollar added to A would increase the benefits by more than the benefits lost by taking the dollar away from B. As A is increased, MB_A decreases; and as B is decreased, MB_B increases. As dollars continue to be reallocated, a point must be reached where the marginal benefit of the last dollar spent on A equals the marginal benefit of the last dollar spent on B ($MB_A/P_A = MB_B/P_B$).

Let's assume that a combination of A and B is chosen so that the entire budget is spent but the inequality is reversed:

$$\frac{MB_A}{P_A} < \frac{MB_B}{P_B}.$$

Following the same line of reasoning as above, dollars should be taken away from A and added to B. The lost benefit from the reduced A is less than the added benefit from increased B. In this way, total benefit is increased while the budget constraint holds. As A decreases and B increases, MB_A rises and MB_B falls until the marginal benefit from the last dollar spent on A equals the marginal benefit from the last dollar spent on B.

Thus we have ruled out each inequality as the combination of A and B that yields the maximum benefit obtainable under the constraint. Only if the equality holds ($MB_A/P_A = MB_B/P_B$), will the decision maker maximize the benefit forthcoming under the given constraint.

The same rule is true when there are more than two activities that can only be obtained at a cost; a budget constraint must be met, and each activity has positive but declining marginal benefits. Any time the inequality $MB_i/P_i \lessgtr MB_j/P_j$ holds for any pair of activities, dollars should be taken away from the activity yielding less marginal benefit per dollar and added to the activity yielding more. In this way total benefit increases while the budget constraint is met.

The following principle has been established:

Principle

With a given budget constraint and prices of activities $X_1, X_2, \ldots X_n$ of $P_1, P_2, \ldots P_n$, maximization of the total benefit obtainable within the given budget requires that

$$\frac{MB_1}{P_1} = \frac{MB_2}{P_2} = \cdots = \frac{MB_n}{P_n}.$$

The marginal benefit from each dollar spent on the last unit of each activity employed must be equal for all activities.

We might digress to consider a case where it is optimal to use none of a certain activity even though the first unit of the activity has a positive marginal benefit. Let's continue using the two activities, A and B, and a given budget. Suppose the *entire budget is spent only on A* and we have the inequality

$$\frac{MB_A}{P_A} > \frac{MB_B}{P_B}.$$

Now, reallocation would not increase benefits. You cannot reallocate dollars away from B and add to A, because nothing is being spent on B. In this case the entire budget should be spent on activity A. If the inequality is reversed and the entire budget is being spent on B, no A will be used. Such cases are called corner solutions to the constrained optimization problem. While such corner solutions can be important, we will concentrate on the situation where positive amounts of all relevant activities are being employed and ignore all unused activities.

In the general case described we have shown the optimization process under the assumption of an income constraint. But other types of constraints are certainly possible. Let's consider an example with a time constraint—the optimal allocation of study time.

Suppose a student has allocated nine hours to study for three examinations scheduled for the next day—statistics, economics, and mathematics. The student's objective is to allocate the study time to maximize the total of the scores on the three exams (and therefore maximize the average score). The student's assessment of the grade in each exam for each amount of study time is shown in the following table.

Study time (hours)	Grade in		
	Statistics	*Economics*	*Mathematics*
0	50	53	65
1	63	65	75
2	73	73	80
3	80	78	84
4	85	81	87
5	89	83	89
6	92	84	90

From the table we can see that if the student spent no time studying, the grades would be 50 in statistics, 53 in economics, and 65 in mathematics. If one hour of study were spent on a subject, that hour could add 13 points to the statistics grade, 12 points to the economics grade, or 10 points to the mathematics grade. So, the first hour of study would be allocated to statistics, where the return is highest. The second hour would be allocated to economics, since it would add 12 points in this subject but only 10 in each of the others. The third and fourth hours are spent studying statistics and math, since the grade increases are 10 points in each of these subjects, but only 8 in economics. Following this allocation rule, the fifth hour would go to economics and the sixth to statistics. The student's nine-hour study time constraint leaves three more hours of study time. We can see that the added test points from an additional hour of study time in each subject are now the same—five. Thus the student would allocate one more hour to each course.

Therefore, optimal allocation of the nine hours would have the student spend four hours studying statistics, three hours studying economics, and two studying math. The total expected points would be 243, with an average grade of 81. This is the highest average possible with the nine-hour study constraint. (You can verify this by trying to reallocate the nine hours in different ways.)

This allocation decision is simply a specific application of the principle set forth above for constrained optimization. The cost (in hours) of allocating an additional hour to a particular course is what you give up during that hour. The marginal benefit of allocating an additional hour to a particular course is the grade increase that would result. As we know, the optimization rule is to allocate so that

$$\frac{MB_S}{P_S} = \frac{MB_E}{P_E} = \frac{MB_M}{P_M},$$

where P_S, P_E, and P_M are the implicit prices of using time to study. They are simply the cost in time (one hour lost to other alternatives) of spending the hour studying statistics, economics, or mathematics.

Using the above table with the allocation we have proposed, the ratios of marginal benefits to marginal costs for the last hour spent in each course are

$$\frac{5}{1} = \frac{5}{1} = \frac{5}{1},$$

where 5 is the number of points that can be added to the test scores in any of the three subjects, and 1 is the hour of time given up to study. The marginal benefit for the last unit of expenditure in time is the same for all three subjects, and the nine-hour constraint is met. The student maximizes the total, and the average grade possible, given the constraint. Many other examples of such constrained maximization problems abound in economic theory, and many are developed much more completely in later chapters of this text.

A very important case involves a firm trying to obtain the maximum output under a given level of cost, using several inputs, denoted as X_1, X_2, . . . X_n, with the cost of the ith input being P_i. From the above analysis, it should be clear that the firm would spend the entire budget and choose the input mix so that for each input employed

$$\frac{MB_1}{P_1} = \frac{MB_2}{P_2} = \cdots = \frac{MB_n}{P_n},$$

where MB_i is the addition to total revenue from the addition of one more unit of the ith input.

Other examples would be consumers who wish to obtain the maximum level of satisfaction (utility) obtainable from a given money income. The consumer obtains satisfaction or utility from the goods and services purchased at given prices with the fixed income. Following our above analysis, the consumer would choose the bundle of goods and services that meets the income constraint, and for all goods and services purchased the additional benefit (called marginal utility) per dollar spent on the last unit is the same. In this way total utility is maximized.

Other examples involve departments or agencies that are given a fixed budget and charged with obtaining the maximum benefit possible under that budget. An advertising department might try to allocate a fixed advertising budget among the various media—newspapers, TV, radio—to maximize total sales. Obviously the department would choose the media mix where the marginal increase in sales for the last unit purchased per dollar spent on that unit is equal for all media used and the budget constraint is met.

Nonprofit organizations would be faced with similar decisions. A hospital would choose among various inputs that contribute to health care (however defined) in order to maximize health care under the given budget. A university wants to maximize education (again however defined) subject to an imposed budget. The same rule applies. Each activity would be used so that the marginal benefit per dollar spent on the last unit is equal for all activities employed.

As implied in the example of allocation of study time, constraints other than money are often relevant—time is frequently an important constraint. A manager would allocate a fixed amount of available time among activities that contribute to the firm's profit. The additional profit from each activity per unit of time spent should be the same for all activities. You can probably think of many other examples where time is the relevant constraint.

Constrained Minimization

Another economic process, constrained minimization, involves decision makers who want to minimize the cost—in dollars or time—of carrying out some objective under a constraint. Now the goal is to minimize cost and the constraint is the fixed or given level of the objective. The minimization rule is the same as the rule for maximization.

To illustrate this principle, let's assume that a firm produces a product using only two inputs, capital (K) and labor (L). Capital cost per unit is r and the wage rate of labor is w. The firm wishes to produce 1,000 units of output per period at the minimum cost possible. The objective is to minimize total cost (TC), where

$$TC = wL + rK$$

subject to the constraint that output equals 1,000 units.

We call the additional output forthcoming from one more unit of labor or capital, holding the other constant, the marginal benefit of the input—MB_L and MB_K. In later chapters when we discuss the demand for inputs, we will give the marginal benefit of inputs a special name. Assume that over the relevant range the marginal benefit of each input is positive but decreases with increased usage.

Following the procedure described above, given that 1000 units of output are being produced, it may be that the amounts of labor and capital used are such that

$$\frac{MB_L}{w} < \frac{MB_K}{r}.$$

In this case the firm could decrease its usage of labor, increase capital, and, while holding output constant at 1,000 units, reduce its total cost.

To see why this is true, suppose that from the above inequality

$$\frac{MB_L}{w} = \frac{20}{\$6} < \frac{10}{\$2} = \frac{MB_K}{r}.$$

The marginal increase in output from the last unit of labor is 20 units. The price of a unit of labor is $6. The last unit of capital increases output by 10 units, but costs only $2 per unit. Because the per dollar benefit of labor is less than capital at the margin, we know that more capital and less labor should be used. Reducing labor by one unit would reduce output by 20. Cost would decrease by $6, the wage of the unit of labor released. To keep output constant, capital must be increased by two units, since the marginal benefit of capital is 10. At $2 each, the two additional units of capital would add $4 to cost. But the net result would be a cost decrease of $2, while output remains constant at 1000.

As long as the above inequality holds, the firm can reduce labor, increase capital, and reduce the cost of producing the 1000 units. As labor usage is reduced and capital increased, the marginal benefit of labor rises while the marginal benefit of capital falls. As the input reallocation continues, an input mix will be reached so that $MB_L/w = MB_K/r$. Next assume that

$$\frac{MB_L}{w} > \frac{MB_K}{r}.$$

By the same reasoning set forth above, capital usage should be reduced and labor increased until $MB_L/w = MB_K/r$. We have established that under the above assumptions, producing a fixed output at minimum cost requires that the marginal benefit of labor per dollar must equal the marginal benefit of capital per dollar, i.e.,

$$\frac{MB_L}{w} = \frac{MB_K}{r}.$$

If this equality holds for any two inputs in the production process, it holds for all inputs employed. Therefore if the firm uses n inputs—$X_1, X_2,$ . . . X_n—to produce a given level of output, X, and the prices of the inputs are $P_1, P_2,$ . . . P_n, the lowest possible cost of producing this output is attained when input usage is allocated so that

$$\frac{MB_1}{P_1} = \frac{MB_2}{P_2} = \cdots = \frac{MB_n}{P_n}.$$

We can further generalize these results. Assume that a particular level of benefits, $\overline{B}$, can be produced using activities, $A_1, A_2, \ldots A_n$. Denote the marginal benefit of an additional unit of the ith activity as MB_i. Let the total cost of producing benefits depend on the levels of usage of the n activities. The marginal cost of the ith activity—the addition to total cost of using one additional unit of that activity—is MC_i. Cost minimization subject to the constraint that the level of benefits is $\overline{B}$ requires that for any activities, i and j,

$$\frac{MB_i}{MC_i} = \frac{MB_j}{MC_j}.$$

To see this, suppose that it is not true at first and

$$\frac{MB_i}{MC_i} = \frac{100}{20} < \frac{50}{5} = \frac{MB_j}{MC_j},$$

and the required level of benefits is being produced. The decision maker could reduce activity i by one unit. Since $MB_i = 100$, total benefit would fall by 100 units, and because the marginal cost of the dismissed unit is $20, the total cost would decline by $20. To keep the total benefits constant, an additional two units of the jth activity would increase total benefits 100 units ($MB_j = 50$) and replace the 100 units lost by the one-unit reduction in activity i. These additional two units of j would cost $10 ($MC_j = $5), assuming marginal cost does not change for the additional j units. Thus benefits would remain constant, but cost would decline by $10 ($20 − $10 = $10). The decision maker should continue to reallocate until

$$\frac{MB_i}{MC_i} = \frac{MB_j}{MC_j}.$$

If this equality holds for any two activities, i and j, it must hold for all activities. We have established the following principle:

Principle

If benefits can be produced by n activities, $A_1, A_2, \ldots A_n$, and the total cost of producing any given level of benefits depends on the level of usage of each activity, to produce a fixed level of benefits at the minimum cost, the marginal benefit of the last unit of each activity divided by the marginal cost of that unit must equal the marginal benefit of the last unit of every other activity used divided by its marginal cost, or

$$\frac{MB_1}{MC_1} = \frac{MB_2}{MC_2} = \cdots = \frac{MB_n}{MC_n}.$$

This relation must hold for any constrained minimization problem.

Recall that in constrained maximization we considered costs other than dollar costs—the same holds for constrained minimization. In many optimization problems, time is the relevant variable. When we discussed time in the constrained maximization context, a student was trying to maximize the average grade on three tests, subject to a constraint on total study time available. We concluded that the marginal benefit from an additional hour of study time (marginal increase in grade) should be equal for all three subjects. Or the last hour spent studying each subject should lead to the same grade increase.

We can also deal with this problem within a minimization context. Suppose that another student is preparing for the same three tests in statistics, economics, and mathematics. This student, rather than attempting to maximize the average grade from a fixed amount of studying, wants to attain an average grade of 90 with a minimum amount of time spent studying. Like the first student, this student has a good idea of how much an additional hour of studying will increase the expected grade in each subject. Thus the student wants to minimize study time subject to the constraint that the expected grade average is 90. As you would expect, the student should allocate time among the subjects so that the average grade is 90, and

$$\frac{MB_S}{1} = \frac{MB_E}{1} = \frac{MB_M}{1},$$

where MB is expected grade increase from an additional hour spent studying each subject.

Proceeding as before, assume that $MB_S > MB_E$ for the last hour of studying each subject. This means that if one hour is taken away from economics and added to statistics, the total grade on the three exams, and therefore the average grade, could be increased. By assumption, the average grade from this allocation is 90. The student could take an hour from economics and add less than an hour to statistics, while maintaining the same average grade. That is, if one hour is taken from economics, that grade would fall by MB_E. If the full hour is added to statistics, that grade would rise by MB_S which is greater than MB_E, and the average grade would increase. Since only a grade of 90 is desired, the student adds only enough time to offset the grade reduction in economics. Given our assumption that $MB_S > MB_E$ for an hour of study, that added time on statistics is presumably less than one hour.

Therefore we see that for both the constrained maximization and minimization problem the same marginal conditions hold: the marginal grade increase for the last unit of time spent studying should be the same for all subjects. You might go back to the original example and verify that if the student had wanted to attain the average grade of 81 with a minimum time spent studying, a total of nine hours would be spend studying and the time would be allocated in exactly the same way among the three subjects.

In summary, whether discussing maximization or minimization of some objective, the same principle applies. If there are n activities used to increase benefits and each of the activities contributes to cost, total benefit is maximized subject to a given level of cost or total cost is minimized subject to a given level of benefit when

$$\frac{MB_1}{MC_1} = \frac{MB_2}{MC_2} = \cdots = \frac{MB_n}{MC_n}$$

for the last unit of each activity used and the constraint is met.

4.4 MULTIPERIOD ANALYSIS

We have analyzed optimization within the context of a single period. Many optimization problems involve a stream of benefits or costs over time. Some examples are capital investments, durable goods that give benefits to consumers over time, and saving or lending. In such problems a crucial variable in the decision-making process is the rate of interest. To see why this is so we introduce the concepts of future and present value.

The Role of Interest

The decision to spend or save, or to buy now or later, depends critically on the rate of interest. Interest income is the cost of spending now. Income could be saved and spent in the future along with the interest payment. Interest is foregone when income is spent.

Interest payments are closely connected with the process of capital accumulation. If people are willing to defer consumption now and invest in a production process, they may be able to consume more at a later time than the amount originally foregone. If C is invested in an activity and $(C + R)$ is earned in the next period, R is the return on the investment of C and represents the cost of consuming now. The rate of return on investment and interest are indeed two sides of a coin. To illustrate this point, consider a very simple example.

Suppose that, in a very primitive society, most of the people earn their living by fishing. The state of technology is so primitive that everyone fishes from the bank of a lake. One family deduces that if they had a boat, they could fish farther out in the lake and catch more fish. In order to build the boat, the family must sacrifice time that could be spent fishing and must, therefore, reduce consumption now in order to consume more later. This reduction in consumption represents an investment. Foregone consumption promises an uncertain but higher return later. The cost of continued fishing from the bank is the extra fish that could be caught in a boat. The individuals who took the risk and decided to build a boat would be called *entrepreneurs*.

The family might decide that they do not want to decrease the amount of fish they consume while building the boat. They can still eat if other families will reduce their current consumption and give some of their fish to them. The problem is persuading other people to sacrifice some of their fish.

One method of persuasion is to agree to repay the fish after the boat is built and the catch becomes larger. But if they prefer consumption now to consumption in the future, the boat builders must agree to repay more fish than they receive while building. The "lenders" of the fish require an additional amount to compensate them for the present consumption given up. The "borrowers" of the fish would, they hope, be able to repay more than they borrowed, because future catches should be larger. The additional amount of fish repaid represents the interest paid for the fish consumed now.

The fact that productive processes take time and people prefer to consume today rather than tomorrow results in a positive interest rate in most societies. Furthermore, the rate of interest will be determined by the increase in output made possible by deferring consumption and the risk of a particular venture. Interest rates are necessary to compensate lenders for giving up present income and for the risk they take if borrowers default on their promise to pay later. Remember that the family building the boat was not absolutely sure more fish could be caught by getting away from shore. Interest rates are affected by the possibility of foregoing consumption without any return at a later time. The more risky the venture, the higher the interest rate.

Future Value

To introduce the role played by interest rates in making multiperiod decisions we begin by considering the rate of appreciation of a monetary asset over time. This rate of appreciation determines the future value of an asset.

Suppose you have $100 today and the interest rate is 12 percent. If you invest the $100 at 12 percent interest, in one year you would have

$$\$100 + .12(\$100) = \$100(1.12) = \$112.$$

The future value of $100 in one year is $112. Obviously if the interest rate is higher (lower), the future value is higher (lower). If you hold the investment for two years, the future value would be

$$\$112 + .12(\$112) = \$112(1.12) = \$125.44,$$

since you had $112 at the end of one year and invested this amount again at 12 percent. We can rewrite this expression for future value by substituting for the $112 you had at the end of the first year. Combining the above equations we have

$$(1 + .12)\$112 = (1 + .12)(1 + .12)\$100 = (1 + .12)^2\$100 = \$125.44.$$

Similarly, the future value of the investment in three years is

$$(1 + .12)\,[(1 + .12)^2\,\$100] = (1 + .12)^3\$100 = \$140.49.$$

More generally, in n years the value of the investment would be

$$(1 + .12)^n\$100.$$

Generalizing further, the future value of investing $\$A$ at an interest rate r for n years is

$$FV = \$A(1 + r)^n.$$

Table 4–1 shows a comparison of future values of $100 over a 25-year period for four different rates of interest. The future values increasingly diverge for higher interest rates as the period of time becomes longer. This divergence shows the importance of the interest rate in making decisions involving time.

One such decision involves the cost of holding an asset. For simplicity, assume that you own an asset strictly for financial reasons. You keep the asset for its increasing market value and not because it provides you with a service. Such commodities are called sterile assets. Examples might be a bar of gold or a ton of coal. The question is: Should you keep the asset, which is appreciating, and sell it later or sell it now? The answer depends on the future value of the asset. For simplicity we assume that the asset costs nothing to store.

Suppose this asset could be sold now for $10,000 or could be held for one year and sold for $11,000, an increase in value of 10 percent. It is obvious that if the interest rate is above 10 percent, you should sell the asset. For example, if the interest rate is 12 percent, you could sell the

TABLE 4–1   **Future values at different interest rates**

Interest rate (percent)	Future value of $100 at the end of				
	5 years	10 years	15 years	20 years	25 years
3	$116	$134	$ 156	$ 180	$ 209
8	147	216	317	466	685
12	176	311	547	965	1,700
20	249	619	1,541	3,834	9,540

asset now, invest the $10,000 at 12 percent, and have $11,200 at the end of the year. You would be $200 better off than if you had held the asset. The cost (called opportunity cost) of holding the asset is the potential $1200 that could be earned as interest.

On the other hand, if the interest rate is below 10 percent, the asset should be held. If, for example, the interest rate is 8 percent, the $10,000 would bring only $10,000 (1.08) = $10,800, or $200 less than the potential gain from keeping the asset.

For sterile assets, the rule is: Hold the asset if it is expected to appreciate at a rate greater than the relevant rate of interest. Sell the asset if it is expected to appreciate at a rate less than the rate of interest.

Present Value

Now that we have the concept of future value, we can translate future values to present values. Consider how much you would be willing to pay for the right to receive $1,000 one year from now. Clearly, $1,000 one year in the future is worth less to you than $1,000 today. If you had $1,000 now, you could invest it at some rate of interest and have more than $1,000 in one year. How much less than $1,000 would you be willing to pay? At a 12 percent rate of interest, if you invest $892.86 now you would receive $1,000 in one year, because

$$\$892.86(1 + .12) = \$1,000.$$

Therefore, you would be willing to pay no more than $892.86 for the right to receive $1,000 one year in the future.

At the same 12 percent rate of interest, you would be willing to pay no more than $797.19 for $1000 received in two years, because

$$\$797.19(1 + .12)^2 = \$1,000.$$

These amounts, $892.86 and $797.19, are the present values of $1,000 for one and two years, respectively. Generalizing, for the right to receive $1,000 n years in the future with an interest rate of 12 percent, a person would be willing to pay no more than the present value (PV), where

$$PV(1 + .12)^n = \$1,000,$$

or

$$PV = \frac{\$1,000}{(1 + .12)^n}.$$

The $1,000 in the above ratio is a specific amount promised in the future, or what we have been calling future value. We can generalize a little further by writing the equation for present value as

$$PV = \frac{R}{(1 + r)^n}.$$

This is the present value of some future return (R) in n years with an interest rate of r.

Present value is the "discounted value" of a future income payment. As you can see, discounting means dividing the return by $(1 + r)^n$. The concepts of present and future values are linked by the rate of interest.

Let's expand our analysis to consider the present value of a *stream* of future income payments. How much would someone pay for the following stream of income payments (each payment payable at year end)?

Year	Income
1	$1,500
2	2,000
3	2,200
4	3,000
5	3,400
Sum	$12,100

No one would pay $12,100, the sum of the yearly incomes. The amount someone would be willing to pay depends on the present value of the income stream. Suppose the relevant rate of interest is 10 percent. Then the present value of this income stream is

$$PV = \frac{\$1,500}{(1 + .10)} + \frac{\$2,000}{(1. + .10)^2} + \frac{\$2,200}{(1 + .10)^3} + \frac{\$3,000}{(1 + .10)^4} + \frac{\$3,400}{(1 + .10)^5}$$

$$= \$1,363.64 + \$1,652.89 + \$1,652.89 + \$2,049.04 + \$2,111.13$$

$$= \$8,829.59.$$

Generalizing, let R_t be the income in the tth year and r be the rate of interest. The present value of the stream of income is

$$PV = \frac{R_1}{(1 + r)} + \frac{R_2}{(1 + r)^2} + \frac{R_3}{(1 + r)^3} + \cdots + \frac{R_n}{(1 + r)^n} = \sum_{t=1}^{n} \left(\frac{1}{1 + r}\right)^t R_t.$$

We have established the following principle:

Principle

The future value of investing $A for n years with an interest rate of r is

$$FV = \$A (1 + r)^n.$$

The present value (the maximum amount that would be paid for) of a future payment of $R in n years is

$$PV = \frac{\$R}{(1 + r)^n}.$$

The present value of an income stream over n years is

$$PV = \sum_{t=1}^{n} \frac{R_t}{(1 + r)^t},$$

where R_t is the income to be received in year t.

The more heavily weighted toward the future are the income payments, the lower is the present value of a stream of income. For an example illustrating this point, consider the following two streams of income, both of which sum to $10,000.

Year	Stream 1	Stream 2
1	$ 1,000	$ 4,000
2	2,000	3,000
3	3,000	2,000
4	4,000	1,000
Sum	$10,000	$10,000

At a 10 percent rate of interest the present value of Stream 1 is

$$PV_1 = \frac{\$1,000}{(1 + .10)} + \frac{\$2,000}{(1 + .10)^2} + \frac{\$3,000}{(1 + .10)^3} + \frac{\$4,000}{(1 + .10)^4} = \$7,547.98,$$

and the present value of Stream 2 is

$$PV_2 = \frac{\$4,000}{(1 + .10)} + \frac{\$3,000}{(1 + .10)^2} + \frac{\$2,000}{(1 + .10)^3} + \frac{\$1,000}{(1 + .10)^4} = \$8,301.34.$$

The present value of Stream 2 is almost $1,000 more than that of Stream 1, even though the sums of the incomes are equal. The high incomes are closer to the present in Stream 2. This means that they are discounted by a lower number than the high incomes in Stream 1. For example, in Stream 1, the $4,000 income is divided by $(1.1)^4 = 1.464$ while the $4,000 in Stream 2 is divided by 1.1. Income closer to the present is worth more now than the same income further into the future.

As additional evidence of the increased impact of interest as the number of time periods increases, Table 4–2 shows the present value of $100 from the present to 25 years from now at four selected rates of interest. By comparing the rows of values, we notice that both time and increased interest have dramatic effects on present value.

Let's now apply our theory of present value to the determination of the market value of an income producing asset. When we speak of the asset's value, we generally mean the price that the asset can be sold for in the market. In the case of an income-generating asset, this value is deter-

TABLE 4–2   **Present values for different interest rates**

Interest rate (%)	Present values of $100 to be received at the end of				
	5 years	10 years	15 years	20 years	25 years
3	$86	$75	$64	$55	$48
8	68	46	32	21	15
12	57	32	18	10	6
20	40	16	6	3	1

mined by the present value of the stream of income the asset can be expected to yield over the relevant time horizon. Unless the asset has some other personal value to its owner in addition to the expected income, no one would pay more for the asset than the present value of its income stream. If the price of the asset is greater than its present value, a prospective purchaser could simply invest the money at the relevant interest rate and derive a net return greater than that expected from purchasing the asset. On the other hand, if the price is lower than the present value, the asset is expected to yield a net return greater than could be acquired from investing the money at the market rate of interest. The market price of the asset will be bid up or down until it is equal to its present value.

We can see the importance of present value in the following example. Suppose a real estate firm can buy a building for $1 million, then lease office space in the building to generate a net income of $50,000 a year for five years. (For analytical simplicity, assume that the rent is paid at the end of each year.) It is estimated that the wear and tear from use of the building (depreciation) will exactly offset appreciation in value due to inflation and that the building will sell for $1 million at the end of five years.

If the market rate of interest is 10 percent, the present value of the building is

$$PV = \sum_{t=1}^{5} \left(\frac{1}{1.1}\right)^t 50,000 + \frac{1,000,000}{(1.1)^5} = \$810,461.$$

The asking price of this asset exceeds the value of the asset—the present value of the income stream. At a 10 percent interest rate, the firm would pay no more than $810,461 for the office building. Unless the present owner is willing to lower the price of the building, the real estate firm would be better off investing the $1 million in an asset yielding a higher return.

Discounting and Consumption Expenditures

We have emphasized the importance of discounting in decisions concerning investment, but discounting is also important in many consumption decisions. People purchase goods that are consumed over several periods and involve expenditures over several periods. For example, certain durable goods, such as automobiles or household appliances, have an initial purchase price and involve operating expenses over the consumption life of the good. In such cases, the rate of interest is important to determine what good to purchase and what method of payment is the least costly.

Consider someone trying to decide between two types of a household appliance—an air conditioner. The two air conditioning units are identical in every way except one costs more and is more energy efficient, meaning the yearly operating costs are lower. Each unit has an expected life of 10 years, with no resale value.

The more expensive unit costs $4,000, and the operating expenditures are $900 a year. The other unit costs only $3,000, but will cost $1,000 a year to run. The total payment in each case is the same over the life of the appliance:

$$\$4,000 + \quad \$900 \times 10 = \$13,000$$
$$\$3,000 + \$1,000 \times 10 = \$13,000.$$

We know that the relevant figure to use is the present value of the payment stream, not the undiscounted dollars. Assuming an interest rate of 10 percent, the air conditioner with the lower price and higher operating cost should be purchased since

$$PV_1 = \$4,000 + \sum_{t=1}^{10} \frac{\$900}{(1 + .10)^t} = \$4,000 + \$5,530 = \$9,530,$$

and

$$PV_2 = \$3,000 + \sum_{t=1}^{10} \frac{\$1,000}{(1 + .10)^t} = \$3,000 + \$6,145 = \$9,145.$$

We can see that when making decisions involving payments over time the present value of the stream of payments must be considered. As we will see in the following application, the same thing is true when deciding whether to rent or purchase a durable.

APPLICATION

Lease or Buy an Automobile?

Leasing as an alternative to buying is becoming increasingly popular at many U.S. automobile dealerships. Many people prefer to obtain a new car without the down payment required to purchase it. In fact, at some dealerships leases represent half of their new car volume. A recent newspaper story presented the following table to help consumers decide if they should lease or purchase a representative automobile, in this case a 1984 Buick Regal. We can use this newspaper story to explain why leasing is popular at relatively high interest rates and point out a serious shortcoming in the advice given by the newspaper writer.

1984 Regal two-door (value: $12,400)

Cost	Buy		Lease
Down payment	$ 1,240		$ 0
Monthly payments			
(36 at $345)	+ $12,420	(36 at $290)	+ $10,440
Subtotal	$13,660		$10,440
Value of car			
(after three years*)	− $ 5,400		− $ 0
Total	$ 8,260		$10,440

* Well-maintained car with average of 45,000 miles.
Source: *Dallas Morning News,* July 17, 1984, p. 21.

According to this table, if consumers decide to buy the automobile, they make a 10 percent down payment of $1,240 then 36 monthly payments of $345. The total cash payment is $13,660 (36 × $345 + $1,240). At the end of three years the owner can sell the car for $5,400, so the net cash outflow according to the newspaper article is $8,260. By leasing, a consumer simply makes 36 payments of $290 then returns the car to the dealer at the end of three years. The total cash outflow under the lease arrangement is $10,440. The numbers in this example seem to show that if customers can come up with the down payment, they should buy rather than lease. The saving is $10,440 − $8,260 = $2,180. The article warns that this decision depends critically on the book value of the car at the end of three years. The less the market value, or the greater the rate of depreciation, the better leasing compares to buying.

An important variable has been omitted—the net sum of the payments is not that important; rather the two present values of the payment streams *over time* should be compared in making the decision. Amazingly, it is not unusual for newspaper articles such as this to not even mention discounting.

Let's begin by calculating the rate of interest implicit in the newspaper's presentation. We know that after a 10 percent down payment the consumer owes $12,400 − $1,240 = $11,160 at the time of purchase. This is the unpaid present value of the car. We also know monthly payments are $345 per month; so to find the interest rate charged by the dealer we set up the problem

$$\$11,160 = \sum_{t=1}^{36} \frac{\$345}{(1 + r)^t},$$

and solve for *r*, giving us a *monthly* interest rate of .59 percent. The *annual* rate of interest is therefore 7.08 percent, which seems extremely low for most car dealerships and banks providing loans.

With this interest rate we can now calculate the correct cost of buying and leasing. We know that the resale price of the car three years later ($5,400) must be discounted. Adding everything up, the true cost of buying is

$$\$1,240 \quad + \quad \$11,160 \quad - \quad \frac{\$5,400}{(1 + .0708)^3} = \$8,001.86.$$

(Down payment) + (Discounted − (Selling price = (Present
            stream of   of the car   value of
            payments)   after three years)   buying)

We also know that the true cost of renting is the discounted sum of the payments. This present value, which can be compared to the present value of buying, is

$$\sum_{t=1}^{36} \frac{\$290}{(1 + .0059)^t} = \$9,380.96.$$

Both cost amounts are considerably different than those reported in the newspaper article. Fortunately, the advice to the consumer is still the same as that reported. Buying is less costly than renting. However, the true savings are not the same as those reported. By buying, the consumer saves $1,379.10 in present dollars, not the amount of $2,180 we calculated earlier.

We might ask ourselves: at what interest rate would it be economical to lease rather than buy? Let's first examine the effect of different rates on the present value of buying. Clearly, as the interest rate rises, the 36 payments needed to pay off the balance of $11,160 will increase, but this present value remains constant if the purchaser makes a 10 percent down payment. The only thing that changes as the interest rate rises is the present value of the resale price of the car; it, of course, declines. The discounted present value of buying at different rates of interest is shown below:

Annual interest rate	Cost of buying
5.0%	$7,735.28
10.0	8,342.90
12.0	8,556.39
15.0	8,849.41
20.0	9,275.00
25.0	9,635.20

Obviously, the cost of buying rises as the interest rate increases.

Turning to the value of leasing, suppose the dealer always wants the discounted stream of lease payments to remain constant at $9,380, whatever the rate of interest. Clearly, the payments must increase as the interest rate increases, in order to keep this present value constant. This assumption oversimplifies things a bit, because a dealer would want the higher present value of the lease payments to compensate for the lower present value of the car when it is returned in three years. But, to keep things simple, we will continue to use a present value of $9,380. Using this figure as the rough dollar amount sought by the dealer and comparing it to the figures in the table, we see that the cost of leasing does not fall below the cost of buying until interest rates rise to about 20 percent.

You might think about buyers who keep their cars longer than three years. How would the calculations change, assuming the person who leases has to write a new contract on another automobile? Is leasing even less attractive?

4.5 SUMMARY

In this chapter we provided some tools of analysis that should prove useful to you throughout this course. Since a large number of the problems you will encounter involve optimization decisions, we developed and set forth the two fundamental rules for maximization and minimization.

If a decision maker wishes to maximize or minimize something that depends on the level of one or more activities, and if these activities can only be employed at a cost, each activity should be used up to the level where the marginal benefit from the activity equals its marginal cost. This process is unconstrained optimization.

Constrained optimization involves maximizing some benefit or minimizing some cost subject to a constraint. In this process the activities should be allocated so that the constraint is met and, for all activities used, the marginal benefit divided by the marginal cost (the marginal benefit per unit of cost) of the last unit of each activity must equal that of every other activity. If there are n activities in the optimizing process then a maximum or minimum is obtained by setting

$$\frac{MB_1}{MC_1} = \frac{MB_2}{MC_2} = \cdots = \frac{MB_n}{MC_n}.$$

This relation must hold for any constrained problem.

When analyzing decision making over time the crucial variable is the rate of interest. The future value of an asset A, invested for n years at an interest rate of r is

$$FV = \$A \, (1 + r)^n.$$

The amount one would pay now for a return in some period in the future is the present value of the return. The present value of a return, R, payable in n years is

$$PV = \frac{R}{(1 + r)^n}$$

assuming an interest rate of r. The present value of a stream of returns over n years is

$$PV = \sum_{t=1}^{n} \frac{R_t}{(1 + r)^t},$$

where R_t is the expected return in the tth year. These concepts are frequently employed in maximization and minimization involving time.

TECHNICAL PROBLEMS

1. A manufacturing firm believes that it can increase labor productivity and, therefore, net revenue by decreasing air pollution in the plant.

It estimates that the marginal cost function for reducing pollution by installing new capital is

$$MC = 50P,$$

where P represents a reduction of one unit of pollution. It also feels that for every unit of pollution reduction the marginal increase in net income *(MB)* is

$$MB = \$800 - 30P.$$

How much pollution reduction should the firm undertake?

2. A firm making auto parts is having quality problems along its assembly line. The marketing division estimates that each defective part that leaves the plant costs the firm $20, on average, for replacement or repair. The engineering department recommends hiring quality inspectors to sample for defective parts and reduce the number of defective parts shipped. After extensive research, a management team comes up with the following schedule showing the number of defective parts that would be shipped for several levels of inspection.

Number of inspectors	Average number of defective parts per day
0	120
1	85
2	55
3	35
4	22
5	12
6	6
7	3
8	1

The daily wage of people qualified to be inspectors is $150.
   a. How many inspectors should the firm hire?
   b. What would your answer be if the wage rate were $100?
   c. What would your answer be if the average cost of defective parts is $10 and the wage rate remains at $100?

3. A firm has the option of advertising on TV, radio, and in newspapers. It has a weekly advertising budget of $2,300 and wishes to maximize the number of units sold. Its estimates of the *increase* in

weekly sales from ads in each of the three media are in the table below.

| | | Increase in units sold | |
Number of ads	TV	Radio	Newspaper
1	40	15	20
2	30	13	15
3	22	10	12
4	18	9	10
5	14	6	8
6	10	4	6
7	7	3	5
8	4	2	3
9	2	1	2
10	1	0	1

The prices of each type of ad are

TV	$300 each
Radio	$100 each
Newspaper	$200 each

a. How should the firm allocate its advertising budget among the media?

b. Show that the allocation you suggest satisfies the condition for constrained optimization.

c. If the advertising budget is reduced to $1,100, how many ads should be purchased in each of the media?

4. A firm has calculated its marginal income or revenue from selling more output (X) as

$$MB = \$1,700 - 2X.$$

It goes down as more units are sold because prices fall. The additional or marginal cost of producing and selling additional units increases as more units are sold. The marginal cost is

$$MC = \$100 + 6X.$$

a. How many units should the firm produce and sell?

b. Does the firm make a profit or loss or can you tell?

c. If you cannot tell, what other information would you need to answer part b?

5. A large shipping firm has established a minimum standard of necessary truck maintenance and repair. It can use a combination of skilled mechanics and unskilled labor to perform the maintenance. The maintenance supervisor believes that any of the following com-

binations of unskilled and skilled labor would achieve this minimum maintenance requirement.

Skilled mechanics	Unskilled labor
2	30
5	22
8	15
12	8

For the table, we see that if less unskilled labor is used, more skilled mechanics must be added, and vice versa. Clearly the two are substitutable.

Assume the going wage for skilled mechanics is $180 a day and the wage for unskilled labor is $40 a day.

a. Which combination results in the least cost for the required maintenance?

b. If the combination you suggest is the optimal and the marginal benefit of a skilled mechanic is 90, what is the marginal benefit of unskilled labor?

c. If the price of unskilled labor rises to $80 a day, what combination would the firm choose?

6. Assume that in this high tech world you can measure the additional or marginal satisfaction of individuals for each unit of any good purchased and consumed. Suppose you test some person who consumes 12 pizzas and 14 burgers a week, and find that the last unit of pizza consumed has a marginal satisfaction rating of 18 while the last burger adds 12 to the happiness index. When you ask the cost of each you learn that pizzas cost $6 apiece and burgers cost $3. What would you advise this person to do? Why? What advice would you give if the price of burgers were $4?

7. Assume an interest rate of 10 percent.

a. What is the future value of $500 three years from now? Six years from now?

b. What is the present value of $500 to be received three years from now? Six years from now?

c. What is the present value of the following income streams?

d. Since both streams total $9,000, what accounts for the difference?

e. What would be your answers to *a, b,* and *c* if the interest rate were 5 percent?

Year	Stream 1	Stream 2
1	$5,000	$1,000
2	3,000	3,000
3	1,000	5,000

8. Suppose you own a sterile asset worth $1,200. You believe that the asset will appreciate $200 a year for the next 10 years. The interest rate is 12 percent.
   a. When would you plan to sell the asset?
   b. How would your answer change if the interest rate is 15 percent?
   c. How might your answer to a and b change if the asset is not sterile but is a fine painting you have in your apartment?

9. A student entering college has $50,000 and is deciding whether to use this money to purchase a duplex and live in half while leasing the other for $300 a month ($3,600 a year) during the four years of college. At the end of four years the duplex would be sold. The student thinks this would be a good investment since the duplex could be sold for the same amount as its price today. Also, there would be no rent paid during the four years in college, and the income on the lease would be $3,600 a year. The interest rate is 12 percent. What would you advise the student to do?

10. A recent newspaper article compared the Beatles' earnings for a concert in 1964 to how much the Jacksons' concert earned in 1984. The following table compares the income of the Beatles and Jacksons when the groups visited Dallas, Texas, nearly 20 years apart.

Beatles vs. Jacksons

	The Beatles	The Jacksons
Concert dates	Sept. 19, 1964	July 13–15, 1984
Location	Memorial Auditorium	Texas Stadium
No. of performances	1	3
Capacity	10,000	65,100
Price per ticket	$7	$28*
Gross concert receipts	$55,000	$1,822,800†

* plus $2 handling fee
† assumes 65,100 seats sold per concert at $28 per ticket
Source: *Dallas Morning News*, June 20, 1984.

It appears that the Jacksons earned considerably more than the Beatles, but take the following steps for a more appropriate income comparison:

a. Take account of inflation. Making 1964 the base year, the consumer price index (CPI) in 1984 is 325. (Hint: divide the inflated 1984 dollars by 3.25.)

b. Suppose the Beatles invested their $55,000 per concert at an 8 percent rate of interest. How much would they have had in 1984. Compare this amount to the Jacksons's earnings. Do you think the real costs of production were equal?

ANALYTICAL PROBLEMS

1. How much does it cost to keep money in a checking account that earns no interest as opposed to a savings or money market account that does? Why would people keep money in a checking account?

2. During the energy crisis *Consumer Reports* evaluated refrigerators and made the point that "by choosing one that's thrifty with electricity, you may save almost $400 over the appliance's lifetime." This $400 figure was arrived at by summing monthly savings in electricity of $2.20 over the 15-year lifetime of a refrigerator. What's the problem with this calculation? How would you go about determining how much more you would pay for a "thrifty" refrigerator?

3. Interestingly, when gasoline prices went up, so did prices of smaller, fuel-efficient automobiles relative to larger, less efficient cars. Suppose an automaker produces two automobiles exactly alike except for the number of miles they travel per gallon of gas. Which automobile will be more expensive? Explain.

4. In the past, government pushed programs designed to subsidize households that converted their heating systems from oil or gas to solar power.

   a. Under what conditions would households voluntarily convert?

   b. If households would not voluntarily convert, but government subsidizes the conversion, the fact that discounting represents the opportunity cost of capital means that subsidization is not optimal from a social point of view. Explain.

5. Suppose you are a lawyer representing a person whose spouse was killed at work through proven negligence of the employer. The firm obviously cannot measure, and therefore compensate for, the grief of the survivor. It will compensate for the economic loss because of the lost earnings of the deceased, who was 50 years old at death. Mandatory retirement is at age 65. The firm is willing to make a flat cash settlement now if you can show the economic loss. What information

do you need? How would you figure the economic loss if you had the information?

6. Bonds have a printed coupon rate and a face value. The face value is the amount the borrower pays the lender when the bond matures. Equal periodic payments are made to the lender. The amount of the payments is the coupon rate multiplied by the face value of the bond. If the market rate of interest is equal to the coupon rate, the bond sells for face value. If the market rate of interest is higher than the coupon rate, what happens to bond prices? What happens if the market rate is below the coupon rate?

7. Many charitable organizations pay celebrities to appear on their behalf. For example, a hospital in Denver spends thousands of dollars annually staging celebrity benefit dinners [*The Wall Street Journal*, June 1, 1984]. One organizer of the affair points out "Some people say the money would be better spent on research, and I'm wondering whether they're right." Evaluate this argument. How should charities decide whether to pay celebrities for benefits?

8. According to the National Safety Council, mandatory seat belt laws could save more than 10,000 lives a year. In New York violators who do not fasten their seat belts can be fined up to $50. Discuss the costs and benefits of the law. On balance is the law worth the cost?

PART III

CONSUMER BEHAVIOR

■ *Theory of Consumer Behavior: Preferences and Constraints*

■ *Theory of Consumer Behavior: Changes in Income and Price*

■ *Applying Consumer Behavior Theory*

Chapter 5

Theory of Consumer Behavior: Preferences and Constraints

5.1 INTRODUCTION

In the discussion of demand and supply in Chapter 2, we simply assumed downward sloping demand curves without formally deriving them. Since demand is derived from the way consumers act in the market, we must understand consumer behavior to fully understand the determinants of demand. This chapter and following chapters describe the theory of consumer behavior and the relations between this theory and the theory of demand. First, the tools of analysis are developed; then these tools are used in the next chapter to analyze the way consumer behavior determines demand, with particular emphasis on explaining why market demand curves are negatively sloped.

Determinants of Consumer Choice

This chapter presents the determinants of consumer choice behavior. We will explain why a consumer chooses a particular bundle of goods and services and not some other bundle. Why does one person consume none of some good, such as a motorcycle, while someone else with nearly the same income may own two or three?

The theory of consumer choice is quite simple. You, as a consumer, have a given income and desire goods. Your income probably prohibits you from purchasing everything you desire. Therefore, you must make decisions about what goods to purchase during a given week or any other period of time. Essentially you have an allocation problem: how to make the most of your income.

If you wish to consume more of some good in the future than you are consuming now, you must give up other goods. A new car this semester will cost you your trip to Europe next summer. An additional movie will cost you a trip to McDonald's. Assume you are now seeing two films a month. Why not see another? The obvious answer is that you value the third movie less than you value what you would have to give up to purchase the additional ticket. Similarly, you value the second movie more than you value what you could purchase instead.

If your alternatives are a new car or a trip to Europe, the decision is the same. If you value the new car more than you value the trip, you give up the trip; if not, you give up the car.

If you would like a new 10-speed bike, why would you choose not to purchase one? Don't say you can't afford it. You could if you gave up enough other things. The reason you don't purchase a bicycle is that the added value or satisfaction received from owning one is not sufficient to compensate you for what you would be forced to give up.

The fundamental analytical tool in this chapter is the concept of *marginal utility*. Marginal utility means the change in consumer satisfaction given a small change in the amount of a good consumed. For someone to choose more of one good and less of others, the marginal gain must outweigh the marginal loss from giving up the other goods. Consumers start at a particular plan of consumption, then make changes in order to reach more preferred levels.

This is our basic theory. Consumers are constrained or restricted by limited incomes and the prices that must be paid for the goods. They attempt to reach the most preferred level of consumption possible, given these constraints. Once they attain this level, they cannot become better off by giving up some goods in order to get others.

As you have probably deduced by now, the theory of consumer behavior is a straightforward example of the principle of constrained maximization set forth in Chapter 4. An individual maximizes something, given a constraint, when the additional or marginal benefit from the last unit of each choice activity per dollar spent on that activity is the same for all activities. In the theory to be developed here, the consumer wishes to maximize utility under the constraint of a limited income. Maximization occurs when the marginal utility from each good or service purchased per dollar cost is equal for all goods and services chosen.

5.2 BASIC ASSUMPTIONS

The theory of consumer behavior makes some simplifying assumptions in order to go directly to the fundamental determinants of behavior. These assumptions allow us to abstract away from less important aspects of the decision process.

Information and Ranking

First, we assume that each consumer has complete information on all matters pertaining to consumption decisions. A consumer knows the full range of goods available in the market, the exact price of each good, and that these prices will not be changed by his or her actions in the market. Finally, the consumer knows what his or her income will be during the planning period. Given all this information, each consumer tries to maximize satisfaction from consumption *given* a limited income. More precisely, economists say a consumer maximizes utility subject to an income constraint. Utility, a term frequently used in this chapter and Chapter 6, is defined as follows:

Definition
Utility is a consumer's perception of his or her own happiness or satisfaction.

Admittedly, to assume perfect information is an abstraction from reality. Consumers have only a fairly accurate notion of what income will be for a reasonable planning period, not perfect knowledge, and they can only estimate some prices, not quote them exactly. No consumer actually succeeds in the task of spending a limited income to maximize satisfaction. Usually this failure is attributable to the lack of accurate information. Yet a more or less conscious effort to attain maximum satisfaction, given imperfect information, determines an individual's demand for goods and services, so the assumption of complete information does not distort the relevant aspects of the economic world but allows us to concentrate on how consumption choices are made.

Second, we assume that each consumer is able to rank all conceivable bundles of commodities. That is, when confronted with two or more collections of goods, a consumer is able to determine an order of preference among them. For example, assume a person is confronted with two choices: (a) five candy bars, six pints of ice cream, and one soft drink; or (b) four candy bars, five pints of ice cream, and three soft drinks. The person can say one of three things: I prefer the first bundle to the second; I prefer the second to the first; or I would be equally satisfied with either.

Therefore, when evaluating two bundles of goods, an individual either prefers one bundle of goods to the other or is indifferent between the two. Since we will use the concepts of preference and indifference frequently, it is essential to understand them thoroughly now. If a consumer prefers one group of goods to another, he or she obviously believes a higher level of satisfaction will be gained from the preferred group. The less preferred bundle would, in the opinion of the consumer, give less utility than the other. If a person is indifferent between two bundles, he or she would be perfectly willing to let someone else (or perhaps the flip of a coin) determine the choice. In the consumer's mind, either bundle would yield the same level of utility.

Much of what follows is based on the consumer's ability to rank groups of commodities. This is a relatively weak requirement. We can see why by listing some of the things we are *not saying* about consumer preferences and indifference. First, we do not say that the consumer estimates *how much* utility or *what level* of satisfaction will be attained from consuming a given bundle of goods. Only the ability to *rank* is required. Second, we do not imply that an individual can say *how much* one bundle of goods is preferred to another. Admittedly, a consumer might say that one group of goods is desired a great deal more than another group, and perhaps just a little more than still another group. But "great deal" and "just a little" are imprecise terms—their meanings differ from one person to another. Third, we do not say that consumers *should* choose one bundle over the other, or that they will be better off if they do. It is only necessary that the individuals who do the consuming rank bundles in their own order of expected satisfaction.

More explicitly, when a consumer can rank bundles of goods, we assume that the consumer's preference pattern possesses the following characteristics. Given three bundles of goods (*A*, *B*, and *C*), if an individual prefers *A* to *B* and *B* to *C*, then *A* is preferred over *C*. Similarly, if indifferent between *A* and *B* and between *B* and *C*, the individual must be indifferent between *A* and *C*. Finally, a consumer indifferent between *A* and *B* but who prefers *B* over *C*, must prefer *A* over *C*. This assumption obviously can be carried over to four or more different bundles. If individuals can rank *any pair* of bundles chosen at random from all conceivable bundles, they can rank *all conceivable bundles.*

A real-world consumer who *purchases* one good rather than another does not necessarily prefer the chosen good. If you drive a Ford rather than a Rolls Royce, we cannot infer that you prefer a Ford to a Rolls. If the Rolls costs less than the Ford at the time of purchase, and you were aware of this, we can make this inference. If, as was probably the case, the Rolls costs more, we can say nothing. If the two goods are presented at equal cost, and you choose one over the other, we can say that you prefer that good. Or, if two goods are priced differently and you choose the higher-priced good, we can again deduce that you prefer that good. But if you choose the lower-priced good, we can say nothing.

Ordinal versus Cardinal Utility

Before concluding our discussion of the basic assumptions used in consumer behavior theory, it is useful to contrast what is called ordinal and cardinal utility. The present theory of consumer behavior went through a long period of development. The earliest psychological approaches to the theory of demand were based on the notion of a subjective and precisely measurable utility. The early theorists also assumed that any good or service consumed provides utility. In contrast to modern theorists, however, they took it for granted that utility was cardinal, additive, and independent of the rate of consumption of any other good.

Cardinal measurability implies that the difference between two numbers is itself numerically significant. For example, how many apples someone possesses is cardinally mesurable; four apples represent twice as much as two apples. On the other hand, measurement is ordinal if items can only be ranked. For example, if one item is ranked second and another fourth it does not mean the item with a rank of two is twice as desirable as the item with a rank of four. Both ordinal and cardinal measures rank items. The difference is that, in an ordinal system, one can say only that x is greater than y, whereas in a cardinal system, it is possible to say by how much x exceeds y.

Later economists objected to the additivity assumption. They argued that while utility was cardinally measurable, it was not simply the sum of the independent utilities obtained from the consumption of each good. These theorists related the level of total utility to the rates of consumption of all goods simultaneously. For example, the utility from eating ice cream depends on the amount of pie consumed and the kind being served.

A development directly from the work of these later economists on cardinal utility theory is the notion of marginal utility. Each additional unit of a good consumed per unit of time adds to total utility, but it is generally assumed that each unit adds less to a consumer's satisfaction than the previous one. For example, a scoop of ice cream might yield five units of utility; two scoops, nine units, and three, 11 units of utility. The marginal utility of the second scoop is four, while the marginal utility of the third scoop is two units of utility. Marginal utility declines as consumption increases. More formally, we define marginal utility as follows:

Definition

Marginal utility is the addition to total utility that is attributable to the addition of one unit of a good to the current rate of its consumption. The marginal utility of good X depends on its rate of consumption as well as the rates of consumption of other goods.

This definition will be very helpful in later sections of this chapter, as we develop the theory of utility maximization.

The last major step in the development of modern utility theory enabled economists to use the concept of utility without resorting to the assumption of cardinal measurability. It can be shown that cardinal utility is an unnecessary condition for the theory of consumer choice. All that is needed is an ordinal measure. This final step led to the use of *indifference curves* in analyzing consumer behavior. As we turn to a study of such curves, it is important to keep in mind that indifference curves depend only on ordinal preference measures. That is, their existence comes from consumers having a preference pattern that:

1. Establishes a rank ordering among all bundles of goods.
2. Compares bundles of two and indicates that A is preferred to B, B is preferred to A, or the consumer is indifferent between the two goods.
3. In three- (or more) way comparisons, if A is preferred (indifferent) to B and B is preferred (indifferent) to C, A must be preferred (indifferent) to C.

5.3 INDIFFERENCE CURVES

Using the assumptions set forth above, we can now analyze two concepts that are fundamental to the theory of consumer behavior: indifference curves and indifference maps.

Definition

An indifference curve is a locus of points—or particular bundles or combinations of goods—each of which yields the same level of total utility or satisfaction. Thus a consumer is indifferent between any two bundles on the curve.

Definition

An indifference map is a graph that shows a set of indifference curves.

For analytical purposes, let us consider a consumer who can choose between only two different goods, X and Y, each continuously divisible or infinitesimally variable in quantity.[1] Figure 5–1 shows a portion of this consumer's indifference map consisting of four indifference curves labeled I–IV. Our consumer considers all combinations of X and Y on indifference curve I to be equivalent (for example, $20X$ and $42Y$, and $60X$ and $10Y$); these combinations yield the same satisfaction, and the consumer is indifferent among them. Because of indifference between the two specified combinations, the consumer is obviously willing to substitute X and Y in order to move from point a to point b. In other words, he or she is willing to give up 32 units of Y to obtain 40 additional units of X. Conversely, if the present bundle of goods is situated at b, the consumer is willing to forego 40 units of X to obtain an additional 32 units of Y, and is willing to substitute at the *average* rate of 4/5 units of Y per unit of X.

All combinations of goods on indifference curve II (say 30 Y and 50 X) are superior to *any* combination of goods on I. Likewise, all combinations

---

[1] Admittedly, the possibility of continuous variation in quantity *is* perhaps less frequently encountered than "lumpiness", but this assumption permits a great gain in analytical precision at the sacrifice of very little realism. The assumption that bundles consist of no more than two separate goods enables us to analyze the problem of consumer behavior with two-dimensional graphs. This assumption is made, therefore, purely for simplicity of exposition. With the use of the differential calculus, bundles of any number of different goods can be handled. But the analytical results based on two goods are exactly the same as those based on more than two. Here, again, the gain in simplicity outweighs the loss of realism.

FIGURE 5-1   **Indifference curves**

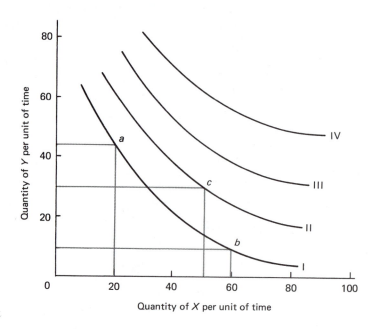

on III are superior to any combination on II. Each indifference curve that lies above a given indifference curve represents combinations of X and Y that are considered superior to, or capable of yielding more utility than, every combination on the lower curve. At every utility level designated by a particular indifference curve, the consumer is willing to substitute X for Y or Y for X at some rate to remain on the same curve (that is, with the same satisfaction or utility level) but consuming different combinations of goods.

Since X and Y are assumed to be continuously divisible, each indifference curve specifies an infinite number of combinations that yield the same amount of satisfaction. It is important to note that the specific utility numbers attached to I, II, III, and IV are immaterial. The numbers might be 5, 7, 12, and 32, or 96, 327, 450, and 624, or any other set of numbers that *increase*. For the theory of consumer behavior, only the position and shape of the indifference curves matter. Only the ordinal ranking of commodity bundles is important. Since a precise measurement of utility is unnecessary the theory of consumer behavior does not have to be based on the stronger concept of measured or cardinal utility. The indifference curves and the capability to order preferences are all that are required in choice theory. All bundles of goods situated on the same indifference curve are equivalent; all combinations lying on a higher curve are preferred.

Relation

A consumer regards all bundles yielding the same level of utility as equivalent. The locus of such bundles is called an indifference curve because the consumer is indifferent to the particular bundles consumed. The higher, or further to the right, an indifference curve, the greater is the underlying level of utility. Therefore, the higher the indifference curve, the more preferred is each bundle situated on the curve.

5.4 CHARACTERISTICS OF INDIFFERENCE CURVES

Indifference curves have four characteristics that are important in our discussion of consumer behavior. All but the fourth property are based on the consumer's ability to rank consumption bundles and on the assumption that the consumer always prefers more to less.

For simplicity, assume once again that there are only two continuously divisible goods, X and Y. The X–Y plane is called the *commodity space*. The first property is that each point in the commodity space lies on one, and only one, indifference curve. This is because each point in the commodity space represents some specific combination of the two goods and therefore some level of utility. Beginning at any point, it is possible to take away Y and add X or take away X and add Y in an infinite number of ways and leave the consumer with the same level of satisfaction. So each point in the plane must lie on an indifference curve, and since all bundles can be unambiguously ranked, each lies on only one indifference curve. For obvious reasons, when graphing an indifference map, only a relatively few curves are used to represent the entire map. But remember, an infinite number of indifference curves lie between any two indifference curves that are drawn.

A second property of indifference curves is that they are negatively sloped. This property is based on the assumption that a consumer prefers a greater bundle of goods to a smaller one. An upward sloping indifference curve would indicate that a consumer is indifferent between two combinations of goods, one of which contains more of *both goods*. The fact that a positive amount of one good must be added to the bundle to offset the loss of another good (if the consumer is to remain at the same level of satisfaction) implies negatively sloped indifference curves.

A third characteristic is that indifference curves cannot intersect. This property is a logical necessity, as illustrated in Figure 5–2. In this graph, I and II are indifference curves, and the points P, Q, and R represent three different bundles (or combinations of X and Y). R must clearly be preferred to Q because it contains more of both goods. The points R and P are equivalent because they are situated on the same indifference curve.

FIGURE 5–2   **Indifference curves cannot intersect**

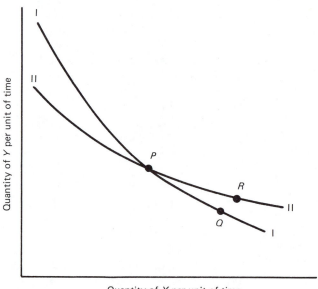

Quantity of *X* per unit of time

In like manner, the consumer is indifferent between *P* and *Q*. Recall that if a consumer is indifferent between *A* and *B* and between *B* and *C,* he or she must be indifferent between *A* and *C*. In our case, *R* and *P* are equivalent, as are *P* and *Q,* so *R* must be equivalent to *Q*. But, as previously mentioned, *R* is preferred to *Q* because it contains more of both goods. Intersecting indifference curves, such as those shown in Figure 5–2, imply that consumers are not consistent about ranking bundles of products.

The fourth and final property is that indifference curves are *convex*— an indifference curve must lie above its tangent at each point, as illustrated in Figure 5–3. The convexity of indifference curves does not follow from the capability of consumers to rank consumption bundles consistently, but comes from empirical observations showing that consumers value diversity and consume a number of different commodities. If the indifference curve were not drawn as pictured in Figure 5–3, utility maximization would lead to specialization rather than diversification in consumption. The predictions of our model would then contradict observation.

It is worthwhile to observe that we could apply the definition of

FIGURE 5–3   **Indifference curves are convex**

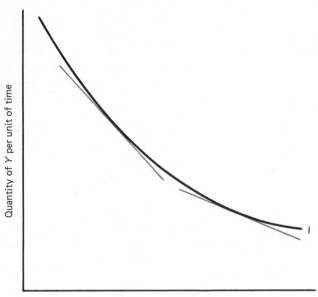

marginal utility and get convex indifference curves. If we assume that the more of a commodity a consumer has, the less valuable an additional or marginal unit becomes—that is, the ratio of marginal utilities declines—preferences would have to be described by convex indifference curves. As the consumer moves along a particular curve, he or she would require increasingly more of the abundant good to maintain the same level of utility. For example, a person at a football game with four hot dogs and one soft drink might be willing to trade two hot dogs for another soft drink. On the other hand, if the same person had two hot dogs and two soft drinks, he or she would be much less willing to give up one hot dog. In all likelihood, several soft drinks would be required to coax a hot dog away.

The results of this section may be summarized in the following way:

Relation

Indifference curves have the following properties: (a) some indifference curve passes through each point in commodity space; (b) indifference curves slope downward to the right; (c) indifference curves cannot intersect; and (d) indifference curves are convex.

5.5 MARGINAL RATE OF SUBSTITUTION

One essential feature of utility theory is that different combinations of commodities can give rise to the same level of satisfaction. In other words, the consumer is indifferent to the particular combination obtained. Therefore, one commodity can be substituted for another in the right amount so that the consumer remains just as well off as before, or remains on the same indifference curve. An important concept in utility theory is the *rate* at which a consumer is willing to substitute one commodity for another in consumption. A consumer attains maximum satisfaction from a limited money income when choosing a combination of goods such that the *rate* at which he or she is *willing* to substitute goods is the same as the *rate* at which market prices *permit* substitution. Therefore, to understand utility maximization, one must understand the rate of substitution in consumption.

Substitution in Consumption

Consider Figure 5–4. An indifference curve is represented by I where the consumer is indifferent between bundle R, containing 4 units of X and 18 of Y, and bundle P, containing 11 units of X and 8 of Y. At point P the consumer is willing to give up 7 units of X for 10 more units of Y. At point R, the consumer is willing to give up 10 units of Y for 7 more units of X. The *rate* at which the consumer is willing, on average, to substitute X and Y is therefore

$$\frac{\Delta Y}{\Delta X} = \frac{RS}{SP} = \frac{18 - 8}{4 - 11} = -\frac{10}{7},$$

where, again, Δ means "the change in." This ratio measures the average number of units of Y the consumer is willing to forego in order to obtain one additional unit of X (over the range of consumption pairs under consideration).[2] The consumer is willing to give up ($1\frac{3}{7}$) units of Y in order to gain one more unit of X. Stated alternatively, the ratio measures the amount of Y that must be sacrificed ($1\frac{3}{7}$ units) per unit of X gained to remain at precisely the same level of satisfaction.

In our subsequent use, we would find it very cumbersome to have the minus sign on the right-hand side of the above equation. We define this rate of substitution as

$$-\frac{\Delta Y}{\Delta X} = \frac{10}{7}.$$

---

[2] The ratio is, of course, negative, since the change in Y associated with an increase in X is negative. This type of relation results directly from the postulate of negatively sloped indifference curves.

FIGURE 5–4   **The marginal rate of substitution**

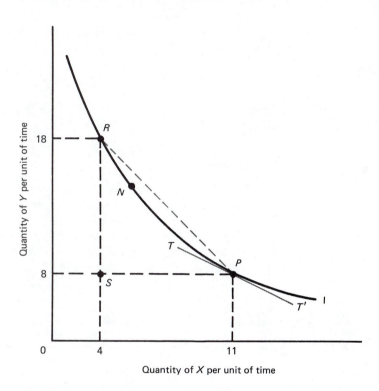

The rate of substitution given by the ratio above is obviously the negative of the slope of the broken straight line joining points R and P. The ratio could be quite different between two alternative points, say N and P. But, as point R moves along I toward P, the ratio RS/SP approaches closer and closer to the slope of the tangent TT' at P. In the limit, for extremely small movements in the neighborhood of P, the negative of the slope of I, which is the negative of the slope of its tangent at P, is called the *marginal rate of substitution of X for Y*.

Definition

The marginal rate of substitution of X for Y measures the number of units of Y that must be sacrificed per unit of X gained so as to maintain a constant level of satisfaction. The marginal rate of substitution is given by the negative of the slope of an indifference curve at a point. It is defined only for movements along an indifference curve, never for movements among curves.

We will use the letters *MRS* to denote the marginal rate of substitution of *X* for *Y* in consumption or, more generally, the marginal rate of substitution of the variable plotted on the horizontal axis for the variable plotted on the vertical axis. Also, since we wish the *MRS* to be positive, and since $\Delta Y/\Delta X$ is necessarily negative, the minus sign must be attached. We write

$$MRS_{x\,for\,y} = -\frac{\Delta Y}{\Delta X},$$

where the subscript *"X for Y"* indicates that the consumer is taking more *X* for less *Y* along an indifference curve.

Diminishing *MRS*

The requirement that indifference curves be convex implies that the *MRS* of *X* for *Y* diminishes as *X* is substituted for *Y* along an indifference curve. This is illustrated in Figure 5–5.

I is an indifference curve; *R*, *N*, *Q*, and *P* are four bundles situated on this curve. Consider a movement from *R* to *N*. In order to maintain the same level of utility, the consumer is willing to sacrifice slightly more than two units of *Y* to gain one unit of *X*. Now consider the consumer situated

FIGURE 5–5   **Diminishing marginal rate of substitution**

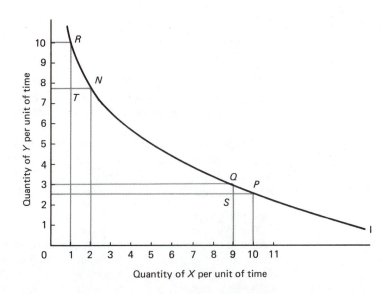

FIGURE 5–6   Diminishing *MRS*

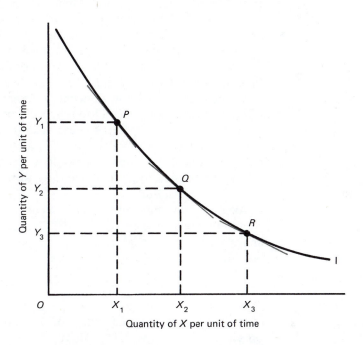

Quantity of *Y* per unit of time

Quantity of *X* per unit of time

at Q. To move to P and gain one unit of X, the consumer now is willing to give up approximately ½ unit of Y.

Diminishing *MRS* is further illustrated in Figure 5–6, this time without actual numbers. I is an indifference curve, and P, Q, and R are three bundles situated on this curve. The horizontal axis is measured so that $OX_1 = X_1X_2 = X_2X_3$. Let's look first at the movement from P to Q. We see that if P is very close to Q, or the amount X_1X_2 is very small, the *MRS* at Q is

$$\frac{OY_1 - OY_2}{OX_2 - OX_1} = \frac{Y_1Y_2}{X_1X_2}.$$

Similarly, for a movement from Q to R, the *MRS* at R is

$$\frac{OY_2 - OY_3}{OX_3 - OX_2} = \frac{Y_2Y_3}{X_2X_3}.$$

By construction, $X_1X_2 = X_2X_3$, but, very obviously, $Y_1Y_2 > Y_2Y_3$. The *MRS* is less at R than at Q. This is also shown by the decreasing (in absolute value) slopes of the tangents at P, Q, and R.

Marginal Utility Approach

Earlier approaches to the theory of consumer behavior, as noted above, used the concept of cardinal utility. The earliest economists who developed the theory of consumer utility assumed that utility was actually measurable and that one could assign actual numbers to its value. They reasoned that the more of one good consumed, the greater the total utility associated with it. Each *additional* unit of the good consumed per unit of time adds to total utility, but each adds less than the previous unit.

We can easily relate the concept of marginal utility to the marginal rate of substitution along an indifference curve. Always keep in mind that marginal utility can be: (a) the increase in utility attributable to a small increase in the rate of consumption of a commodity, holding the level of consumption of all other commodities constant; or (b) the decrease in utility attributable to a small decrease in the rate of consumption under the same assumption.

Assume now that utility (U) is measurable and depends on the consumption rate of two goods, X and Y. Next, let the consumption of both X and Y change very slightly. We can represent the total change in utility resulting from the changes in X and Y as

$$\Delta U = [(MU \text{ of } X) \times \Delta X] + [(MU \text{ of } Y) \times \Delta Y].$$

The terms in parentheses, *MU* of *X* and *MU* of *Y*, refer to the marginal utility of X and marginal utility of Y. Later we will shorten these expressions to MU_x and MU_y, where the subscript refers to the good being consumed. What this entire expression means, for example, is that if X increases by two units, and the average marginal utility of each is five, while Y increases by three units and the average marginal utility of each is four, utility increases by 22 units—$(2 \times 5) + (3 \times 4)$. If X increases by four units and Y decreases by five units, total utility remains constant; i.e., $(5 \times 4) + (4 \times (-5)) = 0$.

Since an indifference curve represents the locus of all combinations of X and Y that the consumer is indifferent to, utility must remain constant along any indifference curve. Thus, ΔU equals zero for any movement along an indifference curve. From the equation above, if, for very small changes in X and Y, ΔU equals zero we can derive the equality

$$\frac{MU_x}{MU_y} = -\left(\frac{\Delta Y}{\Delta X}\right),$$

where ($\Delta Y/\Delta X$) is the slope of the indifference curve. The absolute value of the slope of an indifference curve is the marginal rate of substitution; therefore we can write

$$MRS_{x \text{ for } y} = \frac{MU_x}{MU_y},$$

after substituting for ($\Delta Y/\Delta X$). Thinking of X and Y as specific goods may help us interpret this expression. Suppose we have hot dogs (Y) and soft drinks (X). Remember that we always assume the marginal utility of any commodity is smaller the greater its rate of consumption. Now picture a graph (or construct one for yourself) where the number of hot dogs is plotted on the vertical axis, and the number of soft drinks on the horizontal.

When a football fan has a large number of hot dogs, the marginal utility of an additional hot dog is relatively low. Similarly, when the number of soft drinks is low, their marginal utility is relatively high. Thus, the *MRS*, the ratio of the marginal utility of soft drinks to that of hot dogs, is relatively high. Now the football fan substitutes soft drinks for hot dogs (X for Y, in the previous notation). Increasing the rate of consumption of soft drinks decreases their marginal utility, while reducing the rate of consumption of hot dogs increases the marginal utility of hot dogs. The substitution of soft drinks for hot dogs must lead to a decrease in the *MRS* of soft drinks for hot dogs.

The Value of Indifference Curve Theory

Although the theory of indifference curves is very useful in developing the theory of demand, measuring and plotting actual indifference curves for real people is extremely difficult. Economists have attempted such measurement—with both people and animals—with varying levels of success. But the *actual measurement and graphing* of indifference curves are not really important to those who use economics in business, government, or other everyday decision making.

It is the *concept* of these curves that is most useful in decision making. A decision maker in a business must recognize that employees, for example, have subjective rates of trade-off between income and working conditions. It is possible to obtain certain goals by trading off between the two types of employee benefits. To be more specific, some of our recent Ph.D. graduates have gone to work in business departments such as finance and management, while others have joined economics faculties. The teaching load—number of classes to be taught—for a young Ph.D. has been on average higher in business schools than in economics departments, but the total income earned has been somewhat lower in the economics departments. There is a trade-off between the faculty working conditions and income. University officials recognize that faculty members are willing to trade some amenities, such as preferred seating at football games and preferred parking facilities, for income. These trade-offs result from different tastes reflected in the shape of each individual's set of indifference curves. Any business that seeks to maximize employee benefits with limited resources for compensation must make its decisions based on a comparison of its employees' marginal values.

Government decision makers must also attempt to balance utilities. Consumers of government products—constituents—do not want zero schools and perfect streets or perfect schools and no streets. Government officials must realize that there is a trade-off between the two that would be preferred. Even within a school system, there is a trade between teaching and classroom facilities.

Perhaps most important, any student of economics must realize that all goods have some substitutes. There are very few goods—probably no goods—that you are now consuming that you would not give up some amount of in order to obtain other goods. Don't say I would not give up food because I would die. You wouldn't have to give up *all consumption* of a large group of goods. We only said that there is some group of other goods for which you would be willing to give up some amount of the food—or some type of food—you are now consuming. Virtually all consumers make trade-offs among goods. In very few cases is it *essential* that someone consume exactly the same amount of a particular good. We can think of some examples, of course, mostly medical, such as a given amount of medicine without which the patient would die, or a weekly treatment on a kidney machine. But these absolute essentials are rare.

Therefore, don't make the mistake, unless you are trying to convert someone to your point of view, of making statements like, "It is essential that the school increase classroom space by 20 percent" or "The city must double its recreational area in five years." Each of these "essentials" has some substitutes in the minds of consumers. The concept of the indifference curve allows us to analyze this concept of substitution.

5.6 BUDGET LINES

In this chapter we have set forth a method of analyzing what a consumer is willing to do or wishes to do. Recall from Chapter 2 that demand indicates both what consumers are *willing* or wish to do and what they are *able* to do. We will now discuss a way to analyze what a consumer can do, given a limited budget.

Income Constraints

If all consumers had an unlimited income—in other words, if there were an unlimited pool of resources—there would be no problem of "economizing," nor would there be "economics." Since this utopian state does not exist, even for the richest members of our society, people are compelled to determine their behavior in light of limited financial resources. For the theory of consumer behavior, this means that each consumer has a maximum amount that can be spent per period of time. The consumer's problem is to spend this amount in the way that yields maximum satisfaction.

Continue to assume that there are only two goods, X and Y, bought in quantities x and y. Each individual consumer is confronted with market-determined prices, p_x and p_y, of X and Y respectively. Finally, the consumer in question has a known and fixed money income *(M)* for the period under consideration. M is the maximum amount the consumer can spend, and we assume that it is all spent on X and Y.[3] The amount spent on $X(x \cdot p_x)$ plus the amount spent on $Y(y \cdot p_y)$ is equal to the stipulated money income. Algebraically,

$$M = x \cdot p_x + y \cdot p_y. \tag{5-1}$$

This equation can be expressed as the equation for a straight line. Solving for the quantity y—since y is generally plotted on the vertical axis—one obtains

$$y = \frac{M}{p_y} - \frac{p_x}{p_y}x. \tag{5-2}$$

Equation 5-2 is plotted in Figure 5-7. The first term on the right-hand side of Equation 5-2, M/p_y, shows the amount of Y that can be purchased if no X is purchased at all. This amount is represented by the distance OA in Figure 5-7; thus, M/p_y (or point A) is the ordinate intercept of the equation.

In Equation 5-2, $-p_x/p_y$, the negative of the price ratio, is the slope of the line. To see this, consider the quantity of X that can be purchased if Y is not bought. This amount is M/p_x, shown by the distance OB in Figure 5-7. Since the line obviously has a negative slope, its slope is given by

$$-\frac{OA}{OB} = -\frac{\dfrac{M}{p_y}}{\dfrac{M}{p_x}} = -\frac{p_x}{p_y}.$$

The line in Figure 5-7 is called the *budget line*.

Definition

The budget line is the locus of combinations or bundles of goods that can be purchased if the entire money income is spent. Its slope is the negative of the price ratio.

Because the consumer spends all income on X and Y, the bundle purchased by an individual must lie on the budget line.

---

[3] In more advanced models, saving may be considered as one of the many goods and services available to the consumer. Graphical treatment limits us to two dimensions; thus, we ignore saving. This does not mean that the theory of consumer behavior precludes saving—depending on preference ordering, a consumer may save much, little, or nothing. Similarly, spending may, in fact, exceed income in any given period as a result of borrowing or from using assets acquired in the past. The M in question for any period is the total amount of money to be spent during the period.

FIGURE 5–7   **Budget line**

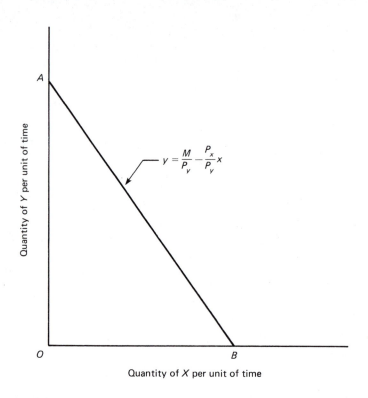

Quantity of Y per unit of time

$$y = \frac{M}{P_y} - \frac{P_x}{P_y} x$$

Quantity of X per unit of time

Shifting the Budget Line

In much of the analysis that follows, we are interested in changes in quantities purchased resulting from changes in price and money income, both represented graphically by shifts in the budget line. Consider first the effect of a change in money income, prices of goods remaining constant.

Any given budget line represents the set of all possible consumption bundles for a consumer at a given set of relative prices and money income. If the consumer has an increase in money income at the original set of commodity prices, the set of possibilities must increase. Since the increase in money income allows the consumer to buy more goods, the budget line is pushed outward, and since prices are not changed, the slope of the budget line does not change. Therefore, an increase in money income causes an outward parallel shift in the budget line. Similarly, a decrease in money income, the price ratio held constant, causes a parallel

FIGURE 5–8   **Changing money income**

Quantity of X per unit of time

inward shift in the budget line. In Figure 5–8, budget line AB is associated with a lower income than is budget line $A'B'$. Because the slopes of AB and $A'B'$ are equal, the price ratio remains constant as the change in money income shifts the budget constraint upward or downward. Note that the intercepts of the budget line are income divided by the prices of X and Y. So the distance OA' is greater than OA because $M'/P_y > M/P_y$, where M' is the larger income. Likewise the distance OB' is greater than OB because $M'/P_x > M/P_x$.

Figure 5–9 shows what happens to the budget line when the price ratio changes with money income held constant. Assume that money income and the prices of X and Y are such that the relevant budget line is AB. The slope of the line is $-(p_x/p_y)$. Hold money income and the price of Y constant, then let the price of X increase. Since p_x increases, p_x/p_y increases also. The budget line becomes steeper, in this case the line AB'. The intercept on the Y axis remains the same because M/p_y remains constant. In other words, if income and the price of Y remain constant, the consumer can purchase the same amount of Y by spending the entire

FIGURE 5–9   **Changing the price of** X

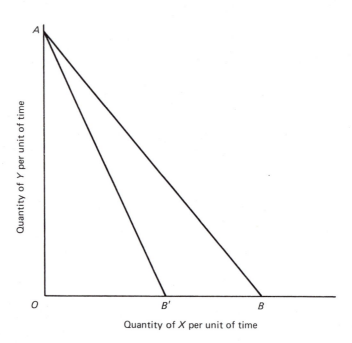

income on Y regardless of the price of X. We can see that an increase in the price of X rotates the budget line backward, the Y-intercept remaining fixed. Of course, a decrease in the price of X pivots the budget line outward, in Figure 5–9, from AB' to AB.

Alternatively, and perhaps more directly, the price change can be explained as follows. At the original price, p_x, the maximum purchase of X is M/p_x, or the distance OB. When the price rises to p'_x, the maximum purchase of X is M/p'_x, or the distance OB'. An increase in the price of X is shown by pivoting the budget line to the left around the ordinate intercept. A decrease in the price of X is represented by a rotation to the right.

Relation
An increase in money income, prices unchanged, is shown by a parallel shift of the budget line—outward and to the right for an increase in money income, and in the direction of the origin for a decrease. A change in the price of X, the price of Y and money income constant, is shown by rotating the budget line around the ordinate intercept—to the left for a price increase, to the right for a decrease.

5.7 UTILITY MAXIMIZATION

All bundles of goods (combinations of X and Y) on the budget line are available to consumers in the sense that their income allows them to purchase these bundles if they wish. This line is established by the fixed money income and the given prices of the commodities available. A consumer's indifference map shows the rank ordering of all conceivable bundles of X and Y. The principal assumption on which the theory of consumer behavior is built is that a *consumer attempts to allocate a limited money income among available goods and services so as to maximize satisfaction or utility*. Given that assumption and the concepts developed in this chapter, it is a relatively simple matter to determine the way a consumer will allocate income; that is, select the most preferred bundle of goods available with the given level of income and prices.

Maximizing Satisfaction Subject to a Limited Money Income

Graphically, we can visualize the consumer as being constrained by a limited money income that permits consuming only bundles of goods along the budget line. The consumer chooses the particular bundle along the line that is on the highest attainable indifference curve. In this way, the highest possible preference level is achieved.

The problem is depicted by Figure 5–10. The portion of the indifference map represented by the four indifference curves drawn in that figure indicates preferences among different combinations of goods. Similarly, the budget line specifies the different combinations the consumer can purchase with the limited income, assuming all income is spent on X and Y. The choice of combinations is limited by the given income.

The consumer cannot purchase any bundle lying above and to the right of the budget line and, therefore, cannot consume any combination lying on indifference curve IV. Some points on curves I, II, and III are, however, attainable. Moreover, as already observed, an infinite number of indifference curves lie between curves I and III. Therefore, all points on the budget line between Q and S are touched by some indifference curve, and if we extend the map to include curves below I, all points above Q and below S are touched by some curve. Each point on the budget line yields some specific level of utility. Four of the infinite number of attainable combinations are represented by points Q, P, R, and S.

Suppose the consumption bundle is located at Q. Without experimenting, the consumer cannot know for certain whether Q represents a maximum position or not. Let the individual experimentally move to combinations above and below Q, along the budget constraint. Moving upwards lowers the level of satisfaction to some indifference curve below I, but moving downward puts the person on a higher indifference curve.

FIGURE 5–10   **Consumer optimization**

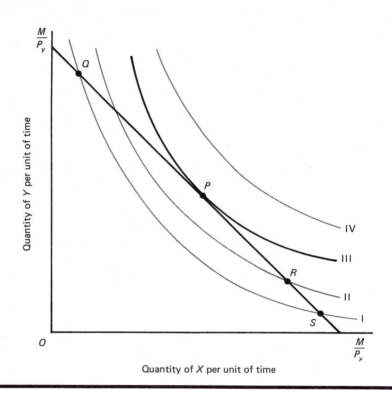

Continued experimentation will lead the consumer to move at least as far as *P*, because each successive movement down the budget line moves him or her to a higher indifference curve. Continuing to experiment, however, by moving away from *P*, the consumer would locate on a lower indifference curve with its lower level of satisfaction and would accordingly return to the point *P*.

Similarly, if a consumer were situated at *R*, small movements would cause the substitution of *Y* for *X*, thereby moving this person in the direction of *P*. No point except *P* is optimal, because each successive substitution of *Y* for *X* brings the consumer to a higher indifference curve until point *P* is reached. The position of maximum satisfaction—*or the point of consumer optimization*—is attained at *P*, where an indifference curve is just tangent to the budget line.

As you will recall, the slope of the budget line is the negative of the price ratio, the ratio of the price of *X* to the price of *Y*. Also recall that the slope of an indifference curve at any point is called the *MRS* of *X* for *Y*.

The point of utility maximization is defined by the condition that the *MRS* must equal the price ratio.

The interpretation of this proposition is very straightforward. The *MRS* shows the rate at which the consumer *is willing to substitute X for Y*. The price ratio shows the rate at which prices permit substitution of *X* for *Y*. Unless these rates are equal, it is possible to change the combination of *X* and *Y* purchased to attain a higher level of satisfaction. For example, suppose the *MRS* is two—meaning the consumer is willing to give up two units of *Y* in order to obtain one unit of *X*. Let the price ratio be unity, meaning that one unit of *Y* can be exchanged for one unit of *X*. Clearly, the consumer will benefit by trading *Y* for *X*, since he or she is willing to give up two *Y* for one *X* but only has to give up one *Y* for one *X* in the market. Generalizing, unless the *MRS* and the price ratio are equal, some exchange can be made to move the consumer to a higher level of satisfaction.

Principle

The point of consumer equilibrium—of the maximization of satisfaction subject to a limited money income—is defined by the condition that the *MRS* of *X* for *Y* must equal the ratio of the price of *X* to the price of *Y*.

Marginal Utility Interpretation of Optimization

At the beginning of this chapter, we gave a rather simplified intuitive explanation of utility maximization subject to a budget constraint. We argued that, if a consumer could give up some good and gain more satisfaction from purchasing other goods for the same total expenditure, such substitution would occur. We can set forth this explanation a bit more formally now, using the marginal utility interpretation of indifference curves.

Recall from Section 5.5 that, along an indifference curve

$$MRS_{x\,for\,y} = \frac{MU_x}{MU_y}.$$

Writing the condition for utility maximization symbolically,

$$MRS_{x\,for\,y} = \frac{p_x}{p_y}.$$

Therefore, in equilibrium

$$\frac{MU_x}{MU_y} = \frac{p_x}{p_y},$$

or

$$\frac{MU_x}{p_x} = \frac{MU_y}{p_y}.$$

This relation provides an alternative view of the condition for consumer equilibrium. Dividing the marginal utility of a commodity by its price gives the marginal utility per dollar's worth of the commodity bought. In this light, we can restate the condition for utility maximization as the following:

Principle

To attain maximum satisfaction, a consumer must allocate money income so that the marginal utility per dollar spent on each commodity is the same for all commodities purchased.

This principle is certainly plausible and follows directly from the analysis set forth in Chapter 4. Suppose, at the current allocation of income, the marginal dollar spent on X yields a greater marginal utility than the marginal dollar spent on Y. That is, suppose

$$\frac{MU_x}{p_x} > \frac{MU_y}{p_y}.$$

Reallocating one dollar of expenditure from Y to X will, therefore, increase total utility; and it must do so until the marginal utility per dollar's worth is the same for both commodities. This equalization will occur as X is substituted for Y because, as X increases, MU_x declines, while MU_y increases as the amount of Y falls.

Alternatively, if

$$\frac{MU_x}{p_x} < \frac{MU_y}{p_y},$$

a dollar taken away from X will reduce utility less than the increase in utility obtained from spending the dollar on additional consumption of Y. The consumer will continue to substitute away from X toward Y until the marginal utility per dollar expenditure is equal.

Zero Consumption of a Good

To this point, the discussion has implied that the consumer chooses to consume some positive amount of both X and Y, regardless of relative prices. This circumstance obviously need not be the case. Some consumers might choose to spend their entire income and purchase none of some specific good.

One set of theoretical circumstances under which a consumer would choose to spend the entire income on (say) good Y and none on X is depicted in Figure 5–11. Given the budget line, *LM,* and the indifference map represented by curves I, II, III, and IV, the highest level of satisfaction attainable from the given money income is at point L on indifference curve III. The consumer chooses to purchase L units of Y and no X. This point need not be a point of tangency where the *MRS* equals the price

FIGURE 5–11   **Corner solution**

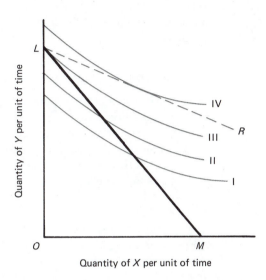

Quantity of *X* per unit of time

ratio (although it could be such a point). In the figure, an equilibrium situation exists even though there is no point (at both non-negative *X* and non-negative *Y*) where the *MRS* equals the price ratio. Economists call such a situation a *corner solution*. Note, however, that for a sufficiently large decrease in the price of *X* relative to the price of *Y* (say to a price ratio depicted by budget line *LR*), the budget line could become tangent to some indifference curve above III (curve IV) at a point where both *X* and *Y* are purchased. The consumer will purchase some positive amount of *X* if its relative price decreases sufficiently.

In other words, a corner solution, where the consumer purchases none of good *X*, results when

$$\frac{MU_x}{p_x} < \frac{MU_i}{p_i} = \cdots = \frac{MU_j}{p_j},$$

for all goods *i*, *j*, etc., where the *i*th and *j*th goods are purchased in positive amounts. The consumer spends the entire income, yet the marginal utility per dollar of *X* is less than the marginal utility per dollar spent on any other good that is purchased. This is generally what we mean when we say that "we cannot afford something." Perhaps you do not own a Cadillac—you say you cannot afford one. Conceivably you could buy one (perhaps by borrowing). So, if you do not own one, it must be that the alternative expenditure on goods that you consume gives more utility *per dollar* than a Cadillac would, even though a Cadillac would give *more* total utility than your present automobile. Stated differently, one does not consume some good X when the $MRS_{x\,for\,y}$ (where Y is any other good that is consumed) is less than the price ratio, p_x/p_y, and total income is exhausted.

Unusual Preference Maps

Earlier it was mentioned that, empirically, consumers prefer variety in their consumption bundle. Theoretically this does not always have to be true; in fact, we have just used indifference curves and budget constraints to show that corner solutions can exist. We illustrated in Figure 5–11 a situation where only good Y was consumed, but it remained possible, given a change in relative prices, that the consumer maximized utility by consuming both X and Y. If we did not have convex indifference curves, utility maximization would necessarily occur at the corner, if there was a unique maximization point at all.

For example, consider some indifference maps that are not strictly convex. Figure 5–12 shows two such maps. In Panel A, the indifference curves are strictly *concave*—they lie below their tangent lines at each point. The budget line in each figure is represented by LL'. The consumer optimizes by seeking the highest indifference curve touching the budget line. Usually, this is where the indifference curve and income line are tangent; but at point E, the tangency of indifference curve I and LL' in Figure 5–12 (Panel A), the consumer actually minimizes utility. The

FIGURE 5–12   **Indifference maps that are not convex**

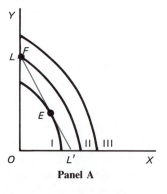
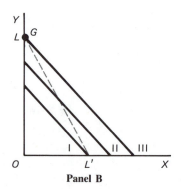

Panel A   Panel B

highest indifference curve is reached by moving to the left along LL' until the consumer eventually hits F on indifference curve II. At this point, the consumer purchases no X and only Y. It will always be the case when indifference curves are strictly concave that corner solutions are the point of consumer equilibrium. Consumers will never choose a variety of products when they maximize satisfaction. This is not a reasonable way to model behavior considering the way people actually behave.

Panel B shows some linear indifference curves. The budget line is dashed to avoid confusing it with an indifference curve. Here, the marginal rate of substitution is constant—that is, the consumer is always willing to trade X and Y at the same rate no matter how much the consumer has of each good. Since both the constraint and indifference curves are linear, there can be no optimizing tangency. If the lines have different slopes, the consumer maximizes utility at a corner, like point G. The problem becomes unmanageable if the budget line and indifference curves have the same slope. Imagine the situation; one indifference curve perfectly superimposed over the budget line. No other indifference curves would even touch the constraint. Our consumer would certainly know what level of utility was optimal but would not know what mix of goods to consume on that indifference curve, because there would be an infinite number of optimal consumption bundles. Our theory would therefore predict indeterminant behavior. This does not accurately describe the real world—most consumers have definite ideas about what they want to purchase.

Panels A and B of Figure 5–12 are the two basic forms that indifference curves might take other than the smooth convex shapes we have been using in our discussion. The result of our analysis is that the indifference maps in Figure 5–12 allow consumers in equilibrium little (or no) variety and/or substitution in their consumption of goods and services. We know this is generally not true of most consumers, so we will continue working with the convex schedules introduced at the beginning of this chapter.

APPLICATION

Fringe Benefits and Taxation

Fringe benefits—goods and services received by employees and paid for by employers—are an important part of employees' total income. In recent years, they made up approximately one third of the average employee's compensation. We can use the tools developed here to analyze why employees might prefer increased fringe benefits to an equivalent increase in salary.

FIGURE 5–13   **The effects of fringe benefits on utility maximization**

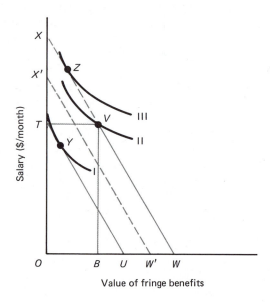

In Figure 5–13, an employee's salary is measured along the vertical axis, while the value of fringe benefits (in dollars) is measured along the horizontal. For simplicity, we assume that the employee could purchase these benefits—insurance, automobile usage, education, travel, etc.—at a price equal to their value. Initially, assume there are no fringe benefits and a worker has a total monthly salary of *T*. The employee, who can purchase these fringes as desired, faces a budget constraint of *TU*. Some benefits are purchased, and the employee maximizes utility at point *Y* on indifference curve I.

Now let the salary remain at *T* but let the employer give fringe benefits equal in value to *B*. Since the employee could receive *B* units of fringe benefits without spending income, the new budget line is *TVW*. The employee can now reach a higher indifference curve and is, therefore, better off. If the employee chooses to purchase no additional benefits, equilibrium is attained at point *V* on indifference curve II. Would the employee be better off receiving the value of the benefits in salary or in the fringe benefits themselves? Under the assumptions made here, the employee would not be worse off and might be better off receiving money rather than benefits.

To see this, assume the value of the benefits, *B,* is paid in salary. The employee receives additional salary of *TX* and no fringes. Extend the budget line above point *V* making the new budget line *XW*. The person who previously maximized utility at *V* is now better off, attaining equilibrium at *Z* on the higher indifference curve III. Anyone who chose a solution at *V* under the benefit package can be made better off by receiving the value of the benefits as income. These people will choose some point on the segment *XV*. Anyone who chose a combination on the segment *VW* with the benefit package will continue to maximize at that position even if the benefits are paid as salary.

Why would employers sometimes prefer to offer fringe benefits rather than more salary? The answer could be, in part, because employers can purchase the fringe benefits at lower prices than employees; for example, group insurance plans are less expensive than individual policies. A more

TABLE 5–1   **Weekly earnings and fringe benefits for workers in the United States, 1969–1979**

Benefits	1969	1979	Percent change
Old-Age, Survivors, Disability and Health Insurance (FICA taxes)	$6.44	$16.87	+162%
Insurance (life, hospital, surgical, medical, etc.)	5.00	16.56	+231
Pensions (nongovernment)	5.88	15.87	+170
Paid vacations	6.17	13.63	+121
Paid rest periods, coffee breaks, lunch periods, etc.	4.12	10.37	+152
Paid holidays	3.85	9.27	+141
Workers' compensation	1.29	4.90	+280
Unemployment compensation taxes	1.10	4.40	+300
Profit-sharing payments	1.63	4.15	+155
Paid sick leave	1.25	3.60	+188
Christmas or other special bonuses, suggestion awards, etc.	0.67	1.23	+ 84
Salary continuation or long-term disability	n.a.	0.88	n.a.
Thrift plans	0.23	0.83	+261
Dental insurance	n.a.	0.77	n.a.
Employee education expenditures	0.12	0.48	+300
Employee meals furnished free	0.29	0.44	+ 52
Discounts on goods and services purchased from company by employee	0.17	0.27	+ 59
Other employee benefits	1.25	2.40	+ 92
Total employee benefits	39.46	106.92	+171
Average weekly earnings	141.44	292.13	+107

n.a. = Data not available.
Source: *Nation's Business,* October 1980, p. 78.

important answer is taxation—fringe benefits are not usually subject to taxation. The effect of income taxes can be seen by returning to Figure 5–13. Let's begin with the employee receiving fringe benefits of *B* and choosing the combination represented by point *V*. Assuming no taxation on benefits, the increase in salary, if fringe benefits are relinquished, is taxed at a rate of 25 percent. The employee receives only the additional *TX'* after taxes rather than *TX*. The new budget line is *X'W'*. Clearly, since the employee prefers combination *V* to any combination along *X'W'*, the fringe benefits are preferred to the increased salary.

As income rises the relative value of untaxed fringe benefits will tend to increase because an employee's marginal tax rate increases. Whenever the tax rate increases, *X'W'* moves closer to *TU*. Employees whose salaries are increasing and are therefore moving into higher tax brackets would probably take larger proportions of the increased compensation in untaxable fringe benefits. Or to put it another way, as income rises, employers are in a position to make their employees better off with fringe benefits than with equivalent salary increases.

Table 5–1 presents some evidence showing that this has occurred. This table shows that the estimated value of fringe benefits for the typical employee during the 1970s rose 171 percent, and certain benefits had much larger increases. Employee education and workmen's compensation, for example, increased by 300 percent. Average weekly earnings, on the other hand, rose by 107 percent; that is, fringe benefits increased by about 62 percent more than earnings during this period. Part of the reason for this increase was certainly the fact that increased salaries moved people into higher tax brackets.

5.8 SUMMARY

In this chapter, we have developed the basic tools necessary to analyze consumer demand theory. Foremost are the concepts of indifference curves and budget lines. An indifference curve shows combinations of goods among which consumers are indifferent. Several indifference curves make up an indifference map. The slope of an indifference curve shows the rate at which a consumer is willing to substitute one good for another in order to remain at a constant level of utility. The slope is called the marginal rate of substitution.

The marginal rate of substitution can be related to marginal utility, which is the addition to total utility attributable to the addition of one unit of a good to current consumption. The marginal rate of substitution between two goods is the ratio of the two marginal utilities.

The budget line indicates combinations that the consumer is able to purchase with a given money income. The price ratio given by the market is the slope of the budget line. An increase in money income moves the budget line outward, parallel to the old line. A change in commodity prices pivots the budget line.

From this relation we develop the following principles:

Principle
The point of consumer optimization—or the maximization of satisfaction subject to a limited money income—is defined by the condition that the MRS of X for Y must equal the ratio of the price of X to the price of Y.

Alternatively,

Principle
To attain maximum satisfaction, a consumer must allocate money income so the marginal utility per dollar spent on each commodity is the same for all commodities purchased.

We can state this principle in terms of a ratio. For all goods X and Y a consumer maximizes utility by operating at a point on his or her preference map where

$$\frac{MU_x}{p_x} = \frac{MU_y}{p_y}.$$

TECHNICAL PROBLEMS

1. Assume that an individual consumes three goods, X, Y, and Z. The marginal utility (assumed measurable) of each good is independent of the rate of consumption of other goods. The prices of X, Y, and Z are respectively $1, $3, and $5. The total income of the consumer is $65, and the marginal utility schedule is as follows:

Units of good	Marginal utility of X (units)	Marginal utility of Y (units)	Marginal utility of Z (units)
1	12	60	70
2	11	55	60
3	10	48	50
4	9	40	40
5	8	32	30
6	7	24	25
7	6	21	18
8	5	18	10
9	4	15	3
10	3	12	1

    a. Given a \$65 income, how much of each good should the con-
        sumer purchase to maximize utility?
    b. Suppose income falls to \$43 with the same set of prices; what
        combination will the consumer choose?
    c. Let income fall to \$38; let the price of *X* rise to \$5 while the
        prices of *Y* and *Z* remain at \$3 and \$5. How does the consumer
        allocate income? What would you say if the consumer main-
        tained that *X* is not purchased because he or she can no longer
        afford it?

2. In Figure E.5–1, suppose a consumer has the indicated indifference
    map and the budget line designated *LZ*. You know the price of *Y* is
    \$5 per unit.
    a. What is the consumer's income?
    b. What is the price of *X*?

FIGURE E.5–1

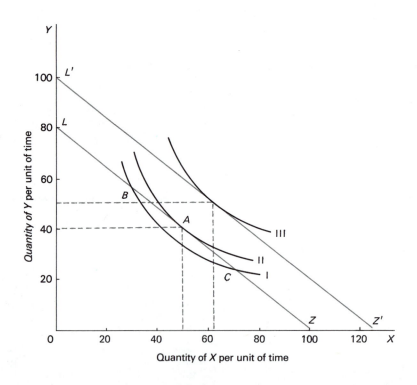

  c. Write the equation for the budget line *LZ*.
  d. What is the slope of *LZ*?
  e. What combination of *X* and *Y* will the consumer choose? Why?
  f. What is the marginal rate of substitution in equilibrium?
  g. Explain precisely in terms of *MRS* why the consumer would not choose combinations designated by *B* or *C*.
    Suppose the budget line shifts to *L'Z'*.
  h. At the same prices, what has happened to money income?
  i. What combination is now chosen?
  j. Draw the relevant budget line if money income remains at the original level (designated by *LZ*), the price of *Y* remains at $5, but the price of *X* rises to $10.
  k. Draw an indifference curve showing the new equilibrium.
  l. What are the new equilibrium quantities?

3. Suppose $MU_x = ay$ and $MU_y = ax$; $M =$ Income $= p_x x + p_y y$.
  a. Fill in the following columns with answers that maximize consumer utility.

	(1)	(2)	(3)	(4)	(5)
	$M = 100$ $P_x = 10$ $P_y = 10$	$M = 200$ $P_x = 20$ $P_y = 20$	$M = 150$ $P_x = 10$ $P_y = 10$	$M = 150$ $P_x = 10$ $P_y = 20$	$M = 150$ $P_x = 10$ $P_y = 30$
x					
y					
x/y					

  b. Using a preference map, graph each of the five utility-maximizing equilibria.
  c. Explain your results when prices and income double between columns (1) and (2).
  d. Explain the change in consumption between columns (1) and (3) when income is increased by 50.
  e. In columns (3), (4), (5), do your results seem reasonable after the price of *Y* is doubled and then tripled?

4. Use budget lines and indifference curves to analyze the effect of the following policies on the quantity demanded of some good, *X*.
  a. Government gives the individual $500.
  b. Government places a 5 percent tax on good *X* only.
  c. Government places a 5 percent tax on both goods.

5. If $MU_x/MU_y < P_x/P_y$, the individual would (increase, decrease) the consumption of *X* relative to *Y*. Explain your answer.

6. Suppose the following table represents points on one indifference curve.

Point	Quantity of pizzas	Quantity of hamburgers
A	10	1
B	8	3
C	6	6
D	4	10
E	2	15

a. Draw this indifference curve, putting quantity of pizzas on the vertical axis and quantity of hamburgers on the horizontal axis. Label points A, B, C, D, and E.

b. Does this indifference curve show diminishing *MRS?* Defend your answer by calculating the *MRS* between points A and B and between B and C.

7. Let Mary Jones have the utility function $U = X + Y$; her spending is limited to $100 per period, while the price of X is $10 and the price of Y is $5. Mary's behavior is one of extremes; she detests variety. Does utility maximization support this assertion? (Hint: MU_x is the change in utility when X changes by one unit. $MU_x = \Delta U/\Delta X = [(X + 1) + Y] - (X + Y) = 1$. The same is true for Y.)

8. An individual consumes two goods, A and B. The price of A is $5 per unit; the price of B is $7 per unit. The marginal utility of A is 10; the marginal utility of B is 21. The consumer spends the entire income on A and B.

a. What should the consumer do?

b. The marginal utility of B falls to 14; what should the consumer do now?

9. Explain why indifference curves might turn upward or bend backward, as shown in Figure E.5–2. Why would people never choose a combination on these portions of their indifference maps?

10. A person's marginal rate of substitution between X and Y ($-\Delta Y/\Delta X$) is four. The person is in equilibrium with the price of X at $12 and the price of Y at $3. The price of X rises to $15 and the price of Y rises to $5. Income is varied to restrict the consumer to the same indifference curve. Does the consumer substitute more X for Y or more Y for X? Explain.

FIGURE E.5–2

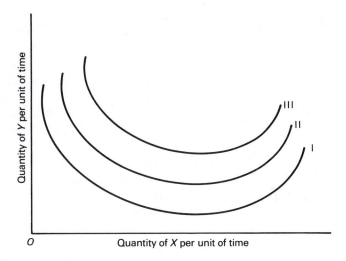

11. There are two goods consumed by an individual: honey and butter. In a preference map the amount of butter consumed is on the horizontal axis.
    a. Suppose both goods have the same price per unit and both axes are scaled similarly. Sketch the budget line in a diagram.
    b. Will the consumer necessarily consume equal amounts of honey and butter? Why?
    c. Choose a point on the budget line and draw an indifference curve that makes this a utility-maximizing equilibrium. Label this point A.
    d. Now assume that the price of butter drops, while the price of honey does not change. Draw the new budget line.
    e. Pick a point on the new budget line and draw a new indifference curve that shows the consumer choosing more butter.
    f. Pick a point on the new budget line where the consumer chooses less butter than at point A. Is it possible to do this?

12. Suppose that consumers in Dallas pay twice as much for grapefruit as for oranges, and consumers in Los Angeles pay three times as much for grapefruit as for oranges. If consumers in both cities maximize utility, how much larger will the marginal rate of substitution of oranges for grapefruit be in Dallas relative to Los Angeles?

13. Nearly all indifference curves are drawn on the assumption that the consumer prefers more of any product to less of that product. Suppose, however, that the consumer reaches a point where additional units of one commodity yield no additional pleasure or satisfaction. What would happen to indifference curves in such an area on the indifference map? Illustrate graphically.

14. What would the budget lines look like if consumers received a progressively lower price as they purchased more during a particular period? The reduction varies continuously over the entire range of quantities of the good. Would the utility-maximizing equilibrium condition be substantially changed from those that prevail under fixed prices?

15. Economists admit that people have greatly differing taste patterns. But they say that, for any two goods consumed by any two people picked at random, the marginal rates of substitution must be equal even though tastes differ. How can this be so?

16. "Increasing the price of things a consumer buys is *equivalent* to reducing the consumer's income." Discuss and illustrate geometrically. Show when this assertion is correct and when it is not.

ANALYTICAL PROBLEMS

1. Business executives generally receive their salary in money income and in goods in kind, such as stock options, nice offices, free trips, and so on. If the income tax is replaced by a sales tax, how do you think the general ratio of money income to nonpecuniary income would change? Explain.

2. "Researchers are intrigued by the fact that many of those moving to small towns or into the country have willingly ignored economics to do so—passing up both better jobs and bigger paychecks. A lot of people are putting other concerns above jobs—quiet place, scenic, safe for children, less noise and congestion, a slower pace of life" (*Newsweek,* July 6, 1981). Are those people who move to small towns really ignoring economics? Use a preference map, plotting income on the vertical axis and small-town quality of life on the horizontal axis, to show how tastes are changing. Could you argue that the "price" of income is rising relative to quality of life in a small town?

3. If a higher sales tax was imposed on all automobiles in a particular state, *every one* of the automobile salespeople in the state would be opposed to the tax increase. Evaluate the conclusion under the following conditions:
   a. The tax is a fixed dollar amount per car sold.
   b. The tax is a given percentage of the purchase price.

c. The tax is progressive. The rate the percentage increases with the price of the automobile.

4. Suppose government is considering a lump sum tax on cigarette smoking. Anyone who smokes must pay a flat amount regardless of the amount smoked. Use cigarettes as one good and expenditures on all other goods as the other.

a. What would the new budget line under the lump sum tax look like? (The price of cigarettes remains constant.)

b. What would probably happen to the amount of cigarettes purchased?

c. Compare the conclusion with those under the assumption of a per unit excise tax.

5. Increasingly, employees are being allowed to choose benefit packages from a menu of items. For instance, workers may be given a package of benefits that includes "basic" and "optional" items. Basics might include modest medical coverage, life insurance equal to a year's salary, vacation time based on length of service, and some retirement pay. But then employees can use credits to choose among such additional benefits as full medical coverage, dental and eye care, more vacation time, additional disability income, and higher company payments to the retirement fund. How do you think flexible benefit packages will affect the employee's choice between higher wages and more benefits? Before you answer, review the application on fringe benefits in the text.

6. In *The Wall Street Journal* (August 10, 1984, p. 1), HUD Secretary Pierce made the following statement in favor of rent vouchers rather than cash payments for housing aid to the poor. "Some of these people will take the money, spend it on liquor, whiskey; they'll never get their rent paid." Evaluate this statement.

a. Draw the budget line with other expenditures on the vertical axis and rental payments on the horizontal axis—first with a voucher and then with a cash payment equivalent to the market value of the voucher.

b. Is it possible to put a convex indifference curve in your figure that makes a consumer better off with the voucher?

7. In many Western states part-time ranchers raise cattle as a hobby. They work full-time at blue or white collar jobs during the week, and run the ranch during their spare time. Most lose money on their venture. Illustrate the utility-maximizing equilibrium for these people with income (or profit) on the vertical axis and "ranching" on the horizontal axis. Are these people profit maximizers? [For more discussion of this hobby see *The Wall Street Journal*, January 8, 1985, p. 1.]

8. In a *Chicago Tribune* story (March 5, 1985) it was estimated that by 1990 there will be 70,000 more doctors than the estimated number needed. Many doctors worry that unnecessary surgery will increase. Can medical surgery be either necessary or unnecessary? Isn't medical care like any other service; when the price falls the quantity sold increases? Using an indifference curve and budget line show that when the price of medical care falls more will be purchased.

9. Perhaps because the national mood is shifting toward sobriety, fueled by activists against drunk driving, overall consumption of distilled spirits dropped 1.5 percent in 1983 and 2.6 percent in 1984. Consumers prefer beverages that are perceived to be lighter—such as beer and wine. Model this change in preferences with an indifference map. For a given income and fixed prices, put "light beverages" on the vertical axis and distilled liquors on the horizontal axis. Show the change in the indifference curve to reflect the described change in tastes.

Chapter 6

Theory of Consumer Behavior: Changes in Income and Price

6.1 INTRODUCTION

Having developed the concept of utility maximization, we are now prepared to analyze the effect of changes in two important determinants of quantity demanded—the consumer's income and the price of the good. In Chapter 2 we emphasized that the theory of demand is concerned primarily with the effect of changes in price, other things held constant. One factor held constant is income; but we know that when prices change, there is a change in purchasing power. When we discussed the budget line, the maximum amount of good X a consumer could purchase with income M was M/p_x. If prices fall to p'_x, then he or she could purchase more—M/p'_x units—creating an increase in purchasing power (real income). With a constant money income, real income cannot be held constant when prices change, and, as a consequence, when a price does change, economists identify an *income* effect as well as a *substitution* effect.

In this chapter, we will examine these two types of change in some depth, and discuss the reasons economists assume demand curves slope downward.

Basic Principles

The effects of changes in income and price can be analyzed simply. First, consider the effect of an increase in money income, prices held constant. This increase is modeled as a parallel shift outward in the budget line. If the consumer was in equilibrium before the increase in

163

income, after the increase there will be a new equilibrium on the higher
budget line tangent to a higher indifference curve. The increase in income
extends the set of the consumer's consumption possibilities, thereby
making the consumer better off. The new equilibrium on the higher
indifference curve is attained under the same conditions—the marginal
rate of substitution equals the price ratio. The effect of a decrease in
money income is analyzed similarly; the budget line shifts downward, and
equilibrium is attained on a lower indifference curve since the set of
consumption opportunities is decreased.

A change in the price of a good, money income held constant, rotates
the budget line—outward for a decrease in price, inward for an increase.
This adjustment principle for a consumer was described in Chapter 5.
This chapter will explain the consumer's reaction to a price change in
more detail. Begin in equilibrium, then let the price of the good decrease.
Since the budget line rotates outward, the set of consumption opportunities available to the individual is increased. In other words, the
consumer is made better off. The good with the reduced price is now less
expensive relative to other goods. The consumer will tend to substitute
consumption away from other goods to the now relatively cheaper good.
Economists call this effect on consumption the "substitution effect." The
fall in price also increases the consumer's total consumption opportunities—more goods can be bought with the same money income. This
includes all goods, but in particular the less expensive commodity. Economists call this part of the price effect the "income effect."

The combination of these two effects leads to a new equilibrium situation, where the new budget line, which has rotated outward, is tangent to
a higher indifference curve. The entire change is a combination of both
the income and substitution effects. After the adjustment, the marginal
rate of substitution equals the new price ratio.

The effect of an increase in price is symmetrical. The budget line
rotates inward, leading to a new tangency on a lower indifference curve.
The income effect follows, because the consumer now has a smaller set of
consumption possibilities and is, therefore, worse off. Since the price of
the good increases relative to that of other goods, the substitution effect
involves a shift in consumption away from the now more expensive good
to other goods.

You can see that the principles involved in analyzing the effects of
changes in income and prices are quite straightforward. There are, however, several implications of the theory that are made more apparent with
the use of graphical analysis, particularly the relation of the principles
discussed above to demand theory. We will devote considerable space in
this chapter to developing the connection between utility maximization
and demand curves to see why economists assume demand slopes downward.

6.2 CHANGES IN MONEY INCOME

To analyze graphically the effect of changes in money income we will plot the quantity of some good, X, along the horizontal axis. Rather than plot the quantity of some other good, Y, along the vertical, we plot expenditure on all goods other than X. The unit of measure along the vertical axis is dollar expenditure. In Figure 6–1, each indifference curve, I–IV, indicates the various combinations of X and expenditures on other goods that yield the same level of utility. Higher levels of utility are indicated by the higher-numbered indifference curves. Assume that the price of X is fixed at \$10 per unit and that, initially, the consumer has an income of \$1,000, indicated by budget line $L''Z''$ A consumer can spend all income on X and purchase 100 units, buy no X and spend all income on other goods, or can purchase any combination along $L''Z''$. We know

FIGURE 6–1   **Income-consumption curve**

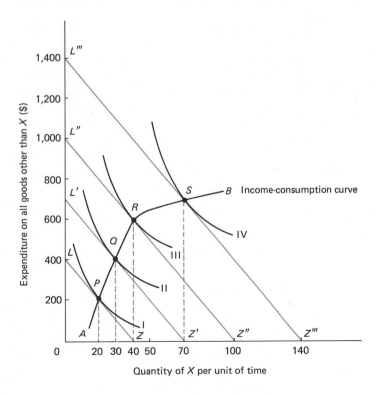

from Chapter 5 that utility is maximized at R on indifference curve III, indicating that the highest available level of utility comes from 40 units of X and \$600 spent on other goods.

When we decrease income to \$700, the new budget line is $L'Z'$. Equilibrium is now at Q, with 30 units of X and \$400 spent on other goods. An income of \$400 causes the consumer to purchase 20 units of X and spend \$200 on other goods. Finally, if income is increased to \$1,400, the budget line is tangent to IV at 70 units of X and \$700. As income changes, the point of consumer equilibrium changes as well. The line connecting the successive equilibria is called the *income-consumption curve,* indicated by AB in Figure 6–1. This curve shows the *equilibrium combinations* of X and expenditures on goods other than X at various levels of money income, nominal prices remaining constant throughout.

Definition

The locus of points showing consumer equilibria at various levels of money income with constant prices is called the *income-consumption curve.*

Engel Curves and Income Elasticity

Engel curves, named for a 19th-century German statistician, show the relation between money income and the consumption of some good, other things, including the price of the good, held constant. These curves are closely related to a good's income elasticity and are important for applied studies of economic welfare and for the analysis of family expenditure patterns. We can relate the income-consumption curve to an Engel curve.

The Engel curve derived from the income-consumption curve in Figure 6–1 is constructed in Figure 6–2. Here, the quantity of good X is plotted along the horizontal axis, money income along the vertical. Point P' in Figure 6–2, showing that with an income of \$400 the consumer purchases 20 units, is associated with point P in Figure 6–1. It follows that Q', 30 units of X at an income of \$700, is associated with point Q. Likewise, R' and S' are equivalent to R and S, respectively. Not all income-consumption curves and Engel curves have the same general slope as this. In some cases, the income-consumption curve may bend backward, in which case the Engel curve will slope downward.

Definition

An Engel curve is a locus of points relating equilibrium quantity of some good to the level of money income. Such curves are readily derived from income-consumption curves.

The responsiveness of quantity demanded to changes in income, other things remaining the same, is measured by the coefficient of income elasticity (E_m). Specifically, the income elasticity of demand is the ratio of the percentage change in quantity demanded to the percentage change in money income. We write this as

FIGURE 6–2   **Engel curve**

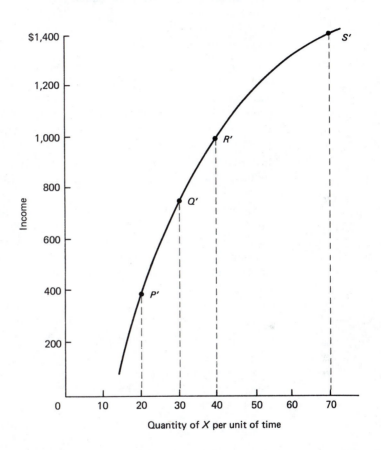

$$E_m = \frac{\Delta X/X}{\Delta M/M} = \frac{\Delta X}{\Delta M} \cdot \frac{M}{X} \gtreqless 0.$$

Note that we do not know the sign of E_m. It depends on the sign of the term $\Delta X/\Delta M$, which may be positive, negative, or zero. We can write this term somewhat differently as

$$\frac{\Delta X}{\Delta M} = \frac{1}{\Delta M/\Delta X}.$$

The denominator in the right-hand ratio is the slope of the Engel curve. Thus, E_m is positive or negative, whenever the slope of the Engel curve is positive or negative.

Principle

The sign on the slope of the Engel curve and the sign on the elasticity of income coefficient, E_m, are always the same.

Normal and Inferior Goods

Looking at Figures 6–1 and 6–2, we can see that the relation between money income and the amount of the good consumed is such that, as income increases, the amount of the good consumed increases, the prices of all goods held constant. That is, in this case, the income-consumption curves do not bend backward, and the Engel curve does not slope downward. Such a good is called a *normal good* over the relevant income levels. Because more X is purchased as money income increases, the income-consumption curve and the Engel curve are positively sloped for a normal good.

In the case of a normal good, the income elasticity of the good is also positive. Using the formula for income elasticity shown above, we have $(\Delta X/X) \div (\Delta M/M) > 0$. Normal goods are given that name because economists in the past believed that an increase in income usually caused an increase in the consumption of a good—they believed this was the "normal" situation. However, an increase in income may well cause a decrease in the consumption of certain commodities at certain price ratios. These commodities are called *inferior* goods. We contrast normal and inferior goods in the following definitions.

Definition

A good is normal if its income elasticity is positive; it is inferior if its income elasticity is negative. A normal good's Engel curve is positively sloped. The Engel curve for an inferior good is negatively sloped over its range of inferiority.

Figure 6–3 illustrates a good that is inferior over a certain range of incomes. In this figure, the quantity of Y, rather than expenditure on all goods other than X, is plotted on the vertical axis. The analysis is the same in either case. Begin with an income shown by budget line LZ. Point P indicates x_1 is the point of equilibrium for the consumer. Next, let income increase to the level shown by $L'Z'$, prices held constant. After the change, the position of consumer equilibrium shifts from point P to point Q. The consumer is better off on a higher indifference curve. But the increase in income leads to a *decrease* in the consumption of X. For this reason, we say that X is inferior over the range of incomes denoted by LZ and $L'Z'$. Over this range, the income-consumption curve bends backward. Since this curve bends backward, the income elasticity of demand $(\Delta X/\Delta M)(M/X)$ is negative. Over some ranges of income, the good may be normal for the consumer, such as movements from A to P and from Q to B.

FIGURE 6–3   **Illustration of an inferior good**

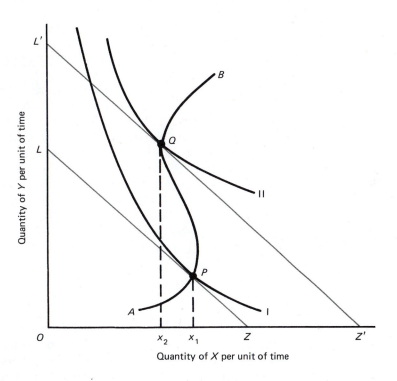

Quantity of *Y* per unit of time

Quantity of *X* per unit of time

Inferiority and normality—and therefore, of course, income elasticity—vary over different ranges of income. Hamburger may be a normal good for one family over a particular range of incomes. It may be an inferior good over another range of incomes. Furthermore, the classification of goods as inferior or normal depends on the price ratio, which changes the slope of a budget line. At one price ratio, a good may have an income elasticity substantially different from the income elasticity at another price ratio. Economists frequently point out examples of inferior goods—margarine, hamburgers, and subcompact cars. As income increases, many people may reduce their consumption of these goods, but others may not. Therefore, remember that inferiority and normality are not inherent properties of the goods themselves. Income elasticities depend on preference patterns of consumers, prices, and the range of incomes.

APPLICATION

Income Elasticities of Housing

Branches of the federal and state government are quite interested in the demand for private housing. This demand directly determines the growth of the construction industry, which in turn is a leading indicator in forecasting business cycles. In order to project housing demand, government officials must take into account the income elasticity of demand for housing. A study published in 1971 estimated the elasticity of rental expenditure with respect to income between 0.8 and 1.0. The estimated elasticity for owner-occupied housing was estimated to lie between 0.7 and 1.5.[1]

In making projections over the next 10 years, people who work for government might wish to predict the increase in the demand for housing (rental and owner-occupied) due to increases in yearly real per capita income, expected to increase between 2 and 3 percent a year. Those making predictions generally realize that they cannot come up with a precise single estimate. Using your knowledge of elasticities and the above figures, how would you estimate the increase in housing demand due to the expected increase in real income?

First, we must estimate the expected increase in real per capita income 10 years hence. If income increases 2 percent per year, income at the end of the first year will be 1.02 times that at the first of the year; at the end of the second year it will be (1.02) times (1.02) times income at the beginning of year one. To generalize, in 10 years income will be $(1.02)^{10}$ times income at the beginning of the period. Since $(1.02)^{10}$ equals 1.218, real per capita income will increase by 21.8 percent, if income increases 2 percent a year.

If income increases 3 percent a year, income in 10 years will be 34.3 percent higher, since $(1.03)^{10}$ equals 1.343. Using estimates for elasticity, we can solve for the percent increase in the demand for rental housing because of income increases over the 10-year period with the formula

$$E_m = \frac{\%\Delta X}{\%\Delta M}.$$

We can summarize the results for rental housing in a table showing the percentage change in quantity under each possible combination.

---

[1] See F. de Leeuw, ''The Demand For Housing: A Review of Cross Section Evidence,'' *The Review of Economics and Statistics,* 53 (February 1971), pp. 1–10.

		Percent increase in income	
		21.8%	34.3%
Income	0.8	17.4%	27.4%
elasticities	1.0	21.8%	34.3%

The range of increase lies between 17.4 percent and 34.3 percent.

The estimates of the percent increase in the demand for owner-occupied housing due to increases in income are summarized in the following table.

		Percent increase in income	
		21.8%	34.3%
Income	0.7	15.3%	24.0%
elasticities	1.5	32.7%	51.5%

The range of estimation is far greater in the case of owner-occupied housing, because the range of elasticities is greater.

We must emphasize that these are estimates of the increase in the amount that would be demanded at a given real price. A person trained in economics would hedge by pointing out that increases in price would curtail, to some extent, the increase in quantity demanded.

6.3 DEMAND CURVES

The effect of price on the consumption of goods is even more important to economists than the effect of changes in income. In this section, we hold money income constant and let price change to analyze the effect on consumer behavior.

Price-Consumption Curves

As with Engel curves, demand curves are derived by moving the budget line and observing the various points of tangency to indifference curves. In this case, rather than a parallel shift in the budget line, there is a rotation of the line, as mentioned in the introduction to this chapter.

Figure 6–4 contains a portion of an indifference map for a consumer who can consume X (measured in units along the horizontal axis) and goods other than X (measured along the vertical axis). The total expenditure on these other goods is measured in dollars. The consumer has a

FIGURE 6–4   **Price-consumption curve**

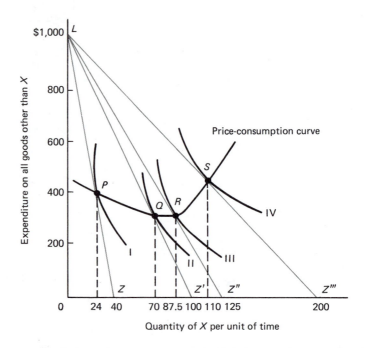

money income of $1,000. When X is priced at $25 per unit, the consumer's budget line is LZ. He or she can spend the $1,000 on other goods, spend the entire $1,000 on 40 units of X at $25 per unit, or spend at any point along LZ. We know by now that the consumption bundle represented at point P, where LZ is tangent to indifference curve I, is optimal. The consumer purchases 24 units of X, spending $600 on this commodity. The remaining $400 is spent on other goods.

Assume that the price of X falls to $10. Now, if the consumer wishes to spend all income on X, he or she can purchase 100 units. The budget line at the new price is LZ', with a slope of -10 rather than -25. The new equilibrium point of tangency is designated by Q, where the individual consumes 70 units of X at a total expense of $700 and spends the remaining $300 on other goods. If price falls to $8 per unit, other things remaining the same, the new budget line is LZ'', with a slope of -8. At equilibrium point R, a consumer purchases 87.5 units of X. Note that $700 is still spent on X and $300 on all other goods. Finally, when the price of X falls to $5, the new budget line, LZ''', is tangent to indifference curve IV at point S. The maximum utility level is attained by spending $550 on 110 units of X

and $450 on goods other than X. Therefore, each price decrease causes the consumer to purchase more units of X. The line joining points P, Q, R, and S (and all other equilibria) is called the *price-consumption curve*. For a given money income, it shows the amount of X consumed as its price changes, other prices remaining the same.

Definition

The price-consumption curve is a locus of equilibrium points relating the quantity of X purchased to its price, money income and all other prices remaining constant. In the case treated above, the price-consumption curve also shows how expenditure on all goods other than X changes as the price of X changes.

Derivation of Demand Curves from Price-Consumption Curves

The individual's demand curve for a commodity can be derived from the price-consumption curve, just as an Engel curve is derivable from the income-consumption curve. The price-quantity relations for good X at points P, Q, R, and S, and presumably for all other points on the price-

FIGURE 6–5   **Demand curve**

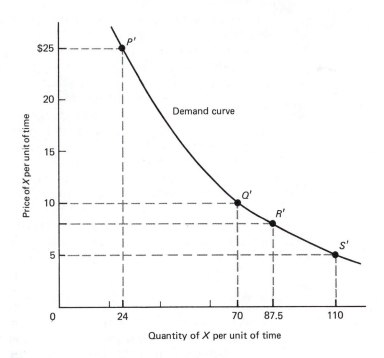

consumption curve in Figure 6–4, are plotted in Figure 6–5. The horizontal axis is the same (units of X), but the vertical axis now shows the price of X. When the price of X is given by the slope of LZ, 24 units of X are purchased, indicated by point P' in Figure 6–5. If the price is $10, 70 units are purchased (point Q'), and so forth. All other points on the curve are derived similarly. The locus of these points is called the demand curve for X.

Definition

The demand curve of an individual for a specific commodity relates the equilibrium quantities purchased to market price, money income and nominal prices of all other commodities held constant. The slope of the demand curve illustrates the law of demand: quantity demanded varies inversely with price—income and the prices of other commodities held constant.

Demand Elasticity and the Price-Consumption Curve

Using our knowledge of the relation between the change in total expenditure on a good and whether that good's demand is elastic, inelastic, or unitary, we can show from the shape of the price-consumption curve in Figure 6–4 that the demand curve in Figure 6–5 is elastic between $25 and $10, has unitary elasticity between $10 and $8, and is inelastic between $8 and $5.

If the price of a good falls, total expenditure on the good increases (decreases) if the demand is elastic (inelastic). Total expenditure remains constant if the demand curve is of unitary elasticity. When price falls from $25 to $10, money income remaining constant at $1,000, equilibrium moves from point P to Q. From Figure 6–4, it is clear that the movement involves a *decrease* in expenditure on all goods other than X. Since money income remains constant, expenditure on X must rise and demand must be in the elastic range. The fall in price from $10 to $8 moves the equilibrium from Q to R. Since expenditure on all other goods stays the same, with money income constant, expenditure on X must stay the same as well. This means elasticity is unitary over the range $10 to $8. The fall in price from $8 to $5 moves equilibrium from R to S; expenditure on all other goods now increases. Hence, expenditure on X decreases and demand is necessarily inelastic over this range. The demand curve in Figure 6–5 is elastic at higher prices, becomes unitary, then becomes inelastic at lower prices.

6.4 SUBSTITUTION AND INCOME EFFECTS

Let us now turn to a more complete analysis of why demand curves slope downward. Recall from the introduction that there are two effects of a price change. If price falls (rises), the good becomes cheaper (more expensive) relative to other goods, and consumers substitute toward (away from) the good. This is the substitution effect. Also, as price falls (rises), the consumer's purchasing power increases (decreases). Since the set of consumption opportunities increases (decreases), the consumer changes the mix of his or her consumption bundle. This effect is called the income effect. Let us analyze each effect in turn, then combine the two in order to see why demand is assumed to slope downward.

Substitution Effect

We begin our analysis of the substitution effect with a definition:

Definition
The substitution effect of a price change is the change in the consumption of a good resulting from a price change while the consumer stays on the same indifference curve.

Consider Figure 6–6, Panel A. Assume LZ is the original budget line, giving an equilibrium at point A on indifference curve I. The equilibrium quantity of X is x_1. From here let the price of X *decrease* so that the new budget line is LZ'. We know from our theory that the consumer will now move to a new equilibrium tangency on the new budget line LZ'.

But suppose we place the following restriction on the consumer: After the decrease in the price of X, we reduce the consumer's money income just enough to force a tangency to the original indifference curve I. That is, at the new price ratio given by the slope of LZ', reduce income so that a budget line with the same slope (same price ratio) as LZ' is tangent to I. This new budget line is shown as RS, parallel to LZ' and tangent to I. With the new budget line RS showing the new price ratio, the consumer maximizes utility at point B, consuming x_2 units of X. The consumer is neither better nor worse off, being on the same indifference curve as before. The movement from A to B, or the change in consumption from x_1 to x_2, is the pure substitution effect, designated by the arrow labeled S.

Considering the impact of price along an indifference curve, a decrease in price must lead to increased consumption of the good. That is, a fall in the price of X reduces the slope of the budget line. Because of the convex shape of indifference curves, the less steeply sloped budget line must become tangent to the original indifference curve at a greater quantity of X.

Panel B shows the substitution effect for an *increase* in the price of X. As in Panel A, begin with budget line LZ tangent to indifference curve I at point A; x_1 units of good X are consumed in equilibrium. The price of X now rises, causing the budget line at the given money income to rotate to LZ''. Again we know that, money income held constant, the new equilibrium will be along LZ''.

Now we *increase the consumer's income* at the new price ratio, shown by the slope of LZ'', until a budget line with the new slope is just tangent

FIGURE 6–6   **Substitution effects**

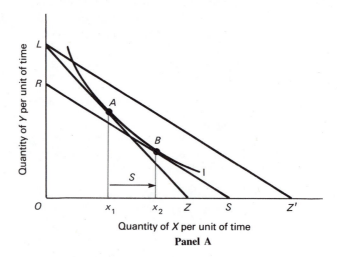

Panel A

Panel B

to the original indifference curve I. This is shown by the budget line *ED*, tangent to I at point *C*. In this case, the consumption of *X* is x_3 units. The pure substitution effect is the movement from *A* to *C*, or the change from x_1 units of *X* to x_3, designated again by the arrow labeled *S*.

Considering the substitution effect only, the *increase* in the price of *X* causes a reduction in the consumption of *X*. This must always be the case. An increase in the price of *X* makes the budget line steeper, so the new point of tangency must come where the indifference curve is steeper. After a price increase, tangency must come at a lower consumption of *X*.

We have established the following principle:

Principle

The substitution effect is the change in the consumption of a good after a change in price, when the consumer is forced by a change in money income to consume at some point on the original indifference curve. Considering the substitution effect only, the amount of the good consumed must vary inversely with its price. That is, utility held constant, $(\Delta X/\Delta P_x) < 0$.

Income Effect

While we have established the direction of the substitution effect, we cannot be as certain about how the income effect influences the quantity of *X* purchased. Before we study the income effect, let us define it:

Definition

The income effect from a price change is the change in the consumption of a good resulting strictly from a change in purchasing power, i.e., a change in real income.

In Figure 6–7, begin with budget line *LZ*. The consumer is in equilibrium at point *P* on indifference curve I, consuming x_1 units of *X*. Let the price of *X* fall, causing the budget line to rotate outward to *LZ'*. We can isolate the substitution effect by reducing money income and forcing the new budget line at the new price ratio to move back until a new line with the same slope as *LZ'* is just tangent to I. Such a budget line is *AB*, tangent to I at *Q*, where the consumer chooses x_2 units of *X*. In this case, the substitution effect of the price decrease shows an increase in the consumption of *X* from x_1 to x_2, shown as *S* in Figure 6–7.

Now that we have isolated the substitution effect, let us return the money income to the original level by shifting the budget line from *AB* back to *LZ'*. Assuming that good *X* is normal, the increase in money income from the level shown by *AB* to that shown by *LZ'* causes the consumption of *X* to increase. This result is shown by the movement from *Q* on indifference curve I to *R* on indifference curve II, or the increase in *X* from x_2 to x_3. This is the income effect. The income effect shows that the consumption of *X* increases from x_2 to x_3—the distance *M* in Figure

FIGURE 6–7   **Substitution and income effects for a decrease in the price of *X***

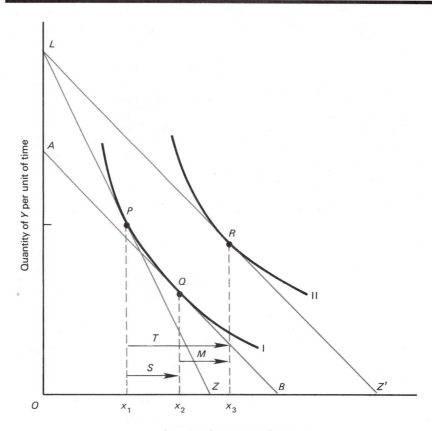

6–7. Whenever the income effect causes more *X* to be consumed and, therefore, reinforces the substitution effect, we know the good is normal.

The total effect of the decrease in price that rotated the budget line from *LZ* to *LZ′* is the increase in consumption of *X* from x_1 to x_3. The total effect is broken up into the substitution effect (the distance x_1x_2) plus the income effect (the distance x_2x_3), resulting from returning the money income we pretended to take away when isolating the substitution effect.

In this example, the income effect reinforced the substitution effect because the good was assumed normal. Had the good been inferior, however, the shift from *AB* back to *LZ′* would have caused a reduction in the consumption of *X*; that is a decrease from x_2. This situation is shown

FIGURE 6–8   **Substitution and income effects for an inferior good**

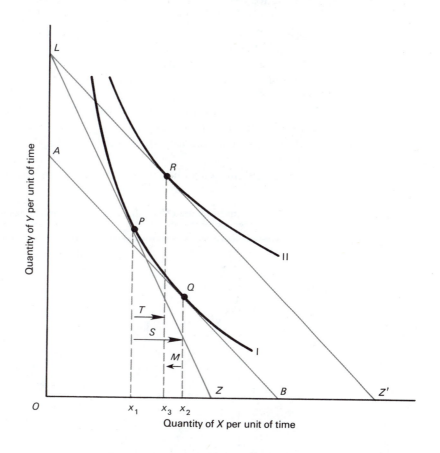

in Figure 6–8, where X is inferior over the relevant range. Again, begin with budget line LZ and equilibrium P, with x_1 being consumed. The decrease in the price of X, as before, rotates the budget line to LZ', and, as before, the substitution effect of the decrease in price is the increase from x_1 to x_2, or the movement from P to Q. Next, let the income be returned for the inferior good. As the budget line shifts from AB back to LZ' the consumption of X is reduced from x_2 to x_3 by the return of the money income. The income effect is the movement from Q back to R. The total effect is the change in X from x_1 to x_3. But the total effect is less than the substitution effect alone because the income effect, to some extent, offsets it.

Let's review this complicated analysis by briefly considering the effects of a price increase. First, take the case of a normal good, illustrated in Figure 6–9.

The original price ratio is indicated by the slope of LZ. The consumer attains equilibrium at point P on indifference curve II, purchasing x_1 units of X. When the price of X rises, as indicated by pivoting the budget line from LZ to LZ', the consumer moves to a new equilibrium position at R on indifference curve I, purchasing x_3 units of X. The total effect of the price change is indicated by the movement from P to R, or by the reduction in quantity demanded from x_1 to x_3, shown as T in the Figure. In other words, the total effect is $x_1 - x_3 = x_1x_3$. This is a negative total effect, because quantity demanded is reduced by x_1x_3 units when price increases.

Coincident with the price rise, suppose the consumer is given an

FIGURE 6–9   **Substitution and income effects for a normal good in case of a price rise**

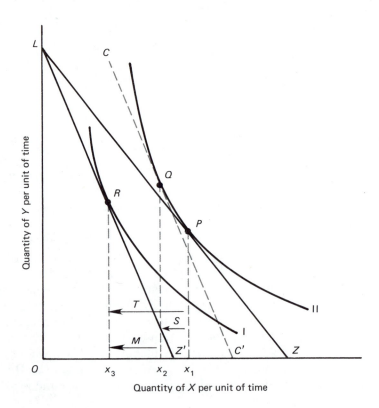

amount of additional money just sufficient to compensate for the loss in real income otherwise sustained. That is, compensatory payment is given that is just sufficient to make the consumer choose to consume on indifference curve II at the new price ratio. This new imaginary budget line is CC'; it is tangent to the original indifference curve II at point Q, but it reflects the new price ratio.

The substitution effect is shown by the movement from P to Q, or by the reduction in quantity demanded from x_1 to x_2. Now, let the consumer's real income *fall* from the level represented by the fictitious budget line CC'. The movement from Q to R (the decrease in consumption from x_2 to x_3) indicates the income effect. Since CC' and LZ' are parallel, the movement does not involve a change in relative prices. It is once more a real income phenomenon, since the reduction in quantity

FIGURE 6–10   **Substitution and income effects for an inferior good in case of a price rise**

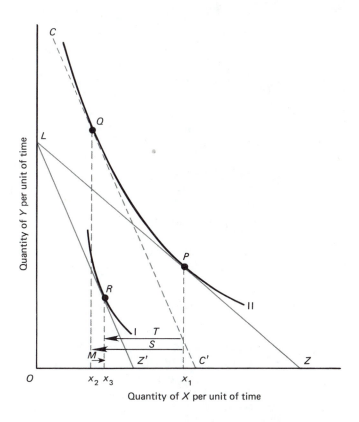

demanded measures the change in purchases attributable exlusively to the decline in real income. The change in relative prices already has been accounted for by the substitution effect. In the figure we can see that X is a normal good; the decrease in real income causes a decrease in consumption. In this case, the income effect reinforces the substitution effect, as is always the case for a normal good.

Consider a situation with an inferior good. In Figure 6–10, an increase in price rotates the budget line from LZ to LZ'. Following the familiar analysis, the consumer moves from point P to point R, decreasing consumption of X from x_1 to x_3 (the total effect—T). The substitution effect, derived by giving the consumer just enough additional money income to compensate for the decrease in real income occasioned by the price rise, is from P to Q (from x_1 to x_2). The income effect is from Q to R (an *increase* in consumption from x_2 to x_3). This partial offset to the substitution effect is to be expected, since X is an inferior good and a decrease in income causes an increase in the consumption of X.

We have established the following principle:

Principle

Considering the substitution effect alone, an increase (decrease) in the price of a good causes less (more) of the good to be demanded. For a normal good, the income effect—from the consumer's being made better or worse off by the price change—adds to or reinforces the substitution effect. The income effect for an inferior good offsets or takes away from the substitution effect to some extent.

6.5 WHY DEMAND SLOPES DOWNWARD

In Ph.D. theory courses a popular test question asks the student to explain why demand curves slope downward. Many argue incorrectly that the principle of declining marginal utility, or a convex indifference curve, is all that is necessary. A better answer is that demand slopes downward because the good is normal or, if the good is inferior, the substitution effect is larger in magnitude than the income effect. Theoretically we cannot prove this is always true, but no contradictory examples have ever been found.

Demand for Normal Goods

In the case of a normal good, it is quite clear why price and quantity demanded are negatively related. From the substitution effect alone, a decrease in price is accompanied by an increase in quantity demanded, and an increase in price decreases quantity demanded. As we have shown, for a normal good, the income effect must add to the substitution effect. Both effects change quantity demanded in the same direction, and demand must be negatively sloped.

Demand for Inferior Goods

In the case of an inferior good, the income effect does not move in the same direction as, and therefore to some extent offsets, the substitution effect. As long as the substitution effect dominates or is larger than the income effect, demand is downward sloping. Could the income effect dominate the substitution effect, causing price and quantity demand to be directly rather than inversely related? In other words, in Figure 6–8, could the indifference map be such that the income effect is so great that the equilibrium point on budget line LZ' falls to the left of x_1 rather than at R? In this case, could the income effect dominate the substitution effect, causing demand to slope upward?

Theoretically at least, such a circumstance is possible. Economists call such theoretical cases, where the domination of the income effect for an inferior good causes an upward sloping demand, *Giffen's Paradox*, named for a 19th century British civil servant who collected data on the effect of price changes.

But just because such cases are theoretically possible doesn't mean that they are likely or occur frequently—or that they occur at all in the real world. Some economists have noted that one way a young economist could advance rapidly in the profession is by discovering a Giffen good (no one has yet!). Cases involving positively sloped demands are probably just theoretical curios—they certainly are not important in the real world.

It is easy to see that in most, if not all, conceivable cases, the substitution effect would tend to dominate the income effect. An increase in the price of a good makes this good more expensive relative to all other goods. In the sense that all goods compete for a consumer's income, all other goods are substitutes. Even more directly, it would be extremely unusual if a good did not have reasonably close substitutes. People can and do change consumption patterns in response to changes in relative prices by substituting to and from other goods.

It would be unusual if an increase in the price of a good consumed substantially reduced a consumer's real income. The effect of the reduction in real income would be felt not only by the good with the increase in price, *but it would be spread over all other goods as well*. The impact of the change in real income from a price change for *any single good* would be rather small, if not minute. Therefore, it appears that the slight change in real income from price changes in inferior goods, combined with the slight change in real income being spread over all goods, would make it extremely unlikely that the income effect could overcome the substitution effect and cause demand to slope upward.

The Law of Demand

Economists feel so strongly about the domination of the substitution effect over the income effect that they speak of the *law of demand*, where quantity demanded varies inversely with price, other things remaining the same.

Marketing experts have pointed out several examples from the business world that supposedly violate the law of demand. Evidence of these alleged departures is that some goods have sold better at higher prices than at lower prices. Marketing experts call such alleged departures from the law of demand "psychological pricing." Let's take a look at a few examples, then analyze them.

A new nasal spray did not sell well when introduced at a price lower than the price of well-known national brands. An increase in the price of the new spray increased sales. Another case of a firm's raising price to increase sales involved pantyhose manufactured by a national hosiery firm. A particular brand of pantyhose sold better when the price was increased to the price range of the competition. There was a marketing experiment where a particular brand of ink was displayed at 25 cents and 15 cents—only the price and the name were different. The ink sold better at 25 cents than at 15 cents.[2] There are many other examples available.

Do these and similar examples mean that the law of demand does not hold under these circumstances? These examples imply no such thing. The problem is one of ignorance.[3] Again, ask yourself the question: Is there anything you buy that you would buy more of at a higher price? Your answer is probably no—but, when uncertain (ignorant) about product quality, you may judge quality by price. This is not irrational behavior and it is easy to explain why products that sell better at higher than at lower prices do not violate the law of downward sloping demand.

First of all, your time is valuable. Since time is scarce, no one uses it to become an expert on every item available. While you are shopping around gaining information about products, you could be working or consuming leisure. The time spent shopping has value in the sense that you are allocating time (a scarce resource) away from other activities. Economists say that the time spent shopping has an opportunity cost, and the total cost of a good is the price of that good plus the value of the time spent shopping for it.

Second, people realize from past experience that price and quality are frequently, although not always, directly related. Price is often used in lieu of quality research as an indicator of product quality. This would be expected when the monetary saving expected from buying the lower

---

[2] For these and other instances, see F. C. Sturdivant et al., "Demand Curve Estimation and Psychological Pricing," in *Managerial Analysis in Marketing* (Glenview, Ill.: Scott, Foresman, 1970), Chapter 10.

[3] Do not equate ignorance with stupidity. Ignorance means lacking knowledge about something. Even the smartest people are ignorant about many things, possibly through lack of interest. If we value the use of our time more in some other alternative than in learning about the diet of the ancient Incas, we will remain ignorant in that area. As in all things, overcoming ignorance has a cost.

rather than the higher-priced item is small compared to the cost (in time) of gaining information. When absolute price variations among products are low relative to income, as would be expected in the case of relatively low-priced items, we expect people to do less systematic research and to judge quality more by prices. For more expensive goods, on the other hand, the absolute price variation is greater. This will make the cost of judging quality by price greater, relative to the cost of systematic quality research, for higher-priced goods. We expect consumers to depend more on research and less on price as an indicator of quality when purchasing high-cost (relative to income) items, such as housing, automobiles, and major household appliances. In other words, when the cost of taking price as an indicator of quality rises, fewer consumers judge quality by price.

As the returns to quality research rise, people will rely more on research and less on price as an indicator of quality. This again would be the case for higher-priced goods where the cost of making a purchasing mistake is greater. The penalty for misjudging quality in an automobile is greater than that for misjudging a $1 bottle of ink. All of the examples given are for low-priced goods—if the price of the goods had been increased much above the "going" price, sales would have fallen substantially. The ink at $3 a bottle would not have sold well when other brands were selling at around $1. In almost every example, the lower-priced good was well below the average price of similar goods, leading consumers to think it was not as good. The price was increased only to about the going price, never well above it, or the price increase was accompanied by a vigorous marketing campaign.

Finally, when consumers believe that quality differences among different brand names are great, they will be more likely to buy higher-priced brands than when they expect little quality difference. That is, when consumers believe they will gain little quality at higher prices, they tend to pay lower prices. Marketing experiments on brands of razor blades, floor wax, cooking sherry, mothballs, salt, aspirin, and beer tend to verify this hypothesis.

We can easily explain apparent exceptions to the law of demand. If consumers *know* two goods are exactly alike in every way (including prestige) and choose the higher-priced good, it would be an exception. For some goods, the imputed quality is judged by price when the cost of research on quality is high relative to expected return. These are different goods at different prices in the minds of some consumers, and the cases cited are not violations of the law of demand.

6.6 SUMMARY

The basic principles of consumer behavior and demand have now been developed. The fundamental point of this chapter is that, if consumers maximize satisfaction from a limited money income, quantity demanded (with one relatively unimportant exception) will vary inversely with price.

An Engel curve is a locus of points relating equilibrium quantity to the level of money income at a specified set of relative prices. The Engel curve slopes upward if the good is normal over that range. If the good is inferior, the curve slopes downward. Income elasticity is an alternative way of determining whether a good is normal or inferior. If the elasticity is positive, the good is normal; otherwise, it is inferior. We have a principle relating the slope of the Engel curve to income elasticity.

Principle
The sign of the slope of the Engel curve and the sign on the elasticity of income coefficient, E_m, are always the same.

The total effect of a price change on consumer behavior can be divided into a substitution and income effect. The substitution effect is always negative; that is, quantity demanded varies inversely with price. If a good is normal, the income effect reinforces the substitution effect. If a good is inferior, the income effect offsets the substitution effect to some extent. In the text two important principles were emphasized:

Principle
The substitution effect is the change in the consumption of a good after a change in price, when the consumer is forced by a change in money income to consume at some point on the original indifference curve. Considering the substitution effect only, the amount of the good consumed must vary inversely with its price. That is, utility held constant, $(\Delta X/\Delta P_x) < 0$.

Principle
Considering the substitution effect alone, an increase (decrease) in the price of a good causes less (more) of the good to be demanded. For a normal good, the income effect adds to or reinforces the substitution effect. The income effect for an inferior good offsets or takes away from the substitution effect.

TECHNICAL PROBLEMS

1. Consider the following table showing income, the quantity of the good demanded, and the price of the good.

Quantity	Income	Price
100	$5,000	$16
120	6,000	16

Compute the income elasticity of the good. Next, suppose the price of the good changes so that the schedule is now as follows:

Quantity	Income	Price
150	$5,000	$10
130	6,000	10

Compute again the income elasticity of demand. Why has it changed even though the change in income is the same?

2. If there is a single "all-important" commodity that absorbs all of the individual's income, what is its income elasticity? Explain your results using the definition of income elasticity.

3. Consider Figure E.6–1. Begin with the consumer in equilibrium with an income of $300 facing the prices $P_x = \$4$ and $P_y = \$10$.

    a. How much X is consumed in equilibrium?
        Let the price of X fall to $2.50; income and P_y remain constant.

FIGURE E.6–1

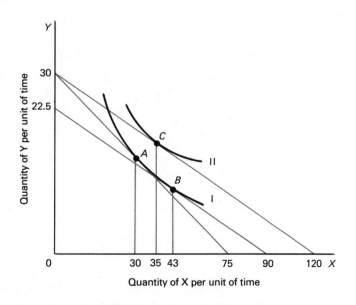

Quantity of Y per unit of time

Quantity of X per unit of time

    b. What is the new equilibrium consumption of *X*?

    c. How much income must be taken from the consumer to isolate the income and substitution effects?

    d. The total effect of the price decrease is _____. The substitution effect is _____. The income effect is _____.

    e. The good *X* is _____, but not _____.

    f. Construct the consumer's demand curve for *X* with income constant.

4. In Figure E.6–2 the indifference curves have a concave shape. For an income or price change, Panels A and B show that the consumer always optimizes at the corner, putting all income into the consumption of *Y*. Based on this information draw

    a. The income-consumption schedule. What is the income elasticity of *Y*?

    b. The demand curve for *Y*. What is the demand elasticity of *Y*?

5. For the entire United States, assume that real per capita income rises over the next few years. Assume also that all *relative* prices remain the same. Draw what you think would be the appropriate Engel curve for the following commodities. Explain why you drew them with the shape you did.

    a. Toyotas.

    b. Cadillacs and Lincolns.

    c. Water.

    d. Fish.

    e. All food.

    f. College education.

    g. Television sets.

    h. Black and white television sets.

6. Explain the statement: "It is possible for all goods and services to be normal, but never can they all be inferior."

7. Graphically derive a demand curve for a normal good. Start with indifference curves for goods *X* and *Y*. Let the price of *X* fall. Identify the income and substitution effects of this price decline on the graph. Identify two points on the resulting demand curve, showing where you got each of the points. Explain each step. Draw and label your diagrams clearly.

8. Draw an income-consumption curve and an Engel curve for good *X*, assuming that the price of *X* is $10 and the price of *Y* is $25, by examining incomes of $100, $200, and $300. Show your work. (Use conventionally shaped indifference curves.)

9. Prove that in any consumer indifference map where the income-consumption curve is a straight line passing through the origin, the income elasticity of demand for each commodity is equal to unity.

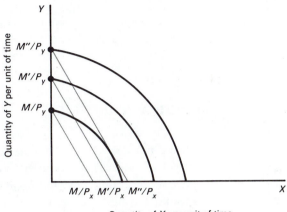

Quantity of X per unit of time
Panel A

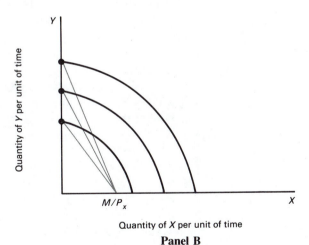

Quantity of X per unit of time
Panel B

10. A consumer has a choice of buying red marbles or blue marbles. The marbles are identical except for color, but can have different prices.
   a. Assume that the only use the consumer has for marbles is to put them at the bottom of a flower pot for drainage. Since dirt will cover the marbles they will not be visible. Draw the consumer's *indifference map* and *a demand curve for red marbles*.
   b. Assume that the only use for marbles is in producing light

glitters which require one red marble and two blue marbles to correctly filter the light. Draw the consumer's *indifference map* and a *demand curve for red marbles.*

c. Assume that this consumer is superstitious and believes that owning marbles that are not all the same color will bring bad luck. That is, he or she prefers more marbles to less, but prefers any bundle containing only one color to any bundle containing two colors. Draw this consumer's *indifference map.*

ANALYTICAL PROBLEMS

1. Family size in the United States decreased for 50 years after 1900 while per capita income increased. Given constant tastes, children must be an inferior good. Evaluate.

2. Charitable contributions are deductible from income taxes. How would an increase in the tax rate affect charitable contributions? (Hint: consider both income and substitution effects.)

3. During the Great Depression, while per capita income was falling, movie theater receipts steadily rose. What does this tell you about the income elasticity of films? Are they normal goods?

4. Suppose you operate a very successful liquor store, and you are thinking about opening a second store elsewhere.
   a. If the income elasticity of liquor is positive and large, in what kind of neighborhood would you want to put your new store?
   b. Imagine that the area in which you sell is in a recession; what kind of income elasticity would you want your product to have?
   c. As a business owner, would you want the income effects on your product to be small or large?

5. In 1985, Kartes Video Communications test marketed the prices of video cassettes. For film classics it set prices at $14.95, $19.95, $24.95, and $29.95 at different times. The most profitable price was $19.95, but the company actually sold more units at the $24.95 price than when the same cassette was priced at $14.95. Explain why this might happen in a market, especially when most movie cassettes sell at prices between $40 and $80.

6. Suppose we wanted to compare demand curves that took into account both the income and substitution effects with a demand curve that only considered the substitution effect. What demand curve would be less elastic? Does it depend on whether the goods are inferior or normal?

7. Critically evaluate the following statement with analysis: "A downward sloping demand curve means the income effect is always smaller than the substitution effect, and the less elastic is demand the less significant is the income effect."

8. After reading this chapter, two students get into a disagreement over the definition of an inferior good. One argues that an inferior good exists when the substitution and income effects work in opposite directions when prices change in a preference map. The other argues that the definition of inferiority has nothing to do with prices. But on the Engel curve, an inferior good exists when the curve has a negative slope. Who is right?

9. Suppose a consumer is promised enough income to purchase a specified bundle of goods, say x_o and y_o. At present the consumer is unable to purchase these quantities. The consumer has the choice of seeing the price of X decreased until x_o and y_o can be purchased, or having income increased until the bundle can be purchased. Explain which option the consumer would prefer. What does it depend on?

10. Some economists argue that certain consumers buy goods simply because their price is high. Flaunting the product makes other people think the owner is wealthy. This is called the "snob effect." Would the income effect be larger than the substitution effect when goods have snob appeal? What slope does the demand curve have? Are these goods examples of Giffen's paradox?

Chapter 7

Applying Consumer Behavior Theory

7.1 INTRODUCTION

The preceding two chapters set forth the theory of consumer behavior, then used that theory to derive and analyze the determinants of demand. This chapter uses the theory, particularly the concept of indifference curves, to analyze selected economic topics. We first show how price indexes—such as the Consumer Price Index—can and often do overestimate the effect of inflation. Next, we analyze the decisions of workers as to how much of their time is spent working and how much is spent enjoying leisure. After this we explain how advertising affects demand through changes on consumers' budget lines and indifference curves. Finally, we add a time dimension to consumer choice theory to show what determines an individual's decision to borrow and lend between periods. While there are many other topics that can and have been analyzed using consumer behavior theory, we feel these four will give you some insight into the usefulness of the theory in explaining the economic behavior of consumers.

7.2 THE REAL EFFECT OF INFLATION

One frequently encountered—and misunderstood—concept in economics is the Consumer Price Index (CPI), computed by the Bureau of Labor Statistics (BLS). Huge labor contracts hinge on changes in the CPI, as do purchasing and construction contracts; changes in the payment of social security and welfare benefits are based on the CPI; and politicians are elected or defeated on favorable or unfavorable reports of the index. How well do changes in the CPI or other indexes reflect the impact of inflation on consumers? Do changes in a price index overestimate or underestimate the impact of inflation? Because price indexes are extremely important for economic policy, these questions are of paramount importance. We can use the tools developed thus far to see how well increases in the CPI actually measure the impact of higher prices on consumers.

The Consumer Price Index

First, let us define the CPI. In computing this index, the BLS uses a *Laspeyres indexing method*, which takes the ratio of the cost of purchasing a specified bundle of goods in one year relative to the cost of purchasing the same bundle during some specified *base* year. For example, suppose there are two goods X and Y, and the base year is 1970. The amount of each good consumed by a typical household in 1970, the bundle used for weighting, consists of x_0 and y_0. For 1985, a Laspeyres index (L) would be

$$L = \frac{p_x^{85}x_0 + p_y^{85}y_0}{p_x^{70}x_0 + p_y^{70}y_0} \gtreqless 1.$$

Note that the quantities in each year are the same, even though the consumption patterns of people might actually have changed. The superscripts on the prices represent the years. If there has been no change in prices, L would be equal to one, because $p_x^{85} = p_x^{70}$ and $p_y^{85} = p_y^{70}$. If prices, on average, have risen, L would be greater than one; if they have fallen, the index would have a value less than one.

The BLS, of course, uses more than two goods in computing the CPI. In fact, it uses a market basket based on what an averge urban family of four consumed in 1967. More generally, when there are more than two goods, we may write L as

$$L = \frac{\Sigma p_i' x_i^0}{\Sigma p_i x_i^0},$$

where p_i and p_i' are, respectively, the price of the ith good in the base year and its price in the year for which the index is calculated; x_i^0 is the consumption of the ith good in the base period.

Inflation, as measured by the change in the CPI, was approximately 14 percent in 1980, 10 percent in 1981, 6 percent in 1982, and 4 percent in 1983. Looking at 1980, the CPI tells us that it took 14 percent more income to buy the same bundle of goods at the end of 1980 than it did at the beginning of 1980. That is, since the price index rose by 14 percent during 1980, the identical bundle of goods costs 14 percent more to purchase at the end of the year. Does this description give us a very accurate picture of the true effect of inflation? An indifference map and some budget lines will show that the answer depends on how much *relative* prices have changed over the year.

True Effect of Inflation

Let us return to the hypothetical two-good (X and Y) analysis. Figure 7–1 shows a particular individual's or household's equilibrium during the base period at point A on budget line LZ and indifference curve II. Let the prices of both goods increase, but let the price of X rise relative to the price of Y. We know that if money income is held constant and the quantity of X is plotted along the horizontal axis, the budget line will shift backward and become steeper. The backward shift in the budget line reflects the fact that both prices rose; therefore, both the vertical and the horizontal intercepts of the budget line must decrease (move toward the origin). The increase in the steepness of the budget line reflects that p_x/p_y (the slope of the budget line) increases, because by assumption the price of X increased more than the price of Y. This new line is shown as $L'Z'$ in the figure. If the household had the same money income after prices changed, it would choose to consume at combination B on indifference curve I. Compared to point A the household is clearly worse off.

The CPI tells us how much additional income or expenditure the household needs to enable it to consume the *original bundle of goods* at the new prices; i.e., to allow consumption at the old equilibrium, point A. As we noted, in 1980 this would take a 14 percent increase in income. In

FIGURE 7–1   **Inflation and the consumer price index**

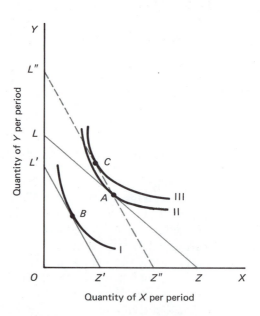

Quantity of X per period

Figure 7–1, an increase in income just enough to shift the budget line to
$L''Z''$ is needed. That is, $L''Z''$ has the same slope as the new line $L'Z'$, but
there is enough additional income to allow the consumer to choose point
A, the original consumption bundle. If this shift requires a 14 percent
increase does this increase in income represent the true incidence of
inflation? In this case the answer is no. It overestimates the impact of
price increases.

We know from our previous analysis that, with budget line $L''Z''$, the
combination shown at A would not be chosen. The household could
increase utility by substituting Y for X, because the price of Y has
decreased *relative* to that of X, even though both prices increased. The
household would choose a point such as C on the higher indifference
curve III and be better off. Because of the possibility of substitution, the
increase in income needed to return to A, would make the household
better off than it was before. In this instance, the change in the CPI
overestimated the effect of inflation.

To carry the analysis further, assume that both prices rise, but this time
the price of Y increases by a greater percentage than the price of X; that
is, p_x/p_y decreases. With money income constant, the budget line moves
downward but now becomes less steep than LZ. Next, move the budget
line with a lesser slope outward so that it passes through the original point
A. The required increase in money income is the change in the CPI. The
household once again can move to a higher indifference curve than II by
substituting X for Y. Once again, the change in the CPI overestimates the
inflationary impact.

Finally, let both prices increase by the same percentage. The budget
line shifts downward, but the slope does not change; p_x/p_y remains
constant. Now increase money income by the change in the CPI so that
the line passes through A. This budget line is the same as LZ. The
household cannot reach a higher indifference curve by substituting. Utility is still maximized at the combination of goods given by A.

The only time the percentage increase in the CPI measures the amount
that income must increase to make consumers exactly as well off as they
were before a price change, is when all prices change in the same proportion. Only then does the increase in income given by the rise in the CPI
exactly equal the increase necessary to make the consumer no better or
worse off than without any inflation. Otherwise, the change in the CPI
exaggerates the impact of inflation, due to consumers' ability to substitute. In such cases, if a consumer's income goes up by exactly as much
as the rate of inflation, inflation actually makes that consumer better off.

Deflation

Paradoxically, if all prices do not decrease proportionately, a fall in the
CPI does not overestimate, but underestimates the impact of deflation—
the decline in income necessary to make a consumer no better or worse

FIGURE 7–2   **The impact of deflation**

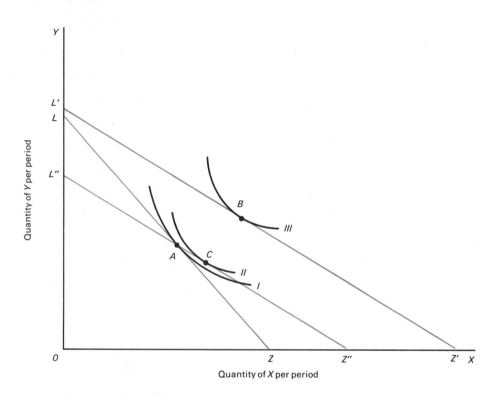

off than before the decrease in prices. To illustrate, begin with budget line *LZ* in Figure 7–2. The consumer maximizes utility by choosing the bundle of *X* and *Y* given by point *A* on indifference curve I. Now let the prices of both *X* and *Y* fall, but the price of *X* falls proportionately more than the price of *Y*. Suppose the price decline represents a fall of 10 percent in the CPI.

The budget line shifts outward to *L'Z'*. Since both prices decreased, both intercepts increase—move outward from the origin—and because the price of *Y* decreased relatively less than the price of *X*, p_x/p_y decreases and the new budget line is less steep than *LZ*. The consumer chooses the bundle given at point *B* on indifference curve III and is clearly better off.

Suppose that after deflation the consumer's income is reduced 10 percent to reflect the 10 percent decline in the CPI. After the 10 percent reduction in income, the budget line shifts backward to *L"Z"*, which has the same slope as $L'Z'$, to reflect the change in relative prices, and passes through the original consumption bundle, A. The line must be shifted this far back so the original bundle can be purchased with the reduced income.

Clearly, A is not a utility-maximizing equilibrium. The consumer substitutes the relatively less expensive X for Y and moves to a bundle such as C on indifference curve II. With a 10 percent decrease in the CPI and an offsetting 10 percent reduction in income, the consumer is better off. The decline in the CPI underestimates the true effect (in this case benefit) of deflation on consumers.

Given a 10 percent decrease in the CPI and in income, the consumer would substitute Y for X, if the price of Y falls relatively more than the price of X. Only if the prices of X and Y fall in exactly the same proportion does the decrease in the CPI exactly show the effect of deflation. The closer the price change is to a proportional change, the more closely the change in the CPI reflects the real impact of both inflation and deflation.

7.3 THE LABOR-LEISURE CHOICE

The tools developed in Chapters 5 and 6 can be easily adapted to analyze the theory of labor supply. We consider a person's total supply of labor time to be the residual of the total time available less the individual's demand for leisure time. The analytical tools pertaining to demand theory are applicable to labor supply and to the economic problems associated with labor supply.

The Labor-Leisure Map

Figure 7–3, Panel A, contains a portion of an individual's indifference map between income and leisure. Instead of depending strictly on the quantity of goods, utility is now regarded as a function of how time is divided between working and leisure. Work, of course, increases an individual's income, measured on the vertical axis. From the shape of the indifference curves in the figure, it is clear that we have assumed both income and leisure are considered desirable by the individual; that is, one does not become satiated with leisure within the relevant range of income.

Before considering the problem of how the consumer maximizes utility, a word of explanation about the unit of measurement for leisure and the vertical line at L_m is in order. The unit of measurement along the horizontal axis can be hours per day, days per year, or any other period of time. Obviously, if the unit is hours per day, the maximum time for leisure is 24 hours. If the unit is days of leisure, the maximum is 7 per week or 365 per year. The line L_m indicates the maximum attainable units of leisure per time period. If the individual chooses C' units of leisure per period, he or she also chooses $C'L_m$ for work; or if L_m units of leisure are chosen, this person does not work at all. The unit of measurement chosen for the

FIGURE 7–3 **Indifference curve analysis of labor supply**

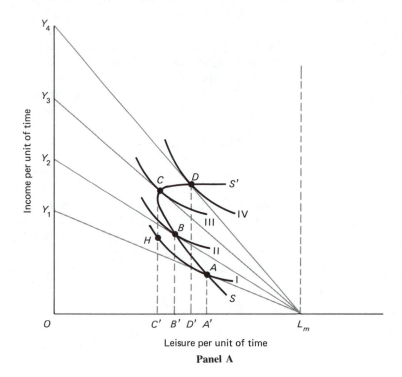

Panel A

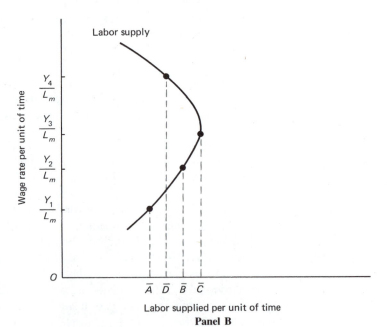

Panel B

horizontal axis clearly specifies the unit for the vertical. For example, when leisure is designated as hours per day, the vertical axis must measure income per day. Each indifference curve specifies the various combinations of income and leisure that yield the same level of satisfaction. For example, the consumer considers C' leisure (and, $C'L_m$ work) and income $C'H$ equivalent to A' leisure (and $A'L_m$ work) and income $A'A$, since both points lie on the same indifference curve. The slopes of the curves indicate the rates at which an individual is willing to trade leisure for income. We assume, for analytical convenience, that both income and leisure are continuously divisible.

The budget lines are determined by the payment per unit of time. If the unit is hours per day, the budget line is determined by the individual's hourly wage rate; if days per year, by the earnings per day. Consider budget line Y_1L_m. If the individual works the entire time period (say 24 hours per day) and consequently takes no leisure, he or she could make Y_1 per time period; with no work, income would be zero, at L_m on the budget line. The slope of the budget line is the relevant wage rate or payment per unit of time. The "cost" of a unit of leisure is the sacrificed earnings for that period of time.[1] Y_2L_m, Y_3L_m, and Y_4L_m are the relevant budget lines for higher wage rates, Y_2/L_m, Y_3/L_m, and Y_4/L_m, respectively.

Labor-Leisure Choices

With a given wage rate, the highest attainable level of utility is at the point where the relevant budget line is tangent to the indifference curve. An individual with the wage rate indicated by the slope of Y_1L_m achieves the highest attainable level of utility at point A. He or she chooses A' leisure, $A'L_m$ work, and receives an income of $A'A$. If the wage rises to that level designated by budget line Y_2L_m, the highest attainable level of utility is at B, where the individual works $B'L_m$ for an income of $B'B$ and enjoys B' leisure time. Points C and D indicate the equilibria leisure, work, and income for the other two budget lines. SS' connects these and all intermediate equilibria. Thus, SS' indicates the amount of time the individual is willing to work (or the amount of labor he or she is willing to supply) at each of a series of wages.

At relatively low wages, the individual is willing to work more and consume less leisure as the wage rate rises. Since an increase in potential earnings causes leisure to cost more (in lost earnings), he or she chooses less leisure and more work. After point C, however, further increases in

---

[1] For simplicity, we assume a constant wage rate regardless of the amount of time worked. Certainly "overtime" work might be at overtime pay or a second job could be taken at a lower wage than the primary job pays. We also assume that the individual is free to choose the amount of working time; sometimes this may not be the case.

the wage rate induce more leisure and less work. Leisure still costs more as the individual moves from C to D, but the income effect causes the individual to consume more leisure with the increased earnings.

Just as we can derive demand curves from the price-consumption curve, we can derive a labor supply curve from curves such as SS'. We may think of labor supply as the reverse of the demand for leisure. Figure 7–3, Panel B, shows the labor supply curve derived from the indifference map in Panel A. The distance $\overline{A}$ in Panel B equals $A'L_m$ in Panel A and is the amount of work associated with wage rate Y_1/L_m, and so on. Since SS' changes direction at C in panel A, the labor supply curve bends backward at C. Although in this case the individual chooses to work less as the wage rate increases at higher incomes, this need not be the case. A person's supply of labor depends on his or her indifference map.

APPLICATION

Effects of Progressive and Flat Rate Income Tax

Many times we cannot obtain a definitive answer to important policy questions using basic economic theory. We can only get the answer "It depends," or "The theory does not say," or "It's an empirical question." This is still, of course, a legitimate use of theory. Certainly, a theory is useful in showing those who assert "obvious" answers that such answers are not so apparent.

Let's consider two important questions concerning proposed changes in the income tax. These questions are presently receiving considerable attention from politicians, policymakers, and the media. The questions being debated are (1) What would be the effect of an increase or decrease in the rate of income tax on the incentive to work; and (2) what would be the effect on incentives if a flat rate (constant percentage) tax were substituted for the presently progressive tax rates (the tax rate increases as income increases)?

We will consider first the changes in the rate of taxation—the easier of the two problems. Many are asserting that a reduction in the tax rate would give people the incentive to work more, because they could keep a greater proportion of income. Conversely, an increase in taxes would decrease the incentive to work. We begin by comparing the budget lines between income and leisure assuming first no tax and then a progressive tax. Consider the individual depicted in Figure 7–4. If there were no income tax, the income-leisure budget line would be $\overline{Y}L_m$, the slope of which would, as discussed already, be the wage rate.

Next we impose a rate of taxation that becomes progressively higher as more income is earned. Assume realistically that persons earning below

FIGURE 7–4   **Income after taxes under progressive rates**

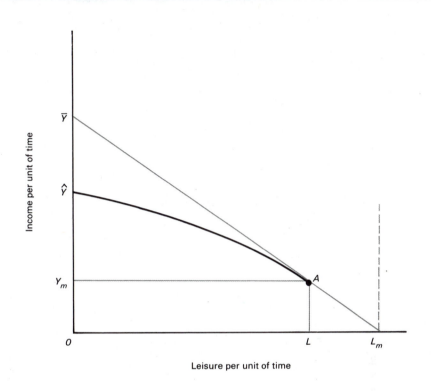

Leisure per unit of time

some minimum income are not required to pay any taxes. In Figure 7–4 that minimum income is Y_m. We picture the relevant budget line as the concave schedule $\hat{Y}AL_m$. This new budget line is the individual's constraint, since after-tax income is all that is available to spend.

Because income below Y_m is not taxed, the before- and after-tax budget lines are the same for incomes between zero and Y_m. For anyone choosing less than L units of leisure and more income than Y_m, the after-tax budget line must lie below $\overline{Y}A$. Also since higher incomes are taxed at a higher rate, the after-tax budget line becomes less and less steep as more income and less leisure are chosen, reflecting a lower after-tax wage rate at higher incomes. The vertical distance between the schedules $\overline{Y}A$ and $\hat{Y}A$ indicates the amount of income tax per period of time paid by this person. Since at higher incomes this person pays more taxes, the after-tax budget line is very close to the before-tax line at incomes slightly above Y_m, but the two lines move further apart as income rises. Thus, the budget line $\hat{Y}A$ has a bend, as shown in the figure.

FIGURE 7–5   **Impact of a progressive tax rate in the incentive to work**

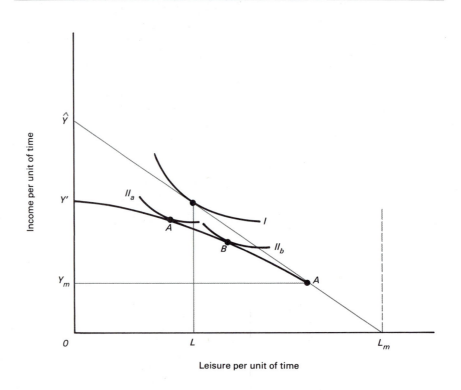

Consider now a change in the tax rate to see how it affects a person's leisure-work decision. In Figure 7–5, let $\hat{Y}AL_m$ be the original after-tax budget line. The individual attains equilibrium on indifference curve I, consuming L units of leisure and working LL_m units of time per period. An increase in the tax rate at each level of income rotates the after-tax budget line downward to $Y'AL_m$. (We continue to assume that no tax is paid on incomes below Y_m.) The vertical distance between the old and new budget lines shows the increase in total taxes paid at any given amount of labor and leisure chosen.

Figure 7–5 indicates that the individual may choose to work more or work less after the increase in the rate of taxation. Point A on indifference curve II_a or B on II_b are equally possible, depending on the indifference map. If the relevant portion of the indifference map is I and II_a, the new income-leisure package chosen is given at A, and more work time is chosen; if I and II_b make up the indifference map, point B is the new equilibrium, and this person chooses to work less and consume more leisure. Certainly, the indifference map would be such that many other points along $Y'A$ are possible.

Unless the person was originally at equilibrium at some point along AL_m, the increase in the tax rate must decrease utility. But our theory does not give a definitive answer as to the effect on work time. Neither can we unambiguously predict the effect of a decrease in the rate of taxation, as should be obvious from the figure. The answer to both questions must be empirical in nature. Theory can only show that the answer is not obvious and what variables are important.

Let's turn to the other question that has also been receiving a considerable amount of attention: What would be the effect of changing from a progressive income tax to a flat rate tax? A flat rate tax is a tax that is a constant percentage of a taxpayer's income regardless of the amount earned. What would such a change do to the work incentive; would tax revenue increase or decrease; would a worker be better off or worse off? It's tempting to say that those people who were paying a lower rate than the imposed flat rate would probably be on a lower indifference curve, pay more taxes, and based on the preceding analysis, work either more or less. One would think that those paying a lower tax rate under the flat rate than under the progressive rate would be on a higher indifference curve, pay lower taxes, and work more or less, depending on their indifference maps. Those who paid exactly the new flat rate under the progressive system would be unaffected. As a first approximation, one might say that if government sets the flat rate at the rate paid by the average taxpayer under the progressive system, tax revenues would be unaffected.

While we have too little space here to analyze all of the ramifications of a flat rate tax, we can get some feel for the problem by using our labor-leisure theory. Let's consider a group of people who are homogeneous in productivity and therefore receive the same wage rate in the market. These people have different preferences as to their trade-off between income and leisure and therefore have different income-leisure indifference maps.

In Figure 7–6, the slope of budget line YL_m gives the before-tax wage rate of all people in this group. The concave line $\overline{Y}L_m$ is the after-tax budget line under the progressive tax system. For convenience, we assume that all incomes above zero are taxed. Assuming that some low incomes are exempt from any taxes, as we did before, would not change the analysis.

Let the average taxpayer be in equilibrium at A on indifference curve I. This person chooses L units of leisure, works LL_m units of time, and earns an income of Y'. A flat rate tax is substituted for the progressive tax, and the rate is set at that rate paid by the average taxpayer. That is, the rate is set so that this taxpayer pays the tax indicated by the distance AB, and keeps Y' income after tax.

The new, after-tax budget line is $\hat{Y}L_m$. This line has a constant slope,

FIGURE 7–6   **The relative impact of a flat and progressive tax on the labor-leisure choice**

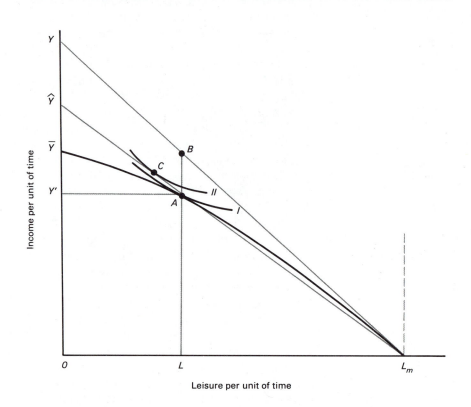

since everyone pays the same tax rate regardless of income earned. The new line must pass through point *A*, because it was set to be equal to the rate paid by this average taxpayer under the progressive system. The amount of taxes paid by anyone who works LL_m and earns Y' would be the same, *AB*, under either system.

It should be clear that this average taxpayer could now, under the flat rate tax, move to a higher level of utility such as point *C* on indifference curve II by working more and earning more income. The average taxpayer would be better off, and so would all persons who worked longer than LL_m and earned more than Y' before the tax change. Since the $\hat{Y}A$ portion of the new after-tax budget line lies everywhere above $\overline{Y}A$ (that portion of the old budget line where these above-average taxpayers were in equilibrium), all who previously chose to work more than LL_m must be able to attain a higher indifference curve under the flat rate tax. Following the line of reasoning used in analyzing the effect of a change in the progressive tax rate, we do not know if people will work more or less under the new tax system.

The effect of a flat tax on taxpayers who originally worked less than LL_m and earned less than Y' is not so straightforward. Consider Figure 7–7 with after-tax budget lines $\overline{Y}L_m$ and $\hat{Y}L_m$ similar to those in Figure 7–6. The flat tax is again set to equal the tax rate paid by a person working LL_m and earning Y'. Let a below-average taxpayer be in equilibrium under the old system at R on indifference curve I. This person works less than LL_m and earns less than Y'. We drew the indifference curve so that this person can, under the flat rate, move to a point such as D on the higher curve II, by choosing to work more and earn more income. Whether this person pays more or less total tax depends on the vertical distances between R and D and the before-tax budget line (not drawn).

The situation shown in Figure 7–7 could probably occur only for those people who were, under the progressive tax, paying a tax rate only slightly below the rate chosen for the flat rate tax; i.e., people who were at

FIGURE 7–7   **The relative impact of a flat tax on a less than average taxpayer**

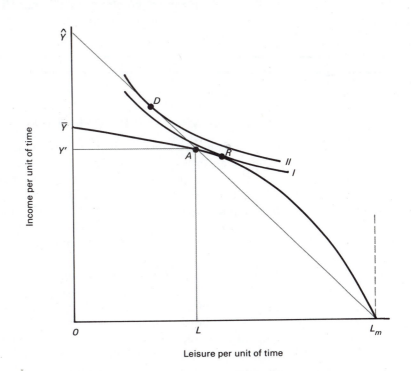

Leisure per unit of time

equilibrium points very close to the point at which $\hat{Y}L_m$ crosses $\overline{Y}L_m$. Others, who worked less than LL_m under the progressive tax, would clearly be worse off by the imposition of the flat rate tax. They would be forced to a lower indifference curve, and could choose to work more or less than before, depending on the indifference map. It could be possible that, with the new budget line, someone would increase the amount of time worked so much that the after-tax income increases—although this person is on a lower indifference curve.

Even with the rate set at the average rate paid under the progressive tax system, we cannot say what will happen to total tax revenue after the tax change. When faced with a different set of constraints, people can and will change the amounts of time spent in labor and leisure. When this occurs, their taxable (before-tax) income changes. The change in the tax structure can be expected to change the tax base. Economic theory doesn't tell us whether this base increases or decreases.

We have only analyzed one small aspect of the effects of a flat rate tax. We have isolated a group of people similar in productivity, with the same wage rate. Their incomes depend solely on the amount of labor time chosen. We have not compared people with different skills, or mentioned the effects on tax-sheltered income or investment and saving incentives. We have only analyzed the effects on the incentive to work and found that in some cases the change can be predicted, but in others it is ambiguous.

7.4 ADVERTISING AND INDIFFERENCE CURVES

Advertising is a topic so diverse that it is impossible for us to give you a complete description or classification of it. Very broadly, we can say that advertising is a paid message about a particular commodity or service, intended to increase the sales of the product. These messages can be divided into two general categories: those intended to convey information about the product and those intended to attach an image to the product. Most ads try to do some of both, but many ads lean more toward one purpose than the other.

We can use the theory of consumer behavior to examine why firms advertise, why different types of advertising are used, and how advertising affects consumer demand through its effect on budget lines and indifference curves. If advertising is to have the intended effect on the demand for a product, it must affect consumer equilibrium on an indifference map, for this is what determines demand. Advertising must, therefore, change preferences and/or the budget line in some way.

Informative Advertising

Purely informative advertising generally conveys pertinent price and quality information. Some examples of this type of advertising are newspaper ads (e.g., food store and drug store ads), catalog ads, and ads in technical publications.

What is the purpose of such advertising? Until now we have assumed in most of our analyses that consumers have complete information about both product price and the ability of goods to satisfy their wants. We know that this is not the case in the real world. People do not always have full knowledge about prices or the quality of all products.

FIGURE 7–8   **Budget lines and indifference curves without complete information**

Quantity of X per unit of time

Panel A

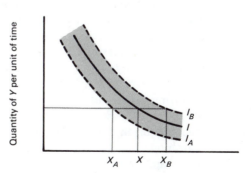

Quantity of X per unit of time

Panel B

We might depict the budget line of a consumer who is only partially informed about the price of a product in Panel A of Figure 7–8. Here we illustrate the situation faced by a consumer who is choosing between a particular good, commodity X, and good Y, representing all other goods. This consumer does not know with certainty the price of product X; instead he or she knows that the price of commodity X lies within a certain range. The upper bound of this range would give the budget line LZ. This is the budget line if the price of commodity X is the highest that the customer believes possible. Budget line LR represents the lowest price of X in the potential range. The true budget line lies somewhere in the shaded area between the two.

Panel B illustrates a similar situation for the indifference curves of a consumer who is only partially informed about the quality of a product. In this figure, we will assume that all three indifference curves depict the same level of satisfaction. Indifference curve I would be relevant if the consumer were completely informed about the quality of commodity X. But, without full information, the consumer can't determine exactly how much X yields this level of satisfaction when y_0 is consumed. The perception of this consumer is that any amount between x_A and x_B may be necessary, which is to say the indifference curve defining a certain level of utility could lie anywhere between indifference curves I_A and I_B. So, the indifference curve under incomplete information is a bounded range rather than a specific schedule.

What would a consumer do when faced with this uncertainty about price and/or quality? One possibility is to purchase (or not purchase) under the limited information available. Alternatively, the consumer might elect to search for price and quality information about the product in order to better determine the true budget line and indifference curve.

If the consumer elects to search for additional information, we have still another economic allocation problem. Gaining additional information about the product takes time, and time is a valuable asset. There are also direct expenses associated with search. How much time would a potential consumer spend acquiring information?

The answer to this search decision is found in the general maximization process described in Chapter 4. A consumer should spend resources acquiring price and quality information as long as the expected benefit exceeds the expected cost of the information. If the expected cost is greater than the expected gain, the consumer should spend no more time searching.

As an example, suppose someone has decided to buy a particular appliance, but knows the price of the appliance varies from seller to seller. This consumer wishes to find the lowest available price and believes that an additional day of price search would probably turn up a lower price. This potential reduction in price is the expected marginal benefit from search. The marginal cost of another unit of search is the value of the person's time and the expense of collecting more information. The value of time is, in general, the wage or salary that could be earned if the person spent his or her time working rather than shopping. This consumer should search an additional day if the expected reduction in price exceeds the cost of that day spent in shopping. While the expected benefits from additional units of search time for quality information cannot be stated in such a straightforward manner, the principle is identical.

We have observed that consumers may spend a considerable amount of time acquiring information about price and quality. How can the manager of a firm benefit from the fact that acquiring information is costly? If the manager can make it less costly for consumers to acquire information about the firm's product, the manager can increase the probability that the consumer will purchase from the manager's firm rather than continue to search.

This is the reason for purely informative advertising. If information about a firm's product is easily available, consumers would be more likely to conserve their valuable search time and purchase this product. The purpose of informative advertising is to lower the search cost of potential purchasers of the product, in the expectation that these people will purchase the advertised product.

To this point, our discussion would imply that informative ads would contain *both* price and quality information. However, as we are all well aware, a lot of informative ads contain only one type of information. Ads for products that consumers have a great deal of experience with tend to concentrate on price information. An excellent example of this can be found in the newspaper ads run by food and drug stores. Ads for products that are less familiar to the consumer, e.g., personal computers, tend to concentrate on quality information, in an attempt to attract consumers for a "test drive."

Image Advertising

While informative and image advertising are frequently combined, image advertising per se is not intended to directly convey information. Image advertising is most often found on television, billboards, and in magazines with a wide and general circulation. Although such advertising presents some information (at the very least telling consumers that a particular product is available), the principal aim of all image advertising is to make consumers associate the advertised image with consumption of the product.

The image is intended to literally become a characteristic of the product. Marlboro cigarettes use the image of the macho cowboy. Consumers buy this image when they buy the product. Calvin Klein advertises to associate sexiness with their jeans. And Cadillac in its advertising tries to make us associate its automobiles with successful middle-aged men.

Generalizing, we might say that image advertising is designed to affect the demand for the product in two ways: (1) make demand less elastic, and (2) increase the demand for the product. Therefore, in most cases, image advertising is intended to change the consumer's preference patterns, i.e., the consumer's indifference curves. To this end image advertising normally has the goal of making consumers think that other products are not good substitutes for the advertised good. However, some image advertising is also designed to increase the amount of expected utility associated with the product. In any case, all successful image advertising will have an effect on the consumer's indifference curves. For analytical simplicity, let us separate the total effect on the indifference map into two parts: (1) a change in the marginal rate of substitution, and (2) a shift in the indifference map. Let's analyze each of these effects separately and look at the resulting effect on the demand for the advertised product.

In Figure 7–9 we have illustrated the desired effect of image advertising on a consumer's marginal rate of substitution. In this figure commodity A

FIGURE 7–9   **Effect of advertising on _MRS_**

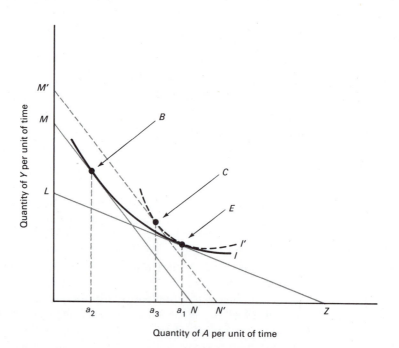

is the advertised good, and good Y on the vertical axis represents all other goods. Let the solid indifference curve I be the relevant curve if A is not advertised, and let LZ be the consumer's original budget line. Equilibrium is attained at E, with the consumer purchasing a_1 units of commodity A. Next we let the price of commodity A increase relative to the price of the composite commodity, p_y.[2] The new budget line, MN, is steeper, because the price ratio, p_A/p_Y, has increased. The budget line MN is tangent to indifference curve I at B. The substitution effect is the movement from E to B, and will result in a decrease in the consumption of good A from a_1 to a_2.

Now let good A be advertised. The desired effect of image advertising for the commodity is illustrated as the change in the indifference curve from I to the dashed curve I'. Note that the only thing that has changed is the shape of the indifference curve. With budget line LZ, equilibrium still occurs at E.

With this new indifference curve after advertising, let the price of A rise relative to the price of the composite commodity. Since the relative price change is the same as in the preceding case, the slope of the new budget line $M'N'$ is the same as MN. Again isolating the substitution effect, the new budget line $M'N'$ is now tangent to indifference curve I' at C. Now the substitution effect is the movement from E to C along indifference curve I', or the decrease in the consumption of good A from a_1 to a_3. The substitution effect is still negative—an increase in the relative price of A causes a decrease in its consumption—but the decrease in the consumption of commodity A is much less with advertising than was the case without advertising.

The reason for the difference is that image advertising increases the marginal rate of substitution, $\Delta Y/\Delta A$. This means that, with advertising, the consumer is willing to give up much less A to obtain an equal amount of the other good. If image advertising is successful in increasing the marginal rate of substitution between the advertised product and other products, the firm can increase price with a much lower decrease in sales than would be the case without advertising. Or, the loss in sales would be reduced if the firm's competitors decrease the price of their product. In other words, image advertising makes the demand for the product less elastic.

Image advertising can have another effect on demand. This effect is shown in Figure 7–10. Let's begin with a consumer facing the income constraint given by budget line LZ. Again, the solid indifference curves I and II make up a portion of the consumer's original (pre-advertising) indifference map. As we know, the consumer attains utility-maximizing equilibrium at E on indifference curve I, consuming a_1 units of good A.

---

[2] We should note that in this analysis we are considering only the substitution effect from a change in price.

FIGURE 7–10   **Demand increasing advertising**

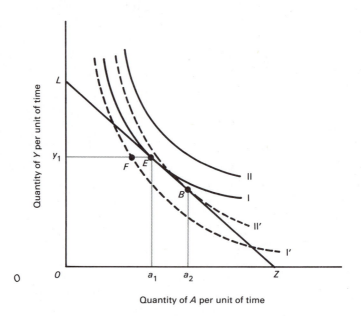

Quantity of A per unit of time

Now suppose that commodity A is advertised and the image advertising is successful in increasing its perceived value. In effect, the advertising shifts the indifference map downward. We have illustrated this new indifference map with the dashed indifference curves I′ and II′. Combinations of goods on the new (post- advertising) indifference curve I′ denote the same level of utility as combinations on the original (pre-advertising) indifference curve I. Likewise, combinations on indifference curve II′ give the same utility level as those on indifference curve II. At any given level of consumption of good A, the consumer attains the same level of utility with less of the Y good when A is advertised. Advertising has increased the perceived value of the advertised good, in the sense that the satisfaction is not reduced from having less of good Y and the same amount of A. With no change in the budget line, the new equilibrium is reached at B on curve II′, with the consumer purchasing a_2 units of commodity A. The advertising increases the demand for the advertised commodity. The MRS still equals the same price ratio, but more A and less Y are consumed at the new equilibrium.

Notice that the distance between the corresponding indifference curves I and I′, and then II and II′, is not uniform. When small amounts of

A are purchased the curves are close together. As larger amounts are purchased they get farther apart. When there is more *A* in the equilibrium bundle of goods, total utility increases by relatively greater amounts since *each unit* of *A* is valued more highly. Therefore, when there are more units in the equilibrium bundle, the distance between indifference curves gets larger. For little or no *A* consumed, advertising will have little or no effect on the shift in the indifference curve. When large amounts of the good are purchased, advertising will shift the curve more because *A* is a larger proportion of the total bundle purchased.

Whenever one good in the consumption bundle has its value altered relative to others it is impossible to shift the indifference curves backward, to reflect higher levels of utility, without also changing the marginal rate of substitution at any quantity of *Y*. For example, at y_1, the $MRS_{A for Y}$ is greater at point *F* than it is at *E*. We know already that increasing the *MRS* makes the demand curve steeper. Hence, when a firm successfully advertises to increase demand, it also makes the demand curve less elastic.

Overall the impact of image advertising can be decomposed into two related effects: One is to increase the marginal rate of substitution, thereby reducing the substitution effect from a change in relative prices and causing the demand for the product to become less elastic. A second effect of image advertising is to shift the indifference map downward, which increases the consumer's demand for the advertised product, enabling the firm to sell a greater amount at a given product price. When this happens the marginal rate of substitution will also increase.

APPLICATION

When Information is Advertising:
The New York Times Best Seller List

We have emphasized that advertising is designed essentially to have two effects: (1) to provide consumers with information, and (2) to change their tastes and therefore their indifference maps. We have also seen that at times it is difficult to separate these two features. In fact, it is somewhat difficult to define what advertising really is, because it is nearly impossible to distinguish the free circulation of information from advertising.

Whether or not a message about a product should be considered advertising depends more on who is providing the message than on what the message is. Certainly, information paid for by the seller of a product should be considered advertising, because the seller has a vested interest in seeing sales increase. On the other hand, some of the media frequently provide information about products that has the same effect as purchased advertising—providing information and changing tastes. Such information is commonly referred to as publicity.

One example that comes to mind immediately is the recommendations and information provided by *Consumer's Report*. Since this magazine has no interest in the success or failure of any particular product, its articles would not be viewed as advertising. But if *Consumer's Report* provides a favorable evaluation about a product this is virtually the same message provided by the seller. Other examples of freely provided information about products are magazines devoted to home computers, automobiles, and boating. The *Mobile Travel Guide* provides information about restaurants and hotels throughout the United States. Certainly, you can think of many other examples.

It would appear then that sellers should be quite sensitive to reports on product performance, because they know that these reports will have a significant impact on their sales—sometimes a favorable report has a greater impact than the firm's own advertising. Of course, an unfavorable report can be devastating.

The above examples have been concerned with freely provided information that is similar to informative advertising. But what about freely provided information that can change the tastes and therefore the indifference curves of potential consumers? Can there be such a thing? A good case in point is *The New York Times* book review section.

The similarity between freely provided information and image advertising has recently been highlighted through a lawsuit filed by author William Peter Blatty (author of *The Exorcist*) against *The New York Times* for mistakenly leaving his new book, *Legion*, off the best seller list. He claimed that the book sold 75,000 copies in its first week, easily qualifying it for the list. (Depending on the time of year, sales of 5,000 to 30,000 copies a week are generally needed to make the list.) The *Times* was said to have been negligent for failing to put the book on its list. Blatty estimated the resulting damages at $6 million. While the newspaper does not admit to making an error, it argues that if an error had been made it was the inadvertent omission of news. Slight errors are always found in newspapers in reporting births and deaths, and book lists are no different. The *Times* claimed that authors view the best seller list as "free advertising."

Why are the claimed damages so high? Any book that reaches the list is guaranteed high sales for at least several weeks, because book readers use the list as a guide to the best new books on the market. When the list was originally published in 1942 as an indicator of what the public was already buying, it quickly became a signal to readers about what they *ought* to buy. Many bookstores also discount the best sellers and give them special display space in the front of the store. This exposure to the casual browser tends to increase sales. As sales rise after the book reaches the best seller list, bookstores will submit larger than usual orders to publishers of the book, anticipating greater sales. Many publishers argue that if a book is stocked and displayed it will be sold. Somewhat cynically, the implication is that availability, not quality, is the most important contributor to the sale of popular books. For all of these reasons, once a book has been put on the list it tends to stay there.

The *Times* compiles its list from sales figures reported by 2,000 bookstores, *not randomly* selected, whose names are held in secret. This practice in part motivated the lawsuit by Mr. Blatty. But he argued that the way bookstores are selected biases the books put on the list. He cannot be sure until he finds out what bookstores are used in making the list, and the *Times* will not reveal the stores. If revealed, the *Times* claims, "ensuing manipulation of sales at selected stores by publishers and authors will render the list meaningless." So the *Times* and Mr. Blatty are at a standoff.

While Mr. Blatty may not win his case, the *Times* is being made well aware of the impact its "information" has on book sales. Undoubtedly, the newspaper will make an effort to improve the accuracy of its reporting. Presently, however, the *Times* accepts all sales figures reported by bookstores as accurate. Because of poor inventory accounting, many independent bookstores simply report their *perceptions* of what is selling. Some even distort their sales reports. Publishers have observed that bookstores, especially the chains, will report high sales figures for books with enormous printings and full inventories. Bookstores are under no legal obligation to be meticulously accurate. Yet they hold tremendous influence over what the public buys for leisure reading, perhaps as much as *The New York Times*.

7.5 CONSUMPTION OVER TIME

Our theory of consumer behavior to this point has been basically static or timeless. Consumers make consumption and purchasing decisions within a single period of time. All income is received and spent during the same period, and no items purchased yield services over multiple time periods. While it is probably safe to say that most economic theory is carried out within a single-period framework, certain problems require multiperiod analysis. This section sets forth a framework that allows us to study how consumers make multiperiod decisions.

We know that consumers do make dynamic decisions. They obviously transfer income and expenditures between different periods by saving some current income and spending in the future, or by borrowing to spend now and reducing future consumption to pay back the loan. The basic principles developed in Chapter 4 on present and future value are used to analyze the principles of allocating consumption over time. We will, for graphical simplicity, restrict our anlaysis to two periods; but the basic points are applicable to consumption allocation over any number of periods.

Income Allocation Over Time

Consider the specific case of a consumer who will receive $10,000 income in period one and $12,000 in period two. The consumer can borrow or lend between periods at a 10 percent rate of interest. In Figure 7–11, consumption in periods one and two is plotted, respectively, along the horizontal and vertical axes. Indifference curves I, II, and III represent a portion of the consumer's indifference map for consumption in the two periods. The marginal rate of substitution along each curve is the rate at which the consumer is willing to trade added consumption in period two for more consumption in period one.

Recall from Chapter 4 that $1 loaned in period one at a 10 percent interest rate will be worth $1.10 in period two. The maximum amount that the consumer could spend in period two, if all income in period one is saved, is

FIGURE 7–11   **Allocation of consumption over time**

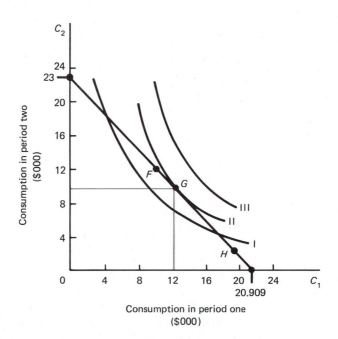

Consumption in period one
($000)

$$\$12,000 + (1 + .10) \, \$10,000 = \$23,000.$$

Again, following the analysis of Chapter 4, if $1 is borrowed in period one, $1.10 must be repaid in period two. Or, if $1 is to be repaid, only the present value of the dollar $1/(1 + .10) = \$0.91$, could be borrowed. If the consumer borrows to consume as much as possible in period one, consumption in period one would be $10,000 plus the present value of $12,000, which is

$$\$10,000 + \frac{\$12,000}{(1 + .10)} = \$20,909.$$

It follows that the straight line in Figure 7–11 between 23 on the vertical axis and 20.909 on the horizontal axis is the budget line. The slope of this line represents the rate at which the consumer can transfer income between periods. The slope of the budget line is $(1 + .10)$ since

$$\frac{23.000}{20.909} = (1 + .10).$$

The consumer's income stream determines the initial location on the budget line. In Figure 7–11. the initial location of a consumer who neither borrows nor lends is point F on the budget line. But consumers can lend or borrow to maximize utility or to match their income stream to their desired consumption stream.

Using the analysis of Chapter 5, optimization is attained where the budget line is tangent to the highest attainable indifference curve, point G in the figure. At this point, the marginal rate of substitution equals $(1 + .10)$, the slope of the budget line. In Figure 7–11, the consumer borrows $2,000 in order to consume $12,000 in period one. In period two, $2,000 plus 10 percent interest on this amount must be repaid leaving $12,000 − \$2,200 = \$9,800$ for consumption.

The general case is shown in Figure 7–12. Let r be the interest rate, M_1 be income in period one, and M_2 be income in period two. If the consumer spends as much as possible in period one, $M_1 + [M_2/(1 + r)]$ can be spent. This amount is the horizontal intercept. If consumption in period two is maximized, $M_2 + (1 + r)M_1$ is spent, which indicates the vertical intercept. The slope of the budget line is therefore:

$$\frac{M_2 + (1 + r)M_1}{M_1 + \dfrac{M_2}{(1 + r)}} = \frac{(1 + r)M_2 + (1 + r)^2 M_1}{(1 + r)M_1 + M_2}$$

$$= \frac{(1 + r)[M_2 + (1 + r)M_1]}{[M_2 + (1 + r)M_1]} = (1 + r).$$

Thus, consumption can be transferred between periods at the rate $(1 + r)$. To put it another way, the price of consuming now rather than later is the principle plus interest.

FIGURE 7–12   **Allocation of consumption over time**

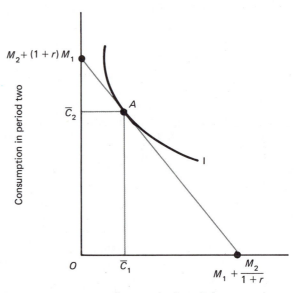

Utility is maximized—the highest indifference curve is reached—at point A on curve I. $\overline{C}_1$ is consumed in period one, and $\overline{C}_2$ is consumed in period two. If the consumer borrows in order to transfer income from period two to one, $\overline{C}_1 = M_1 + B$, where B is the amount borrowed from period one income and $\overline{C}_2 = M_2 - (1 + r)B$, since the loan must be repaid. If the consumer saves the amount S to spend more in period two, $\overline{C}_1 = M_1 - S$ and $\overline{C}_2 = M_2 + (1 + r)S$.

So far in this section we have established the following principle:

Principle

A consumer can transfer income between periods at the rate $(1 + r)$, where r is the rate of interest. Equilibrium is attained and utility maximized where the slope of the indifference curve for consumption in the two periods (the marginal rate of substitution) equals $(1 + r)$, the rate at which the given interest rate permits the income transfer.

We want to emphasize that an income stream can place a consumer anywhere along the budget line. For instance, at point H in Figure 7–11, a consumer receives $19,000 in period one and only $2,000 in period two.

Utility is maximized in this case by lending rather than borrowing. Both borrowing and lending can permit consumers to reach a higher indifference curve.

7.6 SUMMARY

This chapter analyzed several economic topics using the theory of consumer behavior developed in Chapters 5 and 6. As we noted in the introduction, many more topics can be and have been analyzed using these same tools. The material set forth here should give you a feel for the methods that are used.

We first showed that frequently used price indexes, such as the consumer price index, overestimate the true effect of inflation on consumers, unless all prices change in the same proportion, which is seldom, if ever, the case. When relative prices change as the price index changes, consumers substitute away from goods that become *relatively* more expensive toward goods that become relatively cheaper. The ability of consumers to substitute mitigates some of the effect of inflation.

Next, we analyzed how workers decide to allocate their time between work and leisure. Using straightforward indifference curve analysis, we conclude that this allocation is determined at the point where a worker's marginal rate of substitution between income and leisure equals the price of leisure, which is simply the relevant wage rate.

Section 7.4 examined the effect of advertising and how it influences demand. Advertising was classified into two general categories—informative and image—even though at times it is difficult to make the distinction. Informative advertising is designed to establish the budget line or the indifference map more clearly in the mind of the consumer. Image advertising has two interdependent functions: (1) to increase the marginal rate of substitution between the advertised good and other goods to make other goods less substitutable, thereby decreasing the elasticity of the demand for the advertised good; and (2) to shift the indifference map downward, causing the demand for the good to increase.

The final section analyzed the effect of time on the consumption and saving decision. We showed consumers allocate income between two periods so that the marginal rate of substitution between these periods equals $1 + r$.

TECHNICAL PROBLEMS

1. Calculate a Laspeyres price index for an individual who consumes 4 dozen eggs, 60 pounds of meat, 2 pairs of shoes, 1 pair of jeans, and 30 movies per period. The years are 1975 and 1986. Prices are given in the following table:

	1975	1986
Eggs/dozen	$ .60	$ .80
Meat/pound	1.25	1.65
Shoes/pair	25.00	45.00
Jeans/pair	13.00	38.00
Movies	2.50	3.50

What percentage increase in income would this consumer need to buy the same bundle of goods in 1986?

2. Figure E.7–1 shows an individual's indifference map between leisure and income. Ignore indifference curve III for now and assume that curves I and II make up the map. The unit of time is one day of 24 hours. The wage rate is $3 per hour.

    a. How much does the individual choose to work? How much leisure does he or she consume?

FIGURE E.7–1

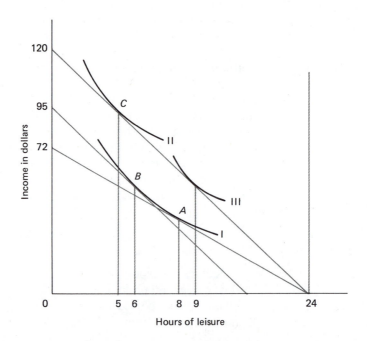

Let the wage rate rise to $5 an hour.
b. Ignoring III, what is his or her work and leisure time?
Suppose, at the wage rate of $5, the individual was taxed just enough to choose a point on the original indifference curve I.
c. What is the substitution effect for the wage change from $3 to $5?
d. Return the taxed income. What is the income effect?
e. What is the total effect?
f. In this example, leisure is a(n) (normal, inferior) good, and the income effect (offsets, reinforces) the substitution effect.
g. Derive the associated supply curve for labor.
Now let the relevant indifference map be I and III.
h. Derive the new supply-of-labor curve.
i. Now the total effect of a wage increase from $3 to $5 is _____; the substitution effect is _____; and the income effect is

_____.
j. Leisure is now a(n) (normal, inferior) good.
k. What can you say about the classification of leisure and a backward-bending supply of labor?
l. Draw an indifference curve IV tangent to the budget line associated with $5 so that leisure is a normal good, but the supply of labor is not backward bending.

FIGURE E.7–2

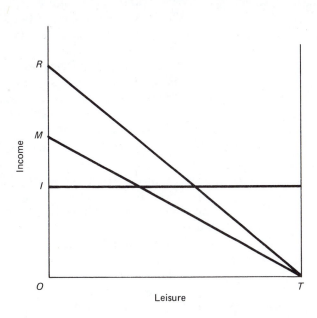

3. An individual can choose between income and leisure as depicted in Figure E.7–2. The maximum amount of time available in the period is *OT*. The first wage rate is indicated by the slope of *MT*; the new higher rate by the slope of *RT*. Regardless of the wage rate, the person works just long enough to earn income *OI*.

    a. Draw in the indifference curves at the two points of equilibrium.
    b. Is leisure a normal or an inferior good to the individual? Prove graphically.

4. On an income of $100 per week an individual can purchase good *X* (horizontal axis) at a price of $5 per unit and a good *Y* (vertical axis) also at a price of $5 per unit.

    a. Draw the budget line, and assume the individual chooses to consume 10 units of each good and call this point *B*.
    b. Price changes occur and P_x is now $4 and P_y is $10. The individual receives a cost of living increase enabling him to purchase the original *B* at these new prices.
        (1) Draw the new budget line.
        (2) Is the individual better or worse off? Will more or less of good *X* be consumed? Explain.
        (3) What is the minimum cost of living increase that will enable him or her to be as well off at the new prices as at *B*? (Your answer will depend on the shape of your indifference curve.)

5. Use Figure E.7–3 to answer the following questions assuming that income in period one is $20,000:

    a. What is the rate of interest?
    b. What is income in period two?
    c. The consumer spends $15,000 in period one and $_____ in period two.
    d. The consumer's marginal rate of substitution between consumption in periods one and two is _____.
    e. Suppose the interest rate increases by 5 percent. What happens to consumption in periods one and two, if consumption in both periods is a normal good?

6. The rate of interest is *r*. A consumer receives $*A* in both periods one and two, and consumes $*A* in each period—i.e., the consumer maximizes utility by neither borrowing nor lending. Use a graphical exposition to answer the following questions. (Note: the consumer can continue to consume $*A* in each period regardless of the rate of interest.)

    a. What happens to the consumer's utility if the interest rate increases?
    b. If the interest rate increases, does the consumer become a net (borrower, lender)?
    c. What happens to the consumer's utility if the interest rate decreases?

FIGURE E.7–3

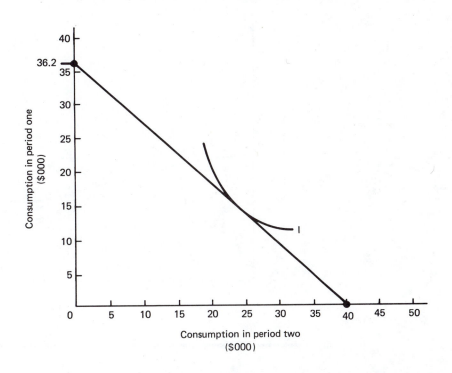

d. If the interest rate decreases, does the consumer become a net (borrower, lender)?

7. Suppose that when a consumer allocates consumption between two periods, with period 1 consumption on the horizontal axis, the slope of the budget line is less than one.
   a. What can you say about the market rate of interest?
   b. Would consumers save under these conditions? Graphically show someone who saves at equilibrium in a diagram similar to Figure 7–12.
   c. Why would consumers save at this interest rate?

8. In Figure E.7–4 the before-tax schedule of income and leisure is YL_m. Answer the following questions, based on this diagram.
   a. What is the income schedule with the progressive tax rate? The flat tax rate?
   b. If the consumer maximizes utility on indifference curve I along $\overline{YL}_m$, the amount of tax paid is distance _____. The after-tax

FIGURE E.7–4

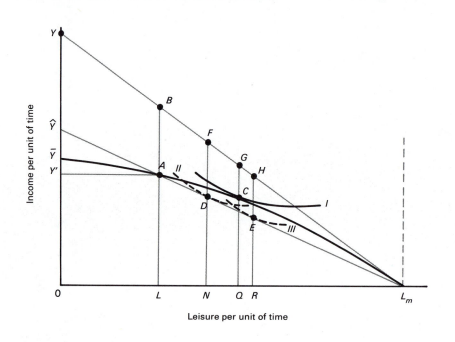

Leisure per unit of time

income is distance _____. The amount of labor supplied is
_____.

c. Suppose a new tax rate schedule, $\hat{Y}L_m$, is put into effect, and the
    consumer optimizes at point D on indifference curve II. The
    amount of tax paid is _____, which is (greater than, less than or
    equal to) distance CG. The amount of labor supplied is _____.

d. Suppose the new tax rate schedule $\hat{Y}L_m$ is put into effect, and the
    consumer optimizes at point E on indifference curve III. The
    amount of tax paid is _____. The amount of labor supplied is
    _____.

ANALYTICAL PROBLEMS

1. What type of country would be more likely to have a backward-
    bending supply of labor for the economy as a whole: an advanced
    industrial country or a much less developed country? Explain.

2. Over the last decade, there is evidence showing that, as more medical
    doctors practice in a community, the real price of medical care rises.

Could this be the result of a backward-bending supply curve among physicians? Can you think of other causes for this trend?

3. Suppose prices increase by 10 percent over a 10-year period in a certain country. Then, during one year, they increase another 10 percent. Would you expect changes in the Consumer Price Index to overestimate the impact of inflation more or less from year to year or over a 10-year period? Explain.

4. In a recent interview a marketer said that when a product is not selling you must either change the product, advertise, or reduce the price low enough to "create a demand for it." Can any of these selling strategies *create* demand? Discuss this question with budget lines and indifference curves.

5. Gone are the days when housekeepers dusted their lightbulbs to perfection and waxed floors to a shine. According to the Good Housekeeping Institute, the new generation of women wouldn't be caught dead on their hands and knees scrubbing a floor, and in a study by Good Housekeeping, 68 percent of the women surveyed said their standards had fallen a great deal. Discuss the economic causes of this observation by using a preference map similar to the labor-leisure diagrams in this chapter. Instead of leisure being traded with labor, make the time trade-off be labor and household activities. Set up an equilibrium and then show:
    a. How less household activity could arise purely by a change in the budget line.
    b. How less household activity could be from a change in preferences.

6. Professors at many colleges and universities are paid a lower wage rate to teach during the summer than they are paid during the academic year. Describe graphically the situation in which an instructor will teach during the summer.
    a. In a labor-leisure preference graph, plot income along the vertical axis and time by months along the horizontal axis. Assume months 1, 2, and 3 are the summer months. Show the budget line in this figure.
    b. Now add indifference curves. Illustrate the case with teaching done during the summer.

7. Social security payments are presently tied to rises in the Consumer Price Index. A given percent rise in the CPI is roughly matched by the same increase in payments to those receiving these benefits. Retired people spend most of their income on food and fuel, and these two items have been the major factor in CPI rises. Taking this into account, are retired people better off if social security payments are increased when the CPI rises? Argue analytically with an indifference map.

PART IV

PRODUCTION AND COST

- **Theory of Production**
- **Theory of Cost**
- **Input Price Changes and Technological Change**

Chapter 8

Theory of Production

8.1 INTRODUCTION

Now that we have completed demand theory, we have developed half of the theory of price. The other half of the story is the theory of supply.

The basic foundation of the theory of supply is production theory. Production, in a general sense, refers to the creation of any good or service that people will buy. While we generally speak of production as being carried out by business firms, the theoretical structure is equally applicable to production of goods and services by agencies of government or by nonprofit institutions, such as hospitals and universities.

Production can be a doctor producing medical care or a city government producing police protection. Ford Motor Company produces automobiles, the Corps of Engineers produces dams, and your university produces educated people. The principles developed in this chapter apply to the production of either goods or services by private firms, branches of government, or nonprofit institutions. In this chapter, however, we will generally concentrate on the production of goods by business firms, only because it is simpler to specify the precise inputs and to identify the quantity of output. It is easier to specify the number of automobiles produced by an auto company or the amount of wheat produced by a farmer than to measure the amount of education produced by your school or the amount of defense produced by the federal government. Keep in mind at all times that the basic principles also apply to production by agencies other than private business firms and to services as well as to goods.

Source of Production Cost

The theory of production illustrates the economic problem faced by every society: the problem of scarcity. For a society to gain additional goods and services of one type, it must give up goods and services of other types. These foregone goods and services make up the cost to society of having more of another good or service.

228

Scarcity, the reason for such trade-offs, results from the fact that goods and services are produced by factors of production, such as labor, capital, natural resources, and so on. At any time in any society, these inputs or factors of production are limited. The limit is at a higher level for very rich societies, but the limit is still there. The basic point is that, in order to have some additional amounts of certain goods, society must use inputs to produce these additional goods. Where do the added inputs come from? They must be taken away from the production of other goods and services.

If society wants more cotton, then resources such as land and farm machinery must be withdrawn from the production of other crops. If government wishes to build more roads, labor and machinery must be taken from the construction of other things—houses, offices, and so on. Scarcity arises because limited resources are available to carry out production. The sacrifice society makes when resources are used for the production of a particular good or service is reflected in the cost of that resource. The problem of giving up some goods (or the inputs needed to produce these goods) in order to produce other goods exists in all economies regardless of their social makeup. The most totalitarian dictatorship, the most open democracy, and all societies in between face the problem of cost in production.

Production-Possibility Frontier

The basic problem of cost is best illustrated with the concept of a production-possibility frontier. This frontier illustrates the way societies must make trade-offs among different goods and services—publicly or privately produced.

To develop the concept of a limit or a frontier for all available goods and services, let us assume, for analytical simplicity, that a society can produce and consume only two goods—food and shelter. Society's finite resources can be used to produce these two goods in many different combinations.

Figure 8–1 shows a hypothetical production-possibility frontier or curve of a typically assumed shape. The curve *FRMS* shows the combinations of the two goods possible for the society with a given amount of productive resources and technology. The figure shows that, if society chooses to produce no shelter, it can have F units of food per period; or if it chooses to produce no food, it can consume S units of shelter. Similarly, it can choose any other point on the curve, such as R, with F_2 units of food and S_2 units of shelter, or M, with a combination of F_1 and S_1 food and shelter.

Furthermore, the society could consume any combination inside of the curve *FRMS*, such as the combination indicated by point A. But at interior points such as A, society is not using all of its resources, or using

FIGURE 8–1   **Production possibilities curve**

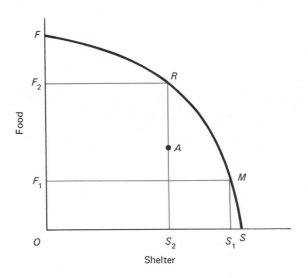

resources efficiently. In this case, the society could increase its food consumption to F_2 without giving up any shelter. Alternatively it could increase shelter with no sacrifice of food, or increase consumption of both goods, moving to some point on the frontier to the right of R. Scarcity exists whenever society operates on the production-possibility frontier, because it cannot consume any combination outside of the curve. To get more of one good, less of another must be produced.

The shape of the curve reflects certain assumptions about the way the output of some goods can be substituted for other goods. In the first place, it is obvious that the production-possibility curve slopes downward. This negative slope reflects the fact that, in order to have more of one good, society must give up some portion of the other good. Note also that the curve decreases at an increasing rate. For example, if the society decreases its food production from F to F_2 units, it can increase shelter from zero to S_2. On the other hand, if there is very little food being produced, say F_1, and society moves from F_1 to zero food, it gains only the very slight increase in shelter from S_1 to S. We have drawn the distance OF_1 to equal the distance F_2F. The increase in shelter from an equal decrease in food diminishes greatly as the amount of shelter rises relative to the amount of food. This means the *cost* of shelter increases as more shelter is produced. For the same sacrifice in food, less shelter is obtainable. Clearly, a similar rise in cost occurs for decreases in shelter relative to increases in food.

The changes in the production of goods, described above, reflect the fact that resources are better adapted to one type of production than to another. As the output of a good rises, less suitable resources must be used to increase its output. Even though we have been concerned here with only two goods, the same principles apply in a multiple-good world.

This chapter and the next deal with the theories of production and cost. As you go through these closely related theories, keep in mind that this body of theory originates with the fundamental principle of scarcity, as illustrated by the production-possibility frontier.[1]

8.2 PRODUCTION FUNCTIONS

Production processes typically require a wide variety of inputs. They are not as simple as "labor," "capital," and "materials;" many qualitatively different types of each are normally used to produce an output. With a given state of technology, the quantity of output depends on the quantities of the various inputs used. The relation between inputs and output is more formally described by a *production function*, that shows the amount of output produced with particular rates of input.

Definition

A production function is a schedule (or table, or mathematical equation) showing the maximum amount of output that can be produced from any specified set of inputs, given the existing technology or "state of the art." In short, the production function is a catalog of output possibilities.

Mathematically, a production function can be written as

$$X = f(L_1, L_2, \ldots, L_m; K_1, K_2, \ldots, K_n; M_1, M_2, \ldots, M_s),$$

where L_i, K_i, and M_i represent the various kinds of labor, capital, and materials that are used in the production of product X.

A hypothetical example of a very simple production function is the production of a student's test score from study time. This might take the form of a table such as:

Expected percentage score	Minimum study time (hours)
90	16
80	9
70	4
60	1
50	0

---

[1] Those students who have already gone through consumer theory will note many similarities between the concepts discussed there and the theory of production. Several users of this text have pointed out that they choose to cover production and cost theory before consumer theory. Therefore, we will not dwell on these similarities in this and the next chapter. For those students who have already studied consumer behavior theory, the relations should be rather obvious.

This table relates the expected score to the minimum time allocated to study. The production function could take the form of a simple equation such as

$$S = 10\sqrt{T} + 50,$$

where S is the expected numerical grade, and T is time spent studying. This function makes product (grade) depend only on one input (study time). Other functions might relate output or product to two or more inputs. Still more complicated functions relate several different outputs to several different inputs. In this chapter we will be dealing primarily with one output produced by either one or two inputs, but the principles we develop apply to any number of inputs.

Economic Efficiency in Production

Most economists are not engineers. When economists work with production functions, they assume a producer knows how to technically derive the greatest amount of output from a given set of inputs. Economists assume that producers are fully aware of the latest technological production processes, and that this technical knowledge is incorporated into the production function when it is described. A change in technology would change the way the production function is written. When producers are presented with input and output prices, the question at hand is not technical but economic: how to produce a certain amount of output at the lowest cost, or, conversely, how to maximize output given total cost.

We wish to distinguish the difference between *technical efficiency* and *economic efficiency*. A producer is considered technically efficient if it cannot reduce the quantity of one or more inputs without increasing others to maintain the same level of production. This kind of efficiency has nothing to do with input prices, but is concerned with minimizing the amount of inputs to reach an output target, whatever prices may be. *Economic efficiency*, on the other hand, seeks the lowest cost combination of inputs for the production of a certain output level. Technical efficiency is taken for granted and prices are given. To be economically efficient a producer seeks the maximization of output under a cost constraint, or the minimization of cost given an output target. These goals have already been presented in Chapter 4 where we discussed optimization in a general context. The optimization rules discussed there, and those we develop with respect to production, lead a producer toward economic efficiency.

We must not be too hasty about labeling a particular production process technically inefficient. A method of production is unquestionably inefficient if another method uses less of one or more inputs and the same amounts of all others. But suppose a second process uses more of some inputs and less of others. Then the less expensive method of production depends on input prices. The technology in the first method of production could be the economically efficient method under one set of input prices and the other process efficient under different prices. Both production processes should be considered technically efficient.

An example will help illustrate the difference between technical and economic efficiency. Consider a very simple production process: Coal is moved from river barges to the loading hopper of a plant by a crane. Let us assume that in this process some coal is dropped into the river. Here it is very likely that the engineer and the economist would differ as to their concept of efficiency. While the engineer might suggest modifying or replacing the crane to eliminate the waste, the economist might take a very different view. If the price of coal is low relative to the price of capital, it could be economically efficient to drop coal into the water. The real problem is to determine the optimal amount to drop. The point is that technical efficiency is concerned with the resource waste no matter what the price of capital and coal may be. Economic efficiency would include input prices to determine the most efficient method of production.

Short and Long Runs

In analyzing the economically efficient choice of productive inputs, it is convenient to introduce an important distinction. At any point in time inputs may be classified as fixed or variable. A *fixed input* exists when the quantity of a factor of production cannot readily be changed, even when market conditions indicate change is desirable. No input is ever *absolutely* fixed, no matter how short the period of time under consideration. Frequently, for the sake of analytical simplicity, we hold some inputs fixed, reasoning that although these inputs could be adjusted, the cost of immediate variation is large enough to put them out of the range of consideration. Buildings, major pieces of machinery, and managerial personnel are examples of inputs that generally cannot be rapidly augmented or diminished. A *variable input*, on the other hand, is a factor of production, the quantity of which may be changed quite readily at any point in time. Many types of labor services and the inputs of raw and processed materials fall into this category.

For the sake of analysis, economists use the presence of fixed inputs to decide when a firm is operating with a short- or long-run production function. The *short run* refers to that period of time when the input of one or more productive factors is fixed. Therefore, changes in output must be accomplished exclusively by changes in the use of variable inputs. If producers wish to expand output in the short run, they must do so by using more hours of labor service with the existing plant and equipment. Similarly, if they wish to reduce output in the short run, they may discharge certain types of workers; but they cannot immediately "discharge" a building or a diesel locomotive, even though its use may fall to zero.

In the long run, however, even this is possible, for the *long run* is defined as that period of time (or planning horizon) where all inputs are variable. The long run, in other words, refers to that time in the future when output changes can be accomplished in the manner most advantageous to the producer. In the short run, a producer may be able to expand output only by operating an existing plant for more hours per day. In the long run, it may be more economical to install additional productive facilities and return to the normal workday.

Fixed or Variable Proportions

Our attention here is restricted mainly to production functions that allow at least some inputs to be substituted for one another in reaching an output target. When there is substitution we say inputs may be used in *variable* proportions. As a consequence, producers must determine not only the optimal level of output to produce but also the optimal mix of inputs.

There are two different ways of stating the principle of variable proportions. First, variable-proportions production implies that output can be changed in the short run by changing the total amount of variable inputs used in cooperation with the fixed inputs. Naturally, when the amount of one input changes while the others remain constant or do not change as much, the *ratio* of inputs will change. Second, when production is subject to variable proportions, the *same* output can be produced by various combinations of inputs—that is, by different input ratios. This may apply to the long run as well as the short run.

Most economists regard production under conditions of variable proportions as typical of both the short and long run. There is certainly no doubt that proportions are variable in the long run. When making an investment decision, for instance, a producer may choose among a wide variety of different production processes. As polar opposites, an automobile can be practically handmade or it can be made by assembly-line techniques. In the short run, however, there may be some cases where output is subject to fixed proportions.

Fixed-proportions production means that there is one, and only one, ratio or mix of inputs that can be used to produce a good. If output is expanded or contracted, all inputs must be expanded or contracted at the same rate to maintain the fixed-input ratio. At first glance, this might seem the usual condition: one man and one shovel produce a ditch; two parts hydrogen and one part oxygen produce water. Adding a second shovel or a second part of oxygen will not augment the rate of production. In such cases, the producer has little discretion about what combination of inputs to employ. The only decision is how much to produce.

In actuality, examples of fixed-proportions production are hard to come by. Certainly some "ingredient" inputs are often used in relatively fixed porportions to output. Otherwise, the quality of the product would change. There is so much leather in a pair of shoes of a particular size and style. Use less leather, and we have a different type of shoe. There is so much tobacco in a cigarette, and so on. In these cases, the producer has little choice over the quantity of input per unit of output. But fixed-ingredient inputs are really only a short-run problem. Historically, when these ''necessary'' ingredients have become very expensive or practically impossible to obtain, businesses, generally under the lure of profits, have invented new processes, discovered new ingredients, or somehow overcome the problem of a given production function and increasingly scarce ingredients. As a consequence, we will direct our attention to production where the producer has some control over the mix of inputs and concentrate on production with variable proportions.

APPLICATION

Fixed-Proportions Production and the Timber Crisis

After the Civil War, the United States began to enjoy the greatest period of economic growth in the history of the world. But, forecasters of that day were predicting an end to this growth in the near future. These forecasts were based on the observation that America was running out of an essential factor of production—wood. The railroads, the driving force behind industrialization, appeared doomed, and without rail transportation, development west of the Mississippi River would halt. The problem was that railroads accounted for 20–25 percent of the annual timber consumption, and wood seemed to be a fixed input in rail transportation.

Trains ran on tracks, and to lay tracks, ties had to be laid every few feet. The distance between ties could be increased and each tie could be cut shorter, but this led to more frequent repairs. Substitution was therefore considered to be impossible, or at best very limited. Trains also used wood as fuel and it was consumed in fixed proportions. If trains reduced their speed, less wood was necessary on a haul, but this conserved a relatively small amount of the resource. Lumber thus appeared to be a fixed input in the production function of railroads, and there appeared to be only two ways for the nation to proceed: (1) reforest the continent, or (2) end the economic growth of the nation.

The feeling in the 1890s was utter gloom. A headline from *The New York Times* summed it up: "Banish Christmas Trees. This Heathenish Practice Denudes Forests." Really, banning Christmas trees to save wood! Was nothing sacred? America, though, was running out of its most important, most necessary, and purportedly most nonsubstitutable natural resource. Why?

In the first half of the 19th century, timber was abundant and therefore cheap. Conversely, because of the relatively small population and opportunities available in the frontier, labor was very expensive. So American business used a lot of wood but conserved labor as it built a nation. To conserve the expensive resource, they used the abundant, and cheap natural resource—timber. By 1880 everyone realized that timber could not continue to be used at the historic rate for very long without a gigantic increase in timber production. If this prevailing trend continued, the nation would run out of wood. No wood meant no growth or prosperity. What happened to the timber crisis? How was such a serious national problem solved? Substitution was the answer.

As timber prices rose, railroads turned to wood preservation and sub-stitutes in order to reduce their use of timber. Many new, more plentiful species of timber were found to be suitable for crossties, after the wood was chemically treated. More efficient methods of sawing ties were found. Iron, steel, and concrete were used more in the construction of bridges. And what about the wood used to fuel locomotives? Most of us are familiar with the evolution of rail power. Wood was the first fuel, replaced with the technically more efficient use of coal, and currently most locomotives run on diesel fuel. Since the wood-burning steam locomotive there has been tremendous technical progress, to a large degree sparked by the increas-ing price of an input used with the old technology.

Was there a crisis? Certainly. Timber use could not have continued at the same rate without total depletion. There was a problem and something had to be done. The primary consumers of wood, lead by the railroads, adapted their levels of consumption through substitution. Wood, once thought of as a fixed input, became increasingly variable as its price increased.

8.3 PRODUCTION WITH ONE VARIABLE INPUT

We will introduce some simplifying assumptions to cut through the complexities of dealing with hundreds of different inputs. Our focus will be on the essential principles of production. To explore these principles, we assume that there is only one variable input that can be combined in different proportions with fixed inputs to produce various quantities of output. This assumption still allows inputs to be combined in *various* proportions to produce the commodity in question. In the short run considered here, all but one input is fixed.

Total, Average, and Marginal Product: Arithmetic Approach

Assume that a firm with a fixed plant can apply different numbers of workers to get output according to columns (1) and (2) of Table 8–1. These columns define a production function over a specific output range.

TABLE 8–1   **Total, average, and marginal products of labor**

(1) Number of workers	(2) Total output per unit of time	(3) Average product	(4) Marginal product
1	10	10.0	10
2	25	12.5	15
3	45	15.0	20
4	60	15.0	15
5	70	14.0	10
6	78	13.0	8
7	84	12.0	6
8	88	11.0	4
9	90	10.0	2
10	88	8.8	−2

They specify the product per unit of time for different numbers of workers in that period. The total output rises to a point (nine workers), then declines. The *total output* is the *maximum* output obtainable from each number of workers with the given plant.

Average and marginal product are obtained from the production function. The *average product* of labor is the total product divided by the number of workers. (Here it rises, reaches a maximum at 15, then declines thereafter.)

Definition

The average product of an input is total output divided by the amount of the input used. Thus, average product is the output-input ratio for each level of output and the corresponding volume of input.

It will later be convenient to see the notation AP_i for "average product of the *i*th input." For labor, AP_L is output per worker or

$$AP_L = \frac{X}{L}.$$

Marginal product is the additional output attributable to a small increase in the variable input with a fixed plant (or with the use of all other inputs fixed). Frequently, as in Table 8–1, we observe marginal product by changing the variable input by one unit. Marginal product first rises, then falls, becoming negative when an additional worker reduces total product.

Definition

The marginal product of an input is the addition to total output attributable to the addition of a small amount of the variable input in the production process, usually one unit, all other inputs remaining constant.

An abbreviation of this definition can be written if we let MP_i be the "marginal product of the ith input." Then for labor

$$MP_L = \frac{\Delta X}{\Delta L}.$$

It is the ratio of the change in output to a change in labor.

It is important to understand that we speak of the marginal product of labor, not the marginal product of a particular laborer. We assume all workers are the same in the sense that reducing the number of workers from eight to seven would cause the total product to fall from 88 to 84—regardless of which of the eight workers is released. The order of hiring makes no difference.

On closer inspection of the table we see that when average product is rising (falling), marginal product is greater (less) than the average. When average product reaches its maximum, average product equals marginal product (at 15). This result is not a peculiarity of the table; it occurs for any production function where average product peaks. To illustrate, if you have taken two tests and your grades are 70 and 80, your average grade is 75. If a third test grade is higher than 75—say 90—your average rises to 80. The 90 is the *marginal addition* to your total grade. If the third grade is less than 75, the marginal addition is below average and the average falls. This is the relation between all marginal and average schedules. In production theory, if each additional worker adds more than the average, the average product rises; if each additonal worker adds less than the average, the average product falls.

The short-run production function set forth in Table 8–1 specifies several common characteristics of marginal and average product in production theory. First, marginal and average products start out increasing, but then decrease, with marginal product becoming negative after a point. Marginal product reaches a maximum before the highest average product is attained. At maximum average product, marginal product equals average product. These relations mean that total product at first increases at an increasing rate, then increases at a decreasing rate, and finally decreases. The graphical exposition in the next subsection will illustrate the relation between average and marginal product.

Total, Average, and Marginal Product: Graphical Approach

The short-run production function in Figure 8–2 shows the maximum output per unit of time obtainable from different amounts of the variable input (labor), given a specified amount of the fixed inputs. In Figure 8–2 and thereafter in this section, we assume that both the output and the variable input are continuously divisible. This assumption sacrifices little realism, yet adds a great deal of analytical convenience. The product curve in this figure embodies the same assumptions about production

FIGURE 8–2   **Derivation of average product from total product**

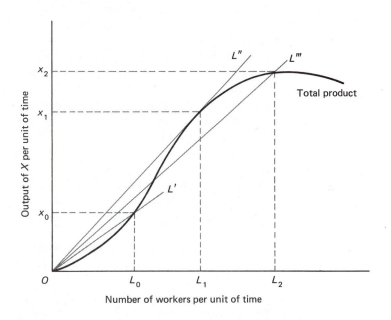

given in the last subsection; both average and marginal product rise then fall, marginal product equalling average product at the maximum point of the latter.

In the figure, x_0 is the *maximum* amount of output obtainable when L_0 workers are combined with the fixed inputs. Likewise, L_1 workers can produce a maximum of x_1, and so forth. Certainly, the specified numbers of inputs could produce less than the amount indicated by the total product curve, but not more than that amount. Figure 8–2 shows the total output increases with increases in the variable input up to a point, in this case L_2 workers. After that, so many workers are combined with the fixed inputs that output diminishes when additional workers are employed. The figure also shows that production at first increases at an increasing rate, then increases at a decreasing rate, until the maximum total output is reached.

The average product of L_0 workers is output per worker, or x_0/L_0. In Figure 8–2 this is equivalent to the slope of the OL', passing through the origin and the point (L_0, x_0). By inspection we can see that this slope is the ratio of the distances Ox_0/OL_0, which is simply the amount of output produced divided by the amount of labor used. In like manner, the average product of any number of workers can be determined by the slope of a ray from the origin to the relevant point on the total product curve; the steeper the slope, the greater the average product. We can see that the slopes of rays from the origin to the total product curve in Figure 8–2 increase with additional labor until OL'' becomes tangent to the total product curve at L_1 workers and x_1 output, then the slope decreases thereafter (for example, to OL''' at L_2 workers). Typical average product curves associated with this total product curve first increase and then decrease.

As with average product, we can derive a marginal product curve from a total produce curve. In Figure 8–3, L_0 workers can produce x_0 units of output and L_1 can produce x_1. L_0L_1 additional workers therefore increase total product by x_0x_1. Because marginal product is defined for small changes in the input, we can let L_1 become very close to L_0. The quantity, x_1 will then get very close to x_0, and $\Delta x / \Delta L$ will approach the slope of the tangent T to the total product curve. Thus, at any point on the total product curve, marginal product, which is the *rate of change of total product* as labor changes, can be *estimated* by the slope of the tangent at that point. By inspection, we see that marginal product first increases; for example, notice that T' is steeper than T. It then decreases, OL'' at point

FIGURE 8–3   **Derivation of marginal product from total product**

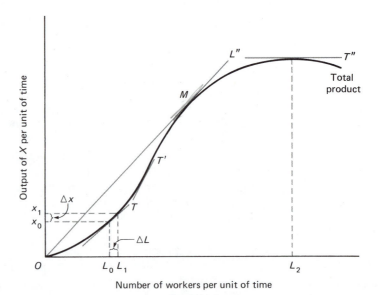

M being less steep than *T'*. Marginal product becomes zero when L_2 workers are employed (the slope of *T''* is zero), and then becomes negative.

At point *M*, the slope of the tangent *OL''* is also the slope of the ray from the origin to that point. As mentioned above, average product attains a maximum when a ray from the origin is tangent to the total product curve. Therefore, marginal product equals average product when average product is at a maximum. To repeat, as long as marginal product is less than average product, the latter must fall. Average product must attain its maximum when it is equal to marginal product.

Figure 8–4 illustrates all of these relations. In this graph, one can see the relation between marginal and average products, and also the relation of these two curves to total product (*TP*). Consider first the total product curve. For very small amounts of the variable input, total product rises gradually. Then it begins to rise quite rapidly, reaching its maximum *slope* (or rate of increase) at point 1. Since the slope of the total product curve equals marginal product, the maximum slope (point 1) must correspond to the maximum point on the marginal product curve (point 4).

After attaining its maximum slope at point 1, the total product curve continues to rise. Since output increases at a decreasing rate, the slope is

FIGURE 8–4   **Total, average, and marginal products**

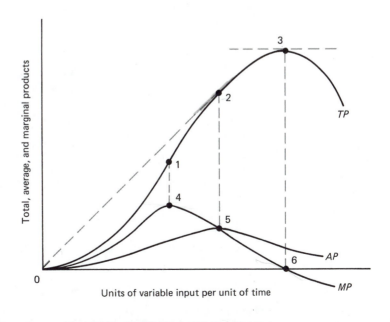

less steep. Moving outward along the curve from point 1, the point is soon reached at which a ray from the origin is just tangent to the curve (point 2). Since tangency of the ray to the curve defines the condition for maximum average product, point 2 lies directly above point 5.

As the quantity of the variable input is expanded from its value at point 2, total product continues to increase. Its rate of increase is progressively slower until point 3 is finally reached. At this point, total product is at a maximum; thereafter, it declines. Over a tiny range around point 3, additional input does not change total output. The slope of the total product curve is zero; thus, marginal product must also be zero. This is shown by the fact that points 3 and 6 occur at precisely the same input value. And, since total product declines beyond point 3, marginal product becomes negative.

Most of the important relations have so far been discussed with reference to the total product curve. To emphasize certain relations, however, consider the marginal and average product curves. Marginal product at first increases, reaches a maximum at point 4, and declines thereafter. It eventually becomes negative beyond point 6, where total product attains its maximum.

Average product also rises until it reaches its maximum at point 5, where marginal and average products are equal. It subsequently declines, conceivably becoming zero if total product itself becomes zero. Finally, one may observe that marginal product exceeds average product when the average is increasing, and is less than average product when the average is decreasing.

Law of Diminishing Marginal Product

The slope of the marginal product curve in Figure 8–4 illustrates an important principle, the law of *diminishing marginal product*. As the number of units of the variable input increases, other inputs held constant, the marginal product of the input declines after a point. When the amount of the variable input is small relative to the fixed inputs (the fixed inputs are plentiful relative to the variable input), more intensive utilization of fixed inputs by variable inputs may increase the marginal output of the variable input. For instance, as you add more labor to a garden plot of fixed size, the marginal increase in vegetables grown may rise. Nonetheless, a point is reached where an increase in the use of the variable input yields progressively less additional product. Each additional unit has, on average, fewer units of the fixed inputs with which to work.

Principle

As the amount of a variable input is increased, the amount of other (fixed) inputs held constant, a point is reached where marginal product begins to decline. This decline is often referred to as the law of diminishing marginal product.

This is a simple statement concerning physical relations that have been observed in the real economic world. While it is not susceptible to mathematical proof or refutation, it is of some worth to note that a contrary observation has never been recorded. That is why it is called a law. Psychologists have found that the law holds true for consecutive study time.[2]

Three Stages of Production

Economists use the relations among average and marginal products to define three stages of production, illustrated in Figure 8–5. Stage I covers that range of variable-input use over which average product increases from zero to A units. Of course, in order for average product to rise, marginal product must be above the average as shown in the figure. Stage II of the production function covers the range of input over which marginal product is less than average product, but positive, the distance from A to B. Finally, Stage III is defined when marginal product becomes negative, amounts of input after B. Negative marginal product means the last unit of input actually causes a *decrease* in total output.

Suppose a producer is unable to influence the market price of the product it sells or the price of the input. We can explain that such a firm would then operate in Stage II of its production function. We immediately know that Stage III is definitely out for any profit maximizer. Whether a firm can influence prices or not, Stage III represents a blatant loss of revenue. More output could be produced by spending less on those inputs beyond point B. Even if the inputs were free, the profit-maximizing producer would still cut back to B since the marginal input in Stage III is actually *decreasing* total output.

At Stage I of the production function the marginal product of an input is always above the average product, so the average is continually rising up to A units of input. Suppose that a producer earned profits in Stage I. Could more profits be earned by moving to Stage II? We will define profits (π) as the difference between total revenue (TR) and total cost (TC), or

$$\pi = TR - TC.$$

Remember that output price and input prices are constant. Because average product is rising in Stage I, if the producer employed more inputs

---

[2] Do not make the common mistake, however, of saying that you stopped studying because diminishing returns set in. The term *diminishing returns* is frequently heard in noneconomic usage and is almost as frequently misused. Diminishing returns may set in with the first unit of study time, but you may continue studying. You cease studying when the marginal utility of the (expected) increase in grade (or of the pleasure of studying) from an additional unit of study time is less than the expected marginal utility of using that time for something else.

FIGURE 8–5   **Stages of production**

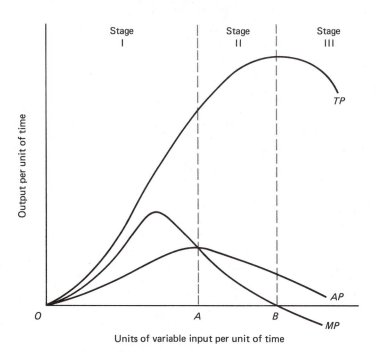

the amount of output *per unit of input* would rise. With constant prices total revenue in the above equation has to rise faster than total costs, and therefore profits will rise. This will always be true as long as average product is rising, and prices are not changing. Profits will increase at least until point *A* is reached in Figure 8–5. In other words, Stage I cannot be a profit-maximizing range of the production function. Profit maximizers must find an equilibrium somewhere in Stage II.

The point can be made another way with a little bit of arithmetic. Suppose the variable input we are talking about in Figure 8–5 is labor. We know that average product (AP_L) is $AP_L = X/L$. We also know that the total cost of this input is the wage (w) multiplied by the number of workers employed. We may write the above profit equation as

$$\pi = TR - TC$$
$$= p \cdot X - w \cdot L.$$

Total revenue is the price, *p*, that the producer gets for its output times the amount of output, X. Both p and w are fixed prices in the market. We may make another change in the equation and write

$$\pi = L \cdot (p \cdot \frac{X}{L} - w)$$

$$= L \cdot (p \cdot AP_L - w).$$

In Stage I of the production function, as more labor is hired, L rises and AP_L rises. The other terms stay constant. As long as we know AP_L is rising, profits will therefore go up. Since average product always increases in Stage I, this part of the production function cannot be profit maximizing.

8.4 PRODUCTION WITH TWO OR MORE VARIABLE INPUTS

Here we consider the more general case of several variable inputs in production. For graphical purposes, we concentrate on only two inputs, but all of the results hold for more than two. One may assume either that these two inputs are the only variable inputs, or that one of the inputs represents some combination of all variable inputs except one.

Production Isoquants

When analyzing production with several variable inputs, we cannot simply use several sets of average and marginal product curves such as those discussed above. These curves were derived holding the use of all other inputs constant and letting the use of only one input vary. When the amount of one variable input changes, the total, average, and marginal product curves of all other variable inputs shift. In the case of two variable inputs, increasing the use of one increases the amount of this input that is combined with the other input. This increase would probably cause a shift in the marginal and average product curves of the other input. For example, an increase in capital would quite possibly result in an increase in the marginal product of labor over a wide range of labor use.

This relation between inputs is shown graphically in Figure 8–6. We show only the situation where labor is in Stage II. TP_0 in Panel A and AP_0 and MP_0 in Panel B are the original total, average, and marginal product curves of labor for a fixed amount of another factor, say capital. If the amount of capital increases, the three curves increase to TP_1, AP_1, and MP_1. This means that, for each amount of labor over the relevant range, total, average, and marginal products are greater. For example, for L units of labor, an increase in capital increases total product from T_0 to T_1, average product from A_0 to A_1, and marginal product from M_0 to M_1.

FIGURE 8-6   **Total, average, and marginal products for two different amounts of the fixed factor**

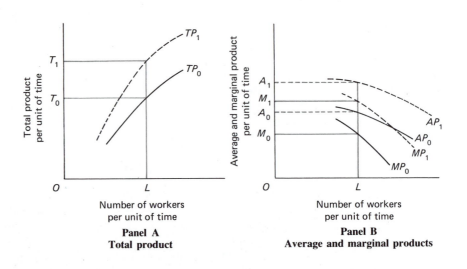

Panel A
Total product

Panel B
Average and marginal products

If both labor and capital are variable, each factor has an infinite set of product curves, one for every amount of the other factor. Therefore, another tool of analysis is necessary when there is more than one variable factor. This tool is the *production isoquant.*

Definition

An isoquant is a curve or locus of points showing all possible combinations of inputs physically capable of producing a given level of output. An isoquant that lies above another designates a higher level of output.

Figure 8–7 illustrates two isoquants of the shape typically assumed in economic theory. Capital use is plotted on the vertical axis and labor use on the horizontal. Isoquant I shows the locus of combinations of capital and labor yielding 100 units of output. The producer can produce 100 units of output by using 10 units of capital and 75 of labor, or 50 units of capital and 15 of labor, or by using any other combination of inputs on I. Similarly, isoquant II shows the various combinations of capital and labor that can produce 200 units of output.

Isoquants I and II are only two of an infinite number of isoquants that are possible. In fact, there are an infinite number of isoquants between I and II because there are an infinite number of possible production levels between 100 and 200 units, provided, as we have assumed, that the product is continuously devisible.

FIGURE 8–7   **Typical isoquants**

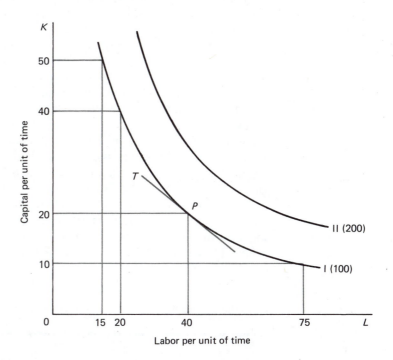

Isoquants have several important properties. First, as shown in Figure 8–7, isoquants slope downward over the relevant range of production. This negative slope indicates that, if the producer decreases the amount of capital employed, more labor must be added in order to keep the rate of output constant. Or, if labor use is decreased, capital must be increased to keep output constant. Thus, the two inputs can be substituted for one another to maintain a constant level of output.

Great theoretical and practical importance is attached to the rate at which one input must be substituted for another in order to keep output constant. The rate at which one input can be substituted for another along an isoquant is called the *marginal rate of technical substitution (MRTS)*, defined as

$$MRTS_{L \, for \, K} = -\frac{\Delta K}{\Delta L},$$

where K is the amount of the input measured along the vertical axis, capital, and L is the amount measured along the horizontal, labor. The minus sign is added in order to make *MRTS* a positive number, since $\Delta K/\Delta L$, the slope of the isoquant, is negative.

Over the relevant range of production, the marginal rate of technical substitution diminishes; that is, as more and more labor is used relative to capital, the absolute value of $\Delta K/\Delta L$ decreases along an isoquant. This can be seen in Figure 8–7. If capital is decreased by 10 units, from 50 to 40, labor must be increased by only 5 units, from 15 to 20, in order to keep the level of output at 100 units. If capital is decreased by 10 units, from 20 to 10, labor must be increased by 35 units, from 40 to 75, to keep output at 100 units.

The fact that the marginal rate of technical substitution diminishes means that isoquants are convex; that is, in the neighborhood of a point of tangency, the isoquant lies above the tangent line. This relation is seen at point P in Figure 8–7. The slope of the tangent T shows the rate at which labor can be substituted for capital in the neighborhood of point P, maintaining an output of 100 units. For very small movements along an isoquant, the negative of the slope of the tangent is the marginal rate of technical substitution. It is easy to see that the slope of the tangent

FIGURE 8–8   **Diminishing marginal rate of technical substitution**

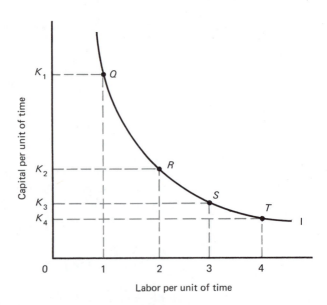

becomes less and less steep as the input combination moves downward along the isoquant.

The concept of diminishing *MRTS* is stressed again in Figure 8–8. $Q, R, S,$ and T are four input combinations lying on isoquant I. Q has the combination K_1 units of capital and one unit of labor; R has K_2 units of capital and two units of labor, and so on. For the movement from Q to R, the marginal rate of technical substitution of capital for labor is, by the formula,

$$- \frac{K_1 - K_2}{1 - 2} = K_1 - K_2.$$

Similarly, for the movements from R to S and S to T, the marginal rates of technical substitution are $K_2 - K_3$ and $K_3 - K_4$, respectively.

Since the marginal rate of technical substitution of capital for labor diminishes as labor is substituted for capital, it is necessary that $(K_1 - K_2) > (K_2 - K_3) > (K_3 - K_4)$. The amount of capital replaced by successive units of labor will decline if, and only if, the isoquant is convex. Since the amount *must* decline, the isoquant must be convex.

Isoquants cannot intersect one another. If they did, then one combination of K and L would yield two different levels of output. The producer's technology is inconsistent; we rule out such events.

Relation of *MRTS* to Marginal Products

For very slight movements along an isoquant, the marginal rate of technical substitution equals the ratio of the marginal products of the two inputs. The proof is straightforward and similar to an exercise we did in Chapter 5 when we discussed indifference curves.

Let the level of output, X, depend on the use of two inputs, L and K. Assume that L and K are both allowed to vary slightly, and consider how X must vary. Suppose the use of L increases by three units and K by five. If, in this range, the marginal product of L is four units of X per unit of L and that of K is two units of X per unit of K, the change in X is

$$\Delta X = (4 \times 3) + (2 \times 5) = 22.$$

In other words, when L and K are allowed to vary slightly, the change in X resulting from the change in the two inputs is the marginal product of L times the amount of change in L plus the marginal product of K times its change.[3] Put in a more general form

---

[3] We have violated our assumption about marginal product somewhat. The marginal product of an input is defined as the change in output per unit of change in the input, *the use of other inputs held constant*. In this case, we allow both inputs to change; and the marginal product is really an approximation. But we are speaking only of *slight*, or very small, changes in use. Thus, the violation of the assumption is small, and the approximation approaches the true variation for very small changes.

$$\Delta X = MP_L \Delta L + MP_K \Delta K.$$

Along an isoquant, X is constant; therefore ΔX equals zero. Setting ΔX in the above equation equal to zero and solving for the slope of the isoquant, $\Delta K/\Delta L$, we have

$$-\frac{\Delta K}{\Delta L} = \frac{MP_L}{MP_K} = MRTS_{L \text{ for } K}.$$

Since, as noted, along an isoquant K and L must vary inversely, $\Delta K/\Delta L$ is negative.[4]

Using the relations developed here, the reason for diminishing $MRTS$ is easily explained. As additional units of labor are added to a fixed amount of capital, the marginal product of labor diminishes. Furthermore, as shown in Figure 8–6, the marginal product of labor diminishes, if the amount of any other input is diminished. Thus, two forces are working to diminish the marginal product of labor: (a) less of the other input causes a downward *shift* of the marginal product of labor curve; and (b) more units of the variable input (labor) cause a downward movement *along* the marginal product curve. As labor is substituted for capital, the marginal product of labor must decline. For analogous reasons, the marginal product of capital increases as less capital and more labor are used. With the quantity of labor fixed, the marginal product of capital rises as fewer units of capital are used. But, simultaneously, there is an increase in labor input, thereby shifting the marginal product of capital curve upward. The same two forces are present in this case: a movement along a marginal product curve and a shift in the location of the curve. In this situation, however, both forces work to increase the marginal product of capital. As labor is substituted for capital, the marginal product of capital increases.

8.5 OPTIMAL COMBINATION OF RESOURCES

The core of production theory is concerned with how a producer should combine inputs when operating under a constraint. Any desired level of output can normally be produced by a number of different combinations of inputs. Nearly every producer has the goal of either maximizing output given an operating budget or minimizing cost given a required output to produce. To pursue either goal is called constrained optimization. This is not profit maximization; a producer cannot maximize profits if cost or output is restricted.

---

[4] It is possible that, as more and more labor is used relative to capital, and labor goes into Stage III, the isoquant bends upward. Or, as more and more capital is used relative to labor, and capital goes into Stage III, the isoquant bends backward. Since both of these regions involve one input in Stage III, production does not take place in that area. Thus, we will ignore these noneconomic regions.

Our task is to determine the specific combination of inputs a firm should select when it is constrained. The analysis is a specific application of the constrained optimization methodology discussed in Chapter 4. We will see in this section that a firm attains the highest possible level of output for any given level of cost or the lowest possible cost for producing any level of output when the marginal rate of technical substitution for any two inputs equals the ratio of input prices.

Input Prices and Isocost Curves

Inputs, as well as outputs, bear specific market prices. In determining the optimal input combination, producers must pay heed to relative input prices if they are to minimize the cost of producing a given output or maximize output for a given level of cost.

Input prices are determined, as are the prices of goods, by supply and demand in the market. For producers who are not monopsonists or oligopsonists (that is, the sole purchaser or one of a few purchasers of an input), input prices are given by the market, and one producer's rate of purchase does not change prices even though many producers as a group could change them. The theory we present applies to a producer who faces fixed input prices, but it could be generalized to optimization with variable input prices.

We will continue to assume that the two inputs are labor and capital, although the analysis applies equally well to any two productive inputs. Denote the quantity of capital and labor by K and L, respectively, and their unit prices by r and w. The total cost, $\overline{C}$, of using any volume of K and L is $\overline{C} = rK + wL$, the sum of the cost of K units of capital at a price r per unit and of L units of labor at w per unit.

To take a more specific example, suppose capital costs \$1,000 per unit ($r = \$1,000$), and labor receives a wage of \$2,500 per month ($w = \$2,500$). If a total of \$15,000 is to be spent for inputs, the equation above shows that the following combinations are possible: $\$15,000 = \$1,000K + \$2,500L$, or $K = 15 - 2.5L$. Similarly, if \$20,000 is to be spent on inputs, one can purchase the following combinations: $K = 20 - 2.5L$. More generally, if the fixed amount, $\overline{C}$, is to be spent, the producer can choose among the combinations given by

$$ K = \frac{\overline{C}}{r} - \frac{w}{r} L. $$

This equation is illustrated in Figure 8–9. If \$15,000 is spent for inputs and no labor is purchased, 15 units of capital may be bought, as shown by the intercept of the lower schedule. More generally, if $\overline{C}$ is to be spent and r is the unit cost, $\overline{C}/r$ units of capital may be purchased. This is the vertical axis *intercept* of the line. If one unit of labor is purchased at \$2,500, then

FIGURE 8–9   **Isocost curves for *r* = $1,000 and *w* = $2,500**

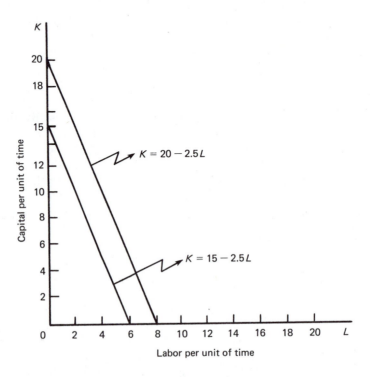

2.5 units of capital must be sacrificed; if two units of labor are bought, five units of capital must be sacrificed; and so on. As the purchase of labor is increased, the purchase of capital must decrease, if cost is held constant. For each additional unit of labor, *w/r* units of capital must be foregone. In Figure 8–9, *w/r* = 2.5. Attaching a negative sign, this represents the *slope* of the line.

The solid lines in Figure 8–9 are called *isocost curves*, because they show the various combinations in inputs that may be purchased for a stipulated amount of expenditure. In summary:

Relation

At fixed input prices *r* and *w* for capital and labor, a fixed outlay, $\overline{C}$, will purchase any combination of capital and labor given by the following linear equation:

$$K = \frac{\overline{C}}{r} - \frac{w}{r} L.$$

This is the equation for an isocost curve whose vertical intercept ($\overline{C}/r$) is the amount of capital that may be purchased if no labor is bought, and whose slope is the negative of the input price ratio (w/r).

Production of a Given Output at Minimum Cost

Whatever output producers choose to produce, they wish to produce it at the least possible cost. Whatever expenditure producers wish to make, they seek the highest output possible with that expenditure. To accomplish this task, production must be organized in the most economically efficient way. The basic principles of efficiency can be shown with the following problem: Suppose that Transport Service, an airline, must produce a certain output of cargo and passenger service per year. The service is confronted with the following combinations of aircraft and mechanics that can be used to yield this required output over its route pattern.

Combination no.	Number of aircraft	Number of mechanics
1	60	1,000
2	61	920
3	62	850
4	63	800
5	64	760
6	65	730
7	66	710

If the cost resulting from the operation of another aircraft is $250,000, and if the mechanics cost $6,000 each, which combination of aircraft and mechanics should Transport Service use to minimize its cost? By trial and error, a solution of combination 4 is obtained. We could be more systematic and use the following method to find the answer. Begin at combination 1. An additional airplane would cost $250,000 to operate, but 80 mechanics could be released at a savings of $480,000. A move to combination 2 would be beneficial. By moving to 3, the firm would save $420,000 in mechanics' salaries and add $250,000 in aircraft expenses. Following the same line of reasoning, the firm could reduce cost by moving to combination 4. It would not move to 5 since the $240,000 saved is less than the $250,000 added.

To analyze the problem graphically, suppose, at given input prices r and w, a firm wishes to produce the output indicated by isoquant I in

FIGURE 8–10   **Optimal input combination to minimize cost subject to a given level of output**

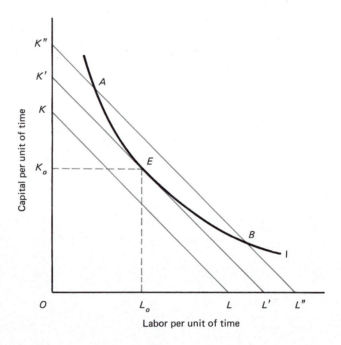

Figure 8–10. Isocost curves KL, $K'L'$, and $K''L''$ represent the infinite numbers of isocost curves the producer can choose at the given input prices. Obviously the firm chooses the lowest one that enables it to attain output level I. That is, the firm produces at the cost represented by isocost curve $K'L'$. Any resource expenditure below that, for example that represented by KL, is not feasible, since it is impossible to produce output I with these resource combinations. Any resource combinations above that represented by $K'L'$ are rejected because the entrepreneur wishes to produce the desired output at *least* cost. If combination A or B is chosen, at the cost represented by $K''L''$, the producer can reduce costs by moving along I to point E. Point E shows the optimal resource combination, using K_0 units of capital and L_0 units of labor.

Equilibrium is reached when the isoquant representing the chosen output is just tangent to an isocost curve. Since tangency means that the two slopes are equal, least-cost production requires that the marginal rate of technical substitution of labor for capital be equal to the ratio of the price of labor to the price of capital. The market input-price ratio tells the producer the rate at which one input can be *substituted for another in the input markets.* The marginal rate of technical substitution shows the rate at which the producer *can substitute in production.* As long as the two are not equal, a producer can achieve a lower cost by moving in the direction of equality.

Principle

To minimize cost subject to a given level of output and given input prices, the producer must purchase inputs in quantities such that the marginal rate of technical substitution of labor for capital is equal to the input-price ratio (the price of labor to the price of capital).

$$MRTS_{L \text{ for } K} = \frac{MP_L}{MP_K} = \frac{w}{r}$$

We can analyze the equilibrium condition in a way described in Chapter 4. Recall that constrained optimization requires that the marginal benefit per dollar spent on each activity be equal. Assume that the above equilibrium condition did not hold, or specifically that

$$\frac{MP_L}{MP_K} < \frac{w}{r}.$$

In other words,

$$\frac{MP_L}{w} < \frac{MP_K}{r}.$$

In this case, the marginal product of an additional dollar's worth of labor is less than the marginal product of an additional dollar's worth of capital. The firm could reduce its use of labor by one dollar, expand its use of capital by less than one dollar, and remain at the same level of output with a reduced cost. It could continue to do this as long as the above inequality holds. Eventually, MP_L/w would become equal to MP_K/r since MP_L rises with decreased use of labor and increased use of capital, and MP_K falls with increased capital and decreased labor. By the same reasoning, it is easy to see that firms substitute labor for capital until the equality holds if the inequality should be reversed.

Production of Maximum Output with a Given Level of Cost

In the above discussion we assumed the producer chose a level of output and then found the input combination that permitted production of that output at the least cost. As an alternative, we could assume the firm spends only a fixed amount on production and wishes to attain the highest level of output possible for that expenditure. Not too surprisingly, the results turn out to be the same as before.

This situation is shown in Figure 8–11. The isocost line *KL* shows every possible combination of the two inputs at the given level of cost and

FIGURE 8–11   **Output maximization for a given level of cost**

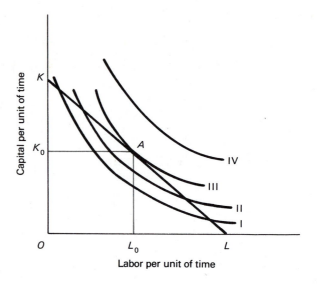

input prices. Four isoquants are shown. Clearly, at the given level of cost, output level IV is unattainable. Neither level I nor level II would be chosen since higher levels are possible. The highest level of output attainable with a given level of cost is produced by using L_0 labor and K_0 capital. At point A, the highest possible isoquant, III, is just tangent to the given isocost schedule. In the case of output maximization, the marginal rate of technical substitution of labor for capital equals the input-price ratio (the price of labor to the price of capital).

Principle

   In order to maximize output subject to a given cost or to minimize cost subject to a given output, the producer must employ inputs in such amounts as to equate the marginal rate of technical substitution and the input-price ratio.

Expansion Path

   The expansion path in production theory shows how factor usage changes when output changes, the ratio of one factor price to another held constant. In Figure 8–12, curves I, II, and III are isoquants depicting a representative production function; KL, $K'L'$, and $K''L''$ represent the least cost of producing the three output levels. Since the factor-price ratio does not change, these isocost schedules are parallel.

FIGURE 8–12   **Expansion path**

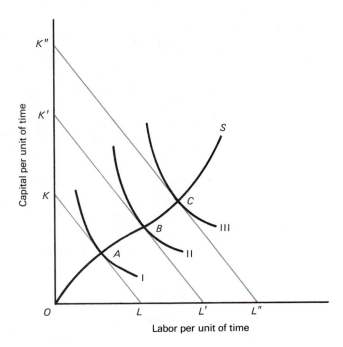

To derive what is defined as a producer's *expansion path*, we first assume factor prices remain constant, and let cost change. Each equilibrium point is defined by the equality between the marginal rate of technical substitution and the factor-price ratio. Since the latter remains constant, so does the former. Therefore, *OS* in Figure 8–12 is a locus of points along which the marginal rate of technical substitution is constant. It is a curve with a special feature—it is the locus along which output will expand when factor prices are constant. We may accordingly formulate this result as a definition.

Definition
The expansion path is the curve along which output expands when factor prices remain constant. The expansion path shows how factor proportions change when output or expenditure changes, input prices remaining constant throughout. The marginal rate of technical substitution remains constant also, since the factor-price ratio is constant.

As we will see in the next chapter, the expansion path gives the firm its cost structure. That is, the expansion path shows the optimal input combination for each level of output at the given set of input prices. Thus, it gives the minimum cost of producing each level of output from the cost associated with each tangent isocost curve.

In Figure 8–12, the two inputs, capital and labor, are called *normal inputs* because, as higher levels of output are produced, more of each input is used. In other words, the expansion path is positively sloped. An input is called *inferior* if, over a range of outputs, the use of this input declines as production increases. Over this range, the expansion path is negatively sloped. In Figure 8–13, labor is inferior over the range of production between the outputs shown by I and II. At the lower output given by I, L_0 labor is used; labor is reduced to L_1 when the higher output represented by II is produced. If capital had been the inferior input, the expansion path would have bent downward as capital became inferior. Clearly, both inputs cannot be inferior at the same time. No firm could increase output by reducing all inputs, therefore reducing total cost.

As mentioned at the beginning of this chapter, a production function could possibly be characterized by production under fixed proportions. In this case, all inputs must be used in the same proportion regardless of output. For example, if two units of labor and five of capital are necessary

FIGURE 8–13   **Expansion path: one input inferior**

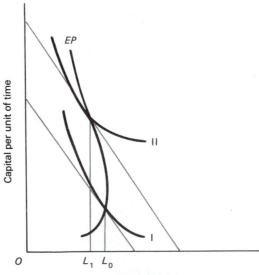

to produce 100 units of output, 200 units of output require four labor and ten capital, 300 units require six labor and fifteen capital, and so on. If labor is limited to two units, no matter how much capital is added beyond five units, only 100 units of output can be produced.

Figure 8–14 shows a set of isoquants and the expansion path for a fixed-proportion production function. The isoquants for outputs X_1, X_2, and X_3 form right angles. Take output level X_1; this level is produced by K_0 capital and L_0 labor. If labor remains at that level while capital is increased, no more output can be produced. An increase in labor cannot increase output while capital remains fixed. Furthermore, X_2, X_3 and all other outputs require labor and capital to be used in the same ratio, K_0/L_0. This ratio is the slope of the expansion path, EP, which is a straight line passing through the corner of each isoquant.

Returns to Scale

Recall in Section 8.2 we wrote output, X, as a function of inputs. Specifically, for just two inputs, K and L, we can write

$$X = f(L,K).$$

Now suppose we increase the inputs by a constant proportion, say λ, and observe the proportionate change (z) in output. We have

FIGURE 8–14   **Production with fixed proportions**

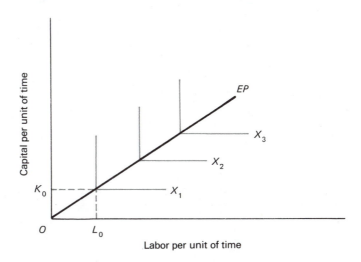

$$zX = f(\lambda L, \lambda K),$$

where λ and z represent proportionate increases in the scale of operation and level of output, respectively.

We have noted that, in the case of fixed-proportions production functions, if inputs are increased by a constant percent, output rises by the same proportion. More concisely, $z = \lambda$ in fixed-proportions production. This phenomenon is called *constant returns to scale*.

But returns to scale are often referred to when dealing with variable-proportion production functions. If all inputs are increased by a factor of λ and output goes up by a factor of z, then, in general, a producer experiences:

1. *Increasing returns to scale* if $z > \lambda$. Output goes up proportionately more than the increase in input usage.
2. *Decreasing returns to scale* if $\lambda > z$. Output goes up proportionately less than the increase in input usage.
3. *Constant returns to scale* if $\lambda = z$. Output goes up by the same proportion as the increase in input usage.

Economists often refer to returns to scale in two contexts. Returns may exist at the plant level or at the firm level, in which a firm may operate several plants. Frequently, there are increasing returns to scale over ranges of output at the firm level, but not for plants. For a proportionate increase in output at the firm level, it often takes proportionately less of an increase in administrative and selling personnel, while, at the plant level, there may be constant or decreasing returns for the increase in output.

Do not deduce from this discussion of returns to scale that, with variable-proportion production functions, firms actually expand output by increasing input use in exactly the same proportion. As we have seen above, the very concept of variable proportions means that they do not necessarily expand in the same proportions; the expansion path may twist and turn in many directions. This concept of returns is of great importance in the theory of cost; returns to scale determine the shape of a producer's long-run total cost schedule.

8.6 SUMMARY

This chapter has set forth the basic theory of production and the optimal combination of inputs under a given set of input prices.

We studied first the production function when only one input could be changed. We developed two important concepts captured by the following definitions:

Definition

The average product of an input is total output divided by the amount of input.

Definition
The marginal product of an input is the addition to total output attributable to a small increase in input.

Both of these definitions were expressed as ratios. If labor is the variable input, we wrote the average product of labor (AP_L) as

$$AP_L = \frac{X}{L}.$$

The marginal product of labor (MP_L) is the change in output (ΔX) from a small change in the labor input (ΔL), or

$$MP_L = \frac{\Delta X}{\Delta L}.$$

Both average product and marginal product at first rise and then decline. The marginal product curve will intersect the average product curve at its highest point. When marginal product declines, a producer is said to experience diminishing marginal returns.

Next we looked at production with two or more variable inputs. Our tools of analysis were the isoquant and the isocost curve.

Definition
An isoquant is a curve or locus of points showing all possible combinations of inputs physically capable of producing a given level of output.

The isocost curve is a linear schedule described by the following relation:

Relation
At fixed input prices r and w for capital and labor, a fixed outlay, $\overline{C}$, will purchase any combination of capital and labor such that

$$K = \frac{\overline{C}}{r} - \frac{w}{r} L.$$

The firm, operating under either a cost or output constraint, maximizes the output that can be produced at any given level of cost, or minimizes cost at any given level of output, when

$$MRTS_{L \text{ for } K} = \frac{MP_L}{MP_K} = \frac{w}{r},$$

or, more generally, when the marginal rate of technical substitution equals the ratio of input prices. The expansion path is the set of all points for which the above equality is met as costs change.

Production functions can be described by returns to scale. A producer experiences increasing returns when output rises by a greater proportion than the proportional increase in all the inputs, constant returns if the proportional changes are equal, and decreasing returns if the increase in output is less than the proportional increase in the inputs.

TECHNICAL PROBLEMS

1. Fill in the blanks in the following table.

Usage of the variable input	Total product	Average product	Marginal product
1	—	20	—
2	—	—	34
3	81	—	—
4	—	26	—
5	—	—	21
6	138	—	—
7	—	21	—
8	—	—	5
9	153	—	—
10	—	15	—

2. Fill in all three columns in the following table. Make your numbers conform to the conditions set forth below. Graph the average and marginal product curves.

Units of variable input	Total product	Average product	Marginal product
1	100		
2			
3			
4			
5			
6			
7			
8			
9			
10			
11			
12			
13			
14			
15			
16			
17			
18	2,000		

Make your numbers meet the following restrictions:

a. Marginal product first increases, reaches its maximum at 5 units of variable input, declines thereafter, and becomes negative after 17 units.

b. Average product first rises, reaches its maximum at nine units, and declines thereafter.

c. Marginal product equals average product at approximately the maximum point of the latter.

3. You are an efficiency expert hired by a manufacturing firm that uses two inputs, labor (L) and capital (K). The firm produces and sells a given output. You have the following information

$$P_L = \$4, \ P_K = \$100, \ MP_L = 4, \ MP_K = 40$$

a. Is the firm operating efficiently? Why or why not?

b. What should the firm do?

4. Use the table you derived in problem 2 to answer the following questions:

a. When average product is rising, marginal product is _____ than average product.

b. When marginal product is increasing, total product is increasing at a (decreasing, increasing) rate.

c. When marginal product is decreasing and positive, total product is increasing at a (decreasing, increasing) rate.

d. When marginal product becomes negative, total product is _____.

e. When average product is falling, marginal product is _____ than average product.

5. A firm can produce a certain amount of a good using three combinations of labor and capital. Labor costs $2 per unit, capital $4 per unit. The three methods are:

	A	B	C
Labor (units).............	5	6	2
Capital (units)...........	7	5	9

a. Which method should be chosen?

b. The price of labor rises to $4 while the price of capital falls to $3; which method should be chosen?

c. Under the second price structure (part *b*) the labor is done by you and you hire capital at $3; now which method should be chosen? Why? (Can you even answer this? What information would you need?)

6. Assume that a curve is drawn showing, along the horizontal axis, the amounts of a factor *A* employed in combination with a fixed amount of a group of factors called *B*, and, along the vertical axis, the amount of physical product obtainable from these combinations of factors (see Figure E.8–1).

a. How can you find (geometrically) the amount of *A* for which the average product per unit of *A* is a maximum?

b. How can you find (geometrically) the amount of *A* for which the marginal product of *A* is a maximum?

c. Between the two points defined in parts *a* and *b*, will the marginal product of *A* increase or decrease as more of *A* is used?

d. Between these two points, will the average product per unit of *A* increase or decrease as more of *A* is used?

e. At the point defined in *a*, will the marginal product of *A* be higher or lower than the average product per unit of *A*? Give reasons.

FIGURE E.8–1

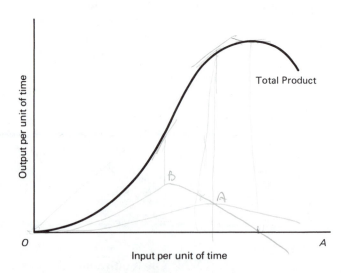

    f. At the point defined in *b*, will the marginal product of *A* be lower or higher than the average product per unit of *A*? Give reasons.

    g. How can you find (geometrically) the amount of *A* for which the marginal product of *A* is zero?

7. In Figure E.8–2, *LZ* is the isocost curve and I is an isoquant. Explain precisely why combinations *A* and *B* are not efficient. Explain in terms of the relation of the ratio of the marginal products to the ratio of the input prices. Explain, in these terms, why the direction of substitution in each case, labor for capital or capital for labor, is optimal. Using the ratio of input prices given by *LZ*, find and label the least-cost combination of labor and capital that can produce the output designated by I. In the above terms, explain why this combination is optimal.

8. Explain precisely why *MP* exceeds (is less than) *AP* when *AP* is rising (falling).

9. In Figure E.8–3, the isoquant turns upward at *OL* units of labor. Explain this upward turn in terms of labor going into Stage III; i.e., negative marginal product.

10. A business executive claims a company should never hire another

FIGURE E.8–2

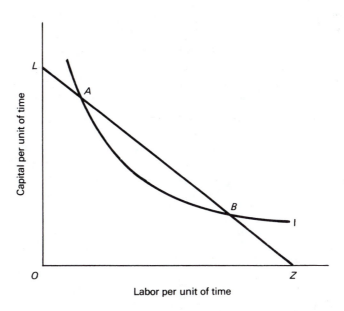

FIGURE E.8–3

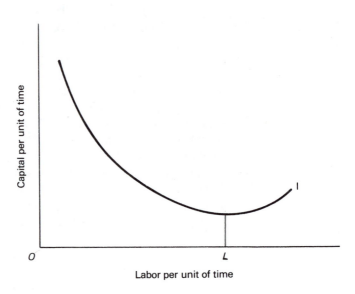

Labor per unit of time

worker if the new person causes diminishing returns. Explain why this person is wrong.

11. Cuddles Toy Company makes stuffed animals. There are two essential ingredients in the production of these animals: sewing machines (K) and machine operators (L). Can you offer any advice on the proper mix of these two factors of production?

12. Suppose that a steel plant's production function is $X = 5LK$, where X is the output rate, L is the amount of labor it uses per period of time, and K is the amount of capital it uses per period of time. Suppose that the price of labor is $1 a unit and the price of capital is $2 a unit. The firm hires you to figure out what combination of inputs the plant should use to produce 20 units. What is your answer? (Hint: $MP_L = 5K$ and $MP_K = 5L$.)

13. In Figure E.8–4, the isoquants I, II, and III are associated respectively with 1,000, 2,000, and 3,000 units of output. The price of capital is $2 a unit and the price of labor is $1 a unit.
    a. Construct an expansion path.
    b. How many units of each input are used to produce each level of output efficiently?

FIGURE E.8–4

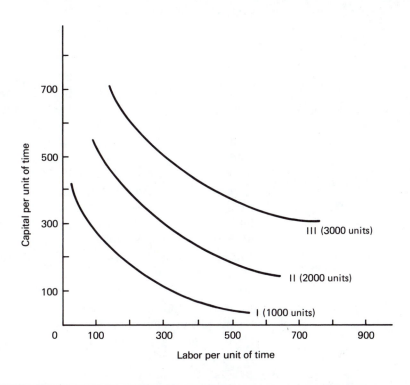

c. What is the minimum cost of producing each level of output?
d. Answer each question under the assumption that the price of labor is now $2 a unit and the price of capital is $1 a unit.

ANALYTICAL PROBLEMS

1. Why do we say that a student should not stop studying after reaching diminishing returns? How much should a student study?

2. The Meadowlark Country Club is a nonprofit organization. It collects only enough revenues from its members to cover the cost of operation. Explain why this club still ought to provide services at the point of tangency between the isocost line and a production isoquant, just like a profit-maximizing enterprise.

3. An efficiency expert who examined a power company's plant said he believed the mill was being operated inefficiently. When the presi-

dent of the company asked for examples, the efficiency expert said that, for one thing, the crane operators who were unloading coal from barges dropped about 10 percent of the coal into the river. If you were the president of the company, would you necessarily consider this circumstance evidence of inefficiency? Why or why not? What questions would you ask?

4. Several years ago, the United States was sending engineers and other technical experts to underdeveloped countries to advise these countries on the latest technological methods in manufacture and agriculture. They also assisted these underdeveloped countries in instituting modern technological methods. Can you explain why, in many of these countries, the advice and help were utter failures, causing great cost to the poorer countries. Why do you think, in many instances, the old-fashioned methods worked better?

5. Explain why the marginal product of any input might become negative; that is, why would additional units of the input cause output to fall? Do not answer that the firm hires inferior inputs. Assume all units of the input are alike.

6. During the past 10 years, more and more business firms have been purchasing small computers and word processors. Provide an economic rationale for this. Can you think of more than one reason?

7. Explain the following statement: "It is possible for a producer to be technically efficient and not economically efficient, but it is impossible for a producer to be economically efficient without being technically efficient."

8. In a recent *Business Week* article dealing with management [October 22, 1984, p. 156] the following account was written. "When he took over the furniture factory three years ago, . . . [the manager] realized almost immediately that it was throwing away at least $100,000 a year worth of wood scrap. Within a few weeks, he set up a task force of managers and workers to deal with the problem. And within a few months, they reduced the amount of scrap to $7,000 worth" Was this necessarily an *economically efficient* move?

9. Highly paid business executives are hiring personal shoppers to buy clothes. Although fees range from $35 to $80 an hour, most shoppers can put together a wardrobe in two to four hours. The shopper, after choosing the clothes, often brings them to the client's home to check the fit. Sometimes the choices are brought to the executive's office for quick approval. In the past decade the number of personal shoppers has increased from a few dozen to more than 1,000 [*The Wall Street Journal*, April 1, 1985, p. 25]. Discuss this trend in terms of the marginal product of business executives. If management skills are so valuable, why doesn't a producer just hire more business executives? Is management an easily measured input?

Chapter 9

Theory of Cost

9.1 INTRODUCTION

As we noted in Chapter 8, the determinants of cost in production theory are the state of technology, characterized by isoquants, and input prices, described by isocost curves. The cost of producing or supplying goods and services is, as we will see, the most important determinant of supply. This chapter develops the underlying theory of cost from the theory of production. It first sets forth the theory of cost in the long run when all inputs are variable, then turns to cost in the short run when some costs are fixed.

Definition of Cost

The cornerstone of cost theory is the concept of *opportunity cost*. Quite frequently, people ignore opportunity cost when discussing total cost. They generally think cost simply means the price that must be paid for the item purchased. To people in business, the cost of producing a good usually means the number of dollars that must be paid for raw materials, labor, machinery, and other inputs. In economics, however, cost means more than these expenses.

Consider the cost of attending college for one year. As a first approximation, you might say that attending college for one year costs a year's tuition, room, board, book purchases, and incidental expenses. Using that approach, it would appear that the expense of attending a particular college is essentially the same for all students. Under most circumstances, this would be an incorrect conclusion. Assume that there are two students at the same school paying approximately the same tuition, board, and so forth. One student, however, is an exceptional tennis player who could turn professional and earn $50,000 on tour in the first year. The *real* cost of attending college is not only the sum of this person's expenses, it is also what he or she must forego to attend college. To go to school, the athlete must *sacrifice* or *give up* the amount that would have been made by playing professional tennis.

Other students also sacrifice something in addition to direct outlays for expenses. Assuming that most students are not so athletically inclined, perhaps the best alternative earning possibility lies in working as a bank teller. If the student would work as a teller instead of enrolling in college, the salary paid to a teller is the sacrifice that is made to attend school. Since bank tellers generally do not receive large salaries, the athlete sacrifices a greater amount; hence, the *real* cost of attending college is greater for the tennis player than for the nonathlete. We say the athlete's *opportunity cost* is greater, which makes the total cost of attending college greater.

An economist would also take a different view of the direct expenses while going to school; tuition, room, board, etc. Some of these expenses occur without attending college, so they should not be counted as a college expense. Room and board is an ongoing expense no matter what activity is pursued. Tuition and books are not; incidentals may or may not be attributed to attending college depending on whether they arise directly because of enrollment at school. Thus, in counting the total cost of education, an economist adds up just those costs that entail foregone opportunities. Often this is a different figure than what is typically thought of as total expenses.

Recall in Chapter 8, when we set out the production-possibilities curve, we emphasized that the cost of having more of one good is the amount of some other good that must be given up. This is the opportunity cost of production. Throughout this chapter, we will attempt to stress the importance of opportunity cost.

Definition

Opportunity cost is the value of the best alternative to resources that must be given up to produce a good or service.

Opportunity Cost and Accounting Cost

We must emphasize that it is wrong to think of the total cost of production as the sum of all accounting costs, which is to say the economist and the accountant think of total costs as two different things. They agree on the *explicit* costs a producer incurs, but differ on what economists call *implicit* costs in production. Total cost is equal to the sum of explicit and implicit costs. Implicit costs exist because accountants overlook opportunity cost for some inputs in production.

To aid in analyzing the nature of implicit costs, consider two firms that produce good *X* and are in every way identical—with one exception. The first firm rents the building where the good is produced, while the second owns the building and, therefore, pays no rent. Whose costs are higher? An economist would say both are the same, even though the second firm makes lower payments to outside factors of production. Costs are the same because using the building to produce X costs the second firm income it could have received from leasing it at the prevailing rent, an opportunity cost. Since these two buildings are the same, presumably the market rental would be the same. In other words, a part of the cost incurred by the firm that owns the building is the payment from the producer (itself) to the owner of the building (also itself).

If you are not convinced that implicit costs should be counted, think of the issue this way. Suppose the building owned by the second firm was destroyed. To continue production, a different structure is rented—and an explicit payment is made to the input. What was once an implicit cost has been turned into an explicit cost.

Similarly, suppose an individual owns and manages a small business alone. At the end of the year, the business earns $60,000. This is not profit if the cost of the manager's time has been ignored. Time is an implicit cost that must be subtracted from earnings to get profit. How should the owner's time be priced? We answer with another question. What would the owner have to pay to hire someone to manage the business equally well? If it would have taken $30,000 to hire a manager who could earn the same amount for the business at the end of the year, then the implicit cost of the owner's time is $30,000.

In sum, there are often inputs in a production process that are not explicitly paid. To an economist, these implicit costs should be valued at the price that would have to be paid to replace their contribution to output. Implicit costs must be added to explicit costs in order to obtain total production costs.

9.2 PLANNING HORIZON AND LONG-RUN COSTS

Let us begin our analysis of production costs by assuming that an individual starts a firm in a particular industry. Since this person is just beginning the firm, it is in the long run. The long run is not some date in the future, but rather means that all inputs are variable to the firm. Therefore, one of the first things that must be decided on is the *scale* of operation, or the *size* of the firm. To make this decision, the entrepreneur must know the cost of producing each level of output. We begin our analysis of cost with the long run rather than the short run, because the scale of the firm must be determined before an entrepreneur decides on different output levels from a fixed plant size.

Derivation of Long-Run Cost Schedules from a Production Function

Let us assume, for analytical purposes, that this new business will never be large enough to affect the prices paid for the resources used in production. Further, assume this person can estimate the technically efficient means of production for each level of output. Using the methods described in Chapter 8, the entrepreneur can therefore derive an expansion path. Assume that the firm uses only two inputs, labor and capital.

TABLE 9–1   **Derivation of long-run cost schedules**

(1) Output	(2) Labor (units)	(3) Capital (units)	(4) Total cost at $5 per unit of labor $10 per unit of capital	(5) Long-run average cost	(6) Long-run marginal cost (per unit)
	Least cost usage				
100......	10	7	$120	$1.20	$1.20
200......	12	8	140	.70	.20
300......	20	10	200	.67	.60
400......	30	15	300	.75	1.00
500......	40	22	420	.84	1.20
600......	52	30	560	.93	1.40
700......	60	42	720	1.03	1.60

The characteristics of the derived expansion path are given in columns (1) through (3) of Table 9–1. Labor costs $5 per unit and capital $10 per unit. Column (1) gives seven output levels and columns (2) and (3) give the optimal combinations of labor and capital for each output level at the prevailing input prices.

Column (4) shows the total cost of producing each level of output. For example, the least-cost method of producing 300 units requires 20 units of labor and 10 of capital. At $5 and $10, respectively, the total cost is $200. It should be emphasized that column (4) is a *least-cost schedule* for various rates of production. Obviously, the entrepreneur could pay more to produce any output by using less efficient productive processes or by paying some factors of production more than their market prices. The firm could not, however, produce any output at a cost lower than that given. Stated precisely in a definition, we have:

Definition
Long-run total cost (*LRTC*) is the least cost at which each quantity of output can be produced when no resources are fixed in quantity or rate of use.

As noted above, the lowest total cost of producing any output consists of two components, the explicit costs and the implicit costs. The explicit costs given in Table 9–1, are the payment entrepreneurs must make to the factors of production. The implicit costs are the market values of the resources they own and use in production, including the wages they pay to themselves. We could assume, in Table 9–1, that the entrepreneur owns the capital and thus incurs implicit costs. We could also assume that implicit costs are zero. Or, we might just ignore them here. In any case, when entrepreneurs plan, they must consider payments to themselves, since this is what they would have to pay to replace themselves.

Two important cost schedules, derived from column (4) are long-run average cost (*LRAC*), shown in column (5), and long-run marginal cost (*LRMC*), shown in column (6). Average cost is simply the total cost of producing a given level of output divided by that output.

Definition

Long-run average cost (*LRAC*) is the long-run total cost of producing a particular quantity of output divided by that quantity.

We can write *LRAC* as the ratio of *LRTC* to output, *X*,

$$LRAC = \frac{LRTC}{X}.$$

Column (5) reflects an important assumed characteristic of average cost: average cost first declines, reaches a minimum, then rises.

Long-run marginal cost shown in column (6) is the change in total cost divided by the change in output. As a definition,

Definition

Long-run marginal cost (*LRMC*) is the addition to long-run total cost attributable to a small increase in output (usually one unit) when all inputs are optimally adjusted. It is thus the change in total cost as one moves incrementally along the long-run total cost schedule.

This cost schedule can also be written in terms of a ratio of a change in *LRTC* to a change in output. That is

$$LRMC = \frac{\Delta LRTC}{\Delta X}.$$

Column (6) of Table 9–1 shows incremental increases of 100 units of output, so the denominator, ΔX, in the above ratio is always 100. Moving from 100 to 200 units of output, for example, raises the total cost from \$120 to \$140. The change in long-run total cost is \$20, and dividing by 100 gives a marginal cost of 20 cents. We see that marginal cost first decreases then increases. Frequently marginal cost is measured as the change in total cost for a *one unit* increase in output. Usually as the change in output gets smaller, the above ratio gives a more precise measure of the change in long-run total cost at the *margin*.

To summarize the situation graphically, consider Figure 9–1, where we assume that output is produced by two inputs, *K* and *L*. The known and fixed input prices give the constant input-price ratio, represented by the slope of the isocost curves $I_1 I_1'$, $I_3 I_3'$, etc. Next, the known production function gives us the isoquant map, partially represented by x_1, x_3, etc., in Figure 9–1.

As is familiar from Chapter 8, when all inputs are readily variable (that is, in the long run), the entrepreneur will choose input combinations that

FIGURE 9–1   **The expansion path and long-run cost**

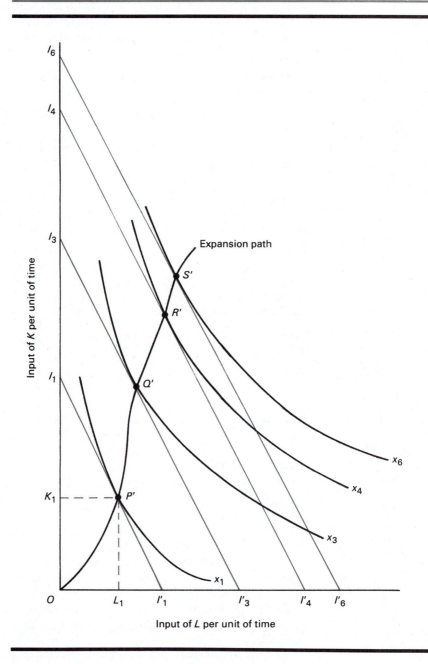

minimize the cost of producing each level of output. This gives us the expansion path $OP'Q'R'S'$. Given the factor-price ratio and the production function, the expansion path shows the combinations of inputs that enable the entrepreneur to produce each level of output at the least possible cost.

Now let us relate this expansion path to a long-run total cost curve with a shape frequently assumed by economists. Figure 9–2 shows graphically the least-cost curve for the good X, derived from the expansion path in Figure 9–1. The least cost of producing x_1 is c_1; of x_3 it is c_3, and so on.

The points P, Q, R, and S in Figure 9–2 correspond exactly to the points P', Q', R', and S', respectively, in Figure 9–1. For example, the cost, c_1, of producing x_1 units of output in Figure 9–2 is precisely the cost of using K_1 units of capital and L_1 units of labor to produce the output x_1 at the point on the isoquant represented by P' in Figure 9–1.

It is important to keep in mind that the firm may use different amounts and combinations of resources. Nothing is fixed except the set of technological possibilities (or state of the arts) and the prices at which the firm can purchase resources.[1] Thus, completely different production processes may be used to achieve minimum cost at (say) x_1 and x_2 units of output. This "planning horizon," where nothing is fixed to the entrepreneur except factor prices and technology, is called the long run, and the associated curve that shows the minimum cost of producing each level of output is called the *long-run total cost curve*. The shape of the long-run total cost curve depends exclusively on the production function and prevailing factor prices. The schedule in Table 9–1 and the curve in Figure 9–2 reflect some of the commonly assumed characteristics of long-run total costs.

Two characteristics are apparent on inspection. First, costs and output are *directly related;* that is, the curve has a positive slope. It costs more to produce more, which is just another way of saying that resources are scarce, or that one never gets "something for nothing" in the real economic world.

The second characteristic is that cost first increases at a decreasing rate and then at an increasing rate. Recall from Table 9–1 that the cost of producing an *additional* 100 units at first decreases, then increases. For example, the first 100 units add $120 to cost, the second 100 units add $20 to cost, but the third 100 units add $60. Each 100 units thereafter add more to cost than the preceding 100.

Figure 9–2 is constructed to reflect that marginal cost first falls, then rises. The schedule is constructed so that for equal output changes,

---

[1] Note that, since the cost curve begins at the origin and not at some positive amount on the vertical axis, we tacitly assume the entrepreneur can readily vary the amount of time and other resources he or she "invests" in the business. All costs are readily variable when one is considering the long run, or planning horizon. It is only in the short run that some costs may be fixed.

FIGURE 9–2   **Long-run total cost curve**

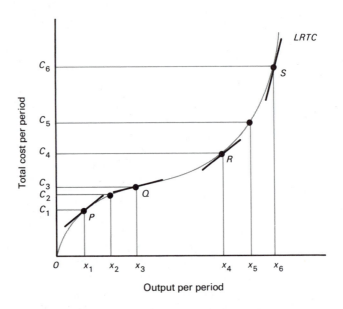

$x_1x_2 = x_2x_3$, c_1c_2 is clearly greater than c_2c_3. This means that the added total cost is greater when the entrepreneur moves from x_1 to x_2, than when output increases from x_2 to x_3. On the other hand, x_4x_5 is equal to x_5x_6, but c_4c_5 is less than c_5c_6—over this range, the additional cost incurred by producing more output increases. Alternatively stated, the slope at P (indicated by the tangent at that point) is greater than the slope at the larger output corresponding to Q. Long-run marginal cost decreases over this range, even though total cost increases. The slope at R is less steep than at S, indicating that marginal cost is increasing in this output interval.

Long-Run Average and Marginal Costs

We are now prepared to examine graphically the relation between the long-run total cost curve and the long-run average and marginal cost curves.

Recall that the long-run average and marginal costs in Table 9–1 first fell then increased. You may have also noticed that the minimum marginal cost was attained at a lower level of output than the level where minimum average cost was reached. We will show that these are results forthcoming from the generally assumed shape of the long-run total cost curve shown in Figure 9–2.

Figure 9–3 shows graphically the relation between total cost (Panel A) and average cost (Panel B). Since average cost is total cost divided by the corresponding output, the long-run average cost of a particular quantity is given by the slope of a ray from the origin to the relevant point on the

FIGURE 9–3   **Derivation of average total cost curve**

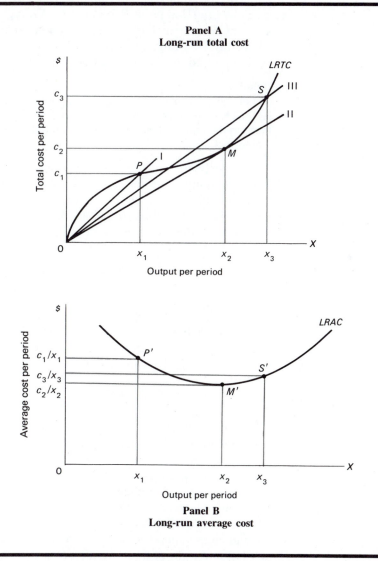

Panel A
Long-run total cost

Panel B
Long-run average cost

$LRTC$ curve. For example, in Panel A, the cost of producing x_1 is c_1. $LRAC$, c_1/x_1, is therefore given by the slope of the ray designated I at point P. Average cost at x_1 is plotted in Panel B at point P'. (Note that the vertical scales of the two graphs differ, but the horizontal scales are the same.)

From inspection of the $LRTC$ curve, it is clear that the slope of a ray to any point on the curve decreases as output increases from zero to x_2. Average cost must fall as output increases from zero to x_2, as shown in Panel B. As output increases thereafter from x_2, the slope of a ray to any point on the total cost curve increases. For example, at x_3 the $LRAC$ is given by ray III at point S in Panel A. Average cost of x_3, c_3/x_3, is plotted at point S' in Panel B. Thus, minimum average cost is reached at x_2, where ray II is tangent to the cost curve at M in Panel A. This average cost is plotted at M'. Notice that the $LRAC$ curve rises thereafter.

Relation

For the generally assumed long-run total cost curve, long-run average cost ($LRAC$) first declines, reaches a minimum, where a ray from the origin is tangent to the long-run total cost curve, and rises thereafter. (These relations are all shown in Figure 9–3.)

The derivation of long-run marginal cost is illustrated in Figure 9–4. Panel A contains a total cost curve shaped similarly to the one in Figure 9–3. As output increases from x' to x'', one moves from point P to point Q and total cost increases from c' to c''. Marginal cost, the additional cost of producing a small increment of output is

$$LRMC = \frac{c'' - c'}{x'' - x'} = \frac{QR}{PR} .$$

As P moves along $LRTC$ toward point Q, the distances between P and Q becomes smaller and smaller, and the slope of the tangent T at point Q becomes a progressively better estimate of QR/PR. For movements in a tiny neighborhood around point Q, the slope of the tangent is the marginal cost of output x''.

As one moves along $LRTC$ through points such as P and Q, the slope of $LRTC$ diminishes until point S is reached at output x_m. Therefore, the long-run marginal cost curve is constructed in Panel B so that it decreases (as the slope of $LRTC$ decreases) until output x_m is attained and increases thereafter (as the slope of $LRTC$ increases).

Notice in Figure 9–4, Panel A, we have brought ray II over from Figure 9–3, Panel A. As indicated in Figure 9–3, the slope of ray II gives minimum $LRAC$. At this point, the ray is tangent to $LRTC$; hence its slope also gives $LRMC$ at point M. Thus, $LRMC = LRAC$ when $LRAC$ attains its minimum value. Consider the relative position of $LRMC$ and $LRAC$ to the left and right of point M. Figure 9–4, Panel B, illustrates the relation between the curves. Since the slope of $LRTC$ is less than the slope of a ray

FIGURE 9–4   **Derivation of long-run marginal cost curve**

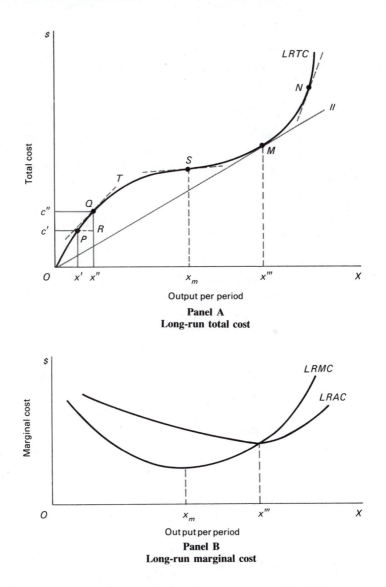

Panel A
Long-run total cost

Panel B
Long-run marginal cost

from the origin to any point on the curve to the left of *M* in Panel A, *LRMC* is less than *LRAC* from the origin to *x'''*, as shown in Panel B. But because the slope of *LRTC* is greater than the slope of a ray from the origin to any point on the curve to the right of *M* (say at point *N*), *LRMC* is greater than *LRAC* at outputs larger than *x'''*.

In a line of reasoning similar to the theory of production, this relation between marginal and average costs would be expected. If an additional unit of output adds more to cost than the average cost, the average must increase. Thus, average cost increases whenever marginal cost is greater than the average. When the marginal cost is less than average, an additional unit of output adds less than the average and average cost must fall. When another unit adds a cost exactly equal to the average, average and marginal cost are equal.

Relation
(1) *LRTC* rises continuously, first at a decreasing rate then at an increasing rate. (2) *LRAC* first declines, reaches a minimum, then rises. When *LRAC* reaches its minimum, *LRMC* equals *LRAC*. (3) *LRMC* first declines, reaches a minimum, and then increases. *LRMC* lies below *LRAC* over the range in which *LRAC* declines; it lies above *LRAC* when *LRAC* is rising.

Economies and Diseconomies of Scale

We now want to draw attention to the long-run average cost schedule. The shape of this curve has far-reaching consequences for the profitability of firms and the level of output they choose. Long-run average costs may be decreasing, constant, or increasing as output increases. If they are decreasing, then the firm is experiencing *economies of scale;* if they are increasing, the firm is experiencing *diseconomies of scale;* and if long-run average costs are constant, the firm is simply said to have neither economies nor diseconomies of scale. We can, therefore, characterize the long-run average cost schedule with the following definition:

Definition
A firm is said to have economies of scale if the long-run average cost schedule is declining as output increases and diseconomies of scale if the long-run average cost schedule is rising.

Figure 9–5 illustrates the ranges of output for which the *LRAC* schedule exhibits economies and diseconomies. The firm experiences economies of scale up to x_0 units of output and diseconomies after x_1 units.

There is a connection between returns to scale and the shape of the long-run average cost curve. Recall from the last chapter, our discussion of increasing and decreasing returns. When increasing returns exist, as output goes up the increase in output is proportionately more than the increase in inputs. Thus, if the prices of all inputs are constant, *LRMC* is falling and this pulls *LRAC* down. Increasing returns to scale will, therefore, lead to economies of scale, because long-run average cost declines if it takes less inputs at the margin to produce more output. Similarly, if a producer experiences decreasing returns to scale, then proportionately more inputs are needed at the margin to increase output. *LRMC* is therefore rising, and eventually this will cause *LRAC* to rise. Decreasing

FIGURE 9–5   **The presence of economies and diseconomies of scale**

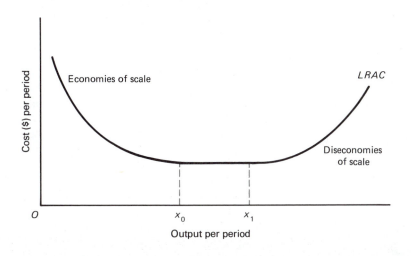

returns yield diseconomies to scale if input prices are again unchanged. This description of the connection between returns is brief, but to be more specific about the relation between returns to scale and the shape of the average cost curve requires mathematics inappropriate for this text.[2] The point is that the state of technology, expressed by the firm's isoquants, is a primary determinant of economies and diseconomies.

What makes unit costs fall as output is increased? Adam Smith gave a major reason in 1776—specialization. Proficiency is gained by the concentration of effort. If a plant is very small and employs only a small number of workers, each worker will usually have to perform several different jobs in the production process. In doing so, workers are likely to move about the plant, change tools, and so on. Not only are workers not highly specialized, but part of their work time is also consumed by moving from one job to another. Important savings may be realized by expanding the scale of operation. A larger plant with a larger work force may permit each worker to specialize in one job, gaining proficiency and decreasing or eliminating time-consuming interchanges of location and equipment. There naturally will be corresponding reductions in the unit cost of production.

[2] See C. E. Ferguson, *The Neoclassical Theory of Production and Distribution* (Cambridge, England: Cambridge University Press, 1969), pp. 79–83, for the derivation of a measure of increasing and decreasing returns. See pp. 158–63 for the relation to cost functions.

Somewhat related to specialization is the evidence from studies that have shown that as labor produces more output, it gains experience that leads to increased output per worker. Experience, or "learning by doing," improves the quality of labor. As cumulative output rises in a business, a direct result is an increase in the productivity of labor. This learning factor, discovered in the 1920s by the U.S. Air Force, is known as the *learning curve,* which shows that on-the-job experience lowers unit labor costs 10 to 15 percent each time output is doubled.[3]

The physical characteristics of related pieces of capital constitute another force giving rise to economies of scale. If several different machines, each with a different rate of output, are required in a production process, the operation may have to be quite sizable to permit proper "meshing" of equipment. Suppose only two types of machines are required, one that produces and another that packages the product. If the first machine can produce 30,000 units per day and the second can package 45,000 units, output will have to be 90,000 per day in order to fully utilize the capacity of each machine.

This example, in essence, shows that investment frequently must be made in "lumps." At the extreme, in some industries nearly all of the capital investment must be made before any production can be undertaken. Such lumpiness can lead to pervasive economies of scale. For example, suppose a railroad builds a line between two cities. Before the first run is made, tracks must be put down, stations built, and locomotives and cars purchased. To make one or one hundred trips per period, the same capital investment is needed. Investment in this case is virtually independent of the output. Clearly, the more trips made per period, the less capital cost per trip. Lumpiness in investment leads to economies of scale.

Another physical element of capital that induces economies is that the cost of purchasing and installing larger machines is usually *proportionately* less than the cost of smaller machines. For example, a printing press that can run 200,000 papers per day does not cost 10 times more than one that runs 20,000 per day—nor does it require 10 times as much building space, 10 times as many people to work it, and so forth. For this reason also, expanding the size of the operation tends to reduce the unit cost of production. A second example of how larger capital investment acts to reduce average cost can be found when pipelines are built to transport crude oil, refined petroleum products, and natural gas. Capacity or volume of a pipeline varies with the square of the radius, while the circumference is a linear function of the radius. Thus, pipelines experience substantial economies of scale, because the capacity to ship liquids rises

---

[3] See *Perspectives on Experience* (Boston: Boston Consulting Group, 1972); and "Selling Business a Theory of Economics," *Business Week,* September 8, 1973, pp. 85–90.

much faster than the amount of steel necessary for construction of a larger cylindrical tube.

A final technological element is perhaps the most important determinant of economies of scale. As the scale of operation expands, there are qualitative changes in inputs. Consider the capital requirements for ditch digging. The smallest scale of operation is one laborer and one shovel. As the scale expands beyond a certain point, you do not continue to add workers and shovels. They are replaced by a modern ditch-digging machine or a backhoe. The capital-labor ratio thus rises with output. In this case, expansion permits the introduction of different inputs that tend to reduce the unit cost of production.

In summary, two broad forces—specialization and technological factors—enable producers to reduce long-run average cost by expanding the scale of operation.[4] These forces give rise to the negatively sloped portion of the long-run average cost curve. Why should it ever rise? After all, possible economies of scale have been realized—why doesn't the curve stay horizontal?

The rising portion of *LRAC* at the firm level generally implies limitations to efficient management. Managing any business entails controlling and coordinating a wide variety of activities—production, transportation, finance, sales, and so on. To perform these managerial functions efficiently, the manager must have accurate information; otherwise, the essential decision making is done in ignorance.

As the scale of operation expands beyond a certain point, top management necessarily has to delegate responsibility and authority to lower-echelon employees. Contact with the daily routine of operation tends to be lost, and efficiency of operation declines. Red tape and paperwork expand, and management is generally not as efficient. This increases the cost of the managerial function and, of course, the unit cost of production.

It is very difficult to determine exactly when diseconomies of scale set in and when they become strong enough to outweigh the causes of economies of scale. In businesses where economies of scale are negligible, diseconomies may soon become of paramount importance, causing *LRAC* to turn up at a relatively small volume of output. Panel A, Figure 9-6, shows a long-run average cost curve for a firm of this type. In other cases, economies of scale are extremely important. Even after the effi-

---

[4] This discussion of economies of scale has concentrated on physical and technological forces. There are pecuniary reasons for economies of scale as well. Large-scale purchasing of raw and processed materials may enable the buyer to obtain more favorable prices (quantity discounts). The same is frequently true of advertising. As another example, financing of large-scale business is normally easier and less expensive; a nationally known business has access to organized security markets, so it may place its bonds and stocks on a more favorable basis. Bank loans also come easier and at lower interest rates to large, well-known corporations. These are only examples of many potential economies of scale attributable to financial factors.

FIGURE 9–6   **Various shapes of *LRAC***

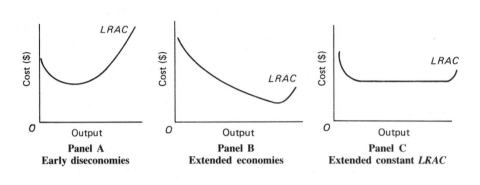

Panel A	Panel B	Panel C
Early diseconomies	Extended economies	Extended constant *LRAC*

ciency of management begins to decline, long-run average cost may continue to fall for technical reasons over a wide range of output. The *LRAC* curve may not turn up until a very large volume of output is attained. This case is illustrated in Panel B, Figure 9–6.

In many actual situations, however, neither of these extremes describes the behavior of *LRAC*. A very small scale of operation may enable a firm to capture all of the economies of scale, however, diseconomies may not be incurred until the volume of output is very great. In this case, *LRAC* would have a long horizontal section, as shown in Panel C. Some economists and business people feel that this type of *LRAC* curve describes many production processes in the American economy. For analytical purposes, we will assume a "representative" *LRAC*, such as that illustrated in Figure 9–5.

APPLICATION

Are Diseconomies of Scale a Real Problem?

We have discussed why expanding firms *could* encounter diseconomies of scale as they grow. But, you may be thinking that there are a lot of giant firms in the world, and they seem to be doing all right. And you would be correct. This is not to say that growth doesn't involve problems. Many firms that have become large and successful have had to find ways to overcome the diseconomies of size.

Let's look at a general trend in American business. Frederick C. Klein, in an article in *The Wall Street Journal* pointed out the declining role of very large companies in the U.S. employment picture.[5] The proportion of people working for firms employing 500 or more workers peaked in 1967 and declined steadily until 1979, the last year for which data were available. Moreover, total employment by U.S. companies that employed 100,000 or more remained constant from 1970 to 1980, while the U.S. work force increased 24 percent. A 1979 study by a MIT research group found that between 1969 and 1976, 66 percent of the net new jobs created came in firms employing 20 or fewer workers, and more than 80 percent from firms employing 100 or fewer. The same research group found that the number of "dying" establishments was significantly greater for acquired firms than for those remaining independent. Thus there appears to be some evidence of diseconomies for large firms that purchase smaller firms.

Klein pointed out that the blame for the laggard performance of many large corporations is focused on their structured and entrenched ways of doing things. He noted that a growing body of opinion has it that the "economies of scale" made possible by bigness often are more than nullified by organization rigidities and bottlenecks. Larry E. Greiner, a professor of business at the University of Southern California, is quoted: "More companies seem to be showing concern that their neat organizational charts don't always reflect reality and certainly don't, in themselves, overcome the tensions between autonomy and control that get worse with size."

The article went on to say that big-corporation management can't always work their wills on large and cumbersome work forces. As Richard C. Edwards, an economics professor at the University of Massachusetts, said, "Big companies tend to react slower to marketplace changes than small ones, and bounce back from adversity slower."

One corporation that is trying to "think small" is Minnesota Mining and Manufacturing Co. (3M). The top personnel officer at 3M said, "We are keenly aware of the problems of large size. We make a conscious effort to keep our units as small as possible because we think it keeps them flexible and vital. When one gets too large, we break it apart. We like to say that our success in recent years amounts to multiplication by "division.""

Even though 3M employed some 87,000 workers, its average manufacturing plant employed only 270 people. Many product management groups consisted of only five people. Despite the declining role of many of the largest firms, 3M's earnings grew almost fourfold during the 1970s, while its work force increased 40 percent. It appears that 3M has successfully overcome the problems brought about by large size by breaking its huge production facility into many smaller, more manageable divisions.

Another corporate giant is attempting to overcome the problems of

---

[5] "Some Fight Ills of Bigness by Keeping Employment Units Small," *The Wall Street Journal*, February 5, 1982. Reprinted by permission of *The Wall Street Journal*. © Dow Jones & Company, Inc., 1982. All rights reserved.

diseconomies of scale in a somewhat different manner. During 1984, General Motors made plans to reorganize its entire corporate structure. According to an article in *The Wall Street Journal,* GM was planning to consolidate its five U.S. sales divisions into one small car division and one large car division.[6] The five sales divisions would remain only as marketing organizations. Chevrolet and Pontiac would sell only the cars manufactured by the small car division while Buick, Oldsmobile, and Cadillac would sell only large cars.

According to GM sources, the idea is to restore more realistic profit centers. The various divisions, originally intended to be self-sufficient, had evolved into a hodgepodge of staff and manufacturing responsibilities that contributed more cost than profit to the bottom line. The 1984 reorganization was intended to eliminate thousands of white collar jobs through attrition. GM officials said that they could do away with the diffusion of responsibility that existed by forming two groups that would be responsible for their own cars from start to finish. They also hoped to eliminate duplication of effort and streamline communication.

The point is that GM had grown so large that the management structure had become unwieldy; and serious diseconomies had been encountered. The reorganization was a way to eliminate or at least reduce some of these problems.

Obviously, a firm does not have to be nearly as large as 3M or General Motors to experience managerial diseconomies of scale when expanding. One example of a smaller company that encountered problems with rapid expansion is Nutri/System Inc., a franchiser of weight loss centers throughout the country. According to *The Wall Street Journal,* when Nutri/System went public in January 1981, it quickly became a "Wall Street star."[7] Revenues and earnings doubled in both 1981 and 1982 and "there seemed to be no end in sight to its growth." Profit had risen from $3.8 million in 1980 to $18.1 million in 1982. But expansion brought problems.

The company made several acquisitions that turned bad, and revenues and profits from the weight loss centers decreased sharply. During 1983 Nutri/System stock fell from $48.18 to $11.25. Several franchises, upset over the high prices being charged for food, were suing the company to allow them to purchase food from alternative sources.

As the *Journal* pointed out, "Like many rapidly growing companies, Nutri/System yielded to the temptation to pursue even faster growth through acquisitions." During its period of rapid growth, Nutri/System purchased an executive placement service, a cosmetics firm, and a chain

---

[6] Jim Koten, "GM Revamp Seeks to Solve Corporate Ills that Persist Despite Rebound in Finances," *The Wall Street Journal,* January 12, 1984. Reprinted by permission of *The Wall Street Journal.* © Dow Jones & Company, Inc., 1984. All rights reserved.

[7] Virginia Inman, "How Nutri/System Developed Indigestion from Its Acquisitions," *The Wall Street Journal,* October 14, 1983. Reprinted by permission of *The Wall Street Journal.* © Dow Jones & Company, Inc., 1983. All rights reserved.

of figure salons. The purchases were based on the owner's belief that "once you know how to handle one business of the service nature and sales nature, you can handle any type business in that field."

The placement service quickly began to lose money and several of the major executives left the firm. Nutri/System's management didn't know the cosmetics business, and the people they hired to run it evidently didn't know either. They soon sold the firm back to the original owners. Furthermore, the techniques that succeeded for Nutri/System didn't work well for the figure salons. Many of the unprofitable salons had to be dropped.

9.3 THEORY OF COST IN THE SHORT RUN

Once entrepreneurs have investigated all possibilities open to them, they can decide on a specific scale of output and build a plant to produce that output at the least possible cost. In order to find out how a firm maximizes profit once a scale of operation is selected, we must study costs in the short run.

Short-Run Total Cost

Prior to investing in buildings, machinery, and so on, the amounts of all resources are variable. That is, the use of each type of resource can be determined so as to obtain the most efficient (that is, the least-cost) combination of inputs. But once resources have been congealed into buildings, machinery, and other *fixed* assets, their amounts cannot be readily changed, although their rates of utilization can be decreased by allowing fixed assets to lie idle. (Note, however, that idle assets cost as much as, perhaps more than, utilized assets.) Therefore, in the *short run* there are certain resources the amounts of which cannot be changed when the desired rate of output changes, and other resources (called variable inputs) the use of which can be changed almost instantaneously.[8]

We can show the relation between the long and short run by returning to a producer's expansion path. Suppose there are only two inputs,

---

[8] It is not quite precise to say that the inputs of some resources cannot be changed. Certainly the firm could scrap a very expensive piece of capital equipment, buy another one twice as large, and have it installed before lunch, *if it is willing to pay the price*. In fact, the firm can probably change any input rather rapidly, given, once more, its willingness to pay. The short run is a convenient but important analytical device. It is frequently helpful in analyzing problems to assume that some inputs are fixed for a period of time. Moreover, it does not deviate too much from reality to make this assumption, since entrepreneurs often consider certain resources as fixed over a period of time. You should not be overly concerned about the time factor in the short and long run. The fixity of resources is the important element.

FIGURE 9–7   **Short-run and long-run expansion**

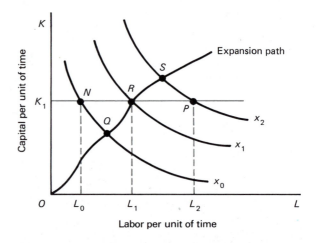

FIGURE 9–8   **Short-run total cost relative to long-run total cost**

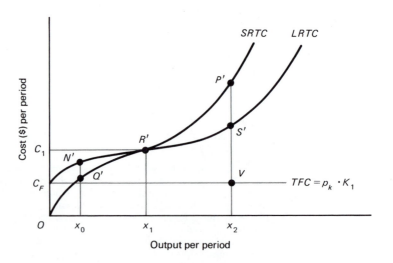

capital and labor. Figure 9–7 illustrates an expansion path with representative points Q, R, and S. These points are the least-cost method of producing outputs x_0, x_1, and x_2 in the long run. They correspond to points Q', R', and S' in Figure 9–8 on the $LRTC$ schedule.

Suppose an entrepreneur, whose $LRTC$ is that indicated in Figure 9–8, builds a plant to produce x_1 units of output. The producer should operate at point R on the expansion path using K_1 and L_1 units of capital and labor as shown in Figure 9–7. Once the plant is built, capital is fixed at K_1; if the producer decides to manufacture only x_0 units of output, L_0 and K_1 units of labor and capital would be necessary. For output x_2, L_2 and K_1 units of input would be needed. As you can see in Figure 9–7, this mix of inputs is not the lowest-cost method of operation since it is not on the expansion path. On the isoquant x_0, point N represents a higher total cost than does Q; similarly, point P is less efficient than S on isoquant x_2.

This explains why the $SRTC$ schedule lies above the $LRTC$ schedule at every point except R' in Figure 9–8. In the short run, the entrepreneur has an input that is invariant to output. The amount and therefore the cost of this input is fixed. If the price of capital is p_k, total fixed costs (TFC) are $p_k \cdot K_1$, as shown in Figure 9–8. At R', K_1 is the right amount of capital, but when more or less of X is produced, it is either too little or too much. Thus, short-run total cost is higher than long-run total cost at every point except at R'. The more output diverges from x_1, the less efficient is the input mix, and the higher $SRTC$ is relative to $LRTC$. Notice that, even if the entrepreneur produces nothing, costs are still the amount C_F or $TFC = p_k \cdot K_1$, in Figure 9–8.

In discussing the short run, $SRTC$ is always divided into total fixed cost (TFC) and total variable cost (TVC):

Definition
    Total fixed costs (TFC) are those costs invariant with respect to output in the short run.

Definition
    Total variable costs (TVC) are the amounts spent for each of the variable inputs used.

Definition
    Total cost in the short run ($SRTC$) is the sum of total variable and total fixed costs.

In Figure 9–7, total variable cost is $w_l \cdot L$, where w is the wage rate and L is the amount of labor employed and depends on the level of output.

Figure 9–8 shows both components of short-run total costs. Total fixed costs, C_F, must be paid regardless of output, and total variable cost (TVC) is the difference between $SRTC$ and TFC at any level of output. At output x_2, for instance, distance $P'V$ is total variable cost. TVC changes as output changes, since variable costs are the payments to the resources that the firm can vary with output. In summary, we may write in symbols

$$SRTC = TFC + TVC.$$

Average and Marginal Costs

The short-run total cost of production is very important to an entrepreneur. However, one may obtain a deeper understanding of total cost by analyzing the behavior of short-run average cost and marginal cost. The method used in deriving these curves is similar to that used to derive long-run average and marginal costs.

We assume at least one input is fixed and identify three distinct average cost schedules. First, consider average fixed cost (AFC).

Definition

Average fixed cost is total fixed cost divided by output. We may write $AFC = TFC/X$.

Since average fixed cost is a constant amount divided by output, average fixed cost is relatively high at very low output levels and falls continuously as output increases, approaching the horizontal axis as output gets very large. We picture AFC in Figure 9–9 along with its associated TFC.

FIGURE 9–9   **Average fixed cost and total fixed cost**

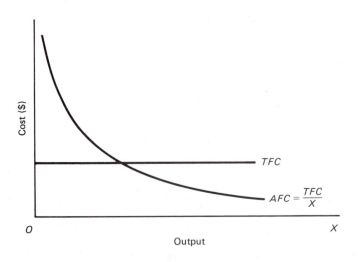

With respect to variable costs we can define average variable cost (*AVC*), a concept completely analogous to long-run average costs, since all costs are variable in the long run.

Definition
Average variable cost is total variable cost divided by output, or $AVC = TVC/X$.

Having spent considerable time developing the concept of long-run average cost, we need not spend much time deriving the average variable cost curve.

Figure 9–10 shows how *AVC* is derived from *TVC*. As is true of all "average" curves, the average variable cost associated with any level of output is given by the slope of a ray from the origin to the corresponding point on the *TVC* curve. As may easily be seen from Panel A, the slope of a ray from the origin to the curve steadily diminishes as one passes through points such as *P*, and it diminishes until the ray is tangent to the *TVC* curve at point *Q*, associated with output x_2. Thereafter, the slope increases as one moves from *Q* toward points such as *R*. This is reflected in Panel B by constructing *AVC* with a negative slope until output x_2 is attained. After that point, the slope becomes positive and remains positive. Although the U-shapes of *AVC* and long-run average cost are similar, the reasons for their decline and rise are different. The explanation for the curvature of *AVC* lies in the short-run theory of production.

Total variable cost at any output consists of the payments to the variable factors of production used to produce that output. *TVC*, therefore, equals the sum of the number of units of each variable input (*V*)

FIGURE 9–10   **Derivation of the average variable cost curve**

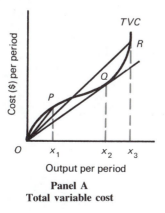

Panel A
Total variable cost

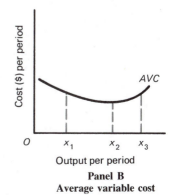

Panel B
Average variable cost

multiplied by unit price (W) of that input. For example, an output X produced by n variable inputs, has $TVC = W_1V_1 + W_2V_2 + W_3V_3 + \ldots + W_nV_n$. For the one-variable case, $TVC = WV$. Average variable cost is TVC divided by output (X), or,

$$AVC = \frac{TVC}{X} = \frac{WV}{X} = W\frac{V}{X}.$$

The term (V/X) is the number of units of input divided by the number of units of output. In Chapter 8, we defined the average product (AP) of an input as total output (X) divided by the number of units of input (V). Thus

$$\frac{V}{X} = \frac{1}{(X/V)} = \frac{1}{AP},$$

and therefore

$$AVC = W\frac{V}{X} = W\frac{1}{(X/V)} = W\frac{1}{AP}.$$

Average variable cost in the one-input case is the price of the input multiplied by the reciprocal of average product. Since average product normally rises, reaches a maximum, then declines, average variable cost will normally fall, reach a minimum, then rise—just the reverse of average product.

This U-shape is also common to average total cost. Figure 9–11 shows the derivation of short-run average total cost ($SRAC$), which is sometimes

FIGURE 9–11   **Derivation of the average total cost or unit cost curve**

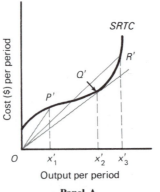
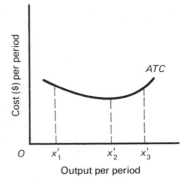

Panel A
Short-run total cost

Panel B
Short-run unit cost

simply called average cost or unit cost. As it was in the long run, *SRAC* is a ratio.

Definition
Average total cost is total cost divided by output.

Exactly the same analysis used for *AVC* holds for Panels A and B, which show the derivation of *SRAC* from the *SRTC* curve in the figure. The slope of the ray diminishes as one moves along *SRTC* until point Q' is reached. At Q', the slope of the ray is at its minimum, so minimum *SRAC* is attained at output level x_2'. Thereafter, the slope of the ray increases continuously, and the *SRAC* curve has a positive slope. It is quite important to notice that the output level x_2, in Figure 9–11 does not represent the same quantity as x_2 in Figure 9–10. *AVC* reaches its minimum at a lower output than that at which *ATC* reaches its minimum.

SRAC may also be computed as the sum of the previously defined average fixed cost and average variable cost. Since *SRTC* = *TFC* + *TVC*,

$$SRAC = \frac{SRTC}{X} = \frac{TFC + TVC}{X} = \frac{TFC}{X} + \frac{TVC}{X} = AFC + AVC.$$

One may calculate average total cost as the sum of two other average cost schedules.

This method of calculation helps to explain the shape of the average total cost curve. Over the range of values for which *AFC* and *AVC* both decline, *SRAC* (the sum of *AFC* and *AVC*) must obviously decline as well. But even after *AVC* turns up, the decline in *AFC* causes the *SRAC* curve to continue to decline. Eventually, the increase in *AVC* more than offsets the decline in *AFC*; *SRAC*, therefore, reaches its minimum and increases thereafter.

Finally, let us examine marginal cost (*SRMC*) in the short run.

Definition
Marginal cost in the short run (*SRMC*) is the change in short-run total cost attributable to a small change in output (usually one unit). This cost schedule can be written in terms of a ratio of a change in *SRTC* to a change in output:

$$SRMC = \frac{\Delta SRTC}{\Delta X}.$$

The definitions we have given for long- and short-run marginal cost are virtually identical. The concepts are not quite the same, however. Long-run marginal cost refers to the change in cost resulting from a small change in output when *all inputs are optimally adjusted*. Short-run marginal cost, on the other hand, refers to the change in cost resulting from a change in output when *only the variable inputs change*. Since the fixed inputs cannot be changed in the short run, input combinations are not optimally adjusted. Thus, the short-run marginal cost curve reflects a suboptimal adjustment of inputs.

Even though the concept of marginal cost differs slightly between the long run and the short run, the process of deriving both marginal cost curves is similar. For example, the marginal cost of the second unit produced is the increase in total cost caused by changing production from one unit to two units, or, $SRMC_2 = SRTC_2 - SRTC_1$. Since only variable cost changes in the short run, however, the marginal cost of producing an additional unit is the increase in variable cost. Thus, the marginal cost of the second unit can also be written as $SRMC_2 = TVC_2 - TVC_1$.

The derivation of short-run marginal cost is illustrated in Figure 9–12. Panel A shows the short-run total cost curve $SRTC$. As output increases from x_1 to x_2, one moves from point P to point Q, and total cost increases from c_1 to c_2. Marginal cost is thus QR/PR. As before, the slope of the tangent at point Q becomes a progressively better estimate of $SRMC$ (QR/PR) as the distance between P and Q becomes smaller and smaller. For small changes, the slope of the total cost curve is marginal cost.

As TC increases, the slope decreases ($SRMC$ decreases) until point S is reached at output x_3. Thereafter, the slope increases ($SRMC$ increases). The $SRMC$ curve is constructed in Panel B so that it decreases until output x_3 is attained, and increases thereafter.

FIGURE 9–12   **Derivation of the marginal cost curve**

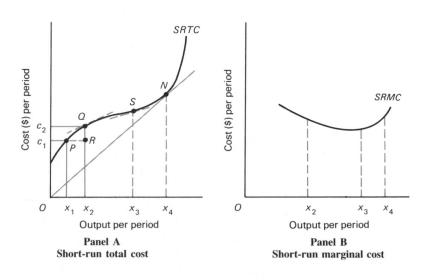

Panel A
Short-run total cost

Panel B
Short-run marginal cost

Just as average variable cost is related to average product, short-run marginal cost is related to marginal product. As before, consider the one-variable case in which $TVC = WV$. The price of the input is W, and V is the amount employed. Therefore,

$$SRMC = \frac{\Delta TVC}{\Delta X} = \frac{\Delta(WV)}{\Delta X} = W \cdot \frac{\Delta V}{\Delta X},$$

where again Δ means "the change in." But, recall from Chapter 8 that marginal product is $MP = \Delta X/\Delta V$. Therefore,

$$SRMC = W \cdot \frac{1}{MP}.$$

From this relation, as marginal product rises, marginal cost falls; when marginal product declines, marginal cost rises. Since marginal product first rises then falls, marginal cost must first fall then rise.

One final point concerning the relation of short-run marginal and the average total and variable cost curves should be noted. As already implied, and as Figure 9–13 again illustrates, $SRTC$ and TVC have the same

FIGURE 9–13   **Relation of *MC* to variable and total costs**

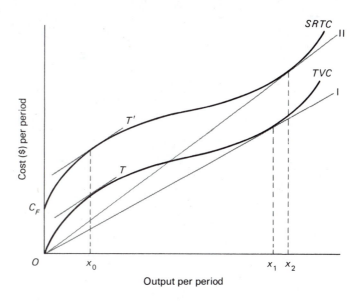

slope at each output level. *SRTC* is simply *TVC* displaced upward by the constant amount *TFC*.

At output x_0, the tangent (T) to *TVC* has the same slope as the tangent (T') to *SRTC*. Since the slopes of the two tangents at output x_0 are equal, the short-run *MC* at x_0 is given by the slope of either curve. The same holds true for any other output level. The slope of ray I from the origin gives minimum *AVC*. At this point (output x_1), ray I is just tangent to *TVC*; therefore its slope also gives *SRMC* at output x_1. Thus *SRMC* = *AVC* when the latter attains its minimum value. Similarly the slope of ray II gives minimum *SRAC* (at output x_2). At this point the ray is tangent to *SRTC*; its slope also gives *MC* at output x_2. Consequently, *SRMC* = *SRAC* when the latter attains its minimum value. Finally, as is easily seen

FIGURE 9–14   **Typical set of cost curves**

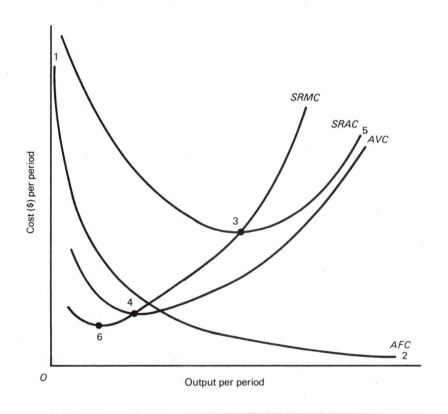

from Figure 9–13, *AVC* attains its minimum at a lower output than the output at which *SRAC* attains its minimum.

The properties of the average and marginal cost curves, as derived in this section, are illustrated by the traditionally assumed set of short-run cost curves shown in Figure 9–14. The curves indicate the following:

Relation

(a) *AFC* declines continuously, approaching both axes asymptotically, as shown by points 1 and 2 in the figure. (b) *AVC* first declines, reaches a minimum at point 4, and rises thereafter. When *AVC* attains its minimum at point 4, *SRMC* equals *AVC*. As *AFC* asymptotically approaches the horizontal axis, *AVC* approaches *SRAC* asymptotically, as shown by point 5. (c) *SRAC* first declines, reaches a minimum at point 3, and rises thereafter. When *SRAC* attains its minimum at point 3, *SRMC* equals *SRAC*. (d) *SRMC* first declines, reaches a minimum at point 6, and rises thereafter. *SRMC* equals both *AVC* and *SRAC* when these curves attain their minimum values. Furthermore, *SRMC* lies below both *AVC* and *SRAC* over the range in which the curves decline; it lies above them when they are rising.

Table 9–2 illustrates numerically the characteristics of the cost curves we have analyzed graphically. As seen in this table, average fixed cost decreases over the entire range of output. Both average variable and average total cost first decrease, then increase, with average variable cost attaining a minimum at an output lower than that at which average total reaches its minimum. Marginal cost per 100 units is the incremental increase in total cost and variable cost. Marginal cost (per unit) is below average variable and average total when each is falling; it is greater than each when *AVC* and *SRAC* are rising.

TABLE 9–2   Short-run cost schedules

(1) Output	(2) Total cost ($)	(3) Fixed cost ($)	(4) Variable cost ($)	(5) Average fixed cost	(6) Average variable cost	(7) Average total cost	(8) Marginal cost (per 100 units)	(9) Marginal cost (per unit)
100	$ 6,000	$4,000	$ 2,000	$40.00	$20.00	$60.00	$ 2,000	$ 20.00
200	7,000	4,000	3,000	20.00	15.00	35.00	1,000	10.00
300	7,500	4,000	3,500	13.33	11.67	25.00	500	5.00
400	9,000	4,000	5,000	10.00	12.50	22.50	1,500	15.00
500	11,000	4,000	7,000	8.00	14.00	22.00	2,000	20.00
600	14,000	4,000	10,000	6.67	16.67	23.33	3,000	30.00
700	18,000	4,000	14,000	5.71	20.00	25.71	4,000	40.00
800	24,000	4,000	20,000	5.00	25.00	30.00	6,000	60.00
900	34,000	4,000	30,000	4.44	33.33	37.77	10,000	100.00
1,000	50,000	4,000	46,000	4.00	46.00	50.00	16,000	160.00

APPLICATION

Refinery Cost Functions from Engineering Data

There are ways to estimate the average cost schedule for a particular firm. The two most popular methodologies employ either accounting data or an engineer's estimate of the production function. This application sets forth an example showing how the engineering approach is used to estimate short-run average cost.

An industry where the engineering technique is used is petroleum refining. A firm considering the construction of a new refinery needs some estimates for the investment (fixed) and operating (variable) costs associated with the proposed refinery. In this application, we present a simplified example of how these estimates are obtained.

At the outset, it must be understood that petroleum refineries are designed to handle a specific type and quantity of crude oil. In this example, let us assume that the refinery is designed to process 30,000 barrels per day (bpd) of a particular crude oil or mix of crude oils. The first process used in refining the crude oils is atmospheric distillation. On the basis of physical evaluation of the specific crude oils to be processed, the

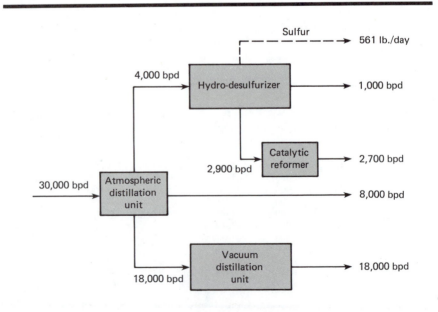

engineers estimate that this process will result in 8,000 bpd of finished products (e.g., gasoline and fuel oils) and 22,000 bpd of materials that require further processing. Part of this amount (18,000 bpd) can be processed via vacuum distillation to yield the final products. The remainder (4,000 bpd) must be sent through a hydro-desulfurizer. As a result of this process, the engineers estimate an output of 561 pounds per day of sulfur, 1,000 bpd of finished products, and 2,900 bpd of materials that require still further processing. These materials are processed in a catalytic reformer to yield 2,700 bpd of finished products. This processing flow is illustrated in the above diagram.

Given this knowledge of the production process, the firm knows what types of capital are required and the necessary capacities for each (e.g., a catalytic reformer with a capacity of 2,900 bpd). It can then use available industry sources to obtain the cost of such capital equipment. In this way, the firm will be able to estimate the capital costs associated with this refinery. Such estimates are summarized below:

Item	Capacity (bpd)	Cost (1973)
Atmospheric distillation unit	30,000	$1,900,000
Vacuum distillation unit	18,000	1,200,000
Hydro-desulfurizer	4,000	625,000
Catalytic reformer	2,900	1,800,000
Total		$5,525,000

The next task is to obtain an estimate of the variable costs associated with this refinery. These are normally calculated on an annual basis, assuming that the refinery is operating at capacity. The major variable inputs are crude oil, labor, cooling water, electric power, royalties, and catalyst replacement. Assuming that the refinery operates 340 days per year, the refinery will require 10,200,000 barrels of crude oil. If the crude oil to be used sells for $7 per barrel (1973 prices), crude oil costs will be $71,400,000. Using data obtained from other plants, the engineers calculate that this refinery will require a staff of 22 workers. Assuming an average annual 1973 wage of $18,000, annual labor costs would be $396,000. Required cooling water and electric power is determined from data on comparable refineries. Multiplying these requirements by the average current costs of the inputs, annual expenditures are obtained. Let us assume that these are, respectively, $16,000 and $14,000. Royalties are paid to patent owners on the basis of the throughput of the refinery. For example, if the royalty rate on the catalytic reformer is 4.5 cents per barrel, the annual royalty is $44,370 (i.e., $0.045 \times 2,900 \times 340 = 44,370$). We will round total royalties to $44,000 annually as shown below. Finally, catalyst replacement is also determined by the amount of crude oil processed. For this we assume that the annual expenditure is $23,000. Combining these, the annual variable costs associated with this refinery are:

Crude oil	$71,400,000
Labor	396,000
Cooling water	16,000
Electric power	14,000
Royalties	44,000
Catalyst replacement	23,000
Total	$71,893,000

Have our estimations of fixed and total variable costs produced a point on any cost schedules? Think about this; we have always defined our cost schedules in terms of one well-defined output. Refineries produce multiple products, and five distinct products are being produced from the crude oil input. What is the fixed cost attributable to each output? We do not even have a common unit measure. Sulfur, for instance is measured in pounds, while the other outputs are measured in barrels. Allocating the fixed costs of the plant will involve some arbitrary decisions.

The same problem arises with respect to the variable costs we estimated. They are plant costs, not product costs. Looking at the above table, we are confronted with a host of questions about how to allocate the costs across products. How much of the crude variable cost should be assigned to the production of gasoline? Jet fuel? Distilled oils? These problems are common in production processes. A physical plant and input quantities are seldom completely devoted to the production of one product. Most produce multiple products, making the accurate estimation of the cost schedules we have defined very difficult.

9.4   RELATIONS BETWEEN SHORT-RUN AND LONG-RUN AVERAGE AND MARGINAL COSTS

Figure 9–8 shows the relation between short-run and long-run total cost curves. Recall that the two curves are tangent at the output for which the

FIGURE 9–15   **Long-run and short-run average and marginal costs**

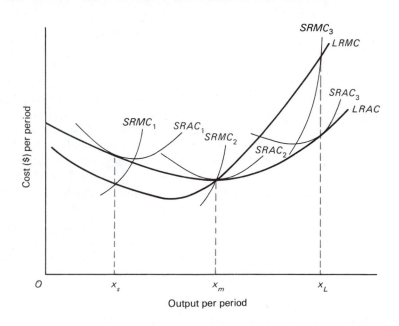

short-run is optimal. At every other level of output, short-run cost exceeds long-run cost.

Figure 9–15 shows a long-run average and marginal cost curve. Three short-run situations are indicated by the three sets of curves $SRAC_1$–$SRMC_1$, $SRAC_2$–$SRMC_2$, and $SRAC_3$–$SRMC_3$. $SRAC_1$ and $SRMC_1$ are the short-run curves for the plant size designed to produce output x_s optimally. Since the short-run total cost curve is tangent to the long-run total cost curve at this output, the cost associated with each is the same. Recall that marginal cost, $\Delta TC/\Delta X$, is shown by the slope of the total cost curve. Therefore, long-run marginal cost equals short-run marginal cost at the output given by the point of tangency, x_s, since both total cost schedules have the same slope. Finally, short-run marginal cost crosses short-run average cost at the latter's minimum point. Since x_s is on the decreasing portion of $LRAC$, $SRAC_1$ must be decreasing also at the point of tangency.

$SRAC_3$ and $SRMC_3$ show another short-run situation. Here, tangency occurs at x_L on the increasing part of $LRAC$, and $SRAC_3$ is increasing at this point also. Again, the two marginal curves are equal at x_L, and $SRMC_3$ crosses $SRAC_3$ at the minimum point on the latter.

Finally, $SRAC_2$ is the short-run curve corresponding to the output level at which long-run average cost is at its minimum. At output level x_m, the two average curves are tangent. The two marginal costs, $SRMC_2$ and $LRMC$, are equal at this output, and since the two average curves attain their minimum at x_m, the two marginal curves equal the two average cost curves. All four curves are equal at output x_m.

In the situation shown in Figure 9–15, the firm must operate with one of the three plant sizes—large, medium, or small. But in the long run, it can build a plant of a size that leads to least average cost for any given output. It regards the long-run average cost curve as a planning device, because this curve shows the least cost of producing each possible output. Entrepreneurs are normally faced with a choice among quite a wide variety of plants. In Figure 9–16, six short-run average and marginal cost curves are shown; but this is really not enough. Many curves could be drawn between each of those shown—these six curves are only representative of the wide variety that could be considered.

These many curves generate $LRAC$ as a planning device. Suppose the entrepreneur thinks the output associated with point A in Figure 9–16 will be most profitable. The plant represented by $SRAC_1$ will be built, because it will allow production of this output at the least possible cost per unit.

FIGURE 9–16   **Average and marginal cost curves**

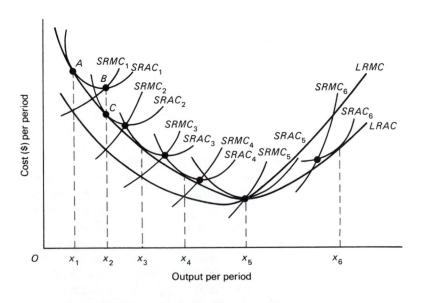

For average cost given by $SRAC_1$, unit cost could be reduced by expanding output to the amount associated with point B (x_2), the minimum point on $SRAC_1$. If demand conditions were suddenly changed so that this larger output was desirable, the entrepreneur could easily expand and would add to profitability by reducing unit cost. Nevertheless, when setting future plans, the entrepreneur would decide to construct the plant represented by $SRAC_2$ because the firm could reduce unit costs even more. It would operate at point C, thereby lowering unit cost from the level at point B on $SRAC_1$.

The long-run planning curve, $LRAC$, is a locus of points representing the least unit cost of producing the corresponding output. The entrepreneur determines the size of plant with reference to this curve, selecting the short-run plant that yields the least unit cost of producing the volume of output desired.

Figure 9–16 illustrates the following:

Relation

(*a*) *LRMC* intersects *LRAC* when the latter is at its minimum point. One, and only one, short-run plant has minimum *SRAC* that coincides with minimum *LRAC* ($SRAC_5$). $SRMC_5$ equals *LRMC* at this common minimum. (*b*) At each output where a particular *SRAC* is tangent to *LRAC*, the relevant *SRMC* equals *LRMC*. At outputs below (above) the tangency output, the relevant *SRMC* is less (greater) than *LRMC*. (*c*) For all *SRAC* curves, the point of tangency with *LRAC* is at an output less (greater) than the output of minimum *SRAC* if the tangency is at an output less (greater) than that associated with minimum *LRAC*.

9.5 SUMMARY

Economists think of cost differently than just out-of-pocket expense. Total cost must be viewed as the value of foresaken opportunities. Opportunity cost can be much larger than accounting entries. In many cases, accounting costs will not reveal the implicit costs of operation, which is another way of saying some opportunity costs are ignored.

The physical conditions of production and resource prices jointly establish the cost of production. If the set of technological possibilities changes, the cost curves change. Or, if the prices of some factors of production change, the firm's cost curves change. Therefore, it should be emphasized that cost curves are generally, although not always, drawn under the assumptions of constant factor prices and a constant technology.

We have distinguished between cost in the short run and in the long run. In the long run all costs are variable. Some inputs are fixed in the short run, leading to fixed costs, as opposed to variable costs. The sum of variable and fixed costs is total cost in the short run. Average cost in either the long run or short run is found by dividing the relevant total cost schedule by output. Marginal cost is the change in total cost per unit change in output. Marginal cost in the long run is not the same as marginal cost in the short run, because some inputs cannot be changed in the short run.

The presence of economies of scale determines the shape of the long-run average cost schedule. When there are economies the long-run average cost curve declines as output increases. Diseconomies of scale tell us that average cost in the long run is rising as output increases. There are numerous technical causes of economies. Generally, capital costs do not rise as quickly as capacity. It is also true because of specialization and experience that labor becomes more productive as size increases. Diseconomies of scale seem to arise from difficulties in communication and coordination as an organization expands.

TECHNICAL PROBLEMS

1. In the accompanying table, total product is given; you must compute average and marginal product. You are also given the following information.
    a. Total fixed cost (total price of fixed inputs) is $220 per period.
    b. Units of the variable input cost $100 per period. Using this information, complete the remaining columns in the table.
    c. Graph the total cost curves on one sheet and the average and marginal curves on another.

Units of variable input	Product			Cost			Average cost			
	Total	Aver-age	Mar-ginal	Fixed	Vari-able	Total	Fixed	Vari-able	Total	Marginal cost
1	100									
2	250									
3	410									
4	560									
5	700									
6	830									
7	945									
8	1,050									
9	1,146									
10	1,234									
11	1,314									
12	1,384									
13	1,444									
14	1,494									
15	1,534									
16	1,564									
17	1,584									
18	1,594									

d. By reference to table and graph, answer the following questions:

(1) When marginal product is increasing, what is happening to:
   (i) Marginal cost?
   (ii) Average variable cost?

(2) When marginal cost first begins to fall, does average variable cost begin to rise?

(3) What is the relation between marginal cost and average variable cost when marginal and average product are equal?

(4) What is happening to average variable cost while average product is increasing?

(5) What is average variable cost when average product is at its maximum? What happens to average variable cost after this point?

(6) What happens to marginal cost after the point at which it equals average variable cost?
   (i) How does it compare with average variable cost thereafter?
   (ii) What is happening to marginal product thereafter?
   (iii) How does marginal product compare with average product thereafter?

(7) What happens to total fixed cost as output is increased?

(8) What happens to average fixed costs as:
   (i) Marginal product increases?
   (ii) Marginal cost decreases?
   (iii) Marginal product decreases?
   (iv) Marginal cost increases?
   (v) Average variable cost increases?

(9) How long does average fixed cost decrease?

(10) What happens to average total cost as:
   (i) Marginal product increases?
   (ii) Marginal cost decreases?
   (iii) Average product increases?
   (iv) Average variable cost decreases?

(11) Does average variable cost increase:
   (i) As soon as the point of diminishing marginal returns is passed?
   (ii) As soon as the point of diminishing average returns is passed?

(12) When does average cost increase? Answer this in terms of:
   (i) The relation of average cost to marginal cost.
   (ii) The relation between the increase in average variable cost and the decrease in average fixed cost.

2. Assume that labor—the only variable input of a firm—has the average and marginal product curves shown in Figure E.9–1. Labor's wage is $2 per unit of labor.

    a. At how many units of labor does average variable cost reach its minimum?

    b. What is average variable cost at this output?

    c. At what level of output does marginal cost attain its minimum?

    d. What is marginal cost at this output?

    e. Suppose fixed cost is $1,000. What is average total cost when average product is 200 and decreasing?

    f. At the same fixed cost, what is average total cost when marginal product is 100 and falling?

3. Why do long-run average cost curves fall, then rise? Why do short-run average cost curves first fall, then rise?

4. Assuming the long-run total cost curve in Figure E.9–2, answer the following questions:

    a. When output is x_0, average cost is the ratio _____ and is (greater than, less than, equal to) marginal cost.

    b. At output x_2 average cost is the ratio _____ and marginal cost is the ratio _____ .

    c. Answer part *a* for output levels x_1 and x_3.

FIGURE E.9–1

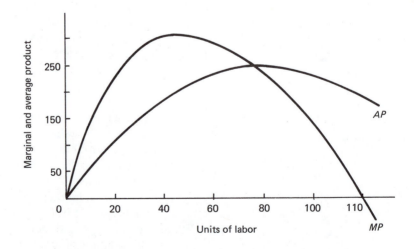

FIGURE E.9–2

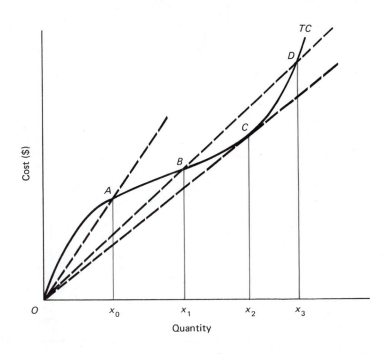

5. Fill in the blanks in the following table:

Units of output	Total cost	Fixed cost	Variable cost	Average fixed cost	Average variable cost	Average total cost	Marginal cost
1.....	$	$100	$ 900	$	$	$	$
2.....					850		
3.....							700
4.....					800		
5.....						900	
6.....							1,500
7.....			7,900				
8.....						1,300	
9.....	14,000						

FIGURE E.9–3

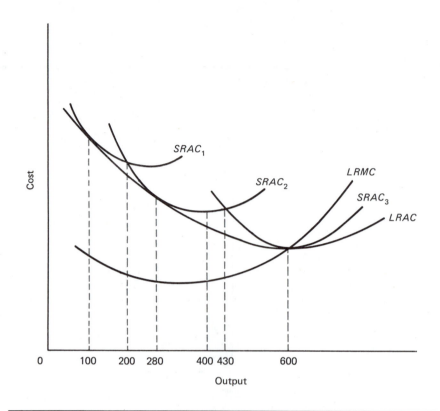

FIGURE E.9–4

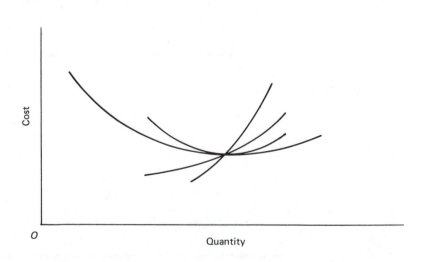

6. In Figure E.9–3, *LRAC* and *LRMC* make up a firm's planning horizon. $SRAC_1$, $SRAC_2$, and $SRAC_3$ are the only three plant sizes available. These are called plant 1, plant 2, and plant 3.

   a. Draw accurately the short-run marginal cost curves associated with each plant. Recall the relation between short and long-run marginal costs.

   b. Plant 1 is designed to produce _____ units optimally, plant 2 is designed to produce _____ units optimally, and plant 3 is designed to produce _____ units optimally.

   c. The firm would produce in plant 1 any output below _____. It would produce any output between _____ and _____ in plant 2.

   d. $SRAC_2$ attains its minimum at 400 units. Suppose there was another plant (say 4) that could produce 400 optimally. Would the average cost curve associated with this plant attain its minimum above, below, or at 400 units?

   e. The lowest possible per unit cost is at _____ units in plant _____. Why would the firm not use this plant to produce every other output since this is least per unit cost?

7. Consider the average and marginal curves shown in Figure E.9–4. Label properly the four curves, *LRAC, LRMC, SRAC,* and *SRMC*.

8. Why does short-run marginal cost rise more rapidly than long-run marginal cost beyond the point where they are equal?

9. If, at every level of output, average cost for a seller is equal to marginal cost, what can we conclude about the presence of fixed costs?

10. If average variable costs are constant, what must be true of marginal costs? Given that there are fixed costs, does the average cost schedule show that there are economies of scale?

11. Is it possible for the *AFC* curve to slope upward? Prove your answer by applying the definition of *TFC*.

12. Explain why short-run total cost can never be less than long-run total cost.

13. a. Suppose you own a commercial lot on a busy street. Your business is located on the lot. Last year your firm earned $100,000. The lot next to you rents for $30,000 a year. What is the implicit cost of your property? What is the opportunity cost?

    b. Now suppose Chris Evert Lloyd left professional tennis and opened a tennis shop that sold rackets and tennis wear. During the first year the shop was open, it earned $200,000. No payments were made to the owner. If Lloyd did not manage the shop, she could choose to continue playing professional tennis and earn at least $500,000 a year. What is the implicit cost of

Lloyd's services to the tennis shop? What is her opportunity cost? In this case, are implicit and opportunity costs equal?

ANALYTICAL PROBLEMS

1. You are the adviser to the president of a university. A wealthy alumnus buys, then gives a plot of land to the university for use as an athletic field. The president says that, as far as the land is concerned, it does not cost the university anything to use the land as an athletic field. What do you say?

2. Does it cost a doctor more to treat a rich person than a poor person? Explain. What information would you need to answer the question?

3. Suppose you could somehow measure the output of education from a college or university. Why might the long-run average cost curve at first show economies of scale? Why, after some size, might diseconomies set in? How can you account for the fact that some of our most distinguished universities are rather small in terms of number of students, while other very distinguished universities are extremely large? How do you measure "distinguished?" The last part of this question may be very difficult to answer.

4. We frequently hear several terms used by businesspersons. What do they mean in economic terminology?
   a. Spreading the overhead.
   b. A break-even level of production.
   c. The efficiency of mass production.

5. Suppose a person is trying to decide whether it is cheaper to drive a car to work or to travel by bus. How could the distinction between fixed and variable costs facilitate the comparison? What difference would it make whether
   a. The person owns a car?
   b. Depreciation of the car is purely a function of time rather than use?

6. In his book on language, *Strictly Speaking,* Edwin Newman points out one of the more famous current cliches in the English language. "If we can fly men to the moon, why can't we eliminate the ghetto?" Or "If we can fly men to the moon, why can't we improve our school system?" Or "If . . . why can't we do something I want done?" Analyze such cliches using the concept of opportunity cost.

7. Suppose you manage a business and have to make business trips of two to four days at least once a month. What factors determine the total cost of a trip? What factors would you consider when deciding whether your salespeople should travel by automobile or airplane? Are these necessarily the same factors that determine the cost of your own travel?

8. Recently, a large number of automobile makers have idled or disposed of assembly plants. Describe the factors that must be considered in making such a decison.

9. A publisher of a new novel has spent $100,000 setting the type. It is now ready to print the book. For practical purposes, as many books as they like can be printed. In deciding how many copies to run, does the cost of typesetting have any influence on the publisher's decision? Explain your answer.

10. Suppose there are a large number of producers in an industry, and all of them produce identical products which sell for the same price. Suppose the firms experience economies of scale. Would they have the incentive to expand? Why? Explain what would eventually happen to the number of producers.

11. Let us return to our application dealing with an engineering cost function in petroleum refining.
   a. Disregarding the output of sulfur, calculate the average variable cost associated with a barrel of finished products.
   b. In such an approach, maintenance expense is normally calculated as a percent of total capital cost. Would such a cost be fixed or variable?
   c. Note that fuel is not included as a cost of operation. This is because the firm does not purchase any fuel oils; rather, it simply burns some of its own output. Comment on such a practice and how it affects cost.

12. The National Association for Gardening argues that home gardens can yield big profits for a relatively low investment. Average material costs, including seeds and gardening tools, amount to as little as 10 percent of the yearly value of the vegetables grown. In 1984, a $32 investment raised $356 worth of vegetables. Is the Association counting all costs when they make these estimates? What costs are overlooked? Would you expect to see more gardens in low-income neighborhoods than those with higher incomes? Why?

13. Tickets to the Super Bowl each January are difficult to get. Suppose you are fortunate enough to purchase a ticket at the $60 window price. Aside from this price, what other *direct outlays* would have to be added into the cost of going to the game? Tickets often will resell at an average price of $500. What is the implicit price of the seat?

14. At Nordstrom Department Stores prices are high, sales and markdowns are infrequent, and advertising is minimal. But they pamper the customer with service. Frequently, a salesperson will assemble coordinated outfits from various departments of the store while their customers do errands. What kind of customers do you expect Nordstrom's to attract? For these customers is the opportunity cost of clothes high?

Chapter 10

Input Price Changes and Technological Change

10.1   INTRODUCTION

Chapter 8 showed how to determine the most efficient, or optimal, combination of inputs for each level of output. Economic efficiency, in this sense, required that the level of input usage be such that the marginal rate of technical substitution between any two inputs equals the ratio of the prices of the inputs; or for any two inputs, L and K, $MP_L/P_L = MP_K/P_K$. Two types of changes can cause the optimal level of input usage to change for a given level of output. These are a change in input prices and technological change.

This chapter first discusses two effects of a change in input prices: a substitution effect and an output effect. These effects are similar to the substitution and income effects derived in our theory of consumer behavior. We then examine the effect of technological change on input usage and on the relative shares of factors of production.

10.2   CHANGES IN INPUT PRICES—SUBSTITUTION EFFECT

In the theory of consumer behavior, the substitution effect from a change in relative prices is the change in a person's consumption of a good, holding the consumer's utility constant. We would expect the same type of effect in production theory. After a change in the relative price of

312

an input, firms would be expected to change their usage of that input, holding output constant. In production theory the substitution effect is defined as follows:

Definition
   The substitution effect is the change in the usage of an input after a change in relative input prices, holding the level of output constant.

Since the substitution effect of a change in input prices is derived holding output constant, we know that the change takes place along a given isoquant. As we would expect, when the ratio of input prices changes, firms substitute away from the relatively more expensive input toward the relatively cheaper input. The extent of substitution depends on the magnitude of the price change and the degree of convexity of the isoquant. We can illustrate the substitution effect and analyze its determinants graphically.

Graphical Analysis

In Figure 10–1, let the output level be given by isoquant X. The original set of input prices is given by the slope of isocost curve KL. Cost

FIGURE 10–1   **Changing input prices**

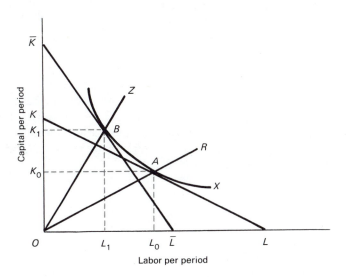

minimization occurs at point A; the firm uses K_0 units of capital and L_0 units of labor. The ratio of input usage is the slope of the ray OR, because, as we can see in the figure, the slope of OR is K_0/L_0. Now let the price of labor rise relative to the price of capital. This could occur if the price of labor rises while the price of capital remains constant, if the price of capital falls while the price of labor remains constant, or if both prices rise (fall) and the price of labor rises (falls) more (less) relative to the price of capital.

After the change in prices, suppose all new isocost lines have the slope of $\overline{KL}$; the steeper slope reflects the relative increase in the price of labor. Tangency and cost minimization must occur on a portion of the isoquant that is steeper than it is at point A. This tells us that if output remains constant, capital, the now relatively cheaper input, is substituted for labor. Equilibrium occurs at point B on X with K_1 units of capital and L_1 units of labor employed. The higher capital-to-labor ratio (i.e., $K_1/L_1 > K_0/L_0$) is shown by the slope of the ray OZ, which is steeper than the original ray OR. The substitution effect is the movement from L_0 to L_1, in the case of labor, and from K_0 to K_1, in the case of capital.

If the price of capital rises relative to labor, the isocost line becomes less steep, and efficiency would then call for labor to be substituted for capital. In general the input demand curve, holding output constant, must be negatively sloped. The firm substitutes away from the input that becomes more expensive when the price ratio changes.

We see evidence of substitution among inputs between various countries. For example, agricultural methods vary greatly from one country to another. The French insist that American farmers are extremely inefficient compared to French farmers. They point out that French farmers plant crops much closer together obtaining a higher yield per acre than American farmers; French farmers fertilize more carefully and weed much better, thereby growing larger vegetables. Americans plant, cultivate, and harvest by machine, which reduces the yield per acre. Are French farmers more efficient than Americans? Clearly, the key point is that land in the United States is cheaper relative to labor; in France, labor is cheaper relative to land. French farmers use a lot of the relatively cheap labor and try to conserve the relatively expensive land. Farmers in the United States use a lot of land and capital to save on the relatively expensive labor. Technical efficiency is not the issue in this example; economic efficiency is. Input prices determine the relative mix of capital and labor. Producers in the United States and France are simply optimizing under different cost conditions.

Relative input prices determine the *relative* input usage in production. Producers use more of the relatively less expensive inputs and less of the relatively more expensive inputs.

APPLICATION

The Effect of Rate-of-Return Regulation[1]

State regulatory agencies regulate public utilities, such as electric companies, using their authority to set prices that allow the regulated utilities to earn only a "fair rate of return" on their investment in plant and equipment. That is, if a public utililty commission regulates an electric company and follows a fair rate-of-return rule, the utility would be allowed to charge prices no higher than those that would give it a normal return on its capital investment. We can use the theory set forth above to show that rate-of-return regulation induces the firm to produce inefficiently.

Suppose the allowed rate of return is 10 percent and the utility uses two inputs, labor and capital. This means that profits can be only 10 percent of the value of the firm's capital. Let D be the depreciation of capital during a period; w and r are, respectively, the prices of labor (L) and capital (K); P is the price of the product the firm sells, X. The regulatory commission sets a price so that

$$.10 \cong \frac{PX - wL - D}{rK}.$$

That is, P is set in the numerator so that the ratio of profit to the value of capital on the right side is approximately equal to .10. The denominator, rK, is often called the rate base. If the rate base increases, a regulator allows P to increase, so the ratio remains close to the 10 percent target rate of return.

In the absence of regulation, we know that the firm would choose capital and labor so that

$$MRTS = \frac{MP_L}{MP_K} = \frac{w}{r}.$$

But, in essence, rate-of-return regulation changes the price of capital to the firm and, consequently, changes the slope of the isocost line.

When a regulated firm buys another unit of capital, the price of the product is allowed to go up in order to give the firm a 10 percent return on the capital, so the price of a unit of capital is really $r - .10(r) = r(1 - .10) = r(.9)$. The firm effectively gets a 10 percent discount on every

---

[1] The theory described here is from H. Averch and L. Johnson, "Behavior of the Firm under Regulatory Constraint," *American Economic Review* 52, no. 5 (December 1962), pp. 1052–69.

FIGURE 10-2   **The Averch-Johnson effect**

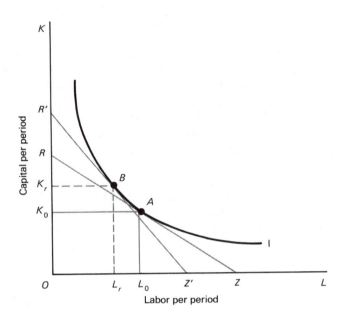

unit of capital it buys. We can easily picture what happens to the isocost line under these circumstances.

Figure 10–2 shows an unregulated firm optimizing at point A, where the isocost curve, RZ, is tangent to isoquant I. This is the efficient point of production, given prices r and w for capital and labor. The firm employs L_0 and K_0 units of labor and capital. Since rate-of-return regulation lowers the price of capital to the producer, the isocost lines become steeper. If the regulated firm produces the same output as the unregulated firm, it would operate at point B, using more capital (K_r) and less labor (L_r), since the now steeper isocost, $R'Z'$, is tangent to I at this combination. Since point A was the true cost-minimizing combination of labor and capital for this level of production, the cost of production must be higher at B than at A. Thus B represents an inefficient level of operation, caused by the distortion in the effective price of capital.

The excessive use of capital among firms subject to rate-of-return regulation is called the *Averch-Johnson (A-J) effect*. Several statistical studies have been done to determine the extent of overcapitalization among regulated firms.[2] The results are mixed; the A-J effect has been difficult to verify in the real world. Part of the problem is that regulators are slow to make price adjustments once a firm has increased its rate base. During this *regulatory lag*, the firm is earning below normal rates of return which may not be recouped. This makes regulated firms cautious about overcapitalizing. Thus it is ironic that if regulatory agencies were quicker about making decisions, the A-J effect would probably be more pronounced.

Elasticity of Substitution

How much or to what extent producers substitute among inputs, while producing the same level of output after a change in relative prices, depends on how easily these inputs can be physically substituted. For some inputs, a firm may be able to reduce its usage of one input by a specific amount, and need only a small increase in the other input (inputs) to produce the same level of output. In other cases a firm might have to increase its use of the other input (inputs) by a larger amount in order to hold output constant. Of course, the substitutability of resources at a given level of output is closely related to the shape of the isoquant—i.e., how the marginal rate of technical substitution changes in relation to changes in the input ratio along an isoquant. More specifically, the ability to substitute one input for another while holding output constant is determined by the *elasticity of substitution,* defined as follows:

Definition
The elasticity of substitution measures the relative responsiveness of the ratio of two inputs to proportional changes in the marginal rate of technical substitution, keeping output constant.

Assuming two inputs, K and L, the elasticity of substitution (σ) can be written as

$$\sigma = \frac{\Delta(K/L) \; / \; (K/L)}{\Delta(MRTS) \; / \; (MRTS)} = \frac{\Delta(K/L)}{\Delta(MRTS)} \cdot \frac{(MRTS)}{(K/L)}.$$

---

[2] See H. C. Petersen, "An Empirical Test of Regulatory Effects," *Bell Journal of Economics and Management Science* 6 (Spring 1975), pp. 111–26; L. Courville, "Regulation and Efficiency in the Electric Utility Industry," *Bell Journal of Economics and Management Science* 5 (Spring 1974), pp. 53–74; R. M. Spann, "Rate of Return Regulation and Efficiency in Production: An Empirical Test of the Averch-Johnson Thesis," *Bell Journal of Economics and Management Science* 5 (Spring 1974), pp. 38–52; W. J. Boyes, "An Empirical Examination of the Averch-Johnson Effect," *Economic Inquiry* 14 (March 1976), pp. 25–35.

FIGURE 10–3   **The elasticity of substitution and the substitution effect**

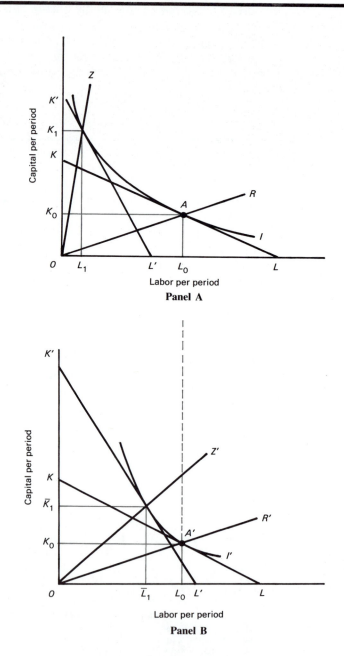

Panel A

Panel B

The elasticity of substitution can take on values between zero and infinity, depending on the slope of the isoquant over a given range. The relation between σ and the slope of an isoquant can be seen in Figure 10–3. In Panel A the slope of isoquant I (*MRTS*) at point A is the slope of the tangent line *KL*. The firm uses L_0 units of labor and K_0 units of capital. Panel B shows a different isoquant but the same *KL* isocost line. At their tangency, the slope of isoquant I′ at A′ is identical to the slope of I at A. This firm uses the same amounts of capital (K_0) and labor (L_0) as the firm in Panel A. Thus, the rays *OR,* in Panel A, and *OR′*, in Panel B, have the same slope, reflecting the same *K/L* ratio.

Now let the marginal rate of technical substitution along each isoquant change identically. In both panels, the new *MRTS* is given by the slope of the tangent *K′L′*, drawn to have identical slopes. In Panel A, the new *MRTS* decreases labor usage to L_1 and increases capital to K_1. The new *K/L* ratio is given by the slope of *OZ*.

In Panel B, the isoquant I′ is much steeper (less flat) than I in Panel A. In this case when the *MRTS* increases to that given by *K′L′*, labor usage falls to $\overline{L}_1$, a much smaller reduction than shown in Panel A; capital increases to $\overline{K}_1$, a smaller increase than shown in Panel A. The ray to the new point of tangency, *OZ′*, is much less steep than *OZ* in Panel A, reflecting a much smaller increase in the *K/L* ratio after the same increase in the *MRTS*.

We can see that the elasticity of substitution is related to the "flatness" or "steepness" of the isoquant. The flatter (steeper) the isoquant, the greater (smaller) is the change in the capital/labor ratio after a change in the *MRTS* and the larger (smaller) is the elasticity of substitution. We can also see that the size of the elasticity of substitution is directly related to the size of the substitution effect for a given change in the price of an input. That is, the larger is σ, the greater is the substitution effect.

This relation simply means that for a given level of output, σ shows how easy or difficult it is for the firm to substitute one input for another. One would expect that the easier (more difficult) it is to substitute inputs, the larger (smaller) the substitution effect would be after a change in the price of an input.

This connection between σ and the ease of substitution can be seen by rewriting the elasticity of substitution ratio to reflect the efficiency condition that requires the *MRTS* to equal the input price ratio, *w/r*:

$$\sigma = \frac{\Delta(K/L) \, / \, (K/L)}{\Delta(MRTS) \, / \, (MRTS)} = \frac{\Delta(K/L) \, / \, (K/L)}{\Delta(w/r) \, / \, (w/r)}.$$

The elasticity of substitution can be thought of as the elasticity of the *K/L* ratio with respect to the *w/r* input price ratio. The larger the value of σ, the greater the relative change in *K/L,* and therefore the greater the substitution effect, after a change in the relative prices of the inputs. If σ is less (greater) than one, the proportional change in the K/L ratio is less (greater) than the proportional change in w/r, implying substitution is relatively difficult (easy).

Elasticity of Substitution and Changes in Relative Input Shares

Elasticity of substitution in production is closely related to the change in the relative share of the inputs. We define the relative share of an input as the proportion of the *total value of output* received by a particular input. The relative share of labor, for example, is

$$S_L = \frac{wL}{PX},$$

where P and X are respectively the price and quantity of the product produced; the relative share of capital is

$$S_K = \frac{rK}{PX}.$$

The ratio of the relative shares is

$$\frac{S_K}{S_L} = \frac{rK}{wL} = (K/L) / (w/r).$$

The relation between this ratio and the elasticity of substitution is apparent. Suppose the relative wage rate increases by 10 percent (w/r increases 10 percent). At a given level of output, firms want to substitute capital for the now relatively more expensive labor—increasing the K/L ratio. Suppose the elasticity of substitution coefficient, σ, is large, meaning labor and capital are good substitutes in the production process, and the capital-to-labor ratio rises by 20 percent. From its definition, this means that σ must be greater than one, since by assumption the percentage increase in the K/L ratio exceeds the percentage increase in w/r. Since K/L increases proportionately more than w/r, S_K/S_L must also increase. The relative share of capital rises and the relative share of labor falls. It follows that anytime K/L increases proportionately more, or decreases proportionately less, than the percentage change in w/r, the elasticity of substitution must be greater than one, and the share of capital rises relative to that of labor. Following exactly the same line of reasoning, if a given percentage increase (decrease) in w/r causes K/L to increase (decrease) proportionately less than w/r, σ must be less than one and S_K/S_L must decrease; the relative share of capital falls and that of labor rises. We can summarize these observations in the following principle:

Principle

In the two-input case with output constant, when the price of one input increases relative to the price of the other, the relative share of the now relatively more expensive input will increase, remain constant, or decrease as the elasticity of substitution is less than, equal to, or greater than one.

10.3 CHANGES IN INPUT PRICES—THE OUTPUT EFFECT FOR A PROFIT MAXIMIZER

We have examined the effect of a change in the price of an input under the assumption that output remains constant. This is useful, because at any given output, the firm must determine the input combination that can produce that output at minimum cost. The most efficient combination results when the marginal rate of technical substitution between each pair of inputs used equals the ratio of the prices of these inputs. We have also established that when the price of an input rises (falls) the firm will decrease (increase) its usage of that input at any given level of output; i.e., the substitution effect of an input price change is negative.

Profit Maximization on the Expansion Path

Another decision the firm must make is how much output to produce in order to maximize profit, given the input prices, the resulting cost curves, and the price of the product it produces and sells. Only one quantity along the expansion path will be the profit-maximizing level of output. In the next chapter, we will analyze extensively the firm's profit-maximizing output decision, but the principles of unconstrained maximization, set forth in Chapter 4, enable us to give a brief preview of this decision. Recall that unconstrained maximization requires a firm to increase any activity as long as the marginal benefit exceeds the marginal cost and decrease the activity if the marginal benefit is less than the marginal cost. In equilibrium the marginal benefit of an input must equal its marginal cost.

In the case of the profit-maximizing output decision, the marginal benefit is the addition to total revenue from producing and selling the additional output from another unit of input. The increased output from another unit of input we know is marginal product. If the firm is a price taker in the market (i.e., it is so small relative to total market output that it cannot affect the product price by producing one more unit), then marginal benefit can be measured by $MP \cdot P$, where P is the constant price of the output. The addition to cost from employing another unit of input is, of course, the price of the input. Thus a firm maximizes profit by equating

$$r = MP_K \cdot P,$$

and

$$w = MP_L \cdot P,$$

for the two inputs capital and labor. Is the profit-maximizing amount of capital and labor on the expansion path? We can see the answer is yes by forming the ratios:

$$\frac{w}{r} = \frac{MP_L \cdot P}{MP_K \cdot P} = \frac{MP_L}{MP_K}.$$

The ratio of input prices is equal to the ratio of marginal products, which is the common characteristic of points on the expansion path. The profit-maximizing level of inputs is therefore economically efficient—as we would expect.

We can show that there is a unique point on the expansion path that is profit maximizing. Since $r = MP_K \cdot P$ and $w = MP_L \cdot P$, we see that

$$\frac{MP_K \cdot P}{r} = \frac{MP_L \cdot P}{w} = 1.$$

Rearranging terms by dividing everything by P gives us the condition that

$$\frac{MP_K}{r} = \frac{MP_L}{w} = \frac{1}{P}.$$

The interpretation of this set of equalities is that at the profit-maximizing point of operation, the per dollar contribution of each input must not only be equal, they must all be equal to the inverse of the product price. This uniquely identifies one point on the expansion path as the profit-maximizing output for any given product price.

The Output Effect

Since a change in input prices is expected to change the firm's cost curves, we expect the profit-maximizing level of output to change also. When output changes the firm will change the level of the inputs it uses. In addition to the substitution effect, there is an *output effect* from a change in the price of an input:

Definition

The output effect of an increase or decrease in the price of an input is the change in input use resulting solely from the change in the profit-maximizing level of output after the change in the cost structure.[3]

Consider a firm using two inputs, labor and capital, to produce the profit-maximizing level of output along its expansion path. Let the price of labor fall. We know that at the same level of output the firm will

---

[3] The output effect in production theory is analogous, but not identical, to the income effect in consumer behavior theory.

substitute the now relatively cheaper labor for the relatively more expensive capital; i.e., from the substitution effect only, the K/L ratio will fall. But what about the change in K and L after the firm adjusts its level of output?

Recall that total cost is $\overline{C} = rk + wL$. With r constant, we would expect the average and marginal cost curves to fall after a decrease in the price of labor.[4] After the decline in costs, the firm would make more profit than before at the original level of output. The decrease in costs will motivate the firm to increase its level of output in order to make even more profit.

In general, this expansion in output will result in the firm using more of both labor and capital to produce the higher output.[5] We would expect that the firm's use of labor would unambiguously increase, since the output effect causes more labor to be hired after its price decreases and, therefore, reinforces the substitution effect. But we see that in the case of capital, the substitution and output effects move in the opposite direction. From the substitution effect only, the usage of capital falls after the price of labor decreases. The resulting increase in output causes more capital to be employed and therefore offsets, to a greater or lesser extent, the substitution effect. If the substitution effect dominates, less capital is used; if the output effect dominates, more capital is used.

The effect of an increase in the price of labor is exactly parallel. From the substitution effect alone, less labor and more capital are used. The increase in the price of labor increases the firm's cost curves. The increase in costs induces the firm to decrease its output. This decrease in output results in the firm's using less of both capital and labor.[6] The use of labor unambiguously declines. The substitution effect increases the amount of capital employed, but the output effect reduces capital. The effects are once more offsetting to a greater or lesser extent. We have established the following principle:

Principle
When the price of an input falls (rises), the substitution and output effects for that input move in the same direction, causing more (less) of that input to be used. In the two-input model, the effect on the other input is ambiguous, since the substitution and output effects move in opposite directions.

---

[4] There is one minor exception to this effect. If labor is inferior over the relevant range—at higher levels of output the use of labor declines—a fall in the price of labor would cause an increase in the marginal cost over this range. This small exception does not affect the analysis.

[5] Again, the minor exception results if one of the inputs is inferior. This exception does not change the analysis.

[6] We once again ignore the minor exception when one of the inputs is inferior.

10.4 TECHNOLOGICAL CHANGE AND INPUT USAGE

We have seen how a change in input prices changes input usage. Another factor that can affect input proportions and input usage is a change in technology. Technological change involves an improvement in the state of knowledge—the knowledge of how to organize factors of production more efficiently. In terms of the production function, any given set of inputs in the relevant range can produce more output after the improvement in technology.

Technological change leads to a shift of the isoquant map toward the origin, because a given level of output can be produced with fewer inputs. This downward shift in the isoquants means that, with given input prices, each level of output can be produced at a lower cost (on a lower isocost curve) than was possible before the change in the level of technology.

Classification of Technological Change

While technological change reduces the amounts of productive inputs necessary to produce any given level of output, it can also change the

FIGURE 10–4   **Neutral technological change**

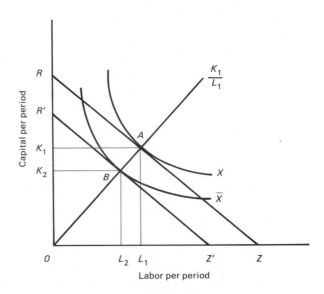

input *proportions* that are used to produce that output at the lowest cost. Technological change is classified as neutral or biased according to its effect on the economically efficient proportion of input usage.

Consider first neutral technological change:

Definition
Neutral technological change reduces the amounts of inputs necessary to produce a given level of output but leaves the cost-minimizing ratios of input usage unchanged.

Figure 10–4 illustrates neutral technological change in the case of labor and capital. Before the change, the firm produces the output represented by isoquant X. The cost-minimizing isocost curve is RZ. Equilibrium occurs at point A, with the firm using L_1 units of labor and K_1 units of capital. The ratio of capital to labor is given by the slope of the ray from the origin, K_1/L_1.

Now let technological change shift the isoquant downward toward the origin. Specifically, the isoquant X is shifted to $\overline{X}$, which represents the same level of output as X. With unchanged input prices, the slope of the isocost lines remains constant; the new equilibrium isocost curve is $R'Z'$, which has the same slope as RZ. Cost minimization for the original level of output is now attained at B, with L_2 and K_2 units of labor capital being used. Since $R'Z'$ is below RZ, this output is produced at a lower cost. But the original K/L ratio is unchanged, since the same ray from the origin passes through the new equilibrium. Because the capital-to-labor ratio remains unchanged, the technological change shown in Figure 10–4 is neutral.

Panels A and B in Figure 10–5 show biased technological change:

Definition
Technological change is biased if for any level of output the ratio of inputs is changed. For production with two inputs, capital and labor, the change is said to be labor saving or capital using if the ratio of capital to labor increases. The change is capital saving or labor using if the ratio of capital to labor decreases.

Panel A shows labor-saving technological change. Before the change, the firm minimized the cost of producing the output represented as X by using L_1 units of labor and K_1 units of capital. The ray K_1/L_1 from the origin through point A on X shows the capital/labor ratio. Technological change shifts the isoquant X to $\overline{X}$. With the same input price ratio, the new cost-minimizing isocost curve is $R'Z'$. Equilibrium is now at B on isoquant $\overline{X}$. For the original level of output, relatively more capital and relatively less labor are used. The capital/labor ratio must increase, as can be seen by drawing a ray from the origin through the equilibrium point B. The slope of this ray must be steeper than the original ray, K_1/L_1. We see then that labor-saving or capital-using technological change must lead to a

FIGURE 10–5   **Biased technological change**

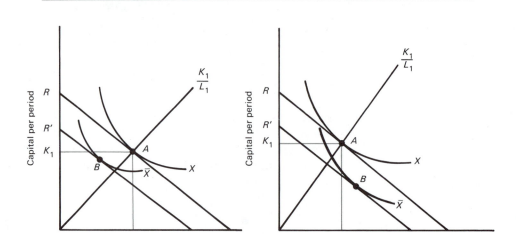

Panel A

Panel B

cost-minimizing equilibrium with a higher capital/labor ratio. In the case shown in Panel A, less of both capital and labor are used, as the K/L ratio increases. But, while it must be the case that less labor is used, the isoquant shift could be such that the usage of capital would have increased above the amount K_1. In this case the change would be extremely capital using.

Capital-saving or labor-using technological change is shown in Panel B, Figure 10–5. The original least-cost equilibrium occurs at point A on isoquant X and isocost RZ, with K_1 and L_1 units of capital and labor being employed. The ray K_1/L_1 shows the capital-to-labor ratio, as before. Technological change then shifts the original isoquant to $\bar{X}$. With unchanged input prices, cost minimization occurs at B in the figure. Drawing a ray from the origin through B shows readily that the ratio of capital to labor declines. In this case, the amount of capital declines, as must be the case for capital-saving change, but the amount of labor actually increases slightly. Notice that the new equilibrium could have occurred to the left of L_1, had the technological change not been quite so labor using. The important point in classifying technological change is not the effect on the actual amounts of the inputs used but the change in the ratio or proportion of the inputs.

Technological Change and Factor Usage

As shown in Figure 10–4, neutral technological change can decrease the amounts of inputs used to produce a given level of output. Figure 10–5 has shown that labor-(capital-) saving technological change decreases the amount of labor (capital) used to produce a given level of output, while increasing (decreasing) the ratio of capital to labor. The absolute effect on the other input is ambiguous. Even though technological change must decrease the amount of one or both inputs used to produce a given level of output, it is not clear that both inputs are used less after the level of output is changed.

Figures 10–4 and 10–5 show that all technological change reduces the cost of producing any given level of output. Because of its effect on the firm's cost curves, the resulting change in the firm's level of output may well have an offsetting effect. Since technological change causes the cost curves to fall, the firm's profit from producing the original level of output will clearly increase. The original level of output will therefore not be profit-maximizing. This is because the marginal cost of another unit of output will decline after the technological change; the output where marginal cost equals marginal benefit will therefore increase—i.e., even more profit can be earned if output is increased.

This expansion in output causes the firm to increase its usage of both capital and labor. For example, suppose neutral change causes less of both inputs to be used to produce the original level of output. The resulting decrease in cost induces the firm to increase its level of output. This effect causes an increase in its usage of both labor and capital, which may more than offset the reduced input usage at any given level of output. The total effect for both inputs is ambiguous. If the output effect is strong enough, even labor-saving technological change could cause more labor to be used, and the same is true for capital-saving change.

Input Price Changes and Technological Change

To this point, we have treated changes in input prices and changes in technology independently. This need not be the case—a change in one may lead to a change in the other.

For example, suppose we have a period of widespread capital-using or labor-saving technological change throughout much of the economy. Many industries are undertaking this technological change and are in the process of substituting capital for labor. During this process one would expect the demand for capital in general to increase while the demand for labor in general decreases. This shift in demand may well cause the price of capital to rise and the price of labor to fall. Then, as firms see the change in relative prices, they would be induced, to some extent, to substitute labor for capital in the manner discussed in Section 10.2.

We should note that, after the capital-using/labor-saving technological change, the demand for labor need not decrease because of the output effect, even though the demand for capital must increase. As we discussed above, technological change lowers firms' cost curves and induces them to expand output, and consequently to increase their usage of both capital and labor. Nonetheless, the technological change, even in this case, may well change the input price ratio and cause firms to substitute further between the resources. The extent of the substitution depends on the relative strengths of the shifts in input demand and the extent of the change in the input price ratio. In practice it is difficult to separate the effect of the technological change from the effect of the resulting change in input prices.

While technological change can bring about a change in input prices, a change in input prices can also bring about technological change. Suppose, for example, that in a two-input economy labor is becoming increasingly scarce, and consequently the price of labor is rising relative to the price of capital. We would expect firms to respond initially by attempting to substitute capital for labor to the extent permitted by the existing technology.

Firms would also be induced to undertake research and development in order to find new ways to produce, using more capital and less labor; that is, they would try to discover ways to bring about capital-using/labor-saving technological change. This effect is called induced technological change. The technological change does not come about because someone happened to discover new methods of production—firms are induced to try to find new technologies in order to conserve the more expensive input. Once again it is difficult to separate the effect of the change in technology from the effect of the change in relative input prices.

Many observers believe that a great deal of the most important technical advances throughout history were induced or brought about in response to increased scarcity of natural resources or some other inputs into the production process. Certainly the 1970s saw a great deal of technological change that enabled people to conserve an increasingly more expensive resource, oil. As oil prices rose, manufacturers found ways to make automobiles more fuel efficient and to substitute other sources of energy for oil. Many argue that the present modernization of U.S. manufacturing, in which capital is being substituted for labor, is in response to higher wage rates for U.S. labor (and, of course, to increased foreign competition).

Others have argued—and we pointed this out in Chapter 1—that the use of petroleum came about because whales were becoming increasingly scarce from overhunting in the 1850s, and whale oil, the previous source of lubrication and illumination, was rapidly increasing in price. There is evidence that a British cartel, which in the 1920s drove up the price of natural rubber from the Far East, led to the discovery of synthetic rubber in the 1930s. Some argue that the depletion of trees and resulting rise in the price of wood in Great Britain brought about the age of coal and the following industrial revolution in that country. And there are many other examples throughout history.[7]

APPLICATION

Adapting to Changes in Technology and Input Prices— The Effect of Time

During the early 1980s social critics maintained that many manufacturing plants in the United States were inefficient, compared to firms in other countries. These commentators pointed out that technology had changed, but many U.S. firms had not followed. Similarly, when gas and oil became increasingly scarce in the 1970s, the federal government began putting pressure on private businesses to convert plants from gas or oil to coal. In fact, many electric utilities were required by law (Section 301 of the Fuel Use Act) to convert from gas by 1989.

If technological change could, in fact, lower costs, why wouldn't firms adopt the new technology? If coal is a cheaper and more certain energy source than oil or gas, wouldn't total costs be reduced by switching to coal and thereby increasing the stream of profits? Why didn't firms convert voluntarily?

The stream of total profits may well be higher, but it still may not be profitable to change. The decision to change technology or the method of production is somewhat more complex than it appears. We must use the concept of present value to analyze the problem in order to see why many firms are reluctant to change technology.

To begin, let's assume that a firm is currently using a somewhat out-of-date technology. The firm owns all of its capital equipment. This plant and other equipment are expected to yield an income stream from the present period (call it year one) through the final period in the horizon, year H. The present value of the income stream under existing conditions is

$$PV_1 = \sum_{t=1}^{H} \left(\frac{1}{1+r}\right)^t (R_t - C_t),$$

---

[7] These and several other examples of such change are documented by Charles Maurice and Charles W. Smithson in *The Doomsday Myth,* (Stanford, Calif.: Hoover Institution Press, 1984).

where

> r is the relevant rate of interest.
> R_t is total revenue in period t, and
> C_t is total cost in period t.

Next, suppose the firm can purchase capital in order to convert to the new technology and increase its profits in future periods. Let's assume the revenues in each period are expected to remain constant over the time horizon, but cost in each period after the capital conversion is accomplished is expected to fall to $\overline{C}_t < C_t$. Cost remains the same during each period that the new technology is being implemented. The time of conversion is expected to be three years, and the expense of conversion in each of these years will be E_t. The expected present value of net returns over the time horizon if the new technology is adopted is

$$PV_2 = \sum_{t=1}^{3} \left(\frac{1}{1+r}\right)^t (R_t - C_t)$$
$$+ \sum_{t=4}^{H} \left(\frac{1}{1+r}\right)^t (R_t - \overline{C}_t) - \sum_{t=1}^{3} \left(\frac{1}{1+r}\right)^t E_t.$$

The decision rule is clear. If $PV_2 > PV_1$, the firm should change technology; if $PV_2 < PV_1$, the firm should continue using the old technology, unless other conditions change. Clearly, the conversion expenditures come in early time periods and are therefore discounted less than the increases in profits because of reduced costs that come in later time periods. It is easy to see that the rate of interest plays an important role in the decision.

To see the effect of the interest rate on the conversion decision, let's take a hypothetical example. Suppose a firm has a time horizon of 10 years. It discovers a new technology that can lower its yearly cost of production about 11 percent. The firm's revenue is expected to be $10 million a year over the horizon. If it does not convert, its yearly cost of production will be $9 million. If it changes technology, it can lower its cost to $8 million in each year after the change is complete. The conversion will take three years to complete and will cost the firm $1.5 million in each of the three years. Cost will remain the same until the conversion is complete. Without discounting, we can see that the technical change will cost the firm $4.5 million but will reduce costs a total of $7 million ($1 million a year) over the last seven years of the horizon. We know, however, that this is not the relevant comparison for decision making. We must compare present values.

Suppose the relevant rate of interest is 12 percent. The present value of the stream of net returns without conversion is (in million dollars)

$$PV_1 = \sum_{t=1}^{10} \left(\frac{1}{1 + .12}\right)^t (\$10 - \$9) = \$5.65.$$

The value of the firm if it does not change technology is \$5.65 million. If the firm does change technology, its present value will be

$$PV_2 = \sum_{t=1}^{3} \left(\frac{1}{1 + .12}\right)^t (\$10 - \$9) + \sum_{t=4}^{10} \left(\frac{1}{1 + .12}\right)^t (\$10 - \$8)$$

$$- \sum_{t=1}^{3} \left(\frac{1}{1 + .12}\right)^t \$1.50 = \$2.40 + \$6.50 - \$3.60 = \$5.30.$$

Since the present value of the firm is approximately \$350,000 higher if it does not change its technology, it clearly should not convert.

Next, let's assume that the relevant rate of interest is 6 percent, so that the present value of the firm (in millions dollars) without converting is

$$PV_1 = \sum_{t=1}^{10} \left(\frac{1}{1 + .06}\right)^t (\$10 - \$9) = \$7.36.$$

If the firm chooses to change technology the present value is

$$PV_2 = \sum_{t=1}^{3} \left(\frac{1}{1 + .06}\right)^t (\$10 - \$9) + \sum_{t=4}^{10} \left(\frac{1}{1 + .06}\right)^t (\$10 - \$8)$$

$$- \sum_{t=1}^{3} \left(\frac{1}{1 + .06}\right)^t \$1.50 = \$2.67 + \$9.37 - \$4.00 = \$8.03.$$

Now since the present value with the change in technology is approximately greater than the present value with no change in technology, the firm should clearly convert to the new technology.

This hypothetical example shows clearly the effect of the interest rate on the decision to carry out technological change. In fact, the extremely high interest rates of the early 1980s explains why so many U.S. manufacturing firms were reluctant to modernize, even in the face of severe competition from foreign firms.

One note of warning might be warranted, however. In the advent of a new technology firms might be forced to adapt, even if they don't want to. In our example, the hypothetical firm assumed that it could continue to earn the same revenues, even if it did not convert to the new technology. The only effect of the new technology was on costs. But, in reality, if other firms selling similar products are able to lower their costs through technological change, they may lower prices and undersell those firms that refuse to modernize. If firms that do not adopt the new technology reduce their prices to meet competition, they may not be able to cover costs. While the more efficient firms make profits, the firms that did not adapt would incur losses. If the losses continue too long, they go out of business. On the other hand, if they do not lower prices to meet competition, they could experience such a loss in sales revenues that they are forced out of business anyway. Competition frequently forces firms to modernize and adopt the most efficient technology. We will return to this point in the next chapter.

10.5 SUMMARY

This chapter has extended the theories of production and cost by considering the effects on cost and input usage of changes in input prices and technological change. We have shown that for any level of output, when relative input prices change, the firm will always substitute away from the relatively more expensive input toward the less expensive input. The extent of the substitution depends on the magnitude of the change in prices and the elasticity of substitution, which indicates how easy or how difficult it is for the firm to substitute.

There is an output effect also. When input prices change, the firm's cost structure changes and causes the firm to change its level of output. If an input becomes less (more) expensive, the output effect reinforces the substitution effect and the use of that input increases (decreases). In the case of the other input, the output effect may, to some extent, offset the substitution effect and the results are ambiguous.

Technological change moves the isoquant map downward toward the origin. Each level of output can be produced with a lower level of input usage and hence at a lower cost. If the technological change does not change the ratio of the inputs that minimizes the cost of producing a given level of output, the change is said to be neutral. If the change increases (decreases) the cost-minimizing capital/labor ratio, the change is said to be capital-using or labor-saving (capital-saving or labor-using).

While technological change generally (though not necessarily) causes less of each input to be used to produce a given level of output, the total effect is ambiguous. As noted above, technologicl change decreases the firm's costs. This decrease in cost lends to an increase in output and to an increase in input usage. The two effects are to a greater or lesser extent offsetting. Even biased technological change can cause more of all inputs to be employed when the total effect is considered.

TECHNICAL PROBLEMS

1. In Figure E.10–1, Isoquants I and II are associated, respectively, with 1,000 and 2,000 units of output. The price of capital is $6 per unit; the price of labor is $3 per unit.

FIGURE E.10–1

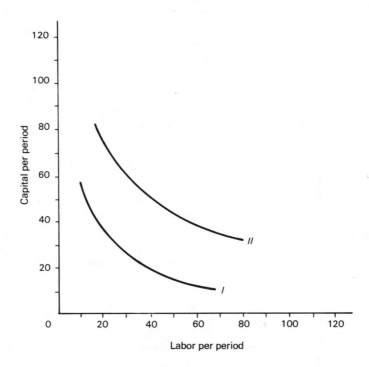

a. Construct the expansion path.
b. What is the cost of producing each level of output? Now let the price of labor rise to $6 while the price of capital remains $6.
c. Construct the new expansion path.
d. How does the cost of production change at each level of output?
e. What is the substitution effect for each input at each level of output?

2. If in a two-input production function the price of labor falls, firms substitute labor for capital.
   a. Explain why, in the case of labor, the output effect reinforces the substitution effect.
   b. Explain why, when the total effect is considered, the firm may use more capital after the input price change.

3. Why does the value of elasticity of substitution determine the extent of the substitution effect after an input price change?

4. The value of the elasticity of substitution in equilibrium on a given isoquant is three. The ratio w/r decreases 10 percent.

      a.   What is the change in the *K/L* ratio at the original output?

      b.   What is the change in relative shares, S_K/S_L.

      c.   Answer questions *a* and *b* under the assumption that the elasticity of substitution is ½ and the *w/r* ratio increases 20 percent.

5. In the application on rate-of-return regulation, we noted that such regulation increases the slope of the isocost lines and causes the firm to operate less efficiently. Explain.

6. In Figure E.10–2, the firm is in equilibrium on isoquant I at point *A*. Draw a new isoquant reflecting technological change that is neutral. Capital saving. Capital using.

7. Explain why technological change that is neutral can cause an increase in the usage of both inputs.

8. *a.* How can technological change bring about a change in input prices?

      b. How can a change in input prices bring about technological change?

9. In the section on the effect of time on technological change, we deduced that a firm would not undertake the change if the interest rate is 12 percent. At approximately what rate of interest would the firm be indifferent between the two choices? You may want to

FIGURE E.10–2

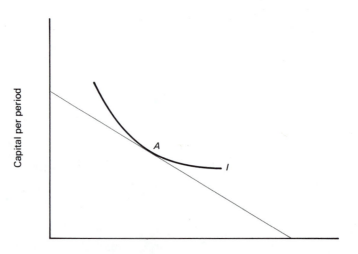

Labor per period

simply set up the problem. The actual solution involves a considerable amount of algebra.

10. Why might a firm be forced to undertake a technological change even if originally the present value of making the change was less than the present value of changing?

ANALYTICAL PROBLEMS

1. After 1973, the price of oil rose relative to the price of most other resources. Clearly, there was substitution. But can you think of any technological change that took place in response to the change in input prices? If the trend had continued, can you think of any additional changes that might have occurred?

2. If, over a long period of time, considerable capital-using (labor-saving) technological change takes place in the agricultural sector of the economy, what would you expect would be the effect on the birthrate for farm families? Explain.

3. Compare the types of manufacturing processes that would be used in a country such as India compared to the processes used in the U.S. or Western Europe.

4. In the Western region of the United States, much of the agriculture uses underground water for irrigation. As the level of the underground water falls, what would you expect to find happening to the methods used for irrigation? Explain.

5. Why would unions sometimes resist technological change? Under what circumstances would they support it?

6. In some manufacturing industries, U.S. firms are being undersold by Japanese goods because the Japanese are producing these products more efficiently. Why might the U.S. firms not wish to modernize and instead lobby strongly for import quotas on these goods? Why might unions support management in this case?

7. Define technological change. What is the difference between your definition of technological change and
   a. An invention that leads to a new product?
   b. Research and development?
   c. Innovation?

8. What kind of industry do you think is more likely to introduce technological change—one dominated by a few large firms or one made up of many small firms? Explain.

9. Suppose a large oil company acquires an electric company that has recently announced the invention of an efficient electric motor. What do you think will happen to the commercial development of that motor? Will it be delayed?

PART V

MARKET STRUCTURES

- *Theory of Perfectly Competitive Markets*

- *The Model of Perfect Competition in Practice and Perspective*

- *Theory of Price under Monopoly*

- *Monopoly Behavior and Performance*

- *Imperfect Competition*

Chapter 11

Theory of Perfectly Competitive Markets

11.1 INTRODUCTION

In Chapter 2, we showed how demand and supply interacted to determine prices and quantities sold in markets. Chapters 5 and 6 then modeled consumer behavior to establish the fundamentals of market demand. Next the foundations of market supply were developed; in particular Chapters 8 and 9 presented the theories of production and cost. This chapter explores the simple theory of the firm. We will use consumer and producer behavior as our building blocks. *Consumer demand* establishes the revenue side of a business operation. *Production theory* has been used to derive the cost conditions faced by a firm. Brought together, revenue and cost determine the behavior of a profit-maximizing business firm. This behavior determines supply for the entire market, which interacts with demand to establish market price and output. We will see, in this and subsequent chapters, an inseparable and sometimes complicated relation between the behavior of the firm and market outcomes.

Why Firms Exist

Before developing the theory of the firm, we should discuss, at least briefly, why firms exist. We pointed out in Chapter 1 that economists, for analytical purposes, divide the economy into two sectors—households and business firms. Households sell their resources to firms in exchange for income with which they purchase goods and services produced by firms.

An economy could, of course, function without firms. Some have in the past; some do today. In the past, households produced practically everything they consumed. Frontier households in the United States, for instance, were virtually self-sufficient. However, this method of production is inefficient because society loses the advantage of specialization. We could go one step further and let households specialize in one part of the production process and then trade their products for finished goods in the marketplace. This method would be more efficient than assembling all resources used to produce the household's goods under a single roof. But there would still be sizable transportation and other trading costs involved in such exchanges. People would eventually discover that these costs could be eliminated by bringing together all of the resources in one place and pooling their efforts in the production of goods and services. This system of production would give the advantages of specialization and division of labor, along with reducing transportation costs and the number of transactions made. If there were economies of scale, this cooperative form of organization would also produce at a lower cost and drive smaller scales of operation out of the industry. Historically, this method of production did develop very quickly in the second half of the 19th century. It is often referred to as the *factory system*.

Cooperation of resources does not necessarily make a firm efficient. To see why, let us take a very simplified example. Suppose four of us chipped in and bought a boat in order to become commercial fishermen. We agree to split the profits equally. Fishing is hard work and if one of us goofs off a little, we catch fewer fish than if all of us worked hard. Every fish the loafer *does not catch* costs the person doing the loafing only one fourth of the value of that fish, because its value is divided into four parts. Since the cost of goofing off is lower than would be the case if we received the full value of our product, we will goof off more, and production per worker will fall off. This incentive problem is common to any jointly owned and operated venture.

Someone would soon see the advantage of separating ownership from the operation of the business. The owners could contract with workers for a fixed amount of their labor per period in return for a fixed payment per period. Then if there was any shirking of duties, the worker could be fired. Separating the owners from the operation of the business offers a better means of control. Owners would claim any residual after the output was sold and the workers were paid, or suffer losses after all factors of production were paid. The owners, as residual claimants, could either assume the task of monitoring the workers to make sure they fulfilled their contract, or they could hire monitors, sometimes called managers, to do the job.

Firms of various types arise in an economy because they have been able to organize production more efficiently than other types of institutions. Generally, we think of the owners of capital contracting with other resources and either hiring managers (monitors) or carrying out this task themselves. While this may be the most prominent form of organization, it is not the only one. In many countries, the labor-managed firm is a frequently used form of organization; ownership and operation are purposely not separated. Sometimes, but less frequently, we find consumer-managed firms. The point here is that most production does take place in business firms. They exist because they offer an efficient way of organizing production. If some other, more efficient, way of organizing production were discovered, that organization would replace firms. Until then, economics texts will treat production of goods and services as generally being organized in the business firm.

11.2 THE CONCEPT OF PROFIT MAXIMIZATION

The fundamental point of this chapter is the way profit-maximizing firms determine their output, both in the long run and the short run. The basic analysis follows the reasoning set forth in Chapter 4. To maximize the total gain, continue producing until marginal benefit is equal to marginal cost. We will summarize the fundamentals here before going into the more formal analysis.

Profit Maximization

Our entire theoretical structure is based on the single assumption that firms try to maximize profits. That is, other things remaining the same, firm owners prefer more profit to less, profit being the difference between total revenue and total cost. This does not mean that business people seek no other goals. An entrepreneur who ignores profits or prefers less profit to more, other things equal, would be rather unusual. In any case, a firm generally cannot remain in business very long unless profits are earned. There have been several criticisms of the profit-maximizing assumption, but this assumption provides a general theory of firms, markets, and resource allocation that is successful both in explaining and predicting firm behavior. In short, the profit-maximization assumption is used, first because it works well, and second because it describes, to a large extent, the way firms actually behave.

The basic principles of profit maximization are straightforward. The firm will increase any activity so long as the *additional* revenue from the increase exceeds the *additional* cost of the increase. The firm will contract the activity if the *additional* revenue is less than the *additional* cost.

Suppose that the activity or choice variable is the firm's level of output. As the firm increases its level of output, each added unit adds to the total revenue of the firm. The change in total revenue from a small change in output is called *marginal revenue*. This term will be used so frequently in this chapter and the next that it deserves to be highlighted in a definition.

Definition

Marginal revenue is the change in total revenue per unit change in output when output is increased by a small amount.

As the firm increases its level of output, each unit of additional output increases the firm's total cost. This added cost per unit increase in output is called *marginal cost*.

The firm will choose to expand output as long as the added revenue from the expansion (marginal revenue) is greater than the added cost of the expansion (marginal cost). The firm would choose not to increase output if the marginal cost is greater than the marginal revenue.[1] Profit maximization is, therefore, based on the following principle:

Principle

Profit is the difference between total revenue and total cost. If an increase in output adds more to revenue than to cost, the increase in output adds to profit. If the increase in output adds less to revenue than to cost, the increase in output subtracts from profit. *The firm, therefore, chooses the level of output where marginal revenue equals marginal cost.* This level maximizes total profit.

We will be concerned in this chapter with the special case where the firm assumes the price of the produced commodity is fixed by the market. In other words, the firm is such a small producer, it could never cause the market price to fall by producing more. In this case, marginal revenue equals price. Suppose, for example, the firm is a cotton farm, and the price of cotton is $500 per bale. The marginal revenue from each additional bale is therefore always $500 and this does not change if the farmer produces and sells more cotton. The owner of the farm would increase production as long as the marginal cost of each additional bale was less than $500. It would not increase production if each additional bale cost more than $500 to produce.

Economic Profit

In economics the term *profit* means return over and above *all costs* including opportunity costs. In Chapter 9 we argued that implicit costs should be included in total cost. For example, if the owner manages the firm, the wages that would be paid to an equally qualified manager need to be included in total cost. Or suppose the entrepreneur has invested his or her own resources in the firm's production process. The return that could be earned from the use of this capital in its next best alternative is an opportunity cost, and consequently an implicit cost to the firm.

Economists frequently refer to the opportunity cost of using the entrepreneur's capital as a "normal return." Any return over and above the "normal" return and all other costs, both explicit and implicit, is called "pure profit" or economic profit. Suppose the entrepreneur has $1 mil-

---

[1] There is one extremely minor exception to this rule of behavior, which will be mentioned later in the text.

lion invested in the firm and the normal or going return in the economy is 6 percent per year. If the entrepreneur earns 10 percent per year, the normal profit, included in the calculation of total cost, is 6 percent; the pure or economic profit is the additional 4 percent return. In this text, when we use the term *profit*, we mean pure or economic profit—profit over and above the normal return on the entrepreneur's resources.

11.3 PERFECT COMPETITION

The theory of the firm set forth in this chapter is based on the exacting concept of *perfectly competitive markets*. Perfect competition forms the basis of the most important and widely used model of firm behavior. The essence of the model is that neither buyers nor producers recognize any "competitiveness" among themselves; no *rivalry* among business agents exists.

This theoretical concept of competition is diametrically opposed to the layman's notion of competition. Someone in business might maintain that the automobile or cigarette industry is quite competitive, since each firm in these industries considers what its rivals will do before making a decision about advertising campaigns, design changes, quality improvements, and so forth. That type of market is far removed from what the economist means by perfect competition. Perfect competition permits no personal recognition among individual firms in a market. All relevant economic magnitudes are determined by broader market forces.

Several important conditions define perfect competition. Taken together, these conditions guarantee a large, impersonal market where the forces of demand and supply, or of revenue and cost, determine the allocation of resources and the distribution of income. Our first assumption is that firms attempt to maximize profits. There are five additional assumptions that make up the model.

Free Markets

We assume that each market is free and operates freely without external controls. One form of external control is government intervention (i.e., farm crop controls or public utility price regulation). Such controls establish artificial market conditions and business firms must adjust to them. Another external control is collusion of firms to raise price and restrict output in a market. Such behavior also limits the free exercise of demand and supply.

Our objective is to analyze the efficiency of resource allocation in free markets. If the market is controlled, one may draw inferences concerning its relative efficiency, and the cost of the imposed constraint. The perfectly competitive market thus serves to measure the performance of more restricted types of market structures.

Small Size, Large Numbers

Perfect competition requires every economic agent to be so small, relative to the market as a whole, that it cannot exert a perceptible influence on price. On the demand side of the market, this means that all consumers taken individually must be unimportant and therefore cannot obtain special considerations (such as rebates or price concessions) from the sellers. There are no special credit terms or free additional services; every buyer is treated the same when markets are perfectly competitive.

On the supply side, perfect competition requires that each firm be so small that it cannot affect market price by changes in output. If all producers act collectively, changes in the quantity produced will definitely change market price. If perfect competition prevails, each producer alone sells such a small amount relative to total market sales that any change by one firm goes unnoticed. In other words, the behavior of an individual seller has an imperceptible impact on market prices and quantities, and the behavior of other sellers.

Homogeneous Products

The product of each seller in a perfectly competitive market must be identical to the product of every other seller. This ensures that buyers are indifferent about the firm from which they purchase.

To an economist, a "product" has a detailed and exhaustive meaning. When we think of an automobile, for instance, we visualize four wheels, a chassis, steering wheel, engine, doors, trunk, etc. To completely characterize the product—any product—we would have to list every conceivable attribute of the good and call that list of attributes the product. All physical features of the good would have to be listed, and items such as the location and reputation of the seller would also be included as part of the product. If any one of the characteristics differed between two lists, the products could not be considered identical.

Of course very few products are homogeneous, or perfectly standardized. For this reason, there are not many perfectly competitive markets. Even slightly differentiated products imply that buyers know who the seller of a certain product is. This leads to brand loyalties and gives sellers a degree of control over their product price. Whenever there is product differentiation, the producer can raise price without losing all its customers. Even the smallest degree of control over price is not allowed in the model of perfect competition.

Free Mobility of Resources

Another condition for perfect competition is that all resources must be perfectly mobile—any productive input must be able to move in or out of the market very readily in response to prices.

This means that firms already in the market can increase or decrease labor and capital instantly without violating labor agreements or having difficulty finding specialized equipment or a buyer for used capital. Free mobility of resources also means that new firms can enter and leave an industry without difficulty. If patents or copyrights restrict the use of some inputs, entry is not free. Similarly, if vast investment outlays are required, the entry of a new producer into an industry may be difficult. In short, free mobility of resources requires free and easy entry and exit of firms into and out of an industry, another condition very difficult to realize in practice.

Perfect Knowledge about Markets

Consumers, producers, and resource owners must know everything about a market if it is to be perfectly competitive. If consumers are not fully cognizant of prices, they might buy at higher prices when lower ones are available. Similarly, if laborers are not aware of the wage rates offered, they may not sell their labor services to the highest bidder. Finally, producers must know costs as well as price in order to attain the most profitable rate of output.

Conclusion

The discussion to this point can be summarized by the following:

Principle
Perfect competition is an economic model of an unimpeded market possessing the following characteristics: each economic agent is so small relative to the market that it can exert no perceptible influence on price; the product is homogeneous; there is free mobility of all resources, including free and easy entry and exit of business firms into and out of an industry; and all economic agents in the market possess perfect knowledge.

These requirements should convince us that no market has been or can be perfectly competitive. Even in agriculture, where most of the requirements are frequently satisfied, perfect knowledge does not exist. We might ask why such a palpably unrealistic model should be considered at all.

For our purposes, the answer is brief. First, generality can be achieved only by means of abstraction. We stressed in Chapter 1 that no theory can be *perfectly* descriptive of *real-world* phenomena. The more accurately a theory describes one specific real-world case, the less accurately it describes all others. In any area of thought, a theoretician does not select assumptions on the basis of their presumed correspondence to reality. For example, physicists often assume away friction even though a frictionless world is incomprehensible; and chemists analyze, as a matter of course, the chemical reactions between two compounds without considering the role of impurities—though impurities are always present. The conclusions of theory, not the assumptions, are tested against reality.

This leads to a second point of great, if somewhat pragmatic, importance. The conclusions derived from the model of perfect competition have permitted accurate explanation and prediction of real-world phenomena. That is, perfect competition frequently works as a theoretical model of economic processes even though it does not accurately describe any specific industry.[2] The most persuasive evidence supporting this assertion is the fact that, despite the proliferation of more sophisticated models of economic behavior, economists today probably use the model of perfect competition in their research more than any other model.

11.4 DEMAND FACING A PERFECTLY COMPETITIVE FIRM

Recall from our previous analysis of consumer behavior that a demand schedule is a list of prices and quantities that would be purchased by a consumer or a group of consumers at each price on the list per period of time. Demand curves are generally assumed to be downward sloping. But a perfectly competitive firm sees its demand curve in a much different way.

Demand for a Price Taker

This difference follows from two of our assumptions about competitive firms—each firm produces a homogeneous product and each firm is very small relative to the size of the total market for the product. Since no firm, acting alone, can affect market price, each firm takes as given the market price set by total industry supply and demand. Any firm can sell all it wants at the going market price. If the market price of the product is $10 each, then the marginal revenue from each additional unit sold is $10. The marginal revenue curve is therefore a horizontal line at $10. Such a curve is shown in Figure 11–1; marginal revenue equals the price, $10, at any relevant output.

The horizontal marginal revenue curve at the market price is called the *demand* for the product of a perfectly competitive firm. We call this demand because any single firm can sell all it wants at marginal revenue or the market price. The demand curve faced by the entire market for the commodity remains downward sloping.

---

[2] Furthermore, the assumptions do not imply that the model of perfect competition is not relevant in predicting the consequence of a disturbance in an economy containing industries that comprise a few interdependent firms (economists call such industries oligopolistic). The competitive model is a useful approach to many problems in which the conditions differ from the assumptions set forth here.

FIGURE 11–1   **Marginal revenue (demand) facing a perfectly competitive firm**

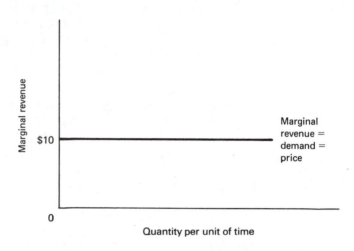

FIGURE 11–2   **Derivation of demand for a perfectly competitive firm**

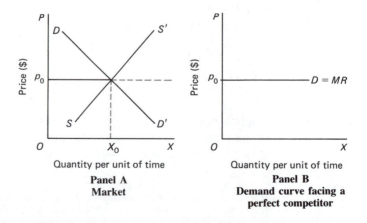

We use Figure 11–2 to illustrate the full picture. Panel A shows the equilibrium price and quantity in the market. Equilibrium price is p_0 and quantity is X_0. The demand curve for any firm in this perfectly competitive industry is shown in Panel B. Each producer knows that changes in the firm's volume of output will have no perceptible effect on the market price. A change in the rate of sales per period of time will change the firm's revenue, but will not affect the market price. The producer's perception is that any number of units per period of time can be sold at the market equilibrium price. If the firm charges a higher price, it could sell nothing. A lower price would result in a needless loss of revenue. This is why we say perfectly competitive firms are *price takers*.

When the demand curve is horizontal, it is perfectly elastic. In Chapter 2, elasticity of demand was defined as the ratio of the percentage change in sales to the percentage change in price. If a competitive firm with a hardly measurable share of total market sales lowered price a very small amount, it could immediately capture all the sales in the market. Products are identical and consumers have perfect information. So every consumer would buy from the lowest priced seller. From the definition of elasticity, this means the percentage change in sales would be virtually infinite for any small change in price. In general we know that demand elasticity depends on the number and closeness of substitutes. As the number of close substitutes increases, a firm's demand curve must become more sensitive to a change in price. The product of a perfectly competitive firm has perfect substitutes, since the products of all other firms in the market are identical. We would expect then that the demand elasticity for a firm's output would be infinite.

The results of this section may be summarized as follows:

Relation

The demand curve facing a producer in a perfectly competitive market is a horizontal line at the level of the market equilibrium price. The output decisions of the seller do not affect market price. In this case, the demand and marginal revenue curves are identical (that is, $D = MR$); demand is perfectly elastic, and the coefficient of price elasticity approaches infinity.

Average Revenue

Frequently, the demand curve of a firm is referred to as an *average revenue curve*. This is true for perfectly competitive firms, as well as firms that do not meet the requirements of perfect competition. At any price, say p_0, the demand curve tells a seller how much can be sold at that price, and therefore total revenue, where total revenue is

$$TR = p_0 \cdot x_0.$$

Average revenue (AR) is simply total revenue divided by total sales so

$$AR = \frac{TR}{x_0} = \frac{p_0 \cdot x_0}{x_0} = p_0.$$

Average revenue is always equal to price. For any quantity, a demand curve reveals the highest price at which the entire amount can be sold. This is simply the average revenue for that quantity.

11.5 SHORT-RUN PROFIT MAXIMIZATION

Let us turn now to the output decision of a firm in the short run. In the short run, the firm has fixed costs, expenses that must be paid regardless of output, and variable costs that vary with the level of output. In the short run, the firm, given its production function and the prices of inputs, must make two decisions. The first decision is whether to continue producing or to close down. If the first decision is to keep producing, the second decision concerns the proper level of output. We analyze these decisions first with a numerical example and then show how they are made with a graph.

Numerical Example

Suppose a hypothetical firm faces the short-run cost situation shown in Table 11–1. The given market price of the firm's product is $42 per unit, and thus the marginal revenue schedule for each unit produced and sold is $42. From the marginal cost schedule shown in column (7), we see that, if the firm produces at all, it will produce eight units of output. That is, each

TABLE 11–1   **Short-run costs**

(1) Rate of output and sales (units)	(2) Fixed cost	(3) Variable cost	(4) Total cost	(5) Average variable cost	(6) Average total cost	(7) Marginal cost
0	$30.00	$ —	$ 30.00	$ —	$ —	$ —
1	30.00	5.00	35.00	5.00	35.00	5.00
2	30.00	15.00	45.00	7.50	22.50	10.00
3	30.00	30.00	60.00	10.00	20.00	15.00
4	30.00	50.00	80.00	12.50	20.00	20.00
5	30.00	75.00	105.00	15.00	21.00	25.00
6	30.00	105.00	135.00	17.50	22.50	30.00
7	30.00	140.00	170.00	20.00	24.29	35.00
8	30.00	180.00	210.00	22.50	26.25	40.00
9	30.00	225.00	255.00	25.00	28.33	45.00
10	30.00	275.00	305.00	27.50	30.50	50.00

additional unit of output through eight units adds less to cost than the marginal revenue received for that unit. The firm would not produce the ninth unit, which adds $45 to cost but only $42 to revenue. The total profit in this case is $8 \times \$42 = \$336$ minus a total cost of $210. This yields a profit of $126 for the period. Since the entrepreneur's opportunity cost is included in the total cost of production, the $126 represents an "above-normal" profit, sometimes called "pure" profit or "economic" profit. In any case, it represents a return over the opportunity cost of all resources. The reader should verify arithmetically that $126 is the maximum obtainable profit.

Now let price fall to $33. Using the same profit-maximizing rule of increasing output as long as marginal revenue exceeds marginal cost, we see that the profit-maximizing output is now six units. With total revenue of $6 \times \$33 = \$198$ and a total cost of $135, the firm earns a diminished profit of $63. It is still an above-normal return, but profits have fallen because price has fallen.

Finally, let us assume that market price decreases to $12. Marginal revenue exceeds price for each of the first two units of production. The third unit costs $15 to produce. Therefore, if the firm produces at all, it will produce two units. Total revenue is $24; total cost is $45, resulting in a loss of $21. Should the firm produce at this loss? The answer is yes, because the $21 loss is $9 less than the $30 fixed cost that would have to be paid if the firm closed down in the short run. In other words, if the firm produces nothing in the short run, revenue is zero, and cost is $30. By producing two units and selling them at $12 each, the $24 would cover all of the $15 variable cost, leaving $9 left over to apply to fixed cost. The net loss is only $21, compared to a loss of $30 at zero production. The reader should verify that the $21 loss is the minimum loss possible at a price of $12.

The firm would not and could not go on for a very long period of time suffering a loss in each period. In the long run, the firm would leave the industry if it could not cover costs, including opportunity cost, at any level of output. Or it would change its short-run situation if all costs could be covered at some optimal level of output in the long run. We will postpone long-run analysis until we analyze the short-run situation graphically.

APPLICATION

Decision Making and Fixed Costs at the Margin

Many businesses occasionally face the decision of whether to extend their operating hours. For example, restaurants that are open 16 hours a day may be thinking about staying open all night. Stores might be extending the number of evenings they stay open. To increase profits service stations could change the number of hours they operate. What factors influence the decision to stay open additional hours?

The answer is deceptively simple. The manager should compare the expected marginal revenue with the expected marginal cost of staying open. *Fixed costs are not spread over the additional hours of operation.* They are irrelevant to decisions at the margin and all decisions made in the short run. To illustrate how hard it is to ignore fixed costs, the following problem was put to the readers of *Business Week* some years ago.[3]

Problem: Should Continental Airlines run an extra daily
                flight from city X to city Y?

Facts: Average total cost of the flights—$4,500.
              Marginal cost of the flight—$2,000.
              Marginal revenue from the flight—$3,100.

On the surface it appears the flight should not be run since the increase in revenue is less than the average total cost of running the flight. But average total cost includes some allocated fixed costs. The decision should be to run the flight. The marginal revenue from the additional flight will be $3,100, while the marginal cost will be $2,000. Continental's income will therefore increase $1,100. Average cost is irrelevant in the decision, because the fixed costs of $4,500 − $2,000 = $2,500 must be paid whether the flight is scheduled or not. Regardless of the fixed cost, the marginal changes are all that matter. Fixed costs should be ignored.

Decision makers in government should and do make decisions based on marginal analysis and ignore fixed costs. Even in the military, if a weapon or piece of equipment does not prove satisfactory in combat, the Pentagon is frequently quick to drop the defective equipment and develop replacements—ignoring the costs already sunk into the equipment. Two such examples are the M-14 rifle and the M-1 tank.

According to a column by Lynn Ashby,[4] the M-14 was a remarkable rifle on the firing range: "It could fire semi-automatically, automatically . . . shoot around corners, under rocks, [and] through walls." The problem was it could not function in combat. Any dampness or dust turned it into a good club. After discovering that the M-14 was too delicate for combat, the Pentagon junked millions of them in favor of the M-16, which, unfortunately is so sophisticated that it breaks down even more easily.

According to Ashby, the M-1 tank can "roll, fire, turn around, leap, sleep five [people], and dance backward." It was a magnificent piece of equipment, except that its computers and calculators kept failing and the crews

---

[3] "Airline Takes the Marginal Route," *Business Week*, April 20, 1963, pp. 111–14.

[4] L. Ashby, "'Bellbottoms' Return May Ring in New Pentagon Era," *Houston Post*, August 6, 1981, p. 1B.

could not fix them. It was simply no good in a war and was, therefore, discarded in favor of another tank.

We might say that these mistakes should not have been made. But, once the mistakes are discovered, the governmental agency responsible should ignore the dollars already sunk in the project and decide what to do, not on the basis of what is wasted, but on the marginal benefits and costs of future activities and undertakings. Once equipment is shown to be unsatisfactory, it might be more costly to remedy the existing problems than to develop new equipment. This was the choice faced by the military.

Graphical Exposition of Short-Run Equilibrium

Figure 11–3 shows a set of typical short-run cost curves; marginal cost (*SRMC*), average total cost (*SRAC*), and average variable cost (*AVC*). Average fixed cost is omitted for convenience, and because it is irrelevant for decision making. The given market price is p_0. Therefore, marginal revenue is the horizontal line at p_0. The firm produces where short-run marginal cost equals marginal revenue, point E on the demand curve. Producing another unit would add more to costs than the firm would

FIGURE 11–3   **Short-run equilibrium**

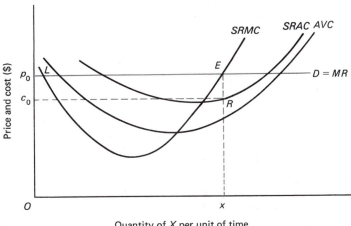

Quantity of X per unit of time

receive from the sale of that unit; hence going beyond x units would mean MC exceeds MR. The firm would not stop short of output x, however, since at lesser outputs, producing another unit adds more to revenue than to cost; therefore, for all units less than x, MR exceeds $SRMC$. Total cost in the figure is the area Oc_0Rx; total revenue is the area Op_0Ex; profit is the difference, the area c_0p_0ER. The firm makes a positive profit over and above opportunity cost.

Note that, at point L in Figure 11–3, marginal cost also equals price. That is not, however, a point of equilibrium. The firm would never choose to produce this output under the circumstances depicted. In the first place, average cost exceeds price at this output so losses would occur, whereas at some other outputs profits could be realized. Second, the firm could clearly gain by producing an additional unit. Price is greater than marginal cost for the next unit of output; thus, the firm would be motivated to increase output.[5]

Profit, Loss, and the Firm's Short-Run Supply Curve

The equality of price and short-run marginal cost guarantees either that profit is maximized or losses are minimized. Whether a profit is made or a loss incurred can be determined only by comparing price and average total cost at the equilibrium rate of output. If price exceeds average total cost, the entrepreneur enjoys a short-run profit; on the other hand, if average cost exceeds price, a loss is suffered.

Figure 11–4 illustrates four possible short-run situations for the firm. First, the market-established price may be p_1; the firm settles at point A where $SRMC = p_1$, produces x_1 units, and, since $SRAC$ is less than price, the firm receives a profit. Second, market price may be p_2. $SRMC$ now equals price at point B and the firm produces x_2 units. Since B is the lowest point on $SRAC$, the firm makes neither profit nor loss, but it does cover opportunity cost, which is included in $SRAC$. Third, if price is p_3, the firm produces x_3 units; price equals $SRMC$ at C. Because average cost is greater than price at this output, total cost is greater than total revenue, and the firm suffers a loss. That loss is CR times x_3 units.

When demand is $D_3 = MR_3$, there is no way the firm can earn a profit. At every output level, average total cost exceeds price. If output were smaller or greater than x_3 units per period of time, the loss would be greater. The firm would not necessarily close down in the short run, even though losses result. A firm incurring a loss in the short run will continue to produce if, and only if, it loses less by producing than by closing the plant entirely. Remember, there are two types of costs in the short run:

---

[5] Economists say that $SRMC = P$ is the *necessary*, or first-order condition for profit maximization and that the second-order condition is that where $SRMC = P$, $SRMC$ must be positively sloped. The two conditions together are *necessary* and *sufficient* for profit maximization.

FIGURE 11–4   **Profit, loss, or ceasing production in the short run**

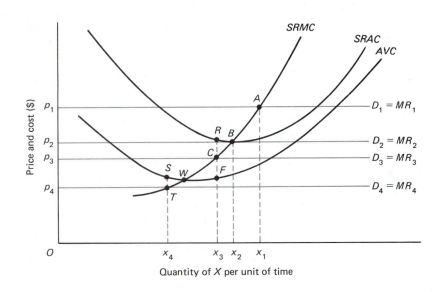

fixed costs and variable costs. The fixed costs cannot be changed and are incurred whether the plant is operating or not. Fixed costs are unavoidable in the short run and are the same at zero output as at any other level of production.

Therefore, at zero output, total revenue would be zero and total cost would be the total fixed cost. The loss would be the amount of total fixed costs. If the firm can produce where $SRMC = MR$ and if at this output total revenue is greater than total variable cost, a smaller loss is suffered when production takes place. The firm covers all of its variable cost and some revenue is left over to cover part of fixed cost. The loss is that part of fixed cost not covered and is clearly less than the entire fixed cost.

Returning to Figure 11–4, one can see more easily why the firm in the short run would produce at C and not shut down. The firm loses CR dollars per unit produced. Variable cost is not only covered but there is an excess of CF dollars per unit sold. The excess of price over average variable cost, CF, can be applied toward fixed costs. Thus, not all of the fixed costs are lost, as would be the case if production were discontinued.

Suppose that market price is p_4; demand is given by $D_4 = MR_4$. If the firm produces, its equilibrium would be at T where $SRMC = p_4$. Output would be x_4 units per period of time. Here, the average variable cost of production exceeds price. The firm would lose all of its fixed costs and also lose ST dollars per unit on its variable costs. The firm could improve its earnings situation by producing nothing and losing only fixed cost. When price is below average variable cost at every level of output, the short-run equilibrium output is zero.

Losses similar to *ST* would occur whenever the market price fell below the minimum point on the average variable cost curve, point *W* in Figure 11–4. If price is less than the minimum average variable cost, the loss-minimizing output is zero; frequently minimum *AVC* is called the *shut-down* point of a firm. For price equal to or greater than minimum average variable cost, the firm should continue to operate with equilibrium output determined by the intersection of marginal cost and price. For a perfectly competitive firm we have the following summary of our discussion so far:

Principle
(1) Marginal cost tells *how much* to produce, given the choice of a positive output; the firm produces the output for which $SRMC = P$. (2) Average variable cost tells *whether* to produce; the firm ceases to produce if price falls below minimum *AVC*. (3) Average total cost tells how much profit or loss is made if the firm decides to produce; profit equals the difference between *P* and *SRAC* multiplied by the quantity produced and sold.

APPLICATION

How Long Can a Firm Suffer Losses?

In our discussion of the short-run decisions of competitive firms, we emphasized that firms should continue producing, even though they are making losses, so long as price exceeds average variable cost. We also noted that such situations cannot continue forever. The firm must either go out of business or find some way to eliminate the losses. For many firms, however, this period of making negative profits can be rather long.

A good example of such a situation was provided in *The Wall Street Journal*.[6] According to the *Journal*, Massey-Ferguson Ltd., a Canadian farm equipment firm, reported losses every year from 1978 through 1983 (when it lost more than $41 million). A spokesman for the company was somewhat optimistic about 1984, partly because of the forecasted improvement in the farm-equipment market. However, even he was not looking for a major resurgence.

The primary reason for the company's guarded optimisim was the effort being made to improve Massey-Ferguson's productivity. In 1984, Massey-

---

[6] "Massey-Ferguson 'Hopes' for Return to Profitability in '84," *The Wall Street Journal*, January, 1984. Reprinted by permission of *The Wall Street Journal*. © Dow Jones & Company, Inc., 1984. All rights reserved.

Ferguson's management was beginning to think of the firm more as a *marketer* of farm machinery than as a *manufacturer*. Although the company was still making large numbers of tractors and harvesters, its implements were increasingly being manufactured by other firms. It had cut its own work force from 58,000 in 1978 to 25,000 in 1983, and its capital assets had declined from $2.57 billion to $1.64 billion over the same period.

These reductions in cost were brought about by the company purchasing many of its component parts overseas, since it could buy them more cheaply than it could make them. They also entered into joint manufacturing ventures with other Canadian firms.

This adjustment process illustrates two points we have made in this chapter. First, Massey-Ferguson continued to operate for a long time—five years—while making substantial losses. It must have been at least covering its average variable costs during this period. In this case the short run lasted for a considerable period of time.

Second, Massey-Ferguson adjusted its scale in the long run in order to attain a more optimal (and they hoped a profitable) size. In this case, it is clear that the company management felt that its former scale of operation was much too large for efficient operation.

Short-Run Supply of the Firm

Using the concepts just discussed, it is possible to derive the short-run supply curve of an individual firm in a perfectly competitive market. The process is illustrated in Figure 11–5. Panel A shows the marginal cost curve of a firm for rates of output greater than those associated with minimum average variable cost. Suppose market price is p_1, the corresponding equilibrium rate of output is x_1. Now, find on Panel B the point associated with the coordinates p_1, x_1. Label this point S_1; it represents the quantity supplied at price p_1.

Next, suppose price is p_2. In this case, equilibrium output would be x_2. Plot the point associated with the coordinates p_2, x_2 on Panel *B*—it is labeled S_2. Similarly, other equilibrium quantities supplied can be determined by postulating other market prices (for example, price p_3 leads to output x_3 and point S_3 in Panel B). Connecting all the points so generated, one obtains the short-run supply curve of the firm—the curve labeled S in Panel B. By construction, the S curve is precisely the same as the short-run marginal cost curve. The following is thus established:

Principle

The short-run supply curve of a firm in perfect competition is precisely its short-run marginal cost curve for all rates of output equal to or greater than the rate of

FIGURE 11–5   **Derivation of the short-run supply curve of an individual producer in perfect competition**

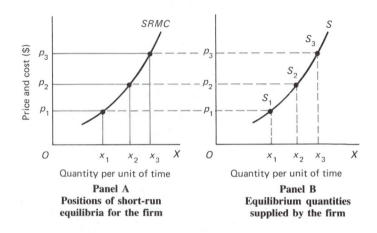

Panel A
**Positions of short-run
equilibria for the firm**

Panel B
**Equilibrium quantities
supplied by the firm**

output associated with minimum average variable cost. For market prices lower than minimum average variable cost, equilibrium quantity supplied is zero.

Short-Run Industry Supply Curve

In earlier chapters it was shown that market demand is simply the horizontal sum of the demand curves of all buyers in the market. The derivation of the short-run market supply curve is similar, but is complicated by the possible change in input prices as market output rises.

As you will recall from Chapter 9, the short-run marginal cost curve of a firm is derived under the assumption that the unit prices of the variable inputs are fixed. This seems a reasonable assumption under perfect competition, because one firm is usually so small (relative to all users of the resource) that variations in its rate of purchase will not affect the market price of the resource.

When *all* producers in an industry *simultaneously* expand output, there may be a marked effect on the resource market. For example, one small cotton textile manufacturer could expand production without affecting the world price of raw cotton. The relatively few additional bales purchased would not have a significant effect on the total demand for raw cotton. If all textile manufacturers in the United States simultaneously attempt to expand output by 10 percent, however, the demand for cotton would probably increase substantially, and the resulting increase in the price of cotton would be significant. When all manufacturers attempt to increase output, raw cotton prices would therefore be bid up; and the increase in the price of a variable factor of production (raw cotton) would cause an upward shift in all firms' cost curves, including marginal cost.

As a consequence, the industry supply curve usually cannot be obtained by horizontally summing the marginal cost curves of all producers. As industry output expands, some input prices normally increase, thereby shifting each marginal cost curve upward and to the left. We may generally presume that the industry supply curve is somewhat more steeply sloped and, therefore, somewhat less elastic when input prices increase in response to an increase in industry output. Without more information on how much input prices increase, it is impossible to be more precise. Nonetheless, doubt is not cast on the basic fact that, in the short run, quantity supplied varies directly with price. The latter is all one needs to draw a positively sloped market supply curve.

11.6 LONG-RUN EQUILIBRIUM OF A COMPETITIVE FIRM

In the short run, the firm is limited by past decisions. In the long run all inputs are variable and the firm is not bound by the past. The long run represents a planning stage. A firm operating in the short run may be at a scale where it is not obtaining maximum possible profits or it may be in a stage prior to entry into the industry. It would then readjust its scale in the long run. Once plans have congealed and some fixed resources are committed, the firm operates in the short run, and continues to do so until it makes another long-run change in the scale of operation.

Profit Maximization in the Long Run

In the long run, just as in the short run, the firm attempts to maximize profits by setting marginal cost equal to marginal revenue. In this case, however, there are no fixed costs; all costs are variable. As before, the firm takes a market-determined commodity price as given. This market price is also the firm's marginal revenue. As above, the firm would increase output as long as the marginal revenue from each additional unit is greater than the marginal cost of that unit, and would not produce more when marginal cost exceeded marginal revenue.

To illustrate, let us take the long-run situation shown in Table 11–2. In deciding the size plant to build, the entrepreneur attempts to achieve maximum profit—the difference between the total receipts from selling the product (total revenue) and the total cost of producing it. The third and fourth columns of Table 11–2 show the long-run revenue and cost schedules of a hypothetical firm planning to enter an industry. Columns one and two show the market price and the attainable rates of output from

TABLE 11–2   **Revenue, cost, and profit in the long run**

Market price	Rate of output and sales	Total revenue	Total cost	Profit (TR − TC)
$5	1	$ 5	$17.00	− $12.00
5	2	10	18.50	− 8.50
5	3	15	19.50	− 4.50
5	4	20	20.75	− 0.75
5	5	25	22.25	+ 2.75
5	6	30	24.25	+ 5.75
5	7	35	27.50	+ 7.50
5	8	40	32.00	+ 8.00
5	9	45	40.00	+ 5.00
5	10	50	52.00	− 2.00

which total revenue (price times output) is derived. Clearly, maximum profit is $8.00, attained at an output of eight units. The entrepreneur would build a plant to produce this output at the lowest cost.

We can examine the long-run decision using demand, long-run average cost, and long-run marginal cost. Table 11–3 shows the relevant average and marginal schedules for the situation set forth in Table 11–2; it indicates the same profit-maximizing condition as before. (Any differences are because of rounding errors.) Maximum profit again corresponds to eight units of output. We also see that profit per unit is maximized at eight units of output, but this is immaterial inasmuch as the entrepreneur is concerned with total profit. Maximization is obtained by producing up to

TABLE 11–3   **Marginal revenue, cost, and profit in the long run**

Output and sales	Marginal revenue or price	Marginal cost	Average cost	Unit profit	Total profit
1	$5.00	$17.00	$17.00	− $12.00	− $12.00
2	5.00	1.50	9.25	− 4.25	− 8.50
3	5.00	1.00	6.50	− 1.50	− 4.50
4	5.00	1.25	5.19	− 0.19	− 0.75
5	5.00	1.50	4.45	+ 0.55	+ 2.75
6	5.00	2.00	4.04	+ 0.96	+ 5.75
7	5.00	3.25	3.93	+ 1.07	+ 7.50
8	5.00	4.50	4.00	+ 1.00	+ 8.00
9	5.00	8.00	4.44	+ 1.80	+ 5.00
10	5.00	12.00	5.20	− 0.20	− 2.00

the point where marginal cost equals marginal revenue (or price). In the table, the producer would not produce beyond the eighth unit because marginal cost is greater than marginal revenue for the ninth.

So long as the firm can sell an additional unit for more than the marginal cost of producing that unit, it can increase profit by producing one more. If price is less than marginal cost, the firm should not produce that unit, because it costs more to produce than would be gained from its sale.

Let us examine these relations graphically. In Figure 11-6, $LRAC$ and $LRMC$ are the long-run average and marginal cost curves. The demand curve indicates the market price (p_0), which is also marginal revenue. As long as price is greater than long-run average cost, the firm can make a profit above the opportunity cost. In the figure, any output between x_0 and x_1 yields some profits.

Maximum profit occurs at point S where marginal revenue equals long-run marginal cost. The firm would not, under these circumstances, try to produce at point M, the minimum point of long-run average cost. At M, marginal revenue exceeds marginal cost and the firm can gain by producing more output. In Figure 11-6, total revenue (price times quantity) is given by the area of the rectangle Op_0Sx_m. Total cost (average cost times quantity) is the area Oc_0Rx_m. Total profit ($TR - TC$) is the shaded area c_0p_0SR.

FIGURE 11-6   **Profit maximization by the marginal approach**

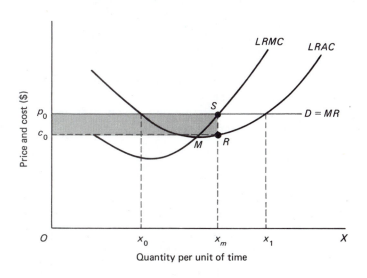

To summarize, the firm will plan to operate at a scale or size such that long-run marginal cost equals price. This is the most profitable situation with the given market price. Of course, if market price changes, the point of long-run profit maximization will change also.

Zero and Negative Profit Situations

If firms in a competitive industry are, in fact, making above-normal returns, there is strong reason to believe that the price in the market will, in fact, fall. Because of free entry, profits attract new firms into the industry, and the increased supply will drive down price. Price may even go below long-run average cost, at least temporarily.

Figure 11–7 shows such a situation. Price (p_L) lies below *LRAC* at every output; no positive profit can result. The minimum loss at a positive output occurs at x_L, where *LRMC* equals p_L. This loss is given by the area of the rectangle $p_L c_0 L'R$, the difference between total cost and total revenue. Firms would no longer wish to enter the industry under these circumstances. In fact, under the assumption that all firms have similar cost curves, firms already in the industry would be induced to exit.[7]

If an increase in the number of firms increases supply and lowers price, a decrease in the number of firms must decrease supply and raise price. When there are below-normal returns, firms would be motivated to leave the industry until market price rises sufficiently to eliminate losses. Let us assume that as exit takes place price rises to p_E in Figure 11–7. At the profit-maximizing output x_E price equals marginal cost and average cost; therefore, total cost equals total revenue. The firm earns just enough profit to cover total costs. In the long run, profits are normal or excess profits are zero. Notice that at any other positive output, average cost is above price, and losses would result.

While no profit results at x_E, no firm is induced to leave the industry since each covers its opportunity cost—the amount the entrepreneur could make in any alternative industry. Neither is any other firm induced to enter, since it would earn only its opportunity cost, which it presumably earns already. Each firm and therefore the market is in a profit-maximizing equilibrium.

---

[7] The student might note that we violate our assumption of perfect knowledge by positing that enough firms enter to drive the price down to P_L. Why would a firm with perfect knowledge enter knowing it would make losses? We could assume that demand suddenly falls and drives prices to p_L. The explanation given, however, is more consistent with the model of long-run industry equilibrium, to be analyzed later in this chapter.

The reason we know all firms are making losses is that the firms in the industry are operating in the short run and, except for the one point where they are equal, short-run average cost is everywhere greater than long-run average cost. If price is less than *LRAC*, it is also at least as far below *SRAC*, if not farther.

FIGURE 11–7   **Zero and negative profit situations**

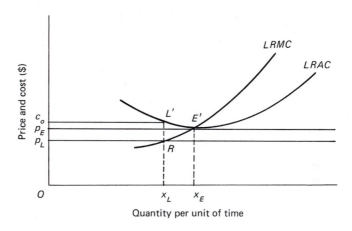

Principle

Long-run equilibrium of a competitive industry involves several equilibrium conditions. Each firm in the industry must be in long-run (and short-run) profit-maximizing equilibrium; marginal revenue equals long-run marginal cost. The entry or exit of firms must compete away all pure profit. Then, all firms must produce the quantity where price equals the minimum long-run average cost.

Graphical Exposition of Long-Run Equilibrium

Consider a firm in a short-run situation in which it possibly incurs a loss, a profit, or just makes normal returns. In looking to the long run, the entrepreneur making below-normal profits has two options: liquidate the business and transfer resources to a more profitable alternative or construct a plant of a more suitable or profitable size and remain in the industry. Suppose the firm is in a profitable short-run position or just earning normal returns. Even here it may build at a more appropriate size in the long run in order to increase profit. It is also true that if profits are obtainable in the industry, new firms will enter. All of these adjustments in the size and number of firms in the industry in response to the profit incentive are key elements in establishing long-run equilibrium.

The process of attaining long-run equilibrium in a perfectly competitive industry is illustrated in Figure 11–8. Suppose each firm in the industry is identical. Its size is represented by $SRAC_1$ and $SRMC_1$ in Panel B. The

FIGURE 11–8   **Long-run equilibrium adjustment in a perfectly competitive industry**

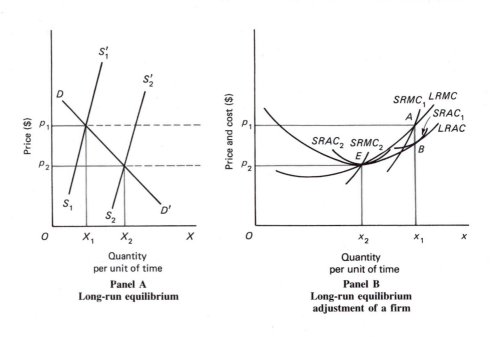

Quantity
per unit of time

Panel A
Long-run equilibrium

Quantity
per unit of time

Panel B
Long-run equilibrium
adjustment of a firm

market demand curve is given by DD' in Panel A, and the market supply is S_1S_1'. Market equilibrium establishes the price of p_1 per unit and total output and sales of X_1 units per period of time. At price p_1, each plant is built to produce x_1 units (the output at which $p_1 = LRMC$) at the lowest possible average cost (x_1B). Each firm receives a profit of AB per unit of output. The number of firms multiplied by x_1 (each firm's output) equals X_1 (total output). Although each firm is in equilibrium, the industry itself is not. As we saw earlier, the appearance of *pure economic profit*, a return in excess of that obtainable elsewhere, attracts new firms into the industry, increasing industry supply, say to S_2S_2', and reducing market price. The process of new entry might be very slow, or it might be very fast. It depends primarily on the mobility of assets in other industries. In any event, as time elapses, capacity will increase in the industry, thereby shifting the supply curve to the right.

When each firm adjusts optimally to the new market price, the output of each will be smaller. The larger number of firms accounts for the increase in output from X_1 in Panel A. Now, all firms produce the output at which p_2 equals $LRMC$ at output x_2. The number of old firms plus the number of new entrants times x_2 equals X_2. Since the new price equals

$LRMC$ and $SMRC_2$ at E, the minimum $LRAC$ and the minimum $SRAC_2$, neither profit nor loss is present for any firm. Both the industry and its firms are in long-run equilibrium.

The long-run equilibrium position of a firm in a perfectly competitive industry is shown in Figure 11–9. As we have seen, if price is above p, each established firm can adjust plant size and earn a pure profit. New firms are attracted into the industry, shifting the supply curve to the right. Price falls, and the horizontal demand curve facing each firm, old and new, falls also. All firms readjust. If "too many" firms enter, market price and each firm's horizontal demand curve may fall below p and each firm incurs a loss. As their plants and equipment depreciate, some firms will leave the industry, thereby causing the market supply curve to shift to the left. Market price, and accordingly, the horizontal individual demand curves rise.

So long as the cost curves do not change, the only conceivable point of long-run equilibrium occurs at point E in Figure 11–9. Each firm in the industry receives neither profit nor loss. There is no incentive for further entry, because the rate of return in this industry is considered normal, or equivalent to other investment opportunities. For the same reason, there

FIGURE 11–9   **Long-run equilibrium of a firm in a perfectly competitive industry**

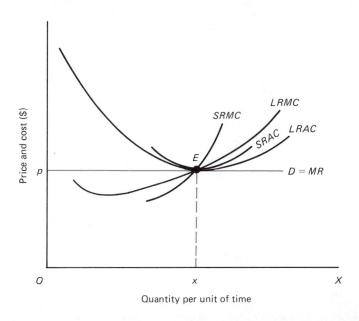

is no incentive for a firm already in the industry to leave. The number of firms stabilizes, each firm operating in the short run with a plant size represented by *SRAC* and *SRMC*.

Firms will only enter or leave the industry if there is either pure profit or pure loss. Since the position of long-run equilibrium must be consistent with *zero* profit (and zero loss), it is necessary that price equal average cost. For a firm to attain its individual equilibrium, price must also be equal to marginal cost. Therefore, price must equal both marginal and average total cost. This can occur only at the point where average and marginal cost are equal, or at the point of minimum average total cost.

The short-run position could conceivably apply to any *SRAC* and *SRMC*. However, unless it applies only to the short-run plant that coincides with minimum long-run average cost, a change in plant size would lead to the appearance of pure profit, and entry would take place to reduce profits to their normal level.

Long-Run Equilibrium and Rent

Some students may object to the model of long-run equilibrium at the minimum point on each firm's long-run average cost curve because the model is based on the assumption that each firm's cost curve is the same as that of every other firm. We have made that assumption for simplicity, but it is probably a reasonable reflection of the real world. Recall that any differences in cost are due to differences in the productivity of one or more resources. Assume that all firms except one are alike; that firm, perhaps because of a more favorable location, has a lower cost curve. The owner of that location (who could be the owner of the firm) could raise the rent to the firm (or if the person is the firm's owner, the opportunity cost would rise) up to the point where the firm's pure profit disappears. The firm would be motivated to pay the rent, since the owner of the firm would continue making the equivalent of its best alternative.

The cost of the previously lower-cost firm would tend to rise because of increased rent. It would not rise above those of other firms, because any higher rent would cause losses and no firm would pay it in the long run. The same type of argument applies to the superiority of other specialized resources, including management. If a superior manager, even a manager-owner, could lower the firm's costs, that manager could presumably lower the costs of other firms as well. The salary would be bid up, or, if the owner of the resource is the owner of the firm, the opportunity cost would rise. At equilibrium, all firm's long-run averge cost curves would, therefore, reach their minimum points at the same cost, and no firm would make pure profit or loss, although some might have differing factor payments or rents.

Firms with even higher cost structures are generally "waiting in the wings" to enter the industry if demand increases and drives up prices sufficiently to cover their costs. These higher-cost firms could cover opportunity cost only at a higher price. If price increases enough to induce their entry, the owners of resources that cause the firms already in the industry to have lower costs than the new firms will receive increased rents. Some firms that were making normal profits prior to the increase in price may begin to enjoy above-normal profits, which will, in the long run, be dispersed as rents to the resources responsible for lower costs.

11.7 CONSTANT-, INCREASING-, AND DECREASING-COST INDUSTRIES

The long-run analysis thus far has been based on the assumption that expanded resource use by the industry does not entail an increase in resource prices. To carry the analysis further and to make it more explicit, constant-, increasing-, and decreasing-cost industries are examined in this section. We will discover that a decreasing-cost industry leads to a downward sloping supply curve. Such an industry is an empirical rarity.

Constant-Cost Industries

Long-run equilibrium and long-run supply price under conditions of constant cost are explained by Figure 11–10. Panel A shows the long- and short-run conditions of each firm in the industry while Panel B depicts the

FIGURE 11–10   **Long-run equilibrium and supply price in a perfectly competitive industry subject to constant cost**

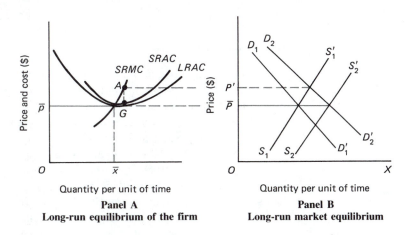

Panel A
Long-run equilibrium of the firm

Panel B
Long-run market equilibrium

market as a whole. D_1D_1' and S_1S_1' are the original market demand and supply curves, establishing a market equilibrium price of $\bar{p}$ dollars per unit. We assume that the industry has attained a position of long-run equilibrium, so the position of each firm in the industry is depicted by Panel A—the price line is tangent to the long- and short-run average cost curves at their minimum points.

Now suppose demand increases to D_2D_2'. With the number of firms fixed, the price will rise to p', and each firm will move to short-run equilibrium at point A. At point A, each firm earns a pure economic profit since price exceeds average cost by the amount AG per unit. New entrants are attracted into the industry, causing the industry supply curve to shift to the right. In this case, we assume that all resources used are so general that increased use in this industry does not affect the market price of resources. As a consequence, the expansion of old firms and entrance of new firms does not increase costs. The *LRAC* curve for all firms remains stationary. Complete long-run equilibrium adjustment to the shift in demand is accomplished when the number of firms expands to the point where the original equilibrium price, p, is restored. This means in Panel B that supply increases to S_2S_2'. The firm in the market operates at the minimum point on *LRAC*, producing the quantity $\bar{x}$.

In other words, since output can be expanded by expanding the number of firms, each producing $\bar{x}$ units per period of time at average cost p, the industry has a constant long-run supply price equal to p dollars per unit. If price were above this level, firms would continue to enter the industry in order to reap the pure profit obtainable. If price was less than p, some firms would ultimately leave the industry to avoid economic loss. In the special case where an expansion of resource use does not lead to an increase in resource price, the long-run industry supply price is constant. This is precisely the meaning of a constant-cost industry.

Increasing-Cost Industries

An increasing-cost industry is depicted in Figure 11–11. The original situation is the same as in Figure 11–10. The industry is in a position of long-run equilibrium and D_1D_1' and S_1S_1' are the market demand and supply curves, respectively. Equilibrium price is p_1. Each firm operates at point E_1, where price equals minimum average cost for both the long- and short-run curves. Each firm is also in a position of long-run equilibrium.

Let demand shift to D_2D_2' so that price rises to a much higher level. The higher price is accompanied by pure economic profit for the producing firms; new firms are consequently attracted into the industry, and the use of resources expands. Now suppose this expansion causes the prices of resources to rise. The cost of inputs will increase for the established firms

FIGURE 11–11   **Long-run equilibrium and supply price in a perfectly competitive industry subject to increasing cost**

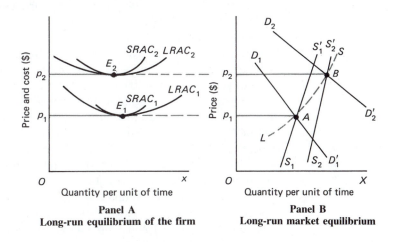

Panel A
Long-run equilibrium of the firm

Panel B
Long-run market equilibrium

as well as for the new entrants. As a result, the entire set of cost curves shifts upward, say, to a position represented by $LRAC_2$ in Panel A.[8]

Naturally, the process of equilibrium adjustment is not instantaneous. The $LRAC$ curve shifts upward as new entrants gradually join the industry. Marginal cost curves of all firms shift to the left as new firms enter and bid up factor prices. Two forces tend to work in opposite directions on the industry's supply curve. The rising marginal cost curve tends to shift the industry's supply curve to the left. But the entry of new firms tends to shift industry supply to the right. The forces causing a shift in the market supply schedule to the right (entry) must dominate those causing a shift to the left (rise in marginal costs); otherwise, total output could not expand and there would not be a new market equilibrium price and quantity.

To see why supply must shift to the right after an increase in demand, let us assume that the opposite happens. In Figure 11–11, demand, as before, shifts to D_2D_2'. In the short run, price and quantity increase along with profits. The profits attract new firms, which, on entering, bid up resource prices. All cost curves rise, as indicated in Panel A. Suppose,

---

[8] As Figure 11–11 is constructed, the minimum point on $LRAC$ shifts to the left as $LRAC$ shifts upward. In fact, minimum $LRAC$ can correspond to either a smaller or a larger output. The analysis underlying the exact nature of the shift involves an advanced concept not treated in this text.

however, that the leftward shift in all marginal cost curves dominates the tendency for an increase in supply caused by entry. Therefore, the new supply curve would lie somewhere to the left of S_1S_1'. If demand remains D_2D_2', price must be greater than p_2; firms must be making pure profits, and entry would continue. If the same process reoccurs, price will rise further, costs will rise, profits will continue, and entry will be further encouraged. Thus, a leftward shift in supply is not consistent with equilibrium. At some point, the entry of new firms must dominate the increase in costs, and supply must shift to the right, though not as much as it would in a constant-cost industry.

The process of adjustment must continue until a position of long-run equilibrium is attained. In Figure 11–11, this is depicted by the intersection of D_2D_2' and S_2S_2', establishing an equilibrium price of p_2 dollars per unit. Each firm produces at E_2, where price equals minimum average cost. The new price is above the original equilibrium price unlike the constant-cost case. In a constant-cost industry, new firms enter until price returns to the unchanged level of minimum long-run average cost. For industries subject to increasing cost, new firms enter until minimum long-run average cost shifts upward to equal the new price.

In the transition from one long-run equilibrium to the other, the long-run supply price increases from p_1 to p_2. This is precisely what is meant by an increasing-cost industry. The long-run industry supply curve is given by a line, LS, joining such points as A and B in Panel B. Thus, an increasing-cost industry is one with a positively sloped long-run supply curve. Alternatively stated, after all long-run equilibrium adjustments are made, an increasing-cost industry is one where an increase in output requires an increase in long-run supply price.

In our discussion of rents, we noted that, possibly because of scarce resources, industry expansion could take place only through the entry of higher-cost firms, perhaps because less productive resources are used. Until now, we have assumed all firms are alike, and the only reason for cost to rise is because resource prices are bid up. If expansion takes place through the entry of higher-cost firms, we could have an increasing-cost industry as well. When demand increases, bidding up the market price, firms that would have been unprofitable at the lower price enter the industry. The lower-cost firms earn pure profits, which are competed away by rents to the scarce resources. The final equilibrium price is, therefore, higher than before, but each firm operates at the minimum point on long-run average cost. The lower-cost firms have their cost curves pushed up by rents.

Decreasing-Cost Industries

A decreasing-cost industry exists when the market price actually falls after the supply curve adjusts to the initial increase in demand. Oddly, the long-run industry supply is downward sloping.

FIGURE 11–12

Long-run equilibrium and supply price in a perfectly competitive industry subject to decreasing costs

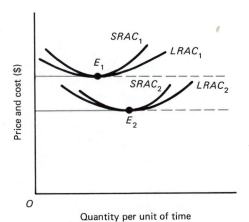

Panel A
Long-run equilibrium of the firm

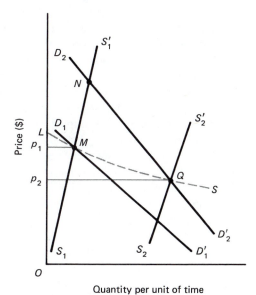

Panel B
Long-run market equilibrium

Such an industry is graphically described by Figure 11–12. Firms begin in equilibrium in Panel A at point E_1, where price is equal to *SRAC* and *LRAC*. All firms in the market make normal returns. The market price is determined by the intersection of supply and demand in Panel B—that is, the intersection of D_1D_1' and S_1S_1' at M. An increase in demand then disturbs this equilibrium so the new intersection of the supply and demand curve is at N. At such high prices, firms make above-normal profits and entry takes place. So far, this is the same story as before.

In contrast to the case of our increasing-cost industry where the cost of production increases as entry occurs, the cost of production decreases in the decreasing-cost industry as entry takes place. The long-run equilibrium of the firm is not restored until prices are lower than before the shift in demand, as shown in Panel A. We see, in Panel B, that supply must have increased relative to demand, reaching a new equilibrium at Q. The long-run market price has fallen from p_1 to p_2, making the long-run supply curve, *LS*, downward sloping. Thus, a decreasing-cost industry is characterized by a long-run supply curve with a negative slope.

Decreasing-cost industries are not common, but they are conceivable. For example, increases in demand may encourage specialization in the industry and consequently lower costs for all producers. As an illustration, in smaller towns, medical care can be relatively expensive when laboratory testing must be done out of town. If the town grows and the demand for medical care increases, laboratories may be set up in the community, allowing tests to be done at a lower cost. As a result of the increase in demand, each doctor can charge patients lower prices for medical tests.

We must be very careful when identifying a decreasing-cost industry. Everyone can think of examples of products that have decreased dramatically in price while experiencing significant gains in sales and quality. One of the most recent examples is the home computer industry—prices have dropped as sales increased. The entire computer industry has experienced the same phenomenon. Earlier, color TV sets dropped in price as sales increased and this was also the case with many household appliances.

These are not examples of decreasing-cost industries in the sense discussed above. In the case of decreasing-cost industries, an increase in output reduces the price of some inputs. For such industries, we stress that costs fall because of reduced input prices. It is likely that technological change caused the prices to fall in the above examples.

Recall that technological change lowers each firm's costs and, consequently, increases industry supply. Two possible situations are depicted in Figure 11–13. In Panel A, the demand for the product, *DD*, remains constant over a reasonably long period of time. We begin with a long-run supply of S_1 and an equilibrium price of p_1. If technological change

FIGURE 11–13   **Effect of technological change**

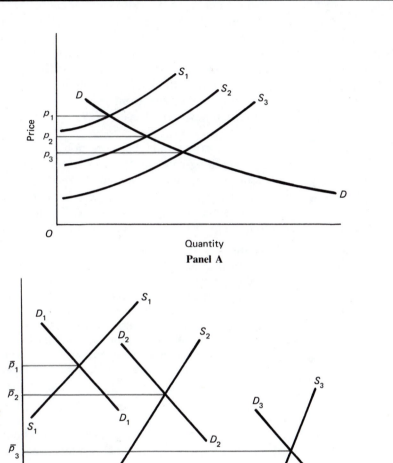

Panel A

Panel B

occurs, the isoquant map shifts toward the origin, causing a reduction in costs. At p_1, profits are earned and entry takes place to increase the supply curve to S_2, lowering price to p_2. Clearly, equilibrium output increases. Technological change continues (induced, spontaneous, or otherwise), increasing supply to S_3, reducing price to p_3, and increasing output. Prices are falling in the market, but not because of declining input prices. In Panel B, the demand for the product increases from D_1D_1 to D_2D_2 to D_3D_3. Because of technological change, not because of a reduction in input prices from increased factor use, supply increases even more, from S_1S_1 to S_2S_2 to S_3S_3. These shifts cause price to fall from p_1 to p_2 to p_3.

Let us stress that these are not examples of decreasing long-run supply. The long-run supply curves were derived under the assumption that technology remains constant. In the situations depicted in Figure 11–13, and in the examples given here, it is the change in technology that is responsible for the shift in supply. To summarize this section, we have the following:

Relation
Constant, increasing, or decreasing cost in an industry depends on the way that resource prices respond to expanded resource use. If resource prices remain constant, the industry is subject to constant cost; if resource prices increase, the industry has increasing costs; and if resource prices decrease, the industry has decreasing costs. The long-run supply curve for a constant-cost industry is a horizontal line at the level of the constant long-run supply price. The long-run industry supply curve under conditions of increasing cost is positively sloped, and the long-run supply curve for a decreasing-cost industry is downward sloping.

11.8 SUMMARY

Perfectly competitive markets exist when there are a large number of buyers and sellers, identical products, easy entry and exit by producers, perfect information, and prices freely determined by the interaction of supply and demand. In the short run, the firm produces the quantity where short-run marginal cost equals price, so long as price exceeds average variable cost. Therefore, marginal cost above average variable cost is the firm's short-run supply. If all input prices are given to the industry, industry short-run supply is the horizontal summation of all marginal cost curves. If the industry's (although not the individual firm's) use of the inputs affects the prices of some inputs, industry supply is less elastic than this horizontal summation. In the long run, the entry and exit of firms force each firm to produce at minimum $LRAC$, where $LRAC = LRMC = SRAC = SRMC$. Profit is zero at this output, although each entrepreneur earns opportunity cost. In a constant-cost industry, long-run industry supply is horizontal line at the level of the firm's minimum long-run average cost. If the industry's use of inputs increases the prices of some inputs, the industry's long-run supply curve increases with output, and it is an increasing-cost industry. If input prices fall, the industry's long-run supply curve decreases with output, and the industry is a decreasing-cost industry.

Up to this point, the salient feature of perfect competition is that, in long-run market equilibrium, market price equals minimum average cost. This means that each unit of output is produced at the lowest possible cost, either from the standpoint of money cost or resource use. The product sells for its average (long-run) cost of production; each firm, accordingly, earns the going rate of return in competitive industries—nothing more or less.

It should be emphasized that firms do not choose to produce the quantity with the lowest possible long-run average cost simply because they believe this level of production is optimal for society and they wish to benefit society. The firms are merely trying to maximize their profits. Given that motivation, the market *forces* firms to produce at that point. If society benefits, it is not through any benevolence of firms but through the functioning of the market.

Finally, it is important to remember that the theory of perfect competition is not designed to describe specific real-world firms. It is a theoretical model that is frequently useful in explaining real-world behavior and in predicting the economic consequences of changes in the different variables contained in the model. The conclusions of the theory, not the assumptions, are the crucial points when analyzing economic problems.

TECHNICAL PROBLEMS

1. Use the output-cost data computed from problem 1 (Technical Problems) in Chapter 9.
   a. Suppose the price of the commodity is $1.75 per unit.
      (1) What would net profit be at each of the following outputs?

         1,314   1,494
         1,384   1,534
         1,444

      (2) What is the output that yields the greatest profit?
      (3) Is there any output that will yield a greater profit at any price?
      (4) How much more revenue is obtained by selling this number of units than by selling one fewer? What is the relation between marginal revenue and selling price?
      (5) If you are given selling price, how can you determine the optimum output by reference to marginal cost?

b. Suppose price is 70 cents.
    (1) What would net profit be at each of the following outputs?

         410   945
         560   1,234
         700   1,444
         830

    (2) Is there any output that will earn a net profit at this price?
    (3) When price is 70 cents, what is the crucial relation between price and average variable cost?
    (4) Consider any price for which the corresponding marginal cost is equal to or less than 70 cents. At such a price, what is the relation between marginal cost and average variable cost?
    (5) When the relation in (4) exists, what is the relation between average and marginal product?
    (6) What will the producer do if faced with a permanent price of 70 cents?
    (7) Why is it not socially desirable to have a producer operating when price is 70 cents?

c. Suppose price is 80 cents.
    (1) What will the optimum output be?
    (2) Can a profit be made at this price?
    (3) Will the producer operate at all at this price?
    (4) If so, for how long?

d. Determine the supply schedule of this individual producer.

Price	Quantity supplied
$0.60	
0.70	
0.80	
0.90	
1.00	
1.10	
1.20	
1.30	
1.40	
1.50	
1.60	
1.70	
1.80	
1.90	
2.00	

FIGURE E.11–1

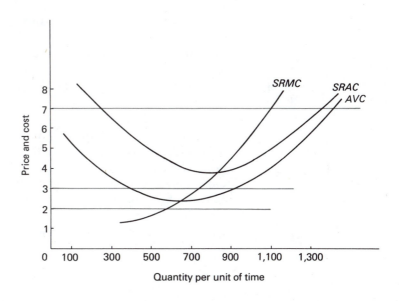

2. Use Figure E.11–1 to answer these questions.
   a. If price is $7 the firm should produce _____ units.
   b. Since average total cost at this profit-maximizing output is $_____, total cost is $_____.
   c. Therefore, the firm makes a total profit of $_____.
   d. Price then falls to $3. The firm will produce approximately _____ units.
   e. Since average total cost at this output is $_____, total revenue less total cost is $_____.
   f. Total variable cost is $_____; thus, the firm's total revenue covers all of variable cost, leaving approximately $_____ to apply to fixed costs.
   g. If price falls to $2 the firm will produce _____ units. Why?

3. Draw precisely and label the following curves: Long-run average cost. Long-run marginal cost. Short-run average cost. Short-run marginal cost. Let the short-run profit-maximizing output be greater than minimum long-run average cost. The firm is a perfect competitor making short-run profits. It could, however, increase profits (maximize profits) by decreasing plant size.

  a. Show the current output price and profit.

  b. Show the profit that could have been earned and the optimal output if, at the same price, the firm was maximizing long-run profit.

  c. Show price and output of this firm after the industry goes into long-run equilibrium.

  d. Explain how this long-run competitive equilibrium situation is attained.

4. Figure E.11–2 shows a graph of a perfectly competitive firm's short-run cost structure.

  a. Label the three curves.

  b. Show a price at which the firm would make a pure profit. Show the quantity it would produce at this price and the amount of pure profit earned.

  c. Show a price at which the firm would continue to produce in the short run but would suffer losses. Show the output and losses at this price.

  d. Show the price below which the firm would not produce in the short run.

FIGURE E.11–2

Price and cost ($)

Quantity per unit of time

5. Show that a perfectly competitive firm would never produce an output at which marginal cost is falling. (*Hint*: Begin where $P = MC$, and examine what happens when one more unit of output is produced.)

6. Explain why the short-run supply curve of a perfectly competitive industry is less if industry usage affects the prices of some inputs than would be the case if all input prices are given to the industry.

7. Suppose a perfectly competitive firm has a total revenue in a particular year of $4 million. Its total payments to factor of production are $3 million. The firm owner also owns $4 million dollars worth of capital used by the firm. The going rate of return on capital is 10 percent. The owner does not manage the firm. What is the owner's rate of return on capital? What is normal profit? What is pure or economic profit?

8. Why might a decreasing-cost industry not have a long-run equilibrium?

9. How can we have a constant-cost industry when any firm that increases output would experience increased costs?

10. Explain how technological change would cause an industry to take on the afferant characteristics of a decreasing-cost industry.

11. Explain the existence of rents in a perfectly competitive industry.

ANALYTICAL PROBLEMS

1. "Economists are silly to say that profits are competed away in the long run. No firm would operate unless it made profits." Explain.

2. "My overhead (fixed cost) at this car dealership is $2,000 per day. So I figure that the best way to make the most money is to sell as many cars as possible, thereby spreading out the overhead so it is only a small part of the cost on each car sold." What is wrong with the reasoning of this person?

3. Explain why, in the case of a decreasing-cost industry, one firm would have the incentive to buy up the competitive firms or to expand, underprice the competitive firms, and drive them out of business.

4. The separation of ownership from the operation of a business has been presented as a better way to control the incentives of workers. An owner cannot be fired for laziness, while a hired worker could. Is it always true that work incentives are improved if owners are not workers? What positive incentives are created when workers are also owners?

5. In a perfectly competitive industry suppose every firm is assessed a lump sum tax of $100.

    a. Since each firm is only earning normal returns, will every firm go out of business? Describe the adjustment process.

    b. Is it likely that prices will go up by an amount that completely covers the tax paid by each firm? If not, how does the firm, earning just a normal return, pay part of the tax?

6. If all of the assumptions of perfect competition hold, why would firms in the industry have little incentive to carry out technological changes or do much research and development? What conditions would encourage research and development in competitive industries?

7. Suppose an excise (per unit) tax is placed on the products sold in a perfectly competitive market. Each firm must pay the government $t per unit for each unit sold. What would be the effect on each firm's marginal cost? Average cost? Output? Industry supply? The price of the product?

8. We have said that the exacting characteristics of perfect competition are not met in real-world markets. Can you think of some real-world industries that approximate the model? What characteristics do you think would most likely be met?

9. In light of problem 8, we might suggest that farming, ranching, and wildcat oil drilling have many characteristics of perfect competition. No firm is large enough to affect price. We say that competition competes away profits, but there are many very rich farmers, ranchers, and oil wildcatters. Explain how this can occur.

10. Grocery stores and gasoline stations in a large city would appear to be an example of competitive markets. There are numerous sellers, each seller is relatively small, and the products sold are quite similar. How could we argue that these markets are not perfectly competitive (leaving out the assumption of perfect knowledge)?

11. Would a perfectly competitive firm advertise? How about a dairy association? A wheat growers' association? Why would a trade association representing a competitive industry want to advertise?

Chapter 12

The Model of Perfect Competition in Practice and Perspective

12.1 INTRODUCTION

We have remarked more than once that no market completely fulfills the conditions of perfect competition. Many markets approximate this model, and, as a consequence, it is a useful tool in predicting the effect of changes in supply or demand, or perhaps the impact of government regulation. In this chapter we will apply the model of perfect competition to specific industries to show its predictive power. In a second application we look more closely at the interaction between total revenue and total cost in a competitive setting. We will explore the relative impact of fixed and variable costs on a competitive producer. Together, these examples are presented to show how the model of perfect competition can be put to work as an analytical tool. Our purpose is to apply the model in ways that help us think the way economists do about markets and help us become better decision makers.

We will also take a more critical look at the model of perfect competition. The assumptions of the model will be questioned. Do we like the underlying conditions of perfectly competitive markets? Is competition something we should desire as consumers, businesspeople and government policymakers? The answers to these two questions are not easy. In this chapter we will bring up some of the important issues, not to give you the answers to the questions, but to tell you that perfect competition may not be all that perfect on closer inspection.

We want this chapter to provide two kinds of transitions. We first want to take the conceptual and abstract competitive model discussed in the last chapter and make it a concrete and practical tool—a device useful to those studying markets and/or working in the marketplace. The second transition is a move from a perfectly competitive world to one of imperfect markets. Most markets are not perfectly competitive, and we will spend the next three chapters talking about other types of market structures. It is important that we do not start these later discussions with the impression that markets are somehow flawed if they are not perfectly competitive. In most cases both costs and benefits are realized when moving away from the perfectly competitive model. In some cases, there is no choice—if the product is to be produced at all, competitive markets may not be possible. At any rate, we do not want to leave our discussion of perfect competition thinking of this market structure as "good" and other market structures as inherently "bad."

12.2 THE ADJUSTMENT PROCESS IN COMPETITIVE MARKETS

In the last chapter we discussed how the model of perfectly competitive markets was a useful predictor of market behavior when there was a large number of sellers. In this section we use the model to show how a price ceiling in the coal industry affects prices and outputs. This discussion is not peculiar to coal markets, but reference to a specific product will emphasize the applicability of the model.

Long-Run Effects of a Price Ceiling on Coal

Suppose the demand for coal at the retail level is elastic over the relevant price range. The government feels that the price of coal is too high and places a price ceiling (maximum price) on coal at the mine. What will happen to the price of coal at the retail level? Will total receipts of retailers increase or decrease?

As a first step, let's consider what happens at the mine (or mining area). Assume, for analytical purposes, that coal mining is a perfectly competitive, increasing-cost industry. Assume also that, before the imposition of the ceiling price, the industry was in long-run equilibrium; each firm produced the quantity at which $P = LRAC$ and, therefore, enjoyed no pure profit. Figure 12–1 shows the market demand and supply for coal at the mine. Demand $(D_m D_m')$ is the demand curve of retailers for coal at the mine. It is derived by holding constant the demand for coal from retailers. (We assume that individual consumers cannot purchase coal directly from the mine.) The equilibrium price at the mine is w_c and equilibrium quantity is x_c.

FIGURE 12–1   **Supply and demand at the coal mine**

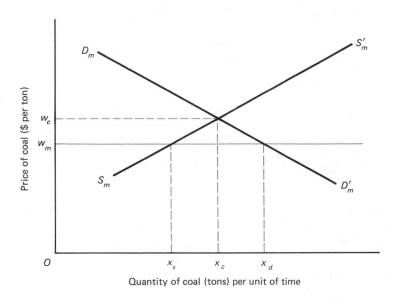

Quantity of coal (tons) per unit of time

Figure 12–2 shows demand and supply conditions in the retail market. $D_r D_r'$ is the consumers' demand for coal. $S_r S_r'$, based on a given cost of coal at the mines to retailers (Figure 12–1, w_c), is the retailers' supply curve. Since coal is an input for the retailers, the supply curve for coal at the retail market level should shift when the price of coal at the mines changes, just as a change in the price of any factor of production changes the supply of the product produced. Specifically, when the price at the mine falls, other things remaining the same, the retail supply curve should shift to the right. If retailers can buy coal more cheaply, they would be willing and able to supply more retail coal at every retail price. Begin with equilibrium in the retail market occurring at a price of p_r (given a price at the mine of w_c) and a quantity sold of x_c, obviously the same as x_c in Figure 12–1, because the retailers sell all that they buy.

Returning to Figure 12–1, assume that the government sets the ceiling price w_m at the mine. Quantity demanded by retailers at the new price is x_d. The new price is below w_c, the price at which neither profit nor loss occurs; thus, firms begin to make losses, and some leave the industry. Since we assume that mining is an increasing-cost industry, the exit of firms and the decrease in quantity produced will lower factor prices and

FIGURE 12–2   **Demand and supply in the retail market for coal**

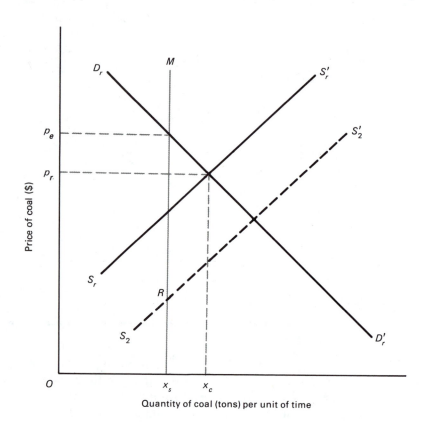

Quantity of coal (tons) per unit of time

lower the long- run average and marginal cost curves of the remaining firms in the industry. Figure 12–3 shows the process. Long-run average and marginal costs fall from $LRAC_1$ and $LRMC_1$ to $LRAC_2$ and $LRMC_2$. The minimum point on $LRAC_2$ equals the ceiling price, w_m. Each remaining firm now produces x_m (the new equilibrium output) rather than x_c, and there are fewer firms and none makes pure profit. The new quantity supplied by the industry, indicated in Figure 12–1, is x_s. Thus, a shortage (excess demand) of $x_s x_d$ occurs at the mines, since retailers now wish to purchase x_d, but the mines are only willing to sell x_s. The mining industry must find some method of allocation (rationing, first come-first served, favoritism, and so on) in order to determine what retailers get the available supply. In any case, only x_s is available to the retailers.

FIGURE 12–3   **Cost curve of a firm**

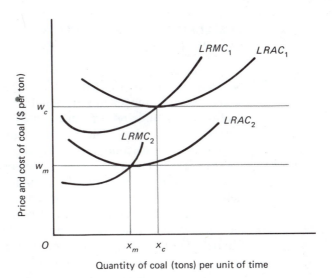

Quantity of coal (tons) per unit of time

The lower price of coal at the mine should cause supply at the retail level to shift to S_2S_2' (Figure 12–2). Retail price should fall, and the quantity of coal sold should increase as determined by the intersection of D_rD_r' and S_2S_2'. Remember, however, that only x_s is produced, so only x_s can be sold. The curve S_2S_2' specifies the quantities that retailers are *willing* to sell if the price of the mine is w_m; the vertical line Mx_s indicates the maximum amount retailers are *able* to sell at that price. The curve S_2RM shows the quantities that retailers are *willing and able* to sell at each retail price when the mine price is fixed at w_m.

The intersection of supply and demand now occurs at the price p_e, clearly higher than the old price. The quantity sold, specified already, is x_s. After the ceiling price at the mine is imposed, consumers pay a higher price for less coal. Since demand was assumed to be elastic, retailers receive less total revenue.

We have traced the effects of a price ceiling in a perfectly competitive setting. The impact of ceiling prices was just the reverse of its desired impact. Ceiling prices are usually imposed to benefit consumers by lowering the price they pay for a product. After the ceiling was put into place, exit from the industry reduced market supply, and in the long run raised the retail price. If price ceilings have just the opposite of their intended effect, shouldn't a price floor lower the price consumers pay? Unfortunately, this is not the case, as you will see after working technical problem 3 at the end of the chapter.

12.3 ALLOCATION OF FIXED AND VARIABLE COST IN A COMPETITIVE ENVIRONMENT

The model of perfect competition is not just a model of business behavior in an environment characterized by a large number of small firms selling homogeneous products. As we stressed in Chapter 4 the profit-maximizing and efficiency rules can be generalized to many non-business applications. The way we think about profit maximization can help us think like economists in many everyday situations. In this section we study the importance of allocating costs to a fixed or variable category when deciding between two short-run total cost curves. This analysis will help us see that when there is uncertainty about the profitability of entering a market, a new firm can reduce potential losses by the way it allocates total costs. Price-taking firms need not be passive toward costs. Though they sell at a given price, some control over fixed and variable costs can have an impact on profits earned in the short run.

This section also presents a new way of looking at cost. We introduce costs in terms of a *break-even* chart that presents a sharper picture of the relation between cost, revenue, and profit. Awareness of the distinction between fixed costs and variable costs will make us better decision makers in many seemingly noneconomic cases.

The Break-Even Chart

When firms in a competitive environment make their production plans, they must choose between several short-run cost schedules. When making these choices firms do not have the luxury of working with the long- and short-run average cost curves and the marginal cost curves we used to study the behavior of competitive firms in the last chapter. Completely estimating these cost curves is very difficult and frequently impractical. We sampled some of this difficulty in Chapter 9 in our discussion of the engineering approach to cost estimation. It was an involved process just to estimate *one point* on the average and marginal cost schedules.

To get around this estimation problem, a firm, for planning purposes, will often use a cost accounting device called the *break-even chart*. For a specific scale of production, the firm makes some simplifying assumptions to study the profit potential of an operation. We know that in the long run all profits are competed away by entry or rents, but competitive firms are continually searching their market environment for new opportunities that generate above-normal returns (as short-lived as they may be). This search is as much a part of the profit motive as the profit-maximizing rule of equating marginal cost with marginal revenue once plans have been put into operation. Firms continually seek the short-run scale that maximizes their return. There is, however, uncertainty about these potential returns at the planning stage.

The break-even chart assumes first that a firm can sell all the units it

FIGURE 12–4   **The break-even chart**

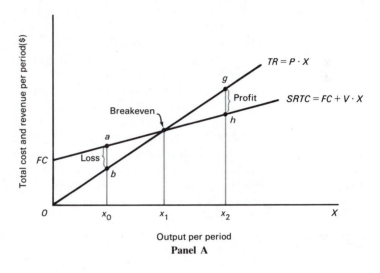

Panel A

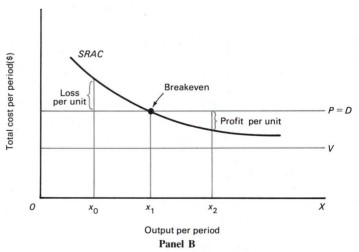

Panel B

produces at a going market price. Total revenue (TR) is a linear schedule $TR = P \cdot X$, with the endpoint at the origin, as shown in Figure 12–4, Panel A. The slope is the price, P. This is the same way we modeled total revenue in the last chapter. There we referred to the constant price as the demand curve, and illustrated demand as the horizontal price schedule. Panel B shows this constant price schedule for the same price.

Short-run total cost in a break-even chart, on the other hand, takes an unusually simple linear form. It is written as $SRTC = FC + V \cdot X$, when fixed costs are given by the term FC and total variable costs are $V \cdot X$. This linear schedule for total cost is also illustrated in Panel A of Figure 12–4. The intercept on the vertical axis is the fixed cost of operation and the slope is the dollar amount V, which we know is marginal cost. Since total variable cost is $V \cdot X$, the average variable cost ($V \cdot X/X$) is also V. Thus, average variable cost and marginal cost are equal.

The break-even point occurs where the $SRTC$ schedule intersects the TR schedule at x_1. If the firm produced less, total costs would be greater than total revenue and the firm would suffer losses. For output x_0, they are equal to the distance ab in the figure. If the firm produced more than x_1, short-run profits would be realized, an amount equivalent to the distance gh at output x_2. Obviously if business planners, given their estimates of fixed costs, variable costs, and the product price, foresaw a profit opportunity in a market they were not in, they would enter that market. It is possible, however, that the $SRTC$ schedule could lie everywhere above the projected TR schedule. In such instances, the firm would not enter the market. The break-even chart helps a competitor decide whether to enter a new market and at what scale it should enter.

Panel B of Figure 12–4 has recast Panel A in terms of the cost schedules that we are more accustomed to. Remember that the linear schedules in Panel A cover a specific range of output and are estimated by firms for planning purposes. In Panel B, $SRAC$ slopes downward because average fixed cost is decreasing while average variable cost is constant. The break-even point in Panel B occurs where $SRAC$ crosses price, at x_1; beyond this level of output, the $SRAC$ curve is below the demand schedule and profits are earned. At x_2, the *profit per unit* is the distance between price and the $SRAC$ curve, while before the break-even point, say at x_0, the *loss per unit* is the distance between $SRAC$ and price.

Choosing a Cost Structure

The competitive planner may not be absolutely certain about the break-even point in Figure 12–4. Both total revenue and total cost are simply estimates; the actual schedules could be different when the firm goes into production. One way to avoid potential losses incurred by not reaching the break-even output x_1 is to rearrange the distribution of costs between those that are fixed and variable. By making some fixed costs variable the firm could reduce potential losses. Alternatively, moving some costs from a variable to a fixed category would increase the potential gains after the break-even point. Hence the entrepreneur has some control over potential gains and losses by the way costs are structured.

An example will help us understand the decision the planner must make. Suppose the decision maker begins with the total cost schedule, $SRTC = 600 + .5x$. Fixed costs are $600 and the average variable cost (equal to marginal cost) is $.50. The estimated price per unit is $1.50; so total revenue will be $TR = \$1.50 \times x$. By setting $SRTC = TR$, we can solve for the break-even point. We show in Figure 12–5 that it is at 600 units.

Now suppose the firm has the opportunity to shift some costs from a fixed category to one that is variable. It may, for instance, be able to put its salespeople on a contract that pays them a commission based on sales rather than a guaranteed salary. Such a move might give the firm a new short-run total cost curve in which $SRTC = 300 + 1.00 \cdot X$. Fixed costs have been cut in half, while the variable cost component has been doubled. The new cost schedule, illustrated in Figure 12–5, is closer to the total revenue schedule at every output, except for the break-even point. This means that at outputs less than 600, the potential loss is smaller; but at quantities greater than 600 the potential gain is also smaller.

FIGURE 12–5   **Potential losses and gains under different cost structures**

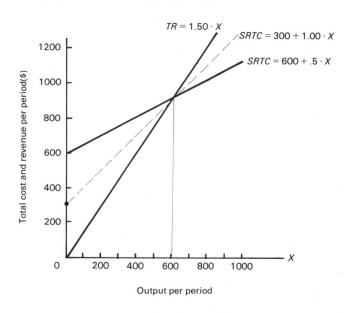

We constructed this example to give the same break-even point when costs were rearranged. Generally when costs are moved between fixed and variable categories the break-even point will change. The principle we illustrate in Figure 12–5 still holds—making costs variable instead of fixed, lowers potential gains and losses. In an uncertain planning environment this could be desirable.

How can costs be shifted between fixed and variable categories? It is a matter of making payments to productive resources dependent or independent of output. Labor, for instance, can either be paid on a "piecework" basis or compensated independent of sales. Sometimes capital can be paid an amount based either on sales or an agreed fixed rate. United Shoe Machinery, for example, sold machinery to shoe-makers for many years at a price based on the sales of shoemakers. For every pair of shoes sold, cobblers would pay United Shoe a royalty until the machinery was depreciated. United also offered its machinery at a lump-sum nonroyalty price.

Universities could operate more conservatively in the contracts they write for faculty, administration, and other employees. They might, for instance, pay football coaches according to the number of victories per season rather than negotiate a fixed contract amount. The coach would be paid very little during a losing season (which might please alumni). Business executives frequently are guaranteed a fixed base salary and a variable "bonus", depending on profits at the end of the year. In this case labor costs have both a fixed and variable component.

Below we present a rather unusual application to show how the decision to choose between fixed and variable costs can arise in "everyday life." It is the major part of a short story about a French farmer who hires a nurse to care for his ailing mother.

APPLICATION

Choosing between a Fixed and Variable Cost

THE DEVIL[1]

by

Guy de Maupassant

The doctor raised his voice and said: "Honoré, you cannot leave your mother in this state; she may die at any moment." And the peasant, in great distress, replied: "But I must get in my wheat, for it has been lying on

---

[1] From *The Best Stories of Guy DeMaupassant*. Copyright 1945 by Random House, Inc. Reprinted by permission of the publisher. Portions of this short story have been omitted.

the ground a long time, and the weather is just right for it; what do you say about it, Mother?" And the dying woman, still possessed by her Norman avariciousness, replied yes with her eyes and her forehead, and so urged her son to get in his wheat, and to leave her to die alone. But the doctor got angry, and stamping his foot he said: "You are not better than a brute, do you hear, and I will not allow you to do it. Do you understand? And if you must get in your wheat today, go and fetch Rapet's wife and make her look after your mother. I *will* have it. And if you do not obey me, I will let you die like a dog, when you are ill in your turn; do you hear me?"

The peasant, a tall, thin fellow with slow movements, who was tormented by indecision, by his fear of the doctor and his keen love of saving, hesitated, calculated, and stammered out: "How much does La Rapet charge for attending sick people?"

"How should I know?" the doctor cried. "That depends upon how long she is wanted for. Settle it with her, by Jove! But I want her to be here within an hour, do you hear?"

La Rapet, who was an old washer woman, watched the dead and the dying of the neighborhood, and then, as soon as she had sewn her customers into that linen cloth from which they would emerge no more, she went and took up her irons to smooth the linen of the living. Wrinkled like a last year's apple, spiteful, envious, avaricious with a phenomenal avarice, bent double, as if she had been broken in half across the loins, by the constant movement of the iron over the linen, one might have said that she had a kind of monstrous and cynical affection for a death struggle. She never spoke of anything but of the people she had seen die, of the various kinds of deaths at which she had been present, and she related, with the greatest minuteness, details which were always the same, just as a sportsman talks of his shots.

When Honoré Bontemps entered her cottage, he found her preparing the starch for the collars of the village woman, and he said: "Good evening; I hope you are pretty well, Mother Rapet."

She turned her head round to look at him and said: "Fairly well, fairly well, and you?"

"Oh! as for me, I am as well as I could wish, but my mother is very sick."

"Your mother?"

"Yes, my mother!"

"What's the matter with her?"

"She is going to turn up her toes. That's what's the matter with her!"

The old woman took her hands out of the water and asked with sudden sympathy: "Is she as bad as all that?"

"The doctor says she will not last till morning."

"Then she certainly is very bad!" Honoré hesitated, for he wanted to make a few preliminary remarks before coming to his proposal, but as he could hit upon nothing, he made up his mind suddenly.

"How much are you going to ask to stay with her till the end? You know that I am not rich, and I cannot even afford to keep a servant-girl. It is just that which has brought my poor mother to this state, too much work and fatigue! She used to work for ten, in spite of her ninety-two years. You don't find any made of that stuff nowadays!"

La Rapet answered gravely: "There are two prices: Forty sous by day and three francs by night for the rich, and twenty sous by day, and forty by night for the others. You shall pay me the twenty and forty." But the peasant reflected, for he knew his mother well. He knew how tenacious of life, how vigorous and unyielding she was. He knew, too, that she might last another week, in spite of the doctor's opinion, and so he said resolutely: "No, I would rather you would fix a price until the end. I will take my chance, one way or the other. The doctor says she will die very soon. If that happens, so much the better for you, and so much the worse for me, but if she holds out till tomorrow or longer, so much the better for me and so much the worse for you!"

The nurse looked at the man in astonishment, for she had never treated a death as a speculative job, and she hesitated, tempted by the idea of the possible gain. But almost immediately she suspected that he wanted to juggle her. "I can say nothing until I have seen your mother," she replied.

"Then come with me and see her."

When they got near the house, Honoré Bontemps murmured: "Suppose it is all over?" And the unconscious wish that it might be so showed itself in the sound of his voice.

But the old woman was not dead. She was lying on her back, on her wretched bed, her hands covered with a pink cotton counterpane, horribly thin, knotty paws, like some strange animal's or like crabs' claws, hands closed by rheumatism, fatigue, and the work of nearly a century which she had accomplished.

La Rapet went up to the bed and looked at the dying woman, felt her pulse, tapped her on the chest, listened to her breathing, and asked her questions, so as to hear her speak: then, having looked at her for some time longer, she went out of the room, followed by Honoré. His decided opinion was, that the old woman would not last out the night, and he asked: "Well?" And the sick-nurse replied: "Well, she may last two days, perhaps three. You will have to give me six francs, everything included."

"Six francs! six francs!" he shouted. "Are you out of your mind? I tell you that she cannot last more than five or six hours!" And they disputed angrily for some time, but as the nurse said she would go home, as the time was slipping away, and as his wheat would not come to the farmyard of its own accord, he agreed to her terms at last.

"Very well, then, that is settled; six francs including everything, until the corpse is taken out."

"That is settled, six francs."

And he went away, with long strides, to his wheat, which was lying on the ground under the hot sun which ripens the grain, while the sick-nurse returned to the house.

At nightfall Honoré returned, and when he went up to the bed and saw that his mother was still alive he asked: "How is she?" just as he had done formerly, when she had been sick. Then he sent La Rapet away, saying to her: "Tomorrow morning at five o'clock, without fail." And she replied: "Tomorrow at five o'clock."

She came at daybreak, and found Honoré eating his soup, which he had made himself, before going to work.

"Well, is your mother dead?" asked the nurse.

"She is rather better, on the contrary," he replied, with a malignant look out of the corner of his eyes. Then he went out.

La Rapet was seized with anxiety, and went up to the dying woman, who was in the same state, lethargic and impassive, her eyes open and her hands clutching the counterpane. The nurse perceived that this might go on thus for two days, four days, eight days, even, and her avaricious mind was seized with fear. She was excited to fury against the cunning fellow who had tricked her, and against the woman who would not die.

La Rapet was getting exasperated; every passing minute now seemed to her so much time and money stolen from her. She felt a mad inclination to choke this old ass, this headstrong old fool, this obstinate old wretch— to stop that short, rapid breath, which was robbing her of her time and money, by squeezing her throat a little. But then she reflected on the danger of doing so, and other thoughts came into her head . . . . So [on the next day] she went up to the bed and said to her: "Have you ever seen the Devil?"

Mother Bontemps whispered: "No."

Then the sick-nurse began to talk and to tell her tales likely to terrify her weak and dying mind. Mother Bontemps, who was at last most disturbed in mind, moved about, wrung her hands, and tried to turn her head to look at the other end of the room. Terrified, with a mad look on her face, the dying woman made a superhuman effort to get up and escape; she even got her shoulders and chest out of bed; then she fell back with a deep sigh. All was over. . . .

When Honoré returned in the evening, he found . . . [La Rapet] praying. He calculated immediately that she had made twenty sous out of him, for she had only spent three days and one night there, which made five francs altogether, instead of the six which he owed her.

This interesting story not only highlights the difference between fixed and variable costs, but also tells us that how labor is paid may influence the incentives of workers. The method of payment, as the story implies, could induce the wrong incentives in workers.

12.4 PERFECT COMPETITION AS A GOAL

One purpose of presenting the theory of perfect competition is to show why many economists and policymakers make perfectly competitive markets an ideal. The model of perfect competition is often used as a yardstick with which to compare real-world markets. Most actual markets violate one or more of the assumptions underlying the model of perfect competition, and the assumption a market fails to meet tells lawmakers and economists how to make the market more competitive. For example, if the price of hearing aids is high because elderly people lack proper information to compare prices, providing consumers with the information they need will probably make the market more competitive. This is not to say that perfect competition is always more desirable than other market structures. This section briefly analyzes the desirable and possibly undesirable features of the model.

Desirability of Perfect Competition

Perfect competition is viewed as a standard of market performance because the assumptions underlying the model guarantee that in the long run a large number of producers operate at the lowest possible point on their *LRAC* curve, and since $P = LRMC = LRAC$, consumers pay the lowest possible price for a good or service.

Perhaps equally important, in a perfectly competitive market the fundamental forces of supply and demand determine who gets what and how it is produced. Goods are produced by the lowest-cost firms. As prices rise, less efficient firms may enter, but if prices fall, it is these same firms that exit. Competition guarantees that the most efficient, lowest-cost producers operate. This is the ''how'' of production.

The ''what'' in production is established by demand. Consumers, not producers, decide this question. Cattle ranchers, for instance, would like to see more beef consumed, but the decision is made by buyers. Consumers decide whether they want beef, pork, poultry, or even meat at all. Free entry into, and exit from, any industry lets consumers make this choice. Finally, ''who'' gets what goods that are produced is determined by the willingness and ability of consumers to pay, which in turn are influenced by tastes, income, and prices.

Taking all of the assumptions of perfect competition into consideration, probably the most important feature of competitive markets is that buyers and sellers are so small relative to the total market that anyone acting alone cannot affect market prices. We will see in the next two chapters that, because of economies of scale, a few or even one firm may have lower costs than would be the case with a large number of producers. These kinds of market structures give producers some control over price. Prices can be higher because consumers do not have a large number of other producers from whom they can buy. What is produced and how to produce it are no longer determined by the impersonal interaction of supply and demand.

In fact, even when it is apparent that the overall cost of production is higher with many producers than with just a few firms, policymakers, by and large, would prefer more producers to fewer, because it is the *market that ultimately* determines prices and output, rather than the *managers* of a few large businesses. In a 1945 court decision that eventually led to a more competitive aluminum industry, Judge Learned Hand wrote in his court opinion:

> It is possible, because of its indirect social or moral effect, to prefer a system of small producers, each dependent for success upon his own skill and character, to one in which the great mass of those engaged must accept the direction of a few.[2]

It must be pointed out, however, that the large number of competing firms goes a long way toward explaining some undesirable aspects of the model of perfect competition.

Incentive Effects of Being Small

In making any decision, a firm or an individual weighs the marginal cost that must be paid to carry out an activity against the marginal revenue or benefit. This decision, of course, is made without any concern given to the impact the activity may have on total market benefits and cost. In the case of competitive firms, or of individuals acting alone, the actions of one economic agent in the market generally have no *perceivable* effect on the market outcome. This realization on the part of each market participant frequently impedes efforts to move a market in a socially desirable direction. Some examples will help illustrate this potentially undesirable trait of perfect competition.

Suppose scientists discover that a certain insecticide used by most farmers is harming the wildlife in a particular state. The governor pleads with farmers to change to a brand of insecticide that is less harmful. Farmers will be reluctant to make the switch (though they may also want to protect wildlife) because the original harmful insecticide is more productive or cheaper. If it were not, farmers would have been using some other brand voluntarily. Would farmers have any reason to comply with the governor's request, knowing that the original brand of insecticide harms wildlife? Probably not! Why not?

In the first place, farmers must realize that each one, acting alone, has an infinitesimal effect on total wildlife killed or damaged, even though all

---

[2] *U.S.* v. *Alcoa Aluminum*, 148 F. 2d 416 (1945).

farmers acting together would have an observable impact. Therefore no individual farmer has the incentive to bear higher costs with zero effect, even though each farmer deplores the fact that wild animals are being damaged or killed. Even if some farmers did decide to comply with the plea, the higher costs in the long run would drive their operation out of business. Furthermore, each farmer, being competitive, knows that the particular brand of insecticide used has no effect on the farm's sales or on the price that can be obtained for the product. The output of any one farm is indistinguishable from the output of any other farm. In this case, voluntary actions by any individual farmer would not help sales *or* the protection of wildlife.

A large farm with an identifiable product and a large share of the market would have different incentives than one that was competitive. Because of its size, the benefit to wildlife would be noticeable if use of the pesticide were discontinued. It may want to advertise to the public that it uses safe chemicals. These ads could increase demand and, therefore, sales and profit to the grower. A large farm could also become the target of public out-cry against the use of harmful pesticides. Its visibility to the community would add to the incentive to make a change. A market composed of fewer and larger firms might therefore have the incentive to use a different pesticide.

We can apply the same analysis to water or air pollution. Any small firm can pollute at close to zero cost to society. Each firm knows that with so many firms polluting, its own polluting activity has practically no effect on total pollution. Therefore, appeals for voluntary restraint are likely to have little or no effect on behavior. Every firm knows that reducing its pollution would raise costs, but would have no effect on the price of its product. As a consequence, firms would not have the incentive to reduce pollution voluntarily. (However, if someone charged for polluting, firms would reduce pollution. This is a problem that belongs in the section on property rights, and will be addressed in the final chapter.)

Similar analysis applies to the behavior of individuals in response to appeals for voluntary actions in the alleged social interest. Take, for example, the national reduction in the speed limit to 55 miles per hour. Do governmental appeals to reduce speed in order to conserve the nation's energy work? What do you think? As you know, time is valuable. If we drive the largest "gas guzzling" automobile 24 hours a day all year at 90 miles per hour, it would have virtually no effect on the nation's total gasoline consumption. For each individual, slowing down costs valuable time and has no perceivable effect on total consumption. Observations tend to confirm our expectations—very few drivers on the nation's expressways abide by the 55-mile-per-hour limit.

What about appeals by the President in the mid-70s to keep homes cooler in winter and use less air conditioning in the summer to conserve the nation's gas and electricity? If all homes complied, certainly the total use would decline. But any household knows that the temperature of its home has absolutely no effect on national energy use. Why bear discomfort if the discomfort has no perceivable effect on the total? Frequently, during water shortages in cities (often caused by too low prices), city officials ask households to cut down water use voluntarily. Again, everyone knows that his or her own use of water has no effect on the city's water use, so why comply?

During World War II, the government imposed price controls and rationing in the case of many goods. National appeals were made to consumers not to deal with black markets in the nation's interest. Yet there was considerable trade in black markets. Appeals to patriotism did not work well, even when the country experienced the greatest period of national purpose and patriotism in its entire history. Why should appeals to national purpose work any better now?

If any competitive firm is doing a social "bad", whatever that is, it would have little incentive to cease doing "bad" if its actions alone have only an infinitesimal effect on the total amount of "bad" and zero effect on sales, but would raise costs. In fact, even if owners of the competitive firms are earning rents on some of their resources, and therefore would not be driven out of business by the increased cost, few owners would be willing to sacrifice income, knowing the sacrificed income has no effect on total "bad". Large firms, on the other hand, have a perceptible effect on market outcomes. For this reason they may have an incentive as profit maximizers to undertake a "socially responsible" action. If they choose not to, profits to the firm could be hurt.

Product Variety

Another characteristic of perfectly competitive markets that may have undesirable consequences is a complete lack of product variety. Products must be identical in competitive markets to be perfectly substitutable—insuring that no seller has any influence over the market price. In some markets, this is not a bothersome imposition. Product variety is not important in agriculture, steel production, and coal. In other markets, however, product homogeneity would make consumers very unhappy. Suppose there was perfect competition in the apparel industry. Homogeneity implies one color, one style, one fabric—you can understand why consumers would not want *perfectly* competitive markets in such cases.

As soon as noticeable quality differences are allowed between products, the products become less substitutable. Because of product differences a Mercedes Benz is not readily substitutable for a Ford in the mind of most consumers. Most consumers would not consider the two automobiles in the same market, though Ford would like you to think so.

Product variety also leads to brand loyalties, which reinforce perceived product differences. Even though product differences may be superficial, brand identification can make certain products less substitutable with other products. For instance, firms like Levi Strauss & Co. and Coca-Cola sell products that have similar alternatives, but because of strong brand loyalties among consumers, they have considerable control over their price. Consumers identify so strongly with Levi Strauss & Co. and Coca-Cola that even substitutes are referred to by those respective registered brand names, Levis and Coke. It is difficult to say exactly how these loyalties develop. Firms attract loyal customers by having a reputation for superior quality, by being the first in the market with a new product, through advertising and creating an image associated with the consumption of their product, by providing good service, and so on.

In any case, there is a cost connected with product variety. Product differentiation, whether real or created by advertising, gives a seller some control over price. A product's price can be raised without the fear of losing all of the product's customers. In other words, the demand curve of the seller is no longer perfectly elastic. As a consequence, we will see in Chapters 13 and 15 that, if the cost curves are not different from those of perfectly competitive producers, prices and the average cost of production will be higher. This outcome should be considered the cost of product variety.

12.5 PERFECT COMPETITION AND CONSUMER'S SURPLUS

An important and desirable feature of the model of perfect competition is that in equilibrium firms produce at the lowest point on their *LRAC*. This means consumers in the market pay prices that just cover the costs of production and distribution. If prices were lower firms would not produce the product in the long run. By using consumer's surplus, it is possible to illustrate the benefit consumers enjoy from these low prices and the incentive of firms to operate in less than perfectly competitive markets.

Competition and Maximum Surplus

Figure 12–6, Panel A, illustrates the long-run equilibrium for a competitive firm. Competition guarantees that prices will be at the minimum point on *LRAC*. If they are any higher, entry occurs until they are restored to this level; if lower, exit from the industry reduces supply in the market until a higher price at minimum *LRAC* is recovered. From society's point of view, prices that are below *LRAC* are as undesirable as those above the minimum point on the curve. When prices are too low, it means too many resources are being devoted to producing the good, and these resources could be better employed in other industries. By the same token, we may say that high prices mean too few resources are used in the industry and society would be better off if output increased.

FIGURE 12-6   **Consumer's surplus in perfect competition**

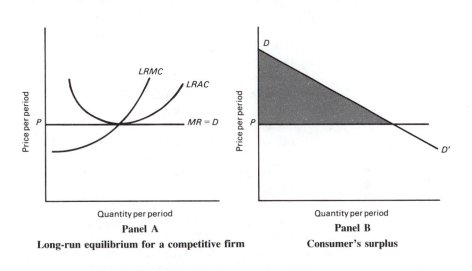

Panel A
Long-run equilibrium for a competitive firm

Panel B
Consumer's surplus

Panel B in Figure 12-6 shows the amount of consumer's surplus enjoyed by a representative consumer in the market. The shaded area between demand, *DD'*, and price represents the net benefit going to a market participant. In the long run it cannot be any greater because firms are producing at their minimum *LRAC*, nor will it be smaller. If price is higher in the short run, entry will restore the level of benefit now shown. Thus we argue that perfect competition maximizes consumer's surplus. When markets are not perfectly competitive, consumer's surplus will fall.

Consumer's Surplus and Imperfect Competition

With the help of Figure 12-6 we can introduce some reasoning for the existence of markets that are not competitive. We will discuss more fully these types of markets in subsequent chapters, but we can get a head start on the discussion by thinking about what a firm gains by not being a perfect competitor.

When a firm is not in a perfectly competitive market it is said to possess *monopoly power*. This is the capability to raise the price of a product without losing all sales. A perfect competitor has no monopoly power. If such a firm should increase price, given its perfectly elastic demand schedule, sales would fall to zero. There are various ways of measuring monopoly power, and all of them tell us that we can be sure that firms possess some monopoly power if their demand schedule is not perfectly elastic. There are basically two reasons firms depart from perfect competition and horizontal demand schedules. One way is through product differentiation, usually by advertising; the other reason for departure arises from restrictions on entry into a market. Restricted entry limits the number of firms in the market, allowing each seller to have a significant market share. When market share is large, a firm can have an impact on the market price charged, and demand for the firm is not perfectly elastic. Product differentiation makes products less than perfect substitutes, and without perfect substitutability the demand curve for a firm must necessarily be less than perfectly elastic.

What do firms gain by having monopoly power? In the short run, profits are possible—in the long run these gains may be competed away. Still, such returns for a short time are better than normal returns all the time. We can adapt Figure 12–6, Panel B, to see these gains and understand the behavior of firms with monopoly power. Figure 12–7 shows what a firm wants to do to increase profit when demand is downward sloping. Suppose a firm has no fixed costs and the price of a product is set at $SRMC = SRAC$ as shown. Total sales are x_0. This represents competitive pricing behavior. The firm earns no profits. If price can be increased to p_1 and sales restricted to x_1, the firm can earn profits equivalent to the shaded region in the figure. A less than perfectly elastic demand schedule gives the firm the opportunity to restrict output and

FIGURE 12–7   **Monopoly price above marginal cost**

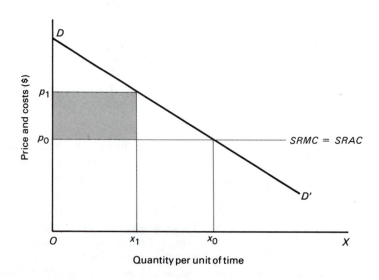

Quantity per unit of time

raise price. Firms with monopoly power tend to produce less than if they were perfect competitors. We will expand on this behavioral characteristic in the next chapter.

12.6 SUMMARY

The profit-maximizing rule is a powerful economic tool. It tells us that any maximizer should continue an activity, whether production or something else, until marginal cost is just equal to marginal revenue. This rule should be the approach used by every decision maker when deciding how much of something should be done. The essence of this rule was discovered earlier in Chapter 4, where we described the general principle of optimization. The concept of equilizing benefit and cost at the margin is a pervasive concept in economics.

The model of perfect competition is another tool widely used by economists. If markets approximate the assumptions of the model, it allows us a basis on which to make predictions about the effects of changes in a market. We worked through the impact of a price ceiling in the coal industry in detail, finding that fixing prices at a low level at the mines will have the long-run effect of making prices higher to consumers. The reasoning used in this application of the theory deserves serious study. The best way to gain experience at applying the model of perfect competition is to practice, and then practice some more.

We extended the applicability of the model of perfect competition by introducing the break-even chart. When a short-run cost structure is being planned, the relative size of fixed and variable costs can affect the size of potential losses and gains. By making more costs variable, rather than fixed, potential losses are lowered, but so are potential gains. Perfectly competitive firms, while having no control over price, do have control over costs in the way they are paid, and the proportion of fixed to variable costs can affect short-run returns.

This chapter has also presented an evaluation of perfectly competitive markets. Most appealing is that competitive firms produce at minimum average cost in the long run and earn only normal profits. The result is that consumers pay the lowest possible prices for goods and services. We have argued that consumer's surplus is maximized under perfect competition. As we will discover, no other market structure offers this much benefit to buyers. But, in reality, "perfect competition" is not unambiguously a *perfect* market structure. Because of their small size, market participants have certain adverse incentives. Individually, the actions of any one buyer or seller have an unnoticeable impact on the market. So market participants react myopically. The total impact of using dangerous pesticides or generating pollutants from production is not considered, since their contribution to the problem and its solution is of little or no consequence. The assumption of homogeneous products in the market is also bothersome. Product variety is, by most standards, a desirable feature of markets. When products are differentiated, firms gain monopoly power or a less than perfectly elastic demand schedule. We now enter a discussion of behavior when demand is no longer the horizontal price schedule.

TECHNICAL PROBLEMS

1. The supply of labor to all firms in a perfectly competitive industry is reduced. Explain the effects on the wage rate, the quantity of labor employed, total industry supply of the commodity produced, and the price of the product.

2. If price falls below average total cost in the short run, the firm, in the long run, will do one of two things. What are these, and under what circumstances will each be done?

3. Similar to our discussion of a price ceiling in the coal industry, trace through the impact of a price floor in the wholesale market. Do consumers pay higher or lower prices in the retail market?

4. In our example of the effect of a ceiling price at the mine on the retail price consumers must pay, we assume that coal from the mine was translated into retail coal in fixed proportions—a ton of coal mined is necessary for a ton of coal to be sold at retail. We know from our theory of production, that inputs can frequently be substituted for other inputs. How, if any, would the analysis change if users of the primary resource on which a ceiling price is imposed could substitute to some extent or use less of the input in the final product? For example, consider a ceiling price on leather and its effect on the price of shoes.

5. Why don't very small wildcat oil producers advertise that they don't pollute the environment, while giants like Exxon and Shell do a great deal of this type of advertising?

6. Explain precisely why consumers have to pay a higher price for product variety than they would if the product is homogeneous and produced in a competitive market.

7. Assume an increasing-cost competitive industry. Discuss the meaning of the area between price and the long-run supply curve.

8. Assume that a price-taking firm is thinking about entering a market. The firm can choose between the two short-run cost curves

$$TC_1 = 100 + 2X$$
$$TC_2 = 50 + 4X.$$

   The projected price of the product is $6.
   a. Identify marginal cost for each of the total cost schedules. What are fixed costs?

    b. In the same diagram, graph total revenue and both *TC* schedules.

    c. Find the break-even point for TC_1; for TC_2.

    d. If projected sales are 10 in the short run, what total cost schedule should the profit maximizer select? What is the loss or gain?

9.   Why is product differentiation desirable in the case of some products but not desirable for other goods?

10.   Explain why turning some fixed costs into variable costs can reduce both potential profit and potential loss. How could it change the break-even point?

11.   Why would firms wish to pay executives a fixed salary plus a bonus based on sales or profits? What about incentives?

ANALYTICAL PROBLEMS

1.   Assume that the peanut industry is a constant-cost industry. Let society's demand for peanuts increase. Explain precisely the steps that must be taken for society to have more peanuts at the same price. Suppose that government becomes alarmed at the first sign of rising peanut prices and imposes a ceiling price on peanuts at the original level. What will occur now? Explain. What will happen if the peanut industry is an increasing-cost industry? Does it matter whether the ceiling is imposed on the farmers' sales or the sales of retailers? Explain.

2.   In the 1960s, hula-hoops were a popular toy, but in a short while, their novelty wore off and prices fell. However, after a few months, they were higher than ever. Given this description, trace out on a graph the fluctuations in supply and demand. What kind of long-run cost industry is this?

3.   During the 1970s, much crude oil in the United States was subject to a price regulation below the world price of oil. When the regulation was removed, most people predicted the price of gasoline would increase dramatically because the price of an ingredient input rose. Gasoline prices in the United States did rise a little at first, but then either fell or remained constant. Explain why predictions of sharply rising gasoline prices were not correct.

4.   The beef market is competitive. During periods of rising prices, ranchers keep more heifers from market to breed them and expand their herds rather than fattening them to slaughter weight for beef. Of course, it takes time for heifers to produce calves. Because of this, would you expect beef prices to fluctuate greatly or remain relatively stable? Explain your answer.

5.   In regard to the situation described in question 4, a U.S. Department of Agriculture economist said that improved goverment information

on cattle numbers and both domestic and export demand will help stabilize the situation. Using your knowledge of the theory of competition, explain why this economist is probably wrong.

6. If all of the assumptions of perfect competition hold, why would firms in a real-world industry have little incentive to carry out technological change or much research and development? What conditions would encourage research and development in competitive industries?

7. A number of apartment buildings in New York are managed by co-op boards elected from building tenants. The board is the arbiter of rules and regulations in the building. Co-op boards can turn away any potential buyer, for almost any reason. Discrimination is prohibited, but boards do not have to provide a reason for rejecting a tenant. Certain tenants are very undesirable to boards. Opera singers, foreign diplomats, psychiatrists, attractive single women, and celebrities are on the undesirable list. On the basis of this information, would you expect co-ops to sell for more or less than an unrestricted condominium dwelling?

8. In the spring of 1985 farmers picketed the White House, demanding higher guaranteed prices and strict production controls. Participants argued that "We've got to have higher price supports so that we aren't forced to sell our products below the cost of production." Many stated that they couldn't make a profit under the present system. One farmer said, "Many of us are shoved out of business by forces beyond our control." (Associated Press, March 5, 1985.) In this context, do you feel the model of perfect competition is working well?

Chapter 13

Theory of Price under Monopoly

13.1 INTRODUCTION

The model of perfect competition provides economists with a very useful analytical tool, even though the exacting conditions of the model never hold entirely in the real world. The same statement applies to the model of monopoly. It is difficult, if not impossible, to pinpoint a true monopolist in real-world markets. Many markets closely approximate monopoly organization, and consequently the model often explains observed business behavior quite well.

A monopoly exists if there is only *one* firm that produces and sells a particular commodity or service and there are no *good* substitutes available. Since the monopoly is the only seller in the market, it has no direct competitors. Yet, as we will see, monopoly does not necessarily guarantee above-normal profits; it only guarantees that the monopolist can make the best of whatever demand and cost conditions exist without fear of new firms entering the market and competing away any profits.

While monopolists have no *direct competitors* who sell the same product, they do have *indirect competition*. In the first place, all commodities compete for a place in the consumer's budget. Thus, to a certain extent, the monopolist's product competes with all other goods and services in the general struggle for the consumer's dollar. Secondly, while there are no close substitutes for a monopoly product at the price charged by the monopolist, some goods could become closer substitutes for the monopolist's product if price is increased. The presence of a monopoly therefore depends on relative prices between the monopoly product and other "poor" substitutes.

Several examples can be cited to illustrate this point. Before 1982, American Telephone and Telegraph was the only firm providing long-distance telephone service in the United States. By virtue of its government franchise, no other firm could provide long-distance telephone connections. There were various substitutes that could be used: mail, telegrams, personal visits, smoke signals, and if the price of long- distance telephone service got too high, these substitutes would become increasingly attractive to consumers. Since deregulation, several direct competitors have entered the market to provide long-distance telephone connections.

As a second example, before World War II, the Aluminum Company of America (Alcoa) was the only manufacturer of aluminum ingots. There were no other producers of virgin aluminum, but it did have indirect competition from producers of other metals and the few firms that recycled aluminum scrap. Competition was not intense, however, because Alcoa kept the price of its raw aluminum relatively low.

For a third example, and depending on prices once again, natural gas can be a fairly good substitute for electricity. However, electric utilities are usually regional monopolies, so consumers cannot choose among producers if they decide to buy electricity. However, as the price of electricity increases, natural gas becomes a better substitute and consumers will switch to the gas fuel. These examples show us that any real-world monopolist has indirect competition to a greater or lesser degree that tends to weaken the monopolist's position. Directly, however, there are no other producers of the monopolist's product, and substitution is limited. To summarize:

Definition
A monopoly exists when there is only one producer in a market, and there are no good substitute products available to consumers.

The term *monopoly* is not very precise because it is difficult and sometimes arbitrary to judge when there are good and poor substitutes available for a particular product. Rather than categorically decide a seller is or is not a monopoly, it is usually more appropriate to describe the degree of *monopoly power* a seller holds. We briefly discussed this concept at the end of Chapter 12. We define it in the following way:

Definition
Monopoly power is the capability to increase price without losing all sales. The more monopoly power the firm has, the fewer sales it will lose after an increase in price.

A perfect competitor has absolutely no monopoly power. The slightest price increase will reduce sales to zero. Any market that is not perfectly competitive is characterized by sellers with some monopoly power. We will occasionally refer to monopoly power as market power in the discussion that follows.

Monopoly and Profit Maximization

The theory of monopoly follows directly from the theory set forth in Chapter 4 and in the introduction to Chapter 11. As in the case of the competitive firm, we assume that the monopolist wishes to maximize profit under the given cost and demand conditions. As you know, any firm can increase profit by expanding output so long as marginal revenue from the expansion exceeds marginal cost. The firm would not expand if marginal revenue were less than marginal cost. The basic principle that profit is maximized by producing and selling the output where marginal cost equals marginal revenue is the same for any firm, monopolist or perfect competitor.

The difference between monopoly and competition is that, for the monopolist, marginal revenue is less than the price the unit sells for, and unlike the competitor, the monopoly cannot sell all it desires at the going market price. Since a monopolist is the only firm selling in the market, the market demand curve *is* the demand curve facing the firm. While additional sales by a competitive firm do not lower the market price, a monopoly firm can sell more only if price falls. Therefore, the marginal revenue from an additional unit sold is the price of that unit less the *reduction* in revenue from lowering the price of those units that could have been sold at the previously higher price. The basic principle of profit maximization is, however, the same for the monopoly as for the competitive firm: *profit is maximized at the output at which marginal revenue equals marginal cost.*

13.2 MONOPOLY POWER MEASURED

In order to identify a monopolist we must know whether there are good substitutes available for a product. There is, for example, only one Hershey's chocolate candy bar, but Hershey is a monopolist *only if* consumers do not think any other candy bar will do in Hershey's place—even if the Hershey bar gets more expensive than the other candy bars. The problem of identifying substitutes for a product boils down to determining what products belong in the same market. Two products should be in the same market only if consumers feel they serve the same purpose and would switch to the other if the price of the one they use now should rise. One way of testing for monopoly is to study how sensitive a firm's sales are to a price increase. If a small increase in price leads to a large reduction in sales, we can be confident that consumers are finding substitutes for the seller's product. This suggests that measures of elasticity can be used to identify a monopoly.

Elasticity of Demand

One measure of elasticity used to identify monopoly and measure monopoly power is the familiar elasticity of demand. The existence of a downward sloping demand curve is evidence that perfect substitutes do not exist for the firm's product. As demand becomes less elastic at any price, fewer consumers are switching away from the product for any price increase. This means that consumers view the product less substitutable with alternative products. Monopoly power can therefore be measured by the firm's elasticity of demand. The less elastic is demand the more monopoly power it possesses. Conversely, as demand becomes more elastic, monopoly power declines.

A rough scale measuring monopoly power may be set up using a seller's elasticity of demand. When elasticity is infinite, meaning demand is horizontal and the firm is a perfect competitor, the firm has zero monopoly power. As demand becomes less horizontal and elasticity declines, monopoly power increases until the firm's elasticity is equivalent to the market's elasticity of demand. At this point, the firm would be considered the only producer in the market and have the maximum monopoly power possible.

Cross-Price Elasticity of Demand

Another helpful measure of monopoly power is *cross-price elasticity of demand*. This measure tells us directly whether two products are good substitutes and therefore if they are in the same market. Cross-price elasticity measures the sensitivity of the quantity purchased of one good to a price change of another. Take two products, X and Y; in terms of a ratio, cross-price elasticity is

$$E_{XY} = \frac{\text{Percent change in quantity of } X \text{ demanded}}{\text{Percent change in the price of } Y} = \frac{\%\Delta X}{\%\Delta P_Y} = \frac{\Delta X}{\Delta P_Y} \cdot \frac{P_Y}{X},$$

holding the price of X constant. This ratio can be positive, zero, or negative. If $E_{XY} > 0$, then a rise in P_Y leads to an increase in the amount of X sold. Consumers switch from good Y to good X; therefore, X and Y are *substitutes*. As E_{XY} gets larger, the two goods are better substitutes. It may be the case that when P_Y rises, less X is purchased. In this case, when consumers buy less Y, they also buy less X. The two goods are then, by definition, *complements*. Examples of goods with negative cross-price elasticities are automobiles and gasoline, bread and butter, shoes and socks, and so on. Finally, the price of Y may have no perceptible effect on the amount of X sold, in which case $E_{XY} = 0$; these goods are said to be *demand independent*.

The important reason for introducing cross-price elasticity is that it helps us determine whether two products are in the same market. A large positive elasticity means the goods are easily substitutable. Monopoly power is, therefore, likely to be weak. If a firm produces a product for which we cannot find any other products with a high cross-price elasticity, we can be reasonably sure that the firm is alone in its market, and there are no good substitutes available.

Cross-price elasticity, like elasticity of demand, can be used as a measure of monopoly power. As E_{XY} increases for any product pair, monopoly power falls. For identical products, E_{XY} approaches a large, positive number because any increase in the price of the identical product Y would drive all the sales to X. Monopoly power increases and becomes a maximum, on the other hand, as E_{XY} goes to zero. In this case no other products are viewed as substitutes for the product consumers presently purchase.

APPLICATION

United States v. E. I. du Pont de Nemours & Company[1]

On December 13, 1947, the Department of Justice brought suit against E. I. du Pont de Nemours & Company with the charge it had violated the Sherman Antitrust Act by monopolizing the sale of cellophane. Cellophane is a clear plastic wrap developed by Du Pont in the 1920s. The product was hailed as a major innovation in packaging. It was the only wrap "clear as plate glass, flexible, easily ripped open, [and] moisture-proof. . ."[2] By 1949, cigarette manufacturers would use nothing else, and 47 percent of all fresh produce, 35 percent of all meat and poultry, 34 percent of frozen foods, and 27 percent of crackers and biscuits were wrapped in the substance.[3]

There were, nevertheless, a number of other wrapping materials available in the post-World War II period—foil, glassine, paper, and films, such as Saran and polyethylene. Together, these alternative packaging substances were used more than 50 percent of the time by food processors.

The case was finally decided in 1953, six years after the suit was filed. Paul Leaky, Chief Judge of the U.S. District Court for the District of Delaware, wrote that the charge against Du Pont rested on two questions: "(1) does Du Pont possess monopoly powers; and (2) if so, has it achieved such powers by 'monopolizing' within the meaning of the Act. . ."[4] Only if the answer to the first question was yes should the second be answered. The Department of Justice argued that cellophane had no good substitutes, and since Du Pont produced and sold 75 percent of all the cellophane in the United States, it possessed an illegal amount of monopoly power. Du Pont, on the other hand, claimed that all flexible wrapping materials should be included in the market because they were substitutes for cellophane. If the market was defined in this way, the company would

[1] 351 U.S. 377 (1956).

[2] G. Stocking and W. Miller, "The Cellophane Case and the New Competition," *American Economic Review* 45, no. 1 (March 1955), p. 52.

[3] Ibid., p. 53.

[4] 118 F. Supp. (D. Del. 1953) at 54.

have only 14 percent of the market. Judge Leaky based his decision on the cross-price elasticity of cellophane with other packaging materials. He concluded that the "facts demonstrate Du Pont cellophane is sold under such intense competitive conditions, acquisition of market control or monopoly power is a practical impossibility."[5]

The Department of Justice, not satisfied with this decision, appealed the case to the Supreme Court. A decision was reached in 1956 upholding the District Court. A majority of Justices defined the market broadly to include all flexible packaging material. The decisive evidence supporting the court's opinion was cross-price elasticity of demand. In their written opinion:

> If a slight decrease in the price of cellophane causes a considerable number of customers of other flexible wrappings to switch to cellophane, it would be an indication that a high cross- elasticity of demand exists between them; that the products compete in the same market. The court below held that the 'great sensitivity of customers in the flexible packaging markets to price or quality changes' prevented Du Pont from possessing monopoly control over price. . . . We conclude that cellophane's interchangeability with other materials mentioned suffices to make it a part of this flexible packaging material market.[6]

High cross-price elasticity with several other products implies that there are good substitutes available and that the product in question is not alone in the market.

13.3 DEMAND AND MARGINAL REVENUE UNDER MONOPOLY

The fundamental difference between a monopolist and a competitor is the demand and marginal revenue curves they face. Let us use a numerical example to show the relation between demand and marginal revenue for a monopoly. Suppose a firm has the demand schedule shown in columns (1) and (2) of Table 13–1. Price times quantity gives the total revenue obtained from each level of sales. Marginal revenue, in column (4), shows the change in total revenue, column (3), per unit change in output. The only time marginal revenue equals price is for the first unit sold. That is, at zero sales, total revenue is zero; for the first unit sold, total revenue is the demand price for one unit. In going from zero to one unit, the change in total revenue is therefore the same as price. Since the monopolist must reduce price to sell additional units, at every other level of output, marginal revenue is less than price.

[5] Ibid., at 179–98.
[6] 351 U.S. 378 (1956).

TABLE 13–1 **Monopoly demand and marginal revenue**

(1) Units of sales	(2) Price	(3) Total revenue	(4) Marginal revenue
1	$2.00	$2.00	$2.00
2	1.80	3.60	1.60
3	1.40	4.20	0.60
4	1.20	4.80	0.40
5	1.00	5.00	0.20
6	0.70	4.20	−0.80

This principle can be more concisely stated with the help of Figure 13–1. A monopolist is thinking about lowering price a small amount from p_0 to p; output will increase slightly by Δx units, or from x to $x + \Delta x$ units. The change in total revenue (ΔTR) is the revenue the monopolist gets for the extra Δx units less area A in the figure which is $\Delta p \cdot x$. Area A is the revenue lost by selling the original x units for less than p_0. Area B is the revenue gained by selling the additional units at p. Thus change in total revenue may be written as:

$$\Delta TR = \text{area } B - \text{area } A = p \cdot \Delta x - \Delta p \cdot x, \qquad (13\text{–}1)$$

FIGURE 13–1 **Marginal revenue when demand is downward sloping**

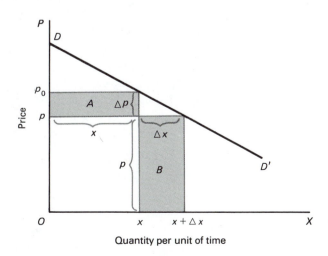

Quantity per unit of time

FIGURE 13–2   **Total revenue, marginal revenue, demand**

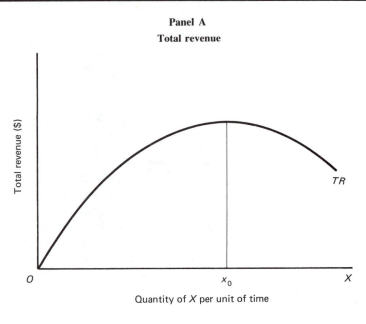

Panel A
Total revenue

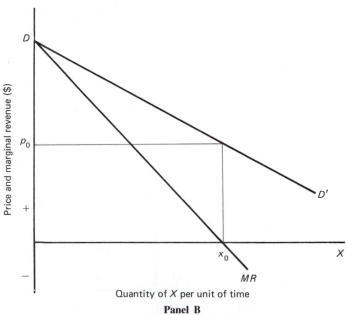

Panel B
Demand and marginal revenue

where Δp is the absolute value of the change in price (in this case, the change in price is negative). Since marginal revenue is the change in total revenue per unit change in output, we divide (13-1) by Δx to obtain

$$\frac{\Delta TR}{\Delta x} = MR = p - \frac{\Delta p}{\Delta x} \cdot x, \qquad (13\text{--}2)$$

where $\Delta p/\Delta x$ is the absolute value. Equation 13–1 or 13–2 tells us that marginal revenue is less than price.[7]

Relation

Marginal revenue is the addition to total revenue attributable to an additional unit of output or sales per period of time. After the first unit sold, marginal revenue is less than price. In general we may write marginal revenue as

$$MR = \frac{\Delta TR}{\Delta x}.$$

Figure 13–2 illustrates the relations between demand, marginal revenue, and total revenue for a monopolist with a linear demand curve. In Panels A and B, the scales of the vertical axes differ, but the horizontal axes are measured in the same units. Total revenue (Panel A) first increases when price is reduced and sales expand; it reaches a maximum at x_0 and declines thereafter. Panel B indicates the relation between marginal revenue (MR) and demand. As mentioned above, MR is below price at every output level except the first. (Since we have assumed continuous schedules, the two are equal infinitesimally close to the vertical axis.) The demand curve gives price at any output level; therefore, marginal revenue is always below the demand curve. Finally, when TR reaches its maximum, MR is zero (at output x_0, price p_0). At greater rates of output, MR is negative, since total revenue is falling.

We can use Equation 13–2 to describe in more algebraic detail the relation between demand and marginal revenue. Since Equation 13–2 is correct in general for any small change in X, we may rearrange some terms and write the equation using the formula for the elasticity of demand. Recall that $E = -\Delta x/\Delta p \cdot p/x$. Hence,

$$MR = p \left(1 - \frac{\Delta p}{\Delta x} \cdot \frac{x}{p}\right) = p \left(1 - \frac{1}{E}\right), \qquad (13\text{--}3)$$

where E is the absolute value of demand elasticity at any quantity. From Equation 13–3 it is apparent that when marginal revenue is negative,

---

[7] We can use Equation 13–2 to derive the equation for marginal revenue when demand is linear. Suppose the demand curve is of the form $p = a - bx$. Then the slope of demand is $\left(\frac{\Delta p}{\Delta x}\right) = -b$. Also we can substitute $(a - bx)$ for p in Equation 13-2 to write

$$MR = a - bx - bx = a - 2bx.$$

Marginal revenue has the same p- intercept, but twice the coefficient for slope.

TABLE 13–2   **Relations among marginal revenue, elasticity, and changes in total revenue**

	(1)	(2)	(3)
Marginal revenue	Positive	Negative	Zero
Demand elasticity..............	Elastic	Inelastic	Unitary
Change in total revenue for an increase in quantity	Increase	Decrease	No change

demand is inelastic ($E < 1$). When marginal revenue is positive, demand is elastic ($E > 1$). Finally, when marginal revenue is zero, demand has unitary elasticity ($E = 1$).

The movement from positive to negative marginal revenue as one moves down the demand curve follows from the definition of the elasticity of demand. As you will recall from Chapter 2, changes in total expenditure are related to demand elasticity. When demand is elastic, an increase in quantity (decrease in price) causes an increase in total expenditure. Over an inelastic segment of demand, an increase in quantity occasions a decrease in total expenditures, while in the unitary portion, total expendi-

FIGURE 13–3   **Relations among marginal revenue, elasticity, and demand**

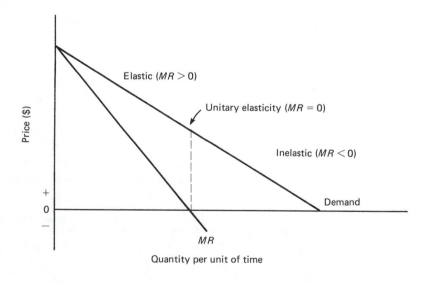

ture remains unchanged. Since total consumer expenditure on a commodity is the same as the monopolist's total revenue, the relation of elasticity to marginal revenue follows directly from the above relations. If marginal revenue is positive (negative), a small increase in sales leads to an increase (decrease) in total revenue. If marginal revenue is zero, a small change in sales does not change total revenue. A positive (negative) marginal revenue indicates that demand is elastic (inelastic) at that quantity. Zero marginal revenue means unitary elasticity. These relations are summarized in Table 13–2. They can also be seen in Figure 13–3, which shows a straight-line demand curve.

Relation

When demand is negatively sloped, marginal revenue is negatively sloped and is less than price at all relevant quantities. The difference between marginal revenue and price depends on the price elasticity of demand, as shown by the formula $MR = p(1 - 1/E)$. The maximum point on the total revenue curve is attained at precisely that rate of sales where marginal revenue is zero and elasticity is unitary.

13.4 SHORT-RUN MONOPOLY PROFIT MAXIMIZATION

The theory of monopoly is based on the profit maximizing principle discussed in the theory of perfect competition: optimize by setting marginal revenue equal to marginal cost. Though certain other features of the model of monopoly differ from competition, the profit-maximizing conditions are similar. Now that we have derived the marginal revenue conditions under monopoly, we are able to describe the short-run equilibrium for a profit-maximizing monopolist.

Cost under Monopoly

Short-run cost conditions confronting a monopolist are similar to those faced by a perfectly competitive firm. The theory of cost follows directly from the theory developed in Chapter 9. Cost depends on the production function and input prices. The chief difference for a monopolist lies in the potential impact of output changes on factor prices.

In the theory of perfect competition, we assume that each firm is very small relative to the total input market and can change *its own* rate of output without affecting input prices, just as any one consumer can change the amount of a good purchased without affecting its price.

However, if *all firms* in the industry change output and therefore the use of all inputs, the prices of some of those inputs may change, unless the industry is a constant-cost industry. The output of the monopolist, the sole firm in the industry, is the output of the industry. Certainly a monopolist, just as a competitive industry, may be so small relative to the demand for all inputs that its input use has no effect on prices. Even a very large monopolist could purchase some inputs (such as unskilled labor) whose prices would not be affected by the monopolist's rate of use. On the other hand, there is a high probability that when a monopoly purchases certain inputs, the firm's rate of purchase will have a definite influence on the prices of these factors of production.

Notwithstanding the monopolist's possible effect on factor prices, the cost curves are assumed to have the same general shape as those described in Chapter 9. The primary implication of rising supply prices of variable inputs is that the average and marginal cost curves rise more rapidly or fall less rapidly than they would if the input supply prices were constant. For example, marginal cost may rise not only because of diminishing marginal productivity, but also because input prices rise with increased use.

FIGURE 13–4 **Short-run equilibrium under monopoly**

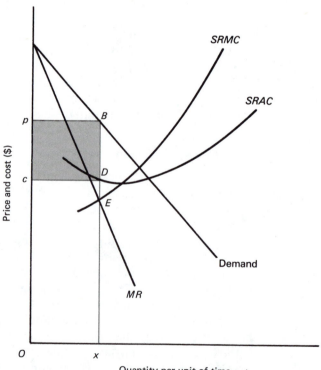

Short-Run Equilibrium

A monopolist, just as a perfect competitor, attains maximum profit (or minimum loss) by producing and selling at the rate of output where the positive (negative) difference between total revenue and total cost is greatest (least). This condition occurs when marginal revenue equals marginal cost (even though for the monopolist, MR does not equal price). Using this principle, the position of short-run equilibrium is easily described. Figure 13–4 shows the relevant cost and revenue curves for a monopolist. Since AVC and AFC are not necessary for exposition, they are omitted. The profit maximizer produces at E where $SRMC = MR$. Output is x, and, from the demand curve, we see that price must be p per

FIGURE 13–5   **Short-run losses under monopoly**

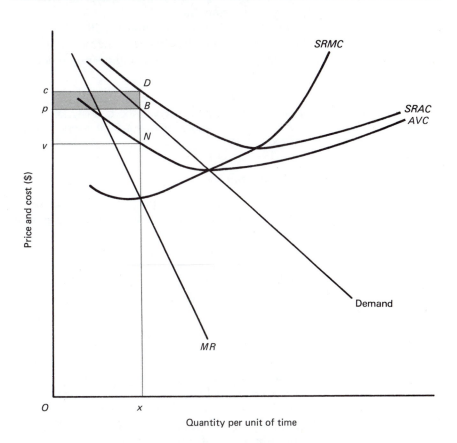

unit in order to ration the x units among those who wish to buy the commodity. Total revenue is $p \cdot x$, or the area of the rectangle $OpBx$. The unit cost of producing this amount is c. Total cost is therefore $c \cdot x$, or the area $OcDx$. Profit is $TR - TC$, or the shaded area $cpBD$.

In the example of Figure 13–4, the monopolist earns a pure profit. This need not be the case, however; a monopolistic position does not always guarantee above-normal returns. If demand is sufficiently low, a monopolist may incur a loss in the short run, just as a pure competitor may. Figure 13–5 shows such a loss situation. Marginal cost equals marginal revenue at output x, which can be sold at price p, but average cost is c, so total cost, $OcDx$, exceeds total revenue, $OpBx$; hence, the firm makes a loss of $pcDB$. The monopolist would produce rather than shut down in the short run, since total revenue exceeds variable cost $(OvNx)$; there is still some revenue $(vpBN)$ left to apply to fixed cost. If demand decreases so that the monopolist cannot cover all of variable cost at any price, the firm would shut down and lose only fixed cost. This situation is analogous to that of the perfect competitor.

In the short run, the primary difference between a monopolist and a perfect competitor lies in the slope of the demand curve. Either type of firm may earn a pure profit; either may incur a loss.

Principle

If a monopoly produces a positive output, in the short run it maximizes profit or minimizes losses by producing the quantity for which $SRMC = MR$. Since the monopolist's demand is above MR at every positive output, equilibrium price exceeds $SRMC$.

Monopoly Supply

The supply curve for a perfect competitor was the marginal cost curve. It is tempting to say the same is true for a monopolist, but a monopolist does not have a supply schedule.

To understand why, recall the definition of supply from Chapter 2: a list of prices and the quantities that would be supplied at each price on the list per period of time. For a monopolist, any number of prices may be associated with a given level of output, depending on the position of demand at that output level.

To illustrate this point, assume first that demand and the associated marginal revenue are $\overline{D}$ and $\overline{MR}$ in Figure 13–6. (Remember marginal revenue depends on the elasticity of demand.) In this case, $\overline{MR}$ equals $SRMC$ at output x and price is $\overline{p}$. Next, let marginal revenue and demand be $\hat{MR}$ and $\hat{D}$. While the marginal revenue again equals marginal cost at x, in this situation, the commodity price is $\hat{p}$. By changing the slope of the demand and, therefore, MR curves, the same output, x, can be sold at an infinite number of different prices. Thus, the monopolist has no supply curve.

FIGURE 13–6 **Why a monopoly has no supply curve**

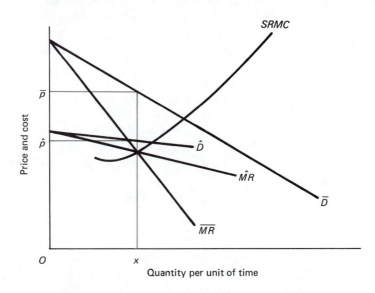

Numerical Illustration

A numerical example can illustrate the principal points of the short-run equilibrium for monopoly. In Table 13–3, the demand schedule in col-

TABLE 13–3 **Marginal revenue-marginal cost approach to profit maximization**

(1) Output and sales	(2) Price	(3) Total revenue	(4) Total cost	(5) Marginal revenue	(6) Marginal cost	(7) Profit
5	$2.00	$10.00	$12.25	—	$0.45	− $2.25
13	1.10	14.30	15.00	$0.54	.34	− 0.70
23	0.85	19.55	18.25	.52	.33	1.30
38	.69	25.92	22.00	.42	.25	3.92
50	.615	30.75	26.25	.35	.35	4.50
60	.55	33.00	31.00	.23	.48	2.00
68	.50	34.00	36.25	.13	.66	− 2.25
75	.45	33.75	42.00	− .03	.82	− 8.25
81	.40	32.40	48.25	− .23	1.04	− 15.85
86	.35	30.10	55.00	− .46	1.35	− 25.10

umns (1) and (2) yields the total revenue schedule in column (3). We can subtract the total cost of producing each relevant level of sales from total revenue to obtain the profit from that output. Examination of the profit column shows that maximum profit ($4.50) occurs at 50 units of output. Marginal revenue and marginal cost, shown in columns (5) and (6), give the same result. Since we make such large changes in the units of output produced, we are really estimating marginal revenue and marginal cost over the output interval by looking at the change in total revenue and total cost *per unit of* sales. Even with these estimates we see that the monopolist can increase profit by increasing sales, as long as marginal revenue exceeds marginal cost. If marginal cost exceeds marginal revenue, profit falls with increased sales. Therefore, the monopolist produces and sells 50 units, the level where marginal cost and marginal revenue are equal.

13.5 LONG-RUN EQUILIBRIUM UNDER MONOPOLY

A monopoly exists if there is only one firm in the market. This statement implies that entry into the market is closed. If a monopolist should earn a pure profit in the short run, no other producer can enter the market in the hope of sharing whatever profit potential exists. Therefore, pure economic profit is not eliminated in the long run through entry, as in the case of perfect competition. The monopolist will, however, have short-run profits capitalized into long-run costs. Just as the rents of a perfect competitor lead to higher factor costs, the rents earned by a monopolist are also captured in the long-run market value of the firm.

Long-Run Equilibrium Process for a Monopoly

A monopolist faced with the cost and revenue conditions depicted in Figure 13–7 would build a plant to produce the quantity at which long-run marginal cost equals marginal revenue. In each period, x units are produced, costing c per unit and selling at a price of p per unit. Long-run profit is $cpBE$. This is the maximum profit possible under the given revenue and cost conditions. The monopoly operates in the short run with plant size indicated by $SRAC_1$ and $SRMC_1$.

Demand or cost conditions can change for reasons other than the entry of new firms, and such changes cause the monopolist to make adjustments. Assume that demand and therefore marginal revenue decrease. At first, the firm will adjust without changing plant size. It will produce the quantity at which the new MR equals $SRMC_1$, or it will close down in the short run if it cannot cover variable costs. In the long run, the monopolist can change plant size.

Long-run equilibrium adjustment under monopoly must take one of two possible courses. First, if the monopolist incurs a short-run loss, and

FIGURE 13–7   **Long-run equilibrium under monopoly**

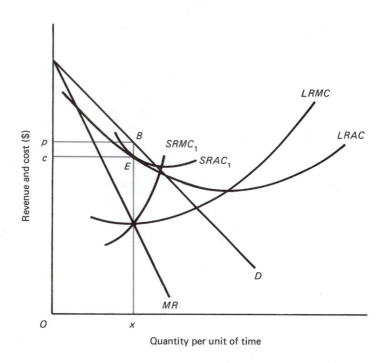

if there is no plant size that will result in pure profit (or at least, no loss), the monopoly goes out of business. Second, if it suffers a short-run loss or earns a short-run profit with the original plant, the entrepreneur must determine whether a plant of different size (and, therefore, a different price and output) will lead to a larger profit.

The first situation requires no comment. The second is illustrated by Figure 13–8. DD' and MR show the market demand and marginal revenue confronting a monopolist. $LRAC$ is the long-run average cost curve, and $LRMC$ is the associated long-run marginal cost curve. Suppose, in the initial period, the monopolist built the plant exemplified by $SRAC_1$ and $SRMC_1$. Equality of short-run marginal cost and marginal revenue leads to the sale of $\bar{x}_S$ units per period at price A. At this rate of output, unit cost is I; short-run monopoly profit is represented by the area of the shaded rectangle $ABCI$.

Since a pure economic profit can be reaped, the monopolist would not consider discontinuing production. Now the long-run marginal cost be-

FIGURE 13–8   **Change in long-run equilibrium for a monopolist**

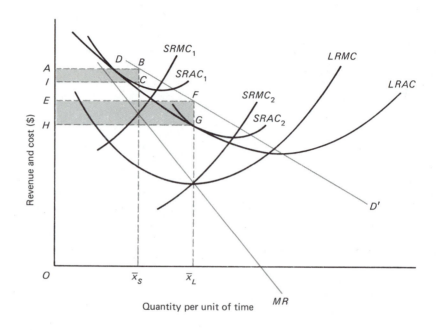

comes the relevant consideration. The long-run profit maximum is attained when long-run marginal cost equals marginal revenue. The associated rate of output is $\bar{x}_L$, and the price is E.

By reference to $LRAC$, the plant capable of producing $\bar{x}_L$ units per period at the least unit cost is the one represented by $SRAC_2$ and $SRMC_2$. Unit cost is accordingly H, and long-run maximum monopoly profit is given by the area of the shaded rectangle $EFGH$. This profit is obviously (visually) greater than the profit obtainable from the original plant.

Generalizing, we have the following:

Principle

A monopolist maximizes profit in the long run by producing and marketing the rate of output for which long-run marginal cost equals marginal revenue. The optimal plant is one for which the short-run average cost curve is tangent to the long-run average cost curve at the point corresponding to long-run equilibrium output. At this point, short-run marginal cost equals marginal revenue.

The profits reached by following the above principle are the highest the monopolist can attain; and they *can* be attained because, in the long run, plant size is variable and the market is effectively closed to entry.

Capitalized Profits

Even though it has been repeatedly stressed that monopoly profits are not competed away through entry, most monopoly owners will probably not enjoy excessive returns. This is because profits become *capitalized* into the value of the business. If assets earn above normal returns in the long run, the market value of these assets will increase until their return is normal, just as they did in competitive markets.

As an example, suppose you were the inventor of the popular board game *Trivial Pursuit*. After you made the invention you immediately had it copyrighted and you are the only person who can manufacture and sell this game. The copyright protects your business from entry for seventeen years. As the owner of the rights to this game, you can do one of two things to capture the profits from the product. First, you can go into production and marketing and earn above-normal profits as long as your copyright protects you and the game is popular. Another way to realize these profits is to sell the rights to your game.

This may sound like the wrong thing to do, but think about the price you would charge for these rights. Price should be equal to the present value of the profits for as long as the game would earn profits. Certainly, the prospective buyers would bid the price up to this level. That is,

$$\text{Price} = PV = \sum_{t=1}^{T} \frac{\pi_t}{(1 + r)^t},$$

where π_t is profit in the tth period, t is the period of time, r is the rate of interest, and T is the end of the time horizon. We assume the game earns above normal returns for T periods. In theory it should not make any difference to you whether you operate the business yourself or sell it at its present value. Selling the business at its present value is what is meant by capitalizing the profits. In practice, however, snags may arise that do not make you indifferent to this choice. You and a potential buyer of the game may not agree on the future profitability of the game, and both of you have incentives to either over- or under-estimate the game's value. Because of this problem you may not find a suitable buyer, and you end up going into production yourself.

If you do sell the business at its capitalized value, what will the profits of the new owner be? Only normal returns will be earned if foresight was correct. The price of the copyright to the new owner was high enough that only a normal rate of profits is earned on assets. Even though the new owner of the game continues to have a monopoly, the business does not earn above-normal profits.

13.6 MULTIPLANT MONOPOLY

In this section we explore the theoretical issues associated with a monopolist operating several plants in the production of a particular product. While this analysis is straightforward, it has strong implications on how we should treat plants that have higher costs. Interestingly, less efficient plants have the impact of shifting portions of a firm's marginal cost curve downward. This result holds for any multiplant firm in a competitive or monopolist market.

Suppose a monopolist produces output in more than one plant, with different cost structures. Consider first how a firm would allocate a given level of output among several plants. From the analysis set forth in Chapter 4, you have probably already deduced that the firm allocates a given output between two plants so that the marginal costs in both plants are equal.

Assume there are two plants—A and B. In the short run, at the desired level of output, the following situation holds

$$SRMC_A < SRMC_B.$$

Clearly, the firm should transfer output out of the higher-cost plant B into the lower-cost plant A. If the last unit produced in B costs \$10, but one more unit produced in A adds only \$7 to A's cost, that unit should be transferred from B to A. In fact, output should be transferred from B to A

FIGURE 13–9   **Multiplant monopoly**

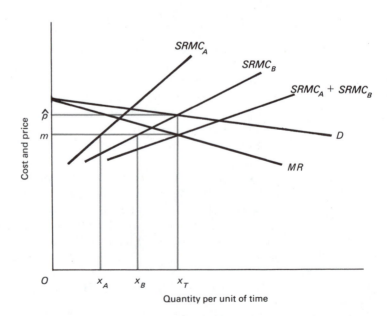

until

$$SRMC_A = SRMC_B.$$

We would suspect eventual equalization because of increasing marginal cost. As output is transferred out of B into A, the marginal cost in A rises, and the marginal cost in B falls. It is simple to see that exactly the opposite occurs in the case of

$$SRMC_A > SRMC_B.$$

Output is taken out of A and produced in B until

$$SRMC_A = SRMC_B.$$

The total situation is pictured graphically in Figure 13–9. Demand for the product is D, and marginal revenue for the firm is MR. Total short-run marginal cost for the firm $SRMC_A + SRMC_B$, equals marginal revenue at output x_T. The product price is p, and marginal cost in each plant is m. Plant A produces x_A units; plant B produces x_B units. Because of the way that the curves were derived, $x_A + x_B = x_T$. The firm is in equilibrium. Exactly the same principles apply for firms producing in more than two plants.

Suppose the monopolist did not have the high-cost plant A. What would happen to prices in Figure 13–9? The intersection of MR and $SRMC_B$ tells us that this price would have to be above p. Ironically, the high-cost plant actually helps keep the monopolist's price down.

APPLICATION

Nonconventional Mineral Extraction[8]

Presently there is a considerable amount of discussion about the implementation of new types of technology in mineral extraction, particularly in energy-related areas. The government established a synthetic fuels commission to investigate new sources of energy and technology. Most discussions of these new technologies and sources of energy make one fundamental mistake—they assume the new, higher-cost technology will increase the price of the mineral.

Suppose a natural gas producer can pump gas from the Permian Basin in Texas at an average cost of C_1 per million cubic feet *(MCF)*. The company also has some leases in the Rocky Mountains. These mountain

---

[8] S. C. Maurice and C. W. Smithson, "The Assimilation of New Technology: Economics versus Technological Feasibility," in *Advances in the Economics of Energy and Resources*, ed. J. R. Moroney (Greenwich, Conn.: JAI Press, 1980), pp. 173–98.

FIGURE 13–10   **The optimal use of technologies**

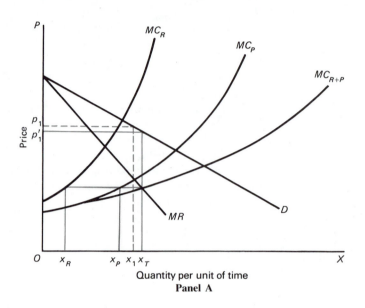

Panel A

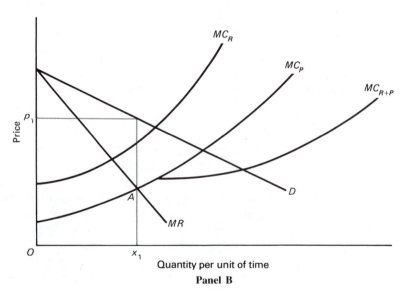

Panel B

deposits are of such low permeability that the firm must use a more expensive, special type of stimulation—perhaps nuclear stimulation—in order to extract the gas. The average extraction cost for a certain quantity, using the new technology, is C_2 per MCF, where C_2 greatly exceeds C_1.

Now, suppose that gas from Texas and gas from the Rockies are mixed, then pumped through the same pipeline to the East Coast. Texas gas makes up 80 percent of the total and gas from the Rocky Mountains, 20 percent. The total cost of the gas is, therefore,

$$C = .8\ C_1 + .2\ C_2,$$

which is, of course, more than C_1, because $C_2 > C_1$. For this reason, people argue that the new technology must raise the price of the gas.

We can adapt our theory of the multiplant monopolist to show that this analysis is not correct. In doing so, we will show how a firm decides on the proper mix of technology.

In Figure 13–10 Panel A, let MC_P be the firm's marginal cost of extraction in Texas. Given the demand and marginal revenue conditions, if the firm pumped only in Texas, it would sell x_1 MCF per period at a price of p_1. The marginal cost of pumping gas in the Rockies using the more expensive technology is the curve MC_R. The horizontal summation is MC_{R+P}. Using the new technology, the firm produces and sells x_T at a price of p_1'. The firm produces x_P in the Permian Basin—a reduction from the previous amount—and $x_P x_T$ from the Rocky Mountains. It is easily seen that, if the new technology is used at all, MC_R must intercept the vertical axis below the value where MC_P intersects MR. The new, but more expensive, technology will not raise prices. This is the same as the above conclusion that, if a multiplant monopolist uses a more expensive plant, price must be lower.

In Panel B, Figure 13–10, MC_R intercepts the vertical axis above point A. The new portion of the marginal cost curve, MC_{R+P}, is not relevant for decision making, and all of the gas sold comes from the Permian Basin. For both fields of gas to be profitable, demand must increase.

13.7 SUMMARY

A monopoly exists if there is only one seller in a market and there are no close substitutes for the seller's product. Few monopolies exist in the real world. It is more appropriate to speak of firms with monopoly power. Monopoly power is the capability to set price above marginal cost. It is frequently assessed in terms of the firm's price elasticity of demand and cross-price elasticity, which measures the degree of substitutability between two products.

Marginal revenue is the addition to total revenue obtained from selling an additional unit of output. For a perfect competitor, marginal revenue is price. Since a monopolist must lower price to sell more output, marginal revenue is less than price. In particular, the relation is given by $MR = P(1 - 1/E)$, where E is demand elasticity. If demand is elastic (inelastic), marginal revenue is positive (negative). Notice that a monopolist always maximizes profits on the elastic portion of demand. Since $MC > 0$, setting MC equal to MR requires $MR > 0$, which requires that E be greater than one.

The monopolist chooses the output at which $MC = MR$. In contrast to perfect competition, the market does not force the monopolist in the long run to produce the quantity at which long-run average cost is at its minimum and to charge a price equal to minimum long-run average cost and marginal cost.

This does not mean that a monopolist will earn profits in the long run. Since above-normal returns can be capitalized in the value of the firm, profit should not be observed in the long run. Any accounting returns represent a rent, just as they did in competitive markets. In the short run a monopolist can suffer a loss or make a profit depending on average cost and demand. If demand is nowhere above the average cost curve, the monopolist does not earn a profit and may even shut down if variable costs are not covered.

Finally, a multiplant monopolist will utilize less efficient plants to reduce the marginal cost schedule and increase profit. Any multiplant profit maximizer will utilize plant capacity in such a way to equate the marginal cost of production in each plant.

TECHNICAL PROBLEMS

1. Assume a monopoly with the demand and cost curves shown in Figure E.13–1. It is in the short run with the plant designed to produce 400 units optimally.
   a. What output should be produced?
   b. What will the price be?
   c. How much profit is made?
   d. If the firm can change plant size and move into the long run, what will be output and price?
   e. Will profit increase? How do you know?
   f. Draw the new short-run average and marginal cost curves for the new output.

2. Explain why a profit-maximizing monopolist always (in theory) produces and sells on the elastic portion of the demand curve. If costs were zero, where would the monopolist produce?

FIGURE E.13–1

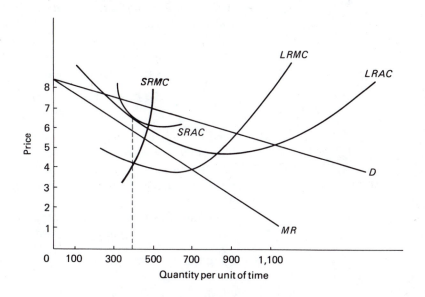

3. Compare the perfectly competitive firm and the monopolist as to how each makes the following decisions:
   a. How much to produce.
   b. What to charge.
   c. Whether or not to shut down in the short run.
   d. What happens in the long run if losses persist.

4. Suppose a monopolist has the demand curve $P = 40 - X$ and marginal costs are constant and equal to 10. There are no fixed costs.
   a. Find the profit-maximizing price and quantity. (Hint: $MR = 40 - 2X$.)
   b. Find profit.
   c. What is the elasticity of demand at the profit-maximizing output and price?

5. If a monopolist is not making enough profit, it can simply raise price until it does. Comment critically.

6. There are two industries; one is composed of one firm, the other of 1,000 firms. At the point of equilibrium, the demand elasticity is 1.75 for one industry and .86 for the other. What industry has what elasticity? Why?

7. The consumption of cigarettes is relatively insensitive to changes in price. In contrast, the demand for individual brands is highly elastic. In 1918, Lucky Strikes sold for a short time at a higher retail price than Camel or Chesterfield and rapidly lost half their market. Explain why the demand for a particular brand is more elastic than the demand for all cigarettes. If Lucky Strike raised its prices by 1 percent, what was its elasticity of demand in 1918?

8. A monopolist has the following total cost and demand functions

$$SRTC = (1/3) X^3 - 7X^2 + 111X$$
$$P = 111 - X$$

   a. Find average cost and graph this function.
   b. Note that marginal cost is $SRMC = X^2 - 14X + 111$. Graph this function.
   c. Graph the demand curve and the marginal revenue curve, where $MR = 111 - 2X$.
   d. Find the profit-maximizing output and price. Are there two possibilities? If so, defend the correct equilibrium.

9. By using the equation $MR = P\left(1 - \dfrac{1}{E}\right)$ and the profit-maximizing condition $MR = MC$, show that as a firm's elasticity of demand E becomes less elastic, a higher price is charged.

10. Suppose we have two substitute products X and Y. Sales of X are 100 and sales of Y are 1,000.
    a. Let the price of Y rise by 10 percent and suppose 30 more units of X are purchased. Calculate the cross-price elasticity E_{XY}.
    b. Let the price of X fall by 10 percent and sales of Y fall by 30 units. Calculate E_{YX}.
    Why are these numbers different? Are the products X and Y good substitutes? Is Y a good substitute for X, but X a poor substitute for Y?

11. Suppose a monopolist takes over a perfectly competitive industry composed of many plants. There can be no entry into the industry after the takeover.
    a. How would the monopoly allocate output among the various plants?
    b. What happens to output?
    c. Does supply elasticity increase or decrease?

ANALYTICAL PROBLEMS

1. You are an adviser to a local government agency. The agency will grant a monopoly license to a firm to operate a profitable business.

You are asked to set a price at which the government will grant the license. How would you advise setting the price?

a. Assume you wish to maximize the government's revenue.

b. Assume government will not set a price. How would you make the decision as to who gets the license?

2. The patent system conveys monopoly rights to some good or process. It is often claimed to be beneficial to economic growth because it encourages research. Are monopolies more likely to do research than perfectly competitive firms? Discuss.

3. Consider a monopolist with the labeled curves shown in Figure E.13–2. Where would the monopolist produce and what output would be sold? Note that they need not be the same. Does the solution tell us anything about why economists do not even consider the case of decreasing total cost as production increases?

4. In what sense is the only bank in a small town a monopoly? In what sense is it not? In what sense is GM or Exxon a monopoly? In what sense is it not? How about the U.S. Postal Service or your local electric company? If you were an adviser to a Supreme Court justice, how would you decide what does or does not constitute a monopoly? How could cross-price elasticity help you decide?

FIGURE E.13–2

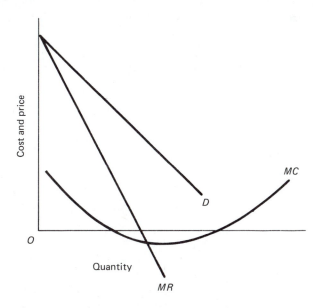

5. Evaluate the following claim: "If a firm earns above-normal profits in the long run it must be a monopolist. One way to measure monopoly power is by the amount of profits earned over a normal return. The greater is profit, the greater is monopoly power in the market."

6. If the cross-price elasticity between two products is 10, would the two products be in the same market? What if the cross-price elasticity is 5? 3? .5? How do *you* define a market?

7. It has been suggested by a student that a monopoly would not advertise; one way of identifying firms in a strong monopoly position is by their advertising budgets. As monopoly power increased, advertising should decrease. Comment on this idea.

8. "Some entrepreneurs will start a successful business only to sell it." Is this reasonable behavior? Are such people forfeiting profits when the business is sold?

9. There are two cable television companies in a city. A third company buys both of them to form a monopoly. Each company was paid 10 times its replacement value to sell. Will the monopoly necessarily earn above-normal profits? Do you think prices in the community will rise?

10. American Motors Corporation has two of its oldest automobile assembly plants in Kenosha, Wisconsin and Toledo, Ohio. It is considering two new plants to "replace" the older ones. If the new plants are built, should the older ones be closed? What does your answer depend on?

Chapter 14

Monopoly Behavior and Performance

14.1 INTRODUCTION

■ The reason firms have monopoly power is that other producers cannot enter the market and make at least normal returns. They are blocked by *barriers to entry*. Although there is some controversy over what constitutes a barrier to entry, for purposes of discussion, we will say that an entry barrier is any impediment that might prevent a firm from producing a particular product.

Barriers to entry may arise for technical reasons. Entry into a market may involve fixed costs so large that only one firm can produce in the market and pay them. Not all barriers are connected with the technology of production, however. In some markets, for instance, the brand loyalty of consumers can be an impossible hurdle to overcome. In this chapter we will describe several methods of fostering monopoly. Some barriers to entry can be *strategically* erected by the firm already producing in the market. We specifically discuss the strategy of entry limit pricing to illustrate such behavior.

Once monopoly power is secure in a market, a firm can undertake more sophisticated pricing strategies that increase returns above the profit-maximizing practice of setting $MR = MC$. The price determined by the intersection of marginal revenue and marginal cost is the price charged to everyone buying from the monopolist. However, a monopolist can often increase profits by charging different prices to different groups of consumers. This is referred to as *price discrimination*.

Finally, we will discuss the market performance of monopoly relative to more competitive market structures. We cannot say whether monopoly is "good" or "bad," but we can acquaint you with some of the issues involved in evaluating monopoly behavior.

14.2 EXAMPLES OF ENTRY BARRIERS

It is impossible to enumerate every reason a potential producer might not be able to enter a market since what constitutes a barrier depends on the market context in which it arises. We will cite several examples of how barriers have actually led to monopoly.

Economies of Scale

Economies of scale exist when the long-run average cost curve is declining over a wide range of output levels. Figure 14–1 shows a case where there are pervasive economies of scale; the *LRAC* curve declines at every level of output. If we let one firm operate in the market, profit maximization leads to output x_m and price p_m.

Suppose a smaller firm enters the market, producing output x_c. The lowest price this firm can charge without making long-run losses is $p_c = LRAC$ at x_c. Profits are normal, but this suggested price is higher than the monopoly price already charged. For identical products, the entrant will not make any sales. At the higher price the entrant might attempt to

FIGURE 14–1   **Monopoly and competitive equilibria with economies of scale**

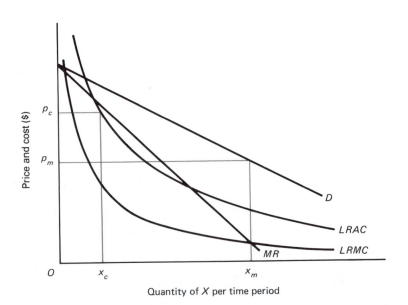

convince buyers its product is better, but this usually means either increased costs for advertising or higher production costs. In both circumstances costs will be higher and this makes successful entry all the more difficult.

Notice that the entrant's problem is intensified after it enters the market. Once its output, x_c, is added to the monopoly output, x_m, the total market output is greater. Price in the market must fall below p_m in order for the entire output to sell. The entrant is always looking at a greater price difference than $p_c - p_m$ after entry has been made.

When pervasive economies like those in Figure 14–1 exist, it is very difficult to maintain a competitive market, even if a number of producers begin at a small scale. In fact, competition could only exist if producers were strictly prohibited from expanding. Imagine what would happen if they were not. Every firm would have the incentive to expand and move down the *LRAC* curve where unit costs would be lower, and, as a consequence, prices could be lower. The larger firm could always undersell smaller firms and drive them out of business. Bigger firms would continue getting bigger until only the largest firm remained. Pervasive economies of scale are not conducive to the existence of perfect competition, because profit-maximizing incentives naturally lead each firm to try to dominate the industry. Eventually the largest firm will drive the smaller ones out of the market. Frequently, when a monopoly exists because of economies, it is said to be a *natural monopoly*.

Fixed Costs

Large fixed costs relative to variable costs can also lead to firms with monopoly power. Once again, the cause of monopoly power lies in the cost structure of production. To illustrate, in the short run let $SRMC = AVC$, so that average variable and marginal costs are constant. Fixed costs (FC) exist and are large. Figure 14–2 shows the cost schedule along with demand and marginal revenue. If the monopolist had to behave as a perfectly competitive firm and set $P = MC$, price would be p_c and output would be x_c. Profits would be negative, because variable costs are just covered, so there is no revenue to pay fixed costs. Such behavior would continually cause losses and therefore the firm would not produce in the long run.

The only way a firm can manage to break even is if it has some monopoly power, or more precisely, if the firm can raise price above marginal cost. If the firm behaves like a monopolist by setting $MR = SRMC$, then revenue above total variable cost equivilent to area p_mABp_c is earned, and this may be enough to cover fixed costs. Another firm could not enter the market and earn normal returns. Output would increase from entry and cause price to fall. Neither firm would then earn

FIGURE 14–2   **Monopoly with fixed costs**

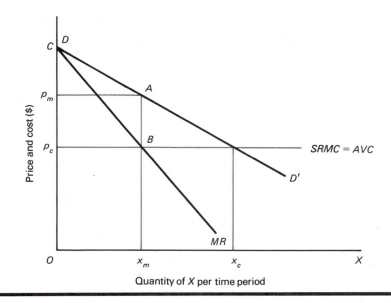

normal returns and one or both would exit from the market in the long run. The single firm acting like a monopolist has no threat of entry in the market, because excessive profits are not earned.

Barriers Created by Government

An obvious entry barrier is government. Allocations, licensing, and franchises are ways monopolies are created by fiat. Allocations, for instance, are granted to growers of many agricultural commodities to prevent the free entry of farmers into a crop market. The allocation tends to restrict output and raise the price of a foodstuff, because entry cannot take place when short-run profits are earned. Licenses are granted to radio and television stations by the Federal Communications Commission, and only those stations possessing a license are allowed to operate. Locally, this confers immense monopoly power on those stations that have FCC approval. Entrants can petition the FCC for a license to operate, but if those who are operating protest to the commission, the petition is usually denied. Governments also grant exclusive franchises for city, county, and state services. For example, local telephone and cable television utilities have ultimate monopoly power in that they are the only regional producer of the product. By law, no other producer can exist.

Another legal barrier to competition lies in the patent laws of the United States. These laws make it possible for a person to apply for and obtain the exclusive right to produce a certain commodity, or to produce a commodity by means of a specified process that provides an absolute cost advantage. E. I. du Pont de Nemours & Company enjoyed patent monopolies over many commodities, cellophane being the most notable. The Eastman Kodak Company continues to hold numerous patents on its camera equipment.

Despite examples to the contrary, holding a patent on a product or production process may not be quite what it seems in many instances. In the first place, the holder of a product patent may choose not to exploit the monopoly position in the production of the product. If diseconomies of scale set in at a low level of production, the patent holder may find it more profitable to sell production rights to a few firms, or to many. Second, a firm that owns a patented lower-cost production process may have a cost advantage over other firms in the market, but sell only a small part of the industry's total output at the equilibrium position. The new technique will lead to patent monopoly only if the firm has the capability to supply the entire market, or finds it profitable to do so. Third, a patent gives one the exclusive right to produce a particular, meticulously specified commodity, or to use a particular, meticulously specified process to produce a commodity. A patent does not preclude the development of closely related substitute goods or closely allied production processes. International Business Machines has the exclusive right to produce their patented computers, but many other computers are available and there is competition in the computer market.

Input Barriers

Historically, an important reason for monopoly power has been the control of raw-material supplies. If one firm (or perhaps a few firms) controls all of the known supply of a necessary ingredient for a particular product, the firm or firms can refuse to sell that ingredient to other firms at a price low enough for them to compete. Since no others can produce the product, monopoly results. For many years the Aluminum Company of America (Alcoa) owned almost every source of bauxite, a necessary ingredient in the production of aluminum, in North America. The control of resource supply, coupled with certain patent rights, provided Alcoa with an absolute monopoly in aluminum production. It was only after World War II that the federal courts effectively broke Alcoa's monopoly in the aluminum industry.

Another frequently cited input barrier arises in capital markets. Established firms, perhaps because of a history of good earnings, are able to secure financing at a more favorable rate than new firms. Imagine how far a typical person would get by walking into a bank and requesting a loan for $20 million to start a mainframe computer company. Most bankers would take a very dim view of this new company's survival. Knowing that you would be in the same market as IBM and other well-established companies, bankers would probably turn down the loan application. If the loan was made available, the interest rate for a new company would be above that paid by established firms. Capital markets pose a barrier for new firms when a large investment is necessary to enter a market.

Brand Loyalties

On the demand side, older firms may have, over time, built up the allegiance of their customers. New firms might find this loyalty difficult to overcome. No one knows what the service or repair policy of a new firm may be. The preference of buyers can also be influenced by a long successful advertising campaign; established brands, for instance, allow customers recourse if the product should be defective or short of its advertised promises. Although technical economies or diseconomies of scale may be insignificant, new firms might have considerable difficulty establishing a market organization and overcoming buyer preference for the products of older firms. A classic example of how loyalty preserves monopoly power can be found in the concentrated lemon juice market. ReaLemon lemon juice has successfully developed such strong brand loyalties among consumers that rival brands evidently cannot survive in the market. The situation is so serious that the courts recently forced ReaLemon to license its name to would-be competitors.[1]

The purpose of this discussion is to expose you to several of the most common types of entry barriers and to illustrate the diversity of factors that prevent entry into a market and, consequently, foster monopoly power. It is noteworthy that several of the barriers mentioned are somewhat influenced by the monopolist. The control of inputs and the development of consumer loyalties are effective barriers essentially erected by firms already producing in the market. Monopoly power can sometimes be gained by the strategic behavior of incumbent firms. In the next section, we will talk more about strategies that keep potential entrants out of the market.

14.3 ENTRY LIMITING STRATEGIES

We want to address in more detail some of the ways a monopolist can erect barriers to entry by manipulating price, carrying excess capacity, or producing multiple products. The theory in this field, commonly referred to as strategic behavior, is developing quickly in both economics and

---

[1] See Richard Schmalensee, "On the Use of Economic Models in Antitrust: The ReaLemon Case," *University of Pennsylvania Law Review* 127, no. 4 (April 1979), pp. 994–1050.

business. The topics discussed here will serve to introduce you to the analysis rather than give you an in-depth understanding.

Entry Limit Pricing

Under some circumstances, a monopoly might charge a price below that where short-run profit is maximized and, therefore, produce and sell an output greater than that where marginal revenue equals marginal cost. One such circumstance would be the case of a monopolist that, facing *potential* competition, lowers price to block the entry of potential competitors.

Figure 14–3 illustrates an example where a monopolist might lower price to prevent entry. A monopolist's long-run average and marginal costs are $LRAC_M$ and $LRMC_M$. Market demand and marginal revenue are D and MR. The profit-maximizing price and quantity are p_1 and x_1. Assume that, for technological reasons, the most advantaged potential rival would have the average cost curve $LRAC_C$. Even though the competitor suffers a cost disadvantage, entry into the industry could be made

FIGURE 14–3   **Price cutting as a barrier to entry**

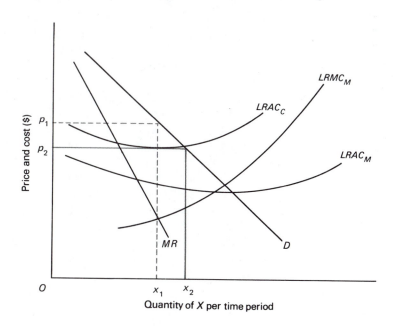

at a price lower than p_1 but above $LRAC_C$. It is, therefore, possible that some of the monopolist's business could be taken away by an entrant.

The monopoly, however, could block attempts to enter the industry by setting a price slightly below the minimum point of the potential competitor's average cost curve. In order for the competitor to realize any potential profit, price in the market must be above $LRAC_C$ over some range of outputs. If the monopoly sets the price p_2 and sells x_2, the competitor would not be able to produce any output where price is greater than average cost and would not have the incentive to enter the market. The monopoly's profit, of course, will be lower in the long run as a result of decreasing price from p_1 to p_2, but probably higher than if entry had actually occurred. If the threat of entry is not great, the monopolist may not wish to sacrifice the stream of higher earnings. If entry is easy, the monopoly firm may well be satisfied with lower profit and the retention of its monopoly position. An analysis of this situation requires the monopolist to compare the discounted future streams of profit with and without entry.

APPLICATION

Entry Limit Pricing

The decision to set price below the point corresponding to the intersection of the marginal revenue and marginal cost curves involves a choice between two discounted streams of profit. Profit maximization depends on relative profits in each period and the discount rate. Let us consider a specific example.

Suppose we have a firm that is currently a monopolist in the production of some good. Assume, for analytical purposes, that the firm has a 10-year time horizon and a choice of two strategies. First, it can set prices to prevent entry and earn a steady stream of profits over its entire planning horizon. Or it can charge a price that enables it to earn higher profits at first but that later encourages entry. After entry, profits are reduced. Figure 14–4 shows the alternative profit streams.

If the firm ignores the threat of entry, it can earn $500,000 a year during years 1 through 3. After entry takes place at the end of year 3, it will earn $250,000 a year in years 4 through 8, and no pure profit in years 9 and 10. With a 12 percent interest rate, the present value of following such a strategy is

$$PV_1 = \sum_{t=1}^{3} \frac{\$500,000}{(1 + .12)^t} + \sum_{t=4}^{8} \frac{\$250,000}{(1 + .12)^t} = \$1,842,000.$$

FIGURE 14-4 **Entry limit profits and profits with entry**

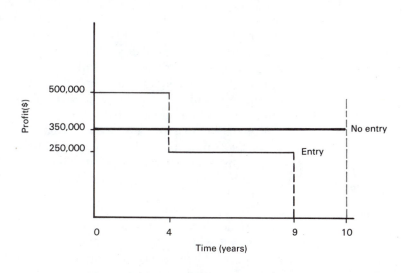

Alternatively, the firm could set an entry limit price and earn $350,000 per year over the entire horizon. Using this strategy, present value is

$$PV_2 = \sum_{t=1}^{10} \frac{\$350,000}{(1 + .12)^t} = \$1,977,570.$$

Clearly the firm would maximize profits by charging the lower price, which discourages entry and ensures the firm's monopoly position. Of course, a different interest rate or a different stream of income could make the first strategy more profitable. For example, if the stream of income under the entry limit price was $260,000 a year, the present value of the stream, using a 12 percent rate of interest, is approximately $1.5 million. In this case, the firm would set a high price during the early years, letting entry drive it down in later periods. The decision is not static, it involves comparing profit streams over time. This discussion of entry limit pricing emphasizes the fact that high monopoly prices encourage the production of substitute products. Potential sellers observe above-normal profits in a market and look for a way to earn them.

Capacity Barriers to Entry

A monopolist does not necessarily have to keep price low to block entry, and may not want to if it can hold excess production capacity in reserve. This capacity signals to other firms thinking about entry that the monopolist has the capability to quickly increase production and lower price if competition threatens. It will take longer for an entrant to build a new factory in order to enter a market than it would for the monopolist to gear up idle capacity. By the time the new firm is ready for business, output in the market would be greater and prices lower from increased production by the monopolist.

Compared to a pricing strategy that blocks entry, it may be less expensive (more profitable) for a monopolist to hold its share of the market by keeping idle capacity. The choice depends on the relative discounted stream of expenditures for capacity against the discounted stream of increased profit from setting price above the relatively low entry limit price—the same sort of comparison made in the above application. If demand is not very elastic in the market, a small increase in production will cause price to fall greatly, whereas a large sacrifice in revenue must be made to keep prices low. Consequently, a small amount of excess capacity may be a much less costly means to block entry.

Multiproduct Cost Barriers

When a firm produces more than one product and uses inputs in the production process that contribute simultaneously to the production of two or more goods, sometimes the total cost of producing the goods together is less than producing each separately. Some obvious examples of cases in which an input produces more than one product simultaneously are cattle used to make beef and leather, a well that pumps crude oil and natural gas, and trees that produce wood for lumber and paper.

Less obvious examples arise from capital expenditures that contribute to the production of more than one product. Railroads, for instance, offer both freight and passenger transportation over the same tracks and between the same depots. These inputs are shared. The postal service shares its capital in sorting and delivering parcels and letters. Finally, telephone companies use the same lines and switching gear to place local and long-distance calls. In these instances, a single investment contributes the production of more than one product. This is a common phenomenon among multiproduct firms.

Whenever it is less costly to produce products together rather than separately, costs are said to be *subadditive*. If we let $C(X)$ be the total cost of producing X, and $C(Y)$ be the cost of producing Y, then cost is subadditive, if, for any amount of X and Y,

$$C(X) + C(Y) > C(X,Y),$$

where $C(X,Y)$ is the cost of producing the goods together.

Subadditivity can create barriers to entry. Suppose we have three products, X, Y, and Z, with the following costs of production for a *specified* number of units:

1. X, Y, or Z produced alone has a total cost of $10 for the specified number of units.
2. Any two products produced together have the cost of $16 for the specified number of units.
3. All three products produced together in the specified amounts have a total cost of $23.

Thus we see that

$$C(X) + C(Y) + C(Z) = \$30$$
$$C(X,Y) + C(Z) = C(X,Z) + C(Y) = C(Y,Z) + C(X) = \$26$$
$$C(X,Y,Z) = \$23.$$

Costs are subadditive because it is less costly to produce two together rather than all three separately, and all three together rather than just two. Notice that the firm producing X, Y, and Z together can undersell any firm that is not. For instance, the seller with a cost of $23 could set $p_X = p_Y = p_Z = \$7.99$ and not be undersold by anyone in the long run. Those producers making two or fewer products together could be driven out of business. A firm must, therefore, produce all three products to successfully enter any one market, thus creating a barrier to entry. Generally, it is more costly to enter all three markets and produce all three products than it is to just enter one.

New Product Development as a Barrier to Entry

Sometimes a monopolist can block entry by introducing new substitutes for its own product in the market. As bizarre as this may sound, such a maneuver is greatly preferred to seeing entrants introduce them. Producing related products crowds the market with choices. As choices proliferate, the demand for each individual product decreases and becomes more elastic. This makes it more difficult for a new firm to enter the market, since it would have a smaller demand. Price and sales would be lower than would be the case if the original firm had not introduced so many substitutes. It therefore becomes less likely under these conditions that total costs will be covered.

Historically, there are some interesting cases where firms with monopoly power sold multiple products expressly for the purpose of blocking entry. In the 1940s, American Tobacco, Liggett and Myers (L&M), and Reynolds, after being found guilty of conspiring to monopolize the cigarette industry, began independently introducing multiple cigarette brands to protect their respective market shares. Before the antitrust suit, the companies were purchasing low-grade tobacco at auctions in an effort to keep new entrants from introducing a low-grade, inexpensive cigarette. Apparently it was not used in cigarette production and nothing was done with the tobacco after it was purchased. When the suit was settled, the companies were ordered to cease and desist from this practice. Soon thereafter, the companies began developing their new brands.

A more recent example of brand proliferation to block entry can be found in the ready-to-eat cereal industry. In the mid-70s the Federal Trade Commission (FTC) began investigating the big three cereal makers—Post, Kellogg, and General Mills—for possible anticompetitive behavior. The accusation made by the FTC was that these companies had generated multiple brands of cold cereal to deter entry. They had introduced a sufficient number of brands to cover the spectrum of tastes consumers had for cold cereals. No new firm could come into the market and carve itself a niche, because any type of cereal the firm could develop would have a close substitute from one of the other makers. Nothing came of the FTC investigation, largely because it was very difficult to prove the intentions of the incumbent cereal makers, but the strategy, for whatever reason it was pursued, was a very effective deterrent to entry.

Summary of Strategies

Strategic behavior on the part of monopoly can arise in numerous forms. We have just scratched the surface of this area of economic theory. We see that firms with monopoly power can take actions to block the entry of additional producers. These actions may take the form of setting relatively low prices, holding excess capacity against the threat of new production, producing multiple products to lower the cost per unit of output, and producing related products in order to reduce demand for a new entrant.

We have not discussed all forms of strategic behavior; many strategies are tailored to the particular market where the monopoly produces. The few mentioned should make it clear, however, that entry into a market is often not "naturally" impeded. It is blocked because those firms already in the market seek to keep new rivals out of the market.

14.4 PRICE DISCRIMINATION

In 1920, A. C. Pigou wrote that, if buyers could be separated into groups with different price elasticities of demand, a monopolist could charge different prices for the same product and raise profits.[2] In general,

---

[2] A. C. Pigou, *The Economics of Welfare* (London: Macmillan, 1920).

the more a seller knows about buyer preferences and the less easily buyers can trade among themselves, the greater the potential profit from setting different prices for the same good.

When consumers in a market do not pay the same price for the same product, the seller is price discriminating. There are two crucial points to note about the definition of price discrimination. First, *exactly* the same products must have different prices. A vacation trip from Boston to Acapulco is not the same as a trip from Houston to Acapulco because transportation costs are different. Timing may also be important—a trip to Acapulco in the winter is not the same as one in summer. Demand is greater in the winter than it is in the summer, and this raises the price of the vacation. Second, in order for price discrimination to exist, production costs must be equal. If costs are different, a profit maximizer who sets $MR = MC$ will usually charge different prices for a product. Costs may differ because of transportation charges, as mentioned. They may also differ because products are produced in different plants. In such cases the vintage of the facility or differing labor contracts may make costs different.

It might seem that price discrimination would rarely exist. Not so. There are many examples of markets with price discrimination. A pharmacy giving senior citizen discounts on prescriptions while other customers pay full price is practicing price discrimination. Theaters discriminate when they charge teenagers a lower ticket price than adults for the same showing. Hardware stores discriminate through their use of retail and commercial accounts. Commercial customers usually receive large discounts. It is important not to confuse the sale of what are actually different products with price discrimination. For emphasis:

Definition
Price discrimination exists when buyers pay different prices for the same product. Products may differ if production costs, delivery expenses, and the time of sale are not identical.

The purpose of this section is to discuss the various types of price discrimination. We begin with an analysis of third-degree discrimination, the most frequently encountered form. Under third-degree price discrimination, sellers charge different prices in separate markets based on the elasticities of demand in the markets. We then describe two more specialized forms of discrimination, commonly called first- and second-degree price discrimination.

Price Discrimination in Theory—Third Degree

In order for a firm to discriminate, markets must be *separable*. If purchasers in the lower-price market are able to sell the commodity to buyers in the higher-price market, discrimination will not exist for long.

TABLE 14–1 **Allocation of sales between two markets**

Quantity	Marginal revenue market I		Marginal revenue market II	
1............	$45	(1)	$34	(3)
2............	36	(2)	28	(5)
3............	30	(4)	22	(7)
4............	22	(6)	13	(10)
5............	17	(8)	10	(12)
6............	15	(9)	8	
7............	10	(11)	7	
8............	7		4	
9............	4		2	
10............	0		1	

Arbitrage, or secondary trading between buyers, will soon restore a single, uniform price in the market. Goods that cannot be easily traded are more apt to have discriminatory prices than are those that can be easily transferred. For example, a patient receiving medical care at a relatively low price cannot resell his or her operation to another patient, but a lower-price buyer of some raw material could perhaps resell it to someone in the higher-price market. Discrimination is more likely to occur in the exchange of services than material commodities.

As a first step in the analysis of discriminatory pricing, let us assume that a monopoly has two separate markets for its product. Demand conditions in each market are such that the marginal revenues from selling specified quantities are as given in Table 14–1. Assume also that the monopoly decides to produce 12 units. How should it allocate sales between the two markets?

Consider the first unit; the firm can gain $45 by selling it in the first market or $34 by selling in the second market. Obviously, if it sells only one unit per period, it will sell in market I. The second unit per period is also sold in the first market since sale there increases revenue by $36, whereas it would only bring $34 in market II. Since $34 can be gained in II and only $30 in I, unit three is sold in market II. Similar reasoning shows that the fourth unit goes to I and the fifth to II. Since unit six adds $22 to revenue in either market, it makes no difference where it is sold; six and seven go to either market. Eight and nine are sold in I because they yield higher marginal revenue there; ten goes to II for the same reason. Unit 11 can go to either market, since the additional revenues are the same, and unit 12 goes to the other. The 12 units should be divided so that the marginal revenues are the same for the last unit sold in each market; the monopolist sells seven units in market I and five in market II.

Principle

The discriminating monopolist allocates a given output in such a way that the marginal revenues in each market are equal. The firm sells any additional unit in the market with the higher marginal revenue.

Intuitively, one would predict that, if there are two separate markets and the firm price discriminates, the higher price would be charged in the market with the less elastic demand, and the lower price would be in the more elastic market. Consumers in the more elastic market have access to better substitutes; therefore, price could be raised only at the expense of a large decrease in sales. In the less elastic market there are poorer substitutes; higher prices bring less reduction in sales. The assertion that the higher price is charged in the less elastic market and the lower price in the more elastic can be proved using the following method.

Let there be two distinct markets for one monopolistically produced good; call these markets A and B. P_A and P_B are, respectively, the prices in markets A and B. MR_A and MR_B are the marginal revenues, and E_A and E_B are the absolute values of demand elasticity. Recall from our discussion of marginal revenue in Chapter 13 that

$$MR = P\left(1 - \frac{1}{E}\right).$$

We can use this relation to prove that if $P_A > P_B$, $E_A < E_B$.

A discriminating monopolist divides output between the two markets so that the marginal revenues are equal in equilibrium. Thus,

$$P_A\left(1 - \frac{1}{E_A}\right) = P_B\left(1 - \frac{1}{E_B}\right).$$

If $P_A > P_B$, then

$$\frac{\left(1 - \frac{1}{E_B}\right)}{\left(1 - \frac{1}{E_A}\right)} > 1.$$

Since the monopolist would never choose a point at which MR is negative

$$\left(1 - \frac{1}{E_B}\right) > \left(1 - \frac{1}{E_A}\right),$$

Manipulation of this inequality yields

$$E_B > E_A.$$

Whenever $P_A > P_B$, $E_B > E_A$ and vice versa. This proves the more elastic market has the lower price.

To analyze the situation graphically, assume that a monopoly can separate its buyers into two distinct markets. The demands and marginal

FIGURE 14-5   **Submarket and total market demands and marginal revenues**

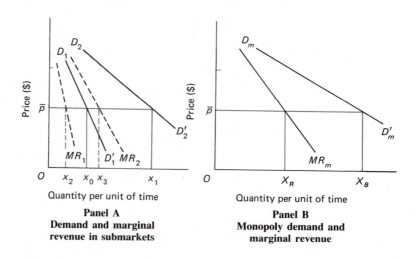

Panel A
Demand and marginal
revenue in submarkets

Panel B
Monopoly demand and
marginal revenue

revenues of each are shown in Panel A, Figure 14–5. D_1D_1' and MR_1 are demand and marginal revenue in the first market; D_2D_2' and MR_2 are demand and marginal revenue in the second. Panel B shows the horizontal summation of the two demand and marginal revenue curves. For example, at a price of $\bar{p}$, consumers in market one would take x_0 and consumers in market two would take x_1. The total quantity demanded at $\bar{p}$ is, accordingly, $x_0 + x_1 = X_B$, shown in Panel B. All other points on D_mD_m' are derived similarly. By horizontally adding we also get marginal revenue for the market. For example, $MR_1 = \bar{p}$ at output x_2; $MR_2 = \bar{p}$ at x_3. Therefore, in Panel B, $MR_m = \bar{p}$ at a quantity of $x_2 + x_3 = X_R$. Other points on MR_m, the total market MR curve, are derived similarly.

The demand and marginal revenue conditions depicted in Panel A, Figure 14–5, are reproduced in Figure 14–6, along with the average and marginal costs of production, which could be short-run or long-run schedules. The profit-maximizing output is $\overline{X}$, the quantity where total marginal revenue equals marginal cost. The marginal revenue (equals marginal cost) associated with this output is $\overline{mr}$.

The previously determined market allocation rule requires that marginal revenue be the same in each submarket. Since the market marginal revenue is the added revenue from selling the last unit in either submarket, it will be equal to $\overline{mr}$. At a marginal revenue of $\overline{mr}$, the quantity

FIGURE 14–6   **Profit maximization under price discrimination**

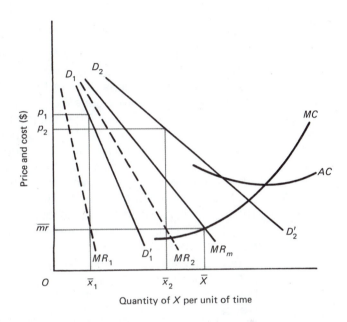

sold in submarket one is $\bar{x}_1$; in submarket two, $\bar{x}_2$. Since MR_m is the horizontal summation of MR_1 and MR_2, $\bar{x}_1 + \bar{x}_2 = \bar{X}$, the total output. Furthermore, from the relevant demand curves in the submarkets, the price associated with output $\bar{x}_1$ in market one is p_1; the price associated with $\bar{x}_2$ in market two is p_2. Because these prices clearly differ and the costs of production are the same, discrimination exists.

Summarizing these results:

Principle

If the aggregate market for a monopolist's product can be divided into sub-markets with different price elasticities, the monopolist can profitably practice price discrimination. Total output is determined by equating marginal cost with aggregate monopoly marginal revenue. The output is allocated among the submarkets so as to equate marginal revenue in each submarket with aggregate marginal revenue at the $MC = MR$ point. Finally, price in each submarket is determined directly from the submarket demand curve, given the submarket allocation of sales.

APPLICATION

Some Examples of Price Discrimination

The typical textbook example of price discrimination is the medical profession. Doctors frequently scale fees according to income. Economists say that this is done in order to increase the income of physicians. The medical profession argues that doctors price discriminate in order to provide service to the poor. They charge high-income patients a high fee to finance the relatively small fees charged low-income patients.

In a classic article on the subject, Reuben A. Kessel tested the hypothesis that doctors price discriminate because of charitable motives.[3] He asked why we do not observe parallel behavior by home builders and grocery stores, since food and shelter are as necessary as medical care. The argument presented is that local communities and states supply food and shelter to the poor but not medical care; therefore, medical charity is up to the profession.

According to Kessel, if the charity motive is correct, there should be no price discrimination among patients with the same income, even if some have medical insurance while others do not. On the other hand, if increased income is the reason for discrimination, those who have insurance should pay, on average, higher fees than do the uninsured. Those with insurance would, other things being equal, have a more inelastic demand than those without, and would pay higher fees. Holding income constant, the evidence cited by Kessel does show that medical fees are higher for the insured than for the uninsured. This evidence comes from unions and from the insurance industry. Kessel pointed out that the effect of insurance on fees, abstracting out variations in income, suggests that medical fees are determined by "what the traffic will bear."

A second bit of evidence that profit, rather than charity, motivates price discrimination in medicine is the stand of the American Medical Association (AMA) on different types of insurance. One type of insurance, cash indemnity plans, has not been opposed by the AMA or by local medical societies. Cash indemnity plans such as Blue Cross and Blue Shield allow doctors and patients to determine fees as though there were no insurance. Doctors are able to discriminate, and under such plans, the price for medical care is increased.

In contrast, the AMA and local medical societies have strongly opposed prepaid plans where an insurance company opens a clinic or hospital to supply medical services directly to patients. The price of medical care

---

[3] R. A. Kessel, "Price Discrimination in Medicine," *Journal of Law and Economics*, 1 (October 1958), pp. 20–53.

under such cooperative plans is independent of the patient's income, and as such, represents a threat to a doctor's ability to discriminate. The opposition of organized medicine to these types of plans is in strong support of the profit-maximizing, discriminating-monopolist hypothesis.

The two conditions necessary for firms to be able to price discriminate in the medical profession are met: differences in income would probably cause different price elasticities, and patients cannot easily sell medical services among themselves. That is, low-price patients cannot resell their operations to high-price patients. But doctors do not have a monopoly. Since there are many, many doctors, why don't some doctors break the agreement, causing the price for high-income patients to fall?

According to Kessel, the reason doctors do not attempt to cut prices individually is the extensive control of the AMA over medical education. Every doctor must undergo an internship administered by a hospital, and only hospitals approved by the AMA are sanctioned for internship and residency. Hospitals value intern and residency training, because they can provide medical care more cheaply with interns and residents than without them. The AMA controls an important resource for hospitals, and its "advice" that hospitals use only doctors who are members of their local medical society is almost always adhered to. It is highly probable that any doctor who is denied hospital services finds the demand for his or her services substantially weakened. It is in the doctor's long-run interest not to lower prices.

First-Degree Price Discrimination—Perfect Price Discrimination

Under first-degree discrimination, the firm treats each individual's demand separately and each consumer represents a separate market. The firm then maximizes its profit given each individual's demand curve. In Figure 14–7, we have illustrated one consumer's demand function with its associated marginal revenue curve and the firm's marginal cost curve. In the normal case, the firm would maximize profit by selling the output where MR is equal to MC (i.e., an output of three units at a price of p_3). However, with first-degree price discrimination, the firm charges a different price for each unit sold to the consumer, depending on what the consumer is willing to pay. For the first unit of the product, the consumer is willing to pay p_1; so the firm makes a profit equal to the difference between p_1 and average cost at this output. For the second unit, the consumer will pay p_2 and so on.

The firm will continue to sell to this consumer as long as the price the consumer will pay is greater than or equal to marginal cost. More specifically, under first-degree price discrimination, the firm will produce and

FIGURE 14–7   **First-degree price discrimination**

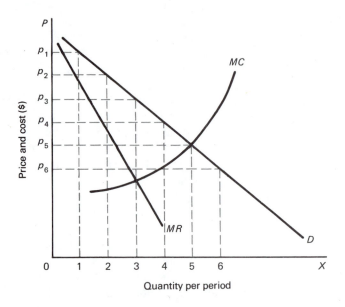

sell to the level of output where the price of the last unit is equal to marginal cost. This is the output where the demand curve intersects the marginal cost curve. Since the monopolist does not have to lower price on every unit sold to sell one more at the margin, the demand curve is the marginal revenue schedule. In other words, since the firm charges a different price for each unit consumed, the addition to total revenue for a unit of the product will be the price charged for that unit. In Figure 14–7 it will not sell the sixth unit, since the price the consumer is willing to pay (p_6) is less than the marginal cost associated with this level of production.

Figure 14–8 provides a comparison of profits with and without first-degree price discrimination. For simplicity, we assume that marginal cost is constant, so $MC = AC$. The consumer's demand and marginal revenue curves are respectively D and MR. Without discrimination, the firm will sell x_s units at a price of p_s. Since average cost is constant, the firm's total profit is indicated by the rectangle p_sABC, the lightly-shaded area shown in Figure 14–8.

Next, let the firm practice first-degree price discrimination. The firm will charge the consumer the maximum price he or she would be willing to pay for each unit purchased. Each unit sells for the highest price that can

FIGURE 14–8　　　**Profit with and without first-degree discrimination**

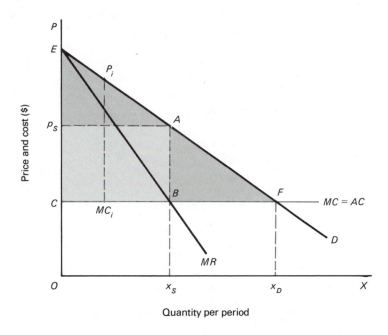

be obtained for that unit. The firm will sell up to the point where the price any consumer is willing to pay equals marginal cost; with price discrimination, the firm will sell x_D units of output. For each unit, the firm charges the price on the demand curve, and profit is the difference between that price and the corresponding point on the marginal cost curve (e.g., $P_i - MC_i$). Total profit to the discriminating firm is the entire shaded section *EFC*. Obviously, price discrimination leads to a substantial increase in profits.

While first-degree price discrimination would increase the firm's profits, it is usually not a realistic practice. Each individual consumer must be isolated and dealt with separately, which places tremendous informational requirements on the monopolist. Learning each consumer's demand curve can be an extremely costly endeavor. Also, once consumers realize that a seller is attempting to price discriminate they may intentionally understate their willingness to pay to get lower prices. Efforts by the monopolist to learn more about what each buyer will pay may be in vain.

Second-Degree Price Discrimination

First-degree price discrimination is expensive to implement, since, at least in theory, the firm must determine each individual's demand function. Second-degree price discrimination is somewhat simpler because it requires the firm to consider groups of consumers, not each individual consumer. This form of discrimination can best be explained using Figure 14–9, where we again employ the simplifying assumption that marginal cost is constant. With second-degree price discrimination, the firm would charge every buyer p_1 for the first x_1 units purchased. If consumers wanted to purchase more, they would then receive discrete discounts. In Figure 14–9, the next x_1x_2 units would cost p_2, then price would fall to p_3 for the next x_2x_3 units, and so on. In effect, buyers are receiving quantity discounts. The discounts are offered as long as the price consumers are willing to pay exceeds marginal cost. The firm will sell a total of x_6 units of its product with the last price tier at p_6 equal to marginal cost. Total profit is again the shaded area. Note the similarity between this case and the profits in first-degree price discrimination. In essence, second-degree price discrimination is an approximation of first-degree discrimination.

FIGURE 14–9   **Second-degree price discrimination**

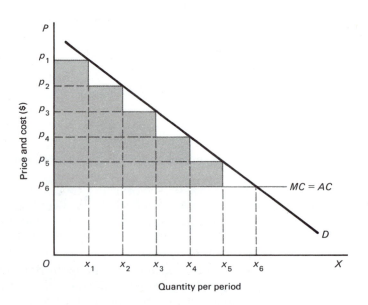

It is particularly crucial in second-degree price discrimination that arbitrage does not occur among buyers. You can easily see that an enterprising consumer could buy cheap at p_6 and sell dear at p_1 or at any price above p_6. Before long, the monopoly would find itself selling only at p_6 and making no profits.

14.5 MARKET PERFORMANCE OF MONOPOLY

Economists have done extensive research, both theoretical and empirical, on the costs and benefits of monopoly relative to perfect competition. By using consumer's and producer's surplus, it is theoretically possible to show, under stylized cost conditions, that there is a total surplus loss as markets become monopolized. We will present some empirical evidence in this section estimating the size of this loss in the United States. However, once we remove ourselves from the familiar U-shaped average cost curves and allow a producer to experience pervasive economies of scale, it is not clear whether a market is better served by monopoly or by perfect competition. Lower costs of production may counterbalance the power of the monopolist to set price, resulting in a monopoly price lower than the price set under perfect competition. Moreover, under some cost conditions, a product may not even be produced unless the market is monopolized. Higher prices and increased revenues may be necessary to cover total costs. The choice is to go without the product or have it produced by a monopolist, which is to say perfect competition is not always a viable market structure.

Comparison with Perfect Competition

The most common criticism of monopoly is that price is higher and output is lower than in a perfectly competitive market. This assertion is based on the following situation.

The monopolist depicted in Figure 14–10 produces x_M per period of time and sells at a price of p_M. If we can also assume that MC represents competitive industry supply, supply equals demand at E. The perfectly competitive industry would sell x_C at a price of p_C. There is some reason to doubt, however, that MC can represent the supply curve of a perfectly competitive industry. The sum of a large number of firms' marginal cost curves is not necessarily the marginal cost curve of a single, much larger firm. In any event, a monopoly is more likely to earn a pure profit because it can effectively exercise some market control; output is restricted and prices are raised relative to perfectly competitive markets.

In long-run industry equilibrium under perfect competition, production occurs at the point of minimum long- and short-run average cost. The monopolist, on the other hand, utilizes the plant capable of producing its

FIGURE 14–10   **Price and output comparisons**

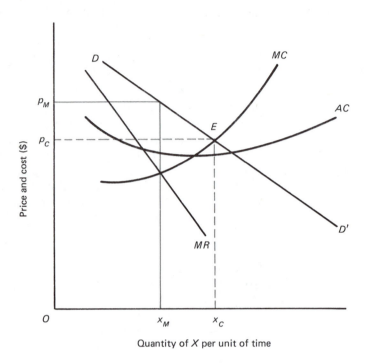

Quantity of X per unit of time

long-run equilibrium output at the least unit cost of producing that output. Only under the extremely rare circumstances in which marginal revenue intersects marginal cost at the output associated with minimum long-run average cost would this plant size be the one chosen by the monopolist.

Surplus Loss from Monopoly

We have shown that, while the perfect competitor produces at the point where marginal cost and price are equal, the monopolist's price *exceeds* marginal cost. Because price exceeds marginal cost, the marginal value of another unit of the good to consumers in the market (and therefore to society) exceeds the marginal cost of its production. Society as a whole would benefit by having more resources used in producing the commodity in question. The profit-maximizing monopolist will not, however, produce more, because producing more would decrease profit. In comparison, the perfect competitor in long-run equilibrium produces the quantity where the marginal cost of production just equals the marginal value of the good to consumers, not because of any innate social consciousness, but because the market forces this outcome on producers.

We can illustrate the loss monopoly causes society by using the tools of consumer's and producer's surplus. Suppose perfect competition forces producers to operate where marginal cost for the industry equals demand. The monopolist, on the other hand, operates where marginal cost equals marginal revenue. In Figure 14–11, we show prices and outputs for both a monopolist (p_m and x_m) and a perfectly competitive industry (p_c and x_c). For the competitive market structure, total surplus is the sum of consumer's and producer's surplus, or $Ap_cC + p_cCF = ACF$. If a monopoly operates in the market, the sum is $ABp_m + p_mBHF = ABHF$. Because monopoly restricts output, the shaded area BCH in Figure 14–11 represents a loss of both consumer's and producer's surplus. The consumer's loss is BCG, while the producer loses GCH. By restricting output and raising price, there is a transfer of surplus from the consumer to the producer equivalent to area p_mBGp_c. In total, the consumer loses the surplus represented by the sum of the areas $p_mBGp_c + BCG$. Since the monopolist gains the area p_mBGp_c, area BCG represents the net loss of consumer surplus.

FIGURE 14–11   **Surplus loss from monopoly**

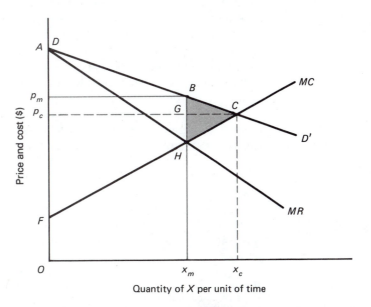

Quantity of X per unit of time

The monopolist is willing to forego the surplus represented by GCH to obtain surplus area p_mBGp_c. The transfer in consumer's surplus, p_mBGp_c, from higher prices, is greater than the loss of producer's surplus, BCH, from restricting output. By setting $MR = MC$ to maximize profits, a monopolist maximizes the difference between areas GCH and p_mBGp_c.

Welfare Loss from Monopoly in the United States

In 1954, Arnold C. Harberger attempted to measure the welfare loss (lost surplus) from all monopoly in the United States.[4] Because of the relative tranquility of the period and the availability of good data, Harberger used the years 1924–28 for his estimation. He assumed that those industries with higher than average returns on capital had too few resources invested (i.e., were monopolized), and those yielding lower than average returns had too many resources. In all industries long-run average cost was assumed constant.

Harberger estimated how much better off society would have been if a transfer of resources had taken place to reduce monopoly price to average cost and increase output. This amount would equal the sum of all increases in consumer's surplus (area BGC in Figure 14–11) due to changing monopolies to competitive markets. There would not be any increase in producer's surplus at the margin since the $LRAC$ curve was assumed horizontal. The total welfare gain estimated from the resource transfer was $59 million; at the time less than $\frac{1}{10}$ of 1 percent of national income. In terms of 1954 income, this averaged to less than $1.50 per person in the United States. When Harberger included certain intangibles in the data, the necessary transfer rose from 1.5 percent to 1.75 percent of national income, and the welfare loss rose to $81 million. (We might note that the welfare change does not consider the reallocation of income from the rest of society to the monopoly, area p_cp_mBG in Figure 14–11.)

In all the estimates, the total welfare loss came to less than $\frac{1}{10}$ of 1 percent of national income, and in most instances, Harberger used assumptions that biased the estimates upward. This extremely low estimate was startling at the time. Aside from the transfer of resources from consumers to monopoly, it appeared that the total welfare cost was quite small.

A little more than a decade later, Gordon Tullock added new insights to the discussion by comparing the welfare loss from monopoly to the economics of theft.[5] While it may be argued that, if one person steals $100

---

[4] See A. C. Harberger, "The Welfare Loss from Monopoly," *American Economic Review*, 34, no. 2 (May 1954), pp. 77–87. For some additional insights into this question, see F. M. Scherer, *Industrial Market Structure and Economic Performance* (Chicago: Rand McNally, 1971), Chapter 17.

[5] See G. Tullock, "The Welfare Costs of Monopolies and Theft," *Western Economic Journal* 5, no. 2 (June 1967), pp. 224–32.

from another, the theft simply involves a transfer of resources, the actions taken to carry out and prevent theft impose a large cost to society. Potential thieves would invest in resources—time, burglar tools, getaway cars, lookouts—until any additional resources would cost more than the marginal return in stolen assets from using these resources. (Even thieves can use a knowledge of economic theory.) Similarly, potential victims wish to protect their wealth. A potential victim would invest in preventive resources—watchdogs, locks, guns, etc.—as long as the expected marginal saving from such resources is expected to exceed their marginal cost. Furthermore, the return to resources used in theft depends on the number of resources used in theft prevention, and vice versa.

In time, society would attain an equilibrium amount of theft, which would probably be positive, since the prevention of all theft would cost too much. Even though the equilibrium amount of theft involves only transfers, the *existence* of theft will cost society considerably. The resources used to steal and to prevent stealing cost the individuals involved, and they cost society the use of those resources that could be used to produce other products. They are *completely wasted* from society's point of view—used only to cause or to prevent transfers of wealth, not to produce wealth.

Similar to theft, monopoly involves a transfer of resources from consumers to the producer. According to Tullock's analysis, the welfare losses estimated using Harberger's technique underestimate the true welfare loss from monopoly. Since the return from establishing a *successful* monopoly is frequently great, one would expect a potential monopolist to expend considerable resources attempting to monopolize a market. In fact, entrepreneurs should be willing to invest resources in attempts to form monopolies until the marginal cost equals the expected discounted return. After the monopoly is formed, others will invest resources trying to break the monopoly, which in turn means that the monopolist must use additional resources trying to prevent the break. Just as successful theft encourages additional theft, successful monopoly encourages additional attempts to monopolize.

As Tullock noted, identifying and measuring the resources used to gain, break, and hold monopoly are quite difficult. It appears that a large amount of a very scarce resource—skilled management—is used toward this end. In any case, the Harberger estimates ignore this cost and therefore underestimate the social cost of monopoly. Establishing the social losses from monopoly is still far from being settled.

A Caveat

In a simple theoretical framework, it is possible to compare monopoly unfavorably to perfect competition. Relative to a perfectly competitive market, monopoly restricts output, charges a higher price, and does not operate at minimum long-run average cost. Furthermore, because monopoly does restrict output, there is a loss of surplus relative to perfect competition.

The comparison between the two market structures is not so clear if production technology is characterized by continuous economies of scale in the long run or high fixed costs in the short run. If economies of scale are present, the profit-maximizing incentive encourages firms to become larger and, as a consequence, fewer in number. A large number of firms could be maintained by making it illegal for a firm to get large, but this has serious disincentive effects for the profit maximizer. More importantly, it is not clear that a few firms (or even a single firm) producing the product is undesirable. Because of lower costs, these firms may charge a lower price than competitive producers. The presence of fixed costs in the short run can also leave no choice in the market structure. Unless firms have monopoly power so that price can be set above marginal cost, the product may not be produced.

As a matter of public policy, economists cannot say that perfect competition is more efficient and, therefore, more desirable than a monopolized market structure. This judgement cannot be generalized. Moreover, if we extended our comparison to the issues of research and development, employment, and inflationary impact, the relative advantages and disadvantages of the two market structures would become even less clear-cut.

14.6 MONOPOLY REGULATION

Since some of the social effects of monopoly behavior are thought to be undesirable, governments sometimes attempt to regulate monopoly behavior by imposing price ceilings and enacting certain forms of taxation. We can analyze some effects of such regulation on the price-output behavior of monopolists.

Price Regulation

If government believes a monopolist is making too much profit, charging too high a price, or restricting output excessively, it can set a price ceiling on the commodity. As you will recall from Chapter 3, a ceiling price under perfect competition causes a shortage, and some form of nonprice allocation of the good will evolve. This may or may not, however, be the case under monopoly.

Consider first the situation in Figure 14–12. Under the cost and revenue conditions depicted, the nonregulated monopoly sells x_m at a price of p_m; obviously making a substantial profit. Let us assume that the government imposes a price ceiling (that is, a price less than p_m), and p_c is the maximum price allowed. The segment $p_c C$ becomes the new demand and marginal revenue up to the output x_c. The monopoly can sell any quantity up to x_c at a price of p_c because, over this range, actual demand lies above

FIGURE 14–12   **Effects of price ceilings under monopoly**

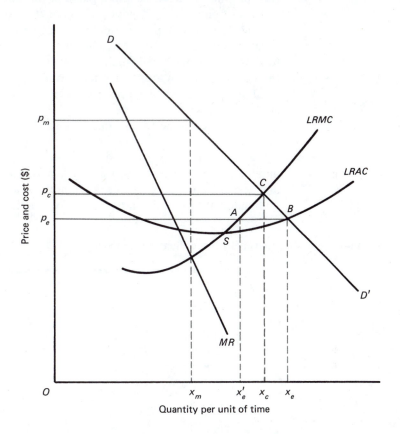

p_cC; it would certainly charge no lower price. The horizontal segment p_cC, represents the monopolist's effective demand. After x_c, the old demand and marginal revenue curves take over. The entire new demand is the line p_cCD'. With the new demand curve, marginal revenue now equals marginal cost at point C; the monopolist sells x_c units per period at a price of p_c. Since C lies on DD', quantity supplied equals quantity demanded and the market is cleared. Profit clearly diminishes; since p_m and x_m gave *maximum* profit, any other price and output combination, including p_c and x_c, must give less than maximum profit.

In this case, demand is equal to marginal cost. If price on the demand curve represents the market's marginal valuation of the commodity, and marginal cost represents the value of producing the last unit, marginal benefit and marginal cost are equal at the margin. In other words, the consumer's and producer's surplus in the market are maximized, and one of the results of perfect competition is obtained even though, in the long run, production need not take place at minimum average cost.

Other ceiling prices would not give this result. For example, at any ceiling price set between p_m and p_c, price would equal *LRMC* at an output greater than the quantity the market would demand at that price. Therefore, the monopolist sells the quantity given by the demand curve (DD') at the ceiling price. Again, price falls from p_m and quantity increases from x_m, but, in contrast to p_c, price exceeds the marginal cost of the last unit sold.

If p_c causes price to fall, quantity to rise, and profit to diminish, why not lower price even further, possibly to p_e? At p_e the monopolist could sell x_e and still cover costs, since $LRAC = p_e$ at x_e. But the new demand and marginal revenue curve up to x_e is p_eB; therefore, $MR = LRMC$ at A, and the firm would produce x'_e, which is *less* than x_e. Since quantity demanded at p_e is x_e, a shortage of $x'_e x_e$ results. In this case, the monopo-

FIGURE 14–13   **Effects of price ceilings under monopoly**

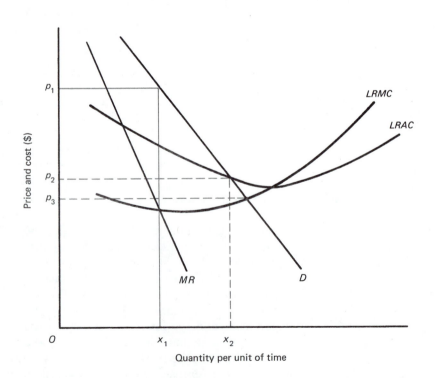

list must allocate by means other than price. In fact, any price below p_c causes a decrease in quantity sold from x_c, and a shortage occurs since quantity demanded exceeds quantity supplied at that price.

Under the conditions assumed in Figure 14–12, the greatest quantity is attained by setting the ceiling price so that the monopolist produces where *LRMC* intersects actual demand. This result may not always be obtainable with a ceiling price. Figure 14–13 depicts such a case. The nonregulated profit-maximizing monopolist in Figure 14–13 sells x_1 units per period at price p_1. If the government sets a ceiling price of p_3, the price where *LRMC* crosses demand, the monopoly in the long run would go out of business since it could not cover total costs. In fact, the ceiling could be no lower than p_2 without forcing the firm to cease production. At p_2, the firm would sell x_2 units per period and make no profit in the long run.

Taxation

An alternative method of monopoly regulation is some type of special taxation. We examine here the effects of three common types: the excise or per-unit tax, the lump-sum tax, and the percentage-of-profits tax.

An excise or per-unit tax means that for every unit sold, regardless of price, the monopolist must pay a specified amount of money to the government. Assume that the monopolist, whose cost curves $LRAC_0$ and $LRMC_0$ are shown in Figure 14–14, is charged a tax of k dollars for every unit sold. Total cost after the tax is the total cost of *production* (presumably the same as before) plus k times output; thus, average or unit cost must rise by exactly the amount of the tax, k dollars. The after-tax *LRAC* in Figure 14–14 rises from $LRAC_0$ to $LRAC_1$, or by the vertical distance k. *LRMC* also rises by k dollars. If it costs $LRMC_0$ to produce and sell an additional unit of output before the tax, after the tax it costs $LRMC_0 + k = LRMC_1$ to produce and sell that unit. This also is shown in Figure 14–14.

Before the tax is imposed, the monopolist produces x_0 and charges a price of p_0. After the imposition of the tax, the cost curves shift vertically by the amount k to $LRAC_1$ and $LRMC_1$. Marginal cost now equals *MR* at output x_1, so price rises to p_1. Some of the tax, $p_1 - p_0$, is shifted to consumers in the form of a price increase, and the rest is borne by the monopolist. This effect differs completely from the effect of the ceiling price that causes price to fall and quantity to rise.

A lump-sum tax has a somewhat different impact on price and quantity. Assume that, instead of imposing an excise tax on the monopolist, the government charges a license fee that remains the same regardless of quantity sold. The license fee is, therefore, a fixed cost to the monopolist. Average cost rises after the fee is imposed; at very small outputs, the curve rises more than it does at larger outputs because, the larger the output, the more units the fee is spread over. Once the fee is paid,

FIGURE 14–14   **Effects of an excise tax under monopoly**

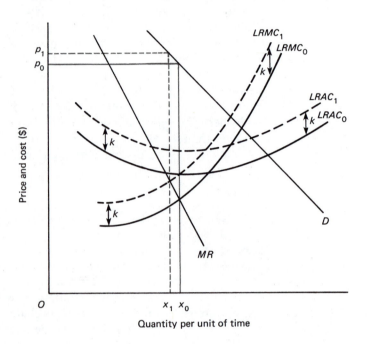

however, no additional tax is charged for an additional unit of production per period—marginal cost remains unchanged. Since *MC* and *MR* do not change after the lump-sum tax, their point of intersection does not change, and price and quantity remain the same after the tax is imposed. The lump-sum tax does reduce profits and cannot be so large that it drives average cost above demand. This would cause a loss and force the monopolist out of business.

A percentage-of-profits tax, just as the lump-sum tax, does not affect quantity or price. Assume that a monopolist must pay *t* percent of profit (regardless of the profit) as a tax. Since *t* is presumably between 0 and 100, the monopolist retains $(100 - t)$ percent of profits after paying the tax. Revenue and cost curves remain the same. Before the tax is imposed, the monopoly chooses price and quantity so as to maximize profit. After the tax, it still chooses the same price and quantity so as to maximize before-tax profit, since $(100 - t)$ percent of the maximum profit is clearly preferable to $(100 - t)$ percent of some smaller amount.

Tax regulation differs from price regulation in several ways, even though profits are reduced in all cases. In particular, taxation, in contrast to some price ceilings, cannot force the monopolist to set price equal to marginal cost.

Before we end this discussion, there is a caveat that should be attached to lump-sum and percentage-of-profit tax theory. Even though the tax, within limits, will not affect short-run profit-maximizing behavior, these taxes will have long-run effects. In energy production, for instance, exploration and other forms of investment are undertaken in the hope of a future stream of profits. Firms would carry out exploration as long as the marginal cost of exploration is less than the expected marginal return. Any tax that reduces the expected return consequently reduces exploration, and anything that reduces exploration reduces future resource extraction (in the case of natural gas, the output of gas would fall in the future). The situation is similar in the case of other forms of investment carried out in the expectation of a stream of returns in the future. A tax that is expected to lower the stream of returns in the future lowers investment. Reduced investment causes a reduction in future output. Therefore, while the tax on profit would possibly not affect current output, such a tax would affect future output, possibly quite significantly.

14.7 SUMMARY

Monopoly can exist only when there are barriers to entry. Certain barriers naturally arise from the technology of production. Economies of scale lead to such types of barriers. Sometimes barriers arise from government. Franchises and patents are in essence government grants to monopolize a market. Finally, other barriers are controlled to some extent by the firms seeking to protect their share of the market. The control of critical inputs and brand loyalties are barriers that can be erected and influenced by an incumbent producer.

We discussed some strategic barriers in detail. Of importance was the practice of entry limit pricing. A firm can block entry by keeping price low and output relatively high. Profits are lower in the short run than if the strict profit-maximizing rule were followed, but in the long run a monopolist may earn a higher, steady stream of profits. A monopolist can also block entry by producing multiple products. In some cases this will give a producer lower costs. If substitute products are made, it may also reduce demand to a potential entrant. In this way, product proliferation allows a monopolist to capture the market share that may have gone to a new entrant.

Price discrimination occurs when different prices are set for the same product. Generally, the practice leads to higher profits for the seller and more output. Third-degree discrimination occurs when buyers are separated into markets with different marginal revenues. The monopolist than maximizes profit in these markets. First-degree discrimination involves treating each consumer as if he or she is a market. All consumers are charged the highest price they are willing to pay for each unit of a product.

This makes marginal revenue equivalent to demand, even though demand is downward sloping. Profits are maximized where $MR = D = MC$, a result very similar to the perfectly competitive outcome. Finally, second-degree discrimination approximates first-degree by setting price tiers or quantity discounts for a product.

The stylized monopolist chooses the output at which $MC = MR$. In contrast to perfect competition, the market does not force the monopolist in the long run to produce the quantity where long-run average cost is at its minimum and to charge a price equal to minimum long-run average and marginal cost. There is some loss of consumer's and producer's surplus. This does not necessarily indicate that price must be higher and quantity lower under monopoly than under perfect competition. We can only say that price under monopoly will not, in the absence of regulation, equal marginal cost.

TECHNICAL PROBLEMS

1. Suppose a seller faces one buyer or a market where all buyers are alike. Let marginal costs (MC) be constant and $MC = 5$; fixed costs are zero. The demand schedule faced by the seller is $P = 20 - X$. Calculate profits when the firm
   a. Sets $MR = MC$. (Hint $MR = 20 - 2X$.)
   b. Practices first-degree price discrimination.
   c. Practices second- degree discrimination and uses $P_1 = 15, P_2 = 10$, and $P_3 = 5$.

2. This question deals with multiproduct economies and is based on the following information about products x, y and z.

$$C(x) = C(y) = C(z) = \$10$$
$$C(x,y) = C(y,z) = C(x,z) = \$16$$

The cost notation $C(\ )$ refers to a constant total cost for a specified amount of the product produced. What can the maximum $C(x,y,z)$ be in order for the technology to be subadditive across all three products?

3. Suppose a monopolist sells one product in two different markets. The demand curves are

$$\text{Market } A\text{: } P_A = 20 - .1X$$
$$\text{Market } B\text{: } P_B = 10 - .1X$$

The marginal cost of production is \$5. Find the profit-maximizing prices and quantities for each market. Again, recall the equation for marginal revenue for the demand curve $P = A - BX$ is $MR = A - 2BX$.

4. Determine which of the following practices should be considered price discrimination. Which are not? Why are some of these pricing strategies not discriminating?

a. Reserved seats are priced higher on airlines than standby seats.
b. First-class accommodations on an airplane are more expensive than coach seats.
c. Long-distance telephone service is more expensive from 8 A.M. to 5 P.M. than it is at other times.
d. Children under 12 sleep free at a hotel.
e. Young faculty members get journals at a lower subscription rate than older members.
f. Consumers pay different interest rates at banks depending on how much they earn.
g. Automobile loans at banks usually have a higher interest rate than home mortgages.

5. When will a discriminating monopolist with two separate markets do the following:
   a. Charge the same price in both markets?
   b. Sell the same level of output in both markets?

6. Assume that a monopolist can divide output into two submarkets, the demands and marginal revenues of which are shown in Figure E.14–1, along with marginal cost. *MR* is the horizontal sum of the two marginal revenue curves.

FIGURE E.14–1.

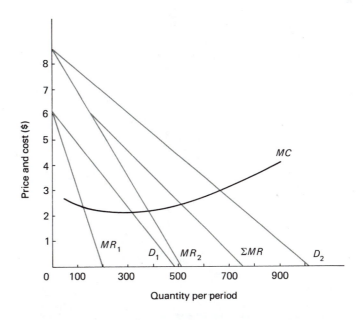

a. Find equilibrium output and price in each market.

b. Which market has the more elastic demand?

c. What would be price and output if the monopolist could not discriminate?

7. Suppose a monopolist faces the demand schedule $P = 50 - 2X$ and the firm's constant marginal cost schedule is $MC = 10$. Marginal revenue for the monopolist is $MR = 50 - 4X$.

a. Graph demand, marginal revenue, and marginal cost in one diagram.

b. Find the profit-maximizing output and price for the monopolist.

c. If the market is perfectly competitive and marginal cost for the market is $MC = 10$, at what output and price would a competitive industry operate?

d. Calculate the loss in total surplus between the market equilibria in problems 7b and 7c.

e. What is producer's surplus under monopoly? Consumer's surplus?

f. What proportion of the welfare loss in problem d was once consumer's surplus? Producer's surplus?

g. Does the monopolist earn a profit if fixed costs are $200? Can the market be competitive when fixed costs are relatively large?

FIGURE E.14–2

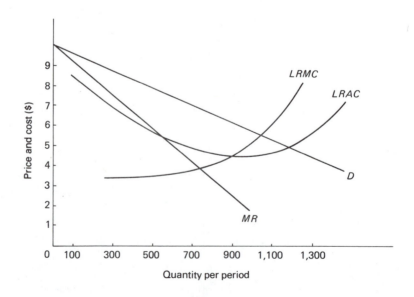

8. Answer the following questions based on Figure 14–8 in this chapter:

   a. What is the sum of consumer's and producer's surplus when the monopolist cannot price discriminate?

   b. What is total surplus when there is first-degree price discrimination?

   c. Do consumers prefer first-degree discrimination because of the change in total surplus?

9. Explain why a percent-of-profits tax on a monopolist will change neither price nor output. Do the same for a lump-sum tax. Explain why such taxes may affect future investment.

10. A monopolist's revenue and long-run cost curves are shown in Figure E.14–2.

    a. Output and price are _____ and $_____.

    b. A ceiling price of $_____ would eliminate profit.

    c. Output and price would change to _____ and $_____.

    d. An excise tax of $2 per unit would change price to $_____ and output to _____.

11. Suppose we have a natural monopoly; economies of scale are experienced over all ranges of output. Show LRAC and LRMC in a graph. Now add a demand curve and marginal revenue. At what output and price does a monopolist maximize profits? If the monopolist were forced to price and produce where LRMC = D, would it continue to operate? Show the profit or loss and, consequently, the subsidy a monopolist would need to operate at this point.

ANALYTICAL PROBLEMS

1. Some bars charge women half price for drinks. Is this consistent with profit maximization? Are all conditions of price discrimination met in this case? Is there an alternative explanation? Speaking of bars, many establishments have a "happy hour," meaning that at a certain time, say 4 to 6 P.M., drinks are served at a reduced price. Is this consistent with price discrimination?

2. Some economists argue that a large number of firms is not necessary to get competitive behavior in the market. All that is really needed is a viable threat of entry in a market where one or a few firms already produce. Evaluate this claim.

3. Why do faculty get discounts from the university bookstore while students do not? (Don't just say price discrimination.) Why can price discrimination exist? Are all conditions necessary for price discrimination met? Discuss.

4. Dr. Hood is a medical doctor who practices first-degree price discrimination. His prices rise with the income of his patients. He

claims that everyone pays a reasonable price, and the poor are helped. Assuming the rich are willing to pay more than poor people for medical services, graphically show how this price discriminating strategy helps the poor. (*Hint:* Suppose the doctor could only charge one price, what would x and p be? Now let the monopolist first-degree price discriminate.)

5. In 1945, Alcoa was found guilty of attempting to monopolize the aluminum market. Up to that time, the company maintained low markups and had a modest profit rate. Ironically, if Alcoa had set high markups and realized a high profit rate before World War II, it probably would have not been found guilty. Can you explain why?

6. For many years, AT&T claimed that it could not provide overseas telephone service at reasonable rates unless it also provided domestic long-distance service. Justify this claim using the discussion of multiproduct monopoly.

7. Section two of the 1914 Clayton Act prohibits sellers from discriminating in price between different purchasers, except where differences in the grade, quality, or quantity of the commodity exist and the resulting lower prices make due allowance only for differences in the cost of selling or transportation, and are offered in good faith to meet competition. As an economist, evaluate this restriction on pricing.

8. Can a firm have any control over the cross-price elasticity of its output with other products? To put the question another way, can a seller lower a high cross-price elasticity? If so, how? Is your answer consistent with an entry limit pricing strategy?

9. In a market characterized by rapid changes in technology, e.g., calculators and computers, would there be less or more incentive to practice an entry limit pricing strategy? Explain your answer.

10. Suppose, because of economies of scale, a community wants one firm to be a monopoly in providing a particular service. The community lets different firms bid on how much they want to be paid for providing the service for a specified period of time. The lowest bidder then gets the contract. Will the monopoly earn profits over the contract period? Is this a good way of eliminating monopoly profits for certain public services?

Chapter 15

Imperfect Competition

15.1 INTRODUCTION

The two stylized market structures we have discussed—perfect competition and monopoly—are extremely useful economic tools, even though neither accurately depicts real-world producers. While not designed to describe actual markets, they are able to help us analyze many economic problems. Nonetheless, there are certain features of real-world markets not addressed by either model. Both models ignore the real-world situation of a large number of firms selling slightly different products. This kind of market structure is known as *monopolistic competition*. It is somewhat monopolistic because product differentiation provides a firm with some monopoly power; it is somewhat competitive because there are many firms in the market and entry is easy. Many real-world markets are of the monopolistically competitive type. Most consumer services, food products, apparel, and household appliances are produced by monopolistically competitive firms.

The assumptions of monopoly and perfect competition also fail to deal with a market structure in which a *few* firms sell either identical or differentiated products. This market structure is referred to as *oligopoly*. Oligopolistic firms characteristically have large amounts of monopoly power, but profit maximization is complicated by the fact that the actions of any firm affect the profits of the others, and this must be taken into account when a firm chooses its price and output. Many capital goods and refined products are produced and sold by oligopolistic firms. Automobiles, heavy machinery, sugar, and aluminum are oligopolistic industries.

We must stress that the distinction between monopolistic competition and oligopoly can become cloudy. The most obvious distinction between the two forms of market structure is that oligopolistic markets have a few firms, while monopolistically competitive markets have many. How do we decide that a market has "many" or "few" firms? In terms of the number of firms in a market, we really do not know when market structures become less like monopolistic competition and more like oligopoly. Whether a market is monopolistically competitive or oligopolistic depends less on the number of firms in a market and more on whether each firm recognizes that its actions will have a discernible impact upon its rivals. Put another way, the difference between monopolistic competition and oligopoly is determined by the degree to which sellers are interdependent. Even so, judging a market as oligopolistic or monopolistically competitive is subjective. The recognition that profit depends on the actions of a producer's rivals is a critical turning point when moving from the theory of monopolistic competition to oligopoly.

This chapter first presents the theory of monopolistic competition and compares the results of the theory with the perfectly competitive model. Since both monopolistic competition and oligopoly frequently use non-price competition to increase profits, we next discuss this type of competitive behavior. Oligopoly models are then presented, with emphasis on why there is no general theory of oligopoly. The chapter ends with a discussion of collusion.

15.2 FUNDAMENTALS OF MONOPOLISTIC COMPETITION

One of the most notable achievements of economists who examined the middle ground between competition and monopoly was done simultaneously by an American economist, Edward Chamberlin, and a British economist, Joan Robinson.[1] They both contributed heavily to the modern development of economic theories of nonperfect competition. At the time they published, neither economist knew of the other's work, but they both based their theories on a solid empirical fact: there are very few monopolies because very few commodities have no close substitutes; similarly, there are very few commodities that are entirely homogeneous. In short, there exists a wide range of commodities that have many good, but not perfect, substitutes.

Chamberlin, who developed the theory of monopolistic competition, noted that, because products are *heterogeneous* rather than homogeneous, perfect competition cannot exist. On the other hand, although heterogeneous, the products are only slightly differentiated. Each is a rather close substitute for the others. Competition does exist, but it is competition among rivals. Unlike perfect competition, it involves sellers who are, to a greater or lesser extent, aware of each other, and buyers who can distinguish among sellers of similar goods.

It is important to note that the only difference between perfect competition and monopolistic competition is product differentiation. In the model of monopolistic competition, there remain large numbers of buyers and sellers, easy entry and exit into the market among sellers, and perfect

---

[1] E. H. Chamberlin, *The Theory of Monopolistic Competition* (Cambridge, Mass.: Harvard University Press, 1933), and J. Robinson, *The Economics of Imperfect Competition* (London: Macmillan, 1934).

information with respect to prices. We will see that this modest change in the assumptions underlying perfect competition has profound effects on the behavior of sellers in the market.

As we discuss the theories of imperfect competition, we must keep in mind the definition of the market. A market is made up of sellers of goods that are easily substituted for one another by consumers. Very often the market is defined by the set of goods that share high and positive cross-price elasticities. In the case of monopolistic competition, a large number of firms sell easily substituted products.

Demand under Monopolistic Competition

Recall that, in the theory of monopoly, one firm supplies the entire market; there are no good substitutes for the producer's product. We can describe the market of a monopolistic competitor by thinking about what happens to a monopoly as entry occurs. We will work in a very simple setting and focus on how the elasticity of demand changes as entry takes place.

Picture the demand for a monopolist as D_m, the linear demand curve shown in Figure 15-1. The curve can be described by the equation for a straight line:

$$P = a - bX.$$

The vertical intercept of D_m is a as shown in Figure 15-1. The slope, $\Delta P/\Delta X$, is $-b$.[2] If we call the elasticity of demand in the market E_M, then

$$E_M = \frac{-\Delta X}{\Delta P} \cdot \frac{P}{X} = \frac{1}{b} \frac{P}{X},$$

where we have substituted $-1/b = \dfrac{\Delta X}{\Delta P}$ from the value of the slope in the above equation. Since $\dfrac{\Delta P}{\Delta X} = -b$, we have inverted the ratio for the substitution in E_M. The market elasticity, E_M, is the same as the elasticity for the monopolist.

Now, let a second firm enter the market and notice what happens to the elasticity of demand. Both firms produce an amount, x_i, where $X = x_1 + x_2$. For the moment, let us assume that the products are alike, so both firms charge the same price. The sum of the amounts each firm produces is total market output; so price in the market becomes

---

[2] The slope $\dfrac{\Delta P}{\Delta X}$ represents the change in P when X changes by one unit. Hence $\dfrac{\Delta P}{\Delta X} = [a - b(x + 1) - (a - bX)] = a - bX - b - a + bX = -b$. Thus $\dfrac{\Delta P}{\Delta X} = -b$ and $\dfrac{\Delta X}{\Delta P} = -\dfrac{1}{b}$ by inverting.

FIGURE 15–1   **Demand shift after entry**

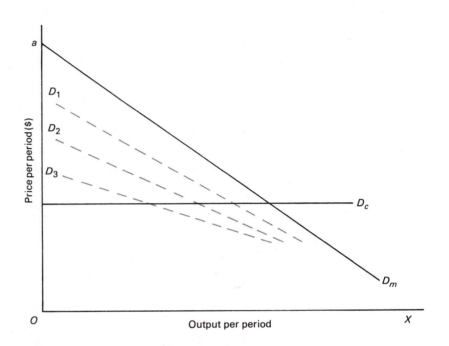

$$P = a - b(X) = a - b(x_1 + x_2),$$

if either firm increases output by one unit $\Delta P/\Delta X = -b$, as before.[3] We have assumed that the two products are such close substitutes that the same price is charged for each. Each firm in the market has elasticity E_i:

$$E_i = -\frac{\Delta x_i}{\Delta P} \cdot \frac{P}{x_i} = \frac{1}{b}\left(\frac{P}{x_i}\right).$$

The quantity produced by the firm, x_i, is in the denominator rather than X.

To see better how E_i relates to E_M, we introduce the ratio x_i/X as the market share of the ith firm. It is the proportion of the total market supplied by a single firm. For convenience, we set $s_i = x_i/X$. For a monopolist, $s_i = 1$, but as firms enter the market, s_i becomes less than one. Under perfect competition, when there are many firms producing

---

[3] Suppose, for example, the second firm expands. Then

$$\frac{\Delta P}{\Delta x_2} = a - b[x_1 + (x_2 + 1)] - [a - b(x_1 + x_2)]$$
$$= a - bx_1 - bx_2 - b - a + bx_1 + bx_2 = -b.$$

identical products, s_i gets very close to zero. We know, therefore, that for imperfect competition, s_i ranges between one and zero.

Using the ratio s_i, we may rewrite the elasticity of demand for the firm (E_i) in terms of the elasticity of demand at the market level (E_m). With some substitution we see that

$$E_i = \frac{1}{b}\left(\frac{P}{x_i}\right) = \frac{1}{b}\left(\frac{P}{x_i}\right)\frac{X}{X} = \frac{1}{b}\left(\frac{P}{X}\right)\frac{X}{x_i} = E_M\left(\frac{1}{s_i}\right).$$

We can verify this equality by supposing that only one seller operates in the market. Then $s_i = 1$, and $E_i = E_M$. The elasticity of demand for a monopolist is the market's elasticity. Suppose we have perfect competition and s_i gets very close to zero. Then $1/s_i$ becomes very large making E_i approach infinity. Once again this verifies what we already know. In perfect competition the firm's demand curve is horizontal, and the elasticity of demand is infinite. Such a demand curve is labeleld D_c in Figure 15-1.

This relation between a firm's elasticity of demand and the market elasticity tells us what demand looks like as a market becomes more competitive. At the extremes, we have D_m and D_c in Figure 15-1. If we allow entry into the market, each firm supplies a smaller share of the market; that is, s_i gets smaller. The firm's demand curve must therefore shift to the left. We also know that as this shift takes place the elasticity of demand increases. As entry takes place, each firm's demand curve both decreases and becomes more elastic than D_m. For illustration, entry shifts demand in the way shown by the dotted schedules in Figure 15-1. Demand goes from D_m to D_1, to D_2, etc., and the more entry, the closer demand gets to the perfectly competitive demand, D_c.

However, product differentiation in monopolistic competition will prevent the firm's demand curve from becoming perfectly elastic. Perceived differences between goods make them less than perfect substitutes. For instance, toothpastes have different flavors and colors, and presumably clean your teeth differently. Because consumers can identify these product characteristics for each producer, toothpastes will never become perfect substitutes. This means that the demand curve for a monopolistic competitor never becomes horizontal; some market power, perhaps only a small amount, is possessed by sellers. Because of product differences, firms capture different shares of the market. That is, s_i is different for each firm. From the formula, $E_i = E_M/s_i$, this means firms face different elasticities of demand. Partly because of this, and partly because costs are different, we see different prices in monopolistically competitive markets.

Short-Run Equilibrium

The theory of monopolistic competition is essentially a long-run theory. In the short run, there is virtually no difference between the model of monopoly and that of monopolistic competition. Each producer is a profit maximizer. With a given demand curve and a corresponding marginal revenue curve, the firm optimizes by equating marginal cost with marginal revenue.

There appears to be very little difference between monopoly and monopolistic competition in the short run. When a longer view is taken, one essential element of monopoly is missing. In particular, a monopoly cannot be maintained if there is free entry. If pure profit is present in the short run for a monopolistic competitor, other firms will enter and produce the product, and they will continue to enter until all pure profits are eliminated.

Long-Run Equilibrium

Knowing that entry will take place until profits are normal, we can proceed immediately to the analysis of long-run equilibrium in a monopolistically competitive market. A zero-profit equilibrium is reached when price equals *LRAC* and the firm cannot increase profits by raising or lowering price. This occurs when demand is tangent to *LRAC*. The *tangency* of demand and *LRAC* is an important feature of the model of

FIGURE 15–2   **Long-run equilibrium in monopolistically competitive markets**

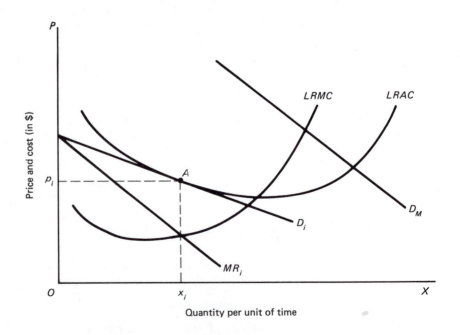

monopolistic competition. We can see from Figure 15–2 that, if demand intersected *LRAC*, prices would exist that could be above average cost allowing firms to make above-normal profits. For instance, if the firm had demand curve D_m, profits would be maximized at a price well above *LRAC*. In a monopolistically competitive market, entry would occur shifting demand to the left and making it more elastic, until the firm had a curve similar to D_i, just tangent to *LRAC*. Long-run equilibrium must exist at a point like *A* in Figure 15–2.

Equilibrium is depicted in Figure 15–2 with a *LRAC* curve that has some economies of scale at first, but diseconomies over larger ranges of output. We know that demand for a monopolistic competitor is not perfectly elastic, which implies that the demand curve is never horizontal. Therefore, equilibrium cannot occur at the lowest point on *LRAC*, but must exist on the downward sloping portion of *LRAC*, before economies of scale are exhausted.

Point *A* must also be described by the intersection of *LRMC* and MR_i, where subscript *i* is used to represent a typical firm in monopolistic competition. The profit-maximizing rule must lead a monopolistic competitor to the highest possible profit, given the demand curve. If the firm produced an amount different from x_i, price would be below average cost, and profits would be below normal. Thus, x_i is the profit-maximizing output.

Principle

Long-run equilibrium in a monopolistically competitive market is attained when the demand curve for each producer is tangent to its long-run average cost curve.

The Long-Run Equilibrium in Comparison with Perfect Competition

In long-run perfectly competitive equilibrium, total output is produced by a large number of small firms, each operating at the minimum point on long-run average cost. The product is sold at a price equal to minimum average cost, and it should be remembered that long-run marginal cost equals both price and average cost at this point. If demand should either increase or decrease, in the long run producers enter or exit, leaving each firm producing at the minimum point on its *LRAC* curve. It is impossible for any firm to lower average cost by either increasing or decreasing output. Therefore, costs are minimized for any level of industry output.

A monopolistically competitive firm is like a monopolist in that it faces a downward sloping demand curve. At the same time, it is like a perfectly competitive firm; it faces market competition that competes away pure profit in the long run. The differences between the model of perfect competition and monopolistic competition result solely from product differentiation. Putting the desirability of product differentiation aside for the moment, we can show that monopolistic competition compares unfavorably with perfect competition on two accounts.

First, since demand is less than perfectly elastic, marginal revenue is different from average revenue. Profit is maximized where $MR = MC$ in the long or the short run, and price is not equal to marginal cost. From our study of monopoly, we know this causes a loss of total surplus (consumer's plus producer's surplus). Figure 15–3 shows this loss as the shaded region between demand and marginal cost. Given the demand for the firm's product, the willingness to pay for the product is greater than the marginal cost of production for $x_e - x_m$ units. Since potential buyers value the product at more than the marginal cost of production, this reduction in output represents a loss to society. A monopolistically competitive firm would never produce x_e in the long run. At x_e, $LRAC$ is greater than p_e, and the firm would need a subsidy to break even and continue production.

The second criticism of monopolistic competition is that the long-run average cost of production is higher than it would be under perfect competition. In equilibrium, a monopolistically competitive firm produces at point A on $LRAC$ in Figure 15–3. A perfect competitor would produce at B where $LRMC = LRAC$ and $LRAC$ is minimized. A monopolistic competitor does not exhaust economies of scale in production as a perfect competitor does.

Frequently, monopolistic competitors are accused of having excess capacity, but this is not the real issue. The firm chooses the most efficient

FIGURE 15–3   **Monopolistic competition versus perfect competition**

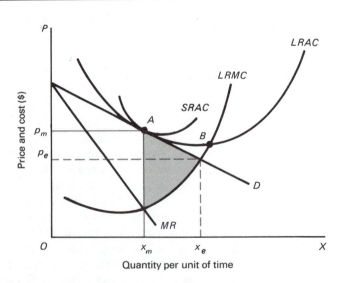

plant size, as described by the *SRAC* curve in Figure 15–3. The average cost of producing quantity x_m cannot be lower whether the market structure is perfect competition or monopoly. The problem with monopolistic competition is that because of the downward sloping demand curve, output is restricted, and, as a consequence, economies of scale are not completely exhausted in the long run.

These two criticisms of monopolistic competition—relatively high long-run average costs and a loss of total surplus—ignore product differentiation. Differences in product characteristics enable consumers to benefit from product variety. A choice between styles, colors, flavors, and qualities is a very desirable feature of market structures. The difference in the average cost of production and loss of surplus is the price society pays for product variety. If consumers did not wish to pay this price, buyers would choose and producers would sell only one product type. Since product differentiation is so common, buyers in markets must be willing to pay the price for product variety. Some would argue that the social cost of monopolistic competition is less than or equal to the social benefit.

15.3 NONPRICE COMPETITION

Imperfect competition—both monopolistic competition and oligopoly—is frequently characterized by competitive behavior not involving price changes. Some examples of nonprice competition are product quality changes and advertising. A perfectly competitive firm would have no reason to resort to nonprice competition, since it can sell all it wants at the going market price. Firms selling in markets with differentiated products frequently have the incentive to use methods other than price changes to increase profits. As we have seen, under monopolistic competition free entry drives profits to zero in the long run. Nonetheless, firms can sometimes delay or reverse this process by further differentiating their product from those of entrants—possibly by advertising or some other marketing strategy designed to increase the demand for their product. If the strategy is successful, the firm will enjoy above-normal profits, at least temporarily.

As we will see in the next section, in oligopolistic markets there is often a great deal of rivalry among firms. At times, because of strong interdependence among the firms, oligopolists hesitate to change prices frequently. Price changes can lead to very unprofitable price wars. Oligopolies may therefore resort to less threatening nonprice rivalry to raise profits, but even this is not a completely safe strategy. Firms are sometimes forced by the actions of their competitors to make nonprice changes (such as expensive changes in styling designs) that they would not have undertaken if their rivals had not initiated the change. In the long run, profits may be normal because of such nonprice strategies.

Product differentiation opens an entirely new dimension of competition, unavailable, by assumption, to perfect competitors. If successsful, such competition increases the demand for the product and, at any given price, causes the elasticity of demand to decline, allowing firms to charge higher prices for their products. This section discusses how product differentiation is a competitive decision variable. Firms can distinguish their products by the characteristics or *qualities* they attach to the goods they sell. Advertising plays a big role in a firm's effort to differentiate its product. It can either accentuate actual differences between products or create differences through the image advertising lends to products.

Product Quality

As we discussed in Chapter 11, under the assumptions of perfect competition, products can be thought of as a collection of attributes. We mentioned that an automobile can be described by its engine size, brakes, transmission, suspension, fuel efficiency, tires, head and trunk room, number of doors, color, and so on. These product features differ among automobiles and can be altered by the maker to differentiate their product. Algebraically, product characteristics are variables (a_i), that are *bundled* in certain ways to make a particular product, X. That is,

$$X = g(a_1, a_2, a_3, \ldots , a_n), \tag{15-1}$$

where n is the number of possible attributes a product may have. How a producer selects these attributes determines the quality and nature of the product and the product's substitutability with other products in the market. The decision of a manufacturer to give an automobile all the product attributes that characterize a Cadillac Sedan De Ville will make the car an unlikely substitute for a Ford Mustang. In general, product differentiation determines the substitutability of products.

The idea that product attributes are a nonprice competitive tool is captured by letting all of the possible preferences consumers may have for a particular attribute be measured along a scale with end-points 0 and 1, as shown in Figure 15–4. Let us say that this product attribute is sugar on breakfast cereal; then 0 is cereal with no sugar and 1 is cereal of virtually pure sugar cubes. The value ¼, ½, and ¾ mark equal distance points along this scale. Suppose that those who buy breakfast cereal are evenly distributed along this scale so that the number of individuals who want no sugar on their cereal is equal to the number who want their cereal half-sugared and is equal to the number who want all sugar.

In the case of the first firm to produce cereal, it does not matter how much sugar is put on its product. It is the only cereal consumers can buy. Thus, we arbitrarily locate firm A on the scale as A_1. Since sugar is expensive, we place A_1 on the lower end of the scale. We subscript the

FIGURE 15-4   **Product quality measure**

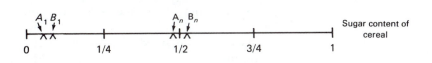

location because the firm may later want to change the sugar content of its cereal when other firms enter the market.

Rivalry begins when firm B decides to enter the market. The new seller knows the preferences of consumers, i.e., the scale in Figure 15-4, and how much sugar A has on its product. The question is, how much sugar should B use to capture the largest share of the market? Market share is very important to profit maximization. We know from Section 15-2 that the larger a firm's market share, the less elastic is demand and, consequently, the higher is price. Also, if there are economies of scale, increased sales allow a producer to move down the $LRAC$ curve and realize a lower average cost of production. Of course, at the margin, higher prices and lower production costs must be balanced against the marginal cost of increasing market share, which may, for example, involve advertising, or, in this case, using more sugar.

In Figure 15-4, we can see that at constant prices firm B could capture most of the market by using a little more sugar than A. The best thing for B to do is enter with a product that is just to the right of A_1. We label this point B_1. Firm B captures all of the market to the right of A_1.

Firm A will, of course, not tolerate this for long. Its market share has been reduced to a very small part of the total market. Only those buyers with preferences between 0 and A_1 remain loyal to A's cereal. The firm could lower price or think about countering B's product by putting more sugar on its cereal. It can regain much of its lost market by moving just to the right of B_1. But then B will move to the right of A again, and A will then move to the right of B a second time. The leapfrogging will continue until one firm drops out of the market, or both firms end up with equal market shares at the midpoint of the preference scale. After a large number of moves, we will find both firms putting approximately the same amount of sugar on their cereal and supplying the amounts desired by the average buyer; i.e., at A_n and B_n.

The situation gets more complicated when a third firm enters the market. With a little experimenting, you will discover that firms will not find an equilibrium; they continually change the amount of sugar on their cereals. This is not so unusual in the real world, considering how many "new" and "improved" labels producers put on their products. Often these improvements are nothing more than a slight adjustment in a product attribute, a change marketers hope will place them near their rival, but on the side of the preference scale that gives them the largest market share.

We have oversimplified things a great deal by allowing product differentiation for only one product variable and assuming price competition does not take place at the same time. Equation 15–1 tells us that there are numerous product attributes for any one commodity. Realistically, there are all sorts of ways attributes can be mixed. Discovering the attributes that capture the largest share of the market requires sophisticated marketing techniques and, at times, just plain luck. The point of our simple model, though, is that product differentiation is a competitive tool that firms use to maximize profits. Differentiation can be as much a part of competition as price.

One further conclusion that we can draw from the discussion surrounding Figure 15–4 is that nonprice competition can lead to the *bunching* of product attributes. In the case of the two firms in this figure, equilibrium occurred at the midpoint of the preference spectrum. Tastes could be better served with more product variety; say *A* moves closer to 0 and *B* closer to 1. Algebraically, it can be shown that, if consumers are evenly distributed along the scale, one firm should locate one quarter and the other three quarters of the distance between 0 and 1 to best serve consumer tastes in the market.[4] But there is no incentive for firms to behave in this way. The incentive to produce product attributes close to those of a rival can be easily seen in the location of businesses, television programming, automobile styling, and fashion apparel. Nonprice competition can frequently lead to what economists call *excessive sameness* in the market. Occasionally, a lack of product differentiation is unavoidable. In some markets, there is little that can be done to change the product. There is, for instance, little or no product differentiation in the facial tissue or aspirin markets, yet these markets fit the monopolistic competition model well. Advertising is a device used to highlight slight differences and, in some cases, even create them in the consumer's mind.

Advertising

Advertising has the capability of impressing a product's image on consumers, and consumers may choose to buy or not buy a product because of its advertised image. For example, people buy Rolex watches partly because of the image that successful, rich people wear these

---

[4] There are some special assumptions about the preference map. See H. Hotelling, "Stability in Competition," *Econonomic Journal* 39 (March 1929), pp. 41–57; F. M. Scherer, "The Welfare Economics of Product Variety: An Application to the Ready-to-Eat Cereal Industry," *Journal of Industrial Economics* 28, no. 2 (December 1979), pp. 113–34.

watches. If consumers are less interested in such a status symbol, they have the option of purchasing another brand. The Rolex status is a product attribute of the watch. The image is literally a characteristic of the product, just as style, color, and size are.

This means that we are likely to observe advertising for one product similar to that of a close substitute. As an example, on television Anheuser-Busch and Miller have very similar types of ads for their beer. Celebrities, in one way or another, endorse the product. Automobile ads tend to either have beautiful, rich people driving down a tree-lined neighborhood street with large, stately houses in the background, or they emphasize performance with a car racing along a speed track or twisting highway. Other advertising similarities may come to mind when you think of products that are in the same market.

Aside from duplicity, it is interesting that from a seller's viewpoint, rivalry can also lead to excessive amounts of advertising. Specifically, if sellers could agree to restrict the amount of advertising they undertake—much of it done in response to a rival's ads in the first place—profits for sellers would rise. Advertising is excessive because it is often a defensive tactic to maintain a seller's market share against the advertising of rivals. In many cases, it is a necessary cost of entry into a market, a cost that would be lower or even nonexistent if firms already selling in the market were not making heavy advertising expenditures.

How rivalry leads to unprofitable amounts of advertising can be illustrated by a model known as the *prisoner's dilemma*. The model is best described by the story that gave it its name. Suppose a crime is committed and two suspects are apprehended and questioned by the police. Unknown to the suspects, the police do not have enough evidence to convict the suspects without one of them confessing. So the police separate them and make each an offer known to the other. The offer is, if one suspect confesses to the crime and turns state's evidence, the one who confesses receives only a two-year sentence, while the other who does not confess gets 10 years. If both turn state's evidence, each receives a two-year sentence. Of course, if neither confesses, the probability is very high both will go free. Each could receive 2 years, 10 years, or go free, depending on what the other does.

Figure 15–5 shows the four possibilities in the dilemma. The upper-left and lower-right cells show the results if both plead innocent or guilty, respectively. The upper-right and lower-left cells show the consequences if one pleads guilty and the other innocent.

The problem is that the suspects cannot *collude* and decide to plead innocent. They must make their decisions based on their conjecture of what the other prisoner will do. If either suspect pleads innocent, each stands a chance of 10 years in prison if the other confesses. However, the worst that could happen if a prisoner confesses to the crime is two years imprisonment regardless of what the other does.

FIGURE 15–5 **Prisoner's dilemma**

		Suspect 1 Innocent	*Suspect 1* Guilty
Suspect 2	Innocent	A 1: 0 years 2: 0 years	B 1: 2 years 2: 10 years
	Guilty	C 1: 10 years 2: 2 years	D 1: 2 years 2: 2 years

How prisoners actually plead depends on a number of factors; for example, whether or not the crime was committed by the accused, how well the prisoners know each other, and the willingness of each to take risks are just a few of the considerations affecting a prisoner's choice. Under many circumstances, however, the safest plea would be guilty, because the *expected* stay in jail would be minimized. Suppose the odds of the other prisoner pleading guilty are even; then your expected stay in jail if you did not confess would be five years ($0 \times ½ + 10 \times ½$). On the other hand, by pleading guilty you know with certainty the term would only be two years. From this calculation we can see that there are incentives for both prisoners to plead guilty, and cell D becomes the equilibrium.

Imperfect competitors are caught in a similar dilemma when it comes to nonprice competition. Suppose the choice is to advertise a little or a lot. The relative advertising outlays determine profits. Low advertising by rivals keeps profits relatively high; any single firm can increase profits at the expense of other firms if it advertises more while the others do not. It is thought by economists that in many imperfectly competitive markets, the *total* amount of advertising by all firms has little effect on *total* sales in the market.[5] That is, total market demand is relatively inelastic with respect to advertising. But, if any firm does little or no advertising while the other firms advertise heavily, that firm loses a substantial share of the market.

To illustrate the situation, assume there are two rival firms. As with the prisoner's dilemma, there are four combinations of choices for the rival firms. In cells A through D in Figure 15–6, the profitability (π) of each combination is shown for the firms. If neither firm undertakes large amounts of advertising, profits are, say, \$100 for each firm. They have

[5] See F. M. Scherer, *Industrial Market Structure and Economic Performance*, 2d ed. (Boston: Houghton Mifflin, 1980), pp. 384–93.

FIGURE 15–6 **Advertiser's dilemma**

		Firm 1	
		Low	High
Firm 2	Low	**A** π_1: 100 π_2: 100	**B** π_1: 60 π_2: 150
	High	**C** π_1: 150 π_2: 60	**D** π_1: 80 π_2: 80

equal costs and market shares. But you can see that there is a big temptation to increase advertising relative to that of the rival. Profits jump to $150, largely because the high advertiser attracts business away from the low advertiser, whose profits fall to $60. To a small extent profits also rise because the total market expands as a result of more total advertising. Cells B and C are not an equilibrium. The low advertiser can at least raise profits to $80 by following with a high advertising budget. In the long run, both firms end up with relatively higher advertising expenditures and lower profits. From each seller's perspective, there is too much advertising.

If firms recognize the long-run effects of high advertising budgets, they might tacitly agree not to increase expenditures. Such an agreement is much more likely to occur when firms recognize their interdependence than when there are many firms with small market shares. An oligopolistic market structure is more apt to prevent advertising excessiveness, as measured by profits, than is monopolistic competition. However, once a rival decides to increase advertising, it is very difficult, regardless of the market structure, to avoid cell D in Figure 15–6. And it is very unlikely that, without an explicit agreement, firms will return to cell A.

APPLICATION

Nonprice Competition in the Decaffeinated Coffee Market

The decaffeinated coffee market is characterized by few sellers. The three largest producers are General Foods, the Nestle Company, and Procter & Gamble. These producers are well acquainted with the products of the others and know their market actions are observed by their rivals. It is safe to say that the decaffeinated coffee market is oligopolistic. Recent behavior in this market offers a showcase for nonprice competition.

Even though there are three main producers, they market, under different names, more than five nationally known products. General Foods leads the decaffeinated market with its Sanka and Brim brands. In September 1980, Sanka brand supplied 40.5 percent of the market. At the same time, Nestle had 17.0 percent of the market with its decaffeinated products, Taster's Choice and Nescafé, while Procter & Gamble held 17.3 percent of the market after the introduction of its new brand—High Point.[6]

Why should firms introduce more than one brand of coffee? Automobile manufacturers sell more than one car model, tobacco companies market several brands of cigarettes, and cereal makers (one of which is General Foods) also sell a variety of brands in which the company's own products have high cross elasticities of demand. One reason was discussed in the last chapter: a firm with monopoly power may want to block entry and protect market share by introducing products that a potential entrant could profitably produce. Another reason for introducing multiple brands is that producers are very uncertain about the product preference spectrum. Recall the product-quality scale in Figure 15–4. When a firm introduces a product, it may be at point A_1 or B_1 without knowing the rest of the scale. Consumers could decide to forego decaffeinated coffee altogether rather than drink something that does not taste good to them. This could be the case for a significant number of potential decaffeinated coffee drinkers, if companies inadvertently located at one end of the scale. So companies explore the market by introducing new brands, hoping to find a flavor that carves out a new market niche.

Before Procter & Gamble introduced High Point coffee, it had 11.8 percent of the decaffeinated coffee market. Its main rival, General Foods, had 49 percent of the market. P&G wanted more than 20 percent of the market with a second brand. To capture this much of the market, Procter & Gamble increased advertising. How would you expect General Foods to react after it sees its share of the market erode? The answer is obvious—it will also advertise more. General Foods is caught in a prisoner's dilemma, as shown below:

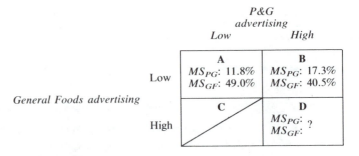

_____
[6] These figures and those that follow are from ''P&G's Campaign to Unseat Sanka,'' *Business Week,* January 26, 1981, p. 65.

In the cells we indicate market share (*MS*) instead of profits, since profits are not reported for specific products. In cell A, High Point has not been introduced yet. Advertising by each of these two large firms was relatively low. After High Point was introduced, Procter & Gamble was reported to have spent at least $30 million on the introduction of the new coffee. In the third quarter of 1980 alone, P&G spent $10 million on advertising for High Point. In cell B, General Foods saw its market share fall and responded by tripling advertising for Sanka. In the last quarter of 1980, it spent $8.4 million on advertising for Sanka. The firms have moved to cell D in the above diagram. The model would predict that neither firm will win the marketing war—market shares will stay roughly the same, but profits will be lower because of the higher advertising expenditures.

15.4 INTERDEPENDENCE IN OLIGOPOLY BEHAVIOR

Oligopoly is said to exist when more than one seller is in the market, but when the number is not so large as to render negligible the contribution of each. A market will have few enough sellers to be considered oligopolistic if the sellers recognize their *mutual interdependence*. In monopoly and competition, firms make decisions and take action without considering how these actions will affect other firms and how, in turn, other firms' reactions will affect them. Oligopolists must take these reactions into account when contemplating a price change, a design innovation, or a new advertising campaign. Ford Motor Comany must anticipate, for example, how GM and Chrysler Corporation will react when it introduces a new model because, without doubt, Ford's actions will affect the demand for Chevrolets and Chryslers.

This, in short, is the oligopoly problem and the central problem in oligopoly analysis. The oligopolistic firm is large enough relative to the total market to recognize (*a*) the mutual interdependence of each firm's demand in the market, and (*b*) the fact that its decisions will affect the sales of other firms, which in turn will cause them to react in a way that requires a new round of adjustments. The great uncertainty is *how one's rivals will react.*

Since so many industries meet the general description of oligopoly, it would, at first glance, seem that a general theory of oligopoly should exist. The problem in developing an oligopoly theory, however, is the same as the oligopoly problem itself. Mutual interdependence and the resulting uncertainty about reaction patterns make it necessary for economists to postulate specific assumptions about behavioral patterns; that is, specific assumptions about how oligopolists *believe* their rivals will react must be made before market outcomes can be predicted.

Therefore, an oligopoly equilibrium depends critically on the assumptions the economist makes in regard to the behavioral reaction of rival entrepreneurs. Since many different assumptions can and have been made, many different solutions can and have been reached. There is no "theory of oligopoly" in the sense that there is a theory of perfect competition or of monopoly.

A second complication encountered when modeling oligopoly is that oligopolists can produce homogeneous or differentiated products. As noted in our discussion of monopolistic competition, product differentiation is a major determinant of demand elasticity. As a consequence, just as a single model cannot simultaneously describe perfect and monopolistic competition, one model cannot describe oligopolies producing identical or differentiated products.

Types of Behavior

Broadly speaking, economists usually posit two contrasting patterns of behavior for oligopolists: they are assumed to be either *cooperative* or *noncooperative*. Cooperative oligopolies tend to accommodate changes made by rival firms. For instance, if a rival should raise price, a cooperative oligopolist would go along with the move and raise price too. Noncooperative behavior, on the other hand, does not accommodate such changes. If another firm raised price, rivals would keep prices low in order to attract sales away from the higher-priced producer.

Because of the possibility of differentiated or identical products, there are four general oligopolistic market structures. One structure consists of a few *noncooperating* firms producing either (1) homogeneous, or (2) differentiated products. Alternatively, there may be a few *cooperating* firms producing either (3) homogeneous, or (4) differentiated products. If oligopolists produce the same products and do not cooperate, the market resembles perfect competition. Each producer's demand elasticity will be high because there are very close substitutes available. If each firm's output exhausts all economies of scale, price will be close to minimum long-run average cost. Cooperating oligopolists producing identical products jointly behave much like a monopoly. For instance, firms tend to act as one in the case of a price increase; since buyers cannot distinguish among products, it appears that industry price has risen as if a monopoly actually controlled production.

Product differentiation makes cooperation more difficult. In a cooperative agreement, price differences must be negotiated to account for differences in product qualities. Instead of settling on one common price for the market, cooperation now essentially entails an agreement on the price of each product sold. Added to this increased difficulty over setting price is the opportunity of nonprice competition over product differences. While oligopolists may have an agreement not to use price as a competitive tool, they may increase product quality to attract business away from rivals. This kind of competition is very difficult to control. Noncooperation would give an oligopolistic market the character of monopolistic competition, while cooperation would tend to result in economic profits. The most visible sort of cooperation when products are differentiated is leadership by a dominant firm in price or model changes. The largest firm in cooperative markets is frequently first to announce price and style changes that other firms in the market follow.

Oligopoly behavior, in general, is determined by the threat of entry. If entry is easy, the gains from cooperation are low. High prices would only encourage new firms to enter the market. Prices in such markets tend to be low and cooperation to increase profits is minimal. If entry is difficult, and oligopolists have relatively secure market shares, over time it is much easier to cooperate and the gains from restricting price, for example, are greater. There is greater incentive to reach a noncompetitive agreement.

Tacit Collusion

Implicitly cooperative oligopolies are often said to be *tacitly colluding*. Tacit collusion is agreement without communication. For instance, steel producers may restrict their sales to specified geographical regions without meeting and openly dividing regions into designated marketing areas. A firm's market is *understood* from the ongoing relations it has had with its rivals over the years. As opposed to the formation of a cartel or a trust in an attempt to monopolize a market, tacit collusion is not per se, or categorically, illegal. However, evidence of communication would quickly tip the legal balance against accused participants.

Examples of tacit collusion are evident among manufacturers of consumer durables. For instance, oligopolists will often act together by changing their models annually at almost the same time. Washing machines, refrigerators, cooking ranges, and lawn mowers have annual changes that are announced by manufacturers at about the same time of the year. The same holds true for fashions when spring and fall designs are announced. For another example, ask yourself why makers of soft drinks and beer all use the same size cans and bottles, or makers of breakfast cereal package their product in the same size boxes. It is not because consumers all have a preference for the 12-ounce size. As far as anyone knows, cereal makers and bottlers have no explicit agreement that only this container size—along with a few others—is allowable.

The strongest examples of tacit collusion come from the prices oligopolists charge. In the service sector of our economy, there is a surprising amount of price uniformity, even though there is a wide variance in the quality of services. For instance, lawyers and real estate agents by and large charge the same prices for their services, even though the quality of services varies from lawyer to lawyer or broker to broker.

Explicit collusuion is illegal in these industries and presumably does not take place, but a substantial amount of price uniformity nevertheless exists.

There is also the appearance of *price leadership* in certain oligopolist markets. At times it has been observed in the tire, oil, steel, and cigarette industries that when one firm announces a price change (usually an increase), the other producers follow along with the same percentage change. Generally in these markets it has been the firm with the largest market share that takes the lead in announcing a change. For instance, General Motors and U.S. Steel were recognized price leaders in the automobile and steel industries during the 1960s. However, as entry into these industries has taken place over the last twenty years, the leadership role of these firms has declined. Price leadership works best as a form of tacit collusion when there are few firms and very little turnover among these firms in the industry.

How does tacit collusion arise? What makes oligopolists cooperate without an explicit arrangement? The answer lies in the consequences of noncooperation. When it comes to selecting competitive strategies, the main difference between a monopolistic competitor and an oligopolist is the realization that what an oligopolist does will cause rivals to react. The expected reaction is likely to leave sellers no better off than they were before the move. Oligopolists know that they are related to rivals in a prisoner's dilemma. Another new style or a lower price on old models may increase profits in the short run, but reduce them in the long run.

Whether or not an oligopolist makes a change depends on the relative present values of making the change or leaving things as they are. Profits may increase substantially at first, but decrease in the long run after rivals react. How quickly rivals react in large measure determines how profitable a change will be. For cases where the discounted stream of profits is expected to be less than it would be without the change, patterns of behavior are established among rivals. Oligopolists cooperate because, given the expected reaction of rivals, long-run profits are maximized by stable behavior. This is particularly true for behavior that, in the long run, will raise the costs of producers, because revenues are not likely to go up after rivals have adjusted.

Competition in Oligopoly

There is a certain amount of debate among economists as to the degree of competition in industries characterized by oligopoly. The discussion boils down to the extent of cooperation that exists in oligopolistic market structures. The less cooperation, the more price and nonprice competition there should be.

Oligopolists are profit maximizers; even when there appears to be a great deal of cooperation among rivals in a market, there is an incentive to make competitive moves that are not easily observed by rivals. Price changes are probably the most obvious moves. Since price is easily observed by rivals, tacit understandings not to lower price often occur. Nonprice competition, on the other hand, is not as easily noticed, and may be very difficult to emulate. Therefore, oligopolists are usually more competitive with respect to non-price variables. For instance, an oligopolist's advertising budget is not widely known; a firm can incrementally increase the budget without inducing a reaction from rivals. Not surprisingly, oligopolists selling differentiated products tend to do a considerable amount of advertising.

Changes in product quality are often less perceptible than changes in price. A wine that is aged longer to give it a better taste, a few added inches between seats on an airplane, or fewer defective parts in a large shipment of equipment are quality changes not easily observed by rivals. Product-quality competition is particularly intense in service oligopolies, where product quality is difficult to judge unambiguously. Doctors and dentists, for instance, do not usually compete over the prices they charge patients, but the quality of their services and the waiting time in their offices vary a great deal. These are the dimensions where professionals usually compete.

Certainly prices do fluctuate under oligopoly, particularly when it is noncooperative. There is controversy over how much price flexibility exists among oligopolists in general. One thing is clear, however, there is more price flexibility under oligopoly than would exist if the market were monopolized. This point has been made in two studies.

In 1947, George Stigler, using industrial data from the 1930s, carried out tests to determine the relative flexibility of prices under oligopoly.[7] As a first piece of evidence, Stigler found that, in seven highly oligopolistic industries (cigarettes, automobiles, anthracite coal, dynamite, oil, potash, and steel), both price decreases and increases by firms in the industry were rapidly followed by other firms. There was no evidence of a lack of price flexibility in any of the seven industries.

Stigler then compared the flexibility of oligopoly prices in many industries with that of prices in industries characterized by monopoly. Even though their outputs varied significantly—more than that of most of the oligopolistic industries tested—two monopolies (aluminum and nickel) were characterized during the period by significantly more price rigidity than was the case for the oligopolies. The oligopolists, who had periods of known explicit collusion, experienced extreme price rigidity during collusion. There was much more flexibility during periods of noncollusion.

Later Julian L. Simon tested the rigid oligopolistic price hypothesis,

---

[7] G. J. Stigler, "The Kinky Oligopoly Demand Curve and Rigid Prices," *Journal of Political Economy* 55 (October 1947), pp. 432–49. Reprinted in G. J. Stigler, *The Organization of Industry* (Homewood, Ill.: Richard D. Irwin, 1968).

using changes in advertising rates in business magazines for the period 1955–64.[8] His data indicate that monopolistic magazines (i.e., magazines with no competitors in the same category) do not change rates any more frequently than magazines with a few close competitors within their classification. In fact, Simon found that, with one exception, magazines in one-magazine groups change price less frequently than magazines in multiple-magazine groups. Also, there was progressively more frequent price change in going from single-magazine to 10-magazine groups. The main results of the test show no evidence that oligopoly changes price less frequently than does monopoly.

15.5 THEORIES OF OLIGOPOLY RIVALRY

There are numerous theories of equilibrium in oligopoly markets, each depending on a key assumption about how rivals will react to a change in either output or price by one firm in the market. By changing the assumed reaction rivals take, the equilibrium in the market changes. These popular models of oligopoly rivalry are not models of collusion; they arise in a noncooperative environment. However, reactions may be quite accommodating. Outlined in this section are some of the market outcomes that may result when oligopolists compete and attempt to maximize profits. All of them will be described in a market setting called *duopoly*—two firms producing a homogeneous product. We also assume that costs are constant, so average cost is equal to marginal cost.

A Pay-Off Table

In Table 15–1 we have what is typically called a *pay-off table*. It is similar to the prisoner's dilemma discussed earlier. The main difference is the number of entries across the top and left side. There are now 10 instead of 2. The numbers along the border in this table can represent either the output sold or the price charged by each duopolist. Inside the table we have the profits earned by one of the duopolists. We have generated these amounts based on the border numbers being output and the demand for the market being $P = 22 - X$, where X is the sum of the outputs for the two firms. Also, marginal cost is constant at \$2. For an example, to interpret the table, suppose you, as a duopolist, select an output of 10 and your rival picks an output of 6; your profit will then be at the intersection of row 10 and column 6 for a profit of 40.

This profit can be calculated from the demand equation and the assumption that unit costs are constant at \$2. Since total output is 16, the market price is $P = 22 - 16 = \$6$. By producing 10 units, your profit is

---

8 J. L. Simon, "A Further Test of the Kinky Oligopoly Demand Curve," *The American Economic Review* 59, no. 9 (December 1969), pp. 971–75.

TABLE 15–1   **Pay-off table**

		Value Selected by the Other Participant									
		1	2	3	4	5	6	7	8	9	10
Y	1	18	17	16	15	14	13	12	11	10	09
o	2	34	32	30	28	26	24	22	20	18	16
u	3	48	45	42	39	36	33	30	27	24	21
	4	60	56	52	48	44	40	36	32	28	24	Collusive
r	5	70	65	60	55	50	45	40	35	30	25
V	6	78	72	66	60	54	48	42	36	30	24	Cournot
a	7	84	77	70	63	56	49	42	35	28	21
l	8	88	80	72	64	56	48	40	32	24	16
u	9	90	81	72	63	54	45	36	27	18	09	Competitive
e	10	90	80	70	60	50	40	30	20	10	00

the total revenue $6(10) = $60 less the total cost of $2(10) = $20, or $40. Profit for your rival selling at 6 units is $6(6) − $2(6) = $24. This is the entry seen by your rival in the pay-off table. It is at the intersection of row 6 and column 10, because your output goes across the top of their table.

However, it is not very likely your rival will stay at 6 units. The other duopolist in the market is looking at a pay-off table just like this and is a profit maximizer. Your rival always sees you as the "other participant" choosing values across the top of the table. If *you* choose a value of 10, your rival will choose a row value to maximize profit and will produce 5 units of output. With your table you observe this choice made by the other participant. Looking down the left side of your table, since the other participant has chosen 5, you take a value of 7 or 8 for profits of 56. The process of adjustment will continue until both duopolists have no further incentive to change their values.

Oligopoly Equilibrium

With respect to Table 15–1, several outputs can be identified as potential equilibria in the market, depending on how much cooperation there is. What actually happens in the market adjustment process is determined by how oligopolists think their rival or rivals will react to market changes in output or price. Expected behavior in economic theory is called a *conjectural variation*. Two firms in the market may think and actually behave like perfect competitors. This will lead to increases in output until a "perfectly competitive" equilibrium is reached in which each firm earns zero profit. In Table 15–1, this occurs at an output of 10 for each participant.

Firms may have a *Cournot* conjecture. In this case, each seller maximizes profit under the assumption the other will hold its output constant. Earlier, when we were describing the pay-off table, we had implicitly made this assumption. Our thinking was that we chose the best value *given* the value already chosen by the other participant. The last choice we discussed was what value to pick if the other person is at 5, and we chose 7 or 8. Continuing in this fashion, both participants will end up at values of 7, and this is called the *Cournot equilibrium* in the market.

Notice that profits are not zero as they were under the competitive assumption. Each seller now earns a return of 42. Also, output is restricted. Under competition, total product sold by both would be 20. A Cournot equilibrium has a total output of 14. When we move from a market that is by and large competitive to one where there are a few firms, profits tend to be higher and output lower. No collusion is taking place, although the outcome may make us suspicious of collusion. When profit maximizers have a recognizable impact on market price and output and know their behavior affects the behavior of other sellers, they realize quite independently of each other that some reduction in output benefits all the sellers. As sellers realize this to one degree or another, the market moves toward the Cournot outcome.

A third potential equilibrium in the duopoly market described by Table 15–1 is called the *collusive* or monopoly equilibrium. It is achieved by the two firms behaving as if they were a single monopolist. We know that a monopolist maximizes profit by setting marginal revenue equal to marginal cost (which is $2 in the Table) for the market. This behavior gives each seller an output of 5, and profit per seller is 50. It is hard to imagine how this equilibrium could exist without some form of cooperation between producers, but cooperation may subtly evolve over time in any number of ways. The history of the market (e.g., how the firms first came to produce and compete with another) and accepted business practices often allow the firms to reach more collusive equilibria without any formal agreement or even communication over prices and output.

The relative outputs of the three oligopoly equilibria we have described so far can be related to each other by observing the diagonal connecting the collusive and competitive profit levels in Table 15–1. The greatest output comes in a competitive environment. It is cut in half if the two firms should behave like a monopolist, and a Cournot equilibrium lies between these two points. Depending on the expected behavior, or conjectures of rivals in a market, an oligopoly equilibrium may exist anywhere along the diagonal line drawn between the collusive and competitive points. In many markets, however, the Cournot equilibrium appears to be a focal point.

We have explored oligopoly behavior in terms of rivals choosing output, but in many markets the value chosen is price. Once price is set, businesses usually try to sell all they can so long as price is greater than marginal cost. Some of the values in the table will change as a result; since the products are identical, the lowest price seller will get all the business. The competitive and collusive outcomes, however, are found in exactly the same way described above. Profits are either zero or maximized as if the firms were a monopoly. A Cournot equilibrium cannot be defined under these circumstances because firms do not choose output. However, it is possible to identify in more specific cases a *Bertrand* equilibrium. Very similar to Cournot, a Bertrand outcome results from each firm setting price assuming rivals will keep their prices fixed. This assumption does not make it as easy as it was in a Cournot world to identify an equilibrium. For homogeneous products, the firm selling at the lowest price captures all of the market and becomes a monopolist. Therefore to attract customers away from this firm, rivals will have to sell at a lower price. Eventually such a "price war" will lead to competitive prices. A Bertrand-type equilibrium will be different from the competitive equilibrium only when there are limits on the capacity of rivals or if the products are differentiated. If rivals cannot meet market demand at the prices they set, the Bertrand outcome will be similar to the Cournot equilibrium in the sense that total output is below a competitive equilibrium.

15.6 OLIGOPOLY AND CARTELS

The firms in an oligopoly may decide to overtly fix price and/or market shares. Explicit collusive behavior, necessary in the formation of a cartel, is illegal in the United States under the Sherman Act and other legislation. But anti-trust litigation flourishes, indicating that such behavior is still thought to continue.

Cartels and Profit Maximization

A cartel is a combination of firms with the common goal of limiting the competitive forces within a market. It may take the form of open collusion where the member firms enter into contracts restricting price and other market variables. The cartel may be based on a secret agreement among members, or it can operate like a trade association or a professional organization. At this time, the most famous cartel is OPEC, a cartel of major oil-producing nations. To be successful, every cartel must have a way of enforcing the agreement members of the group make. European companies can form cartels and write a legally binding contract that courts will enforce. Other means of enforcement are more subtle. In

OPEC, Saudi Arabia is such a large producer of high grade crude that it could increase output at virtually any time to ruin the business of stubborn members. Many cartel agreements are, however, difficult to enforce because they are illegal. Any action taken to punish the violator may expose the whole operation to the authorities.

Let us consider the "ideal" cartel. Suppose a group of firms producing a homogeneous commodity combine their interests. A central management body is appointed to determine the uniform cartel price. The task, in theory, is relatively simple, as illustrated in Figure 15–7. Market demand for the homogeneous commodity is given by DD', so marginal revenue is given by the dashed line MR. The cartel marginal cost curve in the figure is determined by the management body. If all firms in the cartel purchase their inputs in perfectly competitive markets, the cartel marginal cost curve (MC_c) is simply the horizontal sum of the marginal cost curves of the member firms. Otherwise, allowance must be made for the increase in input price accompanying an increase in input usage, and MC_c would stand further to the left than if all input markets were perfectly competitive.

In either case, suppose the management group determines that the cartel marginal cost is MC_c. The profit-maximization problem is identical

FIGURE 15–7   **Cartel profit maximization**

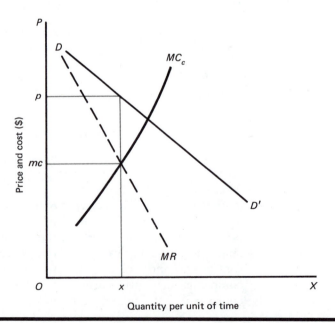

Quantity per unit of time

to that for a monopolist. The cartel should operate where marginal revenue equals marginal cost. From Figure 15–7, marginal cost and marginal revenue intersect at output x; thus, the market price, p, is the price established by the manager. The second, and probably biggest, problem now confronting the cartel management is *how* to distribute the total sales of x units among the member firms. The distribution of sales will determine each member's profit.

Cartels and Market Sharing

Fundamentally, there are two methods of sales allocation. One involves setting the cartel price, then letting firms maximize sales through nonprice competition. The other way of deciding sales is to set quotas. The former is usually associated with "loose" cartels. A uniform price is fixed, and each firm is allowed to sell all it can at that price. Firms cannot reduce price but can compete by other means. For instance, in most localities, doctors and lawyers have associations whose code of ethics is frequently the basis of a price agreement. Patients and clients then select a doctor or lawyer for reasons other than price. In this case fostering and maintaining a good reputation is important to increased sales.

The second method of market sharing is the quota system, which has several variants. Indeed, there is no uniform principle to determine quotas. In practice, the bargaining ability of a firm's representative and the importance of the firm to the cartel are the more prominent elements in determining a quota. Bargained allocations are usually struck on two popular grounds. First, either the relative sales of the firms in some precartel base period or the productive capacities of the firms are used. As a practical matter, the choice of base period or the measure of capacity is also a matter of bargaining among members. The second basis is a geographical division of the market. Many of the more famous examples of cartels involve international market divisions.

While a quota agreement is difficult in practice, in theory some simple guidelines can be laid down. Consider the cartel solution that was shown in Figure 15–7. MC_c is the horizontal summation of all firms' marginal cost curves. The cartel produces and sells at the output level x at a price p. The minimum cartel cost of producing x, or any other level of output, is achieved when each firm produces an output that makes every firm's marginal cost the same and equals the common cartel marginal cost and marginal revenue. Each firm in the cartel shown in Figure 15–7 produces the output where its marginal cost is mc. This may be the way a cartel could allocate sales. Note that this solution is precisely that set forth in the case of the multiplant monopolist, discussed in Chapter 13.

To explain the allocation method in a little more detail, suppose that two firms in the cartel are producing at different marginal costs; that is,

$$MC_1 > MC_2$$

for firms one and two. In this case, the cartel manager could transfer output from the higher-cost firm one to the lower-cost firm two. So long as the marginal cost of producing in firm two is lower, total cartel cost can be lowered by transferring production, and at any given price profits will increase.

But this does not necessarily solve the problem of how profits are distributed. Once total output and its division have been decided on grounds of cost minimization, there may still exist the problem of allocating the profit across firms. If the cost structure for all firms is alike, the firms can, of course, simply share profits equally. But if cost differences exist, letting allocated production determine profit may not be satisfactory. There are sometimes tremendous incentives to increase production once prices are fixed in a cartel.

Short and Turbulent Life of Cartels

Unless backed by strong legal provisions, cartels in the United States are very likely to collapse from internal pressure (before being found out by the Antitrust Division of the Justice Department). A few large, geographically concentrated firms producing a homogeneous commodity may form a very successful cartel and maintain it, at least during periods of prosperity. But the greater the number of firms, the greater the scope of product differentiation, and the greater the geographical dispersion of firms, the easier it is to "cheat" on the cartel's policy. In times of marked prosperity, profit may be so great that there is little incentive to cheat. When profits are low or negative, there are increased incentives to secretly increase output and reduce price. These incentives make cartel agreements unstable.

The typical cartel is characterized by high (perhaps monopoly) price, relatively low output, and a distribution of sales among firms that enables most to operate at an output less than that associated with their minimum average cost. In this situation, any one firm can profit greatly from secret price concessions. Indeed, with a homogeneous product, a firm offering price concessions can capture as much of the market as desired, providing the other members adhere to the cartel's price policy. Secret price concessions do not have to be rampant before the obedient members experience a marked decline in sales. Recognizing that one or more members are cheating, the formerly obedient members must themselves reduce price in order to remain in business. The cartel accordingly collapses. Without effective *legal* sanctions, the life of a cartel is likely to be brief, frequently ending whenever a business recession occurs.

The incentive of cartel members to increase output can be explained by using a *kinked demand curve*. The kink in the curve comes from the incentive structure of members within a cartel. Suppose the collusive organization has fixed a price that maximizes profit for the group. There is no longer an incentive for one oligopolist to cheat by raising price, because the other producers would probably not follow, even if they knew about the infraction. The cheater is imposing a self-inflicted punishment. If it should raise price, sales are rapidly lost to rivals. Thus it is likely that demand is very elastic for a price increase, especially if the products are homogeneous.

There is, however, an incentive for members of an oligopoly to cheat by lowering price. If rivals do not follow the price cut, the cheater quickly gains additional sales from the other sellers. Figure 15–8 shows the potential gain for a member of a price-fixing cartel. Assume the price is fixed at p_0; the oligopolist, in this case, sells x_0, but output may vary among members.

The demand facing the oligopolist, if other members do not follow either price increases or decreases, is the relatively elastic DD' schedule. If a price decrease is not followed, a lower price substantially increases sales. If members in the cartel discover that a rival has lowered price, a reasonable reaction would be to match the lower price. This would protect their market share and punish the violator by reducing that firm's sales. In many cartels this is the only means of enforcement.

If rivals match a price cut, the demand curve below p_0 would be the much less elastic segment AD''. Customers would have no cause to change sellers if all firms sell at the same price. If the cheater is discovered, the gain in sales from the price decrease is relatively small. Output rises from x_0 to x_2 rather than to x_1. This increase is due mainly to

FIGURE 15–8   **The incentive to cheat in a cartel**

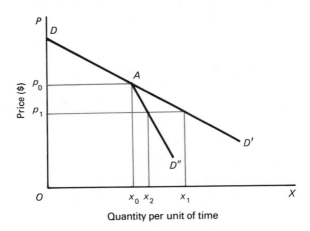

Quantity per unit of time

more total market sales because of the lower price charged by everyone in the cartel. Sales represented by $x_2 x_1$ are those sales that could have been made if the price cut had gone undetected. These sales represent the incentive of a cartel member to cheat on an agreement. The more elastic is DD', the larger the difference between x_2 and x_1, and the greater the incentive to cut price.

Let us suppose that the amount $x_0 x_2$ is very small. The total market demand is so inelastic that total market sales increase very little after price is lowered to p_1. Then sales $x_0 x_1$, for the most part, represent business attracted away from rivals. If this is a noticeable amount, rivals will suspect that someone has lowered prices. A substantial increase in the output of one firm while others are losing sales with fixed prices is another signal of cheating. A potentially large increase in sales from an undetected price cut is the incentive for cheating in a cartel, but, at the same time, it is the signal to other members that prices have been cut. The larger the increase in sales, the higher the probability of detection.

APPLICATION

An Unsuccessful Cartel in Real Estate[9]

A crucial ingredient for the success of a cartel is a barrier to entry. If prices are set to give cartel members above-normal profits, unprevented entry will restore normal profits and result in excess production capacity. The post-World War II history of the real estate industry is a classic case study.

Most real estate agents are members of local real estate associations or boards, professional organizations with a state and a national office. The national association is known as the National Association of Realtors (NAR). Members of the organization (who subscribe to its Code of Ethics) are called Realtors®, a registered trade name. The purpose of the organization is to enhance the professional character of real estate agents by establishing and enforcing a code of ethics. Until 1950, real estate boards set commission rates at 6 percent of a residential sale price. Price competition was considered unethical. When the practice was legally challenged, organizations resorted to "recommending" the 6 percent commission rate. In the late 1970s, a number of antitrust suits found this practice illegal. Presently, the NAR and local boards are prohibited from mentioning any prices in their manuals. Nevertheless, surveys show that nearly 80 percent

---

[9] This application and data are taken from O. R. Phillips and Henry N. Butler, "The Law and Economics of Residential Real Estate Markets in Texas: Regulation and Antitrust Implications," *Baylor Law Review,* Summer 1984, pp. 623–65.

of the homes sold through real estate agents are exchanged at 6 percent commission rates.

For many years, the national association, along with local real estate boards, has acted as a cartel manager. A local board has wide latitude in disciplining members who violate the ethical code; measures range from a reprimand to expulsion. If a member is expelled, he or she loses access to the board's multiple-listing service. This service collects in a catalog all of the available homes a realtor can show. Without the service, agents are at a severe disadvantage compared to those who have the information. Therefore, the cartel had the ability to punish those who cut prices. Historically, there are numerous examples where price cutters were discovered and expelled from the organization.

The cartel has not been successful in raising the income of its members, because as income rises, entry occurs. With entry, each Realtor, on average, sells fewer homes, and income (profit) is restored to a normal

FIGURE 15–9   **Entry in the Texas real estate industry**

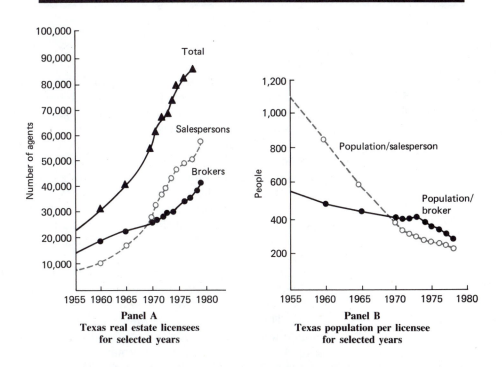

Panel A
Texas real estate licensees
for selected years

Panel B
Texas population per licensee
for selected years

Note: Salespersons are real estate agents who must work under the supervision of a broker.
Source: *Real Estate Atlas of Texas* (College Station, Tex.: Texas Real Estate Research Center, Texas A&M University), July 1979, Sec. 7, p. 3.

level. Data on the number of real estate agents in Texas illustrate the lack of success. Figure 15–9 shows the tremendous increases in agents both in total number and per capita between 1955 and 1980. Panel B, in particular, tells us that the number of agents has been increasing much faster than the population in Texas.

The cause of this influx has been fixed commission rates. As housing prices increase, the amount an agent collects also rises. For example, Realtors collect $3,000 on a $50,000 house at 6 percent commission rates, but $4,500 if the price is $75,000. In Texas, between 1973 and 1979, the average price of a house rose 17 percent each year, while the average annual rate of inflation was 8 percent. Thus, without entry, the real income of agents would have increased. Presently, the income of real estate agents, as reported by the Texas Employment Commission, is slightly below average for all service industries. This evidence indicates that there may be too many agents in the Texas industry. If this is true, the rate of increase should decline in the future.

15.7 SUMMARY

Monopolistic competition and oligopoly are imperfectly competitive market structures that come from a change in the assumptions underlying the theory of perfect competition. Monopolistic competition results from product differentiation. There are a large number of buyers and sellers, easy entry and exit by producers, and market participants have perfect information.

Product differentiation confers a certain amount of monopoly power on sellers. Because of these differences, the demand curve is less than perfectly elastic. However, since entry is easy, under the theory of monopolistic competition, pure profits are competed away. In equilibrium, the *LRAC* curve is tangent to the demand curve at a point higher than minimum average cost.

When products are differentiated, nonprice market strategies become an important competitive tool. Advertising and product-quality changes are two general means that allow a firm to increase market shares and profits. The gains from such strategies are short run under monopolistic competition. In the long run, a successful move is generally matched, and profits in the market return to normal.

Because of interdependence, there is no complete theory of oligopoly. Oligopolies are characterized by few firms in a market. In contrast to perfect competition, there must exist barriers to entry. Also, oligopoly sellers may offer differentiated products. Behavior in oligopoly is determined by how well rivals recognize their interdependence with other oligopolists. Broadly speaking, an oligopolist can be cooperative or non-cooperative with rivals. The degree that oligopolists cooperate with each other determines, to a large extent, market prices and output. Oligopoly can closely resemble perfect competition, or monopolistic competition, if products are differentiated. It can also approach monopoly if cooperation is close among sellers.

The most extreme form of cooperation is a cartel. Oligopolists explicitly agree on output, price, or both. In some cases, firms can be so well organized that behavior is closely akin to multiplant monopoly. But cartels are fragile, because incentives to cheat are inherent within any agreement. A cheater can gain at the expense of other members if the firm is not caught.

Little has been said conclusively about the desirability of oligopoly for two reasons. It is difficult to be very precise about the welfare effects of oligopoly when there is no single theory of oligopoly. Certainly there is no reason to believe that oligopolists will produce at minimum long-run average cost. Oligopoly requires more units of resources per unit of output than are absolutely necessary. Price is frequently higher than both average and marginal cost.

Furthermore, many resources can be devoted to nonprice competition under oligopoly, just as they can for monopolistic competition. If, as some say, many of these resources are "wasted," then too many resources are devoted to the effort. On the other hand, much advertising and many quality and design differentials may be socially desirable. There is no clear evidence on either side. But the welfare criteria imposed are static. Dynamic considerations are also important.

Industrial research and development (R&D) has been essential in the development of our modern industrial economy and is essential to its continued viability and growth. Many argue, with considerable persuasiveness, that R&D usually thrives only in oligopolistic markets. Neither perfect competitors nor pure monopolists have the incentive; moreover, perfect competitors are usually not large enough to support research departments. Oligopolistic firms, on the other hand, always have the incentive. They want to improve the product or reduce its cost of production so as to increase profit relative to that of rivals. Such firms are typically large enough to absorb the short-run cost of R&D in order to reap its long-run payoff. All sorts of static welfare criteria may be violated, more or less with impunity, if the dynamic rate of growth is sufficiently rapid. Some economists, and all oligopolists, hold that oligopolistic market organization is essential for the dynamic growth of the economy.

TECHNICAL PROBLEMS

1. The smaller the seller's share in a cartel, the greater the temptation to cut prices in slack times. Why?

2. Describe the major features of monopolistic competition:
    a. How is it similar to monopoly?
    b. How is it similar to competition?
    c. What characterizes short-run equilibrium?
    d. What characterizes long-run equilibrium?
    e. What is excess capacity under monopolistic competition?

3. Assume that the bituminous coal industry is a competitive industry in long-run equilibrium. Now assume that the firms in the industry form a cartel.
    a. What will happen to the equilibrium output and price of coal? Why?
    b. How should the output be distributed among the individual firms?
    c. After the cartel is operating, are there incentives for the individual firm to cheat? Why or why not?

4. If you were attempting to establish a price-fixing cartel in an industry,
    a. Would you prefer many or few firms? Why?
    b. How could you prevent cheating (price cutting) by cartel members? Why would members have an incentive to cheat?
    c. Would you keep substantial or very few records? What are the advantages and disadvantages of each?
    d. How could you prevent entry into the industry?
    e. How could government help you prevent entry and even cheating?
    f. How would you try to talk government into helping? Under what conditions might this work?

5. Explain why we do not have a general theory of oligopoly. Given the absence of a general theory, what can we say about this type of market structure?

6. Advertising makes the demand curve faced by a seller less elastic. How might this fact be useful to a firm that desires to raise the price of a product without encouraging entry?

7. In many market structures, sellers behave alike without colluding. Use the prisoner's dilemma concept to explain apparent collusion.

8. The key difference between perfect competition and monopolistic competition is product differentiation. How does differentiation affect a market's structure?

9. According to some economists, there are too many gas stations and grocery stores. Is this in keeping with the theory of monopolistic competition? Why or why not?

10. Product variety is a desirable feature of markets, but it leads to market inefficiencies. Explain the costs of product variety.

11. Describe the difference between monopolistic competition and differentiated oligopoly. Do firms in each category behave differently?

12. During the Christmas holidays, the toy industry organized itself into a secret cartel. Use the kinked demand model to describe the incentive of each member of the cartel to cheat.

13. In the text, we noted that the decision concerning whether an oligopolist should break a price-fixing agreement or introduce a new product, knowing that the rivals will follow, is essentially a present-value problem. To illustrate, consider the following case: A cooperating oligopolist is considering introducing a new product. It knows that if it does so, profits will be high at first, but after rivals adapt, the profits will be lower than they were prior to the introduction. If the new product is not introduced, profit will be $100,000 a year for the next 10 years—the length of the horizon. If the product is introduced, profits will be $150,000 in years one through three. After the rivals adapt, profits will fall to $80,000 a year during the next seven years. The rate of interest is 10 percent. Should the firm introduce the new product? Explain.

ANALYTICAL PROBLEMS

1. Du Pont Company and Ethyl Corporation in the late 1970s and early 1980s would give a 30-day advance notice to customers when they raised prices. The companies also had a standing policy that they would match any price their rivals charged. Were the companies colluding to fix prices or behaving in a responsible, competitive fashion?

2. "One sure test that an industry is competitive is the absence of any pure profit." Comment critically.

3. Blue laws in many states restrict the sale of most consumer goods on Sunday. Consumers, by and large, oppose the law because many find Sunday afternoons the most convenient time to shop. Paradoxically retail merchant associations frequently support the law. The Houston Association for instance has filed more than 40 lawsuits against violators, mostly large retailers. Discuss the reasons for merchants supporting Blue laws. Use the prisoner's dilemma.

4. In 1984 a Grand Jury investigated a possible collusive link between Dr Pepper Co. and Coca-Cola. A number of questions were aimed at determining whether the firms had a price-fixing conspiracy. At the hearings one business executive for Dr Pepper is quoted as saying "[We have] a pricing strategy: Whenever Coke and Pepsi went up, we did." (*The Wall Street Journal,* August 13, 1984, p. 3.) Does this practice tell you that the firms are illegally colluding? Might this be price leadership? What about the Cournot model of behavior?

5. By applying the prisoner's dilemma model to advertising, some observers argue that, to avoid the waste of resources on excessive advertising, some collusion should be permitted between firms. Comment.

6. A recent report shows that an aggressive advertising campaign by Pepsi has given the company an increased market share over Coca-Cola in food store sales. In essence, the "Pepsi Challenge" has lowered Coke's profits. Using the prisoner's dilemma model, show how Coke is likely to react to the challenge. What about advertising? What about taste?

7. Television critics frequently argue that TV series are too similar—there is too little variety. Assuming they are correct, explain this phenomenon in terms of the analysis in this chapter.

8. Restaurants in large cities seem to fit the basic model of monopolistic competition. But some restaurants are making substantial profits while others are going broke or barely breaking even. Is this consistent with long-run equilibrium? Why or why not?

9. In states where insurance rates are regulated, how do rate increases affect the income of insurance agents in the short run and in the long run? How does this result differ from the consequences of rate increases for a privately owned municipal electric or gas company? What about a telephone rate increase?

10. Many economists argue that more research, development, and innovation occur in oligopolistic market structures than in any other. Why might this be true? (Consider perfect and monopolistic competition and monopoly.)

11. It has been claimed by economist George Stigler that regulation in industries, e.g., the railroad industry, effectively acts to organize a cartel and foster cooperation among the regulated firms rather than restricting monopoly power. Do you consider this a realistic explanation of industry regulation? Present examples to support your point.

PART VI

INPUT DEMAND

- **Markets for Variable Inputs**
- **Demand for Fixed Inputs: Theory of Investment**

Chapter 16

Markets for Variable Inputs

16.1 INTRODUCTION

We have developed a theory of markets that explains demand, supply, and market prices. A central part of this theory is the marginal cost curve and its reflection in the market supply schedule. Costs, and supply in turn, depend on the technological conditions of production and the prices of inputs. With minor qualification, we have generally assumed that both are given. In this chapter we will continue to assume that the physical conditions of production are technologically given, but now we want to more carefully explore how the prices of inputs are determined.

Broadly speaking, input markets do not differ from any other market. Prices and the quantity sold are determined by the interaction of demand and supply. But there are important differences. First, on the demand side of the market, it is business firms rather than consumers who purchase factors of production. The quantity of inputs used depends on the quantity of output sold by the firm. Sales, in turn, depend on the size of the market and whether producers are perfect competitors or have monopoly power. Input demand is derived from and affected by the market conditions for the commodity. Secondly, supply, at least the supply of labor services, arises from individuals who are not only sellers of labor time, but are also consumers. Furthermore, in many input markets, one determines the price of using the resource for a stipulated period of time, not the price of purchasing the resource.

You have already been exposed to the fundamental elements of input demand. The quantity of input demanded is determined by comparing the marginal cost of another unit to its marginal benefit, as discussed in Chapter 4. Suppose you own a business and a worker applies for a job. Would you hire this worker? The answer depends on how much extra revenue the worker would earn for your business. If the worker is expected to add more to revenue than you must pay in wages, the answer is yes. If the worker is expected to add less in revenue than the wages you must pay, the answer is no. The same reasoning applies to any factor of production. A firm would increase its use of a particular input of any type if the additional unit of input is expected to add more to revenue than it adds to cost. If the additional unit increases cost more than it increases revenue, no more of the input would be added.

It makes no difference whether the input is labor, capital, land, fuel, or something else. A firm increases its use of an input if the additional unit of input adds more to revenue than it adds to cost. The basic theory is simple because you have already learned a great deal about the importance of the margin in decision making.

16.2 ONE VARIABLE INPUT AND PERFECT COMPETITION IN INPUT MARKETS

This section begins the theory of input markets with the simplest case. We assume that only one input, labor, can be adjusted by the firm, and this input is supplied by perfectly competitive agents. The competitive assumption assures us that there are no quality differences in the factor supplied, and individual suppliers do not control enough of the input to affect its price. On the other hand, we will allow the demand side of the market to be first perfectly competitive and then monopolistic. This change affects the marginal benefit of an input and, therefore, the demand for the factor.

The theory developed here is applicable to virtually any productive service that is variable, although the most natural application is to the demand for labor. When we speak of the demand for labor, the demand for any variable factor of production is implied. The demand for capital is somewhat more complicated because investment decisions, as we already know, depend on the rate of interest. Investment will be given special consideration in the next chapter.

Demand of a Perfectly Competitive Firm

Any firm would increase the amount of labor used if the additional unit contributes more to the firm's income than to its cost. Consider the following example: a perfectly competitive firm sells its product at a market price of $1. It can hire one unit of the variable input, labor, at $30 per day. If increasing its labor force by one more worker adds more than thirty units of output per day, the firm would hire the additional worker.

The amount an additional unit of input adds to total revenue is called *marginal revenue product* (*MRP*). That is,

$$MRP = \frac{\Delta \text{ revenue}}{\Delta \text{ input usage}} = \frac{\Delta X \cdot P}{\Delta \text{ input usage}} = MP \cdot P,$$

where P is the given price of the producer's output and MP is marginal product. We can also define marginal revenue product in words:

Definition

The marginal revenue product (*MRP*) of a factor of production for a producer is the additon to total revenue attributable to the addition of one more unit of the factor. Marginal revenue product is equivalent to marginal product multiplied by output price, when output prices are constant.

We will often add a subscript to *MRP* to denote the kind of input to which we are referring. For instance, MRP_L is the marginal revenue product of labor. In the case of a perfectly competitive firm hiring a variable input such as labor, marginal revenue product has a specific name, the *value of the marginal product* (*VMP*).

Since each additional worker in the above example adds $30 to cost, the marginal cost of the input is that wage rate. The marginal price of another unit of input is generally referred to as the *marginal factor cost* (*MFC*) of the input.

If we let the marginal factor cost of labor be the wage rate, *w*, the basic rule for hiring an extra unit is, if

$$MRP_L > w,$$

the producer would add more of the input. If

$$MRP_L < w,$$

the firm would add no more of the input; it would, in fact, decrease its use. Profit maximization requires

$$MRP_L = w.$$

Let us consider another numerical example, this time in more detail. A perfectly competitive firm sells a product for $5 and employs labor at a

TABLE 16–1   **Value of the marginal product (*VMP*) and individual demand for labor**

Units of variable input	Total product	Marginal product	VMP
0	0	—	—
1	10	10	$ 50
2	30	20	100
3	50	20	100
4	65	15	75
5	75	10	50
6	80	5	25
7	83	3	15
8	84	1	5
9	81	−3	−15

wage rate of $20 a day. Table 16–1 lists the daily total product, marginal product, and value of marginal product for zero through nine workers. Note that the value of the marginal product in the last column is simply $5 multiplied by marginal product. Under these conditions, the firm hires six workers. It would not hire fewer than six, since hiring the sixth adds $25 to revenue but only costs $20. It would not hire seven workers, because revenue would only increase by $15 while cost would rise by $20. If, however, the wage rate dropped below $15 (say to $14) the work force would increase to seven (an additional $15 revenue can be gained at a cost of $14). Or if wages rose above $25 but remained below $50, the firm would reduce the labor force to five.

The profit-maximizing rule is illustrated in Figure 16–1. Suppose the value of the marginal product is given by the curve labeled *VMP*. The market wage rate is $\bar{w}$, so the supply of labor to the firm is the horizontal line S_L. The firm can hire as much labor as it desires at the wage rate $\bar{w}$. Suppose the firm employed only L_1 units of labor. At that rate of employment, the value of the marginal product is the distance $L_1C = w_1$, which

FIGURE 16–1   **Demand for a variable resource**

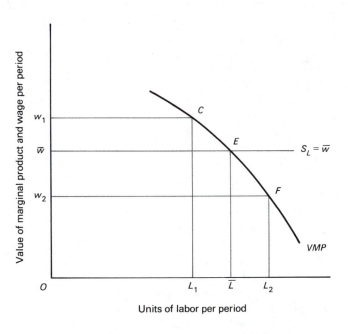

is greater than $\overline{w}$, the wage rate. At this point of operation, an additional unit of labor adds more to total revenue than to total cost. A profit-maximizing entrepreneur should add additional units of labor and, indeed, should continue to add units so long as the value of the marginal product exceeds the wage rate.

Now, suppose L_2 units of labor were employed. At this point, the value of the marginal product, $L_2 F = w_2$, is less than the wage rate. Each unit of labor adds more to total cost than to total revenue. A profit-maximizing entrepreneur should not employ L_2 units, or any number for which the wage rate exceeds the value of the marginal product. These arguments show that employing $\overline{L}$ units of labor leads to profit maximization.

Principle

A profit-maximizing competitive firm will employ units of a variable productive resource until the point is reached where the value of the marginal product of the input (price times marginal product) is equal to the input price.

In other words, given the market wage rate or the supply-of-labor curve to the firm, a perfectly competitive producer determines the quantity of labor to hire by equating the value of the marginal product to the wage rate. If the wage rate were w_1 in Figure 16–1, the firm would employ L_1 units of labor to maximize profit. Similarly, if the wage rate were w_2, the firm would employ L_2 units of labor. By the definition of a demand curve, therefore, the value of the marginal product curve is established as the competitive firm's demand for labor when labor is the only variable input.

Before going further, we should discuss why the demand curve is downward sloping. Recall from our discussion in Chapter 8 that the typical marginal product curve first rises, reaches a maximum, then declines thereafter, crossing the average product curve at its maximum. Since VMP is simply a constant commodity price multiplied by marginal product, it has a similar shape.

A profit-maximizing firm would never choose a level of input usage where marginal product and therefore VMP are rising. To see why, suppose the wage, w, equals VMP where VMP is rising. The firm can add one more unit of labor and the VMP would be greater than the wage. Profits would continue to increase from additional units of labor so long as VMP is rising.

We also argued in Chapter 8 that a competitive firm would always operate in Stage II of the production function, that range of output for which marginal product declines and is below average product. There is a specific range on the downward section of the VMP curve along which a firm will produce. Suppose a competitive firm produced on a range of VMP that was declining, but marginal product was greater than average product. When this happens, price times marginal product (VMP) is greater than price times average product. Recall that average product is output divided by units of labor (X/L). Then since $w = VMP$, for a profit-maximizing enterprise

$$w > P\left(\frac{X}{L}\right),$$

or

$$w \cdot L > P \cdot X.$$

Since $w \cdot L$ is variable cost and $P \cdot X$ is total revenue, we know from Chapter 11 that the firm would shut down. This shows that any points on the marginal product schedule above average product are not profitable. Profits are only positive when the firm operates on that downward sloping part of the VMP schedule that corresponds to marginal product less than average product. This is Stage II of the production function.

Principle
The competitive firm's demand curve for a single variable productive service is given by the value of the marginal product curve of the productive factor over the range where the input is in Stage II of production.

Monopoly in the Commodity Market

The analytical principles underlying the demand for a single variable input are the same for perfectly and imperfectly competitive commodity markets, but marginal revenue product is defined differently. Since commodity price and marginal revenue are different in imperfectly competitive markets, the marginal revenue product will not be price times marginal product.

When a perfectly competitive seller employs an additional unit of labor, output is augmented by the marginal product of that unit. In like manner, total revenue is augmented by the value of its marginal product inasmuch as commodity price remains unchanged. When a monopolist employs additional labor, output also increases by the marginal product of the additional workers. However, to sell the larger output, commodity price must be reduced; total revenue is not augmented by the price times the marginal product of the additional workers. Instead $MRP_L = MR \times MP_L$, where MR falls as output increases.

Definition
Marginal revenue product for a monopolist is the additional revenue attributable to the addition of one unit of the variable input. It is marginal revenue from the product times marginal product.

A numerical example might clarify this point. In Table 16–2, columns (1) and (2) give the output for various amounts of labor. Columns (2) and (3) together, show the demand for the commodity that is produced by labor. Column (4) is the total revenue (product price times quantity)

TABLE 16-2   **Marginal revenue product for a monopolist**

(1) Units of labor	(2) Total product	(3) Commodity price	(4) Total revenue	(5) Additional total revenue per unit additional labor (MRP_L)	(6) Marginal product	(7) Marginal revenue	(8) Marginal revenue product ($MR \times MP_L$)
3 . . .	5	$50.00	$250	—	—	—	—
4 . . .	20	30.00	600	$350	15	$23.33	$350
5 . . .	30	25.00	750	150	10	15.00	150
6 . . .	38	22.00	836	86	8	10.75	86
7 . . .	44	20.00	880	44	6	7.33	44
8 . . .	48	19.00	912	32	4	8.00	32
9 . . .	50	18.50	925	13	2	6.50	13
10 . . .	51	18.00	918	−7	1	−7.00	−7

associated with each level of labor use, and column (6) is the marginal product of labor. The crucial amounts in the demand for labor are shown in columns (5) and (8). Column (5) shows the addition to total revenue (column 4), resulting from increasing labor by one unit. These figures represent the marginal revenue product of labor. MRP_L can also be computed by multiplying marginal product (column 6) times marginal revenue (column 7). We have estimated marginal revenue in column 7 by dividing the change in total revenue (column 4) by the increase in units produced (column 2).

In this example, marginal revenue product falls because *both* marginal revenue and marginal product fall. Marginal revenue product is the *net* addition to total revenue. In Table 16–2, the gross addition to revenue from increasing labor from three to four units is 15 (the additional units of production) times $30 (the selling price of each unit of production), or $450. But to sell 15 additional units, price per unit must fall by $20. The "lost" revenue from the price reduction is 5 × $20 = $100, since five units could have been sold at a price of $50 each. This "loss" must be subtracted from the gross gain, or $450 − $100 = $350 = *MRP*.

Column (5) or (8) of Table 16–2 shows the monopolist's demand for labor. At each wage these columns tell the monopolist how many units to hire. If the daily wage is $25, the monopolist would hire eight workers. Each worker up to the ninth adds more than $25 (the additional daily cost per worker) to revenue. The ninth adds $13, and would cost the firm $25 − $13 = $12 in lost profit. If wages rise to $50 a day, the firm would reduce labor to six units. Both the seventh and the eighth worker add less than $50 to total revenue.

To illustrate the demand for labor graphically, consider the marginal revenue product curve in Figure 16–2. It must quite obviously slope downward, because two forces act to cause marginal revenue product to diminish as the level of employment increases: (a) the marginal product declines (over the relevant range of production) as additional units of the variable service are added; and (b) marginal revenue declines as output expands and commodity price falls. Thus for the monopolist, marginal revenue product falls more quickly than it does for a perfect competitor. Under perfect competition, output price remains constant, so only the declining marginal product causes *MRP* to decline.

By assumption, the monopoly purchases the variable service in a perfectly competitive input market. It views its supply-of-input curve as a horizontal line at the level of the prevailing market price, $\overline{w}$. Given the market price, $\overline{w}$, we wish to show that equilibrium employment is $\overline{L}$. Suppose the contrary, in particular, that L_1 units of labor are used. At the L_1 level of utilization, the last unit adds w_1 to total revenue but only $\overline{w}$ to

FIGURE 16–2   **Monopoly demand for a single variable service: Labor**

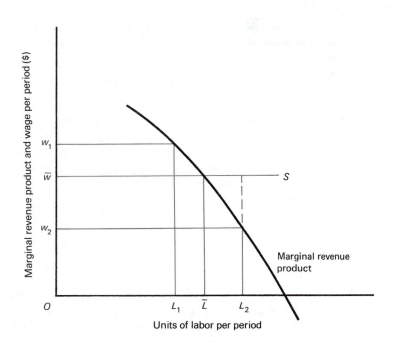

total cost. Since $w_1 > \overline{w}$, profit is augmented by employing that unit. Profit will increase as additional units are employed, so long as marginal revenue product exceeds the market equilibrium price of the input. A profit-maximizing monopolist would never employ fewer than $\overline{L}$ units of the variable service. The opposite argument holds when more than $\overline{L}$ units are employed, for then an additional unit of labor adds more to total cost than to total revenue. A profit-maximizing monopolist will adjust employment so that marginal revenue product equals input price. If only one variable productive service is used, the marginal revenue product curve will be the monopolist's demand curve for the variable service in question.

Principle

An imperfectly competitive producer who purchases a variable productive resource in a perfectly competitive input market will employ that amount of the resource for which marginal revenue product equals the market price of the resource. Consequently, the marginal revenue product curve is the monopolist's demand curve for the variable resource when only one variable input is used. Marginal revenue product declines with output for two reasons: (1) marginal product declines as more units of the variable input are added, and (2) to sell the additional output, the monopolist must lower the commodity price.

APPLICATION

The Marginal Product of Irrigation Water

In order to emphasize that the value of marginal product and marginal revenue product are essentially a demand curve for an input, let's look at a study done by two agricultural economists, Ronald Lacewell and Duane Reneau, who estimated the marginal revenue product of irrigation water on farmland in four Texas High Plains counties.[1] The *VMP* (or *MRP*) curve tells us two things regarding the demand for a particular input. These are:

1. The amount that the use of each additional unit of input adds to the producer's total revenue.
2. How much the producer is willing to pay for the marginal input.

Combined with the price of the input, the *VMP* curve shows how many units of the input a competitive producer will demand. The producer will continue to use more of the input as long as it adds more to total revenue than to total cost.

Lacewell and Reneau's study is particularly interesting for those who

---

[1] "The Value of Groundwater," *Water Currents*, Texas Water Resources Institute and the Texas Agricultural Experiment Station, Summer 1983.

might wish to apply the basic theoretical idea of input demand to real-world situations. In deriving the *VMP* curves displayed below, the agricultural economists took into consideration the following factors that determine the relative benefit of groundwater to an irrigator:

1. The type of irrigation system used.
2. The crop choice and market prices for the crop being produced.
3. The soil type.

In the counties studied by the economists these factors were assumed to be held constant when deriving the demand for irrigation water. Obviously, the *VMP* of water will vary with all three of these factors.

The basic approach used in the study was to estimate the marginal value of each additional acre-foot of water applied evenly over 1,000 acre farms in four different High Plains counties. In order to get a representative *VMP* schedule for the typical High Plains farmer, Lacewell and Reneau used a composite of different crops, combined with a composite average of market prices over a 20-year period. To take into consideration the

FIGURE 16–3   **Value of marginal product curves in four Texas counties**

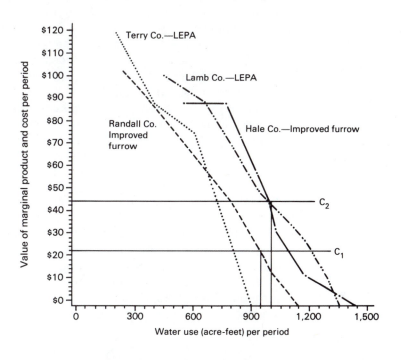

effects of different soil types and irrigation technologies on *VMP,* four different counties were chosen using two different irrigation methods. One is called *improved furrow irrigation,* and is a variation of flood irrigation. The other is referred to as the *LEPA* (low energy precision application) method of irrigation, a drip irrigation technique developed in Israel. The *VMP* curves estimated in Figure 16–3 can be considered fairly representative of those faced by farmers in West Texas using one of these irrigation technologies.

In this study, the price of water is the average cost of pumping groundwater to the surface. The lower the groundwater table, the greater the height it has to be pumped. The price of the input in each of the areas studied varies with different aquifer conditions. The lowest price was $22 per acre-foot in Randall County, and the highest price was $44 per acre-foot in Lamb County.

Figure 16–3 shows the two low and high prices as c_1 and c_2, respectively. The intersection of the horizontal cost schedules and each particular *VMP* curve tells us how much water farmers in each case will use. The Randall County farmer will use the amount of water where the $22 per acre-foot cost schedule intersects the Randall VMP curve. Therefore, the farmer will demand about 950 acre-feet of water per year. If more were used, the farmer would be adding more to total cost than to total revenue. If less were used, the farmer would not be maximizing total profits, since the use of additional acre-feet of water would add more to total revenue than to total cost.

How many acre-feet of water will the farmer in Lamb County, who uses the *LEPA* irrigation technique and faces a cost schedule of $44 dollars, demand? The figure shows a little less than 1,000 acre-feet of water per year. Despite the higher cost schedule, the *VMP* curve is further to the right than that of the Randall County farmer because of the more efficient irrigation technique. We observe that the *VMP* curves literally are demand curves for water from the perspective of the farmer. At any level of cost for groundwater, we are able to determine how much water each farmer demands.

Farmers in all four counties in this study use groundwater from the Ogallala Aquifer, an enormous underground lake stretching across almost all of the U.S. plains states. The level of this aquifer is rapidly falling, and the costs for pumping irrigation water are rising.

Looking again at the estimated *VMP* curves, how much water would each of the four farmers depicted buy if the unit cost of water rises to $150? This does not seem an unreasonable estimate for the cost of each acre-foot of water projected for the year 2000.[2] According to Figure 16–3, the use of the existing technologies would not allow the High Plains

---

[2] Cost per acre-foot in Los Angeles is $250 per acre foot. *Business Week,* March 9, 1984, p. 104.

farmers to use any water at all under such conditions. Some of the options to consider are that farmers may

1. Go out of business.
2. Change to crops or cropping techniques that use much less water.
3. Change to more efficient irrigation techniques.
4. Find a less expensive input.

Alternatives (2) and (3) would both have the effect of shifting the *VMP* curve to the right. Under such conditions, it might be possible for one *VMP* curve to again intersect the unit cost curve of water.

Switching to surface water might be a less expensive substitute for underground water. This would lower the projected unit cost of irrigation water. Undoubtedly, farmers on the High Plains will have to choose some combination of the above options. In fact, they already are making such a transition, and many are changing to more efficient irrigation methods. Agriculturalists are researching new crop strains that use less water. In this, they will be greatly assisted by new genetic engineering techniques. Some farmers are shifting over to surface water by constructing small-scale reservoirs. The Texas Water Plan of 1968 has even considered transporting surface water from the Mississippi River. It is questionable that such an expensive proposition could reduce the marginal factor cost of water, but the dream of such a water plan "resurfaces" periodically in state and national legislative bodies.

16.3 DEMAND FOR A PRODUCTIVE RESOURCE WITH MORE THAN ONE VARIABLE INPUT

We should mention the variables that are assumed to be held constant when deriving the firm's demand for a single variable input. When any one of these *parameters* changes, the *MRP* or *VMP* schedule will shift. After we discuss the parameters held constant when using *MRP* or *VMP* as a demand schedule, we will derive demand when the usage of other inputs can be changed after the price of a particular input changes. From this point on, we will refer only to the *MRP* curve and not distinguish a perfect competitor's marginal revenue product with the special term, value of marginal product.

Parameters for Marginal Revenue Product

Several variables are held constant when the *MRP* schedule is used as an input demand schedule. First, we hold the use of all other inputs constant. Recall from Chapter 8 that, when the rate of use of another input changes, the marginal product curve of the other input shifts. If the use of another input changes, the *MRP* curve for a firm would also shift. We will discuss the derivation of input demand under these conditions more fully as an example of what happens to the demand schedule when the variables underlying the *MRP* curve change. A second variable held fixed is technology, because technological change will also shift the marginal product curves. Thirdly, the demand schedule for the product is held fixed. In the case of the competitive firm this means that the product's price does not change. Finally, until now, we have assumed that the wage bill is the *total* payment to the input; there are no additional or fringe payments, such as contributions to Social Security or to group insurance plans.

All of the conditions held constant except the last are quite apparent. The last point requires some discussion. If you are an employer, you would use the approach described above, but you might look at the wage rate or the price of an input in a slightly different way. In the real world, workers cost an employer more than simply the money wage rate. There are certain *additional* payments to workers required by law or perhaps paid by tradition. The most familiar legal requirement is the employer's contribution to Social Security. Firms also frequently make contributions to the employees' insurance policies or their retirement plans. There are other fringe benefits, such as improvements in working conditions, noise controls, lounge facilities, and so on.

All of these additional payments are costs to the firm. Therefore, the *total wage bill* is the market-determined wage plus the cost of fringe benefits, such as the Social Security payment. At any market-determined wage, if additional payments are made, fewer workers are hired than would be hired in the absence of such payments. The employer does not absorb *all* of the cost of the fringe benefts. As we will see, this is far from the case.

Adjusted Demand When More Than One Input Varies

In Figure 16–4, suppose that equilibrium for a perfectly competitive or monopoly firm initially exists at point A. The market wage rate is w_1; the marginal revenue product curve for labor is MRP_1 when labor is the only input varied. The S_L^1 schedule represents a perfectly elastic supply of labor to the firm. Its intersection with MRP_1 tells us that L_1 units of labor are employed. Let the wage rate fall to w_2, so that the perfectly elastic supply curve of labor to the firm is S_L^2.

When the wage rate falls from w_1 to w_2, the use of labor expands. However, the expansion does not take place along MRP_1. When the quantity of labor used and the level of output change, the use of other variable inputs changes as well. Under these conditions, labor's marginal

FIGURE 16–4   **Individual input demand when several variable inputs are used**

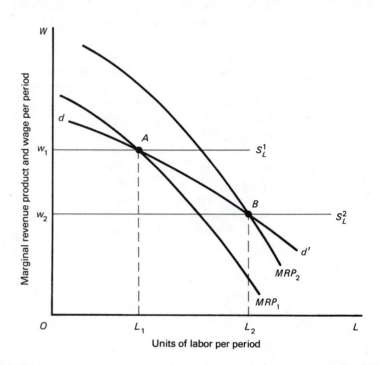

product curve changes, and since marginal revenue product is equal to marginal product multiplied by the marginal revenue of the commodity, the marginal revenue product of labor curve must shift.

Suppose it shifts to MRP_2. The new equilibrium is reached at point B. Other points similar to A and B can be generated in the same manner. The demand curve, dd', can be determined from successive changes in the market wage rate and the marginal revenue product curve. The input demand curve, while more difficult to derive, is just as determinate in the multiple-input case as in the single-input situation. The results can be summarized in the following important principle:

Principle
A firm's demand curve for a variable productive agent or resource when more than one variable input is used can be derived and must be negatively sloped. Even though demand is no longer the marginal revenue product curve, at every point on the demand curve, the wage rate still is equal to marginal revenue product.

16.4 INDUSTRY DEMAND FOR AN INPUT

The industry demand for a variable productive service, in contrast to the market demand for a commodity, is not necessarily the horizontal summation of each producer's demand curve. In general, the process of summation for productive services is considerably more complicated, because when all firms in an industry expand or contract simultaneously, the market price of the commodity changes.

The situation is analogous to the derivation of a perfectly competitive industry's supply curve from each firm's marginal cost curve. Recall that any firm can change its level of output without affecting input prices. When all firms attempt to vary output together, input prices may change and each firm's marginal cost shifts. Therefore, industry supply is the horizontal summation of these "shifted" supplies. In the case of input demand, any perfectly competitive firm can vary its inputs, and thus its output, without affecting commodity price. When all firms attempt to change their use of an input, the product price will change. Since each firm's demand for the input is derived holding commodity price constant, all input demands will shift.

To illustrate the process, assume that a typical employing firm is depicted in Figure 16–5, Panel A. At the going market price of the commodity produced, d_1d_1' is the firm's demand curve for the variable productive service, as derived in Figure 16–4. If the market price of the

FIGURE 16–5   **Derivation of the industry demand for a variable productive service**

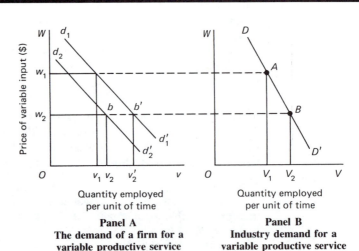

Panel A
**The demand of a firm for a
variable productive service**

Panel B
**Industry demand for a
variable productive service**

resource is w_1, the firm uses v_1 units. Aggregating over all employing firms in the industry, V_1 units of the service are used. Thus, point A in Panel B is one point on the industry demand curve for the variable productive service.

Next, suppose the price of the service declines to w_2 (it may be, for example, that the supply curve of the variable service shifts to the right). Other things being equal, the firm would move along d_1d_1' to point b', employing v_2' units of the service. But other things are not equal. When all firms expand their use of the input, total output expands. Or, stated differently, the market supply curve for the commodity shifts to the right because of the decline in the input's price. For a given commodity demand, commodity price must fall; and when it does, the individual demand curves for the variable productive service also fall.

In Panel A, the decline in individual input demand attributable to the decline in commodity price is represented by the shift leftward from d_1d_1' to d_2d_2'. At input price w_2, b is the equilibrium point, with v_2 units employed. Aggregating for all employers, V_2 units of the productive service are used and point B is obtained in Panel B. Any number of points such as A and B can be generated by varying the market price of the productive service. Connecting these points by a line, one obtains DD', the industry demand for the variable productive service.

If an industry is monopolized by a single firm, the monopoly demand for an input is the same as the industry demand. If several industries demand an input, the total market demand is the horizontal summation of every industry's demand, assuming that we ignore the effect of changes in commodity price in one industry on commodity prices in other industries that demand the input.

We can use the concepts of input demand under monopoly and perfect competition to make a crude comparison between industry employment under the two market structures. We know that, under the same cost conditions, a monopolist restricts output and charges a higher price relative to a perfectly competitive industry. It should, therefore, come as no surprise that, under the same condition, a monopolist hires less of an input relative to the competitive industry. Assuming the monopolist is unable to realize economies, the degree of "inefficiency" attributable to a monopoly employer can be observed by comparing employment at any given wage to that in a perfectly competitive industry.

To make the comparison, we continue with the restrictive assumption that there is only one variable input—in this case, labor. As noted, we assume the same cost curves for both the competitive and the monopolistic structures. The same amount of labor is associated with a given amount of output in either case. And, at any given level of output and labor usage, the marginal product of additional labor is the same under either form of market organization. This might be the case if the monopoly simply organized the firms into individual plants and allocated output

FIGURE 16–6   **A competitive industry and a monopoly employer**

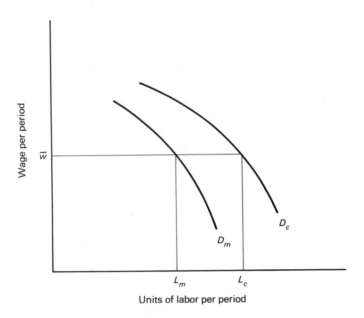

among the plants in the same way output would be divided among firms under competition.

Figure 16–6 compares labor demand under monopoly and competition, using the restrictive assumptions set forth above. Monopoly demand is D_m, which accounts for shifts in *MRP* when more than one input is variable. D_c is the competitive industry's demand for labor. It allows other inputs to be variable and takes account of the declining commodity price as all firms in the industry expand labor usage and therefore increase the quantity sold.

The D_c schedule will be greater than (lie to the right of) D_m, because at any given wage, output will be higher under competition than under monopoly. Or at any given level of labor, price times marginal product in a competitive market will exceed a monopolist's marginal revenue times marginal product. At a wage of $\overline{w}$ in Figure 16–6 the competitive industry will hire L_c workers while the monopoly will hire only L_m.

Keep in mind that this conclusion comes from the assumption that costs are the same under monopoly and competition. If cost advantages were available to the monopoly but not to the competitive industry, more labor might be employed by the monopoly, at a given wage rate.

16.5 SUPPLY OF A VARIABLE PRODUCTIVE SERVICE

Variable inputs may be broadly classified into three groups: natural resources, intermediate goods, and labor. There are other inputs commonly referred to as capital, but in the short run these inputs tend to be fixed. In this section, we briefly describe the shape of the supply curve of these variable inputs.

Intermediate Goods and Natural Resources

Intermediate goods are those produced by one entrepreneur and sold to another, who in turn utilizes them in the productive process. For example, cotton is produced by farmers and sold as an intermediate good to a manufacturer of fabric; the fabric, in turn, becomes an intermediate good in the manufacture of upholstered furniture. The short-run supply curves of intermediate goods are positively sloped because they are the *marginal cost curves* of manufacturers, even if they are variable inputs to others; and, as shown in Chapter 11, marginal cost curves generally have positive slopes. Natural resources may also be regarded as the commodity outputs of extractive operations. As such, they also have positively sloped short-run supply curves. In general, the supply of variable inputs is upward sloping. In most cases inputs are produced like any other good or service. The positive slope of supply tells us that at the margin it becomes more costly to provide another unit of the variable input.

Labor Supply

There are some special features about the supply of labor. In Chapter 7 we showed how an individual's supply of labor is derived from the indifference curves between leisure and income. In that chapter, we showed that, given a wage increase, an individual might choose to work more (sacrifice leisure) or to work less (take more leisure), depending on the shape of his or her indifference curves. Therefore, an individual's supply-of-labor curve may be positively sloped over some range and negatively sloped over other ranges of the wage rate. The crucial question, however, is how the work force as a group behaves—what is the shape of the market supply curve of any specified type of labor?

As an empirical matter a firm, monopolist or competitor, can face two types of supply of labor. In the cases discussed previously in this chapter, the supply of labor has been a horizontal line at the market-determined wage rate, indicating that the firm can hire all of the labor it wishes at the going market wage rate. In certain cases, firms do have some influence on the wage rate. In these instances, the firm faces an upward sloping supply of labor, indicating that, in order to hire more of a certain kind of labor, the firm must pay higher wages. Under this set of circumstances, the firm is called a monopsonist, a situation to be analyzed below.

At the *industry level* the labor supply curve may also be horizontal or have an upward slope. If the industry is small relative to the total supply of labor, the expansion of the industry may have no effect on the wage rate. The wage rate in this instance would serve as the industry's horizontal supply curve. There are, however, situations where the industry demand for labor is relatively large. Suppose an industry uses a specialized type of labor, specialized in the sense that the industry's use of the input affects that input's price. In the long run, the supply to the industry must be positively sloped; if there are a given number of people in a specific occupation and the firms in a particular industry desire more of that type, they must lure them away by paying higher wages.[3]

The situation is similar when more than one industry uses a particular type of labor. If output is to be expanded in one or more of these industries, the wage of workers must increase in order to bid them away from other industries or occupations. When we consider the opportunities for workers in other industries or occupations, the supply of labor to an industry can be assumed to be upward sloping or at least horizonal (if the industry is quite small relative to the total demand) even if many workers in the work force have negatively sloped individual labor supply curves.

APPLICATION

The Shortage of Nurses

Economic theory recognizes that people get different levels of utility from working in different occupations. Economists also observe that people are willing to make trade-offs between less desired occupations and increased incomes. As in the case of commodities, supply and demand determine relative wages and the relative numbers of employees in different occupations, but payment per hour or the salary per month is not the "full wage" of a job from a worker's perspective.

Let us analyze the following facts brought out in an Associated Press report made in February 1981.[4] The shortage of registered nurses was

---

[3] There are two possible exceptions, each leading to a horizontal industry supply-of-labor curve. First, if the industry is small, or if it uses only very small quantities of labor, its effect on the market may be negligible. That is, the industry may be to the market what a perfectly competitive firm is to the industry. Second, if there is unemployment in the particular type of labor under consideration, the supply of labor to all industries may be perfectly elastic up to the point of full employment. Thereafter, the supply curve would rise. The latter is a disequilibrium situation not encompassed in the analysis here.

[4] "Crisis in Nursing: Shortage Nearing Critical Point," *Houston Post,* February 19, 1981, p. 1N.

termed serious to very critical across the nation. Hospitals everywhere were on the edge of unsafe situations. To avoid substandard care, hospitals in Boston, Atlanta, Baltimore, Detroit, Dallas, Milwaukee, and many smaller cities left beds empty and sometimes closed entire units because there were not enough nurses. The shortage of nurses was estimated at 100,000 by the American Hospital Association. Yet, of the nation's 1.4 million registered nurses, only 900,000 were employed, and 300,000 of these were part-time staff. There were at least 500,000 qualified nurses who were not working and 300,000 who could have worked more.

Surprisingly, most hospital administrators do not feel that higher salaries are the answer to the problem. Instead, many hospitals are spending millions on help-wanted advertising and recruiting gimmicks, such as bounties to anyone who recruits a nurse for their hospital. In the report nurses were beginning at a salary of $16,000 a year in a few cities, such as Houston; but the average nurse earned $13,000 annually in 1980. At the same time, the average salary of hospital laundry managers was $16,700 a year. Nurses were earning less than the average unionized grocery clerk.

It a nonsense to assert that salary and fringe benefits are not the answer. If a hospital wants more nurses, the only way to get them is to bid them away from other locations—or, in the long run, to bid them away from other occupations. The higher bids can only be in the form of higher salaries and/or improved working conditions. What else would attract more nurses? Of course, it may be that the hospital administrators do not want to pay higher salaries or to increase fringe benefits. In this sense, higher salaries and benefits may not be the answer for them.

In the story, it was made clear that nurses do not wish to work weekends and nights, when at other jobs they could work just weekdays. What is the problem? Hospitals are not paying a sufficient differential to attract nurses to the less desirable hours. The "full" salary is not enough. If there are jobs with more desirable hours at the same rate of pay, nurses obviously would choose these. With all forms of labor, as with commodities, a shortage will continue in the long run if the wage is below equilibrium. To increase the number of people in a particular occupation or in a particular location, total wages, salary, and/or benefits must be increased.

It is interesting to note that, while salaries of nurses are just keeping pace with the rate of inflation, hospitals are taking steps to increase the fringe benefits of nurses—an implicit rise in payment. Some hospitals are giving cars to nurses who work the late-night shifts. For instance, Eisenhower Medical Center in Rancho Mirage, California, offered nurses use of a Chevrolet Chevette for commuting. Others are offering child care for nurses on duty. During the day there is a charge for the care, while at night the service is free to nurses.

A big change has come in the flexibility of hours a nurse may work. For instance, an Alabama hospital allows nurses to take every other week off. Baylor Medical Center in Dallas hired 100 nurses to work two 12-hour shifts on Saturdays and Sundays for a full week's pay so that the hospital's 1,000 full-time nurses can work Monday through Friday—an unusual schedule in nursing.

Much of the reason for disequilibrium in the nursing market is job dissatisfaction. Certainly dissatisfaction may be overcome with higher salaries. People will do almost anything for the right price, but hospitals have probably learned it would be much less expensive to eliminate the source of dissatisfaction, e.g., schedules, rather than increase compensation directly.

Let us return to the determinants of the supply curves for labor. As population increases and its age composition changes, as people migrate from one area to another, and as education and reeducation enable people to shift occupations, rather dramatic changes can occur in the supply of various types of labor at various locations throughout the nation. These changes represent *shifts* in supply curves and are quite independent of their slopes. To derive the supply curve for a well-defined labor market, we must assume these factors are held constant. In particular some of the parameters underlying a labor supply curve are the population size, age, and education along with the preferences of members of the labor force, which will influence the proportion of the population working and the labor-leisure choice made by individuals.

Given any labor supply curve, the time period of adjustment after a wage change is one of the most important factors in influencing the elasticity of supply. If the salary in a particular occupation rises, people may choose to enter that occupation, but acquiring the needed skills takes time. Therefore, in the short run, supply may be very inelastic. However, given the necessary period of adjustment, an increase in the relative wages in a particular occupation will attract additional people into that occupation, and supply will become more elastic.

In summary, we can say almost unequivocally that, except for the case of an individual worker, the supply of labor to a specific occupation is upward sloping. This reflects the fact that, at least in the long run, higher wages or benefits must be paid in order to attract more persons into the occupation. The longer the time period of adjustment, the more people are induced to enter. The same thing applies to the supply of a particular type of labor in a specific area—city, state, region. When you hear people complaining that a city can't get enough teachers, or a county can't get enough doctors, or a college can't get enough professors, or a community can't get enough garbage collectors—and these are things we hear every day—you should be able to suggest a solution. This is not to say the solution will be acceptable to those paying the bill. What people who make such statements generally mean is they cannot get enough of a particular type of worker at the going price.

16.6   MARKET EQUILIBRIUM AND RETURNS TO INPUTS

The demand and supply schedules of a variable productive service jointly determine its market equilibrium price. We have discussed the demand and supply curves of a variable input separately. By combining the curves we can derive a market equilibrium for input markets. The derivation of this equilibrium and the supply and demand curves is frequently referred to by the general term *marginal productivity theory*.

Market Equilibrium for Variable Inputs

In Figure 16–7, DD' and SS' are the demand and supply curves for a variable input. Their intersection at point E determines the equilibrium price, $\overline{w}$, and quantity demanded and supplied, $\overline{V}$, in a particular input market.

FIGURE 16–7   **Market equilibrium determination of the price of a variable productive service**

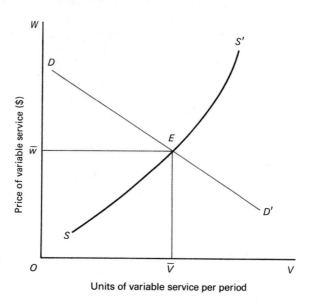

Units of variable service per period

If the price of the variable input (say, labor) exceeds $\overline{w}$, more people wish to work in this occupation than employers are willing to hire at that wage. Since there is a surplus of workers, wages are bid down by the workers until the surplus is eliminated. If the wage rate is below $\overline{w}$, producers want to employ more workers than are willing to work at that wage. Employers, faced with a "shortage" of labor, bid the wage rate up to $\overline{w}$. The analysis is similar to that in Chapter 2. The only features unique to this analysis are the methods of determining the demand for and supply of variable productive services. Because input demand is based on the marginal revenue product of the input, the theoretical derivation of this equilibrium is labeled marginal productivity theory.

Fixed Inputs and Quasi-Rent

Since all resources are variable in the long run, marginal productivity theory applies to all resources. However, in the short run, certain inputs are fixed; they cannot be varied, and a "marginal product" cannot readily be generated for them. The net return attributable to short-run fixed factors is called *quasi-rent*. In competitive markets quasi-rent is the difference between total revenue and total variable cost. It must always be nonnegative since, you will recall, the firm will shut down in the short run if it cannot cover all variable costs. Sometimes, when a pure profit is being enjoyed in the short run, quasi-rent exceeds fixed costs. Occasionally, when the firm operates at a loss in the short run, quasi-rent is less than total fixed cost, and some of the fixed cost must be paid by the entrepreneur, who suffers the loss. Quasi-rent is not profit and should never be confused with the return a firm earns. We can show quasi-rent using the conventional cost curves of the firm. Figure 16–8 illustrates the short-run equilibrium for a perfectly competitive firm. The firm earns zero profits, but to cover fixed costs, there must be positive quasi-rents. Total revenue in the figure is area *OPAX;* total variable costs are represented by area *OCBX*. Therefore, by definition, quasi-rents are area *CPAB*, the shaded region in the diagram.

It should be emphasized that quasi-rent is usually a short-run phenomenon. In the long run, when all factors are variable, quasi-rent is eliminated. Contrived or sometimes natural barriers may prolong their existence. There might be a natural barrier to entry—possibly the ownership of some specialized, highly productive resource that allows these rents to continue. Or the barriers may be artificially set by governmental licensing regulations. For example, in some cities, taxis are issued licenses which are given free or at a very low charge. But the licenses are limited in number. Therefore, entry is prohibited and quasi-rents can persist over a long period. Some land has tobacco allotments, giving the owner the right to grow a certain amount of tobacco on that land. The

FIGURE 16–8   **Quasi-rent for a perfect competitor**

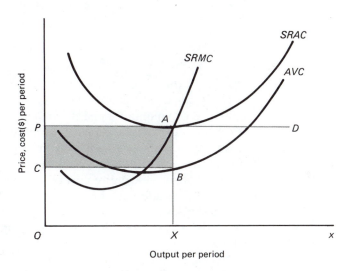

holders of these licenses or permits can continue to receive quasi-rent as long as large numbers of additional licenses or permits are not issued.

However, even these rents will eventually be eliminated. Suppose that, in your city, one must have a city permit to operate a mortuary. There are only 20 mortuaries in operation, and in all likelihood the city will issue no more licenses in the near future. Each of the mortuaries is doing a thriving business because of the prevention of entry as the city grows. Assume you are a young mortician and one of the licensed mortuaries comes up for sale. The license goes with the business. If you purchase the mortuary, will you make positive quasi-rents over a reasonable period of time, because you hold a license to do business in a thriving industry in which entry is prevented?

Probably not. Why? Well, in the first place, other morticians will also be bidding for the licensed business. How high will the bidding go? In all likelihood the business will sell for the value of the equipment *plus* the amount of rent due to the ownership of the license. For example, if the license enables the mortuary to make $100,000 a year *additional,* or pure, profit because of protection from entry, the discounted value of this stream of profit will be added to the selling price. In other words, when you buy a *business and a license,* you pay the value of the business *plus* the value of the license. You, as a new owner, will probably earn no quasi-rent because this rent would be paid to the original owner. Licenses only benefit those who receive them first from government, and only when there is a limit on the number of licenses. This analysis is, of course, similar to the capitalization of monopoly profits in the long run, discussed in Chapter 13.

The Full-Wage Equilibrium

Earlier in this chapter, we spoke of the effect of fringe benefits: either externally imposed benefits such as Social Security payments paid by employers, or voluntary benefits such as improved working conditions or low-cost group insurance plans. Employers simply consider the added cost of the benefits as an addition to wages, and they adjust their use of labor accordingly. From that analysis, you may have the impression that employers absorb the entire cost of such benefits—that the only effect on employees is that fewer workers are hired, but those hired receive higher *total* wage rates (that is, wages plus the value of the benefits). That is only part of the story. We neglected the supply side of the market in that analysis.

Remember that demand and supply determine the wage rates in markets. If working conditions in a particular market improve, or if there are additional fringe benefits paid to workers in this market, jobs in that market become more desirable relative to jobs in markets where conditions do not change. The increased desirability of jobs in that market will, at least in the long run, increase the supply of labor to that market. As we know, the increase in supply will drive down wages in that market relative to what they would have been in the absence of the increased desirability of the occupation. Thus, at least some of the cost of improved conditions is passed on to the workers involved. The proportion depends on demand and supply elasticities and how the curves shift. A somewhat factual, analytical example, using the tools we have developed in this section, may provide more complete insight into the process.

APPLICATION

Effect of Improved Working Conditions in Mining Industries

Let us consider the case of the northern Canadian mining and smelting industry. This industry mines and processes, among other things, zinc, nickel, gold, and lead. The mines and smelters are in rather desolate parts of the country, and the working conditions have historically been quite harsh. Wages have had to be rather high to lure workers away from other more desirable occupations and geographical areas.

FIGURE 16–9   **Effect of fringe benefits**

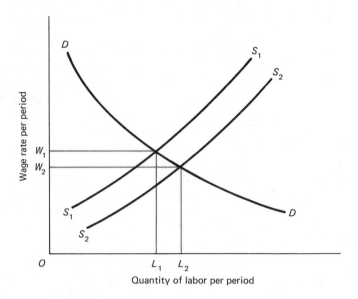

Recently, laws have been passed to make working conditions more amenable. Such laws are pollution control and dust and safety regulations in mines and smelters. In order to attract labor, mining companies have voluntarily improved working conditions in other ways—improved housing, community improvements, etc. These fringe benefits should be viewed as part of the total, or full, wage income for each worker. What is the effect of the additional benefits on the paid wage rate? Who really paid for fringe additions to the wages?

We can use Figure 16–9 to analyze the effect of fringe benefits on the market wage. Let DD be the total demand for labor in the northern Canadian mining industry. This demand reflects the relation between *money wages only* and the quantity of labor hired. That is, the wage rate on the vertical axis is the money wage rate and does not include the value of amenities. As we noted above, employers simply add the cost of fringe benefits to the market-determined wage rate in choosing the amount of labor hired.

Let $S_1 S_1$ be the supply of labor to the industry prior to the imposition of additional benefits. Again, this supply is the relation between money wages and labor supplied; it is obviously upward sloping. The equilibrium wage and quantity of labor hired are, respectively, W_1 and L_1. Now, let fringe benefits be added. These would be improved work conditions, such as added insurance benefits and improved housing. Suppose, just to take a somewhat extreme example, that the government absorbs all of the costs of such benefits. In this case, since the employer does not bear the added cost of hiring workers, we would not see a downward shift in input demand.

But, because of improved working conditions, the supply would increase. That is, at each wage rate, more workers than before would be willing to work in the industry because of improved working conditions. Even though government pays for all of the fringe benefits, the wage rate *falls* to W_2. Workers themselves effectively absorb some of the cost of the benefits in the wage difference $W_1 - W_2$. Of course, the amount of labor hired increases to L_2.

To be more realistic, if the companies themselves pay for most of the added benefits, they would be willing to hire fewer workers at each wage rate. That is, each worker costs more because of the added benefits. In this case, the demand for labor, *DD,* would shift downward and to the left, resulting in even lower wages than W_2 and in fewer than L_2 workers being hired.

Therefore, it is not necessarily the employer who absorbs all of the cost of fringe benefits. If the market works at all, the employees bear some part of the cost in the form of wages below the rate that would exist in the absence of regulations. The extent that wages are reduced because of fringe benefits depends on several factors: (1) the valuation by workers of the fringe benefits, reflected by the extent that supply increases, (2) the elasticity of supply, (3) the extent that demand decreases, and (4) the elasticity of demand.

To some extent, the above application might explain why, in the absence of regulations and labor unions, wages differ from industry to industry. Other things being equal, if the wage rate for the same skill is higher in one industry than in another, workers would leave the low-wage industry and increase the supply of labor to the high-wage industry. In this way, wages would rise in the previously low-wage industry and fall in the previously high-wage industry, until wage rates were the same in both. Therefore, in the absence of external interference, the wages should be approximately equal in the two industries for equal skills. If, over the long run, one industry continues to pay higher wages than another, and there are no external interferences, then the working conditions for some reason or other—location, job risk, amenities, and so on—must differ between industries. The attractiveness of an industry relative to another affects relative wage rates for equal levels of skill.

16.7 EFFECTS OF LABOR UNIONS AND MINIMUM WAGES

The theoretical discussion so far may seem far removed from the dramatic world of General Motors versus the United Automobile Workers. Indeed it is. A more complete understanding of such situations requires one or more *courses,* not chapters in a textbook. For example, there is a substantial body of theory concerning the collective bargaining process, and an understanding of labor markets also requires an extensive knowledge of the institutional framework that labor unions and businesses operate within. This type of knowledge must be acquired in "applied" courses or contexts, just as other applied courses supplement other portions of microeconomic theory.

We can gain considerable insight into the effect of unions on wages and employment by using our simple marginal productivity theory. The basic fundamentals of what unions can and cannot do are easily developed within our general framework. Furthermore, we can use our theory to analyze the effect of external interference in the labor market, such as the imposition of minimum wages.

Labor Unions

Consider any labor market with a positively sloped supply of labor. If the workers in this market are unionized, the union bargaining representative can raise wages in two ways. First, the representative could set a wage rate above equilibrium and guarantee the availability of workers at this price (up to a limit) while offering no workers at a lower price. Second, the union could limit the number of workers below the equilibrium number that would be hired in the absence of a union. This limitation, in effect, allows the market wage to rise.

Let's consider the first strategy. Suppose the labor market in question is perfectly competitive, so there are a large number of purchasers of this type of labor, and there is no union. The situation is depicted in Panel A, Figure 16–10, where D_L and S_L are the demand for and supply of labor, respectively. The market equilibrium wage rate is $\overline{w}$, and $\overline{V}$ units of labor are employed. Each individual firm (Panel B) accordingly employs $\overline{v}$ units. Next, suppose the labor market is unionized. If the union does not attempt to raise wages, the situation might remain as it is. However, gaining wage increases or other benefits is the reason for the existence of unions. Therefore, suppose the bargaining agency sets w_u as the wage rate. Firms can now hire all of the labor they want at the rate w_u, as long as the industry does not hire beyond the point S_u on the labor supply curve. A total of V_u (where w_u equals demand) units of labor are employed, each firm taking v_u units. The result is an increase in wages and a decline in employment.

The fact that the imposed increase in wages causes a reduction in the amount of labor does not necessarily mean a union cannot benefit its

FIGURE 16–10   **Effects of a labor union in a perfectly competitive labor market**

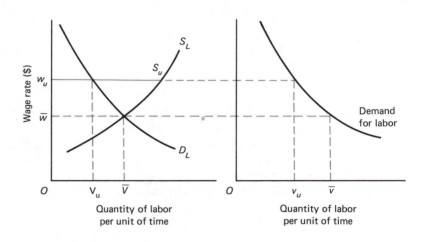

members. If the demand for labor is inelastic, an increase in the wage rate will result in an increase in *total wages* paid to all workers, even though the number of workers employed declines slightly. If the union can somehow equitably divide the proceeds of V_u employed workers among the $\overline{V}$ workers, perhaps by letting the workers work a shorter work week, all the workers will be made better off. The other side of the coin should also be considered, however. Suppose the demand for labor is elastic; then total wage receipts will decline, and the union cannot compensate the $V_u\overline{V}$ workers who are unemployed from the increase in wage rates.

The second option available for a union to raise wages is simply to limit the number of persons in an occupation. In terms of Figure 16–10, if the union could limit the number of union workes to V_u and somehow prevent nonunion workers from working in the industry, pure market forces would cause the wage rate to be bid up to w_u. Thus, limiting entry is an alternative way of raising wages. The problem here, of course, is that nonunion members can offer to work at lower wages and break the union. For this reason, the union must obtain, through threat of strike, boycott, or some other method, a contract with the firms preventing the hiring of nonunion labor. Or the union could get government to issue a limited number of licenses to work in the occupation, thereby restricting entry. The more difficult and time consuming it is to get a license, the more entry is restricted and the higher are wage rates. In either case, under reasonably competitive conditions, wage gains can be obtained only at the expense of reduced employment.

This analysis does not mean that unions deliberately set out to cause unemployment. They do considerable lobbying in Congress to restore full employment by expansionary monetary and fiscal policy and continually support full employment as an economic policy. The fact remains that wage gains in a specific industry are obtained at the expense of employment in that industry.

Minimum Wages

The effect of a minimum wage rate placed above the equilibrium is similar to the effect of a union. Those who retain their jobs in industries covered by the minimum wages are better off with the higher wage. Those who lose their jobs (that is, the "surplus" labor) are worse off. They must find work in other industries at less attractive wages. Therefore, a minimum wage makes some better off and some worse off. The question is, who benefits and who loses?

The amount of unemployment caused by a minimum wage depends on the elasticity of demand as it did for labor unions. To show this relation, let D_1D_1' and SS' in Figure 16–11 be, respectively, the demand and supply

FIGURE 16–11   **The effect of a minimum wage**

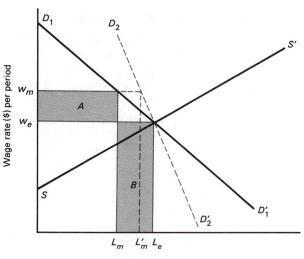

Labor units per period

of labor. In the absence of a minimum wage, equilibrium would occur at a wage of w_e with L_e units of labor employed. Once a minimum wage is imposed, we can see from the figure that the minimum wage of w_m reduces employment to L_m.

Though unemployment is created, labor as a sector can gain from the minimum wage. In other words, it is possible for labor to collectively receive total wages greater than before the minimum wage was imposed. Whether this happens or not depends on the elasticity of demand for workers. The minimum wage increases the total wage bill by area A in Figure 16–11, but decreases it by area B. The labor force as a whole gains if $A > B$, but loses if $B < A$. From Chapter 2 and our definition of elasticity, we know that when demand is inelastic, area A will be larger than area B, and smaller if demand is elastic. It is easy to see that, if we make demand more inelastic as shown by the demand curve D_2D_2', employment would fall by only $L_m'L_e$, which is less than L_mL_e. Area A would get larger and B smaller. Labor therefore benefits more from a minimum wage as demand becomes less elastic.

Of course, even if the total wage bill does increase and labor as a sector is better off, those who are forced into unemployment are worse off unless those who work make transfer payments to those who are unemployed. If all workers were homogeneous, as in our theory, the impact would be randomly distributed. If, as in the real world, workers differ in productivity and in employers' feelings toward them, the least productive workers and those most disadvantaged in their "reputation" with employers are the ones released.

16.8 MONOPSONY: MONOPOLY IN THE INPUT MARKET

We have assumed that firms, whether perfect competitors or monopolists, believe they can acquire as many units of the input as they want at the going market price. In other words, no firm acting alone has a perceptible effect on the price of the input. This obviously is not the case in all situations. There are sometimes only a few purchasers (and in the limit one) of a productive service. When only a few firms purchase an input, each will affect input price by changing input use. We need new tools to analyze the behavior of such firms.

For analytical simplicity, we consider only a single buyer of an input, called a *monopsonist*. However, the analytical principles are the same when there are a few buyers of an input, called *oligopsonists*.

Marginal Factor Cost under Monopsony

Since a monopsonist is the sole buyer of a productive service, the supply curve of the input is upward sloping. In order to hire more of an input, the monopsonist must raise the price of that input. Since each unit of the input hired receives the same price, in order to increase the use of an input, the monopsonist must pay *all* units an increased price. Marginal cost is not simply the price of an additional unit of input purchased, but is this price *plus* the increased payment to the units of input already employed.

Table 16–3 might clarify this point. Columns (1) and (2) indicate the labor supply to the monopsonist. Column (3) is the *additional* expense of increasing labor by one unit. The firm can hire five workers at $10 an hour. To hire an additional worker, the wage rate must rise to $12 an hour as shown in column (1). With five workers, the hourly wage bill is $50 an hour; with six, it is $72. Hiring the additional unit costs an additional $22 an hour, even though the wage rate rises by only $2. The additional worker costs $12, but increasing the wage of the previous five workers from $10 to $12 increases expenses by 5 × $2 = $10. We can use the same analysis to derive each entry in column (3). As we consider the addition of one unit of an input, the increased wage cost is the *marginal factor cost (MFC)*. It includes the price paid to the additional unit *plus* the increase that must be paid to the units already employed. For every unit except the first, the marginal factor cost exceeds price.

The supply curve of a variable input and the marginal factor cost curve are shown graphically in Figure 16–12. Since the price per unit rises as employment increases, the marginal factor cost exceeds supply price at all employment levels except the first unit. The marginal factor cost curve is positively sloped, lies to the left of the supply curve, and typically rises more rapidly than supply.

Definition

The marginal factor cost of an input to a monopsonist is the increase in total cost (and in total variable cost) attributable to the addition of one more unit of the variable productive agent.

TABLE 16–3   **Input supply and marginal factor cost**

(1) Price		*(2)* Quantity supplied	*(3)* Marginal factor cost	*(4)* Marginal revenue product
$10	....	5		
12	....	6	$22	$70
14	....	7	26	50
16	....	8	30	40
18	....	9	34	36
20	....	10	38	34
22	....	11	42	31

FIGURE 16–12

Marginal factor cost

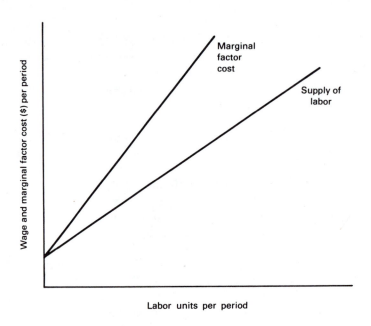

FIGURE 16–13

Price and employment under monopsony

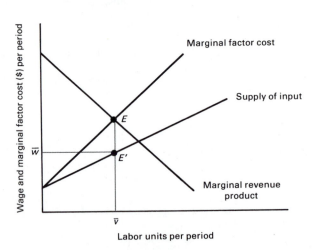

Price and Employment under Monopsony

The relevant curves for price determination under monopsony are the *MFC* and the *MRP* curves, assuming there is one variable input. Suppose a firm is confronted with a positively sloped supply of input curve and the higher marginal factor cost curve. The situation is illustrated in Table 16–3 and in Figure 16–13. Using this table and graph, we will prove the following:

Principle
A profit-maximizing monopsonist will employ a variable productive service until the point is reached where the marginal factor cost equals its marginal revenue product. The price of the input is determined by the corresponding point on its supply curve.

The proof of this principle follows immediately from the definitions of marginal revenue product and marginal factor cost. Marginal revenue product is the addition to total revenue attributable to the addition of one unit of the variable input; the marginal factor cost is the addition to total cost resulting from the employment of an additional unit. As long as marginal revenue product exceeds the marginal factor cost, profit can be augmented by expanding input use. On the other hand, if the marginal factor cost of an input exceeds its marginal revenue product, profit is less or loss greater than it would be if fewer units of the input were employed. Consequently, profit is maximized by employing that quantity of the variable service for which the marginal factor cost equals marginal revenue product.

For example, assume only one variable input in Table 16–3. The marginal revenue product schedule for 6 through 11 workers is given in column (4). Each worker up through the ninth adds more to hourly revenue *(MRP)* than is added to hourly cost *(MFC)*. Thereafter, workers 10 and 11 add more to cost than to revenue. The firm hires nine units.

In the continuous case, the equality of *MRP* and *MFC* occurs at point E in Figure 16–13, and $\bar{v}$ units of the service are accordingly employed. At this point, the supply-of-input curve becomes particularly relevant; $\bar{v}$ units of the variable productive agent are associated with point E' on the supply-of-input curve. This means that $\bar{v}$ units can be hired at a wage of $\bar{w}$ per unit. Therefore, $\bar{w}$ is the equilibrium input price corresponding to market equilibrium employment $\bar{v}$. If the monopsonist is a perfect competitor in the commodity market, the situation is similar, except that the relevant curve is the value of the marginal product curve. In either case the firm employs the variable input until the marginal value of the last unit equals the marginal factor cost of the input.

Recall from Section 16.3 that, at a given wage rate, monopoly in the commodity market led to fewer resources being employed in the input market relative to perfect competition. Each productive service was paid

FIGURE 16–14   **Competition, monopoly, and monopsony in the labor market**

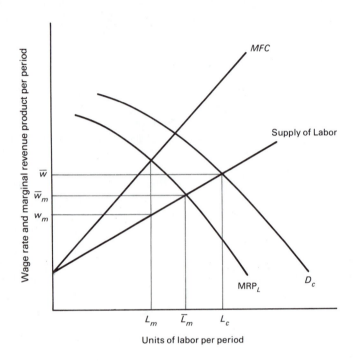

Units of labor per period

its marginal revenue product, which was less than the value of its marginal product. It can now be shown that, when the input side of the market is also a monopsony, still fewer resources are employed than would be in the absence of monopsony. Remember, we are dealing with only one input, and the monopoly faces the same cost curves as the competitive industry.

Figure 16–14 illustrates how monopsony on the demand side reduces employment. As before, let D_c be a competitive industry's demand for labor, the single variable input. MRP_L is the monopolist's marginal revenue product curve for labor, under the assumption of an identical cost structure. The competitive industry equates the supply of labor with D_c; it hires L_c units of labor at a wage $\overline{w}$. If the monopoly faced the same supply curve, it would hire $\overline{L}_m$, which, of course, is less than L_c. If the monopoly is also a monopsony, we can see that the firm reduces the amount of labor hired even more, to L_m, and wages fall to w_m. The monopoly that is also a monopsony therefore hires $L_m\overline{L}_m$ less labor than a firm that is only a monopoly, and pays $\overline{w}_mw_m$ less in wages. Let us note, that, as in most comparisons of monopoly and competition, these conclusions are drawn under quite restrictive assumptions. It is very likely that costs will differ between monopoly and competition, and this could reverse the relative positioning of the MRP_L and D_c schedules. In such cases we could not make unambiguous comparisons between monopoly and competition.

Bilateral Monopoly

An interesting aspect of monopsony behavior arises when the seller of the input is a monopoly. The input market is organized so that a single buyer of labor confronts a single seller of that resource, say a union. This situation, where a monopsonist hires a resource from a monopolist, is called *bilateral monopoly*. Examples of bilateral monopoly would be the United Auto Workers confronting General Motors, or, on a smaller scale, the only textile mill in a small town bargaining with a local union. This market structure yields no single equilibrium price or quantity. We can establish theoretical bounds that price and quantity will range between, but the final results depend on the bargaining and political powers of the negotiating parties.

FIGURE 16–15   **Bilateral monopoly**

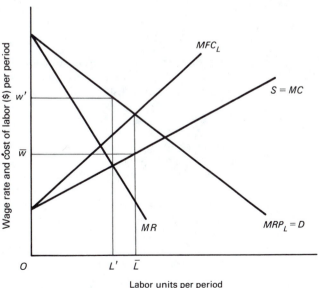

Figure 16–15 helps establish the bounds that price and quantity will fall between. To the union, the demand curve for its labor is the MRP_L curve of the monopsonist. The union takes this as given. We have assumed that the MRP_L curve is linear for the sake of illustration. If this is the demand faced by the union, or labor monopolist, the marginal revenue curve can be easily derived. It is shown as MR in the figure. Suppose the union behaves as a profit maximizer and seeks to maximize returns to its organization, given its labor supply curve S, which represents the marginal cost of hiring another worker.[5] The union will set $MR = S$, offer L' units of labor to the single employer, and ask for wage w'.

We have already discussed the way the monopsonist behaves. It maximizes profits where $MFC_L = MRP_L$; thus, it wants to hire $\overline{L}$ units of labor and pay a wage of $\overline{w}$. The equilibrium wage rate will lie somewhere between $\overline{w}$ and w', and the equilibrium amount of labor between L' and $\overline{L}$.

We can illustrate how bargaining eventually determines the equilibrium wage and employment level. In Figure 16–15, the bargaining could begin with the union refusing to supply more than L' units of labor and the employer refusing to pay a wage higher than $\overline{w}$. Then, if the employer wants more workers, a higher wage must be paid as part of the bargain. Employment moves closer to $\overline{L}$ units for the employer, and the wage rate moves closer to w' for the union. However, it might be the situation that $\overline{L} < L'$. That is, the monopsonist wants to hire fewer workers than the union wants to sell and wants them at a lower wage.[6] In this situation, the bargaining position of the union is weakened. It wants both more workers hired and higher wages. No longer is a *quid pro quo* exchange viable.

16.9 SUMMARY

We have covered a number of topics and developed several theories on the markets for variable inputs in this chapter. The more important points are set forth in the following principles:

Principle

When only one input is variable for the firm, the demand for that resource is its *marginal revenue product*. For the perfectly competitive firm, this is commodity price times marginal product, called the *value of marginal product*. For the monopolist, marginal revenue product is marginal revenue times marginal product. These curves represent the value of additional units of the resource to the firm. Since price exceeds marginal revenue for a monopolist, the value of marginal product exceeds the monopolist's marginal revenue product. When several resources are

---

[5] In Chapter 14, we showed that a monopolist does not have a supply curve. We assume, in this case, that the supply curve is provided by its union members, and the union takes it as given. In other words, the supply curve is outside its control.

[6] This would happen if the demand curve in Figure 16–15 was more inelastic, the supply curve more elastic, or both.

variable, these curves shift when the use of one input changes, but the resource still receives its *MRP* in equilibrium.

Principle

The demand for an input by a perfectly competitive industry is not the horizontal summation of each firm's demand. While any firm can change its level of output without changing commodity price, the industry as a whole cannot. In deriving industry demand, one must take account of the effect on commodity price. The demand of a monopolist is the industry's demand, since the monopolist is the industry.

Principle

Input prices are determined in input markets by the interaction of supply and demand. The supply of an input is generally, though not always, upward sloping to an industry.

Principle

A monopsonist is a firm that is the only buyer of one or more inputs. It hires the quantity at which *MRP* equals the marginal factor cost. The input receives a lower price than its *MRP*. Bilateral monopoly exists when a monopsonist buys an input from a single seller of that input (a monopoly). In such cases, a determinant quantity-price equilibrium does not exist. Quantity and price depend on the relative bargaining and political power of the two parties.

We should end the summary with a warning. Do not simply draw the conclusion that marginal productivity theory says that all workers get what they "deserve" or what they "ought to get." The theory says no such thing. It is a positive predictive or explanatory theory. It enables us to predict the effect of external forces, such as a change in the minimum wage or the unionization of an industry. It enables us to explain differences in wage rates among occupations. It does not allow us to say whether such differences are desirable from a social point of view. We cannot state that a distribution of income based on marginal productivity is somehow more "just" than any other distribution.

Many decades ago economists got something of a bad name because of such moral judgments. People begin with a specific amount of resources that they own—capital, labor skill, social position, and so on. Who is to say that the original distribution of resources is somehow more just than any other?

On the other hand, we can't say that some other method of allocation or distribution may be more just, or may give people more closely what they deserve. We merely want to emphasize that marginal productivity theory doesn't say anything about deservedness. It simply explains to a great extent why people receive what they receive. We can only say that society, or some part of it, believes that the resources owned by individuals are worth a certain amount.

We frequently hear or read someone bemoaning that Marvin Hagler does not deserve $10 million a fight; that Dr. J (Julius Erving), Herschel Walker and other athletes do not deserve their huge salaries; that Robert Redford or Barbra Streisand should not get $3 million a movie; or that Professor X at the University of Y does not deserve his large salary because he teaches only a few students a year. We also hear and read that someone or some group deserves more income. Whether we feel this way or not, our theory, and we, as economists, can say nothing about deservedness. Barbra Streisand and others receive their income because someone thinks the return from hiring them will be greater than or at least as much as, the amount paid out. That is all we, as economists, can say.

TECHNICAL PROBLEMS

1. Analyze some effects of a federal minimum wage. How do these effects differ from a state or local minimum wage?
2. Recall the definition of quasi-rent. Figure E.16–1 shows the short-run cost curves of a competitive firm.
   a. If price is $6, what is output?
   b. What is the amount of quasi-rent?
   c. How much of quasi-rent is attributable to the opportunity cost of the fixed inputs and how much is pure profit?
   d. Answer *a, b,* and *c* in the case of a $4 price.

FIGURE E.16–1

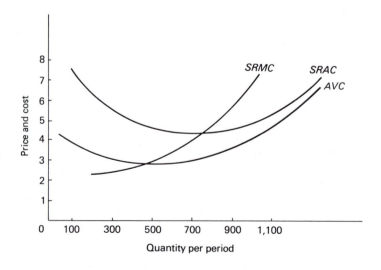

3. Consider a firm using one variable factor of production. The following table gives information concerning the production function [columns (2) and (3)], demand for output [columns (1) and (2)], and supply of labor [columns (3) and (4)] for the firm. Not all information will be used in each section of the problem. Add to the table any columns you wish.

(1) P($ per unit)	(2) X(units)	(3) L(units)	(4) w($ per unit)
10.50	5	5	4.00
5.36	10	6	4.25
5.00	14	7	4.50
4.00	17	8	4.75
3.00	19	9	5.00
2.60	20	10	5.25

a. Suppose the firm is a perfect competitor in the output market and also a perfect competitor in the labor market. Draw a graph showing the demand for labor if the price of output is $3.50 per unit.

b. How much labor would the firm use if the wage is $10.50?

c. Suppose, instead, that the firm is a monopsonist in the factor market facing a supply curve for labor given in columns (3) and (4). This firm is a perfect competitor in the output market and the price of the output is $3.50 per unit. How much labor would be used? What would be the wage? Explain your answers and graph your solution, showing on the graph how you got your answers.

d. Now suppose the firm is a monopolist in the output market and a monopsonist in the input market where the demand for the output is given in columns (1) and (2) and the supply of labor is given in columns (3) and (4). What would be the profit-maximizing amount of labor used by this firm? What would be the market wage? Explain your answer and graph your solution.

4. Consider the monopolist-monopsonist shown graphically in Figure E.16–2. Labor is the only variable input.

a. Show the equilibrium quantity of labor hired and the wage rate.

b. We emphasized in the text that, in a typically assumed case, a union that forces a wage increase will cause some unemployment. Suppose you represent such a union of this firm's employees. You can set any wage that you wish. In effect, you can simply set a wage and say to the firm, "You can hire all the labor you wish at this wage rate, but below this wage you get none." The wage is parametrically given to the firm by you.

FIGURE E.16–2

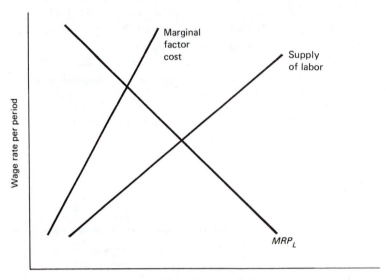

(1) Show on the graph the *highest* wage that you can set and cause no *less* labor to be hired than was hired in part *a* of the question.

(2) Show how much labor would want to work for the firm at this wage but would not be hired.

(3) Show the wage that maximizes the amount of labor hired. (At this wage everyone who wants to work for this firm at the wage you set will be hired.)

Note: This problem shows a minor exception to the point made in the text. The same thing could result from a minimum-wage law. But the analysis in the text generally holds.

5. Explain why the demand of a competitive industry for an input is less elastic than the sum of the demands of all the firms in the industry.

6. Monopolization of an industry will reduce the demand for an input but will not change wages unless the monopoly has monopsony power. Comment.

7. What would be the equilibrium marginal product of an input that is free to a firm; that is, the input costs the firm nothing?

8. After the first unit of an input hired, why is the marginal factor cost of that input to a monopsonist greater than the supply price of the input?

9. The demand for a factor of production depends to some extent on the demand for the products produced by the input. Explain the connection.

10. "Unskilled workers have low wages because their productivity is low." Is this precise? Give a more complete explanation.

11. The wage rate is solely determined by the marginal productivity of labor. In any case, the marginal productivity theory says that all workers get what they deserve. Comment critically.

ANALYTICAL PROBLEMS

1. You are attempting to get a labor union started. What conditions would make your job easier? What would make your job harder? Analyze the case of an individual firm, an industry, and an entire trade or profession.

2. Suppose that a particular firm in a competitive industry had a bigoted manager who refused to hire workers of a particular race even though these workers are as productive as those of other races.
   a. Under what conditions could the firm so discriminate?
   b. Under what conditions could it not?
   c. Would a monopolist be more likely to discriminate? Why or why not?

3. There is a proposal that government should provide an incentive payment to firms that hire unskilled handicapped workers. There would be a fixed amount per unskilled handicapped/hour used. How would this affect the wage and number of unskilled handicapped hired? If the payment is a lump sum regardless of the number hired, how would this affect your answer?

4. The fact that industries must pay a higher wage to get workers to work more means that none of these workers can have a negatively sloped supply of labor. Analyze.

5. Theft is an occupation. How would each of the following circumstances affect the number of thieves and their remuneration. Think in terms of *MRP*.
   a. Higher minimum wages and broader coverage.
   b. Technological advances in the burglar-alarm industry.
   c. Longer sentences for theft.
   d. Economic prosperity.
   e. Recession.
   f. Laws restricting hours of work.

6. A member of Congress was quoted as saying that an increase in the minimum wage will not cause unemployment, since it will raise labor productivity. Comment critically.

7. There is a "shock theory" of minimum wage laws. They supposedly "shock" inefficient firms into becoming more efficient. The evidence is that, after increases in minimum wages, firms purchase new capital equipment to use with labor. Comment. (*Hint:* recall our theory of production.)

8. In many cities, the wages of school teachers are the same in all schools for teachers with similar experience. Why do schools in the wealthier areas of the city generally get the best teachers?

9. A state government has recently spent $3 million of state funds to send units of the National Guard to a riot-torn city. What is the relevant economic cost of sending these troops? What other items should be included?

10. Does it strike you as wrong that we do not compensate the brave men or women who climb a utility pole in a storm to restore electricity at least as much as we compensate the band leader on a television show? What about the nurses, paramedics, and enlisted military personnel who protect our lives and property? Are not these functions of more value to society? Comment.

11. Does Nolan Ryan, a well-known baseball pitcher, make more than a high school teacher because he has more talent?

12. Compare a person's decision to increase his or her human capital by obtaining additional education or training with a firm's decision to invest in physical capital.

13. Professional basketball teams draft the top college seniors each year. If the drafted player wishes to play the sport—at least in the United States—he must sign with the team that drafts him. Most of the better players have agents. How does the theory of bilateral monopoly apply in this case? How are the beginning salaries determined? Would either party benefit if such a draft were declared illegal? Explain.

14. Some people say that, in general, firms do not spend enough time training their employees because management believes the employees will be bid away by other firms at higher salaries after they have been trained and the training expenditure is allegedly wasted. Analyze this argument.

Chapter 17

Demand for Fixed Inputs: Theory of Investment

17.1 INTRODUCTION

Although the last chapter discussed input markets in terms of labor and other variable inputs, we have emphasized that the theoretical tools developed in that chapter apply to all inputs. Conceptually, the firm always maximizes profits by setting the marginal factor cost of an input equal to its marginal revenue product. When the firm is not a monopsony, marginal factor cost is the input price, and, when it is a perfect competitor in the final good market, marginal revenue product is the value of marginal product, where $VMP_i = P \times MP_i$ for the ith input.

In this chapter we focus on some additional considerations involved when inputs yield a stream of services over time. Typically, when such durable inputs are purchased it is called *investment*. Examples of an investment would be the purchase of machines and buildings. Expenditures on such items are often referred to as the purchase of capital. But there are other inputs that meet the definition of investment. Advertising and education are two additional examples of investments in production processes that when purchased will yield a stream of returns to the owner. Whenever an input continues to be valuable over multiple decision periods, interest rates become important in evaluating the benefits and costs of different investment alternatives. This chapter explores the theory of investment.

We have already discussed in Chapter 4 the importance of interest rates in discounting future streams of returns and expenditures to the present. We did this because whenever consumption or production cover multiple periods, discounting is necessary to compare total benefits and costs. We will begin this chapter with a review of present value, but it might be helpful to review the entire discussion at the end of Chapter 4 before continuing.

17.2 THEORY OF INVESTMENT

The objective of any profit-maximizing firm that makes an investment is to obtain a stream of returns, the present value of which exceeds the cost of the investment. The firm first undertakes those available projects with the greatest differential between present value and cost. Since the stream of returns and payments must be discounted, the concept of present value enters into each investment decision. The rate of interest therefore becomes a key determinant of the amount of investment undertaken. It is an important variable in present value calculations, and represents a minimum required return on any investment venture. A firm should invest in a productive asset only if the income stream generated by the asset is larger than investing the same expenditure at the going interest rate in an alternative financial asset.

Investment Decision Making

To show the importance of discounting in investment decisions, consider the following example. A research and consulting firm is thinking about installing a small computer in its office. The total payments on the computer will be $250,000 a year for three years. Beginning in the second year, the net revenue (after subtracting operating costs) generated by the computer is expected to be $90,000 a year for the next 10 years. At the end of that period of time, the firm estimates that the computer will have a salvage value of $50,000. For calculation purposes, the firm uses a discount rate of 5 percent. Should the firm install the computer?

First, calculate the present value of the stream of purchase payments as

$$\frac{\$250,000}{1.05} + \frac{\$250,000}{(1.05)^2} + \frac{\$250,000}{(1.05)^3} = \$680,811.$$

Next, the discounted stream of net returns for 10 years, beginning in the second year, is

$$\frac{\$90,000}{(1.05)^2} + \frac{\$90,000}{(1.05)^3} + \cdots + \frac{\$90,000}{(1.05)^{11}} = \$661,863.$$

Finally, the present value of the salvage or resale is

$$\frac{\$50,000}{(1.05)^{11}} = \$29,230.$$

The research firm should purchase the computer, since the net present value *(NPV)* is

$$NPV(\text{return} + \text{salvage} - \text{cost}) = \$661,863 + \$29,230 - 680,811$$
$$= \$10,282.$$

Of course, a different discount rate would change the present value of a particular investment. For example, keeping the same streams of cost and income as above, let the interest rate go to 12 percent. With a 12 percent interest rate, the present value of the purchase payments of $250,000 over three years is $600,458. The new present value of $90,000 a year for years 2 through 11 is $454,036. Finally, at a 12 percent interest rate, the present value of the $50,000 salvage price at the end of the 11th year is $14,374. With the higher interest rate, the net present value of the investment is

$$NPV = \$454,036 + \$14,374 - \$600,458 = -\$132,048_i$$

Since the net present value now has a negative value, the investment should not be made. The firm could do better by investing in an alternative project or placing the funds available for investment in an interest-bearing account.

This example illustrates an important point. For most investments, the payments are made in early periods, while the returns are spread over a much larger period of time. The higher the interest rate, the lower the present value of benefits, and therefore, high rates of interest tend to discourage investment. We will make this point in much greater detail later.

Discounting and the concept of net present value are helpful for making decisions other than *whether or not* to invest. Importantly, they help firms select among investment alternatives. To take another example, assume the same research firm is considering buying an office building for $1 million or renting office space in the same building at $60,000 a year for five years. For simplicity, assume rent is paid at the end of each year. The firm estimates that, even with inflation, the wear and tear on the building will offset the appreciation in value. The building will sell for $1 million at the end of five years. Should the firm lease or buy the building? Assume in this case the interest rate is 10 percent and, if the firm buys the building, the $1 million is payable immediately from assets owned by the firm.

The relevant stream of benefits and costs to compare is the discounted resale value of the building plus the present value of the stream of saving in rents (these savings add to profit—recall our discussion of opportunity costs) less the $1 million cost of the building:

$$NPV = \sum_{t=1}^{5}\left(\frac{1}{1.10}\right)^t \$60,000 + \frac{\$1,000,000}{(1.10)^5} - \$1,000,000 = -\$151,435.$$

Since the investment has a negative present value, the firm should not make the investment. It should invest the $1 million elsewhere, take the interest, and pay the rent. On the other hand, if the rate of interest is 5 percent, and net present value of the investment is

$$NPV = \sum_{t=1}^{5}\left(\frac{1}{1.05}\right)^{t} \$60,000 + \frac{\$1,000,000}{(1.05)^5} - \$1,000,000 = \$43,295.$$

Since the present value is positive, the firm should purchase the building.

To summarize our discussion, a firm undertakes investment to maximize a discounted stream of net income. Obviously, a profit-maximizing firm wants any new capital purchased to have a flow of returns the present value of which is greater than, or at least equal to, the present value of the flow of costs. Therefore, the discounted income and costs to a firm from an additional unit of capital are key variables in the investment decision-making process. The present value of the expected net revenue from capital depends on several variables such as the market rate of interest, the price of goods produced, the expected lifetime and rate of deterioration of the capital, the flow of services or capital productivity, the prices of other inputs employed, and so forth. A firm should invest in assets that have a lifetime net income stream with a positive (non-negative) present value; it should not invest in assets that have a negative net income stream.

The Firm's Demand for Investment

These principles allow us to develop a firm's demand for capital goods. Assume that a firm, during a particular time period, faces several investment opportunities. The firm may purchase capital goods either by selling debt instruments or by reducing its real money balances. A firm's use of internal funds to finance investments does not change the cost of the investment. The opportunity cost of funds raised internally must be the relevant market rate of interest. We assume the firm may borrow or lend funds at the market rate of interest. While a firm is usually restricted in its borrowing by its overall net worth, we will assume this restriction is not a relevant barrier and ignore it in our analysis.

Even though a firm may know that several investment opportunities are profitable, it must have a way of ranking them in terms of how much profit they earn. The higher the percentage *rate of return* on each unit of capital, the more profitable the overall investment. Projects can be ranked by their rate of return from the highest to the lowest. As long as investment funds are not limited, the firm should continue to purchase capital until the rate of return on the last unit is just equal to the opportunity cost of investment funds.

There is one catch to ranking capital investment projects by their rate of return. What happens if the return in one period is 10 percent, but 12 percent in the next? What is the project's rate of return? To derive the demand curve for investment we introduce the concept of an *internal rate of return,* defined as

Definition

The internal rate of return from a particular investment is the discount rate that makes the net present value of that investment zero.

For example, suppose an investment costing $48,000 is expected to yield a net return (profit) of $20,000 a year for three years. To find the discount rate that makes the net present value zero, set

$$NPV = \sum_{t=1}^{3} \frac{\$20,000}{(1 + r)^t} - \$48,000 = 0.$$

Solving for r, the internal rate of return for this investment is approximately 0.12 (12 percent).

Now suppose the market interest rate is higher than 12 percent. We know from the above calculation that the net present value of the investment would be negative. For example, if the interest rate is 15 percent the net present value is

$$NPV = \sum_{t=1}^{3} \frac{\$20,000}{(1 + .15)^t} - \$48,000 = -\$2,336.$$

Since net present value would be negative, the firm would not undertake the investment. At rates below 12 percent, the stream of returns is not discounted so heavily and the net present value would be positive; e.g., if the interest rate is 8 percent, the net present value is

$$NPV = \sum_{t=1}^{3} \frac{\$20,000}{(1 + .08)^t} - \$48,000 = \$3,543$$

and the firm should undertake the investment.

The firm's investment decision depends on the relation of the internal rate of return for a particular project and relevant market rate of interest. If the internal rate of return is higher than the market interest rate, the net present value at the market rate is positive and the investment should be made. If the internal rate of return is lower, the net present value at the market rate would be negative and the investment should not be made.

Consider another slightly more complicated investment opportunity. This one does not yield the same amounts of revenue per period and thus appears to have different rates of return on the amount of capital invested, depending on the period. Suppose, as before, the project cost is $48,000 paid at the beginning of the venture, but net profit returns are $20,000 for the first two years and $30,000 during the third year. The discount rate that makes net present value on the project zero is that rate for which

$$NPV = \sum_{t=1}^{2} \frac{\$20{,}000}{(1 + r)^t} + \frac{\$30{,}000}{(1 + r)^3} - \$48{,}000 = 0.$$

Because the return in the third period has gone up, everything else remaining the same, the internal rate of return for the entire project life rises to nearly 20 percent. The internal rate of return calculations will give every investment project a rank according to the percentage rate of return earned on each dollar of capital even when returns vary across periods.

We think of the market rate of interest as the return that could be earned if the investment is not made, because that is the return that could be earned if the same amount of funds were put into interest-bearing accounts or financial assets paying that rate of interest. Within this framework, the rate of interest is the opportunity cost of making a capital investment. Using the concept of the internal rate of return, we can derive a firm's demand for investment during a particular period.

Figure 17–1 shows the set of investment opportunities facing a hypothetical firm. In this case, the firm has four possible investment oppor-

FIGURE 17–1   **Alternative investment opportunities**

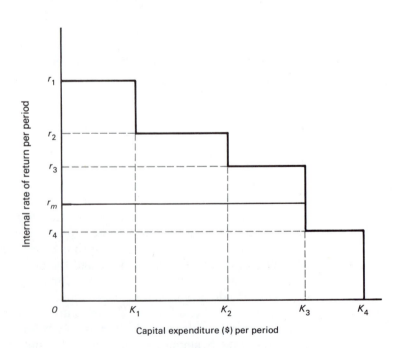

tunities and can rank them according to the internal rate of return on each. The first and most profitable investment project involves a capital expenditure of K_1 dollars and has an internal rate of return of r_1. The second most profitable investment costs K_1K_2 dollars; it has an internal rate of return of r_2. Similarly, the other two investment projects cost K_2K_3 and K_3K_4 with internal rates of return of r_3 and r_4.

We should emphasize that the internal rates of return plotted along the vertical axis are the rates on each *additional* investment project, not the average rate of return on all investments up to that point. For example, r_2 is the internal rate of return for investment project two; i.e., for increasing capital expenditure from K_1 to K_2. It is not the average internal rate of return of the total expenditure of K_2 dollars.

We know from our above discussion that if the firm has no limitation on its capital expenditure, it will undertake all projects that have an internal rate of return greater than the market rate of interest. It would undertake no projects for which the internal rate of return is less than the interest rate. If in Figure 17–1 the interest rate is r_m, the firm would undertake the first three projects. It would not undertake project four, because it could purchase an interest-bearing financial asset with the K_3K_4 dollars and earn a higher return. Thus the firm would invest K_3 dollars during the relevant period. Only if the interest rate falls below r_4, would the firm invest K_4 dollars. If the interest rate rises above r_3 but stays below r_2, investment three would not be made and the firm would invest only K_2 dollars.

We have established the following principle:

Principle
A firm can rank potential investments according to their internal rates of return—the discount rate that would make the net present value of the investment zero. If investment funds are not limited, the firm should undertake those investments for which the internal rate of return is greater than the relevant rate of interest.

APPLICATION

Evaluation of Investment Projects

Argonaut Enterprises, a hypothetical company, has available four potential investment projects that would all begin in 1986. The characteristics of these projects are summarized in the following table.

Project	A	B	C	D
Capital cost	$123,000	$89,200	$56,600	$55,800
Net income*:				
1986	30,000	50,000	20,000	40,000
1987	30,000	50,000	20,000	20,000
1988	30,000	0	20,000	10,000
1989	30,000	0	20,000	0
Scrap or resale value at the end of 1989:	50,000	0	10,000	0

* All income is received at year end.

The question facing the management of Argonaut Enterprises is which—if any—of the projects should be undertaken. Using 15 percent as the relevant market interest rate, the net return for the four investment projects as of January 1, 1986 were calculated. These values are

Project:	A	B	C	D
Discounted profits:	−$8,800	−$7,900	$6,200	$700

Therefore, on the basis of these calculations, only Projects C and D should be undertaken. Note for future reference that project A is the least profitable.

This decision did not "sit very well" with the vice president for operations, for whom Project A was a particular favorite. He argued that the interest rate used in the calculation of the net present values was too high. In response, the board of directors had the staff calculate the internal rates of return for each of the projects. These values are

Project:	A	B	C	D
Internal rate of return:	12%	8%	20%	16%

From these values, the management could see that Project A would be profitable only if the relevant market interest rate was below 12 percent. For interest rates in excess of 12 percent, only Projects C and D should be undertaken.

This application shows us that there are fundamentally two ways to evaluate the relative returns on investment projects. One way is to choose an interest rate—usually the market rate of interest—and evaluate the actual profit of projects at this interest rate. Projects that yield positive profit should be undertaken. Alternatively, the internal rate of return may be calculated. Those projects with an internal rate of return above the opportunity cost of capital should be financed.

The relative ranking of investment projects by their internal rate of return will not change as the market rate of interest changes, but it can change when projects are ranked according to their profitability. For instance, suppose the market rate of interest is 5 percent, rather than 15 percent, the discounted profits of the projects are now approximately:

Project:	A	B	C	D
Discounted profits:	$24,500	$3,800	$22,500	$9,100

All of the projects yield a positive return, but the relative ranking of profits has dramatically changed. Project A, earlier the least profitable venture, becomes the most profitable, followed by projects C, D, and B. The change in the relative profitability of A arises because most of investment A's returns are late in the income stream. At a 15 percent rate of discount they are not wieghted heavily. When the interest rate declines they are given increasing importance in figuring the benefits of the project. Ranking investments by their net present values can be deceptive.

By using the internal rate of return, an investor has a clear picture of when net present value becomes positive. At a 5 percent rate of interest all of the investments should be undertaken according to the above calculation. But because the internal rate of return is 20 percent in investment C, this does not mean it will have the highest *NPV* at 5 percent. We know that the highest *NPV* comes from project A. Thus if capital funds are limited, project A should be taken first and then C. In sum, both procedures for calculating the profitability of investment have pitfalls and must be used carefully. It is usually best to employ both methods in investment decision making, especially if investment funds are limited.

If the firm has only four investment projects available, the firm's demand function for investment looks something like Figure 17–1. However, most (if not all) firms have a wide variety of projects available. As you should be able to see, as more potential projects are available, the "stair-step" demand function gets closer to a smooth—continuous—demand function. If we assume that the investment projects are infinitely divisible, we can talk about the internal rate of return associated with an additional dollar expenditure on capital and we can draw a continuous demand for investment as in Figure 17–2.

This figure shows the internal rate of return for additional (marginal) investment. Capital investment in the relevant time period is plotted along the horizontal axis; the internal rate of return on the marginal investment and the interest rate are plotted along the vertical axis.

Suppose the market rate of interest is r_0. Every additional unit of investment from zero to K_0 has an internal rate of return greater than r_0. From our previous discussion, if the internal rate of return exceeds the rate of interest, the investment is profitable and should be undertaken (if

FIGURE 17–2   **Demand for investment**

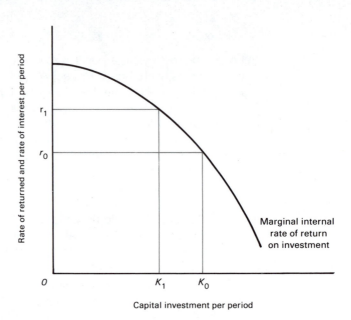

Capital investment per period

there is no limit on the amount of capital that can be raised by the firm). Any additional investment beyond K_0 dollars has an internal rate of return below the rate of interest and therefore should not be undertaken. Thus with an interest rate of r_0 the firm would invest K_0.

By exactly the same type of reasoning, if the rate of interest is r_1, the firm should invest K_1 dollars. Likewise, at every other rate of interest the down-sloping curve, showing the internal rate of return on each marginal investment, provides the optimal amount that the firm should invest at that interest rate. Thus, this internal rate of return schedule is the firm's demand for investment.

Principle

The internal rate of return for additional units of investment is the firm's demand for investment in a given time period. The firm should increase investment until the internal rate of return on the last unit of investment is equal to the rate of interest.

Industry Demand for Investment

The demand for investment by an entire competitive industry is similar to the demand of a firm. We assume that the investment opportunities facing all firms in an industry can be ranked by their internal rates of return, from highest to lowest. Thus, for the industry, the demand curve for investment also slopes downward.

However the curve for the industry slopes downward for an additional reason. As we know, a competitive firm can invest and increase its output without lowering the price of the product. An entire industry cannot. If all firms undertake additional investment, the industry's output will increase and, because of downward sloping product demand, the price of the product will fall. Since the price of the product falls with additional investment, the profitability and therefore the internal rate of return from that investment is less than it would have been had output price remained fixed. While we cannot obtain the industry's demand for investment by simply summing the demands of all firms, its general slope does not change. Firms invest until the marginal rate of return from investment equals the rate of interest. The lower the rate of interest, the more investment undertaken.

As is the case for any type of demand curve, if one of the factors we hold constant changes, the entire curve will shift. To generalize, anything that makes investments more profitable will increase the internal rates of return on investments and consequently increase the firm's demand for investment. Anything that makes investments less profitable will decrease the demand for investment.

For example, a large increase in wage rates would decrease present

FIGURE 17–3   **Effect of taxation on investment**

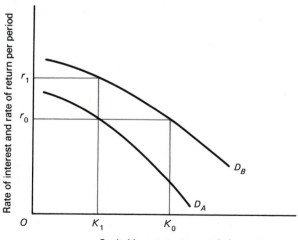

Capital investment per period

values (since it would decrease future net income) and therefore cause a decrease in internal rates of return on investment. Since the amount of investment forthcoming at any given interest rate would decrease, demand decreases. Technological change would have the opposite effect.

The effect of a change in the rate of taxation on investment plans is shown graphically. In Figure 17–3, D_B, showing the before-tax rate of return on investment, is the demand curve for investment if the tax rate is zero. With no taxes and an interest rate of r_0, the industry would, with no credit restrictions, invest in K_0 units of capital. But any taxation lowers the present value of expected income from any investment and, therefore, shifts the demand for investment downward. If taxation shifts this schedule to D_A in Figure 17–3, investment would fall to K_1 units for a rate of interest of r_0. The difference between the two curves reflects the magnitude of the tax and the proportion of the tax that firms can shift to consumers. The larger the tax, other things equal, the greater the effect on investment.

Monopoly in Capital Markets

The type of market in which the firm operates will also have an effect on the firm's demand for capital investment. If the investor is a monopolist, the firm's demand for investment will be the demand of the industry, since the firm is the industry. When considering an additional investment, the monopolist will know that the additional output from the investment will lower the selling price of the product. As the monopolist continues to invest in capital, the marginal return from the investment will be less than the value of the marginal product of the investment for any given amount of investment. Essentially, for the same reason that $MRP_L < VMP_L$ for labor, the marginal return on investment is less than would be the case for a perfectly competitive firm. Nonetheless, the investment decision made by a monopolist is no different than the one made by a perfect competitor. The monopolist will undertake investments so long as the internal rate of return is greater than the market rate of interest.

Monopsony in Capital Markets

Monopsony in capital markets has no effect on our analysis of the demand for capital. Recall that monopsony in labor caused the marginal cost of labor to rise even faster than the slope of the supply curve for labor. The marginal factor cost of another unit of labor increased more quickly than did its price, because it was assumed that all labor received the same wage. For capital, a monopsonist faces an upward sloping supply curve, but there is no *MFC* schedule above the supply curve, as there was for labor. A higher price for the marginal unit of capital does not necessitate paying a higher price for the units of capital already in use. The marginal factor cost of capital is the cost of the last unit purchased.

Demand for Capital in Summary

To summarize, we see that the theory of investment differs in some ways from the theory of labor employment, even though the basics are the same. The profit- maximizing criterion in essence is no different; the firm carries out investment until the marginal return from investment equals its marginal cost. For capital, it is analytically more convenient to make the transition to rates of return, because the input yields a stream of returns. So long as the internal rate of return exceeds the rate of interest, the present value of the stream of net returns is greater than the present value of the cost of the investment. Thus, the optimal level of investment is that at which the internal rate of return equals the market interest rate.

17.3 INFLATION AND INVESTMENT

To this point, we have used interest rates without distinguishing between the *real* rate and the *nominal* rate. The nominal interest rate is the money rate actually paid in the market. The real rate is the rate of interest after an inflation factor is subtracted from the nominal rate. It is therefore net of inflation.

We now show that, under certain assumptions, it is unimportant to specify whether a nominal or real rate is used. For relatively low rates of inflation, as long as inflation has the same effect on interest rates as on the flow of returns, present value is unaffected.

Theoretical Effects of Inflation

To begin, we define r to be the *real* rate of interest and R_t to be the *real* return from investment in period t. These are interest rates and income flows that do not have an inflationary or deflationary factor included. Our analysis has dealt in terms of these real variables. For instance, we have written present value as

$$PV = \sum_{t=1}^{T} \frac{R_t}{(1 + r)^t},$$

where T is the time horizon limit. Now suppose inflation adjusts quoted prices and returns upward. The quoted, or nominal rate of return, includes an inflation factor, π. We will write the nominal rate of interest as the sum of a real and inflationary component. Thus the nominal rate of interest i is

$$i = r + \pi.$$

For example, suppose you have $100 and you want a 5 percent increase in the purchasing power of that money at the end of the year. If the inflation rate is 10 percent during the year, at the end of the year you want

$$100 + .05(100) + .10(100) = (1 + .05 + .10)100 = (1 + r + \pi)100.$$

To increase purchasing power by 5 percent, the nominal rate of interest must be $i = r + \pi = 5\% + 10\% = 15\%$. We will assume that the return to investment or, more generally, the income flow R_t is augmented by the same factor π and increases at this rate each period. If the real return in period one is R_1, the money or nominal return in period two will be $R_1 (1 + \pi)$, and for any period it will be $R_t (1 + \pi)^t$. Thus, the present value of a nominal income stream is written as

$$PV = \sum_{t=1}^{T} \frac{R_t(1 + \pi)^t}{(1 + i)^t} = \sum_{t=1}^{T} \frac{R_t(1 + \pi)^t}{(1 + r + \pi)^t}.$$

Now take a closer look at the denominator in the above equation. Notice that

$$1 + r + \pi = (1 + r)(1 + \pi) - r\pi.$$

The difference between the denominator, $1 + r + \pi$, and $(1 + r)(1 + \pi)$ is the product, $r \cdot \pi$. So, if $r = .05$ and $\pi = .05$, this term is .0025, a relatively trivial amount. In general the lower the rate of inflation, the better $(1 + r)(1 + \pi)$ approximates $1 + r + \pi$. As the inflation rate gets larger, the approximation is poorer. For a 50 percent rate of inflation and a 20 percent real rate of interest, $r \cdot \pi = .10$, which is much larger than .0025. In this case, $(1 + r)(1 + \pi)$ overestimates the discount factor by a significant amount. As a consequence, the discounted present value of investment is underestimated by using $(1 + r)(1 + \pi)$ as the discount factor in the denominator.

Nevertheless, for low rates of inflation, we may write

$$PV = \sum_{t=1}^{T} \frac{R_t(1 + \pi)^t}{(1 + r + \pi)^t} \cong \sum_{t=1}^{T} \frac{R_t(1 + \pi)^t}{(1 + r)^t(1 + \pi)^t} = \sum_{t=1}^{T} \frac{R_t}{(1 + r)^t}.$$

It follows that investors would, under the assumption that inflation rates are low, pay the same amount for a particular stream of returns as they would pay if inflation were zero. We would, therefore, say that under these conditions, inflation is neutral with respect to investment because of the link between the nominal rate of interest and the rate of inflation.

But, with high rates of inflation, the present value

$$PV = \sum_{t=1}^{T} \frac{R_t(1 + \pi)^t}{(1 + r + \pi)^t} > \sum_{t=1}^{T} \frac{R_t(1 + \pi)^t}{(1 + r)^t(1 + \pi)^t} = \sum_{t=1}^{T} \frac{R_t}{(1 + r)^t}.$$

The nominal present value of a particular undiscounted stream of returns is greater than the real present value. We can see that, if the rate of inflation is high, the numerator is increasing faster than the denominator. Since nominal present value increases with inflation, investors would be willing to pay more for a given real stream of income than would be the case with little or no inflation. Investment is, therefore, not neutral with respect to high inflation rates.

Actual Effects of Inflation

The above analysis is not meant to imply that, in reality, the amount of investment and the investment mix in an economy are not affected, or for that matter augmented, by inflation. This is far from the case. In the first place, inflation usually increases uncertainty about projected benefits and costs, and increased uncertainty will generally decrease the demand for investment. Investors may feel, for example, that the returns will not keep up with inflation. Or they may believe that the allowable depreciation rate of capital for tax purposes (which has not changed with inflation) will not be sufficient to cover the replacement cost of the capital when the old capital wears out or is sold for salvage. While we have ignored to some extent capital replacement, this factor does play a significant role in investment decision making, and because replacement must be made when the capital wears out, this cost will tend to have a negative influence on investment.

There is another way in which inflation combined with the current tax structure may have a negative effect on investment. Under our existing tax structure, nominal, not simply real, income is subject to taxation. Therefore, if a firm purchases an asset and resells it later, all gains are subject to taxation even though most or even all of the gains could be due to inflation. For example, suppose a firm purchases an asset for $100,000. The value of the asset increases during a year at the same rate as the rate of inflation, 12 percent. Thus, the firm sells at $112,000, realizing a net gain of $12,000, which is taxed at the 48 percent corporate rate. The after-tax return is $6,240. The firm, in real terms, is $5,760 worse off, however, since the $112,000 is worth only $100,000 in year one dollars. In order to have $112,000 after the inflation and taking account of taxes, the rate of return must be 23 percent, almost double the rate of inflation.

In a world of perfectly anticipated inflation, free of institutional constraints and regulations, the nominal rate of interest and income streams would adjust in an inflationary economy so that firms would realize present values on earning streams approximately equal to those without inflation. The nominal rate of interest would include the rate of inflation and the real rate of interest. But in the actual world with real firms, there frequently is uncertainty leading to constraints on the nominal returns firms may earn. Therefore, in this world, inflation can inhibit private investment. Sometimes, too, the interaction of inflation with the tax structure can compound the adverse impact of inflation.

APPLICATION

The Effects of Inflation on Public Utilities

We have seen that inflation can have very little effect on the present value of an income stream if the discount rate in the denominator and the periodic returns in the numerator are equally affected by the rate of inflation. Often this is not the case for industries whose prices are regulated. Publicly regulated utilities—for instance, electricity and gas companies—must seek permission from a state regulatory board to increase their rates.

"Rate hearings" can last more than a year. For example, in 1978, the average length of time between a request for a price change and a regulatory decision was 13.6 months for electric utilities.[1] Such delays are called "regulatory lags." During this time, costs are rising as a result of inflation, while prices stay fixed unless an interim increase is granted.

Another problem for utilities is that regulators grant price increases at a pace less than the rate of inflation. Table 17–1 shows the price changes allowed several regulated industries compared to unregulated service industries between 1961 and 1977. We assume that the unregulated industries raise prices to keep up with inflation. For each industry, the average increase in price is less than that of the unregulated service sector. Rate-of-return regulation thus distorts the impact of inflation on the earning stream of a utility. While costs rise freely, prices are not allowed to

TABLE 17–1   **Price changes in regulated industries, 1961–1977**

Industry	1961–1965	1965–1969	1969–1973	1973–1977	Average 1961–1977
Electricity and gas	−0.1	0.2	4.3	11.3	3.9
Telephone	−0.5	0.2	2.5	2.9	1.3
Railroad transportation	−2.6	1.0	7.2	8.6	3.6
Motor freight transportation	0.6	2.3	3.6	5.7	3.1
Unregulated service industries	1.7	4.4	4.7	7.8	4.7

Source: Paul MacAvoy, *The Regulated Industries and the Economy* (New York: W. W. Norton, 1979).

[1] Paul MacAvoy, *The Regulated Industries and the Economy* (New York: W. W. Norton, 1979), p. 108.

TABLE 17–2   **Rate of return on assets in regulated industries, 1962–1977**

Industry	1962– 1965	1966– 1969	1970– 1973	1974– 1977	Average 1962– 1977
Electricity and gas	5.0	5.1	5.2	5.7	5.3
Telephone	5.2	5.2	5.4	5.8	5.4
Railroad transportation	3.3	3.3	3.4	4.2	3.6
Motor freight transportation	5.5	5.8	5.9	6.1	5.8
Unregulated service industries	5.9	6.2	6.0	6.6	6.2

Source: Paul MacAvoy, *The Regulated Industries and the Economy* (New York: W. W. Norton, 1979).

adjust as rapidly. In the discount stream, the denominator is going up faster than the numerator.

The immediate implication of such regulation is that the profitability of investment is less in regulated utilities than in unregulated industries. Table 17–2 reveals that this is indeed the case. In the long run, investor-owned utilities will have trouble attracting capital to expand. In the past 20 years, the stock prices of utilities have been depressed, reflecting an unwillingness of investors to finance further utility growth.

17.4 DEPLETION OF NATURAL RESOURCES: PRICING OVER TIME

An important investment decision is the decision to purchase a mineral deposit. During the past decade, the topic of the depletion of natural resources has received a considerable amount of attention. We frequently hear that, because there are finite supplies of certain natural resources, such as oil, gas, and coal, the world will soon run out of these minerals if current rates of depletion continue. Economists assert that market forces can prevent such a disaster. Many policy-makers argue that only governmentally imposed conservation will prevent or at least postpone such a doomsday. We can analyze the situation much in the same way we think about investment.

Rates of Extraction

Assume that a firm owns a mineral deposit such as an ore body or oil field and knows approximately how much of the resource can be extracted. Suppose, also, that the firm expects the price of the natural resource to rise. Should the firm extract and sell some of the resource, or should it hold the resource for future sale? For analytical purposes, we will assume the relevant price for decision-making purposes is the sale price of the resource less the cost of extraction. We will also assume that the decision is simply whether or not to extract and not how much to extract. If the firm chooses to produce, we assume for now that the rate of extraction is predetermined.

We can deduce from our discussion in Chapter 4 on the future value of assets that the decision concerning whether or not to produce depends crucially on the rate of interest. If the price is expected to rise at a rate lower than the rate of interest, the firm will produce. Under these conditions the firm could extract the mineral, sell it, then invest the returns at the market rate of interest and gain a larger return than could be realized by letting the deposit appreciate in value. If the firm expects the price of the resource to appreciate at a rate greater than the interest rate, the best course of action is to withhold extraction until the future.

We can condense the decision-making process into a single rule. If P_t is the future price in time period t, then the future price under which the firm would be indifferent between producing and selling now or producing and selling in period t is

$$P_t = P_0 (1 + r)^t,$$

where r is the rate of interest, and P_0 is the present price of the resource. If price in period t is expected to exceed P_t, the firm should withhold production; if not, it should produce and sell.

Now let us examine what we would expect in the economy as a whole. Suppose the economy has a finite amount of a particular resource and this resource is owned by many private firms. Suppose also that the industry has been producing at some particular rate. Now let some firms notice that the economy is rapidly depleting its supply of the resource. These firms would realize that the reduced supply in the future would probably cause future prices to increase more rapidly; let us say at a rate greater than the rate of interest. The firms would, therefore, withhold extraction in present periods in order to shift it to the future when price is expected to be above the break-even price. Expected prices thus change the rate of extraction.

But the decrease in present supply from the decrease in current production would, as we know, drive up current prices relative to future prices. How much would they be driven up? Suppose enough firms withhold production that the current price rises to the point that the future price is less than $P_0(1 + r)^t$; the future expected price does not exceed the value of the present market price invested for t periods. Some firms would then be induced to increase the current rate of extraction. We would expect the adjustment process to continue until the price expected in each future period equals the present price adjusted for interest.

When the price of the resource increases at the same rate as the rate of interest, firms would have no incentive to increase or decrease production. If there is, in fact, a finite amount of the resource, equilibrium requires price to increase at approximately the same rate as the rate of interest. If price is rising less rapidly than the interest rate, firms will increase production now, driving down present prices relative to future prices. If the price is rising more rapidly than the rate of interest, firms will tend to decrease production, driving up present prices relative to future prices. Market forces tend to force prices along an equlibrium path set by market rates of interest.

Certain factors tend to disrupt this equilibrium path. Discoveries of new deposits of the resource lead firms to believe that future prices will be lower than they would have been otherwise. These discoveries lead to increased production and decreased prices. Also, increases in price tend to decrease the quantity demanded as consumers substitute away from the resource that is becoming more and more scarce and into resources with relatively lower prices.

In fact, the problem with this scenario of finite resource supply with prices increasing at the same rate as the rate of interest is that increasing prices lead to the development of products and technologies that can change the adjustment drastically. As we noted, increasing prices will decrease consumption of the resource. But the increased price will also lead to research to discover substitutes; and, if such substitutes are discovered or invented, the demand for the resource will fall (recall our discussion of price-induced technological change). Alternatively, if increased prices lead to new technologies, the supply of the resource can rise. Moreover, while all resources at any given time are, in fact, fixed in supply, the actual known reserves depend on the price of the resource. Take, for example, oil fields that were uneconomical to exploit when the price was $10 a barrel for crude. When prices rose to $30 a barrel, some of these fields became very economical and quite profitable.

A good illustration of these effects is a field in East Central Texas called the Austin Chalk. When most domestic crude was regulated and this oil was selling at around $6 a barrel, no one could produce profitably from the field. The problem was that the Austin Chalk was of such low permeability that, under the available technology, it was unprofitable to drill in the area even though geologists knew oil was there. After price was allowed to increase, drillers developed a new technology that permitted profitable drilling in a previously unprofitable area. What had not been considered reserves a few years ago are now reserves; the Austin Chalk became one of the more productive fields in the country—and a very profitable one at that.

Oil shale gives us another example. There is a considerable amount of oil shale now in the Rocky Mountains, but with present oil prices and present technology, it is not profitable to extract oil from shale. However, firms are working now to improve the technology because, if oil prices increase rapidly, it will be profitable to do so. Thus shale, not now counted as reserves, may well be considered reserves in the future.

Another function of higher resource prices is that they increase the incentive to explore and develop new reserves. Exploration is similar to other inputs into the production process. Firms will carry out exploration to search for new resources as long as the expected marginal gain exceeds the marginal cost. Given a particular probability of success from exploration, the higher the price of the resource, the higher the expected marginal gain and, hence, the more exploration that will be undertaken. The more exploration, the greater will be the reserves.

Principle

If a mineral resource is known to be in finite supply, market forces will ensure that the price of the resource will increase at the same rate as the rate of interest. But the increasing price has two consequences. The higher price will induce firms to develop substitutes for the resource. Second, the higher price will induce more exploration, more production from previously unprofitable deposits, and the development of new technology to lower the cost of extraction.

17.5 EFFECTS OF RISK AND UNCERTAINTY

With the exception of the brief discussion of the effect of inflation on investment because of the resulting uncertainty, we have ignored the effects on investment when risk and uncertainty exist. Until now, our discussion of investment over time has generally assumed economic decision makers know future incomes, prices, and costs. This assumption is very useful for analytical purposes, but for some types of analysis, we need to assume future economic variables can take several possible values. For instance, a particular investment may have several possible income streams because of uncertainty over the way future prices and costs might behave.

Expected Value

To keep things manageable, we assume that decision makers know the probability of an uncertain event occurring. While even this is not always true, it is a useful approximation in understanding the functioning of most markets under uncertainty. Suppose decision makers know the likelihood of some uncertain event occurring. With this information, investors can determine what will happen ''on average'' or what they can ''expect'' to happen if they had to make the same choice involving uncertain events many times. The expected outcome or the expected value is defined as follows:

Definition

If a particular event has several potential numerical outcomes, designated $X_1, X_2, X_3, \ldots, X_n$ and the probability of each outcome is $p_1, p_2, p_3, \ldots, p_n$ where $0 \leqq p_i \leqq 1$ for all i and $\sum_{j=1}^{n} p_j = 1$, the *expected value* of the event is $\sum_{j=1}^{n} p_j X_j$. Thus, the expected value is the sum of the numerical outcomes weighted by the probability of occurrence.

As an example of expected value, consider how much someone would expect to win from a lottery after playing a large number of times. In the lottery, the probability of winning $10,000 is 1 percent; of winning $5,000, 2 percent; and of winning $1,000, 3 percent. Since the probability of winning some amount is 6 percent, the probability of winning nothing is 94 percent. After a large number of draws, a person could expect to win on average the amount V, where

$$V = .01(\$10,000) + .02(\$5,000) + .03(\$1,000) + .94(0) = \$230.$$

People who played many times should be willing to pay up to $230 for the ticket each time they played.[2] This amount is the expected value of the investment.

Risk Effects in Investment

Business decisions are almost always made under uncertainty. A potential investment could have many possible present values, each with a specific probability of occurrence, depending on external circumstances. When considering potential investments, the firm would not make the decision using only one possible stream of income, but would use the expected present value of the possible streams. The variance, or possible dispersion of the present values, will also enter the decision process.

Consider the following two investments with the possible present values given in Table 17–3. Both investments have the same expected present value, $290,000, but the streams are distributed quite differently. For Investment A, there is little variance around the present value—the minimum return possible is $100,000; the maximum, $400,000. In the case of Investment B, $1 million can be made, but the investment could lose $300,000, or possibly make zero profit. One investor might prefer A, while another would prefer B, depending on the risk aversion of the investors. One may prefer the chance to make $1 million, even with the

---

[2] People do, of course, pay more than the expected value of lotteries (such as in the numbers racket) because they attach more weight (attach more utility) to the possible winnings than to the cost of the ticket.

TABLE 17–3

Investments with different variances of returns

Investment A		Investment B	
Probability	*Possible present value*	*Probability*	*Possible present value*
.10............	$100,000	.10	−$300,000
.80............	300,000	.25	0
.10............	400,000	.25	200,000
		.20	500,000
		.15	800,000
		.05	1,000,000
Expected present value	$290,000	Expected present value	$ 290,000

FIGURE 17–4

Income distributions

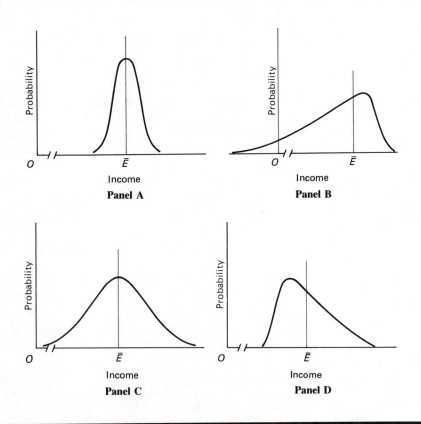

Panel A

Panel B

Panel C

Panel D

greater probability of making nothing or even losing $300,000. Evidence of this type of optimistic behavior is the opening of thousands of small businesses every year, even though the vast majority fail in a year or two. The great success stories, few as they are, encourage the investors.

A few of the many possible distributions of income streams are shown geometrically in Panels A, B, C, and D of Figure 17–4. In each panel, the possible distribution of discounted streams of income from a particular investment is graphed along the horizontal axis. For graphical exposition, we assume that the distribution is continuous. The probability of each stream is plotted along the vertical axis. The expected present value, E, is the same for each investment.

Panel A shows a small symmetrical distribution around the expected value $\overline{E}$. While the investment cannot lead to incomes much above $\overline{E}$, it will not give incomes much below. Panel B shows a distribution that can lead to incomes far below $\overline{E}$, or even losses. Incomes much above $\overline{E}$ are not probable. Panel C indicates a symmetrical distribution around $\overline{E}$. But, in contrast to the distribution in Panel A, incomes much higher and much lower than $\overline{E}$ are possible; that is, the variance is much higher. Finally, the distribution in Panel D is such that incomes much lower than $\overline{E}$ are not too probable, but very high incomes are possible.

Thus, under uncertainty, investors must consider several factors. First, of course, is the expected present value. But they must also consider the variance of the distribution and how the distribution is skewed—i.e., contrast the distributions in Panels B and D. For analytical purposes, the most useful assumption is that investors consider only the expected present value, or that they know the prospective income stream.

17.6 SUMMARY

This chapter has used the concept of present value to develop the theory of investment. We have extended the basic concepts to explore the impact of inflation and uncertainty on the decision to purchase durable inputs. Low rates of inflation will tend not to affect this decision, while uncertainty coupled with risk aversion will tend to decrease investment. To the extent that inflation creates uncertainty about future prices and costs, investment will decline. Finally, we have taken the concept of present value and extended it to the decision producers make about extracting natural resources.

We have generated two basic principles in this chapter.

Principle

Firms would be willing to pay for an investment up to the present value of the stream of income from that investment. An industry's demand for investment is the internal rate of return schedule. Firms invest up to the point where the internal rate of return from the last investment equals the rate of interest.

Principle

If a natural resource is fixed in supply, firms will choose to extract the resource at a rate such that price (that is, selling price less the cost of extraction) rises at the same rate as the rate of interest. If price is expected to rise more rapidly, firms will increase present production, driving down current relative to future prices. The caveat is that resources are generally not fixed in supply. Higher prices lead to new technology, more exploration, and exploitation of reserves that were not previously available.

We cannot overemphasize that few economic choices are made by decision makers knowing with certainty future prices, incomes, and costs. Under uncertainty, consumers and business decision makers are helped by using the concept of expected value. Consumers are concerned with maximizing expected utility, and the variance in possible outcomes will affect the dynamic choices they make. Similarly, investors look at the expected present value of a stream of income from an investment. Variance in earning streams is an important influence on the choice of projects undertaken. A decision maker might make a choice with a lower expected present value over one with higher expectations, depending on the variance.

TECHNICAL PROBLEMS

1. Use the data presented in the application dealing with Argonaut Enterprises to do the following exercises.
   a. Sketch Argonaut's "investment demand function." (Use Figure 17–1 as a guide.)
   b. If it was felt that the relevant interest rate should be 10 percent, what projects would be undertaken? To check your answer, calculate the net present values for the projects, using 10 percent as the interest rate.
   c. The vice president for operations came back to the board of directors with another argument: He believes that the resale value for Project A was underestimated and that the resale value should be $70,000 rather than $50,000. If this is true, should this project be undertaken, using 15 percent as the relevant interest rate? Use the net present value of the project to support your answer.
   d. It turns out that Project B also has a supporter. The director of new product development argues that the capital outlay necessary for Project B is $86,800 rather than $89,200. If this is true, what would be the internal rate of return?
2. An ice cream distributor is thinking about buying another ice cream truck. The price of the truck is $20,000, and it is estimated that the truck will increase profits $4,000 per year for 10 years. Explain how the distributor should decide whether or not to buy the truck.

3. You are hired as an economic consultant to a firm that produces and sells wine. Over a relevant period, the wine gets better as it ages; therefore, the longer it ages, the higher the price the wine maker can get for the wine. Explain precisely the method that you would use in order to advise the wine maker how long to age the wine before putting it on the market. Assume you have all the required technical information.

4. Assume the average price of oil is $30 a barrel and the interest rate is 10 percent. The government wants to stockpile oil in reservoirs (assume they are free). What is the cost of stockpiling this oil over the next 10 years? What if the interest rate is only 4 percent?

5. Explain why the stockpiling cost mentioned in problem 4 is just as real a cost to the government—the taxpayers—as the actual cost of purchasing the oil or of storing the oil if such costs are not zero. Who would benefit and who would lose if this opportunity cost is ignored?

6. If the firm's investment decision is constrained by funding (or credit) limitations, how should it determine what projects to fund? Does your answer conform to the general rule for constrained optimization we set forth in Chapter 4?

7. Suppose you own a deposit of a natural resource, the price of which is $2 a pound (price net of costs). The rate of interest is 12 percent.

FIGURE E.17–1

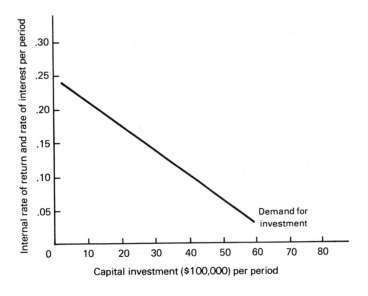

Capital investment ($100,000) per period

What would the price of the resource have to be in five years to make extraction holdbacks economical over this period? Answer the question under the assumption that the interest rate is 5 percent.

8. The current return from an investment is $10,000 per year. The real rate of interest is 5 percent and the rate of inflation is 5 percent. Compare the present value of the return five years from now using the real and the nominal rates of interest. (The return is expected to rise at the same rate as the rate of inflation.) Make the comparison with a 50 percent rate of inflation.

9. A firm can lease a piece of capital equipment for five years at $100,000 a year, or it can purchase the capital now, use it for five years, then sell it at the end of the period for one fourth of the purchase price. If the rate of interest is 10 percent, what is the maximum price of the capital at which it would be economical to purchase rather than lease?

10. Figure E.17–1 shows an industry's demand for investment before taxation. If the interest rate is 10 percent, how much investment will be undertaken? At the same rate of interest, how much will investment decline if a tax of 20 percent is placed on the return to capital? If the interest rate rises to 13 percent and the tax rate increases to 50 percent, what happens to investment?

ANALYTICAL PROBLEMS

1. Nuclear power plants require large capital outlays to build and relatively small amounts of money to operate. During the many years of construction, they are producing no electricity revenues whatsoever. In light of the time lag between money outlays and electricity revenues, explain why long-term interest rates are so important to public utilities in deciding if and when to build such plants. If prices are fixed by regulation, how would you expect inflation to affect the development of power plants?

2. The president of a large chemical firm recently stated that it was more profitable for his firm to pirate the inventions of other companies than it was to engage in original research. How does this behavior affect the value of R&D spending?

3. Use Figure E.17–2 to answer the following questions: investment per period in the U.S. gadget industry is plotted along the horizontal axis. The relevant rate of interest is r_0. Explain what happens to investment in the gadget industry if the following events occur:
    a. The government grants a subsidy to gadget producers.
    b. A high tariff is placed on imported gadgets.
    c. Strict pollution and safety controls are placed on the industry.
    d. The Federal Trade Commission finds that gadgets may be hazardous to your health.

FIGURE E.17–2

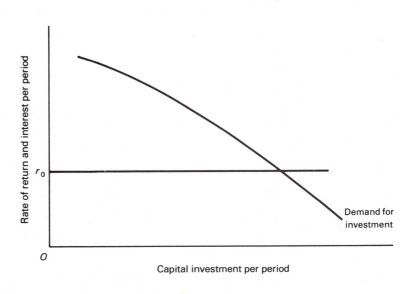

e. Sweeping technological change occurs in the widget industry. (As you know, widgets are a good substitute for gadgets in most uses.)

f. The interest rate falls.

g. The rate of inflation increases.

4. What factors would go into a firm's decision to finance an investment via borrowing or using internal funds?

5. Why would we expect firms that produce capital equipment, e.g., producers of metal-working machines, to lobby Congress for changes in the tax laws asking for more rapid depreciation?

6. At the time we were completing this revision (August 1985), concern about the size of the federal deficit was being voiced by almost everyone. How might a very large federal deficit impact on private investment—investment by firms and individuals?

7. The tools we have developed for the investment decision can also be used in the firm's inventory decision. Why is this so? How would a firm go about deciding on the optimal inventory level?

8. The fact that you are attending a college or university indicates that you have made an investment decision. What kind of investment decision is this? What factors did you (at least implicitly) evaluate when making this decision? In what way would the decision to go to graduate school differ?

PART VII

WELFARE ANALYSIS

- ■ *Welfare and Competition*
- ■ *Exchange Inefficiencies and Welfare*

Chapter 18

Welfare and Competition

18.1 INTRODUCTION

■ In the introduction to this text, we emphasized that economics is the study of choice. Because of scarcity, individuals must choose what goods to consume and decide the allocation of their time. Economics is concerned with the way people make these choices and the results of such behavior. From our theories about consumer behavior we have been able to make predictions and explain the observed behavior of individuals. To study market demand, we combined individual consumers and looked at their behavior as a group. In this way much of our market analysis is based directly on the theory of consumer choice.

Supply theory is also based on the decision-making process of individuals, this time producers. Again, we combine producers into industries or markets, but behavior results primarily from the decisions made by the individual firms, not the group as a whole. One exception we discussed briefly arose when firms combined into groups called cartels and the group as a whole made decisions, or someone made the decision for the group, such as how to distribute production and set price. For the most part, the decisions faced by this combination of firms are the same ones faced by individual producers, and to maximize profits the same decision rules apply.

In the production process, the supply and demand of inputs is also decided by individual decision making. The supply of factors of production results from the choices of separate individuals, as does the demand for inputs by producers. In this context we addressed the behavior of labor through unions, but, as in the case of cartels, we found the choices faced by a union were not much different than those confronted by a single worker. We have stressed and continued to observe that microeconomic theory is basically concerned with the choices of individuals and the economic consequences of these choices.

Economists are, however, concerned with whether or not these individual choices lead to socially desirable outcomes. *Welfare economics* studies how resources should be distributed in order to achieve the maximum well-being of individuals in society. Welfare economics is therefore concerned with what "ought to be" rather than with what "is". To analyze the behavior of economic agents and make predictions is *positive economics;* it deals with what "is". *Normative* or welfare economics focuses on policy changes that will increase the amount of benefit going to members of a community. The recommendations of *welfare* economists are severely limited without their knowing the goals of a community or society. But taking goals as given, the welfare economist seeks the most efficient means of obtaining the desired outcomes. We will see in this chapter that the strongest principles in welfare economics are really conditions necessary for efficiency in production and distribution.

This chapter is only an introduction to the conceptual basis of welfare economics. A thorough study of welfare economics involves one or more courses, frequently at the graduate level, and requires far more rigorous treatment and rather complex mathematical analysis. This chapter is not intended to be analytical in nature but, rather, it should give you a feel for what welfare theory is. We begin with the concepts of social welfare and discuss their limitations. We then analyze the welfare effects of perfect competition. Competitive markets in which consumers maximize utility and producers maximize profits are considered welfare maximizing independent of the distribution of goods and services.

18.2 SOCIAL WELFARE

Groups of people—perhaps society as a whole—are faced with choices much in the way individuals are, and we frequently hear statements that would lead one to believe that a group of people can have a well-defined set of preferences, or a specified indifference map. We even hear statements implying that a nonhuman institution can have preferences.

We read and hear claims such as "The 55 mile-per-hour speed limit is good for the nation," or "Selling grain, arms, or computers to other countries hurts the nation," or "The new tax package will be good for the country." Sports writers have been complaining for years that the repeal of the reserve clause has been bad for baseball and sports in general.

None of these statements, and we are sure you have heard or seen a multitude of assertions similar to these, really makes any sense, outside of a very narrow definition to be discussed below. The problem actually boils down to the fact that populations simply do not have utility maps or preference orderings. Individuals have preference orderings; groups generally do not. Let us analyze why this is the case.

The Concept of Social Welfare

A group's utility function or what is more commonly referred to as a social welfare function is difficult to define or describe. This is largely because preferences within a group encompass so many conflicting interests. In any group, from a nation to a state to a city to a club, a policy or action that benefits one set of people may very well harm another set within the same group. One group in a society may wish to use resources to fight a war, while another wants more spent on highways and schools. Others may want more spent on housing and less on defense. The point is, we cannot say that a particular policy benefits an entire group if some in the group are made better off while others are made worse off. Therefore, we cannot make statements such as those mentioned above. Maybe we prefer a 55-mile-per- hour speed limit because it lowers the highway death toll, while you oppose it because you place a higher value on your time. One person may feel that all pornography must be banned, whereas for other people pornography is their only leisure activity. Many faculty members think the university would be better off with more books and journals in the library at the expense of student study space. Students may think more study space in the library would be better for the university. Who is the university? The faculty, the students, former students, the administration? In fact, could the entire student body ever speak as a unit?

Therefore, because actions taken by groups, or choices made by leaders of those groups, may harm some in the group and help others, we cannot say whether the group is better off or worse off when a certain action is taken. This conclusion comes from the realization that we cannot compare changes in the utility of different people. If you gain 10 hamburgers and someone else loses five six-packs of beer, we can't compare your added utility with another person's loss in utility, because utility is neither mesurable nor comparable. Even in the case of a social decision that takes $1,000 from you and gives it to a poorer person, one cannot say that society's utility increases. No one has ever proven that the marginal utility of income diminishes with increased income. In economics, we do not recognize the concept of a social utility function or group preference ordering.

Any collective decision, whether the action of private producers or consumers acting together or governmental decision makers representing an electorate, that benefits some people at the expense of others cannot be said to benefit or harm society as a whole, since we cannot compare changes in utility.[1] For the reasons given, it is therefore virtually impossi-

---

[1] This statement is not quite accurate but is very close to being so. Say a social action harms one person and benefits another. If the one who is benefited is willing to bribe the one who is harmed sufficiently to compensate for the harm, both can be better off. This entire process is part of the subject matter in more advanced courses.

ble to define social welfare accurately, and in particular, it is impossible to define *maximum* social welfare.

To specify maximum welfare or increases in welfare, we would have to specify a utility function for society as a whole. Certainly a society could vote on all possible organizations and distributions, but even this leads to complications. Consider the following simple hypothetical case. Suppose there are three individuals in a society who will vote on three possible events, A, B, and C. The preference orderings of individuals 1, 2, and 3 are as follows:

1. (ApB) (BpC) (ApC)
2. (BpC) (CpA) (BpA)
3. (CpA) (ApB) (CpB)

In the listing, (ApB) denotes that situation A is preferred to situation B. Note that each individual is rational in the sense that, if A is preferred to B and B to C, then A is preferred to C. If this three-person society voted on events A and B, A would get a majority, as would B if they chose between B and C. But note that society would vote for C over A, and this would be inconsistent with the other two outcomes. If for society as a whole (ApB) and (BpC), then consistency would imply (ApC). But we see that this is not the case; thus society seems to behave irrationally, while individual members maintain well-ordered preferences.

In any case, this simplified example shows that there can be inconsistency in determining social welfare by voting. Moreover, even with consistency in voting, we cannot say that majority rule must specify maximum social welfare. This method would involve interpersonal utility comparisons, and, as you know, economists cannot make such value judgements.

Pareto Optimality

Many, if not most, problems in public decisions, such as those discussed above, involve economic choices; so surely economists must be able to say *something* about them. Actually they can say very little. Economists cannot establish the goals of a society, nor can they say what is "good" for one person or for a collection of people. In general, economists can only address the issue of efficiency when individuals are aggregated and goals have been established. Efficiency within groups reduces to one prescriptive statement: If a change can be made such that one or more people are made better off and *none* worse off, the society's welfare will be increased if the change is made. "Better off" in this statement has a precise meaning.

Definition

A person is said to be better off in situation A than in situation B if he or she moves to a higher indifference curve.

This assertion is known as the condition of *Pareto optimality*. Whenever it is possible to increase the utility of one member of a group without hurting anyone else in the organization Pareto optimality *does not exist*. Such changes are considered *Pareto superior*. It is when the distribution of goods and services within the group can be rearranged only by harming someone that Pareto optimality is finally achieved. To summarize:

Definition
A social organization is said to be Pareto optimal if there is no change that will benefit some people without making some others worse off. Changes that benefit one or more people in a group while leaving everyone else indifferent are Pareto superior moves.

This is admittedly a very weak concept in social welfare economics. To illustrate, suppose a new transcontinental highway is to be constructed. This will benefit millions of travelers. But it also forces the government to condemn (under the right of eminent domain) the homes of a few families. These families, of course, are paid a "fair market price" for their property. However, some of the families may be unwilling to sell for a fair market price; yet they must by law, and as a consequence are made worse off. Millions may benefit and one may be harmed. Economists as economists can therefore not say that the new highway increases or decreases social welfare. For this reason, economists are primarily interested in Pareto optimality because it expresses efficiency, and not because it serves as a social goal. The condition of Pareto optimality is the major component of what economists call welfare economics.

To summarize the implications of the concept of Pareto optimality:

Principle
(a) If a change will benefit one or more people without making *anyone* worse off, the change is socially desirable; (b) is a change helps some and hurts others—the *numbers* are immaterial—no conclusion can be reached.

Consumer's Surplus and Pareto Efficiency

When economists analyze the effects of policy changes—for example, in cost-benefit analysis—they frequently find it impossible to use the Pareto rule. Unless consumers have identical preference patterns, in general, some benefit and some lose with any kind of social change. A much stronger tool in welfare analysis, and one that we have already introduced, is the concept of consumer's surplus. Recall that it is defined as the difference between what a consumer is willing to pay for each unit purchased and the actual market price. Graphically it is represented by the area between the demand curve and price. In the market if this area goes up for any sort of policy change, the change is considered beneficial to consumers as a group; if the area goes down the change is harmful to them. We know from Chapter 3 that producer's surplus can be used in the same way to judge the impact of a market change on producers as a group.

The use of consumer's and producer's surplus goes beyond the definition of Pareto optimality by looking at the *net gain* to consumers or producers from a change. Even though some consumers and producers might lose from a price increase, for example, if on balance there is a gain in total sum of consumer's and producer's surplus, the move is beneficial.

Let us be more specific and focus on consumer's surplus to see how surplus analysis violates the conditions of Pareto optimality. Suppose a certain commodity has an effective price ceiling; i.e., price is set below

FIGURE 18-1   **Welfare consequences of a price ceiling and floor**

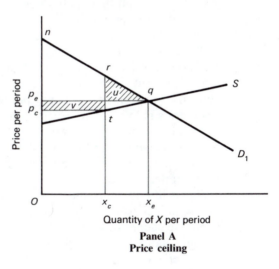

Panel A
Price ceiling

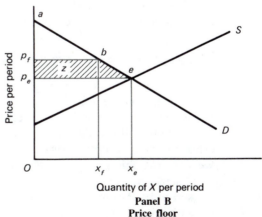

Panel B
Price floor

the equilibrium market price. Panel A in Figure 18–1 illustrates the situation. With a price ceiling at p_c, consumer's surplus is $p_c nrt$. If prices were allowed to rise to the equilibrium price p_e, surplus would be $p_e nq$. Consumer's surplus would increase when prices rose if area u were greater than area v, and fall if area u were less than area v.

The reason we cannot use the concept of Pareto optimality to analyze the results of eliminating the ceiling is because the ceiling causes shortages. Some consumers get the product at p_c; others who want to purchase it at this price do not. If the ceiling is eliminated, those who got the product at p_c would be hurt, while those who could not buy it would be helped. On balance, it is impossible to use the Pareto criterion to say whether welfare rises if the ceiling is removed. Economists, however, frequently do compare areas u and v for the market demand curve, knowing full well that such a comparison is inconsistent with the definition of Pareto optimality.

The use of consumer's surplus is not always at odds with the definition of Pareto optimality, however. For instance, in Panel B of Figure 18–1, we show a price floor at p_f. Consumer's surplus is the area $p_f ab$ when prices are kept at p_f. If the floor is eliminated, price would fall to p_e, and consumer's surplus would be $p_e ae$. Surplus rises by area z. In this case, since price is lowered for every consumer, everyone who buys the product can buy more at the lower price. Because no consumer is harmed, the price decrease is also beneficial to consumers by the Pareto criterion.

Of course, in each diagram we have ignored whether producers are made better or worse off by the policy change. In Panel A, when the ceiling is lifted, all producers are unambiguously helped. All can sell their output at higher prices and sell more on average. In Panel B, on the other hand, we cannot be certain of the effect of relaxing the price floor. Sellers produce more, but now prices are lower. Thus, the use of consumer's and producer's surplus requires great care at the market level. When surplus changes, some gain and some lose—we cannot determine whether welfare increases in the Pareto sense.

18.3 PARETO OPTIMALITY IN CONSUMPTION AND PRODUCTION

While the concept of Pareto optimality is a weak one, it does establish some useful guidelines necessary for the maximization of welfare in society. Pareto optimality is an efficiency condition and a move toward Pareto optimality, a Pareto superior change, is simply a move to a more efficient allocation of goods and services. If an action is Pareto superior, we can unambiguously say that a group is made better off. We must emphasize, however, that an infinite number of resource allocations can be said to be Pareto optimal, in the sense that no one can be made better off without making someone else worse off. None of these allocations can be said to maximize social utility or be socially preferable to other Pareto optimal distributions. In this section, we want to discuss how economists apply the notion of Pareto optimality to market efficiency. We introduce the Edgeworth Box diagram, and then discuss the conditions necessary for Pareto optimality between two consumers and two producers in a market setting.

The Gains from Exchange

Markets exist in an economy because individuals have different marginal rates of substitution between goods. Let us consider the following example. Two people consume only two goods, an endowment of which they receive every week. These goods are X and Y. Given preferences and the endowment to each person, the marginal rate of substitution for one person, say person A, is three X for eight Y or $MRS^A_{x\ for\ y} = 8/3$. That is, the individual would be willing to exchange three units of X for eight units of Y and remain on the same indifference curve. Figure 18–2, Panel A, pictures the marginal rate of substitution for person A. At point G on the indifference curve, this consumer is willing to substitute at the rate of $8Y$ for $3X$. This ratio, in essence, reflects an exchange rate between X and Y. As far as individual A is concerned $8Y = 3X$. The second person, person B, has a different marginal rate of substitution. Suppose person B would exchange three X for six Y. He or she has an indifference curve

FIGURE 18–2   **The marginal rate of substitution for two consumers**

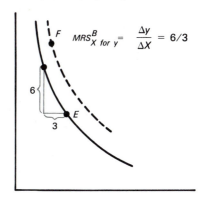

An indifference map for person A

$MRS^A_{X\ for\ y} = \dfrac{\Delta y}{\Delta X} = 8/3$

Quantity of Y per period

Quantity of X per period

Panel A

An indifference map for person B

$MRS^B_{X\ for\ y} = \dfrac{\Delta y}{\Delta X} = 6/3$

Quantity of Y per period

Quantity of X per period

Panel B

slope such that the $MRS^B_{x\,for\,y} = 6/3$. As shown in Panel B of Figure 18–2, this indifference curve at point E is not as steep as it is for Person A. At point E on person B's indifference curve he or she will substitute as little as $6Y$ for $3X$. Person B's exchange rate is therefore $6Y = 3X$.

Both of these people can benefit from trading. One views $8Y$ equivalent to $3X$, while the other thinks $6Y$ is the same as having $3X$. To start trading, person B could offer person A three units of X and get $8Y$ back. Person A would not be harmed and B would be put on a higher indifference curve, since he or she would have accepted as few as six units of Y. In this trade person B offers $3X$ and gets back $8Y$ from person A who is left indifferent. Person B gets two more units of Y than would have been acceptable, and so is put on a higher indifference curve in the exchange. In Figure 18–2, we can trace through the effect of this trade on the indifference map for the two consumers. Person A receives three more X and gives up eight units of Y; A moves from point G to H and is left indifferent by the exchange. Person B gives up $3X$ and receives $8Y$, and therefore moves to point F in the map and is put on a higher indifference curve. Notice that the trade put A on a flatter part of the indifference curve, while B goes to a steeper segment of a new curve. The trade has lowered the MRS for A and raised it for B. Continued trading would eventually make the MRS for each consumer equal.

Suppose person A returned seven, instead of eight, units of Y to person B in the exchange? Now both people would benefit from the trade and each would go to a higher indifference curve. Even if person A went as low as six units of Y in the trade, person B would still make the exchange. At these rates ($3X = 6Y$), person B is left indifferent, while person A is benefited. As long as person A returns between six and eight units of Y in exchange for three units of X both individuals benefit from trade.

Any voluntary trade however will always be in the same direction. Person A receives units of X while person B receives units of Y. The direction of trading will tend to equalize the marginal rates of substitution between the two traders. Because A is moving down an indifference curve, A's MRS gets flatter. Since B is moving up an indifference curve, B's MRS is getting steeper. The two consumers will continue to trade until their respective marginal rates of substitution are equal. It is only when the $MRS^A_{x\,for\,y} = MRS^B_{x\,for\,y}$ that a trade that helps one or both consumers without hurting one of them cannot be arranged. It is at this point that Pareto optimality is achieved between the two traders. In short, any trade that moves the individuals toward equal MRS's is considered a *Pareto superior* exchange.

What we have done in this description of trading is place the whole notion of market exchange in a slightly more abstract context. Person A or B could be a firm and one of the goods traded could be money. For example, McDonald's is willing to exchange hamburgers of a particular type for \$1.50 each. If you are willing to trade more than \$1.50 for a McDonald's hamburger, both you and McDonald's are made better off by the trade. The same analysis can be applied to any other type of exchange. Markets arise whenever the marginal rates of substitution are not equal. In fact, this is a major principle in economics.

Principle

If two individuals have differing marginal rates of substitution, both can be made better off in the sense of attaining a more preferred level of consumption by exchange. Only when the marginal rates of substitution are equal is Pareto optimality achieved.

The Edgeworth Box

Economists frequently use a graphical method to analyze this principle, from which a certain amount of insight into the benefits of exchange can be gained. We continue to assume only two people and only two goods. Each person has an *initial endowment* of each good, but each does not necessarily have the goods in the proportion that yields greatest satisfaction. To analyze the potential gains from exchange we use a graphical device known as the Edgeworth Box diagram, named for F. Y. Edgeworth, a famous British economist of the late 19th century.[2]

First, consider Figure 18–3. There are two consumption goods, X and $Y;$ these goods are available in absolutely fixed amounts. In addition, there are only two individuals in the society, A and $B;$ they initially possess an endowment of X and $Y,$ but the endowment ratio is not the one either would choose if allowed to specify it. This problem is graphically illustrated by constructing an *origin* for $A,$ labeled $O_A,$ and plotting quantities of the two goods person A possesses along the vertical and horizontal axes as shown. Thus, from the origin $O_A,$ the quantity of X held by A (X_A) is plotted on the horizontal axis and the quantity of Y (Y_A) on the vertical axis. A similar graph for $B,$ with origin $O_B,$ may be constructed beside the graph for $A.$ These two basic graphs are illustrated in Panel A, Figure 18–3.

Next, rotate the graph for the B individual 180 degrees to the left, so that it is actually "upside down" when viewed normally, as shown in Panel B. The Edgeworth Box diagram is then formed by bringing the two graphs together. The length of the X axis is the sum $X_A + X_B,$ while the vertical length of the Y axis is the sum $Y_A + Y_B.$ The two graphs will form

---

[2] It has been pointed out to us by a reader of the manuscript, Professor Rodney Mabry, that Edgeworth had nothing to do with the development of the Edgeworth Box diagram; the true originator was V. Pareto. Not being historians, we gratefully acknowledge this but yield to convention in naming the diagram.

FIGURE 18–3   **Constructing the Edgeworth Box diagram**

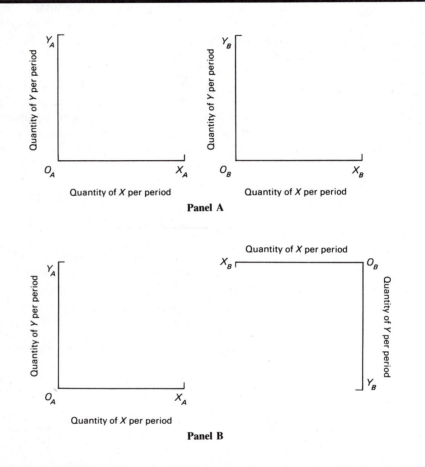

Panel A

Panel B

a ''box'' with a length and height equivalent to the sum of the endow-ments going to both individuals. Figure 18–4 illustrates the Edgeworth Box.

Point D in Figure 18–4 accounts for the total endowment of X and Y possessed by A and B. Person A begins with x_A units of X and y_A units of Y. Since the aggregates are fixed, individual B must originally hold $x_B = X - x_A$ units of X and $y_B = Y - y_A$ units of Y.

Every point in the Edgeworth Box completely describes the distribu-tion of X and Y. Whatever person A does not have of the total, person B holds. The closer point D is moved toward O_A, the more X and Y person B

FIGURE 18–4 **Edgeworth Box diagram**

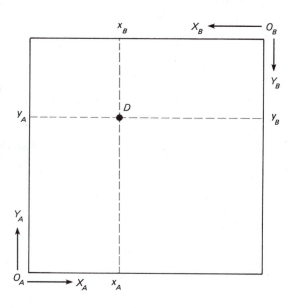

possesses. Moving D toward O_B tells us person A has more of the total endowments.

Equilibrium of Exchange

As a first step toward equilibrium analysis and the determination of Pareto optimality between these individuals, consider an economy in which the exchange of the two goods takes place. If you like, you may think of the problem in the following context. There exists a small country with only two inhabitants, A and B, each of whom owns one half the land area. A and B produce nothing; they merely gather the foods X and Y that grow wild on the land. Each gathers only the food that falls on his or her land; but the two types do not fall uniformly. There is a relatively heavy concentration of Y on A's property and a relatively heavy concentration of X on B's land.

The problem of exchange is analyzed by means of the Edgeworth Box diagram in Figure 18–5. The dimensions of this basic box diagram now represent the scattering of foods, and we have added indifference curves for A and B. The curve I_A shows combinations of X and Y that yield A the same level of satisfaction. As usual, II_A represents a greater level of

FIGURE 18–5   **General equilibrium of exchange**

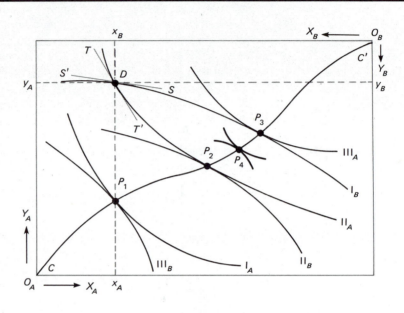

satisfaction than I_A; III_A is preferred to II_A; and so on. In general, A's well-being is enhanced by moving toward the B origin; B, in turn, enjoys greater satisfaction moving closer to the A origin.

Suppose the initial endowment is given by point D; A has x_A units of X and y_A units of Y. Similarly, B has x_B and y_B units of X and Y, respectively. The initial endowment places A on indifference curve II_A and B on curve I_B. At point D, A's marginal rate of substitution of X for Y, given by the slope TT', is relatively high; A would be willing to sacrifice, say, three units of Y in order to obtain one additional unit of X. At the same point, B has a relatively low marginal rate of substitution, as shown by the slope of SS'. Or, turning it around, B has a relatively high marginal rate of substitution of Y for X. Person B may, for example, be willing to forego four units of X to obtain one unit of Y.

A situation such as this will always lead to exchange if the parties concerned are free to trade. From point D, A will trade some Y to B, receiving X in exchange. The exact bargain reached by the two traders cannot be determined. If B is the more skillful negotiator, B may induce A to move along II_A to point P_2. All the benefits of trade go to B, who jumps from I_B to II_B. Or A might steer the bargain to point P_3, thereby increasing satisfaction from II_A to III_A, B's utility level remaining at I_B. Starting from point *D,* the ultimate exchange is very likely to lead to some point between P_2 and P_3, perhaps at a point such as P_4, at which two indifference curves, representing higher levels of utility for each, are tangent. Both are therefore made better off by trade. But the skill of the bargainers and their initial endowments determine the exact equilibrium point. Between points P_2 and P_3 one individual has been made better off without causing the other to become worse off, or both become better off in the sense of attaining a higher level of utility.

In the Edgeworth Box, exchange will continue to take place until the marginal rate of substitution of X for Y is the same for both traders. If the two marginal rates are different, one or both parties can benefit from exchange; neither party need lose. The exchange equilibrium can occur only at points such as P_1, P_2, P_3, or P_4 in Figure 18–5. The locus CC', called the *contract curve in exchange,* is a curve joining all points of tangency between one of A's indifference curves and one of B's. It is the locus along which the marginal rates of substitution are equal for both traders. We accordingly have the following principle:

Principle
The general equilibrium of exchange occurs at a point where the marginal rate of substitution between every pair of goods is the same for all parties consuming both goods. The exchange equilibrium is not unique; it may occur at any point along the contract curve.

The contract curve represents all the possible Pareto optimal distributions between persons A and B in the sense that, if the trading parties are located at some point not on the curve, one or both can benefit by exchanging goods so as to move to a point on the curve. To be sure, some points not on the curve are more preferable to *one or the other* party than are some points on the curve. But, for any point not on the curve, one or more attainable points on the curve are preferable to *both* parties. The chief characteristic of each point on the contract curve is that a movement along the curve away from the point must benefit one party and harm the other. Every distribution of X and Y that leads to a point on the contract curve is said to be a *Pareto-optimal distribution.*

Principle
A Pareto-optimal distribution is one in which any change that makes some people better off makes others worse off. Thus, every point on the contract curve is Pareto optimal, and the contract curve is a locus of Pareto optimal points.

To summarize, the economics behind all of the graphical analysis simply says that people will trade only if the trade makes the participants better off. If each person's *MRS* is the same it is impossible to make both parties better off through trade.

APPLICATION

Uses of the Theory of Trade: Goods-In-Kind and Water Rationing

We can use the Edgeworth Box to analyze the economics of a charity that gives people goods-in-kind instead of money. Take food stamps, for instance. Instead of money, the government gives poor people stamps that can be used to purchase a limited amount but wide range of foods. The stamps effectively lower the price of food to the purchaser.

Whenever individuals pay different prices for a commodity, there is motivation for exchange. Each consumer maximizes utility given the prices paid. Suppose the price of food is p_x and the price of another good is p_y. Each consumer maximizes utility by setting the $MRS_{x\ for\ y} = p_x/p_y$. If consumer A pays a lower price for food because he or she receives food stamps, then $MRS^A_{x\ for\ y} < MRS^B_{x\ for\ y}$, where $MRS^B_{x\ for\ y}$ is the marginal rate of substitution for a consumer B who does not get food stamps. Consumer A would be willing to trade food or food stamps to consumer B for good Y. Both individuals can be made better off by trade, in the sense of being able to reach higher indifference curves. Thus, trade will take place unless it is prohibited by law; and trading food stamps is against the law.

Why aren't food stamps legally traded? Some say that "poor people will sell the stamps and then purchase unnecessary items—beer for instance. If the people are being supported by the taxpayers, they shouldn't buy things that are not good for them. Financial support should go to the purchase of necessary goods and services." But what is necessary? What is unnecessary? An economist would argue that the utility of the food stamp recipient would rise if the stamps could be traded. Trading would increase efficiency in the market and move them toward Pareto optimality. There is a weakness in this, however. The benefactors of the charity may suffer a decrease in utility when they see their gift "wasted". Hence giving income instead of stamps, or allowing stamps to be traded, may not be Pareto efficient.

Another important issue that arises when trading is legally prohibited, is the probable trading of stamps in illegal, or underground, markets. Since the transaction is illegal, food stamps will go at a lower money price in these markets. The stamp sellers may then pay for their beer this way. The individual may give up more food to buy unnecessary items than would have been the case if the stamps were legally traded.

Another application of the Edgeworth Box diagram is the analysis of water rationing. During the winter of 1976–77, a serious drought occurred in the Western United States, causing considerable decreases in the water supplies of many communities. Many of them were rationing water on a daily basis during these years. In his *Newsweek* column of March 21, 1977, the famous economist, Milton Friedman, discussed the rationing plan of one such community, Marin County, California, a prosperous area north of San Francisco.

In response to the drought, Marin County rationed water to 37 gallons per person per day for a household of four. Very stiff fines were imposed for exceeding this level. Furthermore, one household could not legally sell part of its water allocation to another household. No household would have the incentive to sacrifice or cut down on their allocation of 37 gallons.

We can analyze the situation with an Edgeworth Box diagram in Figure 18–6. Let A and B be any two individuals. The origins for A and B are at O_A and O_B. Income is measured on the horizontal axis and water is measured along the vertical axis. The income of A is I_A; B's income is I_B as shown at the top of the Box. Each receives exactly the same amount of water; $W_A = W_B$. Given income, this puts the consumers at point R in the figure. The contract curve is $O_A O_B$, showing the locus of tangent points between A's and B's indifference curves.

If trade were allowed, both individuals could be made better off than they are at point R. Their consumption sets would move to some point on the contract curve between points Z and C. The only circumstances under which trade would not benefit both would be if the incomes of each were precisely such that point D, where the contract curve crosses $W_A W_B$, was the original allocation. Income and water at D are distributed in such a way

FIGURE 18–6   Trade in water

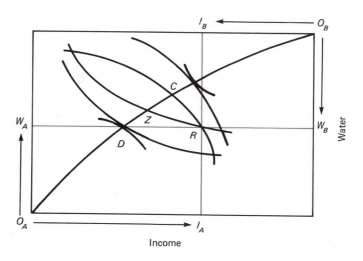

to put the individuals on the contract curve without trading. This would appear to be a rather remote possibility. Otherwise trade would be preferable.

Equilibrium of Production

The analysis of equilibrium and Pareto optimality in production is quite similar to that of exchange. We can model production in the same way we did trade between two consumers. Suppose we have two firms producing two commodities with two inputs. We label the firms X and Y, and the two inputs, K and L, as shown in Figure 18–7.

We form an Edgeworth Box diagram similar to the diagram used to analyze consumer exchange. The X firm has the origin of its isoquant map at O_X; a portion of the map is shown by isoquants I_X, II_X, III_X, and IV_X. The firm producing Y has the "turned around" isoquant map. The origin is at O_Y. The isoquants are shown by I_Y, II_Y, III_Y, and IV_Y, and so forth. The total amounts of labor and capital available to the two firms are,

FIGURE 18–7   **Pareto optimality in production**

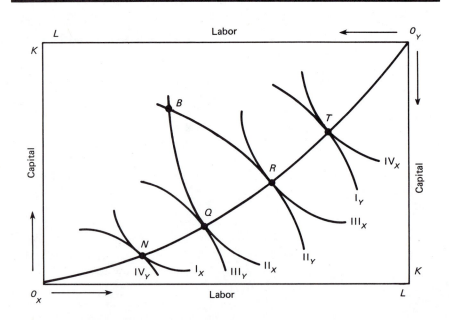

respectively, $O_Y L = O_X L$ and $O_Y K = O_X K$; i.e., labor is plotted along the horizontal axis and capital along the vertical.

Pareto optimality and equilibrium of production occurs at any combination of outputs where the marginal rates of technical substitution between labor and capital are equal for the two firms. This means the isoquants must be tangent so that $MRTS_X = MRTS_Y$. To see why, suppose capital and labor are allocated between the two firms so that production takes place at point B. Firm X is producing the output given by II_X and firm Y, the output given by II_Y. A reallocation of capital and labor between the two firms could move the production point to R—increased output for X with no decrease for Y—or to Q—increased output for Y with no decrease for X. Or both firms could increase output by moving to some combination between II_X and II_Y, say to a point along the line QR. At any point at which the isoquants are not tangent, capital and labor can be reallocated so that one firm can increase its output without reducing the output of the other, or both can increase output.

The locus of points at which the isoquants are tangent is called the *contract curve in production*. If the firms are at a point on the contract curve, one firm can increase production only at the expense of a decrease in production for the other firm. To see this, assume that production takes place at a point such as Q. Next, move in any direction to a point either on or off the contract curve, and note that the output of one firm must fall while the output of the other must rise, or remain constant if the movement is along an isoquant.

It is obvious that the production equilibrium is not unique; it can occur at an infinite number of combinations on the contract curve. But each point on this curve represents a Pareto-optimal equilibrium. Production along the contract curve means that all resources are being used and society is producing on its production-possibilities frontier. As you will recall, the production-possibilities frontier shows the opportunity cost of producing more of some good; that is, the rate at which some goods must be given up in order for society to have more of some other goods.

We can easily derive the production-possibilities frontier from the contract curve in Figure 18–7. Corresponding to each point on the production contract curve is a specific level of output of good X and good Y. For example, at point N in Figure 18–7, firm X is producing the amount represented by isoquant I_X. The production of Y is represented by isoquant IV_Y. A relatively large amount of labor and capital is used in the production of Y. These respective amounts of goods X and Y represent a point on the production-possibilities frontier. We call this point N' in Figure 18–8. As we move to higher isoquants in the production of X, less Y is produced. The isoquants tangent at Q, R, and T represent additional points on the production-possibilities frontier. They are labeled Q', R', and T' in Figure 18–8. Society can choose any point on the frontier, all of which represent efficient production levels.

FIGURE 18-8   **Derivation of production possibilities**

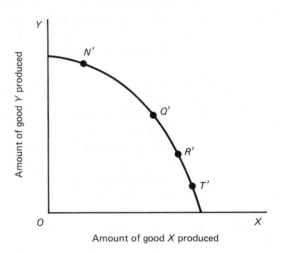

Amount of good X produced

18.4 GENERAL EQUILIBRIUM AND PERFECT COMPETITION

We have described the equilibrium conditions between two consumers and two producers. When consumers maximize utility and are able to trade between themselves they reach an equilibrium that we know is also Pareto optimal. On the contract curve in exchange the marginal rate of substitution for both consumers is equal. A very similar result was discovered for producers. Here optimization led two producers in the Edgeworth Box to operate where their respective *MRTS*'s are the same. If these slopes were different, it would be possible to increase the production of one or both outputs, holding the amounts of inputs fixed. We have observed, in short, that Pareto optimality is really not a condition of welfare as much as it is one of efficiency.

Having described the conditions of efficiency among consumers and these conditions for producers, we now look at efficiency across these two economic groups. Pareto optimality across producers and consumers is referred to as the *general equilibrium* condition.

Pareto Optimality across Consumers and Producers

The *problem* of general equilibrium is as follows: can we find a set of prices at which the demands of consumers are voluntarily fulfilled by the supplies of producers who use all productive resources that are voluntarily supplied at the going set of prices? If so, an efficient general equilibrium exists.

We could provide a fanciful example in which an auctioneer assembles all participants in the economy and "zeros in" on a set of prices in which all markets are in equilibrium. But this process is not even approximately descriptive of any real-world markets. However, competitive bids and counterbids in all markets do tend to push the economy *toward* an efficient general equilibrium. Needless to say, such an equilibrium is never, in fact, even approximately attained. There is a *tendency* toward it; and, it is often useful to analyze the situation that would exist if markets were in general equilibrium.

General equilibrium occurs when we have equilibrium in both exchange and production. We can effectively combine the Edgeworth Boxes for production and exchange by placing the exchange box inside the production-possibilities frontier, which is derived from the production contract curve. Each point on the frontier is a point on the production contract curve. It determines what is available for exchange in our two-producer, two-consumer model. As Figure 18–9 shows, a tangent to the selected point on the frontier is the slope of the production-possibilities frontier. It is called the *marginal rate of transformation*. Hence, the slope of the tangent at E represents the opportunity cost of producing another unit of X. More exactly, if $\Delta X = 1$, the slope $\Delta Y / \Delta X = \Delta Y$ is precisely

FIGURE 18–9   **General equilibrium in production and exchange**

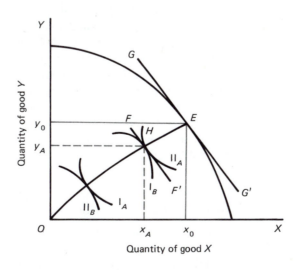

how much of good *Y* society must forego to have another unit of *X*. Production at *E* is Pareto optimal.

Optimality in exchange comes from letting consumers *A* and *B* distribute the x_0 and y_0 output. Pareto efficiency, as we already know, exists along the exchange contract line. Let the Edgeworth Box for exchange be Oy_0Ex_0, with x_0 and y_0 being, from the production-possibilities frontier, the total amounts of *X* and *Y* available. The origin for the consumer with indifference map I_A and II_A is at zero; the consumer with indifference map I_B, II_B has the origin at *E*. Clearly, there are an infinite number of possible allocations along the contract curve. But general equilibrium occurs when the marginal rate of transformation *(MRT)*—the slope of the production-possibilities frontier—is equal to the marginal rate of substitution for both consumers. Because we drop the negative sign on the slope of the *MRS*, we do so also for the *MRT*.

In Figure 18–9, general equilibrium exists at a point like *H*. It is here that the slope of the tangent lines *FF'* and *GG'* are equal. Consumer *A* gets x_A and y_A units of output; consumer *B* gets $(x_0 - x_A)$ and $(y_0 - y_A)$ units. The amount of labor and capital used in production at *E* is found by going back to the point on the production contract curve. Of course, there could be other, perhaps many other, points on the contract curve where the slopes of the indifference curves are equal to the slope of *GG'*. The consumers will settle at such a point, and if there are several such points, the one chosen will depend on the distribution of the two goods.

Why must $MRS_A = MRS_B = MRT$ in general equilibrium? First, we know that if MRS_A is not equal to MRS_B, individuals *A* and *B* could trade and increase the utility of at least one person without decreasing the utility of the other. So, whatever the output, MRS_A must equal MRS_B. Next, suppose MRS_A (or MRS_B) does not equal the *MRT*. For example, let the *MRS* for either consumer be two and the MRT be three. Consumers are willing to take two more units of *Y* for one unit of *X*, while producers can produce three more units of *Y* if they produce one less unit of *X*. It would be possible for the producers to make three more *Y*, give two to consumer *A* (or *B*) for the *X* lost to produce the extra *Y*, and have one unit of *Y* left. The extra unit of *Y* could be given to either person *A* or *B* to increase utility. Thus, welfare rises by the Pareto rule. Welfare can be improved as long as the absolute value of the slope of the production-possibilities curve is not equal to the common marginal rate of substitution in exchange.

Equilibrium in Perfect Competition

We now assume that there is perfect competition in every market, and show that the set of input and output prices that exist will, in general, establish a Pareto-optimal organization for society. Thus, perfect competition is a sufficient condition for the general equilibrium described above.

Let us first consider consumers. If there is perfect competition, all consumers face the same set of commodity prices. Since all consuming units set their *MRS* equal to the price ratio, the *MRS* of any one consumer is equal to the *MRS* of *any other* consuming unit. Since all consumers are just willing to exchange commodities in the same ratio, it is impossible to make one better off without making another worse off. Thus, a Pareto optimum is established among buyers.

Next, consider producers. In maximizing profit, entrepreneurs necessarily arrange the combination of inputs so as to minimize the total cost of production. Under perfect competition, the factor-price ratios are the same to all producers. Since each producer equates *MRTS* to the common factor-price ratio, the *MRTS* is the same for all. Consequently, there is no reallocation of inputs that would increase one producer's output without reducing another's. Again we have a Pareto-optimal outcome.

For general equilibrium, the slope of the production-possibility frontier, or the marginal rate of transformation, represents the opportunity cost of producing another unit of either good. In other words, the opportunity cost of another unit of X is ΔY and the opportunity cost of one more unit of Y is ΔX. Thus the ratio

$$\frac{\Delta Y}{\Delta X} = \frac{\text{opportunity cost of } X}{\text{opportunity cost of } Y}.$$

When perfectly competitive firms maximize profits, they set the marginal cost of producing the good equal to its market price. Assuming that the marginal cost paid by the firm truly reflects the opportunity cost of the resources necessary to produce the last unit of output, we may write

$$\frac{\Delta Y}{\Delta X} = \frac{MC_x}{MC_y} = \frac{P_x}{P_y},$$

where the ratio on the far left is the slope of the production-possibility frontier. This equation tells us that when there is perfect competition, the slope of the production-possibility frontier is equal to the ratio of marginal costs, which in turn equals the ratio of product prices. The second equality between the marginal cost ratio and the price ratio comes from profit maximization.

Since we know that when consumers maximize utility they equate their

$$MRS_{x \, for \, y} = \frac{P_x}{P_y},$$

the marginal rate of transformation must therefore be equal to the marginal rate of substitution because both are equal to the ratio of market prices.

Finally, in this competitive general equilibrium, the number of hours of work voluntarily offered is exactly equal to the number of hours voluntarily demanded. An increase in wages would help some people, but some others would be unemployed. That is, an increase in wages would make some better off, some worse off. A decrease in wages would cause an excess demand. A change in wages from the general equilibrium level will upset both Pareto optimality and general equilibrium.

Let us reemphasize that Pareto optimality does not necessarily indicate maximum attainable welfare or the maximum attainable level of utility for society as a whole. As we stressed in this chapter, to specify maximum welfare, we would have to specify a welfare function for society as a whole. This we cannot do. Perfect competition does lead to *some* final Pareto-optimal equilibrium point, but this is an arbitrary point because any other point on the production-possibilities frontier can also be Pareto optimal in the sense of being efficient. The actual point attained depends on (among other things) the initial "starting point," or the initial distribution of income.

Government may (and generally does) become involved in deciding what the initial distribution of income will be. But, while representatives may decide that the existing income distribution is preferable to any other, or that some other distribution is more preferred, the role of an economist is not to decide what distribution is best, even under perfect competition. An economist's role does include pointing out the economic consequences of changing the distribution. All an economist can say is that, if one or more people can be made better off by an action without anyone else being made worse off, the action makes the group better off.

18.5 SUMMARY

The maximization of community utility or welfare, as we have called it in this chapter, presents difficult conceptual problems. There is no such thing as an aggregate utility function because indifference curves cannot be added across individuals. Indeed any measure of group benefit runs into the problem of interpersonal utility comparison.

Economists have made their greatest contribution to the field of welfare economics through the condition of Pareto optimality. This rule really describes efficient distribution of a scarce resource or product. Pareto optimality exists whenever it is impossible to help someone without hurting another person in the market. This definition led to the Pareto criteria by which economists judge a redistribution of goods:

Principle
(a) If a change will benefit one or more people without making anyone worse off, the change is socially desirable; (b) if a change helps some and hurts others—the numbers are immaterial—no conclusion can be reached by an economist.

In markets, Pareto optimality exists when consumers have the same marginal rates of substitution, and producers similarly have the same marginal rates of technical substitution. These properties were illustrated through the use of Edgeworth Box diagrams. Along the contract curve in an Edgeworth Box it is impossible to improve the welfare of one economic agent without decreasing utility or production of the other. Therefore, all points along the contract curve are Pareto optimal. In markets where economic agents can freely trade, a point on the contract curve is reached; this point depends on the initial distribution of the items traded and to some extent on the bargaining acumen of traders.

General equilibrium exhibits the condition of Pareto optimality between producers and consumers. Markets are efficient, first, if producers operate on their production-possibility frontier, and, second, if the slope of this frontier, or marginal rate of transformation, is the same as the common *MRS* at which consumers trade. General equilibrium is not a unique condition in an economy. There may indeed be many points on the production frontier that satisfy this rule.

Finally and importantly, perfect competition by means of the price mechanism leads to a Pareto-optimal allocation of resources. Again, this allocation is optimal in the sense that it is efficient. This happens when consumers maximize utility facing the same market prices and producers maximize profit when faced with common input prices and set marginal cost equal to the product price they observe in the market. A function of microeconomic theory is to determine the relative efficiency of various types of market organization. The major conclusion of this chapter is that competition can be efficient.

TECHNICAL PROBLEMS

1. Explain why equality of marginal rates of substitution between any two goods for any pair of consumers implies that no consumer can be made better off without making some other consumer worse off. Why does perfect competition guarantee this result?

2. Assume two firms, each using capital and labor to produce two goods. The marginal rates of technical substitution between capital and labor are the same for each firm. *Total* capital and labor are fixed in amount. Explain why one firm cannot increase output without causing the other to decrease output.

3. Explain why there can generally be no social welfare function or social preference ordering.

4. Decide on the Pareto optimal or superior numbers in each of the following situations:

    a. Bill Dance loves bass fishing. It does not matter to him whether or not he catches anything; the important thing is getting out. The more trips, the happier is Bill. Mrs. Dance hates bass. The fewer fish brought home, the happier is Mrs. Dance. On his last outing, Bill caught eight fish. Which sizes of catch (in integer numbers) would be *Pareto superior* for the Dances on the next trip? What is the Pareto optimal number of fish?

b. Suppose two people must work together in the same room. Jane likes the temperature exactly at 72°, her utility declines if it gets any hotter or colder. Ralph likes it hot, the hotter the better for his taste. Is 70° a Pareto optimal temperature? Is 75°? By applying the definition of Pareto optimality list the range of temperatures that could be Pareto optimal.

c. Bob and Jane have three children. Bob would like to have more, but Jane's preferences are not to have any. What number of children is Pareto optimal?

5. There are two individuals, *A* and *B*, who consume two goods, *X* and *Y*. Consumer *A*'s marginal rate of substitution between goods *X* and *Y* is two *X* for one *Y*. *B*'s *MRS* is three *X* for two *Y*. In what direction will trade take place and between what two ratios?

6. In the Edgeworth diagram in Figure E.18–1, point *R* represents the original allocation of goods *X* and *Y* between individuals *A* and *B*. Indicate:

a. The feasible region of exchange and why this range is feasible.

b. All points unacceptable to *A* and why.

FIGURE E.18–1

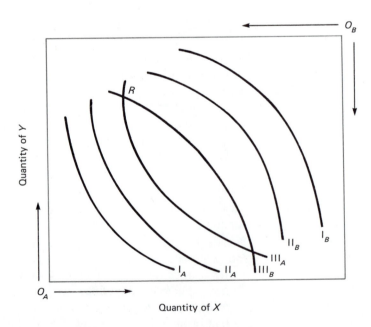

FIGURE E.18–2

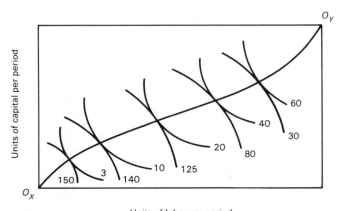

7. Explain how the production-possibility frontier is derived from the production Edgeworth Box.

8. Firm one produces good X and firm two produces Y. Both firms use labor (L) and capital (K) in the production process. For firm one, $MP_L = 10$ and $MP_K = 15$. For firm two $MP_L = 6$ and $MP_K = 12$. What should the firms do from a social point of view?

9. Why is perfect competition desirable according to the Pareto optimality rule in welfare economics? Explain.

10. Given the contract curve for production in Figure E.18–2, construct a production-possibility frontier for X and Y. The numbers attached to each isoquant represent units of output.

11. Discuss the shape of the production-possibility frontier.
    a. Why is it concave (have an outward bulge)?
    b. Graphically sketch the marginal cost of producing X or Y from the production-possibility frontier. What is the relationship between their shapes?

ANALYTICAL PROBLEMS

1. Jill and Jonathan are two children. Jonathan at first is happily playing with a teddy bear. Jill sees it and takes it for herself. This makes Jonathan unhappy; he cries and complains to his mother, who then makes Jill return the bear to Jonathan. But Jill complains that returning the bear is not Pareto superior. Is she right? What weakness is there in the Pareto rule of efficiency?

2. Suppose your professor sets forth the following class policies. Identify those that would make the *class* unequivocally better off, those that would make the *class* worse off, and those for which the conclusion is indeterminate. Explain.
   a. There will be no final exam. Everyone receives as a final grade his or her present average.
   b. The final is optional. You may take your present average or take the final.
   c. The final is mandatory but it only counts if it improves your average.
   d. There will be a final, but points will be taken from the high-grade students and given to the low-grade students until everyone has the same grade.
   e. The professor gives everyone an A, regardless of average.
   f. The final is mandatory, but there will be a makeup final if a student is not satisfied with his or her final grade.

3. Frequently people talk about the goals of a city.
   a. Can a city have goals? Why or why not?
   b. Under what circumsances could you state unequivocally that a city was made better off by a particular activity?
   c. Suppose someone says the goal of a city should be to force the downtown merchants to beautify the downtown area. Can you see any possible trade-off or contradiction?

4. The federal government is very much involved in redistributing income. Programs that transfer income are welfare, social security, and unemployment compensation. Pareto optimality takes the distribution of income as given. Discuss the rationale for income redistribution in light of the Pareto criterion.

5. Pareto efficiency and ''equity'' often work against each other in public policy analysis. For example, a particular distribution of goods may be efficient, but not equitable if one consumer has most of the goods. Should efficiency be sacrificed to obtain more equal distributions of goods and services?

6. Frequently a country's Gross National Product (GNP) is used as a measure of welfare. As GNP increases, the nation is considered to have an improved level of social welfare. Under what conditions, if any, can GNP be used as an indicator of welfare?

7. Some economists are very critical of the Pareto condition as a measure of welfare. The argument made is that utility is not independent of someone else's income. For example, if the Jones family next door gets a new color television, your utility may fall because of envy. The very fact that someone is happier may make another person more or less happy. Is there any validity to this argument? Can you think of examples where this seems to be true?

Chapter 19

Exchange Inefficiencies and Welfare

19.1 INTRODUCTION

In Chapter 18 we explored how perfect competition leads to a Pareto optimal distribution of goods and services. Although we know that perfectly competitive markets are not characteristic of the real world, the competitive general equilibrium model serves as a benchmark to compare the performance of real markets. In this chapter we will examine some of the reasons markets do not achieve Pareto optimality. These reasons fall under the broad heading of *market failure*.

Market failure arises because exchange is impeded. We have studied how markets are less efficient when prices are imposed by the government or firms have monopoly power. Certainly these are two causes of failure. Market failure can also arise from the very nature of certain goods and services. There are peculiar features of consumption and production that make some goods difficult to trade in the market place.

In some instances, consumers of a good or service may not be able to exclude others from consuming the same good or service once it has been acquired. In other cases, producers cannot exclude people from enjoying the benefits of a product when they do not pay for the product. We will see in this chapter that when there are such nonexclusion problems, a market, if it exists at all, does not lead to a Pareto efficient outcome, even when there is perfect competition. When there is the inability to exclude someone from consuming a product, we have a *public good;* the existence of public goods leads to market failure.

Another source of market inefficiency results from *external benefits and costs*. Referred to broadly as externalities, this form of inefficiency arises when the ownership of valuable properties such as air, water, and sometimes land is not well-defined. In such cases, polluted water, air, or land is imposed on others without an agreed on transaction. If individual ownership could be better defined or a designated owner found to represent the interests of those individuals with a collective right to the resource, the transaction might be brought back into the market place and the source of the market failure corrected.

In this chapter we also discuss the inadequacy of information as a source of market failure. When buyers and sellers lack information about prices and product or input qualities, markets will usually suffer. Increased market information will usually generate larger and more competitive market organizations.

19.2 PUBLIC GOODS

The very nature of some goods and services makes it difficult, if not impossible, for markets to function efficiently. The problem centers around either consumers being unable to exclude others from consuming precisely the same good as they do, or producers being unable to exclude consumers from enjoying the benefits of a product once it is produced. Such goods are called *public goods*. The existence of public goods can lead to market failure, because they hamper the incentive to trade.

Most goods do not suffer from the nonexclusion problem. When I eat an apple or drink a Coke, you can't eat the same apple or have the drink I had. If you want these goods, you will have to buy units of them distinct from mine. You pay a price for ownership and consumption that covers the cost of production. It is this exchange that creates and maintains markets. Certain goods, however, do not have the characteristics of apples and Cokes. For example, if your roommate hangs a clock in your apartment, you both gain and simultaneously consume the benefits of knowing what time it is. The clock is a public good. If I consume a public good, you can consume exactly the same good without reducing my consumption of it.

Definition
A public good exists when there is nonexclusion in consumption. That is, person A's consumption is not affected by persons B, C, or D also consuming the same product. The nonexclusion problem may arise once the product is produced, or when it is purchased.

Before we discuss public goods more thoroughly, we should mention that a solution to the problems arising from nonexclusion is generally not straightforward. We must also note that, while this section discusses the provision of goods that do not permit exclusion, it is rarely the case that any good completely satisfies the definition of a public good. At some point, consumption by others does affect your enjoyment of the good. For instance, if everybody in your dormitory or apartment complex came in to your room to look at your clock, your enjoyment of the clock would be affected. The congestion would greatly alter your lifestyle. Also, exclusion may be feasible at some point. You could just lock a door or two. Perhaps the only, and certainly the most widely cited, example of a public good is national defense. But some economists disagree even about this.

The Free Rider Problem

It is easiest to see how nonexclusion can lead to market failure by looking at nonexclusion at the time the good is produced. Nonexclusion in production arises when the producer of a good cannot prevent people who do not pay for the good from consuming it. Obviously, profit-maximizing firms will not produce a good unless they can withhold it if payment is not made. A park without limited access may be an example. A firm must pay the expense of producing the park, but it may have no control of park use after it is built. No control means no revenue. So profit-maximizing firms will stay away from such ventures.

Another frequently cited example is a lighthouse. While it might be technically possible to exclude nonpaying ships from the use of a lighthouse, it would probably be economically infeasible to do so. Or, consider the following example. Suppose that 1,000 families live along a river that floods every few years, causing these people considerable damage. An enterprising person could come along and offer to build a dam, charging these people an amount per year less than the expected value of the damage from flooding. Suppose you lived along the river; what would you say when asked to pay your share of the cost? Probably, "Forget it." There would be no incentive to pay. The dam could not be built to protect everyone else's property and not protect yours. So you could consume the benefits of flood control without paying the cost. You probably would not be the only one to figure this out. The entrepreneur would therefore have trouble collecting enough revenue to cover the cost of construction. Thus, a dam or a lighthouse that would benefit everyone more than it costs would not be constructed because of the inability of private firms to collect from those who do not pay. Or, getting back to the example of national defense, how could someone defend the entire nation from attack without defending St. Louis, Houston, Los Angeles, or any other individual city where the citizens did not choose to pay for defense.

Economists call these and other such examples the *free rider problem*. Little or none of the good will be produced by private firms, because these firms have no way of forcing the people who consume the goods to pay a price. And when firms cannot collect a price for the goods they produce, there is no revenue to cover costs. Market failure results because the cost of these goods to society is less than the value society would place on these goods, but people, because of nonexclusion, have the option of consuming the good without making payment. While value is greater than cost, revenue is not, and the good may not be produced by private enterprise.

To summarize, nonexclusion results when it is impossible, or economically infeasible, to produce and sell a good that has characteristics such that if some people pay for the good, others can consume the same good without paying for it. Once the good is produced no one is willing to pay. Too little, or even none of the good will be produced, and the value of additional units of the good to society will be greater than the social cost of those units. Thus a nonoptimal amount of the good will result.

The absence of exclusion is not the only reason why there is market failure when public goods are demanded. In some cases public goods can be made private. A park for instance can have a fence built around it, so if visitors want in they must pay a toll at a gate. Those who do not pay, do not visit. The publicness of the good has been made more private, and free enterprise will participate in the production of the commodity. But when there is nonexclusion in production and consumption, it is not clear that exclusion should take place. When producers can exclude nonpaying consumers, these people can still consume the good without decreasing its benefits to those who do pay. Within limits, for example, a park visitor who does not pay is not going to disturb others who may have paid. Congestion may be a problem as the park becomes crowded, but at the margin one more visitor could be made better off at *zero marginal cost* to society. In this way strict exclusion in the production of a public good ends up in too little production and prices that are too high.

Public Goods and Marginal Cost

Indeed, an illuminating way of describing public goods is to stress that the marginal cost of letting an additional person consume the good is zero once it is produced. National defense, parks, and television signals are examples of goods that come close to fitting this description. Possibly concerts and fireworks displays are other examples.

If the marginal cost of letting another person consume the good is zero, the optimal price should be zero. It costs society nothing for these ''additional'' consumers to consume the good. If these consumers could have the good at zero price, they would be better off and no one would be worse off, because none of society's resources would have to be used to take in an additional consumer. But the total costs of production are not zero, so how will these costs be paid at a zero price? Private producers must set a positive price to cover costs; hence, price will be greater than marginal cost, and a less-than-optimal amount of the good is consumed. In other words private production does not lead to a Pareto optimal allocation of the good.

To put the issue another way, regardless of the total consumption of the public good, the same amount of society's resources must be used to produce it. It is reasonable to assume that, for some consumers who elect not to purchase the public good, the marginal utility of the good is still positive. That is, for some consumers, in the case of good A, a positive price leads them to a solution in their preference map, such that

$$\frac{MU_a}{p_a} < \frac{MU_b}{p_b} = \frac{MU_c}{p_c}, \text{ etc.,}$$

and $MU_a > 0$. Thus, if a zero price were charged to these consumers, some would consume good A. If A is a public good, they would be better off, and no one would be worse off because no more of society's resources are used when the good is consumed.

Principle

If the production of some public goods is in the hands of private enterprise, social welfare is less than it would otherwise be because some consumers are excluded from the market when price is greater than zero. Since their consumption of the good is "free" to society in the sense that it entails no further resource sacrifice, society as a whole would be better off if these people were allowed to consume the good at zero price; but under free enterprise, they are not allowed to.

Because the marginal consumer can be brought into the market at zero marginal cost, the theory of public goods markets is different from the theory of the market for private goods. Recall that market demand for a private good is found by horizontally adding the demand curves for each individual, as shown in Figure 19–1, Panel A. We show two consumers, A and B. Market demand is DD', the horizontal sum of the two demand curves, $D_A D_A'$ and $D_B D_B'$. For instance, at p_0, $x_T = x_A + x_B$ or the sum of distances $p_0 L + LM = p_0 N$. A competitive market, after horizontally adding the demand curves of all individuals in the market, operates at the intersection of market supply and demand.

Public goods, however, are goods for which the same units of output can be consumed by different people at the same time. Individuals can pay for a good that other individuals are also willing to pay for. Take, for example, public parks. What is the demand for public parks? Ignoring possible congestion, park land is shared; the market demand must therefore be the sum of each person's demand curve for the *same* land.

Consequently, in the case of public goods, demand curves must be summed vertically because each person consumes the same good. To see why, consider the situation shown in Panel B, Figure 19–1. Two consumers, A and B, demand some public good; their demands are, respectively, $D_A D_A'$ and $D_B D_B'$. Consumer A is willing to pay p_A *to use* x_0 units of the public good x. Consumer B will pay p_B for the same units. Thus, the two consumers together will pay $p_A + p_B = p_M$ for x_0 units. Summing the two demands over all amounts of X, we obtain the market demand for the public good, DD'. For example, $x_0 t + x_0 u = x_0 v$ yields market demand. The optimal price and amount of the good are determined by the intersec-

FIGURE 19–1   **The market for private and public goods**

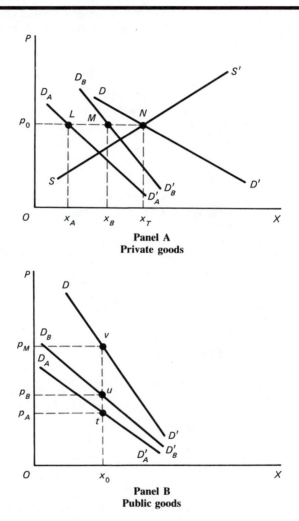

Panel A
Private goods

Panel B
Public goods

tion of marginal cost and market demand. Price should be zero if the marginal cost of an additional unit is zero. But, as noted, this price would not cover total costs.

To summarize, public goods have features that may not permit markets to function efficiently. If producers cannot prevent free riders who do not pay for the good from consuming it, a less than optimal amount of the good will be produced. Or, if producers can exclude those who do not pay, but their consumption of the good would not reduce the consumption of those who do pay, some people could be made better off without anyone being made worse off. Private production is not Pareto optimal. Many economists argue that in such cases government has a role to play in these markets.

The Role of Government

We should note that, sometimes, solutions can be found to the exclusion problem. Building a fence around a park and controlling access is one example of solving the problem. Radio signals, as a second example, also suffer from nonexclusion. Anyone with a radio can consume them, so once the producer of radio waves sends a signal, it cannot be kept from anyone's consumption. We might think that radio stations would be terribly unprofitable businesses, but such is not the case. The problem of nonexclusion has been overcome by stations selling their air time to advertisers. They collect a fee for the commercials they broadcast for advertisers and this covers the cost of producing the signals. In spite of these two examples, solutions to the exclusion problem are not always so straightforward. Governments, recognizing the fact that there may be some goods that are not optimally produced and consumed when the price if set by the competitive market mechanism, will sometimes produce these goods.

Government supplies many goods for which the marginal cost of adding another consumer is close to zero. Many public utilities, public transportation systems, and the provision of education have a cost structure in which the initial investment for production is large, but marginal cost is very low. Efficient prices exist at the point demand and marginal cost intersect, but these prices are not likely to generate revenue that will cover total costs. So government pays the fixed cost or, in the long run, makes the necessary investment, and then charges more efficient prices. The funds used to finance the "subsidized" enterprise are generated by taxes.

There are numerous examples of public goods where consumers pay part of the cost of consumption, but not the whole cost. National parks are one example and the state provision of higher education is another. Even though tourists are charged an entrance fee, national parks are subsidized by tax revenue. At state universities, students pay tuition even though the bulk of a university's expenses are covered by state taxes.

Governments will also supply goods that private firms would produce except for the difficulty or impossibility of collecting a price for them. This is the free rider problem. The previous example of the dam on the flooding river is such a case. No firm could charge consumers who "do not want" the flood protection, but government could collect enough to build the dam through taxation. National defense, police and fire protection, and garbage collection are other examples of people allowing government to assume the role of providing such services, for which there is a free rider.

We should note in closing this section that there is considerable argument among economists about how large the role of the government should be in providing public goods. In many cases, such as the park and radio signal examples, the nonexclusion problem can be overcome. Prices will generally not be efficient when the good is privately produced, but the government financing of these same goods is not distortion free either. The taxes used to pay the cost of public goods will almost always cause market inefficiencies that we have for the most part left undiscussed in this text.

19.3 IMPERFECT COMPETITION

A second reason markets may fail to provide a Pareto-efficient outcome is because of a breakdown in competitive market structures. As markets become more monopolized, there is a strong presumption that they also become less efficient. This point was already discussed in terms of consumer's and producer's surplus in Chapter 14. As firms gain more monopoly power they have an increased capability to set price above marginal cost. This earns them more profit, but causes a loss in total market surplus. In this section we show that imperfect competition violates the conditions for Pareto optimality. We then briefly discuss a caveat concerning making markets more competitive; this warning is widely known as the theory of second best.

Monopoly Inefficiency

In Chapter 18, one of the Pareto rules for efficiency was that, for consumers and producers,

$$MRS_{x\,for\,y} = MRT;$$

that is, the slope of every consumer's indifference curve should be equal to the slope of the production-possibility frontier. The marginal rate of transformation, the slope of the production-possibility frontier, is equivalent to the ratio of marginal costs, MC_x/MC_y. In perfect competition we have this condition satisfied through the set of equalities:

$$MRT = \frac{MC_x}{MC_y} = \frac{P_x}{P_y} = MRS_{x\,for\,y}.$$

Profit maximizers set price equal to marginal cost in competitive markets. Likewise, utility-maximizing consumers equalize the slope of their indifference curves with the same price ratio shown above. Competition thus leads to the equality of the MRT and MRS's of consumers. If we focus on just the middle part of the above equalities, we have

$$\frac{MC_x}{MC_y} = \frac{P_x}{P_y},$$

and rearranging terms we can write this expression as

$$\frac{MC_x}{P_x} = \frac{MC_y}{P_y} = 1.$$

Both ratios are equal to one because competitors set price equal to marginal cost.

This last relation helps us understand why imperfect competition is not Pareto optimal. A firm with monopoly power sets price above marginal cost. Hence for monopoly in both the X and Y markets it is generally the case that

$$\frac{MC_x}{P_x} \neq \frac{MC_y}{P_y} < 1.$$

Not only are the ratios unequal, but they are both less than one. This means two things. First, the slope of the production-possibility frontier will not be the same as the slope of consumers' indifference curves; and, second, since the ratios of marginal cost to price are less than one, the economy is operating inside the production frontier. Too few resources are being devoted to the production of goods in markets that are monopolized.

In summary, we have the following principle:

Principle

If there is imperfect competition, price is usually greater than marginal cost, and the market will not, in general, allocate enough resources in the production of this good.

Theory of Second Best

This seems to say that society can be made better off anytime one or more monopolized markets can be made more competitive. From a policy point of view the implication is that laws against monopoly are beneficial and should be strictly enforced. If there is any way policymakers can move a monopolized market toward one that is more competitive, it would appear to be a Pareto superior action, because prices and marginal costs would get closer together. Some markets may never be competitive, but the more that are, it would seem the more efficient is production. Do we know for sure that Pareto efficiency will go up whenever a market is made more competitive without affecting others?

The answer is efficiency may not necessarily increase, and this is what the theory of *second best* is all about. This theory says that it is sometimes better to move inside the production-possibility frontier than be at just any point along it. Such an idea was made widely known by R. G. Lipsey

FIGURE 19–2   **Theory of second best**

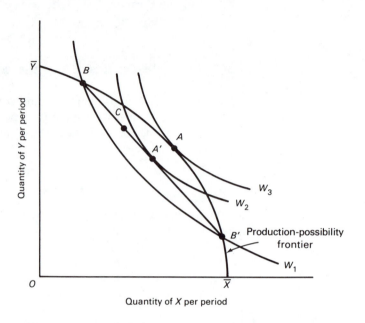

Quantity of X per period

and Kelvin Lancaster[1]. Since then many technical arguments have followed, but the main idea can be explained quite easily with the help of Figure 19–2. Suppose we begin with a production-possibility frontier like $\overline{YX}$ shown in the figure.

Even though we know community indifference curves do not exist in any consistent way, suppose for the sake of argument that society has a set of convex curves that look very much like those for a single consumer. In Figure 19–2 let W_1, W_2, and W_3 be three indifference curves for a society.[2] The curve with the highest level of benefit is W_3, and it is just tangent to the frontier at A. At point A we will assume society's *MRT* equals the *MRS* for all individuals. Thus point A represents an efficient, or Pareto optimal, distribution of resources and outputs.

The presence of monopoly means production is not efficiently organized. Too few resources are in some industries and too many are being used in others. Suppose that both the X and Y industries are monopolized and we move to a point inside the frontier along the schedule BB'. Where

[1] R. G. Lipsey and Kelvin Lancaster, ''The General Theory of Second Best,'' *Review of Economic Studies,* Volume 24 (1), 1956–1957, pp. 11–32.

society is along the schedule will depend in part on the degree of monopolization in each industry. Suppose we are at point C, inside the production frontier. Relative to point A, too much of good Y and too little of X are being produced. If resources were allocated toward industry Y, we could move back to the frontier, perhaps to a point such as B. This point represents a policy that makes the Y industry produce even more than what would be produced at the efficient point A.

However if society has indifference curves like those shown in Figure 19–2, moving back to the frontier is worse than an interior solution. We can see that going to point A' would increase welfare for society from W_1 to W_2. If production is at point C, policymakers should attempt to increase output in industry X relative to industry Y. Given that neither industry is competitive, it is therefore not in the best interests of society to reach just any point on the production-possibility frontier.

There is no uniform agreement among economists concerning the role of government in making markets more competitive. Some argue that piecemeal policies will make matters worse. Others argue categorically for any policy that forces firms to price closer to marginal cost. Proponents of the latter policy maintain that when markets are relatively independent of one another, marginal cost pricing increases efficiency. The theory of second best applies most strongly when markets are closely related; that is, they either produce complementary goods like bread and butter, or one market is an intermediate supplier of another as in the case of tire makers supplying automobile producers.

19.4 INFORMATION AND MARKET FAILURE

Market failure may also occur because of the absence of perfect knowledge among consumers. Perfect knowledge includes knowledge on the part of all consumers of product prices and qualities, including the hazards associated with a product. For the average consumer, this level of knowledge is a practical impossibility. We describe below how this leads to price distortions in markets and possibly too few or too many resources devoted to the production of some goods.

Insufficient Information and Prices

As long as information is costly to obtain, consumers will not gather every piece of information about prices and product characteristics. We know already from a number of discussions in different contexts that the optimal amount of information for consumers occurs when the marginal

---

[2] We cannot, of course, theoretically derive these curves because of our inability to compare levels of utility across individuals. Remember utility is ordinal and not cardinal. We introduce these curves only to discuss relative levels of social welfare, which conceptually must exist even though such schedules cannot be derived.

benefit of its use is just equal to its marginal cost of collection. As long as marginal benefit is greater than marginal cost, more information will be gathered, but because marginal cost is positive, consumers will never collect information until marginal benefit is zero. This means that they will be unaware of higher quality products or the lower prices some sellers charge for exactly the same product they are gathering information about. Knowledge of either might increase a consumer's utility. Also the equilibrium level of information will not be the same across consumers. For some consumers the marginal cost of collecting information will be relatively high. Old age, a handicap, high transportation costs, and the opportunity cost of a person's time all have an effect on the marginal cost of getting information. Marginal benefit will be different across buyers, too. Benefit, of course, will be in part determined by preferences, income and relative prices.

The fact that consumers will not know everything about prices and product attributes tells us that product prices will vary from seller to seller. Considering even a particular product—say a 150 count box of white Kleenex tissue—prices will vary from seller to seller, because all buyers will not go to the seller with the lowest price. The marginal cost of gathering information about the prices all sellers charge is simply too high relative to marginal benefit. Some sellers will, therefore, survive in the market charging relatively high prices, and consumers, when they maximize utility, will not be paying the same prices for all goods. For two consumers, i and j, we can easily see that Pareto optimality is not reached. Because of different costs and benefits of information we have

$$MRS^i_{x\,for\,y} = \frac{P^i_x}{P^i_y} \neq \frac{P^j_x}{P^j_y} = MRS^j_{x\,for\,y},$$

which violates the exchange condition for Pareto efficiency. In addition, firms will not be charging prices equal to marginal cost, because they know information is costly. As long as their prices are not outrageously high, customers will not search for a lower-priced seller. The lack of information gives firms some monopoly power. Insufficient information forces an *inequality* between the marginal rate of transformation on the production-possibility frontier and the marginal rates of substitution for consumers.

Rules of Thumb: The Akerlof Model[3]

Sometimes, when consumers have difficulty gathering information, they will use rules of thumb to judge product quality and the price they are

---

[3] This discussion is based on George Akerlof, "The Market for 'Lemons': Quality Uncertainty and the Market Mechanism," *Quarterly Journal of Economics,* Volume 84 (3), August 1970, pp. 488–500.

willing to pay for a product. These rules of thumb can have grave consequences for a market. As an illustration, suppose someone is in the market for a used car. A strong asymmetry of information in the market may exist between buyers and sellers. What we mean by asymmetry of information is that buyers know little or absolutely nothing about the automobile they see in a used car lot at an asking price, while the seller is fully aware of the car's history—true mileage, accidents, and routine maintenance, would be important pieces of this history.

Buyers, when they do not have very much information about a product, are likely to adopt a rule of thumb to decide whether or not to make a purchase. Consumers use rules of thumb all the time. Brand names are associated with high and low quality products, a busy restaurant must have good food, stocks and bonds are bought and sold by the phases of the moon. Some rules are good, some are not so good. In the example of a consumer buying a used car, suppose buyers know nothing and therefore assume that any car they see is an ''average'' quality used car. They then decide that the highest price they will pay is the price that delivers a car of average quality. The price asked by the seller is never used as a signal of quality.

Sellers who truly know the quality of the car they offer will not sell a high quality car at an average quality price. So the good cars in the used market are taken off the market. After a while, this changes the distribution of quality in the market. Average quality falls. Consumers eventually learn of this shift in overall market quality by consistently over-estimating average car quality. If they continue to hold on to their rule of thumb, they must adjust until prices are brought back in line with average quality. Thus prices fall, and once again, the relatively good cars are pulled off the market; average quality then falls a second time, and so does price. This cycle may continue until the market for used cars eventually disappears. In this example we see that the important thing is not so much the lack of information, as its unbalanced distribution between buyers and sellers. This asymmetry induces peculiar behavior on the part of consumers that can be detrimental to welfare.

Of course, seemingly strange rules of thumb can be overcome by providing consumers with more information. Also, sellers competing with one another to sell their automobiles will have an incentive to supply potential customers with information about their products. Sellers can overcome rules of thumb by offering guarantees, certification by an independent expert, establishing a reputable identity, and so on. We have presented a rather stylized story to illustrate a point. Rarely do consumers not know something about the product they buy. However, the relative amounts of information that buyers and sellers possess may literally determine the existence of some markets. More information is the key in some instances to generating greater exchange and stable equilibrium.

Evaluating Product Quality

The amount and distribution of information are not the only important features of information in a market setting. Consumers, even with information, may not be able to evaluate it. Buyers, for instance, are often unaware of the side effects of chemicals in hair spray or floor wax; foods may contain harmful substances that are listed on the label, but mean nothing to the shopper; and automobiles may have faulty designs that only an engineer can evaluate.

Just as a lack of information distorts the preferences of consumers so will the inability to evaluate available information. When consumers are unaware of the full effects of dangerous products, they may be willing to purchase more of the commodity at the going price than they would under the condition of full knowledge. In other words, information without knowledge causes misperceptions, which distorts the *MRS* between two products for a consumer. Better evaluation of information could bring consumers closer to more efficient exchange.

In some cases, specific governmental bodies such as the Food and Drug Administration (FDA) and the Consumer Product Safety Commission (CPSC) are legislated to evaluate products. For instance, the CPSC annually inspects children's toys and alerts consumers to potentially dangerous features. Beyond this, the government agency may even set standards that eliminate the danger. Usually, the danger involved is reduced, but the cost is a more expensive product to consumers. For example, in the mid-1970s, the Commission determined that baby cribs were unsafe because infants could slip through the crib bars. So it set a maximum distance between the bars of cribs. Manufacturers as a group had to place bars closer together; this took more bars and cribs became more expensive.

Such a change in product quality involves a trade-off to consumers. While standards usually relieve buyers of evaluating the hazards of products, they also make manufacturers conform to designs that restrict product variety and/or make products more expensive. In the specific case of baby cribs, safety standards prevented consumers from buying less expensive cribs that were undoubtedly not as safe as those that conformed to the CPSC guidelines, but the *choice* was eliminated and the less expensive models may have suited some consumers' purposes and budgets.

Whether informational problems necessitate regulation is debatable. Many economists would argue that market failure from the absence of enough of the right kinds of information requires only additional information, not regulation. On the other hand, more is involved than simply acquiring a publication or reading a more informative description of a product. Once information is acquired, it must be studied, and if it is complicated or technically sophisticated, the costs associated with digesting the information can be high. Under these circumstances, many economists argue that safety and quality regulation are beneficial functions of government.

19.5 EXTERNALITIES

We have covered very briefly some circumstances that do not necessarily provide a Pareto-optimal equilibrium for markets. In these cases, arguments have been made for some type of governmental intervention.

Quite possibly, a much more important problem of the market concerns the question of externalities, where the private cost or benefit of some activity does not equal the total cost or benefit of that activity. A very large part of the problem of externalities is closely related to the incomplete assignment of property rights.

In this text, we have generally assumed away the problem of externalities and the incomplete assignment of property rights. In this section, we will examine some aspects of these problems. Because these are complex problems, in this discussion we will be able to merely touch on the major issues involved.

Definition of Externalities

Externalities occur whenever exchange between two economic agents takes place outside the market place. The exchange of some good or service, in other words, is not agreed on by both parties to the transaction, yet the transaction is carried out anyway. Examples of externalities can be found in everyday life. Waking up to your neighbor's crowing rooster is an externality that may be desirable or terribly undesirable, depending on your sleeping habits. Roommates carry on a number of external exchanges which may be good or bad depending on your point of view toward cooking, cleaning, bathing, and use of language. It is most likely that some of the externalities generated by your roommate are desirable and some are not so desirable.

We may think of externalities in terms of costs and benefits. A *private* cost or benefit is defined to be exclusive of any externalities generated by a particular activity. For example, a factory that dumps sewage into a river may not count the cost of water pollution when the costs of production are figured. *Social* costs would consider the cost of pollution and should be thought of as the sum of private costs and the value of any externalities. Thus, we have the relation

$$\text{Social costs} = \text{Private costs} + \text{External costs.}$$

This same reasoning can apply when we think about the benefits of an activity rather than the costs. *Private benefit,* like private cost, is figured exclusive of any externalities. *Social benefit* includes them; so we may imagine a benefit relation in which

Social benefits = Private benefits + External benefits.

The social benefits of education, for example, are greater than the private benefits because of the externalities generated by an educated society. Education is directly related to more responsible behavior, which benefits your friends, neighbors, and co-workers.

Depending on the problem we may be considering, it is frequently more convenient to think of externalities either in terms of costs or benefits. But both of the above relationships represent two sides of the same coin. Whenever there are externalities, social costs or benefits do not equal private costs or benefits.

Definition
An externality exists whenever the social cost or benefit of an activity is not equal to private cost or benefit.

Externalities, depending on their desirability, carry more specific definitions. An *external economy* is said to exist when social benefit at the margin exceeds private benefit. When marginal cost equals private mar-

FIGURE 19–3   **Divergence between marginal private cost and benefit and marginal social cost and benefit**

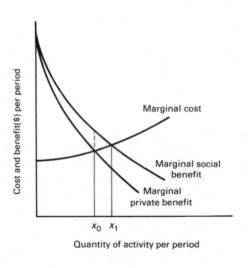
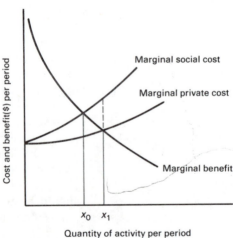

ginal benefit as shown in Figure 19–3, Panel A, marginal social benefit is above marginal cost at x_0. More resources should be allocated to producing the commodity in question. The activity should be increased to x_1, where marginal cost and marginal social benefit are equal. On the other hand, an *external diseconomy* exists when social cost exceeds private cost. In Panel B, Figure 19–3 social cost is above private cost at the margin. When the private cost and marginal benefit curve intersect, marginal benefit is less than marginal social cost. An undesirably large amount of resources is allocated to producing the commodity in question. In Panel B of the figure the activity should be reduced by the amount $x_0 x_1$.

Definition

An external economy exists when social benefit is greater than private benefit. An external diseconomy exists when social cost is greater than private cost.

At this stage, it is quite reasonable to ask *how* private marginal cost and benefit diverge from marginal social cost and benefit. One of the chief answers is that a problem of ownership over a certain resource exists. Briefly, this means that there is some scarce resource owned by a person, but for some reason the owner cannot charge a price for the use of this resource. And when prices cannot be charged, misallocation of resources results.

The now classic example of ownership externalities was originally brought up by the economist J. E. Meade in 1952.[4] A beekeeper raises bees for honey. The ideal location for beehives is in fields with lots of spring blossoms. While bees make honey, they also pollinate blossoms, which, say for apple orchards, generates more fruit in the fall. Hence, both the beekeeper and the apple farmer benefit by being located close to one another. The beekeeper benefits because the apple blossoms are a source of nectar for bees, and the apple farmer benefits from having the blossoms pollinated. But these benefits are not necessarily paid for in the market. Hence, for both the beekeeper and the farmer, social benefit is greater than private benefit. If ownership rights between the two parties were better defined, more efficient exchange might take place, but as it is, too few bees and too few trees exist.

An example of an external diseconomy, because of an improper assignment of ownership rights, might be pollution. Suppose a commercial fishing industry exists at the mouth of a river. Let a factory locate upstream. The factory dumps its waste into the river, killing some of the fish downstream and, consequently, lowering the amount of fish caught each day. Ownership of the stream's resources are often ambiguous, so the polluter is not made to pay for the dirty water. The private cost to the

---

[4] J. E. Meade, "External Economies and Diseconomies in a Competitive Situation," *Economic Journal* 62, no. 245 (March 1952), pp. 54–67.

factory does not include the resulting reduced incomes of the downstream fishermen, and social cost is greater than private cost. Too much factory output is produced. There are many other examples of such external diseconomies—some as simple as this to describe, others much more complex. In all cases, the remedy to the problem is usually difficult.

APPLICATION

Externalities and Urban Renewal[5]

An example of an external diseconomy under private ownership involves the incentive to maintain property. Based on our economic theory, we would expect an individual who owns a piece of property to keep the property developed and repaired so long as the marginal benefits exceed the individual marginal costs of such repairs. There should be no reason for more than the optimal amount of "urban blight" under these circumstances. But, with certain ownership externalities, completely rational people may allow their property to deteriorate.

Note first that the value of a piece of urban property—houses, apartments, and so on—depends to some extent on the condition of other property in the neighborhood. Suppose there are only two properties, one owned by owner A, the other by owner B. Each is attempting to decide whether or not to make an added investment in repair. Both are reaping some return from the property. Each owner has made an initial investment and has an additional sum invested in bonds. Each is making an average return of 7 percent from the property and the bonds, and this return is expected to continue, even if no money is taken out of bonds and put into property repair.

Suppose that if both owners take their money out of bonds and invest in property repair, each will make a return of 10 percent. Clearly, each will be better off. There is a problem, however. Suppose one owner invests the bond money in repairs while the other does not. One property is improved and the other remains run down. The owner who improves the property gives up the return from the bonds, but the property return does not increase much because it remains next to a deteriorated property. In this case, the improving owner's total return falls to 6 percent. The loss of bond income more than offsets the increase in income from improving the property.

[5] This section is based upon a paper by O. A. Davis and A. B. Winston, "The Economics of Urban Renewal," *Law and Contemporary Problems* 26, no. 1 (Winter 1961), pp. 105–117.

On the other hand, the owner who did not improve the property retains the bond income and, in addition, finds that the return on the unimproved property increases since it is next to an improved piece of property. Perhaps the total return from this person's property and bonds increases to 12 percent. These changes in return result no matter who does the repair and who does not. The owner who does not repair the property keeps the bond return and benefits from the better neighborhood.

Suppose both owners know the expected return but do not know what the other will do. If owner A decides to invest, it will be to owner B's advantage not to invest—a 12 percent compared to a 10 percent return. Owner A knows this and, therefore, knows that the investment will cause a decrease in total return from 7 to 6 percent. Owner B knows the same conditions apply to his or her own investment decision also. Therefore, neither invests. However, if both invest, each would be better off.[6]

As the authors of the paper that set forth this example noted, the "neighborhood" effect must be strong enough to get the results set forth. They also noted—and you probably have already deduced it—that there is a solution to the problem. One owner can simply buy out the other owner and improve both properties. Each would be made better off.

But if there were many such properties in the area, the transactions cost, or the cost of "putting the deal together" might very well outweigh the benefits from one individual buying up all of the property. In any case, one owner of a small piece of property might hold out for so large an amount as to thwart the deal.

There is the danger of attributing too many problems to ownership externalities and saying simply that the marketplace does not ever allocate efficiently. One may or may not be happy with the results of the market, but market failures as a result of externalities must be treated carefully. We could, and many do, carry the externality problem to a fallacy of the extreme. Certainly, if a large group of people drive big fast cars, the price of gasoline rises. Some benefit; some lose. Selling wheat to Russia may increase the price of bread; again, some benefit, some lose. If you burn coal, the world has less coal. These activities are not externalities, however, because they are not *external* to the market. Selling more wheat to the Soviet Union is a market transaction, frequently of such large proportions that the world price of wheat is affected. This in turn may cause the price of bread to increase. Events that increase demand or change supply are not externalities since the market is adjust-

---

[6] Such analysis is closely related to the prisoner's dilemma discussed in Chapter 15.

ing. Consumers and producers may not like these adjustments and want government intervention to control them. But in these cases the market is not failing, it is reacting.

Property Rights and Externalities[7]

In most discussions of externalities, the property rights of resource owners are not well-defined. Problems arise because the production, investment, or even consumption decisions of some affect the incomes or utilities of others, through an implicit exchange of property use. No explicit transaction takes place that contracts for this exchange. We wish to stress that the problem of externalities becomes more serious as property rights become more ambiguous, or when no one has property rights in the case of some scarce resources.

The most complete concept of ownership rights, and that which we have assumed to exist throughout the text, is that owners can use their property in any way, subject to laws concerning injury to other parties. A less complete right of ownership is the right to use the property of someone else and to gain benefits from its use, but not to sell it or alter its form. Most rental properties and community-owned properties fall into this category, as do your classroom, our offices, and some government properties, such as national parks.

There are many shades between the various forms of property rights, but these two are the principal categories. The right of ownership is never completely unrestricted. You may own a good but not be able to sell it above a governmentally fixed price. You may own land but not be permitted to build a swimming pool on it unless you build a fence.

As it turns out, most of the problems of externalities result from two situations. The first is incomplete or communal assignment of property rights or even no assignment of property rights. The second problem results when certain uses of one's fully owned property have harmful effects on someone else's property.

Nonowned or Community-Owned Property

A scarce resource that is not owned is both overused and under-produced. Early settlers in the United States had no incentive to postpone chopping down trees or to plant forests. If one group did not chop the trees down, others would. What is the incentive to plant trees if no one owns them? Forests were destroyed. The American Bison were practically wiped out, while cattle, which were owned, were not. Rivers, which were not owned, were polluted. No one owned the valuable

---

[7] This section is in large part based on S. Pejovich, *Fundamentals of Economics* (Dallas, Tex.: The Fisher Institute, 1979), Chapter 2.

whales, and they practically disappeared when whale oil was the major source of light and lubrication. Neither free enterprise nor human greed was the problem per se. The problem was that no one had the incentive to kill fewer whales so that the whales could reproduce at a rate sufficient to maintain the population. If any individuals took upon themselves not to harvest another whale for oil, others would. Similarly, there is no point in individuals planting trees if the ownership of the future forest is not specified.

As we have implied, publicly owned property gives rise to problems similar to those with nonowned property. A government- or community-owned property may not be used efficiently. Suppose a community owned a large piece of property that is better suited for growing vegetables than for cattle grazing. If anyone can use the property, it will probably be used for cattle grazing, because if anyone can harvest the vegetables, growers would have to expend added resources to protect their crops. Cattle owners can drive their cows home from the community property at night.

Publicly owned property may not be put to its most efficient use, but this may not be bad for the society. The society may wish to have free beaches and parks rather than have private ownership of these scarce resources. People may prefer overcrowding to paying for the use of the facilities. Publicly owned resources will be put to uses different from those that would result from private ownership.

APPLICATION

Property Rights and Fishing for Striped Bass[8]

In the case of fishing, property rights are often ill-defined, and over the years a number of controversies have arisen. In the Pacific Northwest the right to fish for salmon has caused conflict between Oregon, Washington, British Columbia, and various Indian tribes. Presently a complex set of interstate and international rules govern fishing seasons and catches in this area. Alaskan and Russian fishing boats have fought over fishing rights near the Aleutian Islands. The international agreement governing these rights appears to be constantly disputed.

The laws of property governing fish are complicated because fish migrate depending on seasons of the year and spawning habits. A community's claim to fish as a resource is made in spite of the migration. Multiple claims arise, causing conflict in the harvesting and preservation of

---

[8] This application is based on David L. Yermack, ''Striped Bass Issue Illustrates Problem of Unclear Jurisdiction,'' *The Wall Street Journal,* July 10, 1984, p. 29.

the resource. The example of striped bass illustrates property rights problems and the consequent externalities present in the fishing industry.

The striped bass, once a common entree on East Coast menus, is disappearing from the Atlantic waters. Over the last fifteen years the population of this fish has fallen 90 percent. The reason for the problem is two-fold. First the spawning grounds of the striped bass are being destroyed, and second, since no state or individual has jurisdiction of the entire East Coast fishing ground, no one can regulate the conditions for catching the fish, and over-fishing has occurred. Both of these problems are discussed in turn.

When not spawning, striped bass roam the Atlantic seaboard from Maine to Florida, but in the spring they return to either the Hudson River or Chesapeake Bay to lay their eggs. Most return to the Chesapeake, and this is the most serious source of the problem. Chesapeake water pollution has severely damaged their spawning ground, which has led almost to the total demise of the fish. Maryland is concerned with the problem but has not been effective in controlling it, because three fourths of the Bay pollution originates in neighboring states. Obviously, Maryland has no legal rights over people in these other states and, therefore, cannot impose restrictions on upstream polluters. The other states, of course, have little incentive to impose restrictions, since the pollution is not directly affecting them. An external diseconomy is thus destroying a valuable natural resource, and management is hampered by the absence of clearcut property ownership and jurisdiction.

To make matters even worse, the small number of bass, roughly 7 percent, that spawn in the Hudson River stand to lose, at least temporarily, this breeding ground. Plans have been made to dredge the river for a $2 billion federally financed highway, housing, and parkland project. Controversy over the impact of dredging on the young bass population has so far slowed development. Seaboard states are pressuring New York to cancel the project, because striped bass in the Hudson are prospering. Environmentalists argue that the River's limestone watershed counteracts acidic pollution, thus protecting the breeding ground. Neighboring states fear the New York development would destroy Atlantic fishing for many years, because at least 2 million young bass grow up in the Hudson waters, before migrating along the New England coast. Upsetting the Hudson breeding grounds would essentially destroy New England fishing.

But no state has offered to help bear the cost of maintaining the Hudson breeding ground. Political pressure is being put on New York to drop their Hudson development project without offer of interstate compensation. Obviously, New York is balking. They feel that the entire cost of maintaining the quality of New England fishing is being put on New York. They are creating an external economy for the other states. While other states will benefit by New York's conservation policy, New York has no way of being compensated by these states. The problem, of course, is created by the absence of property rights over the fish. If New York knew who caught the Hudson Bay bass and therefore benefited from the state's protection of their spawning grounds, a tax could, in principle, be levied to compensate New York for maintaining the spawning grounds of the fish. But New York cannot easily track the fish and legally the state doesn't have the right to tax people in other states.

An additional problem arising from the lack of clear-cut property rights is the difficulty of obtaining uniform regulations on fishing along the Atlantic coast. Such regulations would go a long way to maintain or even increase the bass population. But, because of the characteristics of migratory fish, such uniform regulations have not been set up.

To be sure, a number of states along the coast have begun to protect the bass. But differences in the restriction states put on fishing dilute the effectiveness of any single state's effort. Once again the absence of ownership reduces the incentive of any one state to take strong action, because no one state receives the full benefit of the restrictions it places on its fishing industry. Also, the most lenient state will benefit the most from the regulations of other states. All of the Atlantic States have adopted a minimum set of fishing restrictions written by the Atlantic States Marine Fisheries Commission. The guidelines, aimed at reducing each state's catch by 55 percent, ban fishing on certain dates, set minimum keep sizes, and regulate the use of nets and other equipment. Some states, notably Rhode Island, have gone far beyond these rules. In Rhode Island no one is allowed to catch a striped bass for three years. Maryland and Virginia, on the other hand, have kept the minimum standard. Other states regard this as lenient, given the size and importance of the bass population around those states. "All of the states are playing the game of not wanting to give up more than anyone else," says Fred Schwab, New York's representative to the Interstate Striped Bass Management Project. Schwab is simply pointing out what we know will happen when there are no clear property rights in a valuable resource; there will be overuse of the resource.

The Assignment of Property Rights and Externalities

A fundamental economic and legal problem is the efficient assignment of property rights when the marginal social cost or benefit of some activity exceeds the private cost or benefit. For example, when a factory or group of factories pollutes a publicly owned river, as noted above, the owners of property along the river downstream are damaged by this externality. We could have the same problem with air pollution. As mentioned previously, the polluting factories do not pay the full cost of pollution. The social cost is the total private cost plus the cost of the pollution to the property owners downstream. Or the full cost of production of a factory that is polluting the air is the total private cost of production plus the lowered values of the other people's property that is damaged by the smoke.

In some cases the property rights problem is solved by adjustments in the marketplace. For example, mergers between firms across industries may internalize an externality. Recall the example of the beekeeper and apple farmer. Both provided each other with an external economy. The bees pollinated the apple blossoms, and the blossoms allowed the bees to make honey. Once it is understood by the farmer or the beekeeper that their work provides the other with a valuable benefit, there is an incentive to bring the externality into the market in order to produce more efficiently. The beekeeper, for instance, might begin a pollination service and offer to locate bees closer to apple orchards for a fee, or might offer to pay the apple farmer for the right to keep bees near the trees if the beekeeper benefits more from the arrangement than the farmer. Presently, pollination services do exist and flourish, for example, in the state of Washington.[9] If such transactions prove difficult to arrange, the beekeeper or apple grower might buy the other out. The two firms become one and the benefits of the externality are in this way internalized. Thus contractual arrangements in the market or a merger can eliminate externalities and a source of market failure.

In other cases the legal system can encourage a more specific definition of property rights. Class action suits, in which groups of harmed individuals are represented in civil suits against a polluting factory, help redefine the ambiguous ownership of a resource. Through class action, the owner (owners) of property along the river might be compensated by the factory for polluting and, in this way, make up the loss in their property values. But this does not have to be the only legal solution to the property rights problem. Suppose the factory was given property rights to the river. Then the downstream property owners could go to the factory and pay the owner to reduce pollution if the marginal cost were less than the marginal gain to them.

In either legal assignment of property rights, the pollution problem would be internalized by the market. When the rights are defined, compensation can be arranged to more efficiently take account of the externality. And regardless of how the property rights are assigned, the market will properly adjust to account for the externality. Whether the factory owner must pay downstream landowners or the landowners pay the factory owner, pollution has an explicit opportunity cost attached to it. To pollute more, the owner must either pay the landowners or give up the payment received from them not to pollute. It really does not matter how

9 S. N. S. Cheung, "The Fable of the Bees: An Economic Investigation," *Journal of Law and Economics* 16, no. 1 (April 1973), pp. 11–34.

the property rights are assigned so long as they are clearly defined. This conclusion is referred to as the *Coase Theorem*. [10]

The Coase Theorem critically depends on there not being transactions costs once property rights are assigned. What transpires after property rights have been assigned is affected by the number of parties involved. If 1,000 factories are damaging 10,000 fishermen downstream, it would be very difficult and expensive to work out a transaction. Or, if 9,999 downstream property owners agree to bribe the factories not to pollute and one party does not agree, how could the nonpayer be excluded from the benefits? This is our old familiar free rider problem. In the case of one damager versus one damagee, the solution would be simple if property rights are assigned. But the more parties involved, the greater the cost of making the transaction.

Another option is for government to force a "solution" by charging the damagers and possibly compensating those damaged. An emission tax on all waste dumped into the air or water, for instance, would raise the private marginal cost of production to a level closer to the social cost. Taxes will tend to equate social cost with private cost, while subsidies will bring social and private benefit closer together. Surely a goal of zero air and water pollution is ridiculous. If there are diminishing marginal social benefits and increasing marginal social costs from reducing pollution, the solution is to have pollution at some optimal, but nonzero, rate. It is frequently the task of economists and engineers to determine that rate. Marginal costs are not easily measured, and, in the absence of a social utility function, marginal benefits are also generally impossible to measure.

We have merely touched on the problem of external ownership effects. Many more examples and solutions could be discussed. The economics profession is certainly not in agreement about the problem or the solution. Neither is the legal profession. The sole purpose of this discussion is to make you aware of the problem and some possible solutions. We want you to think about the problem of externalities in economic terms.

APPLICATION

Subsidizing Organ Transplants: The Case of an External Benefit

One of the great medical miracles of recent years is the increasing use of an organ transplant—a heart, liver, or kidney—to save human lives. These miracle operations receive a lot of attention in the press. Frequently

---

[10] In a very famous article by Ronald Coase, "The Problem of Social Cost," *Journal of Law and Economics* 3 (October 1960), pp. 1–44, it was shown that, if one party is damaging another through its productive activity, the optimal amount of damage is the same regardless of the party to whom property rights are assigned, given zero transactions cost.

the local or even national media will call the public's attention to the impending death of a child unless an organ donor can be found.

Transplanting human organs is an incredibly expensive operation for recipients and most families must obtain financial support for the operation. To get some idea of how expensive transplant operations are: in 1984, a cornea transplant was priced between $3,000 and $5,000, a heart transplant cost from $50,000 to $250,000, a new liver $75,000 to $250,000, and the most simple kidney transplant started at $25,000.[11]

If a patient needs a new organ to survive, who should pay for the operation? This is an important question, because who can pay usually determines who gets the operation. At the present time local and federal governments have played a limited role in financing transplants. The one area of exception is kidney dialysis and transplantation, funded heavily through the Social Security Administration. By and large, however, transplant operations have been financed by the private sector, and families have relied on the donations of friends and relatives to pay for an operation. What role, if any, should the public sector have in providing organs to recipients who demand them? Part of the answer lies in thinking about the external economies involved in organ transplants.

Certainly there is tremendous private benefit from a transplanted organ. A patient without hope of living may go on to lead a healthy productive life. Leading a productive life also benefits society; that is, some social benefit comes from an incapacitated member of the community returning to a normal lifestyle. The individual contributes as a citizen and as a productive input and consumer in numerous markets. Thus society has an interest in the health of its members. This is why hospitals and medical research are frequently funded by local, state and federal governments.

Suppose the government has decided to impose a more efficient equilibrium in the supply of and demand for organ transplants. Society has decided to move the equilibrium closer to the point where marginal cost and the social marginal benefit of a transplant intersect. How should the government subsidize operations?

We can illustrate graphically two kinds of public funding in paying for organ transplants. In Figure 19–4, Panels A and B each show two demand schedules, D_P and D_S. The lower schedule labeled D_P is the private demand for transplants; the higher schedule D_S is the social demand curve, which includes both the private and external benefit from a transplant. Disregarding for a moment any external economy from a transplant operation, equilibrium would occur at p_0 and x_0 in both panels. If all benefits, private and external, were counted, more operations would of course be undertaken. Using the D_S schedule as a measure of the social

---

[11] These figures are taken from "Organ Transplant Questions Remain," *Houston Chronicle,* September 2, 1984, Section 3, p. 1.

FIGURE 19-4   Organ transplants as an externality

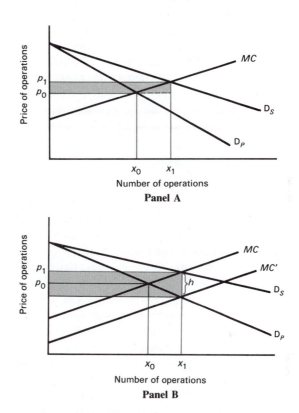

value of transplants, the equilibrium should be at p_1 and x_1. The increase in operations is therefore $x_1 - x_0$. How does a market reach the higher equilibrium output?

One way, and in most cases the least expensive method, is for the government to subsidize the patients by the amount $p_1 - p_0$; then x_1 operations would be made and the government would pay $x_1 \cdot (p_1 - p_0)$ total dollars for transplants. This amount is shown as the shaded region in Panel A of Figure 19-4. The government directly pays each patient the difference between p_1 and p_0 when the operation is completed. This is usually the way most private insurance companies pay claims.

Panel B shows a second means to reach x_1, but it will always be more expensive than the payment method in Panel A. Here the government subsidizes the hospital cost of the operation. The original marginal cost schedule for operations is *MC*. To move patients down their demand schedule, D_P, until x_1 operations are reached, a new marginal cost schedule *MC'* is necessary. This requires that each operation at the hospital have a subsidy of *h* as shown in Panel B. By comparing the panels we see that *h* is greater than $p_1 - p_0$, and since the number of operations is the same, the government spends more by paying hospitals part of the cost of the operation. Unless administrative costs are greater, it is less costly to pay patients rather than hospitals.

19.6 SUMMARY

There are some goods for which exchange in the marketplace does not work well. Public goods have the characteristic that exclusion of consumption cannot be prevented once the good is produced or purchased. The principle of nonexclusion makes it difficult or impossible for a producer to collect revenue to cover the cost of production. Consumers, while enjoying the good, have no incentive to pay, since they can continue to consume without making payment. Public goods encourage consumers to become free riders. Ironically, however, we discovered that the efficient price of some public goods should be zero. Because the marginal cost of letting another person consume the good, once it is produced, is zero, the price at the margin should be zero. Public goods are not a profitable venture for private enterprise. As a consequence, government produces many of the public goods we observe in our society.

Externalities are another cause of market failure. They occur when exchange takes place outside of a market. Usually individuals consume something good or bad, depending on preferences, without paying or being compensated. Social benefit is greater than private benefit if there are external economies. Social cost is greater than private cost if there are external diseconomies. Most externalities result from an absence of property rights. Usually when property rights are better defined the market is able to adjust and *internalize* the externality. It can be difficult to define property rights. As a consequence the government taxes or subsidizes parties to bring social cost and benefit closer to the private counterparts.

In this chapter we have addressed other reasons for market failure. Imperfect competition often stands in the way of Pareto efficient production and distribution, but the theory of second best tells us that making one market more competitive while others remain imperfect may reduce community welfare. The absence of market information or the inability to evaluate it properly can also reduce exchange in markets. Asymmetry in information between buyers and sellers can even lead to the disappearance of a market.

TECHNICAL PROBLEMS

1. Why would a community owned forest be depleted more rapidly than a privately owned forest?

2. Explain in what sense a national park is a public good and in what sense it is not.

3. Is your school library a public good? Could the time of year affect your answer?

4. Your roommate has a stereo. In what sense could this stereo have both positive and negative externalities to you?

5. Other than national defense, can you think of any pure public goods—goods with both producer and consumer nonexclusion?

6. What is the free-rider problem connected with the existence of public goods? How can it lead to a market solution that is not Pareto optimal?

7. Why isn't every point on society's production-possibility frontier preferable to any interior point?

8. Explain why monopoly or oligopoly will not lead to a Pareto optimal equilibrium. Explain why forcing a monopoly to produce more can reduce society's welfare.

9. What problem arises because of asymmetry of information in markets?

10. What is the difference between external economies and diseconomies? Give an example of each. In what case are too few goods produced? Explain. In what case are too many goods produced? Explain.

11. In the Coase Theorem, it does not make any difference to society how property rights are assigned as long as they are. Does it make any difference to the parties involved how property rights are assigned, however? Would a polluting factory rather pay landowners to pollute or be paid by landowners not to pollute as much?

ANALYTICAL PROBLEMS

1. Suppose the social return to education is 8 percent and the return to other investment is 10 percent. This shows too many resources are being used in education. Comment.

2. Suppose from time to time a certain theater has long lines for a particular movie and sometimes has to turn away customers. Is this evidence of market failure? Why or why not?

3. Suppose there are two classes made up of very similar students. In one class, each student receives the grade made on each test. In the other class, each student receives the class average on each test. These policies are known by all. In what class would you expect the

higher average grade? Explain in terms of externalities, or the free rider problem.

4. In Texas, the state owns all the beaches. Analyze the following statements and determine whether they are true or false.

    a. If private individuals owned the beaches, poor and middle-income people would be denied access.

    b. Since the state can afford to clean the beaches, there is less litter than if they were privately owned.

    c. Since the state can regulate the beaches, it can keep off sleazy merchants, and the people using the beaches are better off.

    d. Since the state owns the beaches, more people use them, and the people are better off because a beach is a public good.

5. If bridges and highways are public goods, why do we see private enterprise building them and charging a toll? Do toll roads and bridges maximize consumer's and producer's surplus? Is a toll road or a toll-free publicly financed road better? (In your answer, consider the problem of congestion and the argument that "those who use the road should pay.")

6. In the bee-apple orchard example of externalities is there an incentive for one to buy out the other? Explain. What would be the externality problem if bees were bad for apples, but apple blossoms increased honey production by bees?

7. In our example of a factory polluting fisheries downstream, would the amount of property damage depend on when the fisheries were begun relative to the opening of the factory? Explain.

8. Other things equal, would a monopolistic industry or a competitive industry that is producing an external diseconomy produce more of the diseconomy? Explain.

9. Airport noise is certainly a negative externality. Why would people choose to live near airports?

10. In Wanendale, Pennsylvania, a local restaurant owner took the prices off his menu and told customers to pay him what they thought their meal was worth. According to the owner he isn't "losing a penny" by the new system (Associated Press, December 16, 1984). Has this owner created a public good with his restaurant? Do you expect him to stay in business by letting consumers decide value?

11. Many prison systems are becoming privately owned and operated institutions. Once a criminal is sentenced to serve, the state or Federal government pays a corporation to hold the prisoner. (See *Newsweek*, May 7, 1984, p. 80 for a more detailed description.) Do you think private prisons can detain criminals as well as public institutions? Are prisons public goods? Do they have externalities that cannot be captured by the market? Why does the government own and operate prisons?

INDEX

A

Accounting cost, 270–71
Additivity assumption, 128
Ad valorem tax, 67–69
Advertising, 480–83
  demand increasing, 212
  image, 209–13
  and indifference curves, 206–15
  information as advertising, 213–16
  informative, 207–9
  New York Times best seller list, 213–16
Akerlof model, 616–17
Allocation decision, 98–99
Allocations, 434
Aluminum Company of America (Alcoa),
    404, 435
American Medical Association, 448–49
American Telephone and Telegraph, 403–4
American Tobacco, 441
Anheuser-Busch, 481
Argonaut Enterprises, 555–57
Average product
  arithmetic approach, 236–37
  graphical approach, 238–42
  with two different amounts of fixed fac-
    tor, 246
Average revenue, 347–48

Averch, H., 315
Averch-Johnson effect, 316

B

Barriers to entry, 431
  capacity barriers, 440
  examples, 432–36
  multiproduct cost barriers, 440–41
  new product development, 441–42
  price cutting, 437–39
Brand identification, 395–96
Brand loyalties, 436
Break-even chart, 384–86
Budget lines, 140–44, 196–97
  and advertising, 207–9
  definition, 141
  shifting, 142–44
Budgets, and constrained maximization, 97
Bureau of Labor Statistics (BLS), 192–93
Butler, Henry N., 498

C

Capital market
  monopoly in, 560
  monopsony in, 560–61
Capitalized profits, 421

Cardinal utility, 127–29
Carlyle, Thomas, 3, 14
Cartels, 338–39, 493–500
  incentive to cheat, 497
  life cycles, 496–97
  and market sharing, 495–96
  and profit maximization, 494
  in real estate, 498–500
Cereris paribus, 17
Chamberlin, Edward, 470
Cheung, S. N. S., 628
Clark, Lindey, 47
Coal
  cost curves of firm, 383
  price ceiling on, 380–84
  supply and demand, 381
Collusive equilibrium, 492
Commodity market, monopoly in, 511–17
Competition
  adjustment process, 380–84
  allocation of fixed and variable cost, 384–91
  and consumer surplus, 396–99
  cost structure, 386–91
  and demand, 345–48
  equilibrium in perfect competition, 598–600
  free markets, 342
  and general equilibrium, 596–600
  imperfect, 469–504, 612–15
  monopolistic, 469–77
  monopoly inefficiency, 612–13
  nonprice, 477–85
  nonprice in the decaffeinated coffee market, 483–85
  oligopolistic, 469, 488–90
  perfect, 342–45, 379–402, 475–77, 507–17
  perfect competition as a goal, 392–96
  product variety, 395–96
  and rivals, 485
  supply side, 343
  theory of second best, 613–15
  and welfare, 578–603
Competitive markets, 338–78; *see also* Markets
Conjectural variation, 491
Constant-cost industries, 365–66
Consumer behavior, 124–61
  and advertising, 206–15
  applying theory, 192–225
  basic assumptions, 125–29
  changes in income, 165–71
  changes in income and price, 163–91
  determinants of choice, 124–25
  fringe benefits and taxation, 151–54
  information and ranking, 126
  labor-leisure choice, 197–206
  over time, 215–19
Consumer equilibrium, 147

Consumer price index (CPI), 192–93
  original bundle of goods, 194
Consumer Product Safety Commission (CPSC), 618–19
Consumer's Report, 214–15
Consumer's surplus, 71–75, 396–99
  application, 73–75
  definition, 73
  gasoline rationing tickets, 73–75
  and pareto optimality, 582–84, 585–95
Consumption expenditures, 111
Contract curve, 591, 595
Corner solution, 149
Cost, 3
  average fixed, 290
  average total, 293, 354
  average variable, 291–92, 354
  definition of, 269
  fixed and variable, 386–91
  marginal, 293–96, 354
  under monopoly, 413–14
  planning horizon and long-run, 271–87
  refinery cost functions, 298–300
  relation between short-run and long-run average and marginal costs, 300–303
  short-run, 287–300
  subadditive, 440–41
  theory of, 269–311
  total fixed, 289
  total variable, 289
Cost-benefit analysis, 69–70
  and surplus, 77–79
Cost structure, 386–91
Cournot conjecture, 492–93

D

Davis, O. A., 622
Decaffeinated coffee market, 483–85
Decision makers, 93
Decision making, 82
  and fixed costs at the margin, 349–51
  and indifference curves, 139–40
Decreasing-cost industries, 368–72
Deflation, 195–97
de Leeuw, F., 170
Demand, 14–53
  changes in, 18–19
  elasticity, 20–33
  facing a perfectly competitive firm, 345–48
  for fixed inputs, 549–75
  industry demand for input, 520–22
  industry demand for investment, 558–61
  inferior goods, 182
  for labor, 513
  law of demand, 183–85
  and marginal revenue, 446
  under monopoly, 408–13

Demand—*Cont.*
  normal goods, 182
  of a perfectly competitive firm, 507–11
  for a price taker, 345, 347
  for a product resource with more than one
      variable input, 517–19
  and time, 30
  for a variable resource, 509
  when more than one input varies, 518–19
Demand curves, 171–74, 182–85
  and consumer's surplus, 71
  downward, 182–85
  kinked, 496
  price-consumption curve, 171–75
Demand elasticities; *see also* Elasticity
  and automobile industry, 31–32
  factors affecting, 29–31
Demand schedules, 14–19
  estimating, 81–86
Demand and supply; *see also* Supply and
      demand
  and cotton market, 45
  and laws, 44
Deregulation, 30
Diminishing marginal product, 242–43
Diminishing marginal rate of technical sub-
      stitution, 248–50
Diminishing returns, 243
Discounting, 550–52
  expenditures, 111
Diseconomies of scale, 280–87
Dismal science, 3
du Pont de Nemours & Company, E. I., 435

E

Eastman Kodak Company, 435
Economic efficiency, 232–33
Economics
  science of, 3–6
  uses of, 6–7
Economies of scale, 280–87, 432–33
Edgeworth box, 587–89
  and trade in water, 592–93
Edwards, Richard C., 285
Efficiency, 232–33
Elasticity, 20–33
  computation, 22–29
  cross-price elasticity of demand, 406–7
  of demand, 405–6
  graphical computation, 25–28
  income, 166–68
  income elasticity of housing, 170–171
  and marginal revenue, 412–13
  and monopoly, 405–7
  and natural gas, 30–31
  substitutability, 30
  and taxes, 66
Elasticity of demand, 22–29; *see also* De-
      mand elasticities

Elasticity of substitution, 317–21
  and changes in relative input shares,
      320–21
Elasticity of supply; *see* Supply elasticity
Employment, under monopsony, 539–41
Energy, 394–95
Engel curves, 166–68
Entrepreneurs, 105
Equilibrium
  of exchange, 589–91
  in perfect competition, 598–600
  of production, 594–95
Equilibrium, general; *see* General equi-
      librium
Estimating
  demand schedules, 81–86
  problems, 83–84
  procedures, 84–86
  token economy in mental hospital, 86
Excessive sameness, 480
Exchange inefficiencies, and welfare,
      605–34
Excise taxes, 64–69, 461–63
Exclusion, 607–8, 611
Expansion path, 256–59
  and long-run cost, 274–76
External benefits and costs, 605
External economy, 621
Externalities, 619–32
  assignment of, 627–29
  definition of, 619–22
  and property rights, 624
  and urban renewal, 622–23

F

Factory system, 339
Federal Communications Commission
      (FCC), 434–35
Federal regulation, of natural gas, 79–81
Federal Trade Commission (FTC), 441–42
Ferguson, C. E., 281
Firm
  profit-maximizing competitive, 510
  theory of, 338–40
Fishing, and property rights, 625–27
Fixed costs, 349–51, 433–34; *see also* Cost
Fixed input, 233; *see also* Inputs
  demand for, 549–75
Fixed proportions, 234–35
  and timber crisis, 235–36
Flat-rate income tax, 200–206
Food and Drug Administration (FDA), 618
Franchises, 434
Free markets, 342; *see also* Market(s)
Free rider problem, 607–8
Friedman, Milton, 2, 593
Fringe benefits, 518, 530–31
  and taxation, 151–54

Full-wage equilibrium, 530–32
Future value, 105–7

G

Galbraith, John Kenneth, 3
Gasoline rationing, 73–75
General equilibrium
  and perfect competition, 596–600
  in production and exchange, 597
General Foods, 483–85
General Mills, 442
General Motors, 286–87
German Bayer Company, 4–6
Giffen's Paradox, 183
Goods; see also Normal goods and Inferior
    goods
  in kind, 592–94
  normal and inferior, 168–69
Government revenue, 68–69

H

Hand, Judge Learned, 393
Harberger, Arnold C., 456
Hershey's, 405
Homogeneous products, 343
Hotelling, H., 480
Housing
  income elasticity, 170–71
  market, 47–50
Howard, F., 5

I

Incentive, 339
  effects of being small, 393–95
Income, 165–71
  allocation over time, 216–19
Income-consumption curve, 165–66
Income effect, 163–64, 177–82
  definition, 177
  principle, 182
Income elasticity, 166–68
  of housing, 170–71
Increasing-cost industries, 366–68
Indifference curves, 128–33
  and advertising, 206–15
  characteristics of, 131–33
  labor supplies, 198
  value of indifference curve theory, 139–40
Indifference map, 129–31, 150–51
Industry demand, 520–22
Inferior goods, 168–69
  demand, 183
  and income effect, 179, 181
Inferior input, 258
Inflation
  actual effects of, 563
  and consumer price index, 194
  effects on public utilities, 564–65

Inflation—*Cont.*
  and investment, 561–65
  real effect 192–97
  theoretical effects of, 561–63
Information, and market failure, 615–19
Inman, Virginia, 286
Input barriers, 435–36
Input markets, 507–17
Input prices, 251–53
  changes, 312–35
  graphical analysis, 313–14
  relative, 314
  and technology, 327–32
Inputs; see also Variable inputs
  fixed, 528–30
  returns to, 527–32
Interdependence, and oligopoly, 485–90
Interest, 104–5
Interest rates, real versus nominal, 561
Intermediate goods, 523
Internal rate of return, 553, 558
Investment
  alternative opportunities, 554
  decision making, 550–52
  effect of taxation on, 559
  evaluation of investment projects, 555–57
  firm's demand for, 552–58
  and inflation, 561–65
  lumpiness, 282
  risk effects, 569–71
  theory of, 549–75
Isocost curves, 251–53
Isoquants, 245–49

J–K

Johnson, L., 315
Kellogg, 442
Kessel, Reuben A., 448–49
Kinked demand curve, 496
Klein, Frederick C., 284
Koten, Jim, 286

L

Labor monopoly demand for, 513
Labor-leisure choice, 197–206
  effects of taxes, 200–206
  map, 197–99
Labor supply, 523–27
  indifference curves, 198
  shortage of nurses, 524–26
Labor unions, 533–35
Laboratory experimentation, 86
Lacewell, Ronald, 514
Lancaster, Kelvin, 614
Laspeyres index, 193
Last unit exchanged, 70–71
Law of demand, 14–15, 183–85
  and price, 184–85

Leaky, Paul, 407
Leslie, S., 5
Licenses, 529
Licensing, 434
Ligget and Myers (L&M), 441
Lipsey, R. G., 613
Long run, 234
  versus short run, 288
Long-run costs
  expansion path, 274–76
  long-run average costs, 273
  long-run average and marginal, 276–80
  long-run marginal costs, 273
  long-run total costs, 272
  schedules from a production function, 271–76
Long-run equilibrium, 357–65
  graphical exposition, 361–64
  and monopolistic competition, 473–74
  and monopoly, 418–20
  and perfect competition, 475–77
  and rent, 364–65
Loss, and the firm's short-run supply curve, 352–55

M

Mabry, Rodney, 587
MacAvoy, Paul, 564
Macroeconomics, 8–9
Malthus, 3
Marginal benefit, 93–95
Marginal costs, 93–95, 341; *see also* Cost
Marginal factor cost, 508
  under monopsony, 536–38
Marginal product
  arithmetic approach, 236–38
  graphical approach, 238–42
  relation to MRTS, 249–50
  with two different amounts of fixed factor, 246
Marginal rate of substitution, 134–40
  in consumption, 134–36
  definition, 135
  diminishing MRS, 136–37
  and pareto optimality, 584–87
Marginal rate of technical substituion, 248–50
Marginal rate of transformation, 597–98
Marginal revenue, 340–41
  and elasticity, 412–13
  under monopoly, 408–13
  relation to total revenue, 411
Marginal revenue product, 507–8
  for monopolist, 511–12
  parameters for, 517–18
Marginal utility, 99, 125, 128
  interpretation of optimization, 147–48
Marginal utility approach, 138–39

Market(s)
  free, 342
  government intervention, 55
  mobility of resources, 343–44
  and monopoly, 453–58
  perfect knowledge about, 344–45
  price and quantity, 41–50
  supply and demand, 56–58
  theory of competitive markets, 338–7█
Market demand schedule, 15
Market equilibrium, 41–43, 527–32
  for variable inputs, 527–32
Market failure, 605
  and information, 615–19
Market sharing and cartels, 495–96
Massey-Ferguson Ltd., 354–55
de Maupassant, Guy, 388–91
Maurice, Charles, 329
Maximization
  constrained, 96–100
  and marginal utility, 125
  unconstrained, 93
  utility, 145–54
Medical profession, 448–49
Microeconomics, 8–9
Midgley, Thomas, 5
Minimization unconstrained, 95
Miller, 481
Miller, W., 407
Mineral extraction, 423–25
Minimum wages, 535–36
Mining industries, 530–32
Minnesota Mining and Manufacturing Co. (3M), 285–87
Mobile Travel Guide, 214
Monopolistic competition, 469–77
  demand under, 471–73
  elasticity, 473
  product differentiation, 473
Monopoly, 55
  behavior and performance, 431–67
  bilateral, 541–42
  in capital markets, 560
  in the commodity market, 511–17
  comparison with perfect competition, 453–54
  and competition, 403
  and cost, 413–14
  definition of, 404
  and demand, 408–13
  demand for labor, 513
  and elasticity, 405–9
  equilibrium, 492
  inefficiency, 612–13
  and long-run equilibrium, 418–20
  and marginal revenue, 408–13
  market performance, 453–58
  multiplant, 421–25
  natural, 433

Monopoly—*Cont.*
  versus perfect competition, 457–58
  power, 397–98, 404, 405–8
  price ceilings, 459
  profit maximization, 404–5
  regulation, 458–63
  and short-term equilibrium, 414–16
  and short-run losses, 415
  short-run monopoly profit maximization,
      413–18
  strategic behavior, 436–42
  and supply, 416–17
  and surplus loss, 454–56
  and theory of price, 403–29
  and welfare loss, 456–57
Monopsony, 536–42
  in capital markets, 560–61
  marginal factor cost, 536–38
  price and employment, 439–41
Multiperiod analysis, 104–14

N

National Observer, 32
Natural gas, 79–81
Natural resources, 523
  depletion of, 565–68
  rates of extraction, 565–68
Nestle Company, 482–85
Net present value, 551
New York Times, best seller list, 213–16
Nonexclusion, 607–8, 611
Normal goods, 168–69
  demand, 182
  and substitution and income effect, 180
Normal input, 258
Normative economics, 579
Nutri/System Inc., 286–87

O

Oligopoly
  competition in, 488–90
  and interdependence, 485–90
  oligopoly equilibrium, 491–93
  tacit collusion, 487–88
  theories of rivalry, 490–93
  types of behavior, 486–87
OPEC, 493–94
Opportunity cost, 269–71
  and accounting cost, 270–71
Optimization, 91–121
  constrained, 95–104
  constrained and unconstrained, 91
  leasing versus buying an automobile,
      112–14
  marginal utility interpretation of, 147–48
  of study time, 98, 103
  unconstrained, 92–95
Ordinal utility, 127–29

Organ transplants, 629–32
Output effect, 322–23

P

Pareto optimality, 581–95
  and consumer's surplus, 582–84
  in consumption and production, 585–95
Patent laws, 435
Pay-off table, 490–91
Pejovich, S., 624
Perfect competition; *see* Competition
Petersen, H. C., 317
Phillips, O. R., 498
Pigou, A. C., 442
Pollution, 393–94
Positive economics, 579
Post, 442
Preference maps, 150–51
Present value, 107–11
Price(s), 58–63
  "above equilibrium" and "below equi-
      librium," 78–79
  ceiling and floor, 583
  ceilings, 58–59, 80–81, 380–84
  floors, 59–61
  and insufficient information, 615–16
  under monopsony, 539–41
  and output comparisons, 454
  regulation, 458–61
  relative, 193
  and substitution and income effects, 178
  theory of price under monopoly, 403–29
Price changes, estimating, 85–86
Price-consumption curve, 171–75
Price control, in World War II, 395
Price cutting, 437–39
Price discrimination, 431, 442–53
  definition, 443
  examples of, 448–49
  first degree, 449–51
  and marginal revenue, 445
  and profit maximization, 447
  second degree, 452–53
  in theory, 443–47
Price elasticity, 29–30
Price leadership, 488
Price and quantity, 41–50
  and demand and supply shifts, 44–50
  equilibrium, 41–43
  and housing, 47–50
  for peanuts, 62–63
Price taker, 345, 347
Prisoner's dilemma, 481–82
Procter & Gamble, 483–85
Producer's surplus, 76–77
Product(s)
  homogeneous, 343
  heterogeneous, 470
Product differentiation, 478–80

Product quality, 478–80
  evaluating, 618–19
Product variety, 395–96
Production
  economic efficiency, 232–33
  with fixed proportions, 254
  function, 231–36
  of a given output at minimum cost, 253–55
  of a maximum output with a given level of
    cost, 255–56
  with one variable input, 236–45
  optimal combination of resources, 250–60
  and pareto optimality, 585–95
  possibilities curve, 230
  short and long run, 233–34
  sources of cost, 228–29
  theory of, 228–68
  three stages, 243–45
  with two or more variable inputs, 245–50
Production-possibility frontier, 229–31
Profit, and the firm's short-run supply
  curve, 352–55
Profit maximization, 340–42
  and cartels, 494
  on the expansion path, 321–22
  in the long run, 357–60
  marginal revenue-marginal cost approach,
    417
  and monopoly, 404–5
  under price discrimination, 447
  profit-maximizing competitive firm, 510
  in the short run, 348–57
  and short-run monopoly, 413–18
  zero and negative profit situations, 360–61
Progressive taxes, 200–206
Property rights
  assignment of, 627–29
  and externalities, 624
  and fishing for striped bass, 625–27
  non-owned of community-owned prop-
    erty, 624–25
Public good, 605, 606–12
  definition, 606
  and marginal costs, 608–11
  nonexclusion, 607–8
  role of government, 611–612
Public utilities, and inflation, 564–65

Q–R

Quasi-rent, 528–30
Rate of return, 552–58
  on assets in regulated industries, 565
Rate of return regulation, 315–17
Rates of extraction, 565–68
Rationing, 73–75
Real estate cartel, 498–500
Refinery cost functions, 298–300
Regulation
  and monopoly, 458–63

Regulation—*Cont.*
  price regulation, 458–61
  taxation as, 461–63
Relative input shares, 320–21
Reneau, Duane, 514
Rent, 364–65
Resources, 3–4
Returns to scale, 259–60
Reynolds, 441
Ricardo, 3
Risk, 568–71
  in investment, 569–71
Robinson, Joan, 470
Rolex watches, 480–81
Rules of thumb, 616–17

S

Samuelson, Paul, 2
Scarcity, 3, 228–29
Scherer, F. M., 480, 482
Schmalensee, Richard, 436
Sherman Antitrust Act, 407
Short run, 233
Short-run cost, 287–300
  versus long run, 288
  schedules, 297
Short-run equilibrium, 351–52
  and monopolistic competition, 473–74
  and monopoly, 414–16
Short-run supply curve, 352–57
Shortages, 58, 61
Sloan, Alfred, 5
Smith, Adam, 70, 281
Smithson, Charles, W., 329
Social welfare, 579–84
  maximum, 581
Specialization, 281–83, 338–39
Static analysis, 92
Stigler, G. J., 489
Stocking, G., 407
Sturdivant, F. C., 184
Substitutability, 395–96
Substitution effect, 163–64, 174–77, 312–13
  definition, 175
  elasticity of, 317–21
  principle, 177
Supply, 14–53
  changes in, 35–36
  factors influencing, 35
  theory of, 228–68
  of a variable productive service, 523–27
Supply curves, 67–68
Supply and demand
  analysis, 55–90
  and cotton market, 45
  and laws, 44
  markets, 56–58
Supply elasticity, 36–41
  computation, 37–39

Supply elasticity—*Cont.*
  determinants, 39–41.
  and lawyers, 40
  and time, 40
Supply schedules, 33–36
  graphing, 35
Surplus, 58, 71–79, 396–99
  application, 79–81
  and cost benefit studies, 77–79
  surplus loss and monopoly, 454–56
Synthetic rubber, 4–6

T

Tax revenue, 68–69
Taxation, 461–63
  effects of progressive and flat rate,
    200–206
  and elasticity, 66
  excise taxes, 461–63
  and fringe benefits, 151–54
  and monopoly, 461–63
Technical efficiency versus economic efficiency, 232–33
Technological change, 312–35
  biased, 325–26
  classification, 324–26
  and cost, 370–71
  and factor usage, 327
  and input price changes, 327–32
  and input usage, 324–32
  neutral, 324–25
Technological factors, 282–83
  optimal use of, 424
Theory, purpose of, 7–10
Theory of investment, 92
Theory of price; *see* Price(s)
3M, 285–87
Timber crisis, 235–36
Total product
  arithmetic approach, 236–38
  graphical approach, 238–42
  with two different amounts of fixed factor, 246
Trade, theory of, 592–94

Trivial Pursuit, 421
Tullock, G., 456–57

U–V

Unconstrained optimization, 92–95
Unit tax, 64–67
United States v. *Alcoa Aluminum,* 393
United States v. *du Pont de Nemours & Company,* 407–8
Urban renewal, and externalities, 622–23
Utility, 126
  ordinal versus cardinal, 127–29
Utility maximization, 145–54
  with limited money income, 145–47
Value
  future, 105–7
  paradox of, 70–71
  present, 107–11
  versus price, 71
Value of the marginal product, 508–11
Variable inputs, 233; *see also* Inputs
  demand with more than one, 517–19
  markets for, 506–48
Variable proportions, 234–35
VMP curve, 514–17

W–Z

Wall Street Journal, 284–87
Water rationing, 592–94
Wealth of Nations (Smith), 70
Welfare
  and competition, 578–603
  consequences of a price ceiling and floor, 583
  and exchange inefficiencies, 605–34
  social, 579–84
Welfare economics, 579
Welfare loss, and monopoly, 456–57
Wholesalers, 57
Winston A. B., 622
Yermack, David L., 625
Zero consumption of a good, 148–50
Zero effect, 393–95
Zero marginal cost, 608

This book has been set Linotron 202, in 10 and 9 point Times Roman, leaded 2 points. Part numbers are 16 point Times Roman Bold and part titles are 36 point Times Roman Bold. Chapter numbers are 18 point Times Roman Bold and chapter titles are 36 point Times Roman Bold. The size of the type page is 35.5 picas by 49 picas.